Windows
95
Uncut

Windows 95 Uncut

by Alan Simpson

IDG Books Worldwide, Inc.
An International Data Group Company

Foster City, CA ✦ Chicago, IL ✦ Indianapolis, IN ✦ Braintree, MA ✦ Dallas, TX

Windows 95 Uncut

Published by
IDG Books Worldwide, Inc.
An International Data Group Company
919 E. Hillsdale Blvd.
Suite 400
Foster City, CA 94404

Library of Congress Catalog Card No.: 95-78410

ISBN: 1-56884-074-8

Printed in the United States of America

10 9 8 7 6 5 4 3 2 1

1A/QY/QY/ZV

Distributed in the United States by IDG Books Worldwide, Inc.

Distributed by Macmillan Canada for Canada; by Computer and Technical Books for the Caribbean Basin; by Contemporanea de Ediciones for Venezuela; by Distribuidora Cuspide for Argentina; by CITEC for Brazil; by Ediciones ZETA S.C.R. Ltda. for Peru; by Editorial Limusa SA for Mexico; by Transworld Publishers Limited in the United Kingdom and Europe; by Al-Maiman Publishers & Distributors for Saudi Arabia; by Simron Pty. Ltd. for South Africa; by IDG Communications (HK) Ltd. for Hong Kong; by Toppan Company Ltd. for Japan; by Addison Wesley Publishing Company for Korea; by Longman Singapore Publishers Ltd. for Singapore, Malaysia, Thailand, and Indonesia; by Unalis Corporation for Taiwan; by WS Computer Publishing Company, Inc. for the Philippines; by WoodsLane Pty. Ltd. for Australia; by WoodsLane Enterprises Ltd. for New Zealand.

For general information on IDG Books Worldwide's books in the U.S., please call our Consumer Customer Service department at 800-762-2974. For reseller information, including discounts and premium sales, please call our Reseller Customer Service department at 800-434-3422.

For information on where to purchase IDG Books Worldwide's books outside the U.S., contact IDG Books Worldwide at 415-655-3021 or fax 415-655-3295.

For information on translations, contact Marc Jeffrey Mikulich, Director, Foreign & Subsidiary Rights, at IDG Books Worldwide, 415-655-3018 or fax 415-655-3295.

For sales inquiries and special prices for bulk quantities, write to the address above or call IDG Books Worldwide at 415-655-3200.

For information on using IDG Books Worldwide's books in the classroom, or ordering examination copies, contact Jim Kelly at 800-434-2086.

For authorization to photocopy items for corporate, personal, or educational use, please contact Copyright Clearance Center, 222 Rosewood Drive, Danvers, MA 01923, or fax 508-750-4470.

The screen shots in this book are based on Microsoft Windows 95 made public by Microsoft as of June 1995. Because this information was made public before the final release of Windows 95, it is possible that the final interface may be different than illustrated herein. We encourage you to visit your local bookstore after Windows 95 is released for updated books on Windows 95.

About the Author

Alan Simpson

Alan Simpson is a freelance computer guru and veteran author of *digilit* (*digital literature*, a term that the author just now coined, aka *computer books*). Before writing this book, Alan spent about 15 months exploring the 32-bit world of computing that products such as Windows NT, Windows 95, and Microsoft Office for Windows 95 have brought upon us. Rumor has it, he's gotten pretty darn good at using them.

Alan lives and works at home in San Diego, California, with his wife, Susan; their two young children; two dumb dogs; a cat; a dozen or so fish; a crawfish; and an incredible array of computers, printers, modems, and other high-tech gadgets. He can be reached (eventually) at these addresses:

Alan Simpson
P.O. Box 630
Rancho Santa Fe, CA 92067-0630
Fax: (619) 756-0159
Internet: alan@coolnerds.com
WWW: http://www.coolnerds.com/~alan
MSN: coolnerds
America Online: CoolNerds
CompuServe: 72420,2236

ABOUT IDG BOOKS WORLDWIDE

Welcome to the world of IDG Books Worldwide.

IDG Books Worldwide, Inc., is a subsidiary of International Data Group, the world's largest publisher of computer-related information and the leading global provider of information services on information technology. IDG was founded more than 25 years ago and now employs more than 7,500 people worldwide. IDG publishes more than 235 computer publications in 67 countries (see listing below). More than 60 million people read one or more IDG publications each month.

Launched in 1990, IDG Books Worldwide is today the #1 publisher of best-selling computer books in the United States. We are proud to have received 8 awards from the Computer Press Association in recognition of editorial excellence, and our best-selling ...For Dummies™ series has more than 17 million copies in print with translations in 25 languages. IDG Books Worldwide, through a recent joint venture with IDG's Hi-Tech Beijing, became the first U.S. publisher to publish a computer book in the People's Republic of China. In record time, IDG Books Worldwide has become the first choice for millions of readers around the world who want to learn how to better manage their businesses.

Our mission is simple: Every one of our books is designed to bring extra value and skill-building instructions to the reader. Our books are written by experts who understand and care about our readers. The knowledge base of our editorial staff comes from years of experience in publishing, education, and journalism — experience which we use to produce books for the '90s. In short, we care about books, so we attract the best people. We devote special attention to details such as audience, interior design, use of icons, and illustrations. And because we use an efficient process of authoring, editing, and desktop publishing our books electronically, we can spend more time ensuring superior content and spend less time on the technicalities of making books.

You can count on our commitment to deliver high-quality books at competitive prices on topics consumers want to read about. At IDG Books Worldwide, we value quality, and we have been delivering quality for more than 25 years. You'll find no better book on a subject than an IDG book.

John Kilcullen
President and CEO
IDG Books Worldwide, Inc.

WINNER
Eighth Annual
Computer Press
Awards 1992

WINNER
Ninth Annual
Computer Press
Awards 1993

IDG Books Worldwide, Inc., is a subsidiary of International Data Group, the world's largest publisher of computer-related information and the leading global provider of information services on information technology. International Data Group publishes over 235 computer publications in 67 countries. More than sixty million people read one or more International Data Group publications each month. The officers are Patrick J. McGovern, Founder and Board Chairman; Kelly Conlin, President; Jim Casella, Chief Operating Officer. International Data Group's publications include: **ARGENTINA'S** Computerworld Argentina, Infoworld Argentina; **AUSTRALIA'S** Computerworld Australia, Computer Living, Australian PC World, Australian Macworld, Network World, Mobile Business Australia, Publish!, Reseller, IDG Sources; **AUSTRIA'S** Computerwelt Oesterreich, PC Test; **BELGIUM'S** Data News (CW); **BOLIVIA'S** Computerworld; **BRAZIL'S** Computerworld, Connections, Game Power, Mundo Unix, PC World, Publish, Super Game; **BULGARIA'S** Computerworld Bulgaria, PC & Mac World Bulgaria, Network World Bulgaria; **CANADA'S** CIO Canada, Computerworld Canada, InfoCanada, Network World Canada, Reseller; **CHILE'S** Computerworld Chile, Informatica; **COLOMBIA'S** Computerworld Colombia, PC World; **COSTA RICA'S** PC World; **CZECH REPUBLIC'S** Computerworld, Elektronika, PC World; **DENMARK'S** Communications World, Computerworld Danmark, Computerworld Focus, Macintosh Produktkatalog, Macworld Danmark, PC World Danmark, PC Produktguide, Tech World, Windows World; **ECUADOR'S** PC World Ecuador; **EGYPT'S** Computerworld (CW) Middle East, PC World Middle East; **FINLAND'S** MikroPC, Tietoviikko, Tietoverkko; **FRANCE'S** Distributique, GOLDEN MAC, InfoPC, Le Guide du Monde Informatique, Le Monde Informatique, Telecoms & Reseaux; **GERMANY'S** Computerwoche, Computerwoche Focus, Computerwoche Extra, Electronic Entertainment, Gamepro, Information Management, Macwelt, Netzwelt, PC Welt, Publish, Publish; **GREECE'S** Publish & Macworld; **HONG KONG'S** Computerworld Hong Kong, PC World Hong Kong; **HUNGARY'S** Computerworld SZT, PC World; **INDIA'S** Computers & Communications; **INDONESIA'S** Info Komputer; **IRELAND'S** ComputerScope; **ISRAEL'S** Beyond Windows, Computerworld Israel, Multimedia, PC World Israel; **ITALY'S** Computerworld Italia, Lotus Magazine, Macworld Italia, Networking Italia, PC Shopping Italy, PC World Italia; **JAPAN'S** Computerworld Today, Information Systems World, Macworld Japan, Nikkei Personal Computing, SunWorld Japan, Windows World; **KENYA'S** East African Computer News; **KOREA'S** Computerworld Korea, Macworld Korea, PC World Korea; **LATIN AMERICA'S** GamePro; **MALAYSIA'S** Computerworld Malaysia, PC World Malaysia; **MEXICO'S** Compu Edicion, Compu Manufactura, Computacion/Punto de Venta, Computerworld Mexico, MacWorld, Mundo Unix, PC World, Windows; **THE NETHERLANDS'** Computer! Totaal, Computable (CW), LAN Magazine, Lotus Magazine, MacWorld; **NEW ZEALAND'S** Computer Buyer, Computerworld New Zealand, Network World, New Zealand PC World; **NIGERIA'S** PC World Africa; **NORWAY'S** Computerworld Norge, Lotusworld Norge, Macworld Norge, Maxi Data, Multimedia World, PC World Ekspress, PC World Nettverk, PC World Norge, PC World's Produktguide, Publish& Multimedia World, Student Data, Unix World, Windowsworld; **PAKISTAN'S** PC World Pakistan; **PANAMA'S** PC World Panama; **PERU'S** Computerworld Peru, PC World; **PEOPLE'S REPUBLIC OF CHINA'S** China Computerworld, China Infoworld, China PC Info Magazine, Computer Fan, PC World China, Electronics International, Electronics Today/Multimedia World, Electronic Product World, China Network World, Software World Magazine, Telecom Product World; **PHILIPPINES'** Computerworld Philippines, PC Digest (PCW); **POLAND'S** Computerworld Poland, Computerworld Special Report, Networld, PC World/Komputer, Sunworld; **PORTUGAL'S** Cerebro/PC World, Correio Informatico/Computerworld, MacIn; **ROMANIA'S** Computerworld, PC World, Telecom Romania; **RUSSIA'S** Computerworld-Moscow, Mir - PK (PCW), Sety (Networks); **SINGAPORE'S** Computerworld Southeast Asia, PC World Singapore; **SLOVENIA'S** Monitor Magazine; **SOUTH AFRICA'S** Computer Mail (CIO),Computing S.A.,Network World S.A., Software World; **SPAIN'S** Advanced Systems, Amiga World, Computerworld Espana, Communications World, Macworld Espana, NeXTWORLD, Super Juegos Magazine (GamePro), PC World Espana, Publish; **SWEDEN'S** Attack, ComputerSweden, Corporate Computing, Macworld, Mikrodatorn, Natverk & Kommunikation, PC World, CAP & Design, Datalngenjoren, Maxi Data,Windows World; **SWITZERLAND'S** Computerworld Schweiz, Macworld Schweiz, PC Tip; **TAIWAN'S** Computerworld Taiwan, PC World Taiwan; **THAILAND'S** Thai Computerworld; **TURKEY'S** Computerworld Monitor, Macworld Turkiye, PC World Turkiye; **UKRAINE'S** Computerworld, Computers+Software Magazine; **UNITED KINGDOM'S** Computing /Computerworld, Connexion/Network World, Lotus Magazine, Macworld, Open Computing/Sunworld; **UNITED STATES'** Advanced Systems, AmigaWorld, Cable in the Classroom, CD Review, CIO, Computerworld, Computerworld Client/Server Journal, Digital Video, DOS World, Electronic Entertainment Magazine (E2), Federal Computer Week, Game Hits, GamePro, IDG Books Worldwide, Infoworld, Laser Event, Macworld, Maximize, Multimedia World, Network World, PC Letter, PC World, Publish, SWATPro, Video Event; **URUGUAY'S** PC World Uruguay; **VENEZUELA'S** Computerworld Venezuela, PC World; **VIETNAM'S** PC World Vietnam.
05/17/95

Acknowledgments

I always say that book writing is a prima donna sport. In football, the quarterback gets to be the prima donna; in baseball, it's the pitcher. In book writing, the author gets the glory (and all the heat as well). But in truth, all these enterprises are team sports, and it's the team — not any individual — that makes it all work.

Nonetheless, it's up to the prima donna to give credit where credit is due. So here goes. First of all, many, many thanks to everyone at IDG Books who made this book happen. You were all very supportive, very professional, and very patient. In particular, I'd like to thank Karen Bluestein, Publisher; Corbin Collins, Project Editor; Greg Croy, Acquisitions Manager; Kathy Simpson, Copy Editor; Mary Bednarek, PC Press Editorial Director; Melisa Duffy, PC Press Brand Manager; Drew Moore, Page Layout Technician; and Tyler Connor, Associate Project Coordinator. Dr. Forrest Houlette made valuable contributions in his technical review. Also thanks to Andy Cummings, Kerrie Klein, and Nate Holdread for helping out during crunch time.

Many thanks to everyone at Microsoft for helping me get an early start on this great product and for all the support and answers that you provided along the way. (By the way, whenever I get one of those cards in a Microsoft product that asks, "Want the address of the most important person at Microsoft?", I expect to open it and see the address of Tracy Van Hoof.)

To Matt Wagner and everyone at Waterside: thanks for getting this opportunity to me and making the deal happen.

And, of course, to my family: thank you, thank you, thank you for your patience and understanding. I *really* had to concentrate on this one, and I appreciate your support.

(The Publisher would like to give special thanks to Patrick J. McGovern, without whom this book would not have been possible.)

Dedication

To Susan, Ashley, and Alec, as always. Sorry this one took so long. Thanks for waiting.

Credits

Publisher
Karen A. Bluestein

Acquisitions Manager
Gregory Croy

Acquisitions Editor
Ellen C. Camm

Brand Manager
Melisa M. Duffy

Editorial Director
Mary Bednarek

Editorial Managers
Mary C. Corder
Andy Cummings

Editorial Executive Assistant
Jodi Lynn Semling

Editorial Assistant
Nate Holdread

Production Director
Beth Jenkins

**Supervisor of
Project Coordination**
Cindy L. Phipps

Supervisor of Page Layout
Kathie S. Schnorr

Pre-Press Coordinator
Steve Peake

Associate Pre-Press Coordinator
Tony Augsburger

Media/Archive Coordinator
Paul Belcastro

Project Editor
Corbin Collins

Editor
Kathy Simpson

Technical Reviewer
Forrest Houlette, Ph.D

**Associate Production
Coordinator**
J. Tyler Connor

Production Staff
Gina Scott
Carla C. Radzikinas
Patricia R. Reynolds
Melissa D. Buddendeck
Dwight Ramsey
Robert Springer
Theresa Sánchez-Baker
Kathie S. Schnorr
Chris H. Collins
Angela Hunckler
Drew R. Moore

Proofreader
Kathleen Prata

Indexer
David Heiret

Cover Design
three 8 creative group

Book Design
Drew R. Moore

Contents at a Glance

Table of Contents

Part II: Have It Your Way   97

Chapter 5: General Housekeeping (Copying, Deleting, and So On) 99

Chapter 6: Personalizing the Screen 115

Chapter 30: Using Microsoft Exchange 561

Chapter 31: Dealing with the Registry 577

Introduction

Welcome to *Windows 95 Uncut!*

A Little History

I started using Windows 95 way back in December of 1993. Like
many first-time users, I was a bit perplexed by the new interface.
Little things that were effortless in Windows 3.x suddenly were
difficult again. I was forever jumping into Help just to figure out
how to perform the simplest tasks. I was stymied by many of the
new features in Windows 95. Some features, I couldn't get to
work; some, I didn't understand; and, some I couldn't even find.

But I got hooked — big-time. I decided that I must know everything about this beast; that I must be able to use it fluently and
effortlessly; that I must learn about, and master, every feature. I
was challenged, enthralled, and consumed. Don Quixote had his
windmills; I had my Windows 95.

As the weeks and months rolled by, I did gain that mastery. I
tackled each and every feature in Windows 95 one by one and
didn't quit till everything worked. And when I say every feature, I
mean *every* feature: Briefcase, the Microsoft Network (MSN),
local-area networking, Microsoft Exchange, Microsoft Fax, Sound
Recorder, Media Player, CD Player, HyperTerminal, Phone Dialer,
DriveSpace, dial-up networking, direct cable connection,
WinPopup, PCMCIA. . .on and on. Yes, indeed, if Windows 95 can
do it, it can do it right here in my office.

Windows 95 really was something of an obsession, because I
certainly wasn't getting paid for using it, and I hadn't signed any
contract to write a "big book" on the product. In fact, I had
actually decided *not* to write a big book on Windows 95 — partly
because I couldn't figure out how I wanted to approach the subject,
and partly because I knew that several hundred other Windows
95 books probably would come out on the same day as mine.

But fate has a way of changing your mind. My literary agent called one day and said, "The author who was going to write IDG's *Windows 95 Uncut* just backed out of the deal. Would you be interested in writing the book?" I thought about it and said, "Ya know, Matt, there are a lot of little features in Windows 95 that really require some explanation. A big book on Windows 95 is going to be a *horrendous* undertaking. And Windows 95 books are going to be a dime a dozen. Sounds like a lotta work with little reward. I'll pass."

Matt, however *really* thought that I should do this book, so he worked on me. Finally, I said, "OK, I'll consider it. But here are my terms. Just because this book is big doesn't mean it's going to be one of those huge, boring manuals full of stuffy formality and infinitely boring details. I must write it in my natural speaking voice, and it must stay that way through the editorial process. I want lots of small chapters. I want each chapter to be sort of a standalone essay about one feature of Windows 95, so readers can just jump in wherever they want. I do not want to talk about any operating-system 'theory' or get into any controversy about 'just how much DOS *is* there in Windows 95?' This will be strictly a practical book, an 'empowering' book for aspiring and accomplished power users. No BS — just 'Here's what it can do, and here's how you make it do that.' And I want to stick in a CD-ROM. If you can get the publisher to agree to those terms, I'll consider it."

I guess IDG Books really needed an author in a hurry, because it did agree to those terms.

So here's the result, right here in your hands. My one and only goal in this book is to empower you — the reader — to take advantage of all the great new things that Windows 95 has to offer and to take advantage of all the amazing advances in computing and communications in general. Personal power, plain and simple.

Whom This Book Is For

I wouldn't recommend this book to an absolute beginner. You should be familiar with basic PC terminology, and you should have some hands-on experience with the mouse and keyboard. But I certainly don't expect you to have any formal training in computer science, and you certainly don't need to know anything about programming to use this book.

If words such as *keyboard* and *click* no longer shoot waves of anxiety through you, you're probably OK. If you actually like the PC and want the productive and creative power that it can give you, so much the better. If you're flat-out "wired," ambitious, and only a little scared — perfect. We'll get along just fine.

Features of This Book

Have you ever noticed that computer books have gotten to be a little like computer programs? The books are very heavy on "features": pictures that you have to read around, characters shouting and waving at you from the margins, little boxes of text here and there, maybe the occasional famous quote from some ancient scholar. I didn't do any of that in this book.

This book is pretty much just me talking on paper (as I like to call it) and showing you pictures. Most of the book is based on personal experience: those umpteen months of bringing Windows 95 to its knees and making it my personal slave. (That's probably not a great sales pitch, I realize. But it's the truth, so what the heck.)

The book does have some margin icons. So I guess I'd better explain what those are about:

 This icon signifies your basic tip: a trick, technique, or other tidbit that's worth calling special attention to, just so you don't miss it.

 When I was struggling with the "unpleasant" portion of the Windows 95 learning curve, a lot of things confused and puzzled me. Eventually, though, I'd discover something that would make me say, "Oh, now I get it." The "Puzzled?" icon is an attempt to predict where you may get that Rubik's Cube feeling and an attempt to bring you the "A-ha!" experience a little sooner.

 This icon refers to a source of additional information on a topic (just in case I didn't already tell you enough to bore you to tears).

 This icon points out a technique that you really need to think about before you act. Tread carefully, because if you make a mistake, it'll be difficult — or impossible — to undo the mistake.

 If there *is* a way to undo a mistake, fix a problem, or get out of a jam, this icon points the way.

About the CD-ROM

The CD-ROM that comes with this book is largely optional. That is to say, if you don't have a CD-ROM drive, don't worry about it. But if you *do* have a CD-ROM drive, by all means take a look. The disc has some really great programs and all kinds of fun and useful stuff. When you feel like taking the CD-ROM for a spin, refer to Appendix D.

How to Use This Book

I recommend that you start by browsing through the table of contents to get a feel for the way that topics are organized. You'll see that the book contains parts on topics such as portable computing and cyberspace, and that each part is divided into chapters that deal with a specific topic or feature, such as the Briefcase or the Internet. Feel free to read any chapter at your convenience; I don't expect you to plow through this book cover to cover.

You need to pay special attention to one part, though: Part I, which is titled "Know This or Suffer." All the stuff that you *really* need to know to get along with Windows 95 is in that part. You may have to bite the bullet and actually read through those chapters — in order — to get some grounding and some skill. Otherwise, the later parts and chapters may be a bit overwhelming.

Know This
Or Suffer

How to Do Anything in Windows 95

Hullo. In the introduction (which you may have skipped), I promised that this book will be an "empowering" book. That is, I don't want to get into the theory or design of Windows 95, don't wanna laud its merits or whine about its shortcomings. You've probably already gotten plenty of that from the trade press. I just want to give you the power to do whatever you want with Windows 95.

Also, I don't want you to feel that you have to read this entire book to use Windows 95 effectively. As I mentioned in the introduction, I'm going to put all the "need to know" stuff up here in Part I. Anything beyond Part I is optional; you can read those chapters at your leisure and ignore any chapters that aren't pertinent to your work. And like any good reference book, this one has a table of contents, glossary, and index, so you can just look up information as needed.

Now, first on the list of things that you really need to know is . . .

How to Start Windows 95

Assuming that you have installed Windows 95 on your machine, there's really nothing special you need to do to start it. Just turn on the computer, monitor, printer, and so forth, and wait. If you're on a local area network (LAN), you may be asked to supply a user name and password. Fill in the blanks with whatever information your network administrator gave you, or just press Esc to get right into Windows 95. (If you press Esc, however, you won't be able to use shared resources on the LAN.)

Installing Win 95

I'm going to start off assuming that you have (or somebody else has) already installed Windows 95 on your PC. If you haven't installed Windows 95 yet and want some help with that, see Appendix A. If you're a corporate information systems manager and need to upgrade lots of PCs on a LAN, see Chapter 32 first. That chapter discusses some of the issues concerning large-scale upgrades to Windows 95.

When Windows 95 is ready to roll, your screen will look something like Figure 1-1, which also points out the names of various desktop doodads.

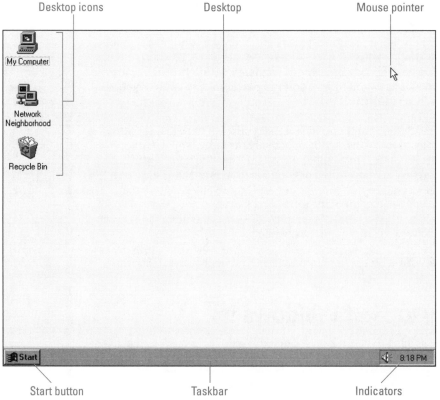

Figure 1-1: The Windows 95 desktop.

When you first get to the desktop, you may see a big *Welcome to Windows 95* window. I'll talk about that window a little later in this chapter. For now, if you're looking at the Welcome window, you can just click on its Close button to make your screen look more like Figure 1-1. The following sections provide a quick overview of what's on the screen to get you started using Windows 95.

Desktop

The desktop is the large blank area that acts sort of like your real (wooden or metal) desktop; it's always there, and it's where you put whatever you're working on at the moment.

 You can right-click on the desktop to display a shortcut menu of commands for rearranging and customizing the desktop.

Mouse pointer

The mouse pointer moves when you move the mouse. To *point to* something on the screen, you move the mouse until the mouse pointer is touching the thing to which you want to point. To *click on* something, you point to that thing and then press and release the main (usually, left) mouse button. To *double-click* on something, point to it and then press and release the main mouse button twice, as fast as you can (click-click!). To *right-click on* something, point to it and then press and release the secondary mouse button (usually, the button on the right side of the mouse).

Desktop icons

You may see a few desktop icons displayed down the left side of the desktop. You can double-click on any one of those icons to open it into a window or right-click on any icon to see what other options are available. After you open an icon into a window, you can click on the X in the upper-right corner of that window to close the window. The desktop icon for that window remains on the desktop.

Taming the mouse

In this book, I'm assuming that you already know how to work a mouse. If you have any problems with the mouse, see Chapter 7, where you'll learn how to control the tracking speed of the mouse, the double-click speed, and so on. If you're a lefty, you can use techniques discussed in that chapter to reverse the mouse buttons so that the main mouse button is below your index finger.

Start button

The Start button is the way that you'll probably start 99 percent of the things you do
in Windows 95. You can click on the Start button to display the Start menu; then you
can point to any option that has a right-pointing triangle next to it to see a submenu. If
an option does not have the right-pointing triangle next to it, then you have to click
(once) on the option to select it.

 You can customize the Start menu and taskbar in many ways, as you'll
learn in Chapter 8.

Taskbar

Although it appears empty in Figure 1-1, the taskbar eventually will contain a button
and icon for every open window on your desktop. If you want to get to a window that's
currently not visible on the desktop (because it's minimized or covered by other
windows), you can click on the appropriate button in the taskbar. You can right-click
on the taskbar to customize it, and you can drag the taskbar to any edge of the screen.

Indicators

The right edge of the taskbar displays the current time and indicators that will change
periodically, depending on what you're doing at the moment. You can double-click on
the current-time display to change the date and time. Typically, you also can click on
any other small icon that appears near the clock to do something with the hardware
that the icon represents. If I click on the little speaker icon, for example, I get the
volume control for my speakers, as shown in Figure 1-2.

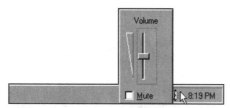

Figure 1-2: Volume control appears when
you click on the Speaker indicator.

Starting Programs

The first thing that most people want to do when they get to an operating system is
launch some other program. I'll discuss how you do that right off the bat. Follow
these steps:

1. Click on the Start button and then point to <u>P</u>rograms.

   A menu of program groups and icons appears, as shown in Figure 1-3. Notice that if you installed Windows 95 over an earlier version of Windows, just about every option in that menu actually is a program group from your old Program Manager.

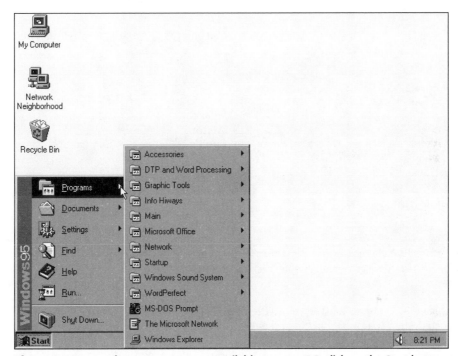

Figure 1-3: To see the program groups available on your PC, click on the Start button and then point to <u>P</u>rograms.

2. To start a program, click on its icon or point to its folder.

For example, suppose you have Microsoft Office (which includes Microsoft Word) on your PC. To start Microsoft Word you would point to (or click on) the Microsoft Office folder and then click on the Microsoft Word icon, as shown in Figure 1-4.

If a right-pointing triangle appears next to a menu item, you really don't have to click on that item to see what's next (although you can if you want to); all you have to do is point to it. If an option *doesn't* have that little triangle next to it, pointing to the item does nothing, and you have to click on the item to open it.

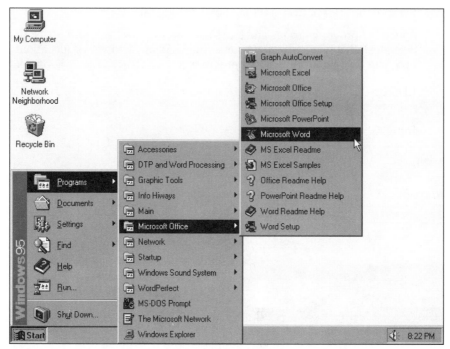

Figure 1-4: Start Microsoft Word by clicking on its icon.

This method seems a little weird when you're getting started, especially if you're accustomed to double-clicking on everything to get to a program, as in Windows 3.x. Also, you'll feel like a mouse klutz for a while, because you have to kind of glide from one menu to another without taking the mouse off the menus for any length of time. Trust me, though, you'll get used to it.

 You can start programs and open documents in Windows 95 in many ways, as I'll discuss in Chapter 3. Using the Start button is just one of many approaches.

I should point out that starting a program and then choosing File⇨Open from its menu bar to open an existing document is somewhat dated now. In Windows 95, a much quicker way to open a recently saved document is to click on the Start button, point to Documents, and then click on the name of the document that you want to open. Or just double-click on the name of the document you want to open.

Closing Programs

When you want to close a program, you use whichever of these three techniques is handiest:

✦ Click on the Close button (X) in the upper-right corner of the window that you want to close.

✦ Double-click on the icon in the upper-left corner of the window that you want to close.

✦ Click on File in the program's menu bar and then click on Exit.

Your options are illustrated in Figure 1-5, which uses Microsoft Word as the example program.

To close a program . . .

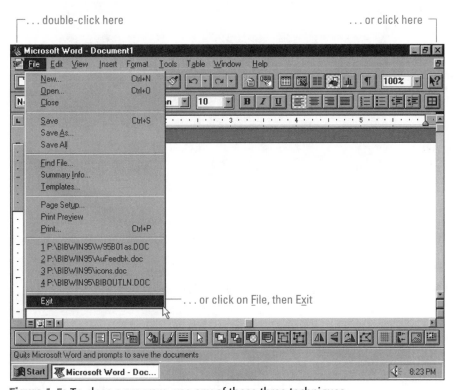

Figure 1-5: To close a program, use any of these three techniques.

Fleeing to DOS

If you're an ex-DOS user, you may feel a little anxiety about being in this new environment. Not to fear though, because you can easily get to the Windows 95 command-line mode, which, for all intents and purposes, is identical to DOS. Follow these steps:

1. Click on the Start button and then point to Programs to display the Programs menu.

2. Click on the MS-DOS Prompt icon (near the bottom of the menu).

   You go to a DOS-like screen, as shown in Figure 1-6.

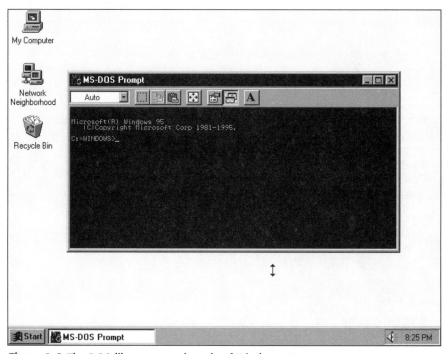

Figure 1-6: The DOS-like command mode of Windows 95.

You can enter any DOS command with which you're familiar and then press Enter, just as you do in "real" DOS.

If you enter the DOS VER command at the C prompt, you'll see that you're not really in DOS after all. (In case you're not near a PC, I'll just tell you what the screen says; it says *Windows 95* where it used to say *MS-DOS*.)

Fleeing from DOS

The little DOS window is pretty much like any other window. If you run a program within the DOS window, however, you typically have to exit that program before you can close the DOS window. Instructions on the screen will tell you if this is the case. Other than that, to close the DOS window, you can do any of the following things:

✦ Click on the Close (X) button in the upper-right corner of the DOS window.

✦ Double-click on the icon in the upper-left corner of the DOS window.

✦ Type **exit** and press Enter at the C:\ prompt.

If you're not already familiar with DOS, you needn't worry; you don't have to know *anything* about DOS to use Windows 95. I included this section only because I know that experienced DOS users probably will want switch to DOS occasionally to do things that they haven't figured out how to do in Windows 95. For example, you might want to use the DOS COPY command to copy some files, or DIR to look for a file.

Take the Guided Tour

A great starting point for getting the hang of Windows 95 is the built-in guided tour. It's only available if you installed Windows 95 from a CD. So if you did, follow these steps to start the tour:

1. If you didn't close the Welcome window described at the start of this chapter, skip to step 3 now.

2. To reopen the Welcome window, click on the Start button, click on Run, type **welcome**, and then click on OK.

3. In the Welcome window (see Figure 1-7), click on the Windows Tour button, and then just follow the instructions on the screen.

 If you have Windows 95 on CD, but your Welcome window doesn't have a Windows Tour button, that component isn't installed on your hard disk. To install it, first close the Welcome window and then see the instructions in "Installing Missing Windows Components" in Chapter 10.

While you're in the Windows tour, be sure to take the Using Help tour. The help system in Windows 95 is *vastly* improved from Windows 3.1. So you'll want to learn how to use the online help as soon as possible. For more information, see "How to Do Anything" a little later in this chapter.

Figure 1-7: The guided tour.

If you're an experienced Windows 3.1 user, you'll probably want to explore the online What's New documentation to ease the transition to Windows 95. To see what's new, follow these steps:

1. If the Welcome window isn't visible on your screen at the moment, click on the Start button, click on Run, type **welcome**, and then click on OK.

2. Click on What's New.

   You see a window titled Windows Help (shown in Figure 1-8) that presents frequently asked questions for experienced Windows users.

3. Follow the instructions on the screen.

This online document is presented in question-and-answer format. Click on any question to view the answer. When you're done, you can click on the Close button (X) in the upper-right corner of the Windows Help window.

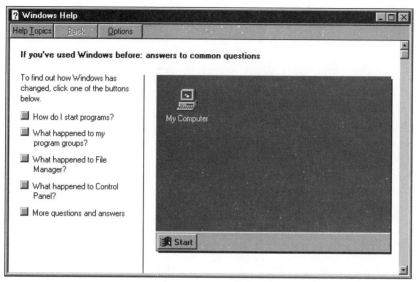

Figure 1-8: If you click on What's New in the Welcome window, you see this window.

How to Do Anything

The Windows tour and What's New online document definitely will help you get your feet wet in Windows 95. But the tours can do only so much. Many new questions surely will arise in your day-to-day use of Windows 95. Obviously, the main purpose of this book is to answer all those questions. But before you become totally reliant on this book (or any other book), you really should master the online help and documentation. These features are much, much better than anything I've seen before and usually are the quickest and easiest way to learn how to do something — even troubleshoot a problem.

I'm not harping on the online help just because it's the hip thing to do these days. The fact of the matter is that I became a Windows 95 "expert" *without any written documentation whatsoever.* From the time I received my first copy of the prerelease version of Windows 95 (in December 1993) until I wrote this chapter (15 months later), I was given barely one stitch of printed documentation. Yet I consider myself to be an expert for the simple reason that I can make Windows 95 do whatever I want it to do, whenever I feel like it. (I assume that making something do whatever you want defines *expertise,* no?)

Now you may be wondering whether you wasted your money buying this book. After all, if I mastered the system without printed documentation, can't you? The answer to that question is "It depends." One of the advantages of going through the online documentation is that I know Windows 95's strengths and weaknesses. I know where more depth would be helpful, what topics are not discussed in detail, and so on. So by writing this book, I can help fill in lots of gaps. Also, other people's experience is always a good thing when you're learning something new. Much of my goal in writing this book is to empower those of you who have less experience than I do by handing you my experience on a silver platter (that is, in a format that I hope you can understand, even if you're not already a hard-core computer whiz).

Anyway, the point is, *don't skimp on learning to use the Windows 95 built-in help and documentation.* Take some time to read the rest of this chapter so that you can learn how to get answers and solve problems quickly.

The following sections show you all the different ways to get help and information right on your screen. You'll start with a quick, simple method and work your way to techniques that require digging.

Instant help

You can use any of the following techniques to get brief but immediate help with just about anything that you see on your screen at the moment:

✦ To get help with a command button, point to it. A tooltip usually appears (see Figure 1-9).

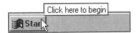

Figure 1-9: Tooltips pop up when you rest the mouse pointer on a button.

✦ To see what options a particular button or icon offers, try right-clicking on that button or icon. You may see a menu of options, as shown in Figure 1-10.

✦ If you're already in a dialog box or window, you typically can press F1 for help. Alternatively, if you see the little Question-mark button in the upper-right corner of the current window, click on that button and then click on whatever item you have a question about.

When you use the last method, a brief help window pops up, as shown in Figure 1-11. After reading the window's contents, click anywhere in that window to remove it from your screen.

In case you're wondering, I double-clicked on the time indicator near the lower-right corner of the screen to get to the dialog box shown in Figure 1-11.

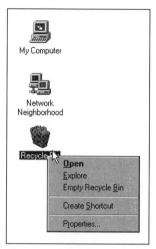

Figure 1-10: Right-clicking
on a button or icon may
display a pop-up menu.

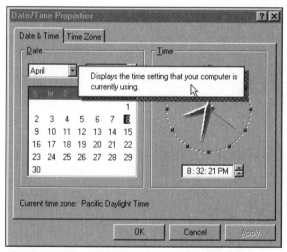

Figure 1-11: To get help, you can press F1 or click
on the ? button and then click on an object.

Your electronic table of contents

For general information or background on a particular topic, try using the table of contents for the online help system. Follow these steps:

1. Click on the Start button, click on Help, and then click on the Contents tab.

2. Open any book by double-clicking on the book, or by clicking on the book once then clicking the Open button.

3. To explore a topic (indicated by a page with a question mark on it), double-click on the topic, or click on it and then click on the Display button (see Figure 1-12).

 When an unopened book is highlighted, the left button at the bottom of the Help Topics menu is labeled Open. When a topic within a book is highlighted, that leftmost button is labeled Display.

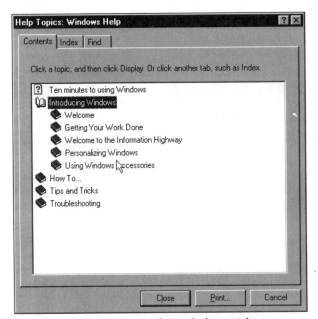

Figure 1-12: The Contents tab in Windows Help.

The table-of-contents technique is most useful when you want to explore a large subject area, such as "How to Use a Network" or "Tips and Tricks for Running Programs." If you want to search for a more specific topic, use the electronic index, as described in the following section.

Your electronic index

The online help system's electronic index is basically the same as the index in the back of a printed book. To use it, click on the Start button, choose Help, and then click the Index tab. Type the word or phrase you want to look up. Then, in the list box, click on the index entry that you want (see Figure 1-13).

You're taken to the help entry for that particular topic, as in the example shown in Figure 1-14.

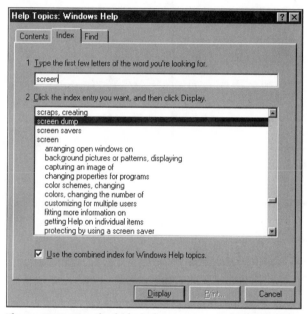

Figure 1-13: Use the help index as you would the index in the back of a printed book.

When you arrive at the help window for a particular topic, you can do any of the following things:

✦ If the help window has a Click Here button, you can click on it to go straight to the appropriate dialog box or folder. (This feature of Windows 95 *alone* justifies making the change from Windows 3.x.)

✦ If the window has a Related Topics button, you can click on that button for information on related topics.

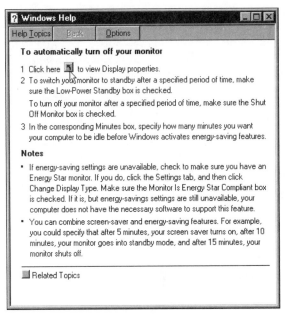

Figure 1-14: A help topic displayed on the screen.

✦ You can click on Help Topics to return to the electronic index (or wherever you came from)

• Or click on Back to move back to the preceding help topic (if any).

• Or click on Options to choose among a variety of options, including keeping the help window on top of other windows.

• When you want to close the help window, click on its Close button (X).

Searching for a word or phrase

When you're in the help window, you may notice that in addition to the Contents and Index tabs, the window has a tab called Find. When you use it, the Find tab may seem to be almost identical to the Index tab, but there are some differences.

For one thing, the Index tab takes you to a professionally prepared index that contains topics (words) that the person who created the Index felt were appropriate for the index. (As I mentioned earlier, the index in Windows Help is virtually identical to the index in the back of a book.) The Find tab, however, takes you to a computer-prepared index, which lists every word that appears in the online document — even words such as *a* and *the*. In short, Find provides a much broader search of the material than Index does.

The word list that Find uses generally is not shipped with a product. Instead, the first time you use a help file, the Find word list is created automatically. During that phase, a little book animation appears on the screen. (In some cases, you may first see a Wizard window. Don't worry about it; just follow the instructions on the screen.)

Another difference is that the Find tab uses a three-step process, rather than a two-step process. In the step 1 section of the tab, you type a word. In the step 2 section, you click on any word to narrow your search, if you like. You also can Ctrl+click (hold down the Ctrl key while clicking the mouse) on several words or phrases to narrow your search. A list appears in the step 3 section of the tab, displaying all related topics.

When you see the topic that you want, you can double-click on the topic to open it immediately. Alternatively, you can click on several topics and then click on the Display button to explore all the checked topics (see Figure 1-15).

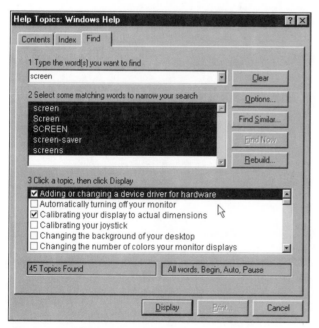

Figure 1-15: The Find tab searches every word in the online help system.

You can customize the way that Find does its thing, if you're so inclined. For example, after you click the Find tab in a help window:

✦ You can click on the <u>O</u>ptions button to specify how Find treats multiple search words and when it performs its search (see Figure 1-16).

✦ After you click on a topic in the step 3 section of the Find tab, you can click on the Find Similar button to review topics that are related to the checked topic(s).

✦ You can click on the Rebuild button to rebuild the word list that Find uses.

The bottom line here is this: if Index doesn't seem to come up with the word or phrase you're looking for, try using Find instead.

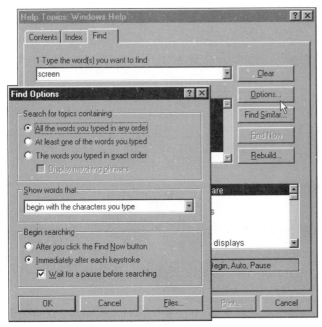

Figure 1-16: The Find Options dialog box.

Instant Troubleshooting

One of the best new features of Windows 95 is its Troubleshooting help feature. I can't even count how many times this feature solved problems for me in the early days of beta testing Windows 95 without written documentation. I *can* tell you with confidence that any time something doesn't work as expected in Windows 95, the first place you should look for a solution is the help system's Troubleshooting feature. Follow these steps:

1. Click on the Start button and then click on <u>H</u>elp.

2. Click on the Contents tab and then double-click on the Troubleshooting book.

    The book opens, as shown in Figure 1-17.

3. Double-click on whichever document is appropriate to your problem.

4. Follow the instructions on the screen.

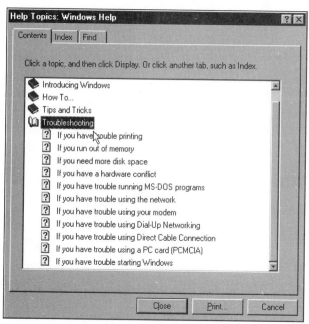

Figure 1-17: Topics in the Troubleshooting book.

Shutting Down Your PC

If you are an ex-Windows 3.1 user, you're probably accustomed to exiting Windows and returning to the DOS command prompt to ensure that all your work is saved before you turn off your PC. In Windows 95, you have no DOS to exit to — but that fact doesn't mean that you can just turn off your PC whenever you feel like it.

To ensure that all your work is saved and no files are corrupted, you should always shut down Windows 95 before you turn off your computer. Follow these steps:

1. Click on the Start button and then click on Shut Down.

   You see the little dialog box shown in Figure 1-18.

2. Click on the first option (if it isn't already selected) and then click on Yes.

3. Respond to any and all prompts that appear on the screen.

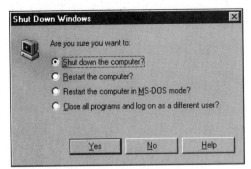

Figure 1-18: Shutting down.

Don't turn off your computer until the screen tells you that it's safe to do so.

Summary

In this chapter you've learned about the following important basic skills:

✦ To start Windows 95, just start your computer.

✦ To get started doing anything in Windows 95, click on the Start button.

✦ To run a program, click the Start button, point to Programs, then choose a program name or program group from the menu that appears.

✦ To exit a program, click the close (X) button in the upper right corner of its window.

✦ The quickest way to get help in Windows 95 is through the built-in help system. And there are several ways to use the help system:

For instant help with whatever you're doing at the moment, press the Help key (F1).

In some windows and dialog boxes, you can click the ? button near the upper-right corner of the window, then just click the item you need help with.

From the desktop, you can click the Start button and then click on Help. In the help window that appears you can choose the Contents (like a Table of Contents), Index (like a book index) or Find (an electronic "super-index") tab to look up the information you need.

✦ You should always exit Windows 95 before you shut down your PC. Just click the Start button, choose Shut Down, then click the Yes button.

✦   ✦   ✦

Getting Around

The guided tours described in the preceding chapter give you a little hands-on practice in the mechanics of managing objects on your screen. In this chapter, I'll review some of those mechanics. But I want to go into more depth, showing you all the many tricks that you can use in managing objects on the desktop. In addition, I want to show you how to actually find things on the computer.

I realize that I've already told you that I assume you have *some* experience with PCs. Therefore, you may feel that much of the material covered here is stuff you already know. Many people, though, have little holes in their knowledge and understanding of these basic concepts; I want to review them all so that I know we're on the same track and using similar terminology.

Understanding Icons

Imagine, for a moment, a desk with all the usual accouterments: telephone, calculator, calendar, pens and pencils, documents that you're using. Now imagine that you have the power to touch any of those objects and shrink it to the size of a pea, just to get it out of the way for the moment. That power would certainly help unclutter your desktop. When you needed to use one of those pea-size objects, you could just tap it with your finger, and bingo — it would open in its natural size.

Of course, no real-world desktop works that way. The *virtual desktop* that is Windows 95, on the other hand, works exactly that way. You can make things appear and disappear just by touching them with your mouse pointer.

A pea-size object on your computer screen is called an *icon*. Initially, you'll see at least two icons on your Windows 95 desktop: one named *My Computer* and another named *Recycle Bin*. As you start opening icons into windows, you'll see that many icons contain still other icons (see Figure 2-1).

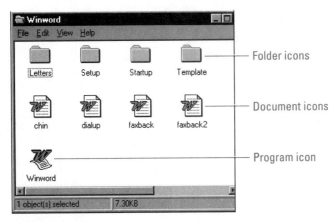

Figure 2-1: Some examples of icons in Windows 95.

The appearance of an icon gives you some clue as to what kind of stuff is inside the icon and, hence, to what will likely appear when you double-click on the icon. The following list summarizes the main types of icons that you'll come across:

✦ *Folder icon:* contains its own set of icons. When you open a folder icon, you see more icons.

✦ *Program icon:* represents a program. When you open a program icon, you start the program that it represents. Double-clicking on the Winword icon in Figure 2-1, for example, would start the Microsoft Word for Windows program.

✦ *Document icon:* represents a document, which typically is something that you can print. The icon typically has a little dog-ear fold in the upper-right corner to resemble a paper document. Opening a document icon typically launches whatever program is required to view/change/print that document, as well as the document itself.

You'll also come across icons that don't fall into any of these categories. Some icons represent disk drives, printers, help files, settings, and so on. But you can manipulate virtually all icons by using the set of basic skills in the following list:

✦ To open an icon, double-click on it. The icon's contents appear in a *window* (discussed in the following section).

✦ To move an icon, drag it to any new location on the screen.

✦ To see all the options available for an icon, right-click on the icon to see its shortcut menu.

✦ To arrange and organize all the icons on your desktop, right-click on the desktop and then choose Arrange Icons or Line Up Icons from the shortcut menu that appears.

Managing Windows

When you click on an icon, it opens into a *window.* You really need to know how to work with those windows to accomplish things. This section discusses what a window really is and what you can do with all windows.

In the olden days of computers, you would run a program, and that program would take over the entire screen. To use a different program, you had to exit the one you were in and then start the other program. That program in turn hogged the entire screen.

The days of running one program at a time ended when Windows was created. With Windows, you can run as many programs as you want (well, as many programs as you can fit into your PC's RAM). Rather than hogging the entire screen, each program occupies only a window on-screen. In Figure 2-2, for example, two programs are running and visible on the screen: Paint (a drawing program) and WordPad (a simple word processor that comes with Windows 95). Each program appears in its own window.

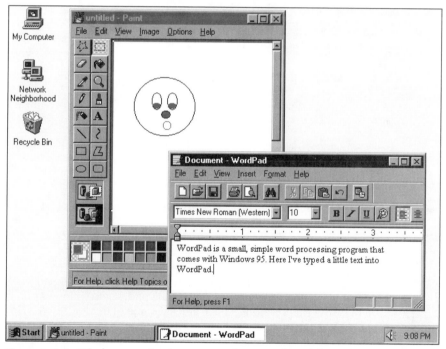

Figure 2-2: In Windows, each program occupies a portion of the screen called a *window.*

Window dressing

Notice that each window in Figure 2-2 has its own unique contents. If you look closely, however, you may notice that the frames surrounding those windows are very similar. The reason for this similarity is simple: all the tools that you use to manage the window are in that frame. This arrangement means that no matter how perplexed you may be by the contents of a window, you can always use the tools on the window's border to manipulate the window. Figure 2-3 shows the tools that frame most windows.

Figure 2-3: Every window has these important tools around its border.

 Not every window has exactly the same set of tools. Some small windows can't be sized and therefore have no sizing pad; some windows don't have toolbars. But most windows have at least some of the tools shown in Figure 2-3.

The following sections describe how you work with each tool.

Title bar

The *title bar* shows the icon and name of the stuff that's inside the window. You can double-click on the title bar to expand the window to full-screen size and to shrink the window back to its previous size. More important, you can move a window anyplace on the screen by dragging its title bar.

Minimize button

When you click on the *Minimize button*, the window shrinks to just a button in the taskbar. To reopen the window, you just need to click on that taskbar button.

Maximize button

Clicking on the *Maximize button* expands the window to full-screen size (a quick way to hide other windows that may be distracting you). When the window is full-screen size, the Maximize button turns into the Restore button. To return the window to its previous size, just click on that Restore button (between the Minimize and Close buttons.)

Close button

Clicking on the *Close button* closes the window, taking it off the screen and out of the taskbar as well. You'll learn more about closing windows in Chapter 3.

 When you open a series of windows, you can close the last window and all the windows that led up to it in one fell swoop. Just hold down the Shift key and then click on the Close (X) button on the last window you opened.

Border and sizing pad

The frame, or *border*, that surrounds a window is a very important tool. You size the window by dragging its border. Many windows have a large *sizing pad* in the lower-right corner; this pad is especially easy to drag.

 To size and arrange all the open windows instantly so that you can see their title bars, right-click on the taskbar between any buttons and away from any indicators. Then click on Cascade in the menu that appears. To bring any open window to the forefront instantly, click on its taskbar button.

Menu bar

Many windows have a *menu bar* just below the title bar. That menu bar gives you access to commands that affect only those things that are inside the current window. The View menu is especially important, because it lets you to arrange the contents of the window in whatever format is most convenient for you at the moment.

 When I'm discussing a series of menu selections, I'll often use the symbol ⇨ to separate menu selections. For example, the phrase "choose View⇨Toolbar" is just an efficient way of saying "Choose Toolbar from the View menu."

Toolbar

Some windows also have a *toolbar* just below the menu bar. The toolbar provides one-click access to the most frequently used menu commands. Sometimes, the menu bar is available but turned off. To display the toolbar, choose View ⇨ Toolbar (see Figure 2-4).

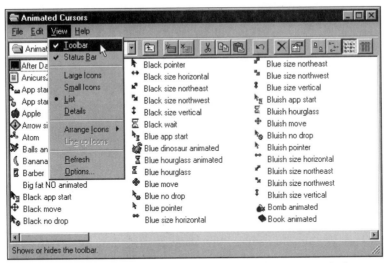

Figure 2-4: The View menu and toolbar are available in many windows.

Status bar

The *status bar* along the bottom of a window shows you the status of various things inside the window. You'll see some examples as you go along in this book. For now, be aware that in many windows, you can hide or display the status bar by choosing View⇨Status Bar.

System menu

The *System menu* lets you move, size, and close the window by using the keyboard rather than the mouse. To open the System menu, click on the icon in the upper-left corner of the window. Or press Alt+spacebar. You also can double-click the System menu icon to close the window.

Scrollbars

If there's more stuff inside a window than can fit into that window, *scrollbars* appear to allow you to move around inside the window. You can use the arrow keys and PgUp and PgDn to move around, or you can use the mouse techniques shown in Figure 2-5.

Top 10 tips for managing windows

If all the various gizmos on the window's border have your mind reeling, perhaps it would be easier to think from the standpoint of what you actually want to do with the windows that are open on your desktop. Following, in a nutshell, are the main things that you need to know how to do:

✦ To open a window, double-click on its icon.

✦ To hide an open window temporarily (to unclutter your desktop a bit), click on the window's Minimize button.

✦ To view an open window that's currently covered by other windows or is minimized, click on that window's taskbar button.

✦ To move a window, drag it by its title bar to some new location on-screen.

✦ To size a window, drag its lower-right corner or any border.

✦ To enlarge a window to full-screen size, so that it completely covers any other windows, double-click on its title bar or click on its Maximize button.

✦ To restore a maximized window to its previous size, double-click on its title bar or click on its Restore button.

✦ To arrange all open windows in a stack with their title bars showing, right-click on any "neutral" area (the space between, above, or below buttons) on the taskbar. Then choose Cascade from the pop-up menu.

✦ To close a window, click the Close button (X) in the upper-right corner of the window.

✦ To reopen a closed window, you need to repeat whatever steps you took to open it the first time, because closing a window also removes its little button from the taskbar.

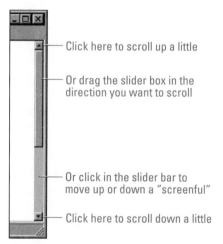

Click here to scroll up a little

Or drag the slider box in the direction you want to scroll

Or click in the slider bar to move up or down a "screenful"

Click here to scroll down a little

Figure 2-5: How to work scrollbars.

Closing versus minimizing a window

Think of minimizing a window as taking some document that's on a real desktop and sliding it into a desk drawer. The document is not cluttering your desk anymore but is within easy reach. Closing a window, on the other hand, is more like putting a real folder back in the file cabinet. You can still get back to the document when you want it, but the process is a little more of a hassle than yanking it out of the desk drawer.

From a technical standpoint, closing a window has two advantages: it frees the memory (RAM) that the program was using, and it gives you an opportunity to save your work. Minimizing a window does neither of those things; it just shrinks the window to a taskbar button to get it out of the way for the moment.

Using the Taskbar

The taskbar at the bottom of the screen contains a button for each open window on the desktop. Figure 2-6 shows an example.

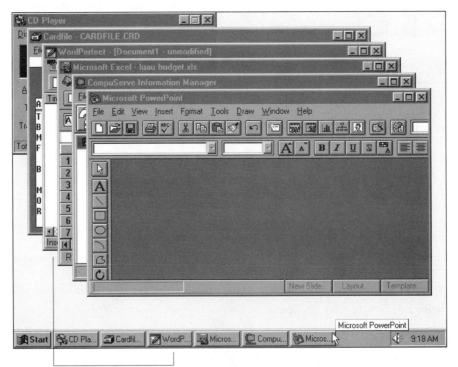

Each open window above has a taskbar button below.

Figure 2-6: The taskbar, showing a button for each open window.

At first, it may seem stupid to show buttons for only *open* windows. If a window is already open, why do you also need to see a button for it? The answer to that question is this: the mere fact that a window is open is no guarantee that you can *see* that window. Windows can (and often do) overlap or completely cover one another. The beauty of the taskbar is that you can bring any open window out of hiding simply by clicking its taskbar button.

You can do many cool things with the taskbar, as summarized in the following list:

✦ To bring an open window to the forefront, click on its taskbar button.

✦ To see the options for a particular window, right-click on its taskbar button.

✦ To arrange all the open windows on the desktop, right-click on the taskbar and then choose Cascade, Tile Horizontally, or Tile Vertically. Feel free to experiment with these options whenever you have two or more open windows on the desktop, to see for yourself how each option arranges the windows.

✦ To see what a taskbar button represents, point to the button and wait for the tooltip to appear. Pointing to the Micros button in Figure 2-6, for example, shows that the button is actually for Microsoft PowerPoint.

Notice that the icon in each taskbar button (CD Pla..., Cardfil..., WordP..., and so on) matches the corresponding icon in the upper left corner of each open window (CD Player, Cardfile, WordPerfect, and so on).

✦ To minimize (or unminimize) all open windows, right-click on the taskbar and then choose Minimize All Windows or Undo Minimize All.

Chapter 8 presents tips and tricks for personalizing the taskbar.

✦ To move the taskbar to some other edge of the screen, drag it to that edge.

✦ To size the taskbar (make it thinner or thicker), drag its inner edge (the edge nearest the center of the screen).

How Stuff Is Organized

Everything that I've talked about so far is vitally important to using Windows 95, because you need to be able to manipulate the various objects on your screen to get anything done. In the real world, managing windows and icons on-screen is as important as managing papers and other objects on your real desktop.

A big difference between your real desktop and your virtual Windows 95 desktop, however, is where you get the stuff that you put on the desktop. In a real-world desktop, most of the documents that you work with are probably stored in a file cabinet. On a computer, all the objects that you can bring to the desktop are stored on a computer disk.

In a real-world file cabinet, you go through the following steps to fetch whatever it is that you're looking for:

1. Go to the appropriate file cabinet.
2. Open the appropriate drawer.
3. Pull out the appropriate file.

On a computer, you do this instead:

1. Go to the appropriate disk drive.
2. Open the appropriate folder(s).
3. Double-click on the appropriate file icon.

You're probably somewhat familiar with these terms from earlier computer experience. To play it safe, though, the following sections define those terms.

Drive

Anything that's in the computer is actually stored on a disk. The disk spins around like a CD in a CD player so that the computer can read and write stuff to the disk. The device that actually spins the disk around is called a *disk drive* (or *drive* for short).

A disk drive generally has a one-letter name. Your floppy-disk drive, for example, is named A; you may have a second floppy-disk drive named B. In general, you use the floppy-disk drives to copy files to and from the hard disk inside your computer, to make backups, or to copy stuff from one PC to another.

Most of the stuff that's in the computer is actually stored on your *hard disk drive,* which usually is named C. Unlike floppy disks, you never actually see the hard disk, because it's hermetically sealed in an airtight compartment within the PC. Typically, a hard disk can hold as much information as hundreds (or even thousands) of floppy disks.

You may have some other drives attached to your computer. If you have a CD-ROM drive, it may be named D.

To see what drives are available on your computer, double-click the My Computer icon on the desktop. When the My Computer window opens, you see an icon for each drive (and perhaps a couple of folders that represent other hardware on your computer). In Figure 2-7, for example, you can see that my computer has a $3^1/_2$-inch floppy drive named A, a $5^1/_2$-inch floppy drive named B, a hard disk named C, and a CD-ROM drive named D.

Figure 2-7: This computer has two
floppy drives (A and B), a hard disk (C),
and a CD-ROM drive (D).

You may notice that my hard disk, C, also has another name: Compaq_hdd.
That name is the disk's electronic *label*. You can create or change your
own hard disk's label, if you like, to any name of 11 characters or fewer,
with no spaces. Right-click on the drive's icon in the My Computer window.
Choose Properties, and fill in the option titled Label. Then choose OK.

Folder

A hard disk or CD-ROM can contain hundreds, even thousands, of files. If you were to
put all those files on the disk without organizing them, finding things later could be
difficult. The process would be sort of like taking all the files out of your file cabinet
and dumping them into a great big box.

Many folders are created automatically when you install new programs. If I were to
double-click on the icon for drive C shown in Figure 2-7, a new window would open,
showing me the names of the folders (and files, if any) on that drive, as shown in
Figure 2-8.

One thing that makes a folder different from a drive or a file is that a folder can
contain other folders. For example, I could have a folder named All My Stuff. Within
that folder, I could have other folders: My Documents, which contains written documents; My Pictures, which contains photos and drawings; and My Clips, which
contains sound clips, video clips, and so on.

In case you're wondering, a *folder* is what we used to call a *directory* or
subdirectory in DOS and Windows 3.x.

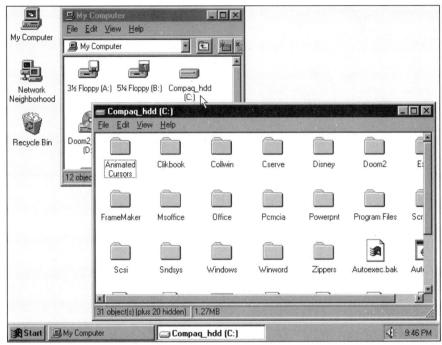

Figure 2-8: Opening a drive icon displays the names of folders and/or files on the disk in that drive.

I'll talk about how you create, manage, and delete folders in Chapter 8. For now, it's sufficient to be aware that a folder can contain many files and also other folders.

Why your screen doesn't look like mine

If you followed along with this section by double-clicking on My Computer and other icons on your own PC, your screen probably won't match mine exactly. That's because every PC starts out as sort of a big, empty electronic file cabinet. You fill that file cabinet by adding whatever folders and files are appropriate to your own work.

One way to create files is to create and save documents, as discussed in Chapter 3. You also can create folders and files by using menu commands, as discussed in Chapters 4 and 5. Also, when you install a new program, the installation procedure automatically creates folders and files for storing that particular program, as discussed in Chapter 9.

Files

A *file* is most like the contents of a manila file folder in a desk drawer. Each item that's in the computer is in its own file. Suppose that you use a word processing program to type a letter. When you save that letter, it's saved in a file.

Programs are also stored in files. When you installed Windows 95, it created a folder named Windows. Within that folder are all the files (and perhaps some folders) that make up the Windows 95 program.

As mentioned earlier, a file's icon gives you some clue about the type of information that's in the file. Program files have icons that represent those programs. Document icons look like dog-eared sheets of paper (refer to Figure 2-1).

Browsing with My Computer

You can find stuff that's in the computer in three main ways: you can use My Computer or Windows Explorer to browse around to see what's available, or (if you happen to know the exact name of the file or folder you want) you can use the Find command on the Start menu to go right to that folder or file. I'll discuss browsing with My Computer first, only because I've already touched on that method.

My Computer is a tool that lets you to browse all the disks that are physically attached to your computer. To start My Computer, double-click on its icon, which opens into a window. In the example shown in Figure 2-7, this window contains icons for two floppy-disk drives (A and B), a hard disk (C), and a CD-ROM drive (D).

Any network drives to which you have mapped a drive letter also appear in My Computer; you can treat them just like drives that are physically attached to your computer. I know, however, that many of you are using standalone PCs, so I won't confuse matters by discussing network drives just now. Part VII of this book discusses local area networks in depth.

Working My Computer is easy. To start My Computer, double-click on its icon. Then you can do any of the following things:

✦ To see what's on the disk in a particular drive, double-click on that drive's icon.

✦ To see what's in a folder, double-click on that folder.

✦ To see what's in a file, double-click on that file's icon.

✦ To back up (close anything that you've opened), click the Close button in the upper-right corner of the window that you want to close.

Changing your view in My Computer

When you first open a window in My Computer, the contents usually are displayed in Large Icons view. You can decide for yourself how you want the contents to be displayed. Your choices — Large Icons, Small Icons, List, and Details — are depicted in Figure 2-9. Notice that the mouse pointer in each example is pointing to the button that I clicked on to select that particular view.

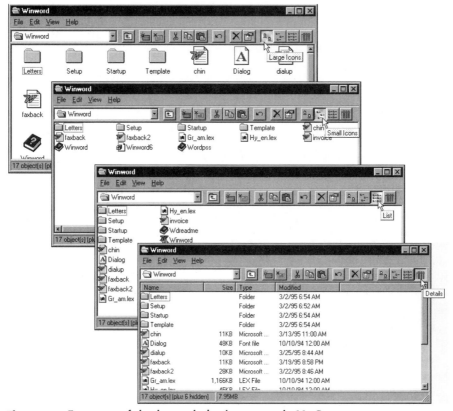

Figure 2-9: Four ways of viewing a window's contents in My Computer.

Keep in mind that each example in Figure 2-9 shows exactly the same files. The size and arrangement of the icons and filenames, as well as the amount of detail displayed about each file, are the only things that vary.

To choose a view, click on <u>V</u>iew in the window's menu bar and then choose Large Icons, <u>S</u>mall Icons, <u>L</u>ist, or <u>D</u>etails, as appropriate. Alternatively, click on the appropriate button in the toolbar. If you can't see the toolbar, first choose <u>V</u>iew➪<u>T</u>oolbar.

Figure 2-10 shows the View menu open.

Figure 2-10: The View menu in a
My Computer window.

Arranging My Computer contents

In addition to deciding the size of the icons in a My Computer window, you can
choose the order in which you want to see those items. The normal order is to list all
the folders (if any) within the current folder in alphabetical order, followed by all the
files (if any) within the current window, also in alphabetical order (see Figure 2-11).

Figure 2-11: By default, folders
and files are listed in alphabetical
order in a My Computer window.

To change the order, follow these steps:

1. Choose View⇨Arrange Icons.
2. Click on one of the following options:
   - by Name: presents folders and files in alphabetical order by name (the usual method).
   - by Type: organizes the folders by type.
   - by Size: organizes everything by size (smallest to largest).
   - by Date: organizes files by date last modified, with most recently modified files listed first. (This option is handy when you're looking for a file that you created recently but can't quite remember the name of.)

Details view (the one that shows all the file details) offers a shortcut for rearranging the icons within the window. Click on the column heading to sort everything by that column; click on the heading a second time to reverse the sort order in that column. If you click the Modified column heading, for example, the icons are instantly arranged in ascending date (newest to oldest). Clicking on Modified a second time reverses the sort order (oldest to newest).

Here's another little trick that pertains only to Details view: you can widen or narrow the columns. Point to the line that separates two column heads until the mouse pointer turns into a two-headed arrow; then drag the column line to the left or right.

Navigating in My Computer

If you think about it, you'll realize that what My Computer really does is let you drill down to more specific areas of the disk. For example, you may open My Computer and double-click on the C drive to just look on drive C. Then you may click on a folder to drill down and see what's in that folder. Within that folder, you may click on yet another folder to drill down and see what's in there.

You also can work your way back up through the drill-down procedure or even jump to an entirely different drive, folder, or whatever without drilling at all. Follow these steps:

1. Make sure that the toolbar is visible in the current window.

   Choose View⇨Toolbar if it isn't.
2. Use the first two buttons in the toolbar as follows:
   - To move up to the parent folder, click on the Up One Level button. The current folder closes, and you return to the previous folder (assuming that you have a "previous folder" to go to).

- The first tool in the toolbar is a drop-down list box named *Go to a different folder* (when you view its tooltip). To jump to another place altogether, you can click that drop-down button then choose a destination from the list that appears. The contents of the current window are replaced by the contents of whatever folder you select.

Figure 2-12 shows an example in which the mouse pointer is pointing to the Up One Level button in the toolbar. The Go to Another Folder drop-down list box is just to the left of that button.

Figure 2-12: The first two buttons in a My Computer window help you navigate.

Ye olde DOS directories and extensions

Three things about using My Computer are especially awkward for people who are familiar with DOS and/or Windows 3.x:

✦ An icon always shows the actual filename (not an alias), which has dire consequences for renaming and deleting things. (I'll discuss all that in detail in Chapters 4 and 8.)

✦ The extension of that filename may be hidden.

✦ The title bar usually displays the name of the current folder (for example, Letters) without showing the full path of how you got to that folder (for example, C:\WinWord\Letters).

For an example, refer to Figure 2-12, which displays the contents of a folder named Letters. That folder contains a bunch of files that apparently have something to do with Microsoft Word for Windows (guessing from the large letter *W* within each icon).

Now suppose that you want to see where this Letters folder is on the disk and what types of files these icons represent. Follow these steps:

1. In any open My Computer window, choose <u>V</u>iew⇨<u>O</u>ptions.

   The Options dialog box appears.

2. Click on the View tab.

   You see the options shown in Figure 2-13.

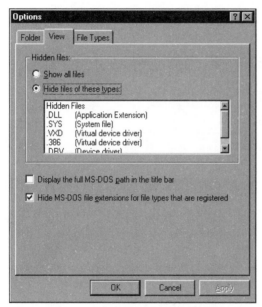

Figure 2-13: The View tab of the Options dialog box.

3. To display the full DOS path name in the title bar of My Computer windows, choose Display the full MS-DOS <u>p</u>ath in the title bar.

4. To display the extension of every filename displayed in a My Computer window, clear (deselect) the Hide MS-DOS file <u>e</u>xtensions for file types that are registered.

5. Click on OK to return to the desktop.

What the heck are registered files?

In Windows 95, certain types of files are automatically identified as belonging to certain programs. Files with the .DOC extension, for example, are registered to Microsoft Word. That means that if you double-click on an icon for a file that has the .doc extension, Windows 95 automatically opens Microsoft Word and then displays the document that you double-clicked on.

This approach has two advantages. For one, you don't need to go through the usual method of opening a program and then choosing File⇨Open within that program to open a specific document. Instead, you just open the document. Also, a naive user doesn't even need to know which program a particular document goes with. Suppose that Kyle Klewless, who knows nothing about computers, wants to see what's in a file named `Please review me Kyle`. He doesn't need

to know what program is required to open that document; he just has to double-click on the document.

Because all the registration business generally is handled behind the scenes, automatically, in Windows 95, there isn't even a reason to display filename extensions. Showing Kyle Klewless the filename `Please review me Kyle.doc` does him no good; the name `Please review me Kyle` is sufficient. So that's the reason extensions on registered filenames are hidden by default in Windows 95.

Of course, the automatic registrations may not always be exactly what you want them to be. You can change them. Chapter 30 discusses this aspect (and others) of dealing with the Windows 95 registry process.

Now the title bar shows the complete path to the current folder, and each icon shows the name and the extension of the file that it represents. Figure 2-14 shows the window from Figure 2-12 after I completed steps 1–5. If you're accustomed to DOS path names and the role of .DOT (document templates) files in Word, this information probably is useful to you.

Other My Computer tricks

The following sections provide some tips and tricks for getting the most out of My Computer:

Refreshing the My Computer icons

If you're on a LAN or using lots of programs and My Computer doesn't show something that it should be showing, choose View⇨Refresh to reread the contents of the folder.

Displaying system and hidden files

Normally, My Computer hides system files, such as dynamic link libraries (.DLL), system files (.SYS), and device drivers (.VXD, .386, and .DRV), the reason being that

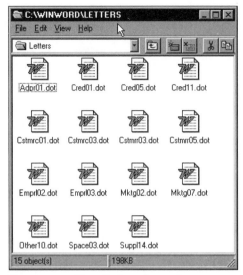

Figure 2-14: The window shown in
Figure 2-12 with the full path in the title bar
and file extensions.

there really isn't any reason for the average user to be messing with them. If you need
to see those files, choose View⇨Options in any My Computer window. Click on the
View tab, and choose Show all files. Then click on OK.

Before you delete an entire folder, remember that there may be some
hidden files on there. As a general rule, you should inspect the folder with
Show All Files turned on, before you delete it, just so you know for sure
which files you're about to delete.

Minimizing window pileups

If you don't want My Computer to stack up so many windows as you drill down
through folders, choose View⇨Options; click on the Folder tab; and then choose the
second option, Browse folders by using a single window....

Piling up *My Computer* windows eats up system resources. If memory is
tight, you'll probably need to use the *Browse folders by using a single
window* option.

Even if you minimize window pileups in My Computer, you still have to drill down
through folders one window at a time. Although this procedure is good for many people,
more experienced users may prefer to use Windows Explorer to browse their PCs.

Browsing with Windows Explorer

Like My Computer, *Windows Explorer* is a tool for browsing around on your hard disk (or on any disk, for that matter) to see what's available. Explorer doesn't use the one-window-at-a-time technique. Instead, Explorer presents your drives, folders, and files in a single window, and you navigate within that window.

 Windows Explorer is virtually identical to the File Manager in Windows 3.x. You may have heard the now-famous quote "Explorer is like File Manager on steroids."

To open Windows Explorer, do any of the following things:

✦ Click on the Start button, point to Programs, and then click on Windows Explorer.

✦ Right-click on the My Computer icon and then choose Explore.

✦ Right-click on the Start button and then choose Explore.

Regardless of which method you use to start Explore, you go to the Explore window, which will look something like Figure 2-15.

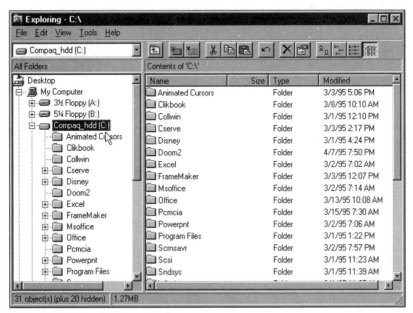

Figure 2-15: The Windows Explorer.

To use the Explorer to go exploring, follow these steps:

1. If the toolbar isn't visible, choose View➪Toolbar.

2. Click the drop-down list button in Go to a different folder (the first tool in the toolbar), and then click on the drive or folder that you want to explore.

3. In the leftmost column, click on the folder whose contents you want to view.

4. If additional folders are within the currently selected folder, you see a plus sign (+) next to the folder name; click on that plus sign to view the names of folders within the folder.

   You can repeat this step until you've drilled down to the folder that you want to view.

5. To see what's in the currently selected folder, look in the pane to the right of the folder list.

6. When you finish exploring, click on the Close button in the upper-right corner of the Explorer window.

Many of the tricks discussed in the My Computer section work in Explorer as well, including the following:

✦ To view large icons, small icons, a list, or details in the rightmost pane of the Explorer window, click on the appropriate button in Explorer's toolbar, or choose View➪Arrange Icons and then click on the arrangement you want.

✦ To update the list of folder and filenames in the Explorer window, choose View➪Refresh.

✦ To display file extensions, DOS path names, and hidden files, choose View➪Options, click on the View tab, and then choose options to view or hide whatever you want.

As you'll learn in Chapters 3 and 4, you can use either My Computer or Explorer to open, copy, move, and delete files and folders.

When you finish with Explorer, you can close it as you would any other window: click its Close button, or choose File➪Exit.

Finding a Specific File or Folder

My Computer and Explorer are fine for browsing around to see what's on a disk and even OK for drilling down to a particular file when you already know what folder that file is in. But in some situations, you may know not know where a file is located. You may know the file's name, the date it was last modified, or something about the folder's contents, but you don't know, or can't remember, *where* that file is.

No problem — you can use the Find feature to search an entire disk (all its folders and subfolders) for a specific file. Follow these steps:

1. Click on the Start button and then point to Find.

2. Click on Files or Folders.

   You're taken to the Find dialog box, shown in Figure 2-16.

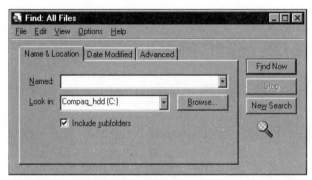

Figure 2-16: The Find dialog box.

3. If you want to search the entire hard disk, leave the Look in setting set to C:, and make sure that the Include subfolders check box is checked. If you want to search some other disk, select the icon or folder, use the Browse button to navigate to that drive or folder. If you don't want to include subfolders in your search, clear the Include subfolders option.

4. Tell Find something about the file that you're looking for, using any of the Search by methods described in the following sections.

5. When you're ready to conduct the search, click on the Find Now button, and wait for the list of file names to appear.

Danger Zone
Never assume that a file has been deleted just because Find doesn't find it right off the bat. You may have searched for the wrong thing or inadvertently narrowed an unsuccessful search. More information on this subject appears under "If Find doesn't find your file" a little later in this chapter.

The following sections describe the various methods mentioned in Step 4.

Search by name

Suppose that you're spearheading a luau for your upcoming convention in Hawaii and have already typed a partial list of people to invite. You need to get back to that file now and add some more names, but you don't remember exactly what you named the file or what folder you put it in. All you know is that you used the word *luau* somewhere in the filename (maybe it was `Luau people` or `Invitations for luau` or something like that).

Not to worry — all you need to do is type the word **luau** in the Named text box and then click on the Find Now button. All the files that contain the word *luau* on the drive that you're searching appear at the bottom of the list (see Figure 2-17).

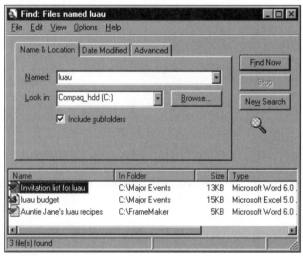

Figure 2-17: Result of a search for filenames containing the word *luau*.

In this example, the file named Invitation list for luau probably is the one you're looking for. To open it and see, double-click on its icon.

Search by date

Suppose that you created and saved an important document yesterday. In your rush to get out of the office on time, you saved and closed the file without much thought. Today, you can't remember where you put the file or even what you named it.

To find the missing file, maybe a good starting point would be to look at all the files that were created or modified yesterday. In the Find dialog box, first click on the Date Modified tab. If today is 11/15/95, you want to see all the files that were created on 11/14/95 (yesterday). So you would fill in the blanks as shown in Figure 2-18 and then click on the Find Now button.

Where are the filenames?

You may be wondering where the filenames are in Figure 2-17. Surprise, surprise — Invitation list for luau and the names below it *are* filenames. Windows 95 accepts filenames up to 255 characters in length, and spaces are allowed.

Be aware, however, that only 32-bit programs (those designed for Windows 95 and Windows NT) allow you to save files with those long names and that those programs are the only ones that let you view the long names.

When you're using a 16-bit program (one designed for DOS or Windows 3.x), you are still limited to eight-character filenames. In dialog boxes that display filenames, you'll see only the first six letters of long filenames, followed by a tilde (~) and a number. When viewing the filename Invitation list for luau in a 16-bit program, you see only Invita~1.doc as the filename.

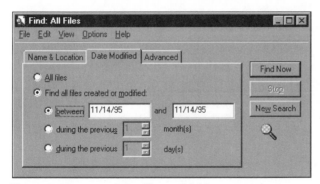

Figure 2-18: A search for files and folders created or modified on 11/14/95.

The list at the bottom of the dialog box shows only the files and folders that were created or modified on that date. Double-click on the one that you want to open.

Search by contents

Suppose that a month or two ago, you typed and saved a letter to a person named Wanda Bea Starr. You need to find that letter now but cannot remember what folder it's in or even what you named the file. It stands to reason, however, that because the file is a letter, her name probably appears in the inside address or somewhere within the letter. You can search the entire disk for files that contain the text *Wanda* or *Starr*.

This method has one drawback: Windows 95 needs to read the contents of every file that's included in the search, and that procedure can take a very, very long time. You can speed things quite a bit if you know what type of document you're looking for. If you're sure that the letter you're looking for is a Microsoft Word document, for example, you can tell Find to search just Word documents.

For starters, click on the Advanced tab in the Find dialog box. If you know what type of file you're looking for, choose that file type from the Of type drop-down list. Then type the word or phrase you're looking for in the Containing text box. In Figure 2-19, I want to search all the Microsoft Word document files for the word *Wanda*.

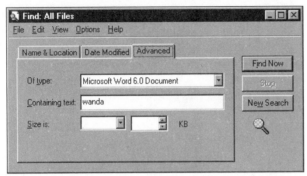

Figure 2-19: A search for Word documents that contain the text *Wanda*.

To begin the search, click Find Now. The list at the bottom of the dialog box will (eventually) show all the Microsoft Word documents that contain the word *Wanda*. Remember that we're talking about the *contents* of the file here, not the name of the file; hence, the word *Wanda* may not appear in the list of filenames that appears. But rest assured that *Wanda* appears somewhere in each of those documents.

If Find lists too many files

In some cases, clicking Find Now produces more filenames than you care to sift through. Fortunately, you can narrow a search easily without starting over from scratch.

Suppose that you searched for all files that were created or modified during the past week and that the result was dozens of files — more than you care to peruse. So you want to narrow the list down to Word documents created during the past week. No problem — click on the Advanced tab, select Microsoft Word documents, and click on Find Now again. The result will be only Word documents that were created or modified during the past week.

If Find doesn't find your file

If clicking F̲ind Now does not help you find the file that you're looking for, the first thing you should do is click on the Ne̲w Search button. Reason: if you don't do so before specifying a new search criterion, all you're doing is narrowing down the previous unsuccessful search. When a search is unsuccessful, you want to *broaden* your search, not narrow it down. You must click on the Ne̲w Search button to dispense of the previous search (even if it resulted in no found files at all) before conducting a new search.

One of the reasons why I emphasize this procedure is that it's very easy to forget this tidbit. No message will ever appear on the screen, saying, "Hey, Einstein, you'll never find what you're looking by narrowing down the same old unsuccessful search!" So this whole business of searches being cumulative is just something you have to log into the "Don't Forget" department within your own brain.

 As you'll learn in Part VII, you can use Find to search disks on other computers in your local area network, not just your own computer.

Whatever you do, don't panic if Find doesn't locate the file that you're looking for. Don't wrongly assume that the file has been deleted; instead, click on the Ne̲w Search button, and try some other means of locating the missing file.

If Find succeeds...

By default, the bottom of the Find dialog box displays folder and filenames in Details view. But just as you can in My Computer and Explorer, you can specify exactly how you want to view and arrange those icons and names. Use any of the following methods:

♦ To view large icons, small icons, a list, or details, click on V̲iew in Find's menu bar and then click on the view you want.

♦ To reorganize names in the list, choose V̲iew⇨Arrange I̲cons and then the sort order you want. In Details view, you can click on the column heading to sort the contents in ascending or descending order within that column.

♦ Although there is no O̲ptions command in Find's V̲iew menu, you can still opt to hide or display file extensions. Open any My Computer window, choose V̲iew ⇨ O̲ptions, click on the View tab, and then check or clear the Hide MS-DOS file e̲xtensions check box.

♦ To open a folder or file in the Find dialog-box list, double-click on the appropriate icon.

In addition to these procedures, you can move, copy, rename, delete, and in all other ways manage any folder or file listed at the bottom of the Find dialog box. As mentioned earlier, we'll get to that information in Chapter 4. First, however, I want to show you all the various ways that you can launch programs and open documents in Windows 95.

Summary

✦ Information in your computer is stored in *files*.

✦ Files are organized into *folders* and *subfolders*.

✦ The thing that stores the folders, subfolders, and files is called a disk drive, or just *drive* for short.

✦ Windows 95 offers three tools for locating files: My Computer, Windows Explorer, and Find.

✦ My Computer offers a simple one-window-at-a-time method of exploring drives, where you can drill down through folders and subfolders to locate a file.

✦ Windows Explorer offers a two-pane method of exploration where a hierarchical tree of folders appears in the left pane, the names of subfolders and files within the selected folder appear in the right pane (much like the File Manager in Windows 3).

✦ Find will search an entire disk (all folders and subfolders) for a file based on whatever information you can provide about the file you're looking for.

✦   ✦   ✦

Launching Programs and Documents

Opening programs and documents are two of those little tasks that you're likely to do dozens of times a day, so Windows 95 offers many different ways to do them. There's no "right way" or "wrong way," of course. Choosing which method you want to use is simply a matter of deciding what's most convenient at the moment.

Understanding Programs and Documents

Before I get into how-to here, I want to take a moment to ensure that we're speaking the same language. When I talk about a *document*, I'm generally referring to something that you create, and save, by using a program. For example, you may use your word processing program to create a typed document or a spreadsheet program to create a spreadsheet document. Text files, such as the readme.txt or readme.doc file that comes with a program that you purchase, also qualify as documents.

When I say "open a document," I mean bring the document to the screen so that you can see it. In most cases, this statement implies that you actually open whatever program is needed to create, change, and view a certain type of document before the document actually appears on-screen.

By *program*, I generally mean something that you buy to run on your computer — for example, a game, a word processing program, or a graphics program. Programs also are called *applications* (or apps, for short). Small programs, such as the accessories that come with Windows, sometimes are called *applets*.

By *opening* or *launching* a program, I mean bringing the program to the screen (and, hence, into memory) so that you can use it. There are many terms for this process — including running, starting, and launching — but they all mean the same thing.

Opening Documents

In earlier versions of Windows, the typical method of opening a document was first opening the program that you used to create the document and then choosing File⇨Open within that program to open a specific document. In some programs, you can click on the File menu and then click on the name of the document that you want to open. You can still use that technique in Windows 95. The only difference is that you start the program with the Start button, rather than the Program Manager.

A great new feature of Windows 95 enables you to skip the step of opening the program first. Instead, you just double-click on the document's icon; the document opens right up.

You can open documents in several ways, as discussed in the following sections.

Open a document from the Documents menu

If the desktop shows an icon for the document that you want to open, just double-click on that icon. Nothin' to it.

 I'll talk about how you put document icons on the desktop a little later in this chapter (and in more depth in Chapter 4).

If no icon for the document appears on the desktop, take a peek at the Documents menu. That menu keeps track of the names of documents that you've saved recently. This feature works only in Windows 95-aware programs, so the menu may not keep track of *every* document that you create and edit, but it's worth taking a peek nonetheless.

To get to the Documents menu, click on the Start button and then point to Documents, as shown in Figure 3-1. If you see the name of the document that you want to open, click on that name. The appropriate program will launch and then automatically load the document you want to work on. (If you don't see the document you want, move the mouse pointer off the Documents menu to get rid of the menus.)

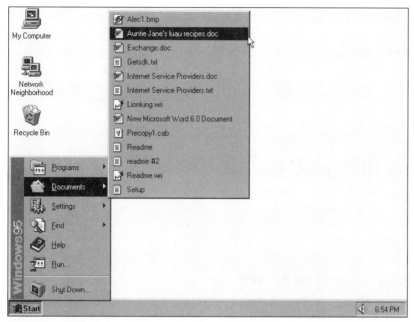

Figure 3-1: The Documents menu keeps track of recently saved documents.

What are ya — document-centric?

If you're an experienced computer user, you may think that Microsoft has gone overboard by offering umpteen ways to open programs and documents. What you're really seeing is a shift from the program-centric operating systems of yesterday to the document-centric operating systems of tomorrow.

Let me explain. In the real world, when you hand a person a document that's printed on paper, she can just start reading it. She doesn't need to know any special magic words to make the document readable. But this isn't true when you hand someone a document that's on a floppy disk. To the contrary, *that* person needs to know quite a bit to actually see the document: what program was used to create that document, how to start that program on his own computer, how to open files

with that program, and generally how to operate that program. It's a lot to know.

The document-centric approach reduces some of that burden by making the operating system aware of what program is needed to open a document. The person who wants to read the electronic document just needs to know enough to get the document's icon on the screen and to double-click on that icon. He or she need not know what type or brand of program is required.

In the future, *documentcentricity* (I made up that word) will be the norm, rather than the exception. PC users may not even be aware that there are things called programs and operating systems; instead, they'll see the PC as being simply a machine for creating and reading documents stored on disks.

Browse to a document's icon

If neither the desktop nor the Documents menu shows an icon for the document that you want to open, you need to do a bit more clicking to get to the icon. Use My Computer, Windows Explorer, or Find to get to the document's icon (refer to Chapter 2). When you see the icon, just double-click on it. If the document doesn't open, the document type probably isn't registered. For details on what to do in that case, see the next section.

Opening Unregistered Documents

In a perfect world, you could double-click on any icon that you come across, and the document would open. But in case you haven't noticed, this is not a perfect world. (Insights such as this are what separate the *real* authors from the amateurs.) The question is, what are you gonna do about it? One possible solution is to . . .

Register a file type on the fly

One way to deal with a document that won't open when you double-click on it is to register the file type as you're trying to open the document. As an example, suppose that I'm browsing around a disk and come across an icon named readme.wp. When I double-click on that icon, I get the dialog box shown in Figure 3-2.

Figure 3-2: The .WP extension isn't registered to any program on my PC.

What this dialog box is telling me, in a roundabout way, is that the document I'm trying to open is actually named README.WP and that no program on my PC is registered to automatically open files that have the .WP extension. The dialog box is also showing me a list of programs that *are* on my computer. Now it's up to me to guess which of those programs is most likely to be capable of opening a .WP file.

In this example, I guess that .wp stands for WordPerfect. First, I could type a plain-English description, such as **WordPerfect Documents**, in the Description of '.WP' files box. Then I could scroll through programs in the Choose the program you want to use list box. When I get to the WordPerfect program (WPWIN in the list), I can click on that icon and then click OK. The document will open in WordPerfect for Windows.

A simple way to open an unregistered document type is to open the program that you normally would use to edit that type of file and then choose File⇨Open in that program. This method, however, does not register that file type with that program.

Looking back at Figure 3-2, you may notice an option titled Always use this program to open this file. Because that option was selected as I proceeded through the dialog box, the .wp extension now is registered to the WordPerfect program. That means from here on out, any time I double-click on the icon for a file that has the .WP extension, Windows 95 will automatically launch WordPerfect and open that document. I have created a registration on the fly.

By the way, I could have registered the .WP extension to any program that is capable of opening a WordPerfect document. If I had Microsoft Word on this PC instead of WordPerfect, I could have assigned the .WP extension to WINWORD rather than WPWIN.

Getting past a bad registration

The whole business of registering (also called *associating*) file types to programs is pretty automatic in Windows 95. But in this less-than-perfect world, you occasionally may have a hiccup. Consider an example in which double-clicking on a document *almost* opens the document, and then something goes wrong. Suppose that someone gives me a floppy disk and says, "Take a look at this." I put the floppy in drive A of my computer, open My Computer, double-click on the icon for the A drive, and see a file named ClayAlan on the floppy. I double-click on that icon. After a few seconds, my screen looks like Figure 3-3.

Figure 3-3: Can't seem to open this document on drive A.

Although I can't see the document, the dialog box does give me three pieces of useful information:

✦ The file that I'm trying to open has the extension .PCX (as in A:\ClayAlan.pcx).

✦ Apparently, .PCX files are registered to the Microsoft Paint program, because that's the program that Windows 95 launched after I double-clicked on the icon.

✦ For some reason, though, Paint can't read this particular .PCX file.

Before giving up hope, I think, "Hmmm. I wonder whether I have some other program that can open a .PCX file." It just so happens that I *do* have a program, named HiJaak PRO, that's especially good at opening all kinds of graphics files. I'll try using that program to open the mysterious .PCX file.

For the moment, I have to forget all about documentcentricity and go back to the old way of doing things. In this example, I would fire up HiJaak PRO, choose File⇨Open, specify a:\ClayAlan.pcx, and hope. Lo and behold, it works! I can see the contents of the file, as shown in Figure 3-4.

Figure 3-4: HiJaak PRO opened the .pcx file.

Trying to determine why Paint couldn't open this .PCX file probably would be more trouble than it's worth. A simpler solution would be to change the registry so that files with the .PCX extension are associated with HiJaak, rather than with Paint. Thereafter, double-clicking on a .PCX file would put me in HiJaak automatically. Chapter 31 discusses how to change the registry manually.

 Before you go messing with the Windows 95 Registry, keep in mind that for the most part, the procedure is automatic. You want to manually mess around with the Registry only when some file association is giving you a hard time.

Create New Documents

In the past, the typical method of creating a new document was to start the program that you needed to create that document and then either start typing or choose File⇨New to start a new piece of work. You can still use that method in Windows 95. But you also can use an alternative technique that enables you to create and name the document, give it a desktop icon, and launch the appropriate program, all in one fell swoop. Follow these steps:

1. Right-click on the desktop and then click on New.

   A menu of document types that you can create this way appears, as shown in Figure 3-5.

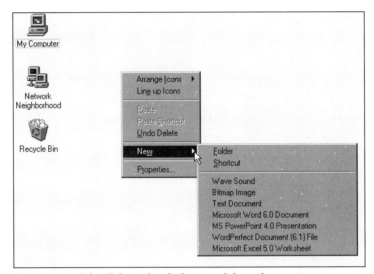

Figure 3-5: Right-click on the desktop and then choose New.

2. If you see an option for the type of document that you want to create, click on that option.

   If you don't see such an option, you can go back to the Start-button method to start the program and create the document.

3. An icon for the document appears on the desktop, along with a suggested name (for example, `New Microsoft Word Document.doc`).

4. If you want to change the name of this new document, type the new name.

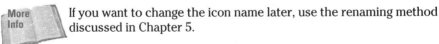 **More Info** If you want to change the icon name later, use the renaming method discussed in Chapter 5.

5. To launch the program needed to edit the new document, double-click on the new desktop icon.

   The program appears with a new, blank editing window, and the document is already saved under the name that you specified in Step 4.

You can just start using the program normally to create the document. When you finish, close the program (click on its X button or choose File⇨Exit). When you are asked about saving your changes, choose Yes. The icon for the new document stays on the desktop, as shown in Figure 3-6.

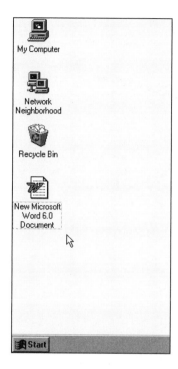

Figure 3-6: Desktop icon for a new document created by right-clicking on the desktop.

To resume work on that document, double-click on its desktop icon. Optionally, you can right-click on that icon to display a menu of options that are available for that document.

To tidy up your desktop icons, right-click on the desktop and then choose Line Up Icons from the pop-up menu. Alternatively, choose Arrange Icons from the same menu and then specify how you want the icons arranged.

Initially, the new document is stored in a folder named C:\Windows\Desktop and appears only on the desktop. When you no longer need immediate access to the icon and want to clear it off the desktop, you can move it into a regular folder. Follow these steps:

1. Use My Computer or Windows Explorer to open the folder in which you want to place the icon.

2. Position the folder window so that you can see both the icon you want to move and the folder contents.

3. Right-drag the icon into the folder.

By *right-drag*, I mean hold down the secondary mouse button (usually, the button on the right side of the mouse) while moving the mouse.

More Info   This right-dragging is just a hint of things to come. Chapter 5 explains the many ways of moving and copying files.

4. Release the mouse button and then choose <u>M</u>ove Here from the pop-up menu that appears.

Figure 3-7 shows an example in which I used My Computer to open the WinWord folder. After sizing and positioning the open windows so that I could see the desktop icons, I right-dragged the icon titled New Microsoft Word 6.0 Document from the desktop into that Winword folder. The figure shows the screen just after I released the right mouse button but before I chose <u>M</u>ove Here to complete the move.

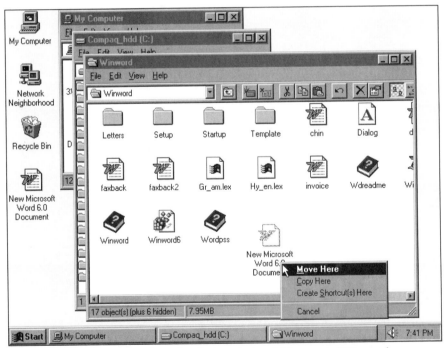

Figure 3-7: Moving an icon from the desktop into a folder named Winword.

Launching Programs

Not all programs involve documents. Games and multimedia titles are just a couple of examples of programs that usually don't allow you to create and edit documents. Also, you sometimes may want to fire up a program without having any particular document in mind. In those situations, you can use any of the techniques discussed in the following sections to launch the program of your choosing.

Launching from the desktop

If you have already opened the program today, look at the taskbar to see whether the program is still open. If you see the program's icon, click on that taskbar button to bring the program back to the forefront.

 In Chapter 4, you learn how to create your own shortcuts to frequently used programs.

Some programs have a *shortcut icon* on the desktop, even when the program isn't open. If you see such an icon, just double-click on it to start that program.

Launching from the Start menu

Chapter 1 showed you how to launch a program from the Start menu. For a quick review, here are the steps:

1. Click on the Start button.

   If you see an icon for the program that you want to start, click on that icon instead, and skip the remaining steps.

 Chapter 4 discusses techniques for creating and using shortcuts, including how to get a program's icon in the Start menu and how to create desktop shortcut icons for launching frequently used programs.

2. Point to (or click on) Programs.

3. If you see the program's icon, click on it.

   Alternatively, point to the program's group icon until you find the icon for the program that you want to start, and then click on the program's icon.

Figure 3-8 shows an example in which I'm about to launch the Hearts game. To get to that icon, I had to click on the Start button and then choose Programs⇨Accessories⇨Games.

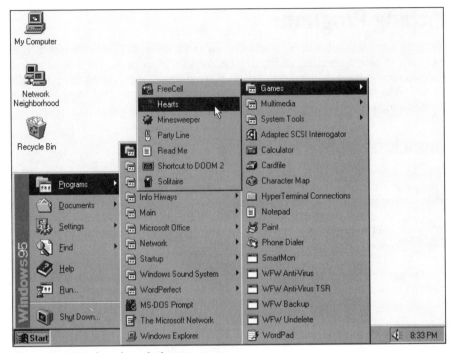

Figure 3-8: Ready to launch the Hearts program.

After you're in a program, you can use it normally. If the program allows you to create documents, you generally can use commands in the File menu to create, open, and save documents. Although some variation exists among programs, the usual commands are as follows:

✦ File⇨New: creates a new document within this program.

✦ File⇨Open: opens a document previously created and saved with this program.

✦ File⇨Close: closes (and, optionally, saves) the current document without leaving this program.

✦ File⇨Save: saves all recent changes to this document and leaves the document on the screen.

✦ File⇨Save As: saves the current document under a new name and possibly as a different type. This command often is used for exporting a document from one program (for example, Microsoft Word) to another (for example, WordPerfect).

✦ File⇨Print: prints the document that's currently on-screen in this program.

✦ File⇨Exit: closes (and, optionally, saves) the current document and closes the current program.

My instructions say to choose Run from the File menu

When you're running or installing a program that was designed for Windows 3.x, your instructions may tell you to go to Program Manager, choose <u>R</u>un from Program Manager's <u>F</u>ile menu, type something, and press Enter.

Windows 95 has no Program Manager per se. But all you have to do to complete your instructions is click on the Start button, choose <u>R</u>un from the Start menu, and then follow the written instructions for your Windows 3.x program.

Launching a program without the Start menu

If, when you go through the Start menu, you can't find an icon for the program that you want to start, you can use any of the following techniques to start the program:

✦ Use My Computer, Windows Explorer, or Find to locate the program's icon; then double-click on that icon.

✦ Click on the Start button and choose <u>R</u>un; then type the command needed to start the program. You can include the DOS path. For example, type **c:\wp51\wp** to launch WordPerfect 5.1 for DOS, assuming that the program is in the WP51 folder (directory).

✦ If you specifically want to run a SETUP.EXE or INSTALL.EXE program from a floppy disk or CD-ROM, try using the Add/Remove Programs wizard, as discussed under "Starting Programs on CD-ROM" later in this chapter, and in Chapter 9.

Auto-Start Favorite Programs

You can have Windows 95 automatically start any program as soon as it finishes starting itself. If you have Microsoft Office, for example, you may want Windows to start the Office Manager program automatically so that the Office toolbar appears on-screen.

To auto-start a program, follow these steps:

1. Click on the Start button and then click on <u>S</u>ettings.

2. Click on the <u>T</u>askbar option in the menu.

3. Click on the Start Menu Programs tab.

   You see the dialog box shown in Figure 3-9.

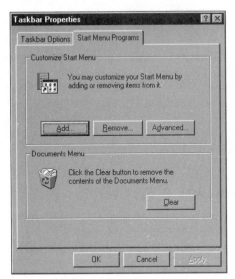

Figure 3-9: The Start Menu Programs tab
of the Taskbar Properties dialog box.

4. Click on the Add button and then click on the Browse button.

5. Browse (double-click your way to) the folder that contains the program you
   want to auto-start, and then double-click on the startup icon for that program,
   just as though you were going to start the program now.

   The path and program name for the program that you want to auto-start appear
   in the Command line text box of the Create Shortcut wizard.

6. Click on Next and then click on the folder titled Startup (see Figure 3-10).

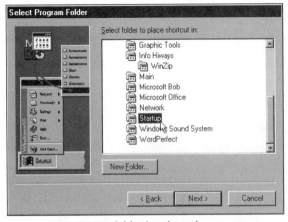

Figure 3-10: Startup folder is selected.

7. Click on Next, click on Finish, and then click OK.

The program won't start right now; all you've done is put its icon in the Startup folder. To verify, click on the Start button, point to Programs, and then point to Startup. You should see the icon for your program in the submenu that appears.

 Here's another way to get to the Startup folder to add, change, or delete icons. Right-click on the Start button, and choose Open. Double-click on the Programs icon and then double-click on the Startup icon. The icons in that folder are the icons for programs that will be auto-started.

From now on, any program(s) listed in your Startup folder will run automatically as soon as Windows 95 starts.

Starting Programs on CD-ROM

CD-ROMs can be a little tricky, because different kinds are available. Some CD-ROMs can auto-start, whereas others require you to go through a setup procedure. Then again, some CD-ROMs are just collections of files, so you use them as though they were king-size read-only floppy disks.

The easiest way to install and/or use a CD-ROM is simply to follow the instructions in the little manual that came with it. But if that's not possible at the moment (or if you hate to read instructions), you can experiment with the methods discussed in the following sections.

Launching an auto-start CD-ROM

Many Windows 95-aware CD-ROMs include a hidden auto-launch feature. These CD-ROMs offer the ultimate in ease-of-use. To use one, follow these steps:

1. Stick the CD-ROM into the CD-ROM drive, per the drive manufacturer's instructions.

2. Sit back and watch the screen, and then follow any instructions that appear.

That's it. *Anyone* can do it — maybe even your boss.

Installing a CD-ROM

Many CD-ROMs include programs that need to be copied to your hard disk before you can actually use the CD-ROM. In some cases, the CD-ROM is just a medium for getting the program to you. After you installed the programs, you don't really need the CD-ROM anymore, except as a backup. Either way, you usually can follow this procedure to install programs from a CD-ROM to your hard disk:

1. Put the CD-ROM in the CD-ROM drive, per the drive manufacturer's instructions.

   Be sure to remove any floppy disks from your floppy drives.

2. Click on the Start button, click on Settings, and then click on Control Panel.

3. Double-click on the Add/Remove Programs icon in the Control Panel.

4. Click on the Install button, and then follow the directions on the screen.

Most likely, the installation procedure will create a program icon (and perhaps even its own program group). For example, I followed the preceding steps to install Microsoft Bob — which, in case you haven't heard, is a talking cartoon interface. Bob is sort of a Windows shell designed to make the PC easier and less intimidating for beginners, kids, the technically challenged, and business executives.

While I was installing Bob, the screen asked where I wanted to put its programs. I chose the default directory (folder), Microsoft Bob. I also opted *not* to auto-start Bob, because I personally don't need a talking dog to help me use a PC (humpf, humpf).

Anyway, when the installation was complete, I had a new program group and icon for starting Bob. In other words, to start Bob from now on, I just need to go through the standard ritual: click on the Start button, click on Programs, click on the Microsoft Bob group icon, and then double-click on the Bob icon (see Figure 3-11).

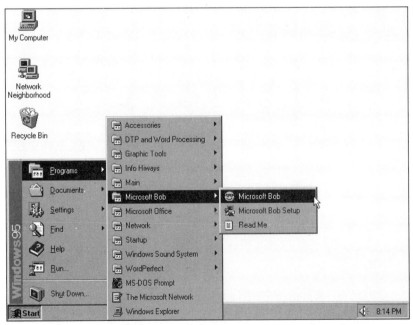

Figure 3-11: After installing a CD-ROM program, I can run it from the Start button.

The Bob example is one in which the CD-ROM is just a transport medium — that is, I don't need to put the disc in the CD-ROM drive to use Bob in the future. But that's not the case with most games and multimedia titles. For those programs, you need to put the CD-ROM in the drive and then launch the program from the Start menu. If you forget to load the disc first, a friendly message appears on-screen, telling you to put in the right CD-ROM.

CD-ROMs that have no setup program

I suspect that just about every consumer-oriented CD-ROM title will have some kind of auto-start or setup program that you can run by using Add/Remove Programs. Some CD-ROMs, however, are just collections of files with no single setup program. Clip-art collections, fonts, demo programs, and shareware programs are often distributed in this manner.

If no single setup program is provided, you can browse the CD-ROM as though it were a hard disk. Put the CD-ROM in the CD ROM drive, start My Computer or Windows Explorer, and then double-click on the icon for the CD-ROM drive (typically, D) to see the folders and icons on that drive. Figure 3-12 shows an example in which I'm using My Computer to browse a CD-ROM that contains screens and wallpapers.

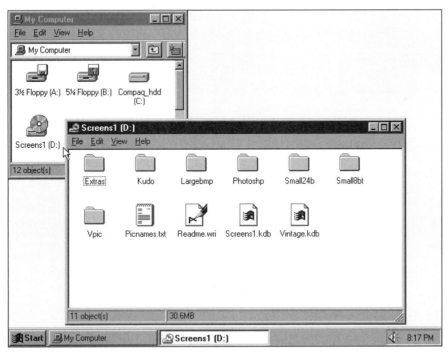

Figure 3-12: Using My Computer to browse the CD-ROM in drive D.

The *ROM* in *CD-ROM*

Don't forget that the *ROM* in *CD-ROM* stands for read-only memory. That means that you can only read stuff from the disc; you cannot copy files *to* the disc or delete files *from* the disc. Neither can you change a file that's on a CD-ROM. You can, however, open a document that's on a CD-ROM, change the document, and then save the changed version to your hard disk. Exactly how you do that depends on the program that you use to change the file. But in most cases, you just need to choose File⇨Save As and then specify a folder that's on your hard disk, rather than on the CD-ROM.

You can open folders, view documents, and launch programs on the CD-ROM by using the standard technique: just double-click on the icon that you want to open. You also can copy stuff from the CD-ROM to your hard disk by using the various methods described in Chapter 5.

Starting and Using DOS Programs

DOS programs may not show up anywhere in your Start menu, but you can start a DOS program in a couple of ways. Use My Computer, Windows Explorer, or Find to locate the icon for the DOS program; then just double-click on that icon, as usual, to launch the program.

Optionally, if you want to use the tried-and-true command-line method to start the program, follow these steps:

1. Click on the Start button, click on Programs, and then click on MS-DOS Prompt.

2. At the C> prompt, enter the appropriate DOS command to start that program.

If you're trying to start WordPerfect 5.1 for DOS, for example, you would type **cd\wp51** to get to the appropriate directory (folder) and then press Enter. Then, to start the program, type **wp** and press Enter.

Program won't run in a DOS window

Some DOS programs will refuse to run in a window. They'll insist that you run from "plain DOS." This is a bit tricky in Windows 95, since there is no "plain DOS" mode to exit to. There is, however, a mode that does a great job of mimicking plain DOS. And even programs that refuse to run in a window will run there.

To get to this "plain DOS" mode you need to click on the Start button, choose Shut Down, and then click on the *Restart the computer in MS-DOS mode?* option. Click the Yes button, and you'll be taken to a C> prompt. From there you can run any DOS program by entering its normal startup command. When you've finished with the DOS program and are back to the C> prompt, you can type **exit** and press Enter to return to Windows.

Be aware that you should use the "Shut Down" method *only* when your DOS program refuses to run in a window. The Start⇨Programs ⇨MS-DOS Prompt method is preferred, when you can use it, because that method offers your DOS programs more conventional memory (RAM).

Using a DOS program

When you have your DOS program running, use it exactly as you use it in DOS. You need to keep a few things in mind, however. For one, the toolbar that appears across the top of the DOS window (see Figure 3-13) belongs to Windows 95, not to DOS. If you don't see that toolbar, it may be turned off. Click the system icon in the upper-left corner of the DOS window; then choose Toolbar (if available) to display the toolbar. Buttons in that toolbar enable you to mark and copy text inside the DOS window. You then can paste that text into any DOS or Windows 95 window.

Figure 3-13: The Windows 95 toolbar near the top of a DOS window.

To switch between full-screen "windowless" DOS and windowed DOS, press Alt+Enter. Optionally, when you're in the windowed view, you can click the Full-Screen button in the toolbar to expand the DOS window to full screen.

Be aware that some graphics-intensive DOS applications can run only in full-screen mode. If the program that you're trying to run falls into that category, you'll see a message indicating that the DOS program will be suspended when you leave full-screen mode.

When you're in a DOS screen, you can do the following things:

✦ Press Alt+Esc to return to Windows 95.
✦ Press Ctrl+Esc to get back to Windows 95 with the Start menu open.
✦ Press Alt+Tab to switch to another program.

Each of these techniques leaves a button for the DOS window in the taskbar. To get back to your DOS program, just click on that taskbar button.

The toolbar also provides options for changing the font used in the DOS window. This procedure is not at all similar to the procedure for changing document fonts in Windows. In the DOS window, a font change affects the entire screen, rather than just the selected text, and has no effect on anything that you print from that window. A DOS-window font change is simply a way to size the screen text in a way that is comfortable for your eyes.

You can use the techniques described in Chapter 8 to add icons for starting DOS programs to your own Start menu. In fact, if you refer to Figure 3-8, which shows some Start menus, you'll see that I have a Shortcut to Doom 2 icon in my Games menu. As you may know, Doom is a DOS program, so this is living proof that you *can* add DOS programs to the Start menus.

Unlike earlier versions of Windows, Windows 95 does not require that you create a PIF (Program Interface File) for each DOS program that you use. In fact, you should be able to run any DOS program that you throw at Windows 95. If you do have problems or need to tweak the memory performance of a DOS program, you can change the program's properties.

First, get the DOS program running. If you're in full-screen mode, switch to windowed mode (press Alt+Enter). Then click on the Properties button in the toolbar, or click on the System menu in the upper-left corner of the DOS window and then choose Properties. Use the Memory and Misc tabs in the Properties dialog box to fine-tune your settings.

Closing a DOS window

You can use the standard title bar, the borders, and the Maximize, Minimize, and Restore buttons to size and shape the DOS window. You won't have as much freedom in sizing the window as you do with regular windows, however, and you may not be able to click the Close button on the window's border to close a DOS window. Instead, you may need to exit the DOS program by using whatever exit procedure is appropriate for that program.

Don't forget to save any unsaved work before you exit. Also, keep in mind that DOS can read and write only 8.3-character filenames; you cannot enter a longer filename in DOS. Doing a DIR at the command line shows the long filenames. When a DOS program does display a long filename, it shows only the first six characters (with any spaces removed), followed by a tilde and a number. A Windows 95 document named `Morph me baby.txt`, for example, would appear as `morphm~1.txt` to a DOS program.

If, after exiting your DOS program and saving your work, you end up at the `C>` prompt inside the DOS window, you can type **exit** and press Enter to close the DOS window and return to Windows 95.

Summary

✦ A program is typically something you purchase to run on your PC.

✦ A document is typically something you create, yourself, using a program.

✦ The easiest way to start a program is to click the Start button, point to Programs, then locate and click the icon for the program you want to start.

✦ If you're starting a program to resume work on a document you saved earlier, you might find it easiest just to click the start button, click on Documents, then click on the name of the document you want to work on.

✦ If the Start menus don't offer an icon for the program you want to start, you can browse to the program using My Computer, Windows Explorer, or Find. Then just double-click the icon for the program you want to start.

✦ You can use the DOS-like C> prompt to start DOS programs. Click the Start button, point to Programs, then click on MS-DOS Prompt to get to the C> prompt.

✦   ✦   ✦

Shortcuts and Other Cool Tricks

In This Chapter

Creating shortcuts with drag-and-drop

Putting shortcuts on the desktop, in the Start menu, and in documents

Creating shortcuts to folders, documents, programs, and printers

You're sure to love these scraps

Tips and tricks at your fingertips

Without a doubt, shortcuts are one of the best new features of Windows 95; they're easy to create and easy to get rid of. So you can make lots of shortcuts on the fly for whatever you're working on at the moment. Then, when new projects take precedence, you can dump the old shortcuts and create new ones.

As you'll see in this chapter, *drag-and-drop* is the easiest way to create a shortcut. And drag-and-drop, in turn, is useful for other handy features, such as *scraps.* When you carry these relatively simple techniques into other areas — networking, e-mail, editing, and so on — things get *really* interesting. You may want to put on your thinking cap and fasten your seat belt for this chapter; you're in for a wild ride.

How to Create a Shortcut

A shortcut offers quick double-click access to any folder, program, or document on your PC. Creating a shortcut is simple. All you have to do is follow these steps:

1. Use My Computer, Windows Explorer, or Find to get to the icon for the folder, program, or document to which you want to create a shortcut.

2. Hold down the right mouse button and drag the icon to the desktop (or to another folder or the Start button, as discussed later in this chapter).

3. Release the right mouse button, and choose Create Shortcut(s) Here from the menu that appears.

The only other thing you really need to know about shortcuts is that you can get help creating them at any time by looking up *shortcut* in the online manual. Click on the Start button and then click on Help. Click on the Index tab, and type **shortcut**. You'll find many ways to create and manage short-cuts.

For the rest of this chapter, I'll mainly present examples of useful shortcuts, with specific instructions wherever possible. But if all you remember from this chapter is what I've just told you, you're already on your way to being a true master of the Windows 95 shortcut.

Creating Desktop Shortcuts

You can put shortcuts to folders, programs, documents — and even to other comput-ers — right on your desktop. My favorite technique is putting a shortcut to a folder on the desktop, so I'll present an example of that first.

Desktop shortcut to a folder

My example creates a shortcut to the folder containing files that I created while writing this book. Obviously, you don't have that folder on your PC, but you probably do have one or more folders of documents that you need to access frequently. Anyway, here's how I create the shortcut to my Windows 95 Bible folder:

1. Using My Computer, Windows Explorer, or Find, I get to the icon for the folder to which I want to create a shortcut: Windows 95 Bible, as shown in Figure 4-1.

2. Next, I hold down the right mouse button and drag that icon to the place on the desktop where I want the icon to appear.

3. I release the right mouse button; a menu appears.

4. I choose Create Shortcut(s) Here.

   A copy of the icon, with a little shortcut arrow, appears on the desktop.

5. To tidy up, I close the My Computer windows.

   Optionally, I can right-click on the desktop and choose Arrange Icons and by Name to put my desktop icons in alphabetical order.

 Originally we had planned to title this book *Windows 95 Bible*, and that's why I titled the folder and shortcut as I did. Later we discovered that someone else wanted to use that title, so we changed the title of this book at the last minute. So when you see a folder or shortcut to Windows 95 Bible, just keep in mind that that's where I originally stored all my files while writing this book.

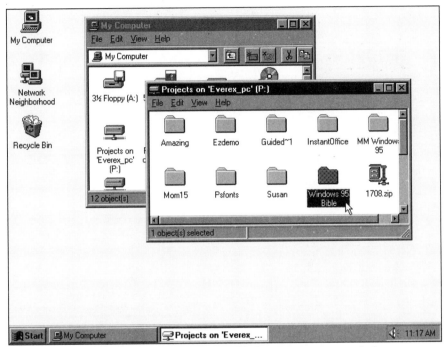

Figure 4-1: The Windows 95 Bible icon is visible in a My Computer window.

What's really cool is the fact that to get to any file in my Windows 95 Bible folder, I just double-click on that desktop icon. The files in that folder appear in a window, as shown in Figure 4-2.

Cooler still is the fact that I can view or change any document in that folder just by double-clicking on its icon (because Windows 95 is document-centric, remember?). I don't need to go through the Start menu or launch any programs; a couple of double-clicks is all it takes.

 Chapter 5 discusses moving and copying files in detail.

Finally, I can move and copy stuff to and from this shortcut as though it were the actual folder. Suppose that I need to copy some files from a floppy disk to my Windows 95 Bible folder. I can drag the icon for those files from the My Computer window for drive A right to the shortcut on the desktop; I don't have to go navigating down to the actual folder.

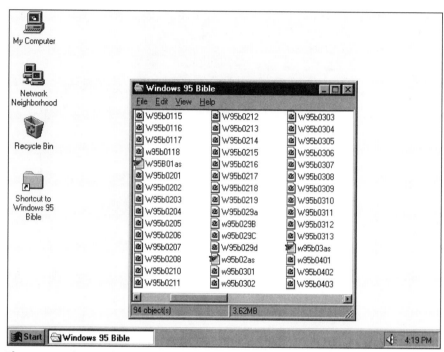

Figure 4-2: The Windows 95 Bible folder open on the desktop after its shortcut icon is double-clicked.

Why the awful filenames?

You may look at Figure 4-2 and wonder why I came up with such weird, seemingly meaningless filenames, especially when Windows 95 allows me to use long filenames with spaces. Let me explain.

First, I sent the files to the publisher of this book as I completed my work. The publisher uses many 16-bit applications that don't support long filenames, so I've stuck with the eight-character names for the publisher's convenience.

As strange as the names look, they are meaningful. The w95b that starts each filename is a code for *Windows 95 Bible* — the title of this book. That latter part — 01as, 02as, and so on — identifies that chapter number and the fact that this is the copy that I (Alan Simpson) submitted. The files that have 0101, 0102, and so on in the filename are figures. For example, w95b0101 is the file that contains Figure 1-1.

If you're into local area networks (LANs), you may be interested in knowing that in this example, the Windows 95 Bible folder isn't even on my PC. Even though the shortcut to the folder is on my PC, the folder itself is on another PC in my LAN. I can go to any other PC in my LAN and create a shortcut to that folder. So no matter what computer I happen to be sitting at when I open my Windows 95 Bible folder, I'm sure to get to the original documents for this book. I don't need to copy and move files from one PC to another via floppy disks.

 More Info Chapters 24 thru 26 tell you how to set up and use a LAN. Scary as that procedure may sound, it's actually quite easy, because networking capability is built into Windows 95.

Last but not least, thanks to dial-up networking (Chapter 20), I can get to the files in the Windows 95 Bible folder via telephone lines. So as long as I have my laptop and modem with me, I can get to those files from anywhere in the world. Yowza!

Program, document, and printer shortcuts

Using the same simple right-drag-and-drop procedure, I can create shortcuts to other items on my PC, as shown in Figure 4-3.

Figure 4-3: Shortcuts to programs, documents, and a printer added to my desktop.

You create shortcuts in the following ways:

✦ To create a shortcut to a program, browse to the program's startup icon and then drag that icon to the desktop. To launch the program, double-click on its shortcut icon.

✦ To create a shortcut to a document, browse to that document's icon. Right-drag the document to the desktop, release the right mouse button, and choose Create Shortcut(s) Here. To open the document, double-click on its shortcut icon.

✦ To create a shortcut to a printer, click on the Start button, click on Settings, and then click on Printers. Right-drag the icon to the desktop, release the right mouse button, and choose Create Shortcut(s) Here. To print a document, drag that document's icon to the printer shortcut.

Not all programs allow you to print documents by dragging their icons to a printer-shortcut icon, but just about any Windows 95-aware program will. Experiment, and if the procedure doesn't work, check that program's help file or manual to see whether you can implement drag-and-drop printing.

 You also can print a document by right-clicking on the document's icon and then choosing Print from the shortcut menu that appears; again, though, this procedure applies to Windows 95-aware programs. See Chapter 31 for ways to enable this feature.

What does "browse to" mean?

Saying "use My Computer, Windows Explorer, or Find to get to" something is going to get old. Furthermore, now that you know how to create shortcuts, you have a whole new way of getting to documents and other stuff.

So when I say "browse to," I mean *get to the icon so that you can see it on your screen.* It really doesn't matter *how* you get to the icon; a folder shortcut is as acceptable as using My Computer, Windows Explorer, or Find. All that matters is that you get to the icon, because you can't drag it until you can see it.

Putting Shortcuts in the Start Menu

You don't need to clutter your desktop with a zillion shortcuts. If you want to have single-click access to a program, folder, or document from the Start menu, drag the icon to the Start button instead of to the desktop. Before shooting Figure 4-4, for example, I did the following things:

✦ I dragged the icon for a Word document named Fax Cover Sheet (Blank) to the Start button.

✦ I dragged the printer icon for my HP LaserJet from the Printers folder to the Start menu.

✦ I dragged the icon for a folder named Major Events to the Start button.

✦ I dragged the icon for starting Microsoft Word to the Start button.

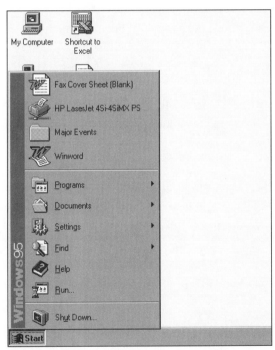

Figure 4-4: Shortcuts to a document, print queue, folder, and program in the Start menu.

Chapter 8 talks about other ways to customize the Start menu, as well as techniques for changing and deleting those shortcuts.

To open any of those items, I click on the item's icon in the Start menu. The printer icon in the Start menu, however, is a little different from the one on the desktop. There's no way to drag an icon to the printer icon in the Start menu. When I click on the printer icon in the Start menu, I'm taken right to the print-queue window for that printer, so I can check the status of print jobs lined up for that printer.

Putting Shortcuts in the Programs Menu

You also can put shortcuts in the Programs menu (the menu that appears after you click on the Start button and then click on <u>P</u>rograms). The procedure for doing so is a little different from the procedures I've discussed so far in this chapter, but it's still pretty easy.

 Actually, you can put shortcuts and submenus in *any* menu that's accessible from the Start button, as you'll learn in Chapter 8.

To put shortcuts in the Programs menu, follow these steps:

1. Right-click on the Start button, and choose <u>O</u>pen from the menu that appears.

2. Double-click on the icon for the Programs folder.

   The Programs folder window appears.

3. Choose <u>F</u>ile⇨<u>N</u>ew.

4. Click on <u>S</u>hortcut to get to the Create Shortcut wizard. Then use the <u>B</u>rowse button to get to the icon for whatever item you want to create a shortcut to.

5. When you get to that icon, double-click on it.

   You return to the Create Shortcut wizard, and the path to your icon appears in the <u>C</u>ommand line box.

6. Click on Next>, and then type whatever word or phrase you want to appear in the Programs menu.

   The text can be a brief plain-English description of your own choosing.

7. Click on the Finish button.

Now you can close any open windows. Click on the Start button and then click on <u>P</u>rograms. You should see your shortcut in its proper alphabetical position below the icons that lead to folders.

 I talk about methods for changing and refining all these menus in Chapter 8.

Figure 4-5 shows an example in which I browsed to the startup icon for Microsoft Access in Step 4. In Step 6, I typed **Access**. Now, to run Access, I just need to click on the Start button, click on Programs, and then click on Access.

Figure 4-5: An icon for starting Microsoft Access in my Programs menu.

Putting Shortcuts in Documents

Windows 95 allows you to put shortcuts in documents as well. Simply drag into your document the icon for the object to which you want to create a shortcut. This procedure is great for writing notes to other users whose Windows 95 skills are just sophisticated enough that they can double-click on an icon. You can write such a user a note that says something like "Hey, just click here to see [whatever]."

I can't give you exact step-by-step instructions for using this capability, because it may vary from one program to the next. You may need to check the help or manual for whatever program you're using to see whether it allows embedded shortcuts and how to implement them. I can, however, take you through an example using Microsoft Word 6 for NT and Excel 5 for NT, just to illustrate how and why you might embed a shortcut in a document.

Suppose that my name is Homer and that I've been working on a spreadsheet for my boss, Marge. She's a great boss but can't work a computer worth beans. I'm sitting at her PC late at night, because I'm the type of nerd who can't function when the sun is up.

I've finished the spreadsheet, and I want Marge to look at it when she comes to work in the morning. But I don't want to explain to her how to find the worksheet and open it, partly because Marge isn't interested in such technicalities and partly because I'm too lazy. So here's what I do:

I save the spreadsheet in the usual manner (File⇨Save), under the filename Homer's Spreadsheet. Then I exit Excel and fire up Microsoft Word. In Word, I type a document that says, "Good morning, Marge. I think I finally finished that spreadsheet. Double-click the icon to take a look."

Next, I use My Computer to browse to the icon for Homer's Spreadsheet. I right-click on that icon and then choose Create Shortcut(s) Here. Windows 95 immediately creates an icon titled Shortcut to Homer's Spreadsheet in the current folder. I drag that shortcut icon from its folder into my Word document. A few seconds later, a copy of that shortcut icon appears in my Word document.

Next, I save that Word document under the name MARGE Double-click me. Then I exit Word and use My Computer to browse to the icon for the MARGE Double-click me document. Next, I right-drag the icon for that Word document to the desktop to create a desktop shortcut to the Word document. At that point, I also can rename the shortcut icon by right-clicking on it and choosing Rename. Finally, I close everything and go home.

When Marge comes into the office in the morning, she sees an icon on the desktop that says MARGE Double-click me (see Figure 4-6). When she double-clicks on that icon, she sees my note (also in Figure 4-6).

Figure 4-6: The note that Marge sees in the morning, with its embedded shortcut.

Shortcuts to Control Panel and Custom Icons

To create a desktop shortcut icon to Control Panel, or your Printers folder, open (double-click) My Computer. Hold down the right mouse button and drag an icon to the desktop. After you release the mouse button, choose Create Shortcut(s) Here.

To change the icon displayed by any shortcut, right-click the shortcut icon and choose Prop-erties. Click the Shortcut tab, then click the Change Icon button. If a message appears saying that the exe file has no icons, don't worry about it. Just click OK.

Under Current icon, use the horizontal scrollbar to find an icon you like. Then click that icon and choose OK (twice) to return to the desktop.

To see the spreadsheet that I created, she just double-clicks on the Shortcut icon right there in the Word document. Bingo — up pops the spreadsheet. Cool, no?

This example is just a preview of bigger and better things. Before long, you'll be embedding shortcuts to programs, folders, documents, and even Microsoft Network forums (Chapter 21) in your documents. Then you'll e-mail those documents to other PC users all over the world so that they can just double-click on your shortcut icon to get to wherever you want to send them. You won't need to wait till the 21st century, either. You're able to do these things right now, in Windows 95.

You'll Love These Scraps

I'm not so sure that scraps really belong in a chapter on shortcuts, but they are real time-savers and too great to put off until later in the book. I have to confess that I'm walking on rather thin ice, because even though Windows 95 supports scraps, it's up to the people who create the programs that you'll be using to use scraps in those programs. I suspect, however, that all programs designed for Windows 95 or Windows NT eventually will support scraps.

 Not all pre-Windows 95 programs will support scraps. If in doubt, try it out. If the mouse pointer changes to an international NO symbol when you're hovering over the desktop, then the program you're using doesn't do scraps.

Scraps versus the Clipboard

If you're an ex-Windows 3.x user and familiar with the Clipboard, you'll especially appreciate scraps as being a great alternative to the Clipboard. If you're not familiar with the Clipboard in Windows 3.x, don't worry about it; just skip this section and go to "Using scraps" later in this chapter.

To understand why scraps are such a great alternative to the old Clipboard, think about how you used the Windows 3.x Clipboard. Typically, you would select some text or some object and then choose Edit⇨Copy to copy that item to the Clipboard. Then you would go to wherever you want to paste that object and choose Edit⇨Paste. This method is not the most intellectually challenging feat in the world, and it has a couple of weaknesses, as follows:

✦ You can't see what's in the Clipboard at any given time unless you go to the trouble of opening the Clipboard Viewer.

✦ The Clipboard can (usually) hold only one thing at a time. To cut and paste several items, you need to cut or copy from the source, go to the destination and paste, come back to the source and cut or copy, and so on, cutting and pasting one object at a time.

Scraps make the process much easier, because rather than copying the selected text or object to the Clipboard, you just drag it to the desktop (or a folder, or wherever). Whatever you dragged appears as a scrap icon. You can drag as many scraps to the desktop as you want, and you can name the scraps. You're no longer working with an invisible Clipboard that can hold only one thing at a time.

Using scraps

To create a scrap, follow these simple steps:

1. Select the text or object that you want to move or copy.

2. Drag that object to the desktop.

3. Repeat Steps 1 and 2 to create as many scraps as you want.

 Exactly how you select the object that you want to move or copy depends on the program you're using. Typically, you drag the mouse pointer through text or click on an object, such as a picture. If you have trouble, look up "select" in online help or the manual for the program that you're using.

When you finish, each scrap appears on the desktop as an icon. You can name each scrap, if you want. Right-click on the scrap's icon, choose Rename, type the name, and then click somewhere outside the scrap.

Figure 4-7 shows an example of scraps in action. Notice that I have an Excel worksheet on-screen (I used Excel for NT in this example). I dragged the chart from the spreadsheet to the desktop and named the resulting scrap Scrap The Chart. Then I selected the range of numbers and dragged that range to the desktop to create a second scrap. I named that scrap Scrap The Numbers.

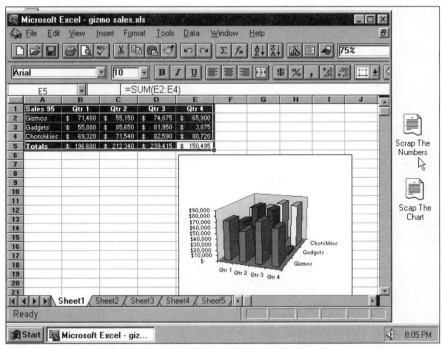

Figure 4-7: A couple of scraps from the Excel spreadsheet on the desktop.

Now suppose that I want to put those scraps in a Word document. I would close Excel (or leave it open — it doesn't matter) and launch Microsoft Word. Next, I would create or open the Word document in which I want to display the numbers and chart. Then I would drag each scrap from the desktop into the Word document. Figure 4-8 shows an example with the two scraps from the desktop pulled into the Word document.

Obviously, the scraps don't look like scraps anymore. As soon as I dragged each scrap into the Word document, the scrap opened automatically, revealing its contents. Thus, the Word document now contains exact copies of the spreadsheet range and chart. Now I can print the Word document or e-mail it to anybody who has Microsoft Word on his or her computer.

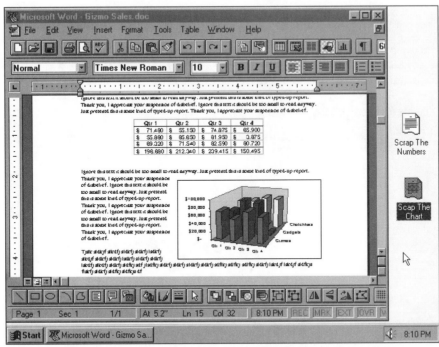

Figure 4-8: The scraps dragged into a Word 6 for NT document.

More amazing feats

You can copy objects from one program to another without scraps, if you want, by dragging the object that you want to embed to the destination program's taskbar menu.

Suppose that I'm typing a Word document, and I come to a place where I want to insert a chart from Excel. I can leave the insertion point at that spot and minimize Word's window, so that it becomes a button in the taskbar. Next, I can open Excel and select the chart that I want to put into the Word document. I drag that chart to the taskbar button for Word, and I'm done. To see my achievement, I click on Word's taskbar button to reopen its window; I see my chart right where the insertion point was. Awesome!

Scraps are OLE-aware

I should point out that scraps are OLE-aware, which means that each scrap knows where it came from. If you double-click on a scrap on the desktop, the scrap opens in its proper program (assuming that the program is on the current PC). You then can see, and even modify, the scrap's contents.

The scrap retains that awareness even after you drag it to some other document. Refer to Figure 4-8, in which you see an Excel spreadsheet range and chart in a Word document. If you were to double-click on the spreadsheet portion of that document, you'd activate *in-place editing* — which means that you'd still be in Word, but Word's menu bar and toolbars would change to Excel's menu bar and toolbar. You'd suddenly have all the capabilities of Excel in your Word document, enabling you to make changes in the little spreadsheet even though you're still in Word. For those of you who are familiar with OLE from earlier versions of Windows, you might realize now that scraps are actually linked OLE objects.

 If I e-mail the Word document shown in Figure 4-8 to someone who also has Word and Excel on his computer, he or she will have instant in-place-editing capability.

If you change the numbers in the spreadsheet during in-place editing, the chart is updated instantly to reflect those changes. Yes, I'm talking about the copy of the chart that's in Word. To get back to the normal Word menu bar and toolbars, simply click on any "regular" portion of your Word document (outside of the spreadheet).

Please keep in mind that like scraps, in-place editing is something that Windows 95 supports, but it's up to the program that you're using to take advantage of that capability. Many Windows 3.x programs already support in-place editing, and I suspect that in-place editing will be built into virtually all programs designed for Windows 95 and NT.

Cutting and pasting to another PC

LAN users will love this little trick. If you want to move or copy an object on your PC to another PC on the LAN, just drag the object from your program into a shared folder on the LAN. The scrap appears in that folder as an icon.

 Part VII of this book discusses LANs in detail.

When other LAN users open that shared folder, they, too, see your scraps. They can drag those scraps right to their own desktops or into whatever documents they are working on at the moment. In other words, you now have a simple way to cut (or copy) and paste multiple objects from one PC to another on a LAN.

Tips and Tricks at Your Fingertips

If you like the kind of time-saving tips and techniques that I've been covering in this chapter, be sure to cruise through the tips and tricks in online help. Click on the Start button, click on Help, click on the Contents tab, and then double-click on the Tips and Tricks book to open it (see Figure 4-9.) Browse at your leisure and enjoy.

Figure 4-9: Browse through the Tips and Tricks book when you have some spare time.

Summary

✦ A shortcut offers quick double-click access to any folder, document, or program.

✦ To create a shortcut, right-drag its icon to the desktop, release the mouse button, and choose Create Shortcut(s) Here.

✦ A scrap is any "cutting" from a document, and can be text, a picture, sounds, or whatever.

✦ To create a scrap, just drag the selection from your document onto the desktop.

✦ Knowing those four things I just mentioned will make your day-to-day work at the PC a whole lot simpler!

✦   ✦   ✦

Have It
Your Way

◆   ◆   ◆   ◆

In This Part

◆   ◆   ◆   ◆

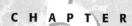
General Housekeeping (Copying, Deleting, and So On)

T his chapter is all about the day-to-day chores of managing files. That term *managing* includes copying, moving, deleting, and renaming folders and files. You should read Chapter 2 before you embark on this chapter. Be especially sure that you understand the concepts of drive, folder, and file. And if you haven't already done so, get some experience with at least one of the three main browsing tools: My Computer, Windows Explorer, and Find. If you have no idea what I'm talking about, I recommend that you go back and read Chapter 2.

Important Concepts for Ex-Windows 3.x Users

If you used Windows 3.x before learning Windows 95, you should be aware that some important differences exist between Windows 3.x and Windows 95. (If you're not an ex-Windows 3.x user, you can skip this section.)

Icons in the Windows 95 browsing tools My Computer, Explorer, and Find are like the icons in the Windows 3.x File Manager. So when you move or delete an icon with a Windows 95 browsing tool, you're moving or deleting the actual file on the disk — not just a pointer to that file. Shortcut icons, on the other hand, are simply pointers, so you can move and delete those icons without disturbing the contents of the disk.

When you delete files from your local hard disk (that is, drive C), the files are moved to a thing called the Recycle Bin. Although they are invisible from outside the Recycle Bin, those files still occupy as much disk space as they did before you deleted them. The space won't become available until you empty the Recycle Bin, as discussed under "Recovering recycled disk space" later in this chapter.

Also be aware that the Recycle Bin keeps track of only the files that you delete from your local hard disk (for example, C). Files that you delete from removable media, including floppy disks and network drives, are *not* sent to the Recycle Bin and, therefore, cannot be undeleted.

Moving, Copying, and Deleting in a Nutshell

Drag-and-drop probably is the most intuitive way to copy, move, and delete files. Following is the general procedure in a nutshell:

1. Use My Computer, Windows Explorer, or Find to get to the drive and/or folder that contains the files that you want to move, copy, or delete.

2. If you're moving or copying, use My Computer, Explorer, or Find to get to the drive and/or folder to which you plan to move or copy.

3. Size the windows so that you can see both the *source* (the files or folders that you want to move or copy) and the *destination* (the place to which you want to move or copy).

4. Select the folders or files that you want to move, copy, or delete, using the techniques described in "Selecting Objects to Copy, Move, or Delete" in a moment.

5. To delete the folders or files, press the Delete key or drag them to the Recycle Bin; then skip the remaining steps.

6. To move or copy the files, point to any of the selected folders or files, hold down the right mouse button, and drag the selected items to the destination.

7. Release the right mouse button and then choose Copy Here or Move Here, depending on what you want to do.

These steps pretty much sum up the procedure. Figure 5-1 shows an example in which I have selected a few files in a folder named Learn to Sail, which I reached by using My Computer. The destination in this example is the floppy disk in drive A. Both the Learn to Sail folder icon and the icon for floppy drive A are visible on-screen. Now I can right-drag the selected files to the drive A icon.

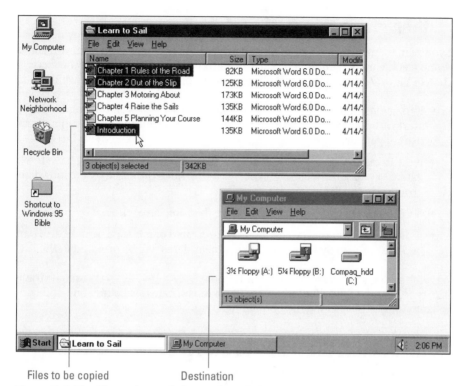

Files to be copied   Destination

Figure 5-1: The files to be copied are selected; the destination-drive icon (A) is visible.

The rest of this chapter focuses on specific parts of each step in the process and presents warnings to help you avoid mishaps.

Selecting Objects to Copy, Move, or Delete

When you want to move, copy, or delete more than one file, you can use the techniques described in the following sections to select those files. It doesn't matter which browsing tool you use to get to those icons: these techniques work the same in My Computer, Explorer, and Find.

First, pick your view . . .

You can decide how you want to view your icons. Your options (discussed in Chapter 2) are Large Icons, Small Icons, List, and Details. You can choose a view from the toolbar or from the View menu.

. . . then group things, if useful . . .

If you plan to manage a group of files that have something in common, you can save yourself some work by bunching those items in a list. Simply arrange the icons. Choose View⬄Arrange Icons and choose an option based on the following examples:

✦ If the items that you want to select have similar names (for example, they all start with the word *Chapter*), choose by Name to put the objects in alphabetical order by name.

✦ If the items that you want to select are of a similar type (they all have the extension .BAK), choose by Type. Files that have the same extension will be grouped in the list.

✦ If the items that you want to select are the same size, choose by Size.

✦ If the items that you want to select were created or modified on or near a particular date, choose by Date. Files with similar dates will be grouped in the list.

Remember that if you use Details view (choose View⬄Details), you can see the name, size, type, and date modified for every file, and you can sort by any one of those columns simply by clicking the column heading.

. . . then select the items to move, copy, or delete

When you see the items that you want to move, copy, or delete, you need to select the specific items. You can select items in the following ways:

✦ To select one item, click on it. Any previously selected items are unselected instantly.

✦ To add another item to a selection, Ctrl+click on it (hold down the Ctrl key while you click).

✦ To extend the selection to another item, Shift+click on where you want to extend the selection.

To see how much space you'll need for all the selected files, look at the status bar at the bottom of the file list.

✦ To create another extended selection without disturbing existing selections, Ctrl+click on the first item in the range and then Ctrl+Shift+click on the last item in the range.

✦ To select all the items in the window, choose Edit⬄Select All or press Ctrl+A.

✦ To deselect a selected item without disturbing the current selections, Ctrl+click on the item that you want to deselect.

✦ To invert the current selection (deselect all the selected files and select all the deselected ones), choose Edit⬄Invert Selection.

Figure 5-2 shows an example in which I have selected several filenames. I started by clicking on the topmost filename. The figure shows the keys that I held down while clicking the mouse button to select other files in the list.

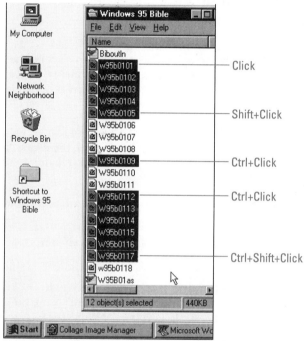

Figure 5-2: To select multiple items, use the Ctrl and Shift keys while clicking.

Yet another way to select multiple items is to drag a frame around them. This is particularly handy when you're using the Large Icons view. Move the mouse pointer to just outside the first item you want to select. Then hold down the mouse button and drag a frame around all of the items you want to select. The items will be selected as you drag and will remain selected after you release the mouse button.

Not sure what's in a file?

Many of your documents will support the Windows 95 Quick View feature, which enables you to peek inside a file without opening the document's program. To see whether that option is available for a certain file, right-click on the file's icon. If you see a Quick View option, you can select that option to peek inside the file. To close the quick view, click on the Close (X) button in its title bar.

Moving or Copying Selected Items

To move or copy selected items, point to one of them, hold down the right mouse button, and drag the mouse pointer to the destination's icon. When the mouse pointer is touching that icon, release the right mouse button. Then choose Move Here or Copy Here, depending on what you want to do.

 If you ever need a reminder of how to do the things discussed in this chapter, click on the Start button, click on <u>H</u>elp, and then click on the Index tab. The index includes the topics files, copying, moving, deleting, renaming, selecting, Recycle Bin, drag and drop, and many others related to general file management.

If you want to save yourself one extra click, you can drag the selected files by using the regular (left) mouse button. When you release the mouse button, the files will either be copied or moved, depending on where the destination is in relation to the source, as summarized in the following list:

✦ If you drag to a different folder on the same disk, the selected items are *moved* to that location.

✦ If you drag to a different disk drive, the selected items are *copied* to that location.

If you drag the files with the left mouse button and aren't sure what Windows 95 intends to do with those items, look at the mouse pointer (without releasing the mouse button). The icon near the mouse pointer tells you what Windows intends to do, as follows:

✦ If you see a plus sign (+), Windows intends to copy the files (*add* them to the disk or folder).

✦ If you see a small arrow, Windows intends to create shortcut icons at the destination.

✦ If you see neither symbol, Windows intends to move the files to that location.

✦ If you see an international "prohibited" symbol, Windows intends to do nothing, because you're attempting a move that's not allowed.

If Windows 95 intends to do something that you hadn't intended, you can force it to copy, move, or create a shortcut by pressing and holding down one of the following keys before you release the mouse button:

✦ Ctrl: copies the selected item(s)

✦ Shift: moves the selected item(s)

✦ Shift+Ctrl: creates a shortcut to the selected files or folder

To remember which key does what, remember that both Copy and Ctrl start with the letter *C* and that both Shortcut and Shift+Copy contain the letters *SC.*

Cancel a drag-and-drop

If you change your mind about a drag-and-drop procedure midstream, drag to any "illegal" destination — for example, the status bar at the bottom of the current window. When you see the international "prohibited" symbol, release the mouse button. Alternatively, tap the Esc key before you release the mouse button. Windows 95 will take no action on the dragged files.

Make a copy in the same folder

If you simply want to make a copy of a file within the current folder, click on the file that you want to copy, or use the techniques described earlier to select multiple files. Choose Edit⇔Copy, press Ctrl+C, or click on the Copy button in the toolbar. Then choose Edit⇔Paste, press Ctrl+V, or click on the Paste button in the toolbar. Each file is duplicated, with the filename *Copy of* followed by the original filename.

Figure 5-3 shows an example in which I selected the first three copies in the list, clicked on the Copy button, and then clicked on the Paste button. The last three files in the list now are copies of the first three files.

The new icons are added to the bottom of the list, so you may not see them right away. If you choose View⇔Refresh or View⇔Arrange Icons⇔by Name, the new files fall into proper alphabetical place in the list.

How to squeeze more onto a floppy disk

A typical 3.5-inch floppy disk can hold about 1.4MB of stuff. But you can squeeze more than that onto a floppy in the following ways:

Use DriveSpace to double the capacity of the floppy before you put anything on it. (See Chapter 10 for information on DriveSpace.)

Use a compression program such as PKZip to compress the files before (or while) copying them. (See Chapter 21 for information on file compression.)

A third technique is to use Backup, rather than Copy, to copy the files to the floppies. Backup can split a single file or group of files across several floppies. If you use Backup, you then need to use Restore to copy the files from the floppies to a hard disk. See Chapter 11 for more information on Backup and Restore.

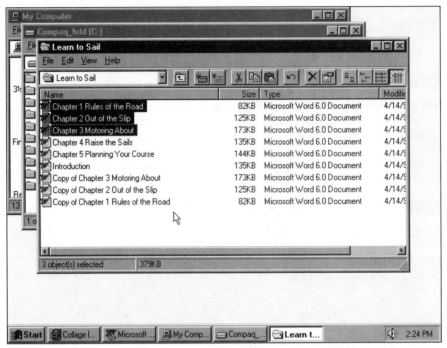

Figure 5-3: Quick copies of a few files made with the copy-and-paste method.

An alternative to drag-and-drop

As an alternative to drag-and-drop, you can cut and paste to move and copy files. Select the items that you want to use. To copy the selected items, choose Edit⇨Copy, press Ctrl+C, or click on the Copy button in the toolbar. To move the selected items, choose Edit⇨Cut, press Ctrl+X, or click on the Cut button in the toolbar.

Next, browse to the folder into which you want to put the moved or copied files. Open that folder; click within it; and then choose Edit⇨Paste, press Ctrl+V, or click on the Paste button in the toolbar.

Undoing a move or copy

If you complete a move or copy operation and then change your mind, you can undo that action as long as you don't do any more moving or copying. To undo a move or copy, choose Edit⇨Undo Copy or Edit⇨Undo Move. Alternatively, right-click on the desktop and then choose Undo Copy or Undo Move from the menu.

Deleting Selected Items

Deleting stuff from a hard disk is always a bit of a risk, because undeleting something is not always easy — in fact, it's often impossible to undelete. So observe the following cautions:

✦ Make sure that you look carefully at the files you're about to delete, and *never* delete a file unless you're sure that you know what you are deleting.

✦ If you're deleting a program, try using Uninstall (see Chapter 9) first. Uninstall does a more thorough job than "Delete" and automatically cleans up the Registry.

✦ When you delete a folder, be aware that you are deleting *everything* in that folder, including all subfolders.

Caution is the key to safe deleting. Always assume a worst-case scenario ("I *won't* be able to undelete this later") so that you don't get cocky and careless. Also, never move things to the Recycle Bin just to get them out of the way temporarily; you may forget about them and permanently delete them later.

✦ Only items that you delete from your local hard disk (typically, drive C) are sent to the Recycle Bin. Files on floppy disks and network drives are permanently deleted right on the spot and can't be undeleted.

✦ If you see the message `Are you sure you want to delete [whatever]?`, the files are going to be deleted immediately — *not* sent to the Recycle Bin. Think before you choose Yes.

✦ Remember that when you delete an icon, you are deleting everything on the disk that the icon represents. The only exception is the shortcut icon, which you can delete without affecting the underlying disk files.

When you're sure that you want to delete the selected items, do any of the following things:

✦ Press the Delete key.

✦ Choose File⇨Delete.

✦ Drag the items to the Recycle Bin. (Once again, only files on your local hard disk will actually be sent to the Recycle Bin.)

To delete a single item quickly, right-click on it and then choose Delete, or click on it and then press the Delete key.

Recovering trash from the Recycle Bin

If you move folders and/or files to the Recycle Bin, and then change your mind and decide to bring them back, you can *restore* them. Follow these steps:

1. Double-click on the Recycle Bin icon on the desktop to view its contents (see Figure 5-4).

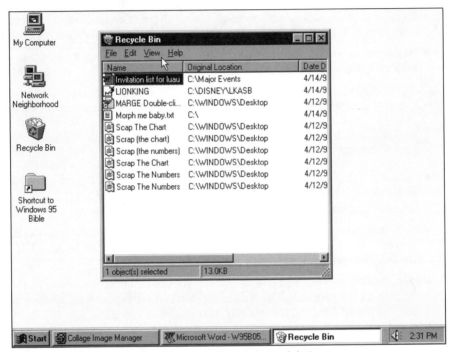

Figure 5-4: The Recycle Bin, with some files ready for deletion.

2. Select the items that you want to bring back to the desktop, using the universal techniques described in "Selecting Objects to Move, Copy, or Delete" earlier in this chapter.

3. Choose File⇨Restore.

If you want to select all the files in the Recycle Bin for recovery, you can press Ctrl+A to select them all.

Another way to undelete

If you send a bunch of files to the Recycle Bin and immediately change your mind, you can take a shortcut to restore those files instantly. Right-click on the desktop and choose Undo Delete from the menu that appears, or choose Edit⇨Undo Delete in the current window.

Recovering recycled disk space

Deleted files and folders that are in the Recycle Bin still occupy as much disk space as they did before you deleted them. In fact, the files are still on your hard disk; it's just that they're hidden from all browsing tools except the Recycle Bin. To use the disk space occupied by those recycled files, you must delete those files permanently. This procedure is called *emptying the Recycle Bin*.

Remember that after you empty the Recycle Bin, you cannot restore the files.

To empty the Recycle Bin, follow these steps:

1. Double-click on the Recycle Bin icon on the desktop.

2. Make sure that *only* files that you want to delete permanently are listed.

   (This is your last chance to change your mind and restore any files in the Recycle Bin.)

3. Choose File⇨Empty Recycle Bin.

 Microsoft should have named the Empty Recycle Bin command something like Burn Recycle Bin, because it permanently deletes the folders and files in the bin. Keep in mind that the command does *not* empty the bin back onto the desktop.

Personalize your Recycle Bin

You can customize the way that the Recycle Bin works on your PC. To see your options, first close the Recycle Bin if it's open; then right-click on the Recycle Bin icon and choose Properties. If you need help with an item, click on the Question-mark button in the menu bar and then click on the item. Alternatively, click on the item and then press F1.

Rename a File or Folder

Before you rename an icon, keep in mind that you're actually doing two things: changing the name that appears below the icon and changing the name of the file on the disk. The only exception to this rule is the shortcut icon, which you can rename (or move, copy, or delete) without affecting files on the disk.

To rename an icon (and its file), follow these steps:

1. Use any of the following techniques to select the icon that you want to rename and get the insertion point in place:

   • Right-click on the icon you want to rename and then choose Rena<u>m</u>e.

   • Click on the icon that you want to rename and then choose <u>F</u>ile⇨Rena<u>m</u>e.

   • Click on the icon (to select it), wait a second or two, and then click on the text that you want to change.

If you don't pause between the first and second click when clicking on an icon to rename it, Windows 95 may interpret your action as a double-click — which, of course, opens the icon. This situation is not a big deal, just potentially confusing. If you open a window by accident, simply click on its Close (X) button.

2. The text is selected, with the insertion point blinking, indicating that Windows is ready to accept your changes.

3. Make your changes, using standard Windows text-editing techniques (see the following section).

4. To save your changes, click on the area just outside the current icon, or click on a different icon within the same window (before you close the current window).

Standard text-editing techniques

The standard text-editing techniques in Windows 95 are the same as they were in Windows 3.x. Notice that you can use these techniques any time, anywhere, in any Windows program — in word processing programs, while filling in the blanks in forms, when filling a tiny text box, or while renaming something.

When text is selected, anything that you type instantly replaces all the selected text. (If you do this by accident, just press Esc.) If you want to change, rather than replace, the selected text, click on the place where you want to make your change, or press the Home, End, left-arrow, or right-arrow key.

The blinking insertion point (also called the I-beam or the cursor) indicates where any new text that you type will be placed. You can press the Delete key to erase the character the follows the insertion point or press Backspace to delete the character to the left of the insertion point.

To select a chunk of text to change or delete, drag the mouse pointer through that text, or hold down the Shift key while you move the insertion point with one of the keyboard direction keys. Then type the replacement text or press Delete to delete the selected text.

If you select the wrong text and need to make a change, drag the mouse pointer through some other text, click anywhere within the text, press Esc, or press any direction key without holding down the Shift key.

Change the name of your C drive

If, for whatever reason, you want to rename your C drive, open My Computer and then right-click on the icon for drive C. Choose P̲roperties, and type the new name in the box titled L̲abel. (This name can be no more than 11 characters long and cannot contain spaces.) Click on OK when you finish.

You can use the same technique to name or rename a floppy disk in a floppy drive, but you can't rename read-only disks (including all CD-ROMs).

Selecting Across Folders and Drives

Both My Computer and Explorer work on sort of a narrowing-down principle — you start by picking a drive and then perhaps a folder on the drive, and you end up seeing files and other folders within that particular folder. Most of the time, this procedure is fine. But once in a while, you may want to do something to all the files on a particular drive, regardless of which folder those files are in.

Suppose that disk space is getting tight, and you want to get rid of old backup (.bak) files that are floating around on your hard drive. You don't really care what folder each file is in; you want to make the deletions on an entire-hard-disk basis. The solution is simple: use Find, rather than My Computer or Explorer, to isolate all the files. Follow these steps:

1. Click on the Start button and then click on F̲ind.

2. Click on Files or F̲olders.

3. In the N̲amed text box, enter some word or phrase that identifies the types of files that you want to delete (or move, or copy).

4. In Figure 5-5, for example, I entered **bak** as the identifying portion of the name.

5. In the L̲ook in drop-down list, select the drive that you want to search (C, in my example), and make sure that Include s̲ubfolders is selected if you want to search all the folders on the drive.

If you want to move, copy, or delete files from all the folders in several drives, choose My Computer rather than a specific drive in Step 5. The resulting list shows files from all the folders from every drive that is physically connected to your PC, as well as from every drive on the LAN to which you have mapped a drive letter. Use caution, however — that's a lot of stuff.

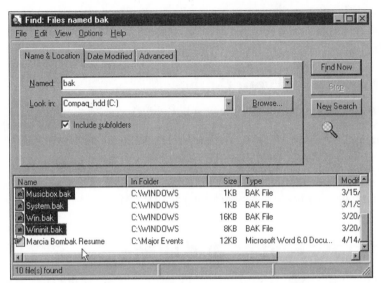

Figure 5-5: Searching drive C for files that have *bak* somewhere in the filename.

6. Click on F̲ind Now.

   The bottom part of the dialog box shows all the matching files.

7. Select the files that you want to delete (or move, or copy), and proceed as usual.

Don't be in too big a hurry when you're about to delete a group of files; look carefully before you leap. In the example shown in Figure 5-5, I chose V̲iew⇨Arrange I̲cons⇨by T̲ype to group all the files that have similar extensions. Then I widened the Name column for the list of filenames so that I could see the entire filenames. Using this method, I discovered that one of the files actually is a Word document named Marcia Bombak Resume (note the *bak* embedded in the filename). To exclude that document from what I was about to do, I didn't select it.

Using DOS Commands to Manage Files

If you're familiar with DOS commands, you may be relieved to hear that you can still use the CD, COPY, ERASE, DEL, MOVE, DELTREE, and RENAME commands to navigate and to move, copy, and delete files and folders.

First, click on the Start button; then click on Programs, and choose MS-DOS Prompt. You go to a C> prompt, where you can enter DOS commands. For brief help with a command, you can enter the command, followed by a space and /? — for example, **deltree /?**.

Where the file type comes from

When you look at a list of filenames in Details view, you'll notice that some files have rather wordy descriptions in the Type column — for example, Microsoft Word Document or Paintbrush Picture. Files that have these wordy Type descriptions are registered files. That wordy description actually is stored on the Windows 95 Registry, which is discussed in detail in Chapter 31.

Other files will have less-glamorous descriptions, such as BAK file or OLD file. Those files are unregistered, and the Type column is simply showing you the file extension followed by the word *file*. Therefore, a file described as the type BAK file is an unregistered file that has .bak as its extension.

When you use the Advanced tab in Find, you may discover that the Of type option allows you to isolate only registered file types. To isolate a nonregistered file type, click the Start button and choose Find⇨Files or Folders. Then click on the Name & Location tab. Then type the extension that you're looking for into the Named box.

When you type folder (directory) and filenames at the C> prompt, use the shortened name — typically, the first six letters, followed by a tilde and a number. Also, spaces should be removed. To get to a folder named Major Events on the current drive, for example, type **cd \majore~1** and then press Enter.

When you use the DOS DIR command, the leftmost column shows the shortened name of each folder and file; the rightmost column displays the long name. You can use that display to discover the short DOS name for any long Windows 95 name. Suppose that you want to determine the short DOS name for a folder or file named Mathilda Misanthrope. You could enter the command **dir mat*.*** to search the current folder or **dir c:\mat*.* /s** to search all of drive C for names that begin with the letters *mat*. For a reminder of all the options that you can use with DIR, enter **dir /?**.

To close the DOS window, enter the **exit** command at the C> prompt.

Summary

This chapter ends Part I of the book — the stuff that you *really* need to know to get along with your PC and Windows 95. If you've read from Chapter 1 to here, I thank you for your patience and hope that I've been of some help.

Keep in mind that practice makes perfect. It takes time to become fluent in the many tricks and techniques that Windows 95 offers for getting around and using your system. And don't forget that whenever you need help, you can always look things up in the online help manual.

Each chapter that follows this part of the book is like an independent essay about a topic that you may (or may not) be interested in. Feel free to skip anything that doesn't interest you.

Here's a quick recap of the most important skills covered in this chapter:

✦ To select an object to move, copy, or delete, just click on the object. To select several objects, you can drag a frame around them. Or use Ctrl+Click, Shift+Click, and Shift+Ctrl+Click.

✦ To move or copy selected object(s), hold down the right mouse button and drag to the destination. Then release the mouse button and choose Copy Here or Move Here from the shortcut menu that appears.

✦ To delete selected objects, press the Delete key. Or right-click on an object and choose Delete from the shortcut menu.

✦ Remember that objects that you delete from your local hard disk (only) are sent to the Recycle Bin, and continue to use up disk space until you empty the bin.

✦ To rename an object, right-click on the object and choose Rename from the shortcut menu.

✦ To "undelete" deleted items, open the Recycle Bin, select the items you want to restore, and then choose File⇨Restore from Recycle Bin's menu bar.

✦ To permanently delete objects in the Recycle Bin and recover their disk space, choose File⇨Empty Recycle Bin.

✦   ✦   ✦

Personalizing the Screen

This chapter looks at all the ways that you can personalize your screen to suit your tastes and needs. Elements such as screen colors, the size of text and objects on-screen, and the appearance of dates, times, and numbers are discussed. But this chapter won't cover techniques for organizing your desktop. Those topics are discussed in Chapter 8, which covers topics such as arranging files in folders, personalizing the Start menu, and customizing the taskbar.

Customizing the Screen: In a Nutshell

Personalizing your screen, wallpapers, and so on is easy in Windows 95. Just follow these simple steps:

Hot Stuff

Always, always, *always* adjust the brightness, contrast, and sizing controls (if any) on your monitor to get the best possible picture before you mess with the Display Properties. Then, if you do adjust the on-screen display settings, adjust those controls again when you finish to get the best possible picture from your new settings.

1. Right-click on the desktop and choose Properties. Alternatively, click on the Start button, choose Settings⊏>Control Panel, and then double-click on the Display icon.

   Either way, you see the Screen Properties dialog box, shown in Figure 6-1.

2. Click on any tab near the top of the dialog box and then choose any options within that tab.

   The sample monitor in the middle of the dialog box gives you a preview of the way your current selection will look on-screen.

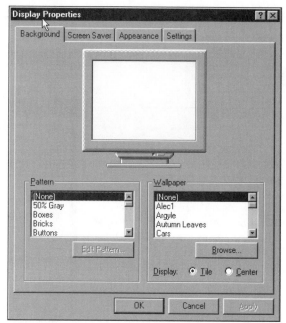

Figure 6-1: The Display Properties dialog box.

3. To apply your selection to the screen without leaving the dialog box, click on the Apply button.

4. When you finish, choose OK to save all your selections, or click on Cancel to save only the settings that you've already applied.

The following sections describe in detail the various options in the Display Properties dialog box. You also can get instant help in the Display Properties dialog box by clicking on the Question-mark button and then clicking on the option you need help with. Alternatively, click on the option you need help with and then press the Help key (F1).

Choosing color depth and resolution

The Settings tab in the Display Properties dialog box may be the most important of the four. Use the options in this tab to set up the general appearance of your screen, as discussed in the following sections.

Change display type

The first thing you want to do is make sure that Windows 95 is taking advantage of whatever features your graphics card and monitor have to offer. To do this, click on the Change Display Type in the Settings tab. Windows 95 displays the Change Display Type dialog box, shown in Figure 6-2.

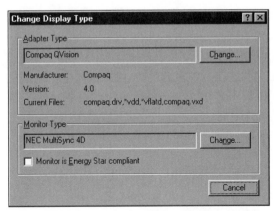

Figure 6-2: The Change Display Type dialog box.

Chances are that Windows 95 has already detected your adapter card and monitor type and that those settings already appear in the dialog box. If that's the case, you can just click on Cancel.

> **More Info** If you do purchase a new graphics adapter, use the Add New Hardware wizard (described in Chapter 10) to install it.

If you recently installed a new graphics card or monitor, the current settings may be incorrect. To choose the correct settings, first gather up your original Windows 95 floppy disks or CD-ROM. If your card or monitor came with disks, keep those disks handy, too. Then click on the Change button for whichever device you want to change. Read and follow the instructions that appear on-screen to install the software for that device.

> **Hot Stuff** If you have a disk for the hardware that you're installing *and* your device appears in the list, choose the driver from the list to ensure that you get the 32-bit Windows 95 driver for your device.

Color palette

The Color palette option in the Settings tab lets you select whatever color depths your graphics hardware offers: 16-color, 256-color, High Color (16-bit), and True Color (24-bit). Only options that are available for your graphics hardware will appear in the list.

The difference among these settings is that the higher you go, the closer you get to true photographic-quality color. The downside, however, is that the higher you go, the longer it takes to repaint the screen when things change. So it's up to you to decide the best tradeoff. I recommend that you not go below 256 colors, because most modern multimedia and graphics programs assume that you're using a 256 (or better) setting.

Desktop area (resolution)

What the Settings tab refers to as the Desktop Area is what the hardware manufacturers usually refer to as resolution. The terms really boil down to how many dots are on-screen (or, in plain English, how much stuff is displayed on-screen). The higher the resolution, the more stuff appears on-screen. The downside of resolution is that the higher the resolution, the *smaller* everything is on-screen.

To change the desktop area option, drag the slider to whatever setting you want. You are allowed to choose only settings that your graphics hardware supports. To get the best picture on-screen, it's especially important to adjust the brightness, contrast, and sizing controls on the monitor after changing the Desktop area option.

You also can change the appearance and size of the mouse pointer on the screen. See Chapter 7 for information.

Figure 6-3 shows three windows — one for Calculator, one for Cardfile, and one for CD Player — on the desktop at the low resolution of 640 × 480 pixels. I need to overlap the windows on this screen because of the small desktop area that I'm using.

Figure 6-4 shows the same three windows on-screen with the desktop area set to 1,024 × 768 pixels. Notice that I now have room to spread things out more, because each item on the screen is smaller.

Graphics-cards manufacturers often recommend that you choose a desktop area based on the physical size of your screen, as summarized in Table 6-1. However, it's really up to you to decide what's comfortable for your eyes. Also, because changing the desktop area on the fly is so easy, you can choose whatever desktop area is most convenient for the work that you happen to be doing at the moment.

Table 6-1	
Physical Screen Size and Recommended Desktop Area	
Screen Type/Size	*Recommended Desktop Area*
Laptop	640 × 480
15-inch diagonal	800 × 600
More than 15-inch diagonal	1,024 × 768

You usually can magnify or shrink the document within a Windows program without fussing with the desktop area setting. Choose View⇨Zoom in the current program or search the program's help system for the word *zoom*.

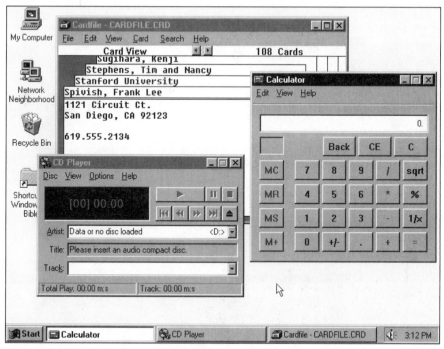

Figure 6-3: Three windows with the desktop area at 640 × 480.

Font size

The Font size option in the Setting tab determines the size of text on the desktop. The name that appears below an icon, for example, is affected by this setting. The options available to you depend on your graphics hardware. Typically, you get to choose between Small Fonts and Large Fonts. If you have trouble reading that kind of text on your screen, try switching to large fonts.

More Info If you're not familiar with fonts, see Chapter 14 for the pertinent concepts and terminology. But keep in mind that in this chapter, I'm discussing only the fonts on the Windows desktop. Settings that you make here have no effect on printed documents.

Some graphics hardware even allows you to define your own custom screen font, as indicated by the button named Custom. If this option is available and none of the other settings works for you, try a custom screen font.

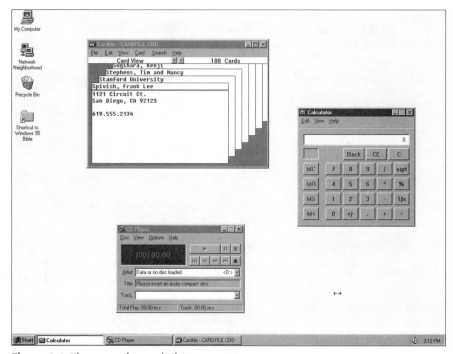

Figure 6-4: The same three windows at 1,024 × 768.

Don't forget that within any program, you usually can change the size of the text on your screen by using Zoom. This method, which simply magnifies the text within the current window, is easy because you don't need to change the resolution for the entire screen.

Choosing a color scheme

You can choose a color scheme for your Windows 95 desktop or make up your own color scheme. In the Display Properties dialog box, click on the Appearance tab. To select one of the predefined color schemes, click on the down-arrow button in the Scheme drop-down list and then click on your preference.

To create your own color scheme, first choose any of the predefined schemes as a starting point. Then choose an option in the Item drop-down list to color individual portions of the screen. For example, you could choose Desktop as the area to color. Then choose a color from the Color drop-down list. Some options also let you choose a Size. If you opt for Icon Spacing (Horizontal), you see the Size rather than the Color option. Enter a size (in pixels).

If the item that you're coloring contains text, you also can choose a Font, Size, and Color for that text. In Figure 6-5, I chose 12-point Lucida Handwriting (a popular TrueType font) as the font for active title bars. You also can choose a color and a weight: Bold (**B**) or Italic (/).

Figure 6-5: Text in active windows set to the 12-point Lucida Handwriting font.

Saving a custom color scheme

As soon as you start changing one of the predefined color schemes, the name for that scheme disappears from the Scheme text box. If you want to save the scheme you created, click on Save As and then enter a name.

Choosing a pattern or wallpaper

The Background tab of the Display Properties dialog box lets you add some texture to the desktop or put a picture (*wallpaper*) on the desktop. If your monitor is slow, you may want to use this option to remove patterns and wallpaper to speed things up. Either way, follow these steps:

1. Open the Display Properties dialog box, as discussed earlier, and click on the Background tab.

2. Do one of the following things:

   • To add some texture (rather than a picture) to the background, choose an option from the <u>P</u>attern list. To remove the current pattern, choose (None) from the top of that list. You also can click on <u>E</u>dit Pattern to change the currently selected pattern (if any).

   • To add wallpaper to the desktop, choose a <u>W</u>allpaper option. If you choose a small wallpaper pattern, you can select the <u>T</u>ile option to fill the screen with that picture.

3. Click on OK to save your selection.

If you choose a pattern and also tiled or full-screen wallpaper, the wallpaper will completely cover the pattern. In that case, you may as well set the pattern to (None).

Create your own wallpaper

You can use any graphic image that's stored on your disk in bitmap (.BMP) format as your wallpaper. If you have a scanner, you can scan a photo, company logo, or whatever into a file in Windows folder and then set the filename for your wallpaper to that file.

If you want the scanned image to fill the screen as wallpaper, be sure to size and scale the scanned image to your screen before you save it. In Figure 6-6, I used the program for my HP DeskJet scanner to scan a photo of my wife. Using options within that scanning program, I scaled the cropped area to 637 pixels wide × 487 pixels high — a close fit for my current desktop area of 640 × 480.

Figure 6-7 shows how my Windows 95 desktop looks with that wallpaper on-screen.

Scanner tips

When you scan an image to use as wallpaper or a screen saver, you should set the unit of measurement to pixels. Then as you scan, crop, and scale the picture, set its size to that of the desktop area. The larger of the two numbers is always the width. If you use 640 × 480 resolution, for example, scan to about 640 pixels wide × 480 pixels high.

To keep the file size of the scanned image small, don't go for extremely high print quality. A setting of 75 *dpi* (dots per inch) probably will do just fine.

If you don't have a scanner, check the phone book for desktop-publishing service bureaus in your area. Call around to see who can do the job and how much they'll charge. When you get there, show them this little sidebar to help explain what you want. Make sure that they save the image to a bitmap (.BMP) file. Warning: If the material you're scanning even *looks* like it's copyrighted, they may not be willing to scan it!

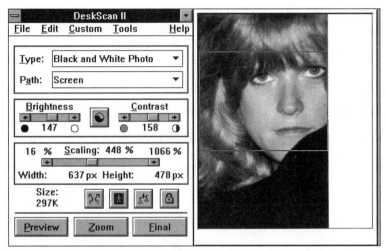

Figure 6-6: A photo scanned, cropped, and scaled for use as wallpaper.

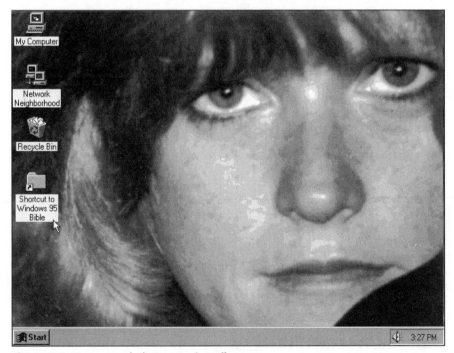

Figure 6-7: My scanned photo now is wallpaper.

Microsoft Plus!, discussed in Appendix F, includes an option to stretch a wallpaper image. So, if you scan a wallpaper image at 640 x 480, and then switch to a higher resolution on your screen, the wallpaper will stretch to fit the new resolution.

Paint a wallpaper

You also can use the Windows 95 Paint program to create wallpaper. To start Paint, click on the Start button, choose Programs➪Accessories, and then double-click on the Paint icon. You can use the Paint program's tools to create a picture from scratch. Alternatively, you can choose File➪Open within Paint to open an existing bitmap image and then use the program's tools to modify that image.

If you don't see Paint in your Accessories menu, maybe it isn't installed yet. See "Installing Missing Windows Components" in Chapter 9 for information on installing it.

To learn to use Paint, click on Help in Paint's menu bar and then click on Help Contents. Click on the Contents tab and then double-click on any book to learn about that topic.

When you're happy with the image that you created in Paint, save it, using the standard File➪Save command. After you save the image, you can set it as wallpaper by clicking on File and then choosing one of the following options:

✦ Set as Wallpaper (Tiled): fills the entire screen with your picture

✦ Set as Wallpaper (Centered): puts your picture in the center of the screen

Figure 6-8 shows an example in which I opened a clip-art image in Paint and used Paint's text tool to add the text *Under Construction* and *PLEASE DON'T TOUCH!*. Then I saved that image and chose File➪Save as Wallpaper (Tiled). The image fills the desktop behind Paint's window.

If you upgraded from Windows 3.x, you still may have the Paintbrush program on your system. You can use that program to create and modify bitmap images, but Paintbrush doesn't have the Set As Wallpaper commands described in this section.

To remove that wallpaper image or select another image, follow the steps described at the beginning of this section: right-click on the desktop, choose Properties, click on the Background tab, and then make your selections in the Wallpaper section.

Choosing a screen saver

A *screen saver* is a moving pattern that moves on your screen after some idle time. By *idle time*, I mean a period in which there has been no mouse or keyboard activity. The purpose of a screen saver is to prevent *burn-in*, a condition caused by keeping an unchanging image on the screen too long. Burn-in causes a screen to become blurry and lose some clarity.

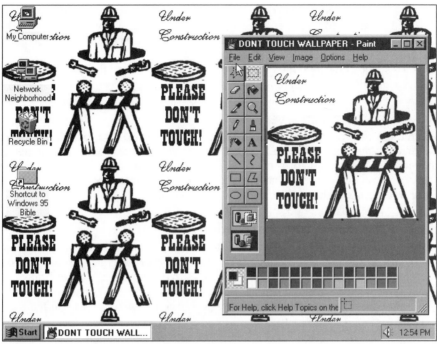

Figure 6-8: A Paint image set as tiled wallpaper.

Windows 95 gives you a few screen savers to choose among. To select a screen saver, follow these steps:

1. If you aren't in the Display Properties dialog box, right-click on the desktop and choose Properties.

2. Click on the Screen Saver tab.

3. Choose a screen saver from the Screen Saver drop-down list.

4. Do any of the following things:

   • To customize the screen saver that you selected, click on the Settings button and then choose among the options that appear.

   • To preview the currently selected screen saver and settings, click on the Preview button. (Move the mouse pointer a little to turn off the preview.)

   • Some screen savers, such as Flying Windows, support password protection. To use that feature, choose Password protected, click on the Change button, and enter a password as you are instructed on-screen.

If you password-protect your screen saver, make sure that you write your password on paper and store it in a safe place. Otherwise, if you forget the password, you won't be able to turn the screen saver off when you need to.

✦ To specify how long the PC needs to be inactive before the screen saver kicks in, specify the number of minutes in the <u>W</u>ait box.

Turning off the screen saver

When the screen saver kicks in, your Windows 95 desktop disappears, and a moving pattern or blank screen appears. To get back to your Windows 95 desktop, just move the mouse pointer a little or press any key. If you password-protected your screen saver, you will be prompted for your password. Type the correct password and press Enter to get back to the regular Windows 95 desktop.

Hacking the screen-saver password

I told a little white lie earlier when I said that after you enter a password for a screen saver, you're doomed if you forget it. Truth is, it's easy to hack (get around) a password-protected screen saver. I'm not telling you this to encourage computer break-ins; I just want to you to know what to do in case you forget your screen-saver password. (Or to get around the prank password left behind by some computer-store vandal.)

Create your own screen saver

Firefly Software Corporation (P.O. Box 782, Jericho, NY 11753, (516) 935-7060) sells a great program for making your own screen savers. The program is called PhotoGenix. It's not cheap (at least, it wasn't when I bought it), but it gets the job done, is simple to learn, and is fun to use. (Rumor has it that Microsoft may soon be releasing a similar program. Though I haven't seen it yet myself.)

First, you need to scan some photos (at least half a dozen, I'd recommend) into files. When you are scanning, scale and crop the photos to your desktop area, and then save them as bitmap files. In other words, create these images just as though you were going to use them as wallpaper (see "Create your own wallpaper" earlier in this chapter).

When you finish scanning, you can use PhotoGenix to assemble the photos into a slide show. You can even pick fancy transition effects from one picture to the next. That slide show then will become a screen saver, which you can select (like any other slide show) in the Screen Saver tab of the Display Properties dialog box. When the screen saver kicks in, you get to see a continuous slide show of your favorite photos.

To make a great computer gift for someone, steal his or her photo album temporarily — just long enough to scan that person's favorite photos — and then make a custom screen saver. Your friend will think that you're some kind of genius. (Don't tell him or her how easy it really was. And don't forget to return the purloined photo album.)

First, in you're stuck in the screen saver and can't get past the password request, you'll need to restart the PC. (I know this is a bummer, but you're stuck.) Either hit the Reset button on the PC, or turn the PC off then back on. Wait to get back to the Windows 95 desktop.

When Windows 95 has fully restarted, right-click the desktop and choose Properties. Click the Screen Saver tab, then click the Change button. Type in a new password, twice (preferably one you'll remember.). Or leave both password boxes blank. Choose OK. Optionally, if you want to get rid of Screen Saver password protection altogether, just clear the Password protected check box. Click on the OK button to return to the desktop. The original password is ancient history and won't bother you again.

If you have a 486 or Pentium PC, and at least a 256 Color monitor, you might want to purchase Microsoft Plus! (discussed in Appendix F). Plus! comes with some fun desktop themes that let you define a wallpaper, screen saver, colors — even sound events in one simple step.

Using Energy Star Features

Did you know that your computer monitor uses far more electricity than anything else in your computer? Even when the monitor is showing only a screen saver or blank screen, it's running up your electric bill. When you multiply your single monitor by the millions of computer screens out there, you've got a lot of screens sucking up a lot of energy, many of them doing nothing. To top it off, the monitors are putting out heat, even while they're doing nothing. According to some scientists, this contributes to global warming (I guess there's *a lot* of monitors out there!)

To curb this high-tech polluting waste of power, the Environmental Protection Agency (EPA) came up with a feature called Energy Star. Energy Star is a feature of many modern computer displays that automatically reduces power consumption — and even turns off the monitor automatically after the computer has been idle for some time. If your monitor complies with Energy Star standards, you'll see an Energy Star logo somewhere on the front or back of the monitor. You can use Windows 95 to put that feature into effect. Follow these steps:

Even if you don't turn off your computer at night, you still should turn off the monitor.

1. If you're not already in the Display Properties dialog box, right-click on the desktop and choose Properties.

2. Click on the Settings tab and then click the Change Display Type button.

3. Make sure that the correct monitor type is selected in the Monitor Type list and that the Monitor is Energy Star compliant option is selected.

If your monitor is one of the generic types (such as Super VGA) and you're sure that your graphics hardware is Energy Star-compliant, choose the Monitor is Energy Star compliant option.

4. Click on Close (if you made a change) or Cancel (if you did not make a change) to get back to the Display Properties dialog box.

5. Click on the Screen Saver tab.

The Energy savings feature of monitor options become available for selection (see Figure 6-9).

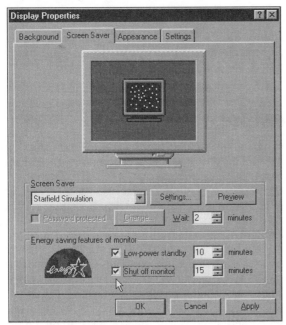

Figure 6-9: Energy Star's Low-power standby and Shut off monitor options are enabled.

6. Select Low-power standby, and then specify how long Windows 95 should wait (in minutes) to activate that feature.

7. Select Shut off monitor, and then specify how much idle time you require before that feature kicks in.

8. Click on the OK button.

In the example shown in Figure 6-9, I set up the screen saver to kick in after two minutes of idle time. I also activated the energy-savings features as follows:

✦ After 10 minutes, the monitor will switch to Low-power standby mode.

✦ After 15 minutes of idle time, the monitor will shut itself off.

Changing the Date and Time

The time indicator in the lower-right corner of the screen shows the current time. When you click on this indicator, it shows the date. If either the date or time is wrong, you can follow these steps to correct it:

1. Click on the Start button and then click on Settings.

2. Click on Control Panel and then double-click on Date/Time to get to the Date/ Time Properties dialog box.

3. In the Date pane (see Figure 6-10), choose the current month and year from the drop-down lists; then click on the current day in the calendar.

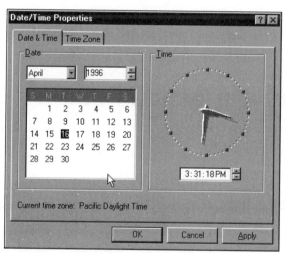

Figure 6-10: The Date/Time Properties dialog box.

4. In the Time pane, click on the hour, minute, second, or AM/PM option; then use the spin box to set the appropriate time.

   Optionally, you can type the correct time.

5. Click on the Time Zone tab, and choose your time zone.

   You can click on your location on the map, or you can press the left-arrow and right-arrow keys to move the highlight to your time zone.

6. If you have daylight savings time in your time zone, select the Automatically adjust clock for daylight saving changes option (see Figure 6-11).

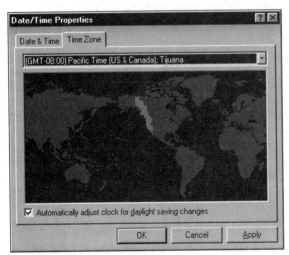

Figure 6-11: Map for telling Windows what time zone you're in.

      7. Click on the OK button to save your settings.

Date, Time, Currency, and Number Formats

The world has many standards for displaying dates, times, numbers, and currency values. In the United States, we use a period as a decimal point, but Great Britain uses a comma. The Regional Settings dialog box in Windows 95 allows you to specify the formats that you want to use on your PC.

To choose regional formats, follow these steps:

      1. Click on the Start button, point to <u>S</u>ettings, and then click on <u>C</u>ontrol Panel.

      2. Double-click on the Regional Settings icon.

         You see the dialog box shown in Figure 6-12.

      3. Click any green region on the map, or select a region from the drop-down list.

 Most Windows programs use whatever date, time, currency, and number format you specify in the Regional Settings Properties dialog box. You don't have to pick the same settings for every program on your system.

      4. To set the Number, Currency, Time, or Date format individually, click on the appropriate tab and then choose among the options provided.

      5. Click on OK to save your changes.

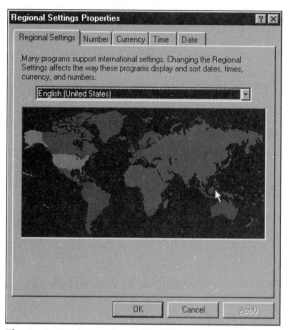

Figure 6-12: The Regional Settings Properties dialog box.

Summary

All right, let's review the most important things discussed in this chapter:

✦ To personalize your screen settings, first right-click the desktop and choose Properties. Then...

✦ To change the background pattern or wallpaper, click on the Background tab.

✦ To change the screen saver, click the Screen Saver tab.

✦ To change the screen colors, click on the Appearance tab.

✦ To change the color palette, resolution, font, and display type, click the Settings tab.

✦ To change the date, time, and format of numbers and currencies, you need to go through the Control Panel (click the Start button, point to Settings, click on Control Panel).

✦   ✦   ✦

Personalizing the Mouse, Keyboard, and Joystick

In this chapter I talk about techniques for tailoring your mouse and keyboard to your own personal work style and habits. If you use a joystick to play games on your PC, you'll find some tips for calibrating the joystick as well. This chapter will also discuss Window 95's accessibility options, which can make using a PC much easier for people with physical disabilities or impairments.

Customizing the Mouse/Keyboard: In a Nutshell

It's easy to personalize your mouse and keyboard, as well as your joystick, if you have one. Following is the general procedure, no matter which device you want to personalize:

1. Click on the Start button, and point to Settings.

2. Click on Control Panel.

3. Do any of the following things:

   • To personalize the mouse, double-click on the Mouse icon.

   • To personalize the keyboard, double-click on the Keyboard icon

   • To personalize the joystick, double-click on the Joystick icon.

4. Make your selections in the tabs provided.

5. Choose OK to get back to the desktop.

As always, you can use the question-mark button (?) or the F1 key to get help with any option in a dialog box. You also can find information in the online manual. From the desktop, click on the Start button, click on Help, and then click on Index. Search for the word *mouse, keyboard*, or *joystick*, depending on your interest.

Personalize the Mouse

When you install Windows 95, it assumes that you're using a standard mouse and a standard desktop monitor, that you're right-handed, and so on. This isn't always the case, though. If the mouse pointer is causing you eyestrain, or if you're just feeling a little klutzy with the mouse, perhaps you should change some of those assumptions.

If your work requires very precise mouse pointing, consider using MouseKeys, which allows you to position the mouse with the numeric keypad. For information, see "Accessibility Options for Physical Impairments" later in this chapter.

To make changes, go to the Control Panel, as described in the preceding section. Then double-click on the Mouse icon to get to the Mouse Properties dialog box, shown in Figure 7-1.

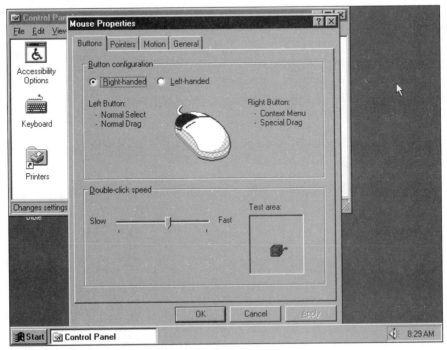

Figure 7-1: The Mouse Properties dialog box.

Tell Windows 95 which mouse you have

The first thing that you want to do is tell Windows 95 which mouse you're using. Click on the General tab. If the mouse displayed in the Name text box is not the mouse that you're using, you should install the appropriate mouse driver. Gather up your original Windows 95 disks or CD-ROM and the disk that came with your mouse (if any). Then click on the Change button, and click on the Show all devices option button.

If you see the manufacturer and model of your mouse, select them, and then choose OK. If you *don't* see the manufacturer and model for your mouse but you *do* have a disk for that mouse, place the disk in the floppy drive, and click on the Have Disk button. Then just follow the instructions on-screen. When you finish, the Name text box in the General tab should show the correct name for your mouse.

Mice for lefties

If you're left-handed and want the main mouse button to be below your index finger, click on the Buttons tab (Figure 7-1) and choose Left-handed. Now you'll need to remember to use the mouse button on the right (the one below your index finger) to click, double-click, and drag. To "right-click" and "right-drag," you'll actually use the button on the left.

Mice and DOS programs

In Windows 3.x, using your mouse in both DOS and Windows programs was kind of a mess. You had to install a separate mouse driver in your CONFIG.SYS or AUTOEXEC.BAT file; and even so, you may have found that the mouse worked in a full-screen DOS session but not in a windowed DOS session.

Windows 95 clears up this mess by having a single mouse driver for all occasions. That mouse driver is installed as soon as you start Windows 95. (In fact, if your mouse isn't plugged in when you start Windows 95 and you plug in the mouse later, the mouse *still* works — a handy arrangement when you forget to plug in your external mouse on a laptop).

Anyway, if you're familiar with DOS and drivers, you may want to peek at your C:\CONFIG.SYS and C:\AUTOEXEC.BAT files to see whether either still loads a mouse driver. If so, you can delete that command (or put a REM statement in front of it) to disable your driver. The next time you start Windows 95, that DOS driver won't be loaded (which saves a little precious RAM), and your mouse should still work fine in every program that you use.

Take control of double-clicking

If you find double-clicking to be a problem, you may want to speed or slow the double-click speed. If you can't seem to double-click fast enough, for example, you want to slow the double-click speed. On the other hand, if you often find yourself accidentally double-clicking when you really meant to make two separate clicks, you want to speed the double-click rate.

The Double-click speed option in the Buttons tab lets you determine how fast two clicks must be to be interpreted as a double-click. To find the double-click speed that works best for you, try the following steps:

1. Drag the slider below Double-click speed all the way to the Fast end of the scale.

2. Double-click on the jack-in-the-box, using your normal double-click speed.

3. If the jack-in-the-box doesn't open, drag the slider bar a little way toward Slow.

4. Repeat steps 2 and 3 until you find a double-click speed that's comfortable for you.

Controlling the mouse motion

If you find it difficult to zero in on things with the mouse pointer, you'll want to slow the mouse-motion speed. Alternatively, if you seem to have to move the mouse too far to get from point A to point B on-screen, the mouse-pointer speed probably is set too slow. On laptop LCD screens (and some others), the mouse pointer may fade or even disappear when you move the mouse. To solve that irritating problem, you need to turn on the pointer trails.

Hot Stuff

When you're using a projector to give a demonstration on the screen, turning on pointer trails makes it easier for your audience to follow the mouse across the screen.

To control the mouse speed and trails, click on the Motion tab in the Mouse Properties dialog box (see Figure 7-2). To adjust the speed of the pointer, drag the slider in the Pointer speed slider bar toward the Slow or Fast end of the bar. To test your current setting, click on the Apply button, and try moving the mouse around. To see your full range of options, apply the slowest speed, and test the mouse. Then apply the faster speed, and try the mouse again.

To turn on pointer trails, select the Show pointer trails check box. The trails turn on immediately and will be visible as soon as you move the mouse. To control the length of the trails, drag the slider to the Short or Long end of the slider bar.

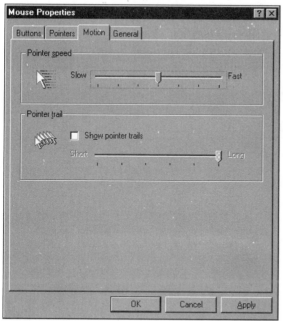

Figure 7-2: Options for controlling mouse speed and pointer trails.

Choosing mouse pointers

If the mouse pointer is hard to see, try a larger pointer. If you just get bored with the same old pointer, you can try some fancy 3-D animated pointers, quite a few of which came with your Windows 95 program. If you haven't already installed these pointers, you can use the general technique for installing missing Windows components (described in Chapter 9) to install them at any time. When you get to the Windows Setup tab, click on Accessories, click on the Details button, and then click on Mouse Pointers.

After you install custom and/or animated mouse pointers on your hard disk, go back to the Mouse Properties dialog box, as described under " Customize the Mouse/ Keyboard: In a Nutshell" earlier in this chapter. Then click on the Pointers tab to get to the dialog box shown in Figure 7-3. From there, you can select any predefined pointer scheme in the Scheme drop-down list or assign a custom pointer to any type of pointer. Double-click on the pointer that you want to change (such as Regular Select) to get to the Browse dialog box for pointers.

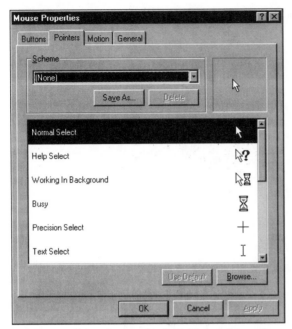

Figure 7-3: The Pointers tab of the Mouse Properties dialog box.

In the Browse dialog box you can click on any cursor that's listed to get a closer look at that cursor. The Preview box shows you the pointer. The filename usually tells you something about the pointer. For example, ARROW_1 is the regular mouse pointer, ARROW_L is the large version of that cursor, and ARROW_M is the midsize one. After making your selection, click on the Open button.

If you have installed animated cursors in any other folder, you can use the Look in drop-down list to browse to the appropriate folder, where you can make your selections.

After you select one or more custom cursors, you can save your selections as a predefined cursor scheme. Click on the Save As button, give your scheme a filename, and then choose OK to return to Control Panel. The cursors that you selected will be in effect from that point on.

Finding animated cursors

Undoubtedly, you'll be able to purchase collections of animated and 3-D cursors at your local computer store shortly after Windows 95 hits the streets. But be aware that hundreds of free 3-D and animated cursors for Windows NT are floating around on bulletin boards and the Internet. These cursors work fine in Windows 95 as well.

Files that contain an animated cursor have the extension .ANI. Files that contain a custom, nonanimated cursor have the extension .CUR. Types of files are displayed automatically in the Browse window in the Pointers tab of the Mouse Properties dialog box.

Personalize the Keyboard

You also can customize the way that your keyboard operates in Windows 95. Follow the steps under "Customize the Mouse/Keyboard: In a Nutshell" at the start of this chapter to get to the Keyboard Properties dialog box (see Figure 7-4). Then use the options discussed on the sections that follow to fine-tune your keyboard.

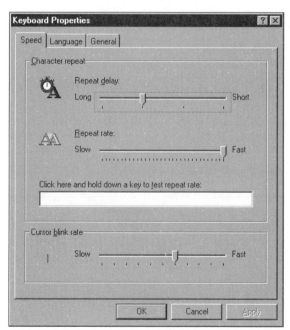

Figure 7-4: The Keyboard Properties dialog box.

Tell Windows 95 what keyboard you have

To make sure that you get the best performance from your keyboard, first make sure that Windows 95 knows what keyboard you're using. Click on the General tab and then look at the Keyboard type setting. If your current keyboard isn't selected, follow these steps:

1. Gather up your original Windows 95 CD-ROM or floppy disks.

   If your keyboard came with a floppy disk of its own, keep that disk handy as well.

2. Click on the Change button.

3. Click on the Show all devices option.

4. If you see your keyboard listed, click on its name and then click on OK.

   Alternatively, put the floppy disk that came with the keyboard into a floppy drive and then click on the Have Disk button.

5. Follow any instructions that appear on-screen.

After you select the appropriate keyboard type, you can use the options described in the following sections to fine-tune your keyboard's performance.

Control the keyboard's responsiveness

Most keyboards are *typematic*, which means that if you hold down a key long enough, it starts repeating automatically. If you're a slow typist, you may find that you accidentally type the same letter two or more times.

To correct the problem, click on the Speed tab of the Keyboard Properties dialog box. Then drag the slider below Repeat delay to the Long side of the slider bar. Click on the text bar below Click here and hold down a key to test repeat rate; then hold down any letter key until it starts repeating.

To shorten the delay between the time when you hold down the key and the time when the key starts repeating, drag the slider toward the Short side of the slider bar.

You also can use the Repeat Rate slider bar to determine how fast the key repeats.

Control the cursor blink speed

The Speed tab of the Keyboard Properties dialog box also allows you to specify how fast the cursor (also called the *insertion point*) blinks. Drag the slider to the Slow or Fast end of the bar, and watch the sample blinking cursor. I guess the idea is to find a speed that's in sync with your own cosmic biorhythms or, perhaps, the pace of life in your locale. In San Diego, for example, people probably like slow-blinking cursors; in New York City, they probably like their cursors blinking at full-on, high-anxiety speed (hurry! *hurry!*).

Multiple-language keyboarding

For people who work in multiple languages, Windows 95 offers some significant improvements over Windows 3.x, including the following:

✦ Easy switching from the keyboard layout used in one language to the keyboard layout for another language

✦ Automatic font substitution when switching among different languages (fonts are discussed in Chapter 14)

✦ Correct sorting and comparison rules for different locales and cultures

 You can set the format of dates, times, numbers, and currency values by using the Regional Settings icon in Control Panel. Look near the end of Chapter 6 for more information.

The following sections examine techniques for installing multiple-language support and using multiple-language keyboard layouts.

Setting keyboard languages and layouts

The first step is to choose specific languages and keyboard layouts that are appropriate to your work. Follow these steps:

1. Windows 95 may need to install specific languages during this procedure, so first close all open programs and save your work; then gather up your original Windows 95 floppies or CD-ROM.

2. Click on the Start button, point to Settings, and then click on Control Panel.

3. Double-click on the Keyboard icon.

4. Click on the Language tab to display the options shown in Figure 7-5.

5. Click on the Add button, and choose a language from the drop-down list.

6. Click on the OK button, and follow any instructions that appear on-screen.

7. Click on the Properties button, and choose a keyboard layout for the currently selected language.

8. Repeat steps 5–8 to add as many languages as you want.

9. To select a default language, click on the language you want and then click on the Set as Default button.

10. You also can choose a shortcut key for switching languages: left Alt key+Shift or Ctrl+Shift.

    Alternatively, choose None for no keyboard shortcut.

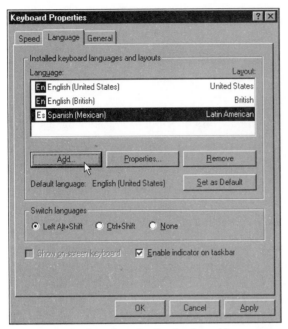

Figure 7-5: Options for selecting keyboard languages and layouts.

11. Optionally, you can choose Show <u>o</u>n-screen keyboard (if you plan to use a keyboard layout that differs from the physical layout of your keyboard) and <u>E</u>nable indicator on the taskbar (if you want to be able to switch between languages simply by clicking on an icon in the taskbar).

12. Choose OK when you finish making your selections.

As usual, if any additional instructions appear on-screen, be sure to read and follow them.

Switching among languages and layouts
After you select one or more foreign languages and layouts, switching among them is easy. If you selected the Enable indicator on taskbar option while you chose layouts, you'll see a two-letter abbreviation at the right end of the taskbar, indicating which language is in use at the moment — for example, you would see En if you're working in English.

To switch to another language and keyboard layout, do either of the following things:

✦ Click on the language indicator in the taskbar and then click on the language that you want to use (see Figure 7-6).

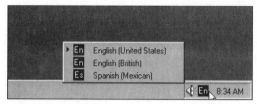

Figure 7-6: Clicking the En indicator to switch to another language.

✦ Press the shortcut keys that you indicated (for example, left Alt key+Shift) and then choose a language.

Now you should be able to fire up your word processing program and type with the currently selected language and keyboard layout. In fact, you can switch to another language and layout on the spot; anything new that you type will use the language, layout, and (if applicable) font for that language. In a true multilingually aware program, you will even be able to move the cursor through existing text to change that text to whatever language and font you're using at the moment.

Programmers: You can use the Win32 NLS APIs (National Language Support Application Program Interface) to build international-language support into all your Windows 95 and Windows NT applications.

Add and Personalize a Joystick

Joysticks are optional input devices used mainly for playing games. Joysticks range from an inexpensive movable stick with a button on top to elaborate steering-wheel and foot-control gizmos for playing simulation games (such as Microsoft's Flight Simulator). I'm more inclined to use my PCs as slave-labor devices than for entertainment, so I won't claim to be an expert on joysticks. I do know, however, that a joystick is fairly easy to install, use, and fine-tune in Windows 95.

To see a list of Windows 95-supported joysticks *before* you buy a joystick, click the Start button, choose Settings⇨Control Panel and double-click the Joystick icon to get to the Joystock Properties dialog. Click on the drop-down arrow under the *Joystick configuration* option, and scroll through the list using the scroll bar or arrow keys. After reviewing the list, choose Cancel to return to the Control Panel without actually installing a joystick.

You install the joystick as you would any other device (see Chapter 10 for instructions). If the joystick is a Windows 95 plug-and-play device, all you have to do is plug it in.

To test and calibrate the joystick, click on the Start button, point to Settings, click on Control Panel, and then double-click on the Joystick icon. If you have several joysticks, select the one that you want to calibrate now from the Current Joystick drop-down list.

Next (if you haven't already done so), assign a specific joystick to the option that you selected. Click on the Joystick Selection down-arrow button, and choose the type of joystick that you have installed from the list that appears. The Rudder, Calibrate, and Test options then will be available, as appropriate.

Remember that if you need help with any option, you can click on the Question-mark button (?) and then click on the option you need help with, or click on an option and then press the help key (F1).

Accessibility Options for Physical Impairments

More than half the corporations in the United States employ people whose disabilities can make using a computer difficult. In its never-ending battle to make computers easier for everyone to use, Microsoft included an enhanced version of its Access Pack in Windows 95. The features of the new Access Pack are called the Accessibility Options.

Installing accessibility options

If you've never used the Windows 95 accessibility options, you may need to install them. Use the standard technique for installing missing Windows components. Save any work in progress, and close all open programs. Gather up your original Windows 95 floppy disks or CD-ROM. Then click on the Start button, point to Settings, and click on Control Panel. Double-click on the Add/Remove Programs icon and then click on the Windows Setup tab. Click on the Accessories option, and click on the Details button. Finally, if the Accessibility Options item is *not* checked, select it and then click on OK. Follow the instructions on the screen.

 For quick online information about accessibility options, click on the Start button, click on Help, then click on the Index tab. Type **accessi** to get to the accessibility topic.

If you have any problems activating the accessibility options later, you may need to restart your PC. Remove any floppy disks, click on the Start button, click on Shut Down, choose Restart the computer?, and then click on Yes. Wait for the Windows 95 desktop to reappear.

Activating accessibility options

When they are installed, you can activate the accessibility options through the Control Panel. Follow these steps:

1. Click on the Start button, point to <u>S</u>ettings, and then click on <u>C</u>ontrol Panel.

2. Double-click on the Accessibility Options icon to display the Accessibility Properties dialog box, shown in Figure 7-7.

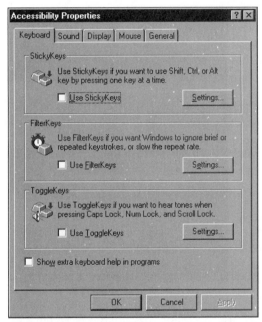

Figure 7-7: The Accessibility Properties dialog box.

The sections that follow describe how to activate and use the various accessibility options. An alternative emergency hot key is available for activating and deactivating each option. Use the hot key if your impairment makes it difficult to get to the Control Panel. For future reference, Table 7-1 shows you how to turn each feature on and off (when the accessibility options are activated) by using the hot keys.

Table 7-1	
Emergency Hot Keys for Turning Accessibility Options On and Off	
Activated Accessibility Feature	*Emergency Hot key*
FilterKeys	Hold down right Shift key for 8 seconds
High-Contrast Mode	Left Alt + Left Shift + Print Screen
MouseKeys	Left Alt +Left Shift + Num Lock
StickyKeys	Press Shift 5 times
ToggleKeys	Hold down Num Lock for 5 seconds

The accessibility options are available even when you're running a DOS program.

Easier mouse/keyboard interaction

Countless physical impairments can make operating the keyboard and mouse difficult. Some of the options for personalizing the mouse and keyboard, described earlier in this chapter, may help. In addition, you can activate options in the Keyboard tab of the Accessibility Properties dialog box, as described in the following sections.

StickyKeys

If you have difficulty pressing two keys at the same time, such as Ctrl+Esc, activate the StickyKeys feature. Choose that option in the Keyboard tab and then click on the Settings button to activate whichever StickyKeys features you want.

For example, you can set StickyKeys so that pressing any modifier key — such as Ctrl, Alt, or Shift — automatically locks down that key. The key stays locked down until you press the second (nonmodifier) key. Optionally, you can make a modified key even stickier, so that pressing the key twice in a row keeps it locked down. To unlock the key, press the modifier key a third time.

When the feature is activated, you can turn StickyKeys on and off by tapping the Shift key five times.

FilterKeys

If you find yourself double-pressing keys by holding them down too long or typing extra characters because your finger just brushes nearby keys, use the FilterKeys option to change the sensitivity of the keyboard. After you select the FilterKeys option, use the Settings buttons to specify which features you want to activate.

To turn FilterKeys on and off from the keyboard, hold down the Shift key on the right side of the keyboard for eight seconds.

ToggleKeys

The ToggleKeys option, when activated, uses high and low tones to tell you when the toggle keys Caps Lock, Scroll Lock, and Num Lock are on or off. To turn ToggleKeys on and off from the keyboard, hold down the Num Lock key for five seconds.

MouseKeys

If you want to be able to control the mouse pointer from the numeric keypad, click on the Mouse tab of the Accessibility Properties dialog box and then activate Use MouseKeys. Click on the Settings button to specify how you want to implement MouseKeys. For example, you can have the keys in the numeric keypad operate the mouse when the Num Lock key is on or when it's off.

When MouseKeys is activated, you can control the mouse as follows:

✦ *Move the mouse pointer.* Press (or hold down) the keys surrounding the number 5 in the numeric keypad.

✦ *Click.* Press the 5 key in the middle of the numeric keypad.

✦ *Double-click.* Press the plus-sign (+) key in the numeric keypad.

✦ *Drag (left mouse button).* Point to the object, press the Insert key to begin dragging, use the number keys to move the mouse pointer, and then press Delete to complete the operation.

✦ *Right-click.* To right-click, position the mouse pointer, and then press and release the minus-sign (–) key or the 5 key in the numeric keypad.

✦ *Right-drag.* To right-drag, point to the object that you want to drag, press the minus-sign (–) key in the numeric keypad, and then press the Insert key to lock down that button. Use the arrow keys to drag; then press the Delete key to complete the drag.

✦ *Click both mouse buttons.* To click both mouse buttons, press and release the asterisk (*) key in the numeric keypad.

✦ *Jump the mouse pointer* in large increments across the screen. Hold down the Ctrl key while pressing a direction key in the numeric keypad.

✦ *Slow the movement of the mouse pointer* (as when you need to position it precisely). hold down the Shift key as you move the mouse pointer with the numeric keypad.

 Even if you're not physically impaired, you may find MouseKeys to be a handy option, especially if you need to position the mouse precisely in your work. It's easier to do that with the numeric keypad than with the mouse.

To turn MouseKeys on and off from the keyboard, hold down the left Alt key, hold down the left Shift key, and then hold down the Num Lock key.

Visual enhancements

If you have any difficulty seeing the screen, or if you find that your eyes fatigue quickly, the first thing that you should do is adjust the knobs on the monitor and personalize the screen display, as discussed in Chapter 6. If your vision is impaired, you may want to select one of the predefined high-contrast color schemes, which are available when you follow the procedure in "Choosing a Color Scheme" in Chapter 6.

If your vision is impaired and you share a computer with another user, you may find it difficult to read the screen when that user leaves his or her settings behind. In such a case, you can set up some emergency hot keys to take you straight to high-contrast mode as soon as you sit down at the keyboard.

To activate the quick switch to high-contrast mode, display the Accessibility Properties dialog box (Start⇨Settings⇨Control Panel and double-click Accessibility Options). Click on the Display tab, and choose Use High Contrast. Click on the Settings button to select a scheme: Black on White, White on Black, or Custom (to choose a different color scheme). Make sure that the check box for the emergency hot key is checked.

When this feature is activated, you can hold down the Alt key, hold down the left Shift key, and press the Print Screen key to turn high-contrast mode on and off.

Sound enhancements

Windows 95 offers visual cues as alternatives to the audio cues that alert the user to some condition. You can activate the sound enhancements by displaying the Accessibility Properties dialog box and clicking on the Sound tab (see Figure 7-8). Then you can activate either or both of the features provided.

If you activate the SoundSentry, you can choose the Settings button to assign visual cues to the warning beep that Windows 95 emits to call attention to the screen. When you activate ShowSounds, you actually activate the closed-captioned capability that's offered in many modern programs that offer speech or other audible cues.

Alternative input devices

Windows 95 also provides built-in support for alternative input devices, including eye-gaze systems and head pointers. Typically, you can plug any such device into any available serial port; you don't need to disconnect the mouse first.

To give an alternate input device its own serial port, install the device according to the manufacturer's instructions and then click on the General tab in the Accessibility Properties dialog box. Turn on the Support SerialKeys devices feature, and use the Settings button to assign the device to the serial port that it's plugged into.

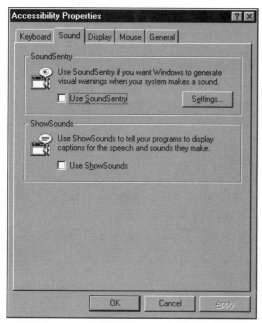

Figure 7-8: Accessibility options for hearing impairments.

Accessibility time-out and status indicator

If disabled and nondisabled users share a PC, you may want to activate the time-out feature and status indicator. The time-out feature turns off the accessibility features, returning to the regular settings, after the PC has been idle for a specified period.

The Accessibility Indicator lets all users see when the accessibility features are active and (optionally) can provide audio feedback when a feature is turned on or off. The indicator also tells MouseKeys and StickyKeys users when a key or mouse button is locked down.

To activate either of these options, click on the General tab of the Accessibility Properties dialog box. Then choose the options that you want to use and the idle time (if any) for turning off the accessibility options.

Summary

All of the techniques for personalizing your mouse, keyboard, joystick, and accessibility options are in the Control Panel. Here's a quick summary of the exact steps required to personalize each device:

✦ To personalize your mouse, click the Start button, choose Settings⇨Control Panel, and double-click the Mouse icon.

✦ To personalize your keyboard, click the Start button, choose Settings⇨Control Panel, and double-click the Keyboard icon.

✦ To personalize your joystick, click the Start button, choose Settings⇨Control Panel, and double-click the Joystick icon.

✦ To activate accessibility options, click the Start button, choose Settings⇨Control Panel, and double-click the Accessibility Options icon.

✦   ✦   ✦

Organizing Your Virtual Office

E arlier in the book, I said that you can think of your
computer's hard disk as being an electronic file cabinet where
you keep everything that's in the computer. The screen is like
your desktop, where you put the stuff that you're working on at
the moment. In a sense, every PC is like a small virtual office with
a file cabinet and a desktop. And as in a real office, the better you
organize things in the virtual office, the easier it is to find things.

Why Folders?

I'll talk first about file cabinets. Imagine a real file cabinet filled with
documents (on paper), but no folders — just sheet after sheet of
paper. What a pain trying to find a particular document would be.

Folders on a disk serve exactly the same purpose as folders in a
file cabinet: to organize stuff so that you can easily find it later. If
you had no folders on your hard disk, you'd continually be
digging through hundreds, maybe thousands of documents
trying to locate whatever document you need at the moment.

Undoubtedly, your hard disk already is organized into folders;
when you install a new program, the installation procedure
(usually) creates one or more folders to put that program's files
in. If you have Microsoft Word, for example, all the files that
make up that program are stored together in a folder named
(usually) WinWord.

Before I start talking about creating and managing folders, I want
to point out that in general, it's *not* a good idea to move or
rename any of the folders created by a program's installation
procedure. Doing so usually is more trouble than it's worth. For
one thing, the Windows 95 Registry keeps track of where various
folders and files are, so when you start moving registered things
around, you run the risk of fouling up the Registry.

Another problem is that any shortcuts you create will continue to point to the original folder. The shortcut won't work anymore, because the folder that it expects to find no longer exists. Older Windows 3.x programs become problematic, because they often put folder (directory) information in several places: initialization (INI) files, and perhaps in the DOS startup files C:\CONFIG.SYS and C:\AUTOEXEC.BAT.

To illustrate why it's not good to mess with the names or locations of a program's folders, let me tell you about a couple of examples from my own experience. Of course, I'll tell you how I fixed the problems that I'd created for myself.

Folder problem 1

One day, I was browsing around my hard disk and came across a folder named Waol15. I couldn't remember what was in the oddly-named folder. I did a little exploring and discovered that it contained the programs I use to interact with America Online (an online information service). Thinking myself clever, I renamed that folder America Online so that I wouldn't forget its contents in the future.

Whoops — that wasn't a good move. The next time I tried to use America Online, I had nothing but problems from the get-go — not because of anything that was wrong with America Online's program, but because I had renamed its folder. My America Online program still expected to find things in a folder named Waol15 (the C:\WAOL15 directory, in DOS terminology). But because I'd renamed that folder, I had no folder named Waol15 anymore.

Fixing the problem was simple, once I realized what was wrong. I changed the name of the America Online folder back to Waol15, and all was well again.

Folder problem 2

Another time, I moved a folder from its current location to a new location in a different folder. I'd made a slightly different mistake, but one that had the same unpleasant results.

Here's what happened:

I had installed Microsoft Access 2, and its installation procedure had put all the programs for Access in a folder named Access (C:\ACCESS, in DOS terminology). Later, I installed Microsoft Office. The installation procedure for Office created a folder named MSOffice; it also created a couple of subfolders inside the MSOffice folder. One of these subfolders was named WinWord (C:\MSOFFICE\WINWORD, in DOS terminology); Office used that folder to store Microsoft Word. The second subfolder, named Excel (C:\MSOFFICE\EXCEL), was where Office stored Microsoft Excel.

It dawned on me that because Access is part of the Microsoft Office suite, I could move Access's folder into the MSOffice folder. So without much forethought, I dragged the Access folder into the MSOffice folder. Not smart. The next time I launched Microsoft Access, I immediately started having problems. As in the preceding example, when the Access program needed something from the disk, it went looking for a folder named C:\ACCESS.

You may think, "Yeah, but you didn't change that name of the folder." True. But by moving the folder, I automatically changed its name as well. In this case, I'd changed the name of the Access folder from C:\ACCESS to C:\MSOFFICE\ACCESS (looking at the names from a DOS perspective). Those names are not the same. So whenever Access needed something from C:\ACCESS, it would bomb.

Once again, the cure was simply to drag Access's directory back to its original location.

The moral of these stories is: when a program gets situated on your hard disk, it's best not to move or rename any of the folders. It's better to live with whatever organization and names the installation programs have created — even if they are the yucky old eight-character DOS names.

Why Create Folders?

After boring you to tears with stories of stupid things that I've done, why am I about to tell you how to create (and manage) folders? Answer: even though you don't want to mess with the folders that your installation programs create, there are plenty of good reasons for creating folders to manage your document files, just as there are plenty of good reasons for managing your paper documents in folders in a file cabinet.

If I can provide a couple more real-world examples, I think you'll see why folders are a good thing when it comes to organizing your documents.

As an author, I usually have a few projects going: a main project, some backburner projects that are just in the idea stage, and perhaps some books that are still in production and that need occasional last-minute checks and changes.

To organize these various projects, I always keep a folder named Projects. Within that folder, I keep a subfolder for each project that I'm working on. For example, right now my Projects folder contains a subfolder named Windows 95 Bible. That folder holds every file that I created for this book. Another subfolder within Projects is called Susans Stuff. That subfolder contains some programs that I've been creating for my wife.

 Yes, I know that the folder I named Susans Stuff should actually be named Susan's Stuff. And in fact, Windows 95 would accept the apostrophe. But the programmer in me senses potential problems with that apostrophe *waaaay* down the road — like when writing Visual Basic code. But I can't verify that suspicion right now because Visual Basic for Applications for Microsoft Office for Windows 95 is not developed yet. Perhaps I'm being unduly pessimistic. Time will tell.

Figure 8-1 shows my Projects folder open on the desktop, with subfolders for all my ongoing projects (in their various stages of disarray).

Figure 8-1: My Projects folder contains a folder for each ongoing project.

The beauty of this organization is that when I need to open a document for any ongoing project, I just open the Projects folder and then double-click on the appropriate project name to see all the documents associated with that project. When I find the document that I'm looking for, I double-click on it. No muss, no fuss, no trying to remember where things are or what program I used to create them.

When I start a new project, I always go right to the Projects folder and create a new subfolder for that project. Then it's just a matter of remembering to put each new document that I create for the project in the appropriate folder so that I can find it later, when I need it.

When I finish a project and don't need immediate access to its documents anymore, I move its subfolder to some obscure place on the disk. Eventually, I may reclaim all the disk space that the folder is hogging by moving that folder to tape or some other storage medium.

Here's another example. I keep a folder named Clip Art that contains thousands of little pieces of royalty-free art. Within the Clip Art folder, I've categorized the files by theme. The Animals subfolder (see Figure 8-2), for example, contains picture of animals. The Business and Travel subfolder contains art related to business and travel, and so on for the other subfolders.

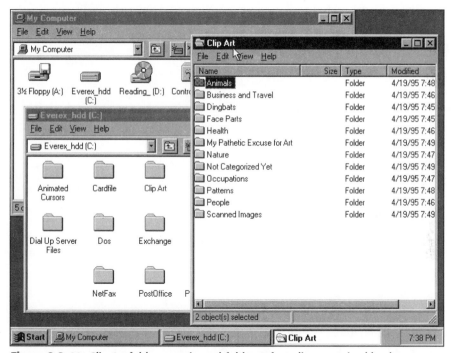

Figure 8-2: My Clip Art folder contains subfolders of art clips organized by theme.

In case you're not familiar with publishing, *clip art* is small "filler" pieces of art that you can put in newsletters, brochures, and other publications. Chapter 14 discusses clip art.

Whenever I need a piece of clip art, I know that I can always start my search simply by opening the folder named Clip Art — a plain, simple, efficient process.

The Projects and Clip Art folders are shared folders on my LAN. I can get to those files from any PC in my house and even when I'm on the road. For more information on LANs, see Part VII.

How to Create a Folder

After this preamble, you may think that creating a folder is a big hassle. Not true — in fact, creating a folder is easy. The purpose of the preamble was just to give you some food for thought about how you might want to organize your own folders, as well as some tips on when not to mess with folders. You can create a folder with whichever browsing tool you prefer: My Computer or Windows Explorer.

Create a new folder with My Computer

To create a folder with My Computer, follow these steps:

1. Open (double-click on) the My Computer icon.

2. Double-click on the icon for the drive on which you plan to put the folder (usually hard disk drive C).

3. If (and *only* if) you want to put this new folder inside an existing folder, open (double-click on) the folder in which you want to put the new one.

   You can repeat this step to drill down as far as necessary to get to the folder that will contain the new folder.

4. You may want to switch to Large Icons view to make it easier to see what you're doing.

   To do so, click the Large Icons button in the toolbar or choose View⇨Large Icons.

5. Choose File⇨New⇨Folder.

   A folder titled New Folder appears, as shown in Figure 8-3. The insertion point is positioned for you to type a new name.

6. Type a name for this new folder.

7. To save the new folder, click on some icon other than the new folder's icon.

If you want to move the folder to its proper alphabetical position within the current window, choose View⇨Arrange Icons⇨by Name. If you don't see the folder right away, try switching to Details view (choose View⇨Details). Then click on the Name button at the top of the first column to put the folders in alphabetical order. The folder icons will be grouped in alphabetical order.

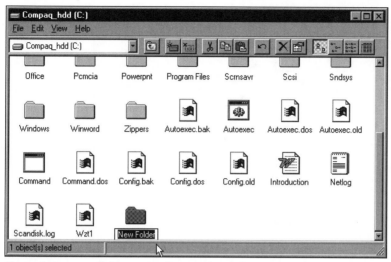

Figure 8-3: A new folder created on my hard drive (C).

Create a new folder with Windows Explorer

If you prefer to use Windows Explorer to browse your hard disk, you can create a folder from the Explorer window. Following is the basic procedure:

1. Click on the Start button, point to Programs, and then click on Windows Explorer. If you don't see a toolbar, choose View⇨Toolbar from Explorer's menu bar.

2. If you want to create the folder on some drive other than the one displayed in the *Go to a different folder* tool in the toolbar, use the drop-down list in that tool to navigate to the appropriate drive (normally A or C).

3. In the left column, click *one level above* where you want to create the new folder.

   If you want the new folder to be at the first level of drive C, for example, click on the icon for the C drive. If you want to create a folder within a folder, click on the folder that will contain the new folder.

A subfolder that's inside another folder sometimes is called the *child folder*. The folder that contains the child is called the *parent folder*. To move from a child folder to its parent, you can click on the Up One Level button in the toolbar.

4. Choose File⇨New⇨Folder.

   A new folder titled New Folder appears at the bottom of the list in the right-hand pane, as in the example shown in Figure 8-4. The insertion point is ready for you to type in a new name.

Figure 8-4: A new folder created with Windows Explorer.

5. Type a name for the new folder.

6. To save the folder with its new name, click on some other folder or files icon.

If you want to shuffle the new folder into proper alphabetical position in the list, choose View⇨Arrange Icons⇨by Name.

Your new folder is just like any other; it's accessible from both the left and right panes of the Explorer window (when you have navigated to a place where you can see the folder). And, of course, it's accessible from My Computer as well.

Managing folders: a quick review

Earlier chapters discussed the many techniques for managing folders and files. Because we're on the subject of folders right now, take a moment to review the main techniques, described in the following list:

✦ *To open a folder,* double-click on it. If a folder is open but covered by other windows on the desktop, click on the hidden folder's taskbar button to bring it to the forefront.

✦ *To close a folder,* click on the Close (X) button in its window.

✦ *To rename a folder,* right-click on it, choose Rename, and then use standard text-editing techniques to create a new name.

✦ *To move or copy items into a folder,* right-drag the selected objects to the folder's icon or the folder's open window, release the mouse button, and then choose Move Here or Copy Here.

✦ *To move or copy items out of a folder,* open the folder, select the items that you want to move or copy, right-drag them to the destination drive and/or folder, release the mouse button, and then choose Move Here or Copy Here.

✦ *To move or copy an entire folder,* navigate to the drive and/or folder that will contain the folder. Then right-drag the folder's icon to that destination, release the mouse button, and then choose Move Here or Copy Here.

✦ *To view the DOS path name for a folder,* open the folder, choose View▷Options, click on the View tab, and select the Display the full MS-DOS path name in the title bar option. Then click on OK.

✦ *To delete a folder,* click on the folder's icon and then press Delete, or right-click on the folder's icon and then choose Delete.

Don't forget that when you delete a folder, *you delete all the files and folders that are inside that folder, including any hidden files.* To bring hidden files into view before you delete a folder, choose View▷Options, click the View tab, and choose Show all files. And remember, only deletions from your local hard disk are sent to the Recycle Bin. You cannot undelete folders deleted from removable media or network drives.

✦ *To create a shortcut to a folder,* drag the folder's icon to the desktop or the Start button.

Find a lost folder

If you lose track of a folder, you can always look it up with Find. Click on the Start button, point to Find, and then click on Files or Folders. If you want to search the entire hard disk, make sure that the C drive is selected in the Look in list and that the Include subfolders option is checked. Type all or part of the folder name, and then choose Find Now.

As discussed in Chapter 2, you can broaden the search beyond the local hard disk by choosing My Computer in the Look in list. As you'll learn in Part VII of this book, you can even search other PCs in your local area network (if you're on a LAN).

Remember that Find is every bit as "live" as My Computer and Explorer. That is to say, Find is *not* like the old Windows 3 Program Manager that showed only iconic "pointers" to objects on the disk. Rather, Find is more like the Windows 3 File Manager. If Find locates your folder, you can open the folder on the spot just by double-clicking on it. You can even move or copy the folder to a new location just by right-dragging its folder from the Find window to the new location. And if you delete a folder in Find, you delete the folder from the disk as well.

Reorganizing Your Start Menu

The Start button is the easiest way to get documents from your virtual file cabinet onto your virtual desktop: the screen. The better you organize your Start menus, the easier it is to get things to the desktop when you need them. The following sections examine ways to organize your Start menu and its submenus.

Top o' the Start menu

We'll take it from the top. For lack of a better term, I'll refer to the options that appear at the top of the Start menu as being *Start-menu shortcuts*. Figure 8-5 shows a couple of examples: one for opening a fax cover sheet and the other for starting Microsoft Word. As I discussed in Chapter 4, to create a Start-menu shortcut, you drag a program's, folder's, or document's icon right onto the Start button.

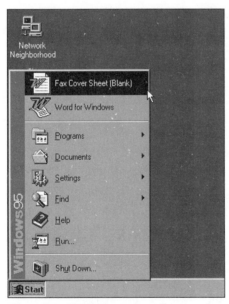

Figure 8-5: Menu shortcuts at the top of the Start menu.

Even though you drag things *onto* the Start button to create shortcuts, you can't drag them back out if you change your mind. But changing or deleting those shortcuts is easy nonetheless. Follow these steps:

1. Right-click on the Start button and then choose Open.

   A window titled Start Menu appears. This window contains a program folder named Programs (discussed in the following section).

Also within the window is one shortcut icon for each item at the top of the Start menu. In Figure 8-6, I've opened the Start Menu window. Notice that the names of the two shortcut icons inside that window match the options at the top of the Start menu.

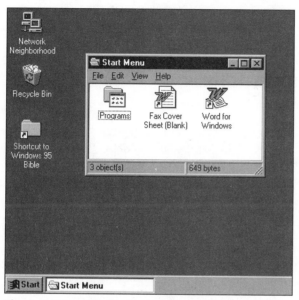

Figure 8-6: Icons in the Start Menu window represent Start-menu shortcuts.

 Remember that when you're working in the Start Menu window, you're working with shortcuts, as indicated by the little shortcut arrows in the icons. You can move, change, and delete shortcut icons without disturbing the underlying files on disk.

2. Do either of the following things:

✦ To delete a shortcut, click on the icon and then press Delete, or right-click on the icon and then choose Delete.

✦ To change the text of an icon, right-click on the icon, choose Rename, and then use standard text-editing techniques to make your changes.

 The longer the name, the wider your Start menu will need to be to display that name. For best results, try to keep the name shorter than 25 characters.

3. Click on some other icon after you change or delete an icon, because changes aren't saved until you move to a different icon.

4. When you're happy with your changes, click on the Close (X) button in the upper-right corner of the Start Menu window.

To see the effects of your changes, click on the Start button and then look at the top of your Start menu. The options in the menu are identical to the names that you assigned to icons in the Start Menu window. That was easy, no?

Customizing the Programs menu

The Programs menu is your lead-in from the Start button to program folders and icons. Figure 8-7 shows an example in which you can see options leading from the Programs menu to program folders named Accessories, DTP and Word Processing, Graphic Tools, and so on. Also, some icons at the bottom of the Programs menu lead directly to programs (MS-DOS Prompt, The Microsoft Network, and Windows Explorer).

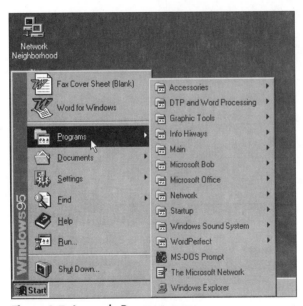

Figure 8-7: A sample Programs menu.

You can arrange items in the Programs menu and all its submenus to your liking, as the following sections explain.

Adding folder options to the Programs menu

If you want to add a new program folder to the <u>P</u>rograms menu, follow these steps:

1. Right-click on the Start button and then choose <u>O</u>pen.

2. Double-click on the Programs icon.

   A window named Programs appears, displaying an icon for each option in the <u>P</u>rograms menu. Figure 8-8 shows an example. Compare that figure with Figure 8-7 to see how each icon in the Programs window relates to one option in the <u>P</u>rograms menu.

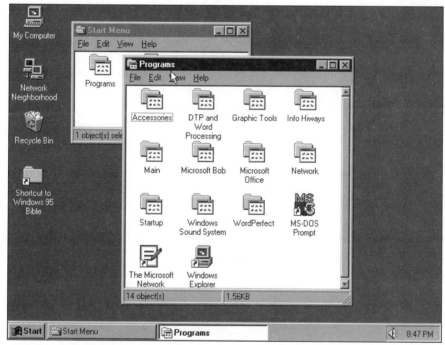

Figure 8-8: The Programs folder opened into a window.

3. To create a new program folder, choose <u>F</u>ile➪<u>N</u>ew.

4. Click on <u>F</u>older and then type a name.

   The name you type is exactly what will appear as the option in the <u>P</u>rograms menu, so you may want to keep the name fairly brief (fewer than 25 characters).

5. After typing the new name, click on some other icon in the window to save the change.

To verify your work, click on the Start button and then point to Programs to see your new folder as a menu item. In Figure 8-9, I just created a new folder named Multimedia Tools. That folder is the last icon in the Programs window. Then I clicked on the Start button and pointed to Programs. Already, there's an option in the Programs menu with the same name. (The folder is empty because I just created it.)

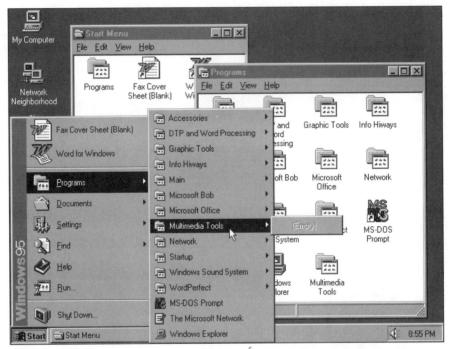

Figure 8-9: The new Multimedia Tools folder, near the bottom of the Programs window and also in the Programs menu.

When you finish adding your new folder, close all the open windows on the desktop by clicking on their Close (X) buttons.

To put things in the new submenu, I can go back to the Programs window, open the Multimedia Tools folder, and then choose File⇨New⇨Shortcut to create shortcuts within that folder (see the following section).

Adding program options to the Programs menu

In addition to folders, your Programs menu can contain an icon to launch any program on your hard disk. As mentioned earlier, many programs' installation procedures automatically add a program folder and startup icon to the Programs menu. But if you need to create your own startup icon for a program that's already installed on your hard disk, follow these steps:

1. Right-click on the Start button and then choose <u>O</u>pen.

2. Double-click on the Programs icon.

3. If (and only if) you want to put the icon in the <u>P</u>rograms menu, rather than in a program file in that menu, skip to step 5.

4. If you want to put the program icon in one of the program folders, open that folder by double-clicking on its icon.

   You can drill down as deep as you want to open a subfolder, sub-subfolder, or whatever.

5. In the current window, choose <u>F</u>ile⇨Ne<u>w</u>.

6. Choose <u>S</u>hortcut.

   The Shortcut wizard appears. Follow the instructions on-screen to create a shortcut to whatever program you want to launch. The easiest way to do this probably is to click the B<u>r</u>owse button and then just navigate to the program's icon.

7. When you get to the last wizard screen, choose the Finish button.

To verify your work, close all open windows, click on the Start button, and then point to <u>P</u>rograms. If you skipped step 4, your new shortcut appears in the <u>P</u>rograms menu. If you put the icon in one of the program folders, point to the appropriate folder. (Repeat this procedure as necessary if you need to go deeper than one folder.) When you point to the folder that contains your program icon, you'll see that icon as an option in the subfolder that appears.

If you drill down to a folder via My Computer, you can close that window, and all the parent windows with one mouse click. Just hold down the Shift key while you click on the Close (X) button of the last window that you opened.

Changing the Programs menu

You can move, change, delete, and copy a program folder or program icon anywhere in the <u>P</u>rograms menu by following these steps:

1. First, to minimize confusion, I suggest that you close all open windows and start with a clean desktop.

2. Be sure that you right-click on the Start button and choose <u>O</u>pen (*don't* try to use any of the other browsing tools, such as My Computer, because they have no effect on the Start button).

3. Double-click on the Programs icon.

4. If you want to change an option in a submenu of the <u>P</u>rograms menu, open (double-click on) the icon that represents that submenu.

   You can repeat this step to drill down as far as necessary.

5. Now use the following techniques to make changes:

Remember that because you started this procedure by right-clicking on the Start button, your changes will affect the contents of the Start menu only — not the contents of the disk.

✦ To delete a menu item, click on its icon and then press Delete, or right-click on that icon and then choose Delete.

If you delete or move an item by accident, or if you change your mind immediately after the fact, choose Edit⇨Undo. To undo a deletion later open the Recycle Bin and look for the item there. The item's original location will be listed in `c:\windows\start menu\programs`.... Click on the icon and then choose File⇨Restore.

✦ To rename a menu item, right-click on its icon, choose Rename, and then type your changes. (Don't forget to click some other icon when you finish, to save your changes.)

✦ To move or copy an item to a different submenu, right-drag the item's icon to the icon that represents that submenu item. Then release the right mouse button, and choose Move Here or Copy Here.

6. When you finish, close all the open windows.

To verify the effects of your changes, click on the Start button, point to Programs, and explore the submenus.

The Programs menu from a Windows 3.x perspective

If you're an experienced Windows 3.x user, you may find it easier to think of the Programs window in terms of the old Program Manager. When you right-click on the Start button, choose Open, and open the Programs icon into a window, that Programs window is, essentially, the old Program Manager.

Any Program folder icon in the Programs menu is what we used to call a program group. Any shortcut icon in the Programs menu is what we used to call an application icon. Unlike the old Program Manager window, the new Programs window can contain both folders (group icons) and shortcuts (application icons), not just group icons.

So why didn't Microsoft stick with the old Program Manager? Because many beginning users had trouble finding Program Manager when it was covered by other windows. By converting the old Program Manager to a menu that the user can get to from the Start button, Microsoft has made the programs more accessible. Beginners and casual users will probably find the menu-like structure of the Start button to be easier and more intuitive than the group icons/application icons in Program Manager.

Other ways to change the Programs menu

Far be it for me to confuse matters, but I would be remiss in my duty if I didn't at least tell you this: if you like Windows Explorer more than you like My Computer, you can use an Explorer-type window to make changes in your Programs menu. To get started, right-click on the Start button and choose Explore. Then double-click on the Programs icon in the right pane. You'll see icons for the program folders and icons in the Programs menu.

You also can use a Find-style window to modify the Programs menu. Right-click on the Start button, and choose Find. Type all, or part of, the menu option that you're looking for; then click on Find Now. You move to the icon that represents that item in the Programs menu.

Confused?

You may be thinking that there's a lot of similarity between the way you create and manage things in the Start menu and the way you create and manage things on disk. As a matter of fact, the techniques are exactly the same — which is good, because you don't need to learn new skills to manage options in the Programs menu.

The downside, however, is the potential for confusion. If you don't keep track of where you started browsing from, you may find yourself wondering, "Am I changing the Start menu now, or am I changing the contents of the disk?" Here are some points to keep in mind to minimize confusion:

✦ When you start browsing from My Computer, Windows Explorer, or Find, you are working directly with the contents of the disk. Anything that you do affects the disk directly.

✦ When you start browsing by right-clicking on the Start menu, you are working strictly with the contents of the Start menu. Nothing that you do affects the disk directly.

✦ The Programs folder is unique in that it's only accessible from the Start button. The only way to modify the contents of the Programs folder is by starting-off with a right-click on the Start button. To use (not modify) the programs folder, you click the Start button and choose Programs. The menu that appears *is* the Programs folder, rearranged to look and act like a menu.

✦ If you're not sure whether an icon represents something on the disk, look closely at that icon. If the icon is a program folder (a folder with a little program window in front) or a shortcut icon (with a little arrow in the lower-left corner, as shown in Figure 8-10), you're safe, because you're not working directly on the disk.

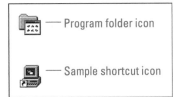

Figure 8-10: Program folder and shortcut icons simply *point* to items on the disk.

To emphasize the last point, keep in mind that program, folder, and document icons essentially *are* the objects that they represent. When you delete, move, or rename one of these icons, you delete, move, or rename the actual underlying folder or file on disk. Program-folder icons and shortcut icons, on the other hand, are just pointers to items on the disk.

I have to confess that it took me a while to get all this straight in my head, so don't feel bad if your brain feels a little fried. (My brain feels fried just *talking* about it.) But like anything else, practice makes perfect. Once you get into the habit of right-clicking that Start button whenever you want to make changes to the menu, it becomes second nature to you.

And the real bombshell is . . .

Now it's time for another confession. I've been saying that when you start a browse session by right-clicking on the Start button, your actions have no effect on the disk. That's virtually true, but with a slight twist. The program folders and icons that you work with after a right-click on the Start button are actually little files on the disk, but they're separate from all your regular folders and files. These files are lumped together in a subfolder named Start Menu in your Windows folder (`c:\windows\start menu`, in DOS path terminology).

The reason why these files are on the disk at all is this: when you shut down your PC, Windows 95 has no way of remembering how you left your Start menu organized. When you start your computer again, Windows 95 reads the program folders in `c:\windows\start menu` to reassemble your Start button's menus.

It's important to remember that `c:\windows\start menu` contains only program folders and shortcuts to items elsewhere on the disk. Your actual programs (such as Microsoft Word) are still stored in their real folders, not in the `c:\windows\start menu` folder.

Whew! Now I just have one more thing — a simple thing — to mention about the Start menu.

Using large or small Start-menu icons

You can choose between large, highly visible icons, or smaller space-saving icons, for your Start menus. Follow these steps:

1. Right-click on the taskbar and then choose Properties.

2. Click on the Taskbar Options tab.

3. To use smaller icons, select the Show small icons in Start menu check box; to use larger icons, clear that check box.

4. Click on the OK button.

This procedure is very easy. (Don't ask me, however, why the icon-size option appears in the Taskbar Options tab rather than the Start Menu Programs tab. Perhaps nobody at Microsoft noticed.)

Clearing the Documents Menu

As I mentioned earlier, the Documents submenu on the Start menu keeps track of recently saved document files (at least, for programs that support that capability). So if you need to reopen that document in the near future, you can click on the Start button, point to Documents, and then click on the name of the document that you want to open.

If your Documents menu gets cluttered with files that you're not opening often anymore, follow these simple steps to clear the Documents menu and start with a clean slate:

1. Right-click on the taskbar and then choose Properties.

2. Click on the Start Menu Programs tab.

3. Click on the Clear button.

4. Click on OK.

That's all there is to that!

Personalizing the Taskbar

The second important tool on your desktop is the taskbar. The following list provides a quick review of the taskbar's purpose:

✦ Every open window has a button in the taskbar. To bring any window to the forefront on-screen, just click on its taskbar button.

✦ To close or resize any open window (even one that's buried in a stack), right-click on its taskbar button, and choose the appropriate option from the menu that appears.

✦ To tidy up (arrange) all the open windows, right-click on the taskbar proper (not on a button in the taskbar), and then choose Cascade or one of the Tile options. You also can minimize all the windows from that menu.

✦ A little clock usually appears in the taskbar, showing you the current time. Point to the clock to see the current date; double-click on the clock to change the current date and time.

✦ Some hardware devices (such as sound cards and printers) display an icon in the taskbar while they are running. Typically, you can click, right-click, or double-click on that icon to get more information about — or even to control — the device.

Handy little gadget, that taskbar. The following sections explain some ways that you can personalize it.

Size and position the taskbar

Sometimes, the taskbar covers the status bar of a program that's running at full-screen size. Fortunately, you can fix that problem simply by dragging the taskbar to some other edge of the screen. When you're using a word processing program, for example, you may want to drag the taskbar to the right edge of the screen so that you can still see your program's title bar and menu bar (see Figure 8-11).

If you have many windows open, the window buttons in the taskbar can become pretty small. One way around this problem is to point to a taskbar button to see its tooltip. The other solution is to change the size of the taskbar. Place the mouse pointer on the inside edge of the taskbar (the edge closest to the center of the screen) so that the pointer becomes a two-headed arrow. Then drag that edge in whatever direction you want to size the taskbar.

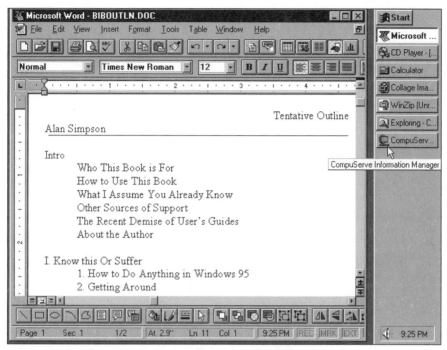

Figure 8-11: Taskbar dragged to the right edge of the screen.

Hide the taskbar

Another way to keep the taskbar out of the way is to hide it until you need it. Follow these steps:

1. Right-click on the taskbar and then choose Properties.

2. Click on the Taskbar Options tab.

3. If you select Always on top, the taskbar never will be covered by a window; if you clear this option, open windows can cover the taskbar.

4. If you select Auto hide, the taskbar shrinks to a thin line along the edge of the screen when it's not in use. To redisplay the taskbar, point to that line. If you clear this option, the taskbar never shrinks to a thin line.

5. Choose OK.

If you want some advice, I suggest that you leave the Always on top option selected; there's no good reason to allow other windows to cover the taskbar. If you feel that the taskbar gets in your way, however, select the Auto hide option so that it'll be tucked away but within easy reach.

Show or hide the taskbar clock

I get to end this chapter with something really, really, *really* easy. If you want to get rid of or redisplay the clock in the taskbar, right-click on the taskbar and then click on Properties. Click on the Taskbar Options tab, select or clear the Show Clock option, and then choose OK.

Summary

Windows 95 has lots of great stuff for organizing your desktop. The techniques involved take some getting used to – especially if you're familiar with the Windows 3 Program Manager which worked in completely different ways. Here are the main points to remember:

✦ When you want to change the Programs menu, or any submenu that follows it, *always* start off this way: right-click on the Start button and choose Open.

✦ When you want to add a new submenu to the Programs menu, right click the Start button, choose Open, and double-click the Programs icon. Then in the Programs folder that appears choose File⇨New⇨Folder and create your folder. Later, when you actually use the Start button, that new folder will become an option on the Prorgams menu.

✦ You can use the same technique as above to create a deeper-level submenu. Just drill down to where you want to create the folder before you choose File⇨New⇨Folder.

✦ To change the size of icons on the Start menu, right-click on the taskbar, choose Properties, and then select, or clear, the Show small icons in Start menu check box.

✦ To clear-out the documents menu, right click on the taskbar, click on the Start Menu Programs tab, and click on the Clear button.

✦ To customize the taskbar, right-click on the taskbar (outside any buttons in the taskbar), and choose Properties.

✦ To size the taskbar, drag its inner edge (the edge nearest the center of the screen).

✦ To move the taskbar, drag the entire taskbar to any edge of the screen.

✦   ✦   ✦

Growth, Maintenance, and General Tweaking

Installing and Removing Programs

CHAPTER

9

◆ ◆ ◆ ◆

In This Chapter

Installing new programs with the installation wizard

Installing new programs with the Run command

Installing missing Windows components

Removing installed programs

Making a startup disk

◆ ◆ ◆ ◆

E very Windows program, whether it is delivered to you on floppy disks or CD-ROM, comes with its own installation program. Installing the programs usually is a breeze, as you'll see in this chapter. Keep in mind that the techniques described here will work with just about any DOS, Windows 3, Windows NT, or Windows 95 program that you purchase. But if you have problems with a particular program or need more information during an installation procedure, you'll need to refer to the installation instructions that came with that program for specifics. I can cover only the general procedures in this chapter.

Installing New Programs

Be aware that in this chapter, I'm talking specifically about installing *programs*. So consider the following guidelines before you begin:

+ If you are trying to install fonts, you should use the techniques described in Chapter 14 rather than the techniques described in this chapter.

+ If you are trying to install a driver for a new piece of hardware, use the Add New Hardware wizard discussed in Chapter 10.

+ If you are trying to copy files, such as other people's documents or clip art, you should use the general copying techniques discussed in Chapter 5.

+ If you are trying to install a program that you downloaded from an online service, you really need to follow the instructions that came with that program. Downloaded files usually require you to decompress them before you install them, and no general procedure applies to all downloaded programs.

So now, assuming that you are indeed trying to install a program, you can use either the Add/Remove Programs wizard or the Run command. I suggest that you try the wizard first.

Using the installation wizard

The Add/Remove Programs wizard makes installing new programs a cinch. To use the wizard follow these steps:

1. Gather up the floppy disks or CD-ROM for the program that you want to install.

2. Click on the Start button, point to Settings, and then click on Control Panel.

3. Double-click on the Add/Remove Programs icon. The wizard starts up.

4. Click on the Install button.

5. As instructed on-screen, insert the installation floppy disk in a floppy disk drive or put the CD-ROM in the CD-ROM drive.

 To make things quick and easy, empty or open the drives that you're *not* going to use during installation.

6. Click on the Next button.

   The wizard searches the floppy and CD-ROM drives for a SETUP.EXE or similarly named file. If it finds such a file, the wizard displays the program, as shown in Figure 9-1.

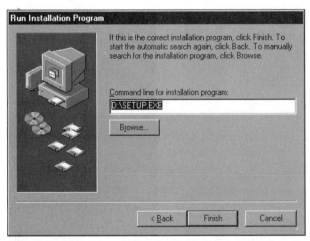

Figure 9-1: The wizard found a SETUP.EXE program on my CD-ROM drive (D).

7. If you're trying to run a setup program that's in a particular folder on the CD-ROM or floppy disk, click on the <u>B</u>rowse button and then navigate to that folder.

If the wizard can't find a setup program, refer to "Programs that have no setup" later in this chapter.

8. Click on the Finish button to launch the setup program.

Now you just need to follow whatever instructions appear on the screen. I can't help you much with this part, because Windows 95 is out of the picture now. The setup program that you ran is in control. Do, however, pay attention to *where* the installation program plans to put the installed program so that you can find it later.

Be sure to complete all the installation instructions on-screen until you see a message indicating that the installation was completed successfully. If you installed from floppy disks, remove the last floppy from the drive, and put the floppies in a safe place for use as backups. If the screen tells you to restart the computer before trying to run the program, click on the Restart button (if any) on-screen. If no Restart button appears, get to the desktop, and choose Sh<u>u</u>t Down from the Start menu to shut down and restart your PC.

Using Run to install a program

The installation instructions for a Windows 3.x or DOS program probably will tell you to start by choosing <u>F</u>ile⟹<u>R</u>un from Program Manager. Windows 95 has no Program Manager, of course, but you still can follow the program's installation instructions by making a detour to the Run dialog box, as follows:

1. Click on the Start button.

2. Choose <u>R</u>un from the Start menu to get to the dialog box shown in Figure 9-2.

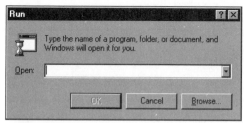

Figure 9-2: Click on Run in the Start menu to get to this dialog box.

Now follow the instructions from your program, starting with the part that tells you what to type (for example, **a:\setup.exe** or **a:\install.exe**). If you have any problems, see the following section for suggestions.

Be sure to follow all the installation instructions until you see a message indicating that the program was installed successfully. If the program requires you to restart Windows, click on the Restart button (if available), or get back to the desktop and choose Sh_u_t Down from the Start menu to shut down and restart the PC.

Programs that have no setup

If the wizard or _R_un doesn't find a setup or install program — or finds the wrong one — don't panic. Just choose Cancel from the error message (then choose Cancel from the wizard window, if you're using the wizard.) Then try the following procedures:

✦ Empty or open all the drives _except_ the one from which you are installing the program, and make sure that the installation disk is fully inserted into the appropriate drive. Then try again, using the Add/Remove Programs wizard.

✦ Check the program's documentation for the name of the program that you need to run to start the installation. That program may not be named setup or install. When you find the name of the installation program, choose _R_un from the Start menu to run that specific program.

✦ If you are trying to run a setup or install program that's in a particular folder on the CD-ROM or floppy disk, you still can use either the wizard or _R_un. Either way, you'll get to a dialog box that offers a B_r_owse button. For example, you can click the Start button, click on _R_un, and you'll come to a dialog box with a B_r_owse button in it. Click that B_r_owse button, and then navigate to the appropriate folder before you proceed.

✦ If you're having problems installing a DOS program, the Troubleshooter can help you. Click on the Start button; then click on _H_elp. Click on the Contents tab; then double-click on the Troubleshooting book. Double-click on If you have trouble running MS-DOS programs; then choose I can't install the program.

✦ Review the list under "Installing New Programs" at the start of this chapter, and think about what type of files you're trying to install to your hard disk. Then proceed to the appropriate chapter.

Running the installed program

When a program is installed, you can use the following standard techniques to run it at any time:

1. Click on the Start button and then point to _P_rograms.

2. Point to the program's folder (group) icon until you find the startup icon for the program.

3. Click on the program's startup icon.

If you can't find the program's startup icon, you can use My Computer, Windows Explorer, or Find (refer to Chapter 2) to locate the program's startup icon. When you do, just double-click on that icon to launch the program. You also can create a shortcut to the program, as discussed in chapters 4 and 8.

Installing Missing Windows Components

When you installed Windows 95 on your PC, the installation procedure made some decisions about which components to install and which not to install. You're not stuck with those decisions, however. If you can't seem to find one of the programs that supposedly comes with Windows 95, you can follow these instructions to install that program:

1. Gather up your original Windows 95 floppy disks or CD-ROM.

2. Click on the Start button and then point to Settings.

3. Click on Control Panel.

4. Double-click on Add/Remove Programs.

5. Click on the Windows Setup tab to get to the dialog box shown in Figure 9-3.

Consumer software alert

Consumer software for the home — including games, "edutainment" programs, and multimedia titles — is notoriously difficult to install and/or run. Some programs assume that you're using a 256-color monitor and a 16-bit sound card. DOS-based programs assume that you have plenty of conventional memory to spare. Those are big assumptions, of course, and plenty of home PCs don't measure up to the required specifications.

Sometimes, the problem is easy to fix. If the program complains that you don't have a 256-color monitor, for example, you may need to activate that capability of your monitor (refer to Chapter 6). Alternatively, you may be able to free some conventional memory. For help with that procedure, click on the Start button,

click on Help, click on the Contents tab, double-click on the Troubleshooting book, and then explore the *If you run out of memory* and *If you have trouble running MS-DOS programs* topics. You also can examine your available hardware by using the Device Manager (see Chapter 10).

If all else fails, you may need to contact the manufacturer of the program. Or check out Michael Goodwin's *Making Multimedia Work*, also published by IDG Books. If it's any consolation to you, the 1994 Christmas season was the biggest season ever for software sales — and also the biggest year ever for returns. The main reason for returns was incompatibility with existing hardware.

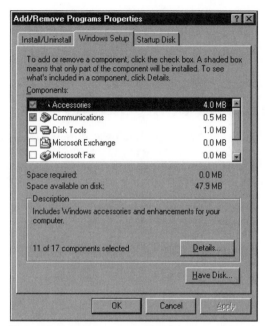

Figure 9-3: This property sheet lets you add and remove Windows 95 components.

Any component in the Windows Setup tab that has a check mark is installed already. A check box that is both checked, and grayed, indicates that some (but not all) of the components in that category are installed. (The Details button lets you see which are, and aren't.) Do not clear any check marks unless you're absolutely sure that you want to remove those components.

6. Scroll through the list of available components; if you see the component that you want to install, skip to Step 10.

7. If you don't see the component that you want to install, check the component's details (that is, click on any component, such as Accessories) and then click on the Details button.

8. If you still don't see the component that you want to install, click on Cancel and then try a different component (for example, Communications).

9. Repeat Steps 7 and 8 until you find the component that you want to install.

10. Click on the component that you want to install, so that its check box is checked.

11. When you've finished choosing components, click OK to leave the Details box (if you're in it). Then click OK to close the Add/Remove Programs Properties dialog. Then follow any instructions on-screen to install the component(s).

Things should go smoothly now. If the installation procedure looks for the components in the wrong place (for example, it looks for a floppy disk in drive A rather than for the CD-ROM in drive D), you can click the Browse button and navigate to the appropriate drive to begin the installation.

Removing Installed Programs

You may want to remove an installed program for many reasons. Maybe you decided that you don't like the program and want to free the disk space that it's using. Or perhaps you bought a competing program from a different vendor and now need to make some room on the disk to install that program.

As a general rule, when you upgrade to a new version of an existing program, you do *not* want to uninstall the earlier version first. The upgrade program will expect the earlier version to be installed; it may even require that version to be installed. If you're in doubt, check the program's upgrade instructions.

Regardless of your motivation for removing a program, you need to exercise some caution. Deleting a program and its folder can have peculiar side effects on files that *expect* that folder and/or program to still be there, especially if you used the Delete key to delete the program's folder. A better practice is to uninstall (remove) the program formally, if possible, to prevent side effects.

Save your work first

Before you remove a program, stop to think about any documents that you may have created and saved within that program's folder. If you're deleting Microsoft Word for Windows, for example, did you ever create and save documents in the `c:\winword` folder or in a subfolder, such as `c:\winword\documents`? If so, are you sure that you want to delete those documents?

If the answer to the last question is no, create a new folder outside the program's folder (refer to Chapter 8); then move the documents that you want to save to the new folder (refer to Chapter 5). Otherwise, when you delete the program's folder, you also delete any documents in that program's folder and subfolders.

Uninstalling with the Add/Remove Programs wizard

Most Windows 95-aware programs register themselves as programs that can be removed automatically. You should always try the following method of removing a program before resorting to one of the other methods:

1. Click on the Start button and then click on Settings.

2. Click on Control Panel.

3. Double-click on Add/Remove Programs.

4. Click on the Install/Uninstall tab.

5. If the program that you want to remove appears in the list, click on that program's name; click on the Remove button; and follow any instructions that appear on the screen.

If, in step 5, you don't see the program that you want to remove, check to see whether it's listed as a Windows component. Click on the Windows Setup tab; locate the component that you want to remove, using the Details button if necessary; and clear the check box for that component. Then choose OK and follow the instructions on the screen.

Uninstalling with SETUP.EXE

If the Add/Remove Programs wizard doesn't find the program that you want to remove, try the following method:

1. Click on the Cancel button, if necessary, to return to Control Panel.

2. Close the Control Panel to return to the desktop.

3. If the program that you want to remove is open, close it.

4. Click on the Start button, click on Programs, and then find the folder for the program that you want to remove.

5. Look for a Setup icon for the program that you want to remove.

   In Figure 9-4, for example, I've located the Setup icon for Microsoft Office.

6. Open that setup program, and look for options that let you remove (or uninstall) programs.

   In Figure 9-5, I've found options that let me Add/Remove individual programs, as well as an option that lets me Remove All programs in Microsoft Office.

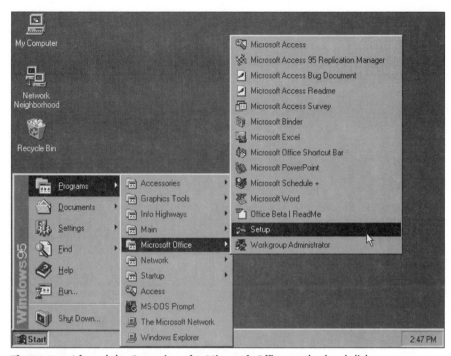

Figure 9-4: I found the Setup icon for Microsoft Office on the hard disk.

Figure 9-5: Microsoft Office's setup offers a couple of *uninstall* options.

7. From here on, the setup program is in control; follow instructions and choose options as appropriate to that program.

 Don't forget that when Windows 95 moves files to the Recycle Bin, those files continue to take up disk space. The space doesn't become free until you empty the Recycle Bin.

If you can't find a setup program or uninstall option for the program that you want to remove, terminate the current installation program and then use the last-resort method described in the following section.

If all else fails

If you can't find an uninstall option for the program that you want to remove, you'll need to remove the program by deleting its folder. First, be sure to move anything that you want to keep outside the program's folder and subfolders. Then you can delete the program's entire folder. Use My Computer, Explorer, or Find to get to that folder; select the folder; and then press Delete.

At this point, the deletion is finished, but you have not deleted references to that program. To tidy up and deal with any problems that arise, consider using the following methods:

✦ If you left behind any shortcuts to the program that you deleted, browse to and then delete those shortcuts.

✦ If you left behind any Program menu options that lead to the deleted program, delete those options, using the techniques described in Chapter 8.

✦ If you experience problems with the Registry in the future, you may need to modify the Registry manually. For instructions, see Chapter 31.

✦ If you have startup problems in the future, your C:\CONFIG.SYS and C:\AUTOEXEC.BAT files may still contain references to the old program. You need to modify those files.

If you feel uneasy about taking any of the preceding actions, *don't* — there's little margin for error, especially when you're dealing with the Registry and with the CONFIG.SYS and AUTOEXEC.BAT files. I strongly recommend against the "wing it and hope for the best" approach here.

Making an Emergency Startup Disk

Keeping an emergency startup disk around is a good idea; you can use this disk in case some problem with your hard disk prevents you from starting your PC in the normal manner. Chances are that you created this startup disk when you installed Windows 95. But if you didn't (or have forgotten where you put it), you can follow these steps to create a new one at any time:

1. Click on the Start button and then point to Settings.

2. Click on Control Panel.

3. Double-click on Add/Remove Programs.

4. Click on the Startup Disk tab.

5. Insert a blank floppy disk (or one containing files that you're willing to trash for all eternity) into the floppy drive.

6. Click on the Create Disk button.

7. Follow the instructions on-screen.

Label the disk Windows 95 Startup Disk (or something to that effect); then put it in a safe place where you'll be able to find it. It's unlikely that you'll ever need the startup disk, but if you do need it, you'll *really* need it.

In a pinch, you can start your PC with a DOS startup disk. To create a DOS startup disk, type a command such as **a: /s** at the DOS prompt.

Summary

Here's a quick recap of the various ways you can install, and uninstall, programs on your Windows 95 PC:

✦ Click the Start button, choose Settings⇨Control Panel. Double-click the Add/Remove Programs icon, click the Install button, and follow the directions on the screen.

✦ As an alternative to the above, you can click the Start button, click on Run, then use the Browse button to locate the setup or install program that you need to run.

✦ To install missing Windows components (programs that come with Windows 95, but are not currently on your hard disk), click the Start button, choose Settings⇨Control Panel. Double-click the Add/Remove Programs icon. Then click the Windows Setup tab.

✦ To remove a program from your hard disk, try the Uninstaller first (click the Start button, choose Settings⇨Control Panel, double-click the Add/Remove Programs icon). If you see the program you want to remove, click its name then click the Remove button.

✦ ✦ ✦

Installing New Hardware

First, I'll define my terms. *Hardware* refers to any physical device that you plug into your computer — devices that plug in from the outside, as well as boards that must be installed inside the computer. Anything that's recorded on a disk is *software*. In this chapter, I'm talking specifically about installing hardware.

When to Skip This Chapter

Not all hardware installations require the elaborate procedures described in this chapter. Following are some tips that may simplify the task you're about to undertake:

✦ If you're installing a PC card in a PCMCIA slot, ignore this chapter and go straight to Chapter 19.

✦ If you're installing a simple fax/modem (no voice-mail or multimedia sound capabilities), ignore this chapter and go to Chapter 15.

✦ If you're installing a printer, plug in the printer, connect it to the PC, and then turn it on. Gather up your original Windows 95 disks or CD-ROM, as well as any disks that came with the printer. Then click on the Start button and choose➪Settings➪Printers. Double-click on the Add Printer icon, and follow the instructions on-screen.

Puzzled? If you have any problems or confusion while installing a new printer, see the sidebar titled "I have no Windows 95 driver" later in this chapter for some advice.

✦ If you're replacing an existing keyboard, mouse, or monitor, shut down your equipment, remove the old device, plug in the new one, and restart the PC. Chances are that the new device will work fine. To select the new device, use the General tab of the Mouse or Keyboard Properties dialog box or the Settings tab of the Display Properties dialog box. You can use other tabs to fine-tune the device. See chapters 6 and 7.

About Plug-and-Play

Historically, adding a new device to a PC was a somewhat haphazard ritual, often leading to hours or days of hair-pulling frustration. If, like most people, you don't know about — or care to learn about — such arcane subjects as IRQ lines, SCSI hosts, and DMA channels, those hours or days of frustration could be for naught. You'd give up and take the new device back to the store or put the device on the shelf, hoping that time would somehow make it easier to install the device later.

One of the most important new features of Windows 95 is support for plug-and-play devices. The idea behind plug-and-play devices is simple: adding a new device to your PC should be as easy as plugging a game into a video-game player or hooking a pair of speakers to a stereo system. You just plug the device in and start playing.

A new breed of PCs and optional gadgets should follow Windows 95 to market, supporting the new plug-it-in-and-go concept. Millions of PCs and other devices, however, aren't plug-and-play-compliant. In this chapter, I'll discuss how to install both plug-and-play and *legacy* (non-plug-and-play) devices in your PC.

How to Install a Plug-and-Play Device

First, a word of caution: the term *plug-and-play* has been used for years, and not all products that claim to be plug-and-play truly are plug-and-play in the sense that I'm discussing here. The installation procedure discussed in this section works for devices whose cartons specifically display the "Designed for Windows 95 Plug-and-Play" logo.

To install a true plug-and-play device, follow these steps:

1. If you have any open program windows on your computer, close them.
2. Gather up your original Windows 95 floppy disks or CD-ROM, the device that you want to install, and the disks that came with the device.

3. Check the instructions for the new device.

   If the instructions tell you to turn off the power to your PC, close Windows 95 and turn off the power.

4. Install the new device, per the manufacturer's instructions.

5. If you turned the PC off in step 3, turn it back on.

6. The screen will notify you when Windows 95 detects the new device and probably will ask you to insert a Windows 95 disk or the disk that came with the device. Follow the instructions on-screen until a message indicates that you are finished.

You're done. Windows 95 automatically notifies all other devices of the new device, and you should be able to start using that device.

If you need to install programs to use the device, do so now, using the Add/Remove Programs wizard discussed in Chapter 9. Then skip the rest of this chapter.

How to Install Legacy Hardware

The term *legacy hardware* refers to any device that doesn't bear the "Designed for Windows 95 Plug-and-Play" logo. This section discusses devices that were designed for DOS and Windows 3.x.

The procedure for installing legacy hardware goes something like this:

1. If necessary, use Device Manager to locate available resources for the device.

2. Follow the manufacturer's instructions for installing the device.

3. When you get to the part about installing DOS/Windows 3.x drivers, ignore them; use the Windows 95 Add New Hardware wizard instead.

4. Install any programs *other than drivers* that came with the device.

If you can complete these four steps on your own, great — you can ignore the following sections. If you need more support, read the sections that follow, which discuss each step in much greater detail. But please be forewarned that I cannot possibly provide detailed instructions for installing every conceivable device on the market. Sometimes, you have to do a little device-specific tweaking, and only the instruction manual that came with the hardware device can help you with that.

Virtual devices versus real-mode drivers

Windows 95 offers a new virtual method of device support that was not available in previous versions of Windows. To understand the advantages, you first need to understand that Windows 3.x used real-mode drivers. These drivers were loaded into conventional or upper memory at bootup time via CONFIG.SYS and AUTOEXEC.BAT. The drivers were static, meaning that after they were in memory, you had no way to get them out, short of changing the configuration files and rebooting. Also, only one program at a time could use the device driver.

Windows 95 virtual device drivers offer significant advantages. For one, these drivers are loaded into extended memory, where they don't consume the conventional memory that DOS programs need. Also, the virtual drivers are dynamic, which means that they can be loaded and unloaded from memory on an as-needed basis. Finally, the virtual driver allows more than one program at a time to access the device.

Virtual device drivers on the disk can be identified by the .VXD file extension. These drivers are never loaded from CONFIG.SYS or AUTOEXEC.BAT; instead, the drivers are loaded after those two files have been processed. Any device driver that's included in CONFIG.SYS or AUTOEXEC.BAT is, by definition, a real-mode driver. When given a choice, you always want to use the virtual driver rather than the real-mode driver.

Step 1: Before you install the device

Before you actually put a hardware device in the PC, you need to determine whether the device requires that you choose an interrupt request line (*IRQ*). To find out, browse through the device's instructions. If the device does *not* require that you specify an IRQ, skip to the section titled "Step 2: Put the device in the machine."

Finding an available IRQ

One of the biggest headaches in using legacy hardware is IRQ conflicts. An IRQ is sort of a voice for the device, telling the computer, "I'm doing something now; pay attention to me." Most PCs have 16 IRQs, numbered 00 to 16. Each device must have its own IRQ. If two devices attempt to share an IRQ, you have what's called an *IRQ conflict,* and neither device will work properly.

Puzzled?

An IRQ conflict can have very strange effects. Your floppy drive may no longer be able to read perfectly formatted floppy disks, for example, or your speakers may crackle madly as you move the mouse pointer across the screen.

The big problem was that some hardware products expect you to specify an available IRQ. But earlier versions of DOS and Windows made it nearly impossible to determine which IRQs were available and which were already being used by some installed device. In some cases, you just had to guess. If your selections didn't work, you had to backtrack, pick another IRQ, and then try that one — on and on until you found one that worked. This situation was not good. (Whenever I hear news stories about some guy going berserk in public, I wonder whether he had been trying find an IRQ just before the mania set in.)

Anyway, if the device's instructions tell you that you're going to have to pick an IRQ at some point, you need not rely on trial and. Follow these steps instead:

1. Click on the Start button and then point to Settings.

2. Click on Control Panel.

3. Double-click on the System icon.

4. Click on the Device Manager tab.

 If your printer is already connected and ready to go, click on the Print button near the bottom of the System Properties dialog box, and then choose an option to get a printed summary of your current system settings.

5. Double-click on Computer at the top of the list in Device Manager.

6. Click the Interrupt request (IRQ) option at the top of the Computer Properties dialog box, as shown in Figure 10-1.

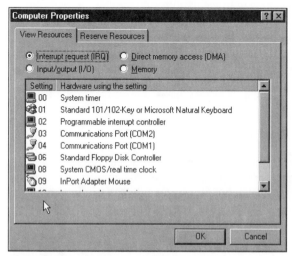

Figure 10-1: A list of used IRQs; any IRQ that's *not* listed is available.

7. Used (unavailable) IRQs are listed in the first column. On a piece of paper, jot down the IRQs that are *not* in the list, because those are the ones that are available.

   In Figure 10-1, for example, 05 and 07 are missing from the sequence 00, 01, 02, 03, 04, 06, 08, and 09. Therefore, 05 and 07 are the available IRQs that you would jot down. You can scroll through the list to see other available IRQs.

8. Although you may not need this information, it can't hurt to write down which DMA channels are in use. Click the Direct memory access (DMA) option, and write down the information that you see in the list.

   You needn't concern yourself with the other resources — Input/Output (I/O) and Memory — unless you are familiar with those concepts and are certain that you need that information.

9. After writing down the necessary information, click on Cancel to leave the Computer properties box. Then click on Cancel again to leave the System Properties box. Close the Control Panel, and then proceed to the following section.

Setting jumpers and switches

The next thing that you need to determine is whether the board requires you to set jumpers or dip switches manually; check the device's instruction manual to find out. Three possibilities exist, as discussed in the three sections that follow.

If you have a jumperless device

Many modern cards are *jumperless*, which means that you don't have to mess with any jumpers or switches on the board. If you have that type of board, skip to the section titled "Step 2: Put the device in the machine."

If your documentation includes written instructions for setting jumpers

If the device has jumpers or dip switches and the instruction manual includes instructions for setting them, follow those instructions now. Make sure that you set the switches or jumpers to an available IRQ, and *write down the IRQ that you decide to use*. Then skip to "Step 2: Put the device in the machine."

If you need to run a program to set jumpers

Some manufacturers do not provide written instructions on how to set jumpers or dip switches to pick an IRQ. Instead, these manufacturers require you to run a program that determines the best setting for your card; the program shows you, on-screen, exactly how to set the jumpers or switches. Typically, you can run the necessary program from the floppy disk that came with the hardware device. The device's instruction manual will tell you what program to run.

If you can run the program from Windows, insert the disk into a floppy drive, click on the Start button, choose Run, and type the appropriate startup command (for example, **a:\comcheck.exe**). Then press Enter.

If you need to run the program from DOS, click on the Start button, click on Shut Down, choose Restart the computer in MS-DOS mode?, and then click on Yes. When you get to the C prompt., type the command required to run the manufacturer's program (for example, **a:\comcheck.exe**), and then press Enter.

After you set the jumpers or dip switches according to the on-screen instructions, proceed to the following section.

Step 2: Put the device in the machine

Now you are ready to install the new device in (or on) the computer. Shutting down everything before you begin is important, so make sure that you carry out this procedure carefully. Follow these steps:

1. Gather up the device that you're installing, any disks that came with that device, and your original Windows 95 floppies or CD-ROM.

2. Close any open programs and then shut down Windows, using the Start button and the Shut Down option.

3. When the screen tells you that it's safe to do so, turn off the PC and any peripheral devices (for example, monitor, printer, modem, and CD-ROM drive).

4. Connect the device to the PC or install the card inside the PC, per the manufacturer's instructions.

   Just install the device; don't worry about installing any software right now.

5. When you finish connecting the device or installing the card, turn on all the peripherals, including the new device (if it has an on/off switch).

6. Make sure that the floppy disk drives are empty.

   If you have a CD-ROM drive, you can put a CD-ROM in it now.

7. Turn on the PC.

If Windows 95 detects the new device as it starts, you go to the Add New Hardware wizard, described in the following section.

Step 3: Install the Windows 95 drivers

You should ignore any instructions for installing DOS/Windows 3.x drivers; the Add New Hardware wizard can install the Windows 95 drivers for you. As mentioned in the preceding section, that wizard may fire up automatically the first time you start the PC after installing the new hardware. If not, you can launch the wizard from the desktop. Follow these steps:

1. Click on the Start button and then point to Settings.

2. Click on Control Panel.

3. Double-click on the Add New Hardware icon.

4. Read the first wizard window and then click on Next.

5. In the second wizard window, choose the Automatically detect installed hardware option (see Figure 10-2) and then click on Next.

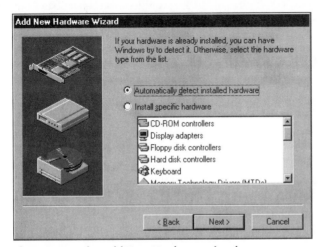

Figure 10-2: The Add New Hardware wizard.

6. Follow the instructions that appear on-screen.

 The Automatically detect installed hardware option in the Add New Hardware wizard window should have been called something like Automatically detect *newly* installed hardware, because the wizard concerns itself only with new devices that have been installed but have no drivers yet. If the wizard doesn't detect a new device, that may be good news; it could mean that your new device is already installed and working fine.

How the wizard proceeds depends on the device that you're installing. For example, if the wizard finds a device, it may install the appropriate drivers from the Windows 95 CD-ROM. If the wizard doesn't find a new device, you'll be given the option to install a specific device. Choose the type of device that you're installing and then proceed through the wizard windows.

If Windows 95 has its own driver for the device, the wizard copies that driver from the Windows 95 CD-ROM or displays a message that tells you which floppy disk to insert. Be aware that if Windows 95 does have its own driver, it will never ask you to insert the manufacturer's disk; this is normal and nothing to be alarmed about. Just keep following every instruction that appears on-screen.

I have no Windows 95 driver

In the worst-case scenario for installing legacy hardware, the device requires a driver, but no Windows 95 driver is available on your Windows 95 disks or on the manufacturer's disk. You may be tempted to try to force the DOS driver or Windows 3.x driver into the system. You can do that, but you won't like the result; most likely, the device won't work, and your whole system will behave strangely.

Your only real alternative is to contact the manufacturer of the device and ask where to get the Windows 95 driver for that device. If you have a modem, you may be able to download that driver, free of charge, from one of the online information services. Otherwise, you may need to wait for the manufacturer to mail you the driver. (Bummer, I know. But life is like that in the PC industry sometimes.)

After the drivers have been copied to the hard disk, the wizard may ask you to shut down the computer. Again, do exactly what the wizard tells you to do. When the installation is complete and the drivers are installed, you should be able to go right to the Windows 95 desktop without a hitch.

Step 4: Install nondriver programs

Many hardware devices come with their own programs. A fax/modem, for example, comes with a faxing program; a scanner may come with scanning and touch-up programs. If such programs came with your device, install those programs now, using the techniques described in Chapter 9.

Once again, make sure that you install only the extra programs — not the DOS/ Windows 3.x drivers.

 If you accidentally install DOS/Windows real-mode drivers or need to get rid of old ones, see "Removing a Device" later in this chapter.

If you have any problems with your newly installed hardware, if a device that worked previously doesn't work anymore, or if you can't get Windows 95 started, try the troubleshooting techniques described in the following sections.

Troubleshooting Hardware Conflicts

Hardware conflicts occur when two or more devices try to use the same IRQ, or the same memory range, to get the computer's attention. The symptoms of a hardware conflict might be strange, erratic behavior of a device. Or, in many cases, one the the conflicting devices won't work at all. Fortunately, Windows 95 offers several tools for tracking down and resolving hardware conflicts.

Using the hardware Troubleshooter

If a new hardware device won't work, or if something that worked before has stopped working properly, you have a device conflict. The quickest and easiest way to resolve a conflict is to use the Troubleshooter. Follow these steps:

1. Click on the Start button and then click on Help.

2. Click on the Contents tab.

3. Double-click on the Troubleshooting book to open it.

4. Double-click on If you have a hardware conflict.

5. Follow the instructions and suggestions on-screen.

As you proceed through the troubleshooting wizard, pay particular attention to any devices whose icons are covered by an exclamation point (!) inside a yellow circle. These devices are conflicting with some other device, and you need to reconfigure them to fix the problem.

If the Troubleshooter doesn't find any conflicts, something else is wrong. Check the manual that came with your new device for specific troubleshooting tips, or try some of the troubleshooting methods described in the following sections.

Getting around startup problems

If starting Windows 95 leads to a slew of error messages, and/or if Windows 95 hangs before you can get to the desktop, you can do many things to get around, diagnose, and fix the problem. Follow these steps:

1. Restart the computer.

2. When you see the `Starting Windows 95` message on-screen, press F8.

My mouse died

Sometimes, the mouse gets involved in a hardware conflict and stops working. To get to the Troubleshooter without a mouse, press Ctrl+Esc and then type **h** to choose Help. When you're in the Help Topics window, you can press Tab and Shift+Tab to move from one area of the window to another. Within an area, you can press the arrow keys to move from one option to another. When you get to the option that you want to use, press Enter to select it. If the option that you want to pick has a *hot key* (an underlined letter), you can hold down the Alt key and tap the underlined letter to select the option.

3. Choose one of the following options:

✦ *Normal:* starts Windows 95 in normal mode, as though you hadn't pressed F8.

✦ *Logged* (\BOOTLOG.TXT): starts Windows 95 normally, but creates a file `C:\Windows\Bootlog.txt` file that contains a transcript of all the events that occurred during startup. Use BOOTLOG.TXT to locate failed startup events.

✦ *Safe mode:* starts Windows 95 but bypasses many startup files; loads only the basic system drivers.

If Windows 95 starts with a blank or funky screen, choose Safe Mode to load only the standard VGA driver.

✦ *Safe mode with network support:* same as Safe mode, but also installs basic networking drivers.

✦ *Step-by-step confirmation:* lets you step through each command in the startup files so that you can identify the commands that are causing problems.

If Windows 95 displays error messages at startup or hangs before it starts, choose Step-by-step confirmation to identify the specific commands that are causing the problem.

✦ *Command prompt only:* processes all startup files and starts Windows 95 at the command prompt only. You can enter DOS commands, such as **edit** to change text files or **win** to start the Windows 95 GUI.

✦ *Safe mode with command prompt only:* same as Safe mode, but doesn't process startup files; loads only the bare-minimum drivers.

If you can't start Windows 95 because of a problem with the hard disk, you can boot from the Windows 95 startup disk, or from any DOS startup disk that has system tracks, in drive A.

Finding all references to a faulty driver

If you discover that the problem is with Windows 95's loading a specific driver, you can delete references to that driver from all initialization files. Starting from the Windows 95 desktop, follow these steps:

1. Click on the Start button and then click on <u>F</u>ind.

2. Click on <u>F</u>iles and Folders.

   In the <u>L</u>ook in box, make sure that all of drive C is selected; also make sure that the Include <u>s</u>ubfolders options is checked.

3. Click on the Advanced tab.

4. Enter the driver name (or some part of it) in the Containing Text box.

   If, for example, a driver named TSBA311.DRV is causing the problem, type **tsba311** as the text to search for.

5. Click on Find Now, and wait for Find to locate every file that contains the text that you typed.

6. To edit a file that Find located, right-click on its icon or name at the bottom of the Find dialog box and then choose Open.

   You especially want to edit any file that's identified as being the Configuration Settings file type.

7. If you are prompted for a program to open the file with, choose Notepad.

8. Within Notepad, choose Search⇨Find and press Find Next (F3) to locate and delete all references to the faulty driver.

9. When you finish, choose File⇨Exit.

10. Repeat Steps 6–8 for each configuration file that you want to edit.

11. Shut down and restart Windows 95 to test your changes.

Using Device Manager to resolve conflicts

If your system starts smoothly but you have problems with specific devices, a hardware conflict is the most likely cause. The Troubleshooter, described earlier in this chapter, takes you step by step through the procedure of finding and fixing the problem. Optionally, you can go into Device Manager yourself and change the settings. Follow these steps:

1. Click on the Start button and then point to Settings.

2. Click on Control Panel.

3. Double-click on the System icon.

4. Click on the Device Manager tab to get to the dialog box shown in Figure 10-3.

Danger! Edit only what you understand

In some of these troubleshooting procedures, I'm assuming that you understand the structure and purpose of initialization (.INI) and similar files (such as C:\CONFIG.SYS and C:\AUTOEXEC.BAT) and that you can use Notepad or DOS's EDIT command to change those files without making a mess of things.

If you are not familiar with those concepts and techniques, I strongly recommend that you *not* make changes in those files. Get help from a more experienced user. There's not much margin for error when you are tampering at this depth, and even the slightest mistake can make matters worse.

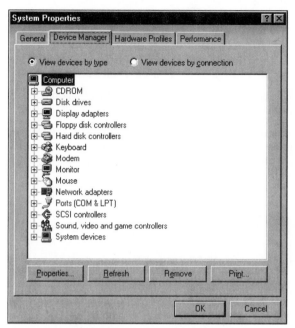

Figure 10-3: The Device Manager tab of the System Properties dialog box.

Within Device Manager, you have enormous flexibility to explore — and change — specific settings for every device that's currently operating in your system. Following are some general guidelines for using Device Manager:

✦ The first items displayed are *classes* of devices. To see the specific devices within a class, click on the class's plus button (+).

✦ If a specific device is conflicting with some other device, its icon is marked by an exclamation point within a yellow circle. If a specific device isn't working, its icon is marked by the international *prohibited* symbol.

✦ To view or change a device's properties, double-click on the device's icon or name, use whatever tabs and options are provided in the dialog box to resolve problems, and then click on OK.

✦ To update the entire list of installed hardware, click on the Refresh button.

✦ To remove a device, click on its icon or name and then click on the Remove button.

The Hardware Profiles tab of Device Manager is discussed under "Hot Docking and Flexible Configurations" in Chapter 17. The Performance tab is covered in under "Are We Optimized Yet?" in Chapter 12.

✦ To print a summary of the hardware list, click on the Print button.

✦ To organize the devices by the way that they're connected, click on the View Devices by connection button.

✦ To view devices by the resources that they're using, double-click on Computer at the tip of the list to get to the Computer Properties dialog box, shown in Figure 10-4; then choose whichever option describes the way that you want the list to be organized.

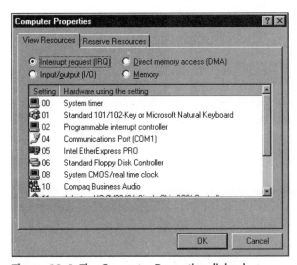

Figure 10-4: The Computer Properties dialog box.

✦ For help with anything in Device Manager, click on the Question-mark button and then click whatever you need help with.

When you are finished with Device Manager, choose OK to close that window. You may need to shut down the PC and restart Windows 95 for your changes to take effect.

Removing a Device

Before you read this section, please be aware that I'm discussing only devices that you want to remove from your system permanently. You can ignore all this information if you're disconnecting a portable CD-ROM drive, modem, network card, or any other device that you plan to plug back in and use later. On the other hand, if you're removing an internal PC card permanently perhaps with the intention of replacing it with some new card, it's a good idea to remove all the drivers for that card first. Follow these steps:

1. If you have any open program windows on the desktop, close them.

2. Click on the Start button and then point to Settings.

3. Click on Control Panel.

4. Double-click on the System icon.

5. Click on the Device Manager tab.

6. Click on the type of device that you plan to remove.

7. Click on the specific device that you plan to remove.

 Do yourself a favor and jot down any settings for the device you're going to remove, before you remove that device. That way, if you need to reinstall it later, you'll know what settings to choose.

In Figure 10-5, for example, I'm poised to remove the Gameport Joystick device.

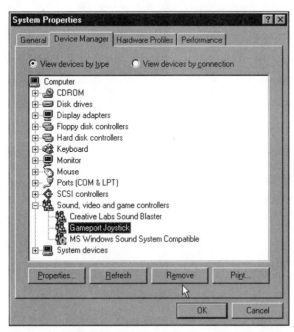

Figure 10-5: Poised to remove the Gameport Joystick virtual device driver.

8. Click on the Remove button, read the dialog box that appears to make sure that you're removing the right device, and then click on OK.

9. Repeat Steps 5–7 as necessary to remove all the drivers that support the device that you plan to remove.

10. Click on the Close button.

If you are instructed to restart your computer, do so. After the computer restarts, you can shut everything down and remove the device from your PC.

If you have any problems when you restart your PC, you may not have removed all the drivers for the device. Repeat the preceding steps, or use Find to find and remove all references to the device, as discussed under "Finding all references to a faulty driver" earlier in the chapter.

More Technical Stuff and Troubleshooting

As I've mentioned, my goal in this book is to empower people to take advantage of what Windows 95 has to offer, not to talk about design philosophy or architectural issues. The topics discussed in this chapter should allow you to install any hardware device successfully. If you encounter problems that you can't solve, don't forget that you can dig around in the online manual for more information.

 To find hardware-related topics and help in the online manual, click on the Start button, click on Help, click on the Index tab, and search for *hardware*.

If you want more advanced technical information or need to go deeper into hardware troubleshooting, you may want to purchase *Windows 95 SECRETS* by Brian Livingston (IDG Books Worldwide, 1995).

Summary

Here are the salient points about installing new hardware:

✦ A new breed of Designed for Windows 95 plug-and-play devices will follow Windows 95 to market. These devices will be the easiest to install and use.

✦ Installing legacy (pre-Windows 95) devices is still a bit rough, but not as bad as it was in Windows 3.x.

✦ If a legacy device is going to ask for an available IRQ, you can easily see which are available. Click the start button and choose Settings➪Control Panel. Double-click the System icon, then click the Device Manager tab. Double-click on Computer at the top of the list to get to the Computer Properties dialog box. From there you can example used (taken) IRQ's, I/O addresses, DMA channels, and Memory ranges.

✦ The typical scenario for installing a legacy device is to shut down everything, and install the device (but not the drivers) as per the manufacturer's instructions. Then...

✦ Restart the PC. If Windows doesn't detect the new device at startup automatically, click the Start button, choose Settings➪Control Panel, then double-click Add New Hardware to start the Add New Hardware wizard.

✦ If at all possible, use the Windows 95 driver for a legacy device, rather than the original DOS/Windows 3 drivers. The Add New Hardware wizard will install the correct drivers for you, if they exist.

✦ If you end up with hardware conflicts, use the troubleshooter to track them down and solve them. Click the Start button, choose Help, and click on the Contents tab. Double-click the Troubleshooting book, then double-click the If you have a hardware conflict topic.

✦   ✦   ✦

Routine Maintenance, General Management

As its title implies, this chapter is about routine
maintenance tasks that you can perform on a regular
basis to keep your hard disk running smoothly and at top speed.
For example, this chapter covers ScanDisk, which finds and
repairs disk errors and also can free wasted space. The chapter
also looks at the Disk Defragmenter, which keeps your disk
running at top speed.

Under the topic of general management, the chapter looks at
ways of backing up your hard disk and formatting floppy disks,
as well a tool called user profiles. User profiles are great when
two or more people share the same PC, because each user can
have his or her own screen settings, desktop icons, and so on.

Find and Repair Disk Errors

The occasional unexpected power loss or fatal error that stops
the PC dead in its tracks can leave behind trash on the hard disk
that does nothing but take up space. To keep your hard disk
working at top speed, you should run ScanDisk from time to time
to clean out the trash. You also can use ScanDisk to search for
and repair damaged sections of the disk.

To use ScanDisk, follow these steps:

1. Click on the Start button and then choose
   Programs⇨Accessories⇨System Tools.

2. Click on ScanDisk to get to the dialog box shown in Figure
   11–1.

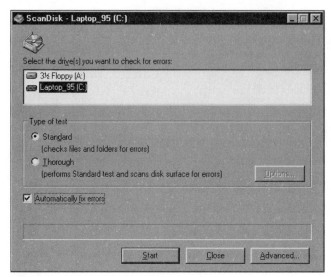

Figure 11-1: The ScanDisk dialog box.

3. Click on the drive that you want to scan (for example, C for your hard disk).

4. If you're just performing routine maintenance, choose Standard, and make sure that the Automatically fix errors box is checked.

5. Click on the Start button.

6. Follow the instructions on-screen.

ScanDisk may take a few minutes to complete its job. When it finishes, you go to the ScanDisk Results dialog box. Review that information if you want; then click on the Close button.

The preceding procedure above is fine for routine (say, weekly) maintenance. If you're having problems with your hard disk, however, you may want to perform a more thorough scan. Follow these steps:

1. Choose Thorough, rather than Standard, in the ScanDisk dialog box.

2. Click on the Options button to further specify what you want to do.

3. Clear the Automatically fix errors check box.

4. Optionally, click on the Advanced button and make additional choices.

Remember that for more information on any option that ScanDisk presents, you can click on the Question-mark button and then click on the option in question. Alternatively, click on the option and then press the Help key (F1). When you're ready to begin the scan, click on the Start button.

Finding lost files

I've often seen people lose a file and then go straight to ScanDisk to try to find it. These people assume that the computer messed up somehow and that the missing file is now floating around in lost fragments, which ScanDisk will reassemble into the missing file. But that's not the way it works. When you're looking for something that's missing, ScanDisk should be your *last* resort.

Ninety-nine percent of the time, a "lost file" really is just a misplaced file. Perhaps you misspelled the intended filename when you saved the file. Or maybe you didn't specify a particular folder, so the file was saved in some folder other than the one you intended. You may even have inadvertently dragged the file, or its folder, to the Recycle Bin.

Before you assume that the PC or hard disk messed up your file, try searching for the file by browsing. Check the Recycle Bin. Also, use Find (refer to Chapter 2) to search the entire hard disk for the missing file and/or for some text within the missing file. Chances are that the file is still intact and that you were a little confused about its exact name and/or location.

Remember, too, that if you're missing a program that comes with Windows 95, you can use the Windows Setup tab of the Add/Remove Programs wizard (refer to Chapter 9) to reinstall that component.

Keep the Hard Disk at Top Speed

In time, files on your hard disk become fragmented, a situation that slows disk activity and, in turn, the entire system. To see how files become fragmented, consider an example: Suppose that your hard disk is nearly full and that you need to delete some stuff to make room for a new program. You drag some old files into the Recycle Bin and then empty the bin. Now you have room. You don't really know, though, how that extra room is split up on the disk. Some of the files that you deleted may have been near the outer edge of the disk, some may have been near the inner edge, and others may have been near the center of the disk. Therefore, you can say that the empty space left by those deleted files is *fragmented* in different areas of the disk.

Now suppose that you install the new program. Windows has to use whatever space is available, so part of your new program might be near the outside of the disk, part near the middle, and part near the center. Now your *program* is fragmented in different areas of the disk. Technically, this situation isn't a problem. Windows can find all the pieces automatically when it needs them; you won't ever know how fragmented the file has become.

But fragmentation has a downside. As time passes, more and more files become more and more fragmented, and the drive head has to move more and more to get things off the disk. From your perspective, opening files and saving your work seem to take longer and longer. If you're near the PC, you may even hear the heavy clickety-clack of the drive head moving frantically about the disk to get to all these fragments.

For best results, delete any unnecessary files, empty the Recycle Bin, and run ScanDisk before you start the disk-defragmentation process.

To get the hard disk back to top speed, you just need to *defragment* the disk. The process takes a few minutes, but it's simple. Follow these steps:

1. Click on the Start button and then choose Programs⇨Accessories⇨System Tools.

2. Click on Disk Defragmenter.

3. Click on the drive that you want to defragment.

4. Choose OK.

Windows 95 first makes a quick pass on the disk to determine how fragmented the files are at the moment. If little fragmentation exists, you'll see a message to that effect, and you'll be given the option to Exit without defragmenting the drive.

 Many laptops have a spin-down feature on the hard disk to minimize battery drain. If you're not dependent on batteries at the moment, you can disable that feature to speed operations — dramatically, in most cases. For instructions, see the user's guide for the laptop computer.

If the drive needs defragmenting, or if you decide to defragment it anyway, you can click on Start. A dialog box appears, keeping you posted on the defragmentation progress (see Figure 11-2). To see what's going on in more detail, click on the Show Details button; to return to the smaller progress dialog box, click on the Hide Details button.

Figure 11-2: The Defragmenting dialog box.

 As you know, you should always shut down Windows before you turn off your PC, especially when the Disk Defragmenter is running.

You can use your PC normally while Windows is defragmenting your disk. Performance may be a little sluggish, however, because of all the disk activity. If you need to do something at normal speed, click on the Pause button in the Defragmenting dialog box. When you finish doing whatever you needed to do, click on the Resume button to resume defragmentation.

Backing Up Your Hard Disk

If you have hundreds or thousands of hours of work invested in the documents stored on your hard disk, or if the data on that disk is critical to operating your business, you really should keep a backup. I don't want to keep you up at night with worry, but you do have to keep in mind that fire, flood, a hard disk crash, theft, or incompetence can wipe out those important files in an instant. In such a situation, an ounce of protection is better than tons and tons of cure.

 Keep your backups in a safe place off-site. After all, backup tapes and floppy disks also can fall victim to fire, flood, and theft.

Windows 95 comes with a program called Microsoft Backup, which greatly simplifies backing up your hard disk. You can back up to and from most media, including floppy disks, hard disks, removable hard disks, network drives, and tape drives.

Starting Microsoft Backup

The first step in making a backup (or restoring from a backup) is inserting a tape into the tape drive or a disk into the disk drive. Then follow these steps:

1. Click on the Start button and then choose Programs⇨Accessories⇨System Tools.

2. Click on Backup.

 If Backup isn't available in your System Tools menu, use the Add/Remove Programs wizard to install the disk tools. See "Installing Missing Windows Components" in Chapter 9.

3. Read and progress through any information windows until you get to the window titled Microsoft Backup (see Figure 11-3).

Buying a tape backup unit

Backing up your entire hard disk to floppies can be a real pain, because the job may require *hundreds* of floppy disks. A tape backup unit, on the other hand, usually can back up an entire hard disk on one or two tapes. Microsoft Backup supports the industry standard QIC (quarter-inch cartridge) 40, 80, 3010, and 3020 standards. For a complete list of supported tape drives, start Microsoft Backup,

choose Tools⇨Redetect Tape Drive, and follow the instructions to get to the list of drives that are supported by Microsoft Backup.

If you want to use a single tape backup drive with two or more PCs, buy a unit that plugs into the parallel printer port, rather than one with a dedicated card. That way, you can unplug the unit from one PC and plug it into another PC.

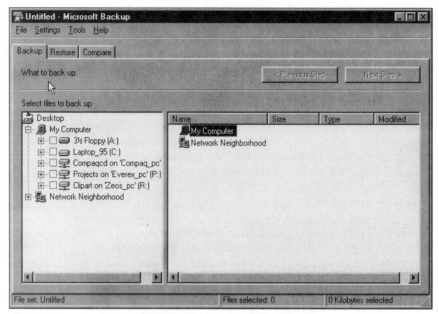

Figure 11-3: Microsoft Backup with the Backup tab selected.

Microsoft Backup is its own little application with its own help file, so when you're looking for information on Backup, you should use the Help option in Backup's menu bar. The sections that follow look at the kinds of tasks that you're most likely to do with Backup.

Backing up the entire hard disk

As mentioned in a previous sidebar "Buying a tape backup unit," if you want to back up en entire hard disk, you should use anything *but* floppy disks. A tape backup unit may be a bit slow, but it's the most cost-efficient way to back up the hard disk. Regardless of which medium you back up to, you'll follow these steps:

1. In Microsoft Backup, select the Backup tab (if it isn't already selected).

   Notice the message What to back up just below the tabs (refer to Figure 11-3).

2. Click on File; then click on Open File Set.

3. Click on Full System Backup, as shown in Figure 11-4.

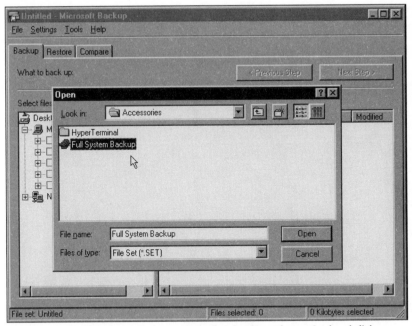

Figure 11-4: Full System Backup selected to back up the entire hard disk.

4. Click on Open, and wait a few seconds while Backup prepares the Registry and files.

   The name Full System Backup now appears in the title bar.

   You can use commands in the Tools menu to format and erase tapes. You also can use the Tools menu to make Windows redetect the tape drive, in case you just plugged it in recently.

5. Choose Settings➪Options.

6. Click on the Backup tab.

7. Choose the Full backup of all selected files option.

8. Click on the Next Step button.

   Notice that now the message below the tabs is Where to back up.

9. Click on the destination for the backup files.

   In Figure 11-5, for example, I clicked on the cassette tape drive icon. That tape's electronic ID label (a long number in this example) is visible on-screen.

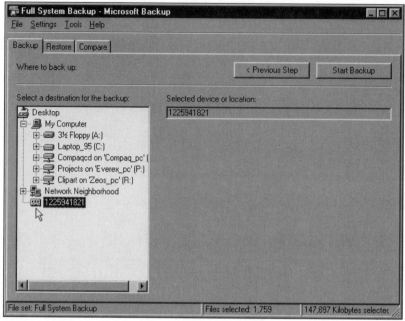

Figure 11-5: I selected the cassette tape icon to back up to.

10. Click on the Start Backup button.

11. Follow the instructions on-screen.

You'll be asked to enter a label for the backup set. You can enter a plain-English description — perhaps something like **Entire Hard Disk, January 1996**. After the backup process begins, you can go about your normal business on your PC. Operation may be a little sluggish, though, until the backup is complete.

LAN professionals: Windows 95 comes with updated versions of Cheyenne ARCServe agent and Arcada Backup agent for backing up to Windows NT Server and NetWare servers. For more information, search Windows 95 help (not Backup's Help) or refer to the *Windows 95 Resource Kit*, published by Microsoft Press.

Backing up new or modified files

It's not necessary to back up your entire hard disk every time you make a backup. In fact, you can save a great deal of time by backing up only the files that you created or changed since the last backup. Follow these steps:

1. Start Microsoft Backup.

2. Click on the Backup tab.

3. Choose File⇨Open File Set⇨Full System Backup.

4. Click on the Open button, and wait a few seconds while Backup prepares to back up the Registry.

5. Choose Settings⇨Options.

6. Click on the Backup tab, and choose the Differential option.

7. Click on the OK button.

8. Click on Next Step, and select a destination for the backup (for example, the tape-drive icon).

9. Click on the Start Backup button

10. Follow the instructions on-screen.

Using Backup instead of Copy

When you want to copy some files from your hard disk to floppies, you can use Microsoft Backup rather than the Copy method described in Chapter 5. Using Backup has a couple of advantages. For one, Backup compresses files as it copies them, so you can squeeze more onto the floppy. For another, Backup can split a large file across two or more floppies — something you can't do with Copy.

A backup strategy

If backups are essential to your business, it's important to come up with a good strategy for making backups. One method that many people use is to back up the entire disk once a week and then to back up only new and modified files for the rest of the week.

To do this on tape, you probably would want to use five separate tapes. If you do your full backup on Friday afternoon, for example, you could label that tape Friday: Full Backup. Label the other tapes Monday, Tuesday, and so on. On Monday through Thursday, you do a Differ-

ential backup to the tape for that day; on Friday, you do a complete backup to the appropriate tape. Thereafter, if a major disk crash occurs, you can restore first from the Friday: Full Backup tape and then restore from the Monday, Tuesday, and other tapes up to the day of the most recent backup.

One disadvantage of this approach is the fact that if you need to restore a single file, you need to search all the tapes for the latest version of that file. Still, this procedure is faster than backing up the entire hard disk every day.

You can use DriveSpace (see Chapter 12) to increase the capacity of a
floppy from 1.4MB to about 2.5MB.

If you're mailing the floppies to someone else, make sure that the recipient has
Windows 95, because he or she needs to use Restore (discussed later in this chapter)
in Backup to copy the files you sent on to his or her hard disk. Anyway, here's how
you use Backup with floppy disks:

1. Start Microsoft Backup.

2. Click on the Backup tab.

    You see the What to back up message.

3. Use either of the following methods to select the specific files and folders to
   browse:

    • Use the plus symbols (+) in the left pane to browse to the folder that you
      want to back up, and then select that folder's check box.

      In Figure 11-6, for example, I'm about to back up a folder named Windows
      95 Bible. You can select multiple folders, if you want.

    • Choose Settings⇨File Filtering to specify files to back up by date modified
      and type.

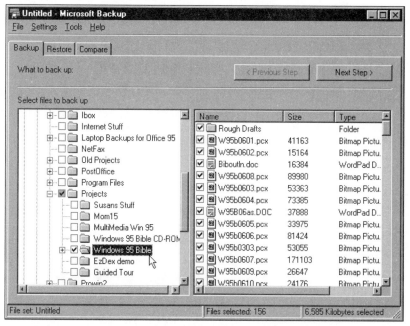

Figure 11-6: About to back up the folder named Windows 95 Bible.

4. Optionally, you can use the right pane of the Backup window to clear the check marks next to files and subfolders that you *don't* want to back up.

The status bar shows you how much stuff is currently selected. In Figure 11-6, I've selected 6,585 kilobytes of data. That comes out to about 6.6MB, because a megabyte is about 1,000 kilobytes.

5. If you want to back up all the selected files, choose Settings⇨Options, click on the Backup tab, choose the Full option, and then click on OK.

6. Click on the Next Step button to display the Where to back up options.

7. Click on the destination for the backup (a floppy disk drive, in this example).

8. If you think that you may back up the same set of files in the future, you can define the selected files as a set. Choose File⇨Save As, enter a name, and then click on the Start button.

9. Click on the Start Backup button.

10. Follow the instructions on-screen.

Notice that if you defined the selected files as a set in Step 8, you can back up the same set of files in the future without first selecting each file individually. Start Microsoft Backup and choose File⇨Open File Set. Click on the name of the file set you want to use, and then choose Open. Don't forget to check the options before you back up the set; choose Settings⇨Options, click on the Backup tab, and then choose the Full option (if you want to back up the entire set) or the Differential option (if you want to back up only files that have changed since the last backup).

Restoring from Backup

If you ever need to restore backed-up files from a tape or floppy disk, follow these steps:

1. Insert the tape or disk that contains the backed-up files into a drive.

2. Start Microsoft Backup.

3. Click on the Restore tab.

4. In the left pane, click on the icon for the drive that contains the files that you want to restore.

5. In the right pane, click on the name of the backup set that you want to restore.

6. Click on Next Step.

7. In the left pane, check each folder that you want to restore.

8. To select subfolders or files within a folder, click the plus symbol (+) next to the folder, and then select subfolders and files in the right pane.

9. After you select all the files that you want to restore, click on Start Restore.

10. Follow any instructions that appear on-screen.

Comparing files with backups

If you need to compare files on the hard disk with copies on the backup tape or disk, follow the same general procedure as in the preceding section, but use the Compare tab. Follow these steps:

1. Insert the tape or disk that contains the backups into a drive.

2. Start Microsoft Backup.

3. Click on the Compare tab.

4. In the left pane, click on the drive that contains the files that you want to compare.

5. In the right pane, click on the backup set with which you want to compare the files.

6. Click on the Next Step button.

7. In the left pane, check each folder that you want to compare.

   You can expand the list by clicking the plus sign (+) and then selecting individual files in the right pane.

8. Click on the Start Compare button.

9. Follow the instructions on-screen.

Formatting Floppy Disks

Floppy disks can be used to back up important documents and to transfer files from one PC's hard disk to another's. Programs that you buy often are stored on floppies. Documents that other people send to you also may be stored on floppies. In both cases, the floppy disk is already formatted, and *you do not want to format it again* — when you format a floppy disk, you also erase everything that's on it.

 If you want to copy files to or from a floppy disk, see Chapter 5. If you want to install a program from a floppy disk or to create a bootable (startup) disk, see Chapter 9.

When you buy a box of floppy disks from your local Comput-O-Rama, those disks may be preformatted for PC use. Those floppies don't need to be formatted, either. In fact, the only times when you *do* want to format a floppy are when the disk has never been formatted or when you want to erase everything on a floppy to make it a blank, formatted disk.

Formatting a floppy is easy. Follow these steps:

1. Put the floppy disk in drive A or drive B of your computer.

2. Open (double-click on) My Computer.

3. Double-click on the icon for the drive in which you put the floppy (usually, A).

4. If the floppy disk has never been formatted, a message appears to inform you so; follow the instructions on-screen to format the floppy disk.

 You can use ScanDisk to test and repair a floppy disk, and you can use DriveSpace (see Chapter 12) to increase the capacity of the floppy disk.

If you don't see a message indicating that the floppy has never been formatted, then you don't have to format it. If you really want to reformat the floppy and erase everything on it, however, close the window that displays the floppy's contents. In the My Computer window, right-click on the floppy drive's icon and choose For_mat. Then click on the Start button to proceed.

Managing Multiple Users on One PC

Every user has his or her own personal preferences in screen colors, desktop icons, and the like. That's why you can personalize Windows 95 in so many ways, as discussed in Chapters 6 to 8. Historically, there was no way for people who shared a PC to set up their own preferences. If you sat down at the keyboard after someone else used the machine, you had two choices: use whatever settings the other person left behind or go through the steps necessary to personalize the screen to your liking.

Those days are over. Thanks to user profiles in Windows 95, each person who uses a PC can have his or her own settings and can turn them on with just a few mouse clicks. To use this feature, every person who uses the PC must come up with a unique username and password. (All users should write that information down and put it in a safe place in case they forget later and need to find that information to get their personal settings back on-screen.) Then one of the users must activate the user-profiles feature, discussed in the following section.

Enabling multiple user profiles

The first step in setting up user profiles is telling Windows 95 that you plan to use that feature. Follow these steps:

1. If you have any work in progress on-screen, save all that work and then close all open program windows.

2. Click on the Start button and then choose Settings⇨Control Panel.

3. Double-click on the Passwords icon.

4. Click on the User Profiles tab to display the dialog box shown in Figure 11-7.

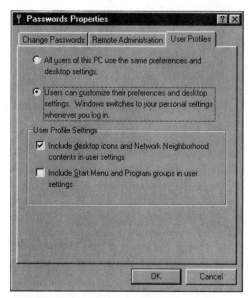

Figure 11-7: The User Profiles tab of the Passwords Properties dialog box.

5. To activate user profiles, click on the second option button.

Each user now can save his or her screen preferences, as described in the following section. In addition, you can allow or disallow individual desktop icons, Start menus, and so on.

- If you want each user to have his or her own set of desktop icons and Network Neighborhood contents, choose the first option.

- If you also want each user to have his or her own Start menu and Program menu options, choose the second option.

6. Click on OK when you finish.

7. Click on Yes to restart the computer.

When Windows restarts, you need to fill in your user name and password and perhaps answer additional questions on-screen. The following section explains how each user creates his or her own profile.

Creating a user profile

Each user of a shared PC can create his or her own user profile by following these steps:

1. To create a new user profile, the current user must log off by clicking on the Start button, clicking on Shut Down, clicking on Close all programs and log on as a different user?, and then clicking on Yes.

   A dialog box appears, requesting a user name and password. The dialog box looks something like Figure 11-8.

Figure 11-8: The login dialog box asks for a user name and password.

2. The new user (the person who's creating the new profile) should type his or her user name and password and then click on OK.

 Whenever you type a password, the screen shows only asterisks to keep nosy bystanders from seeing your password. Also, if your PC is on a local area network (LAN), your login dialog box won't look exactly like the one shown in Figure 11-8, but you still can proceed.

3. The new user is asked to confirm the request and password; he or she should follow the instructions on-screen.

That's all there is to creating a user profile. Any personal preferences that you set from now on are saved as part of your user profile — not as part of anybody else's profile.

 If you need to connect and disconnect devices frequently, as you do on a laptop, look into hardware profiles (see Chapter 20). If you want to limit what other users can do on a PC, look into system profiles.

To keep other people from changing your settings, always remember to log off before you leave the PC, and always remember to log in under your own username and password. If you sit down at the computer and someone else's settings are in effect, click on the Start button, click on Shut Down, click on Close all programs and log on as a different user?, and click on the Yes button. Then log on as you normally would.

Changing your password

If somebody discovers your password, and you want to change it, follow these steps:

1. If you haven't already done so, log on as you normally do, using your current password.

2. Click on the Start button and then choose Settings⇨Control Panel.

3. Double-click on the Passwords icon.

4. Click on the Change Windows Password button.

   The Change Windows password dialog box appears (see Figure 11-9).

5. Follow the instructions on-screen.

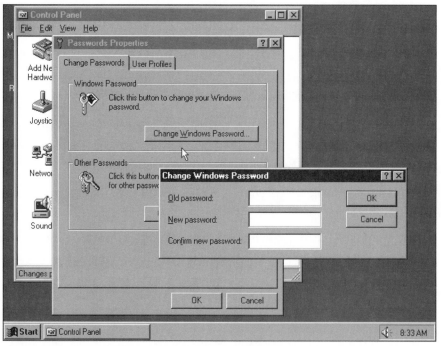

Figure 11-9: The Change Windows Password dialog box.

You can change only your own password (the password for the user name under which you logged in). Also, you must type the old password before you can choose a new one — another good reason to keep a written copy of that password somewhere, in case you forget it.

Summary

This chapter has discussed tools and techniques for keeping your PC tuned up and for dealing with multiple users who need to share a single PC:

✦ To find and repair disk errors, click on the Start button, point to Programs⇨Accessories⇨System Tools and then click on ScanDisk.

✦ Defragment your hard disk occasionally to keep it running at top speed. Just click on the Start button, point to Programs⇨Accessories⇨System Tools, and then click on Disk Defragmenter.

✦ You can use Microsoft Backup to make backup copies of your entire hard disk or just the files you've changed recently. To start Backup, click on the Start button, point to Programs⇨Accessories⇨System Tools, and then click on Backup.

✦ To format a floppy disk, put the floppy disk in drive A or B. Then open My Computer and double-click on the drive's icon. If the floppy has never been formatted, you'll see a message to that effect. And you can just follow the on-screen instructions to format the floppy on the spot.

✦ If several people share one PC, you can activate user profiles so that each user can save his/her own settings and preferences. To activate user profiles, click the Start button and choose Settings⇨Control Panel. Double-click on the Passwords icon and make your selections from the Use Profiles tab.

✦   ✦   ✦

The Zen of Optimization

If there is a Zen of optimizing your PC via Windows 95, it's this:
There ain't much to it. For the most part, Windows 95 is self-
optimizing. If a particular component or process isn't optimized,
Windows tells you so and even helps you fix the problem — kind
of like having a nerdy technician type built right into your PC.

If you love to tinker and experiment, you may find all this rather
disappointing. But as you'll see, you can do a few things on your
own to make sure that your programs are pumping out results as
fast as the hardware allows them to.

Are We Optimized Yet?

The quickest and easiest way to check — and possibly improve — the performance of your PC is simply to have Windows
95 help you do that. Follow these steps:

1. Click on the Start button and choose Settings⇨Control
   Panel.

2. Double-click on the System icon.

3. Click on the Performance tab.

If you can do some specific things to improve the performance of
your system, a message near the bottom of the dialog box offers
suggestions. In Figure 12-1, for example, the dialog box is telling
me that my PCMCIA cards are not using 32-bit drivers. For more
information and instructions on resolving that problem, I click on
that message and then click on the Details button.

When all your components are tuned for optimal speed, no list
appears, and the Details button disappears. Both of these
elements are replaced by the message Your system is configured for optimal performance.

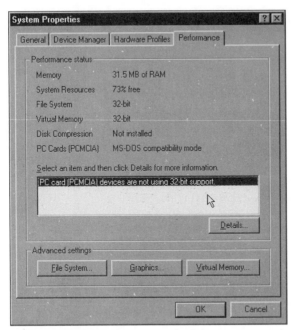

Figure 12-1: The Performance tab of the System
Properties dialog box.

If you love to tinker, however, you may be happy to know that the message isn't
always 100 percent correct. If you do a little exploring, you may be able to squeeze a
little more performance out of your PC. But don't expect your tuning efforts to
produce any dramatic results. You can't fine-tune a 386 into a Pentium any more than
you can fine-tune a Ford Escort into a Ferrari. Such is life.

Careful!

I can't talk about optimizing the PC without getting at least somewhat technical. So
throughout the rest of this chapter, I'll assume that you have a little bit of technical
background. In particular, you should understand that a *real-mode* (16-bit) driver is
one that's left over from DOS/Windows 3.x. Typically, the CONFIG.SYS and
AUTOEXEC.BAT files load those drivers. If you want to remove such a driver, you
need to remove the appropriate command from CONFIG.SYS or AUTOEXEC.BAT,
using a standard text editor such as Notepad on the desktop or **edit** at the C> prompt.
If you're not experienced with editing those files, you really should get some help from
someone who *does* have that experience — or at least review the relevant information
in a book about DOS.

What really dictates performance

The hardware, more than anything else, dictates how fast your PC runs. The most important factor is the processor. A Pentium (or 586) is faster than a 486, which in turn is faster than a 386. Period. Within a class of processor, clock speed determines how fast things go. A Pentium 120 is just flat-out faster than a Pentium 60.

The amount of RAM that you have also plays a role in overall performance — a relatively minor role. But the amount of RAM matters, because accessing stuff in RAM is much faster than accessing stuff on a disk. When Windows 95 runs out of RAM, it starts using the disk as RAM. Given the fact that the disk is slower than RAM, operations slow down.

It stands to reason that the speed of the hard disk counts, too, especially if you have limited RAM and Windows 95 often needs to spill data over to the disk. Performance-tuning your hard disk, then, can have a significant effect on overall speed. In this chapter, I will discuss techniques for optimizing performance in some detail.

The Need for Speed

In day-to-day use, disk accesses tend to be the bottleneck in your PC's performance. The better tuned your hard disk is, the smaller that bottleneck. As I mentioned in the preceding chapter, occasionally defragmenting your hard disk helps keep it running at peak speed. Telling Windows 95 how the hard disk is used on your PC also can help performance. To do that, follow these steps:

1. Click on the Start button, and choose Settings⇨Control Panel.

2. Double-click on the System icon.

3. Click on the Performance tab.

4. Click on the File System button and then choose one of the following options from the first drop-down list:

   - *Desktop computer:* for a normal stand-alone PC or a PC that's a client in a LAN

   - *Mobile or docking system:* for a portable or laptop computer

   - *Network server:* for a PC that plays the role of file server and/or print server in a peer-to-peer LAN

5. Click on OK.

6. Click on Close.

7. Follow the instructions on-screen.

Windows 95 automatically self-tunes to allocate resources according to your selection in step 4. You may need to reboot to activate the new setting.

Disk caching

A *disk cache* (pronounced *cash*) serves as a sort of holding area between RAM and the disk; its purpose is to minimize disk accesses and thereby speed operations. Windows 95 uses a self-tuning cache named VCACHE (the *V* stands for *virtual*). Unlike the caches in earlier versions of Windows, VCACHE does not require you to set its size, because it's dynamic. When demand is high, VCACHE uses whatever resources it can find; when demand is low, VCACHE frees resources for other activities so that they can run faster.

Caching is another reason why more RAM equates to faster performance: VCACHE automatically takes advantage of whatever RAM you have. The more RAM you have, the larger the cache. The larger the cache, the fewer disk accesses. The fewer disk accesses, the faster things go.

Caches are not additive. In fact, a cache within a cache slows operations. You should check your CONFIG.SYS and AUTOEXEC.BAT files to see whether either is loading a real-mode cache, such as SmartDrive (SMARTDRV). If so, remove the appropriate commands or at least comment them out with a **rem** command. While you're at it, you can remove any commands that load the old SHARE program, which is not needed in Windows 95 either. After making and saving your changes, don't forget to reboot the machine.

The swap file

When Windows 95 spills RAM data over to the disk, it uses what's called a *swap file*. In Windows 3.x, you could improve system performance by creating a permanent swap file. But it doesn't work that way in Windows 95. To the contrary, creating a permanent swap file may deteriorate Windows 95's performance.

Like VCACHE, the swap file in Windows 95 is dynamic, automatically using what resources are available, and freeing them when they're not needed. To ensure that you're using the dynamic swap file, double-click on the System icon and then click on the Performance tab. Click on the Virtual <u>M</u>emory button, and choose the first (recommended) option, as shown in Figure 12-2.

Then choose OK and follow the instructions on-screen.

Disk spin-down

Battery-operated laptops offer *disk spin-down* (also called *hard disk timeout*) to prevent the hard disk from running all the time and draining battery power. Unfortunately, spin-down also means slowdown — big time slowdown. If you're not relying on batteries while you use your laptop, by all means disable spin-down (you may have to disable all the power-savings features to do so).

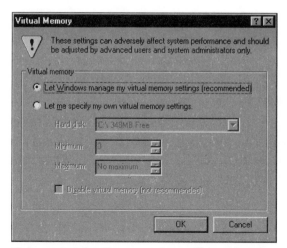

Figure 12-2: Virtual Memory (swap-file) options in Windows 95.

 Don't forget to re-enable your laptop's power-management capabilities when you go back to battery power. Otherwise, you'll drain those batteries before the stewardesses serve the first round of drinks.

You'll need to check the manual that came with your laptop for specific instructions; the exact method varies from one machine to the next. Typically, however, you can control spin-down by using the CMOS setup. On my laptop, I have to shut down Windows and reboot the machine. After the memory test flashes on-screen, I press Del to run setup. Within that setup (called WinBIOS on my laptop), I can enable or disable all the power-management features. Turning all those features off disables disk spin-down and makes the machine run noticeably faster.

Maximize Your Disk Space

For most people, hard disk speed is not nearly as much a headache as hard disk capacity is. Programs get bigger every year. Multimedia files are huge. A 200MB hard drive, which was a fantastic luxury just a few years ago, now is barely enough for your operating system and your favorite programs. It doesn't take long to run out of hard disk space. Luckily, Windows 95 comes with a program named DriveSpace that essentially doubles the capacity of your hard disk.

Disk space is cheap

Another solution to the hard disk-capacity problem is simply to buy a bigger hard drive. A bigger drive costs money, but perhaps less than you think. The day before I wrote this chapter, for example, I bought a 1.2 GB (that's 1,200MB) hard drive for $355. That price works out to about 30 cents per mega-byte — fairly cheap, especially compared with RAM, which costs anywhere from 30 to 50 *dollars* a megabyte.

Installation is fairly easy (for people who know what they're doing), so that part doesn't cost much. The store that performs the upgrade may even take your old drive as a trade-in, knocking the price down even further. It's worth a try to call your computer dealer and find out what it would cost to replace your current hard drive with a much larger one.

DriveSpace terminology

DriveSpace is easy to use but a bit mysterious until you get the hang of it. The way the program works is this: the folders and files on the drive that you're compressing are squeezed into one big compressed file. Your PC doesn't know that the compressed file is a file, however; it thinks that the compressed file is a drive, such as C. In fact, your PC is so convinced that the file is a drive, you won't even know that such a file exists. When you go browsing through your C drive, everything will look normal.

The following buzzwords describe what DriveSpace creates:

✦ *Compressed-volume file (CVF).* The compressed-volume file is the file that contains the compressed data. The CVF *acts* like a drive, *looks* like a drive (to Windows), and is *named* like a drive (such as C). In fact, the CVF is the file that holds all the compressed files.

✦ *Host drive.* The host drive is the actual drive that holds the CVF; it still has a drive letter name, but not the name that it used to have. When you compress drive C, for example, the compressed file *becomes* drive C. The host drive, where that file is stored, will have some higher-letter name, such as H.

At first glance, this naming method may seem to be counterintuitive. You may think that the host drive should get to keep its original name (C) and that the CVF (the fake drive) should be assigned a new name. But it wouldn't work that way, because Windows needs to think that the compressed file *is* the original drive. That's why the CVF gets the original drive name and the host drive takes on a new name.

More Info   Windows 95 DriveSpace is compatible with Microsoft's earlier DoubleSpace and DriveSpace programs. If you're using a disk compression tool from another vendor, such as STAC or AddStor, you should upgrade to the Windows 95 version of that product soon. You want to replace those products' original 16-bit real-mode drivers with 32-bit protected-mode drivers to get the best performance in Windows 95.

Compressing a disk

If you plan to compress your hard disk, be aware that the process can take several hours. You can do other things while DriveSpace is compressing, but your system will seem to be sluggish — as slow as a slug in September snow. You may want to consider launching the compression program just before you go home or before you go to bed. When you see the Compress a Drive dialog box, turn off the monitor and call it a day. Your new double-capacity drive will be ready in the morning.

You follow these steps to compress a disk:

1. Close all open program windows, and save any work in progress.

2. Click on the Start button, and choose Programs⇨Accessories⇨System Tools.

3. Click on DriveSpace to display the DriveSpace dialog box, shown in Figure 12-3.

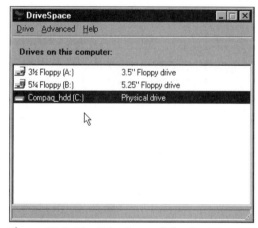

Figure 12-3: The DriveSpace dialog box.

4. Click on the drive that you want to compress.

DriveSpace can't create a hard drive larger than 512MB; typically, it compresses only the first 256MB of a disk to a 512MB drive. If your drive is larger than 256MB, you'll probably end up with some free space on the host drive. You can use that free space to store normal (noncompressed) files. To create larger drives, use DriveSpace 3, which comes with the Microsoft Plus! product (see Appendix F).

5. Choose Drive⇨Compress.

The Compress a Drive dialog box appears, showing you what to expect if you proceed with the compression. In Figure 12-4, for example, DriveSpace estimates

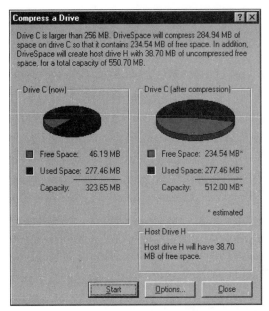

Figure 12-4: A preview of what DriveSpace can do.

that it will be able to increase my free space from about 46MB to 234 MB and my total disk capacity from about 323MB to 512MB.

6. If you want to proceed with the compression, choose Start; otherwise, click on Close to back out and forget the whole thing.

The compression starts, and now it's just a matter of waiting (and waiting, and waiting).

Compressing floppy disks

Compressing a floppy disk takes only a few minutes. You can follow the steps in the preceding section to compress a floppy. When you get to step 4, select the drive that the floppy is in (for example, A). If the disk is empty, you'll end up with almost twice as much space as you had originally. A 1.44MB floppy disk, for example, ends up with about 2.5MB of space.

Recently, I put more than 10MB of graphic bitmap (.PCX) files on one floppy disk. I compressed the files, using PKZIP and then copied the compressed .ZIP file to a 2.5MB floppy disk.

When the compression is done, you can use the floppy just as you would a normal (noncompressed) floppy disk; for example, you can copy other files to that disk. Just be aware that when you're browsing your system, you'll see two icons for the floppy disk: the original A icon and a new icon with some higher letter (such as E). The higher-letter name is for the host drive, which, for all intents and purposes, you can ignore. Be sure to copy files to and from the A: drive.

When you put the compressed floppy in another Windows 95 PC, you should be able to browse that floppy as you would any noncompressed floppy; for example, you can open My Computer and then double-click on the A: drive icon. Again, an icon for the host drive appears in the My Computer window, but you can ignore the host drive.

If the PC can't read the compressed floppy, the browsing window probably will display an icon named ReadThis. Double-clicking on that icon displays text that explains the problem and gives you the solution. As the ReadThis file will suggest, you'll probably want to enable automatic mounting. Go back to the DriveSpace dialog box (choose Start⇨Programs⇨Accessories⇨System Tools⇨DriveSpace). Then choose Advanced⇨Options, and select the Automatically mount option, as shown in Figure 12-5. Click on OK, and follow any instructions that appear on-screen.

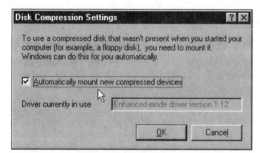

Figure 12-5: Choose this option to mount (read) compressed disks automatically.

Spelunking DriveSpace

The compressed-volume file that DriveSpace creates is hidden from normal browsing modes. But you can do a bit of spelunking if you're curious about what's going on below the surface. All you need to know is the host-drive name (for example, H for a hard disk or maybe E for a floppy disk) and a little bit about the DOS DIR command. In the sample commands that follow, I assume that you're exploring a compressed floppy in drive A whose host drive is named E.

If you pop out to the C:> prompt and enter a command such as **dir a:**, the result would be the same as looking at a noncompressed floppy: a list of files on the disk. The command **dir a: /c** would show the same list of files but would include the compression ratio for each file. A file may show 2.0 to 1.0, for example, meaning that the compressed file is half the size of the original file.

Never, ever try to open or modify the contents of the DBLSPACE.000 file. If you do, you're almost certain to lose everything within that file.

If you enter the command **dir e:** to look at the host drive, you see nothing other than (perhaps) the READTHIS.TXT file on a floppy disk. If you enter the command **dir e: /a** to include hidden files, however, you see a file named DBLSPACE.000. That file is the CVF. On a floppy, the CVF's size will be roughly equal to the capacity of the disk (because it fills the disk). On a hard drive, the CVF will be any size up to 512MB, which is the largest CVF that DriveSpace can create.

Tweaking DriveSpace

Like other mini-applications in Windows 95, DriveSpace has its own help file, which offers more options and settings than I need to discuss here. If you want to explore those options or learn about decompressing a disk, choose Help⇨Help Topics. Alternatively, select an option in some menu other than Help and then click on the Question mark button or press F1 for information about that option.

Optimizing Print Speed

Printing can be another bottleneck in overall PC performance. Even though you can do other things with your PC after the printer gets going, the print job takes up all system resources for a period right after you issue the Print command. All you can do is wait.

That waiting period, called *return-to-application time*, occurs when the PC is creating an image for the printer on the disk. Windows 95 offers a new format called EMF (Enhanced Metafile Format) for that disk image, which it can create quickly. The EMF can't make your printer go any faster than it was designed, but the time required to create the EMF is reduced, so return-to-application time is shorter.

EMF works only with non-PostScript printers and printer drivers. If you're not using a PostScript printer, follow these steps to ensure that you're using the EMF format:

1. Click on the Start button, and choose Settings⇨Printers.
2. Right-click on the icon for any non-PostScript printer driver.
3. Click on Properties.
4. Click on the Details tab.
5. Click on the Spool Settings button and then choose EMF from the Spool data format drop-down list (see Figure 12-6).
6. Click on OK twice to return to the Printers dialog box.

You can repeat steps 2–6 for each non-PostScript printer driver in the Printers dialog box.

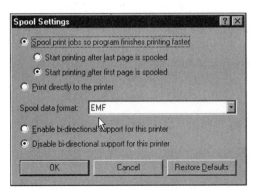

Figure 12-6: The Spool data format set to EMF.

Parallel ECP Ports

Extended Capabilities Port (ECP) is a new standard for the parallel printer port. ECP supports high-speed printers and other devices connected to the printer port; it can even speed the performance of non-ECP devices. Keep in mind that ECP is *hardware*. None of what's discussed in this section applies to a standard parallel printer port.

You need to refer to your computer manual to determine whether you have an ECP port (or whether you can upgrade your existing port to ECP). After you determine that you have an ECP port, follow these steps to enable ECP support in Windows 95:

1. Refer to the computer manual or add-in card documentation to determine the IRQ and DMA settings for each of the ECP ports that you want to use.

   (This information is required, and there's no way to get it from Windows.)

2. Click on the Start button, and choose Settings⇨Control Panel.

3. Double-click on the System icon.

4. Click on the Device Manager tab.

5. Click on the plus sign (+) next to Ports (COM & LPT) and then select Extended Capabilities Port (available only if you have an ECP).

6. Click on the Properties button.

7. Click on the Resources tab.

   The Input/Output range for the port should be listed under Resource Type.

8. Select Basic configuration 2 from the Settings based on options.

9. Under Resource Type, click on Interrupt Request; then click on the Change Setting button.

10. Enter the IRQ value that you determined in Step 1, and click on OK.

11. Click on Direct Memory Address.

12. Enter the DMA value that you determined in Step 1, and click on OK.

These steps configure only one ECP. If you have multiple ECPs, you need to repeat the steps to configure each port's IRQ and DMA settings. The ECP capabilities will be available after you shut down and restart the computer.

Using System Monitor

Windows 95 comes with a System Monitor feature that enables you to assess the speed of various components. System Monitor is sort of a debugger/oscilloscope that technicians and network administrators can use to analyze hardware performance and test for bottlenecks. But even if you don't work at that nitty-gritty level of detail, you may find it interesting to actually see how your system is working.

To start System Monitor, follow these steps:

1. Click on the Start button, and choose Programs⇨Accessories⇨System Tools.

2. Click on the System Monitor option.

The System Monitor window appears, probably nearly blank at first. But as you use your PC, the feature tracks the performance of various components, as shown in Figure 12-7.

 More Info If System Monitor isn't available in your Accessories menu, use the Windows Setup tab of the Add/Remove Programs dialog box to install it (refer to Chapter 9). System Monitor is with the Accessories programs.

Spikes in the chart indicate the amount of time or number of CPU cycles used by a component or process at that point in time. You can use buttons in the toolbar to select components to view and the type of graph to view. If your work requires this kind of detailed analysis of processes, you can learn more by browsing System Monitor's Help options. The *Windows 95 Resource Kit* (Microsoft Press) also describes System Monitor in some detail.

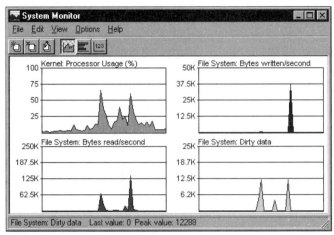

Figure 12-7: The System Monitor.

Summary

This chapter is all about getting the best performance from your PC hardware and Windows 95. In a nutshell:

✦ To check/improve your system performance, click Start and choose Settings⇨Control Panel. Double-click the System icon, then click on the Performance tab.

✦ To maximize file system speed, click Start and choose Settings⇨Control Panel. Double-click the System icon, click on the Performance tab then click on the File System button. Choose an option from the *Typical role of this machine* drop-down list.

✦ To experiment with disk caching, disable SMARTDRV and SHARE in your AUTOEXEC.BAT and CONFIG.SYS files. Then shut down and restart the PC. VCACHE (Virtual Cache) that comes with Windows 95 will take over all caching, which might improve your overall disk performance.

✦ Windows 95 performs best when you *don't* set a fixed swap file (virtual memory) size.

✦ On a portable PC, disabling the disk spin-down feature when you're not relying on batteries will improve disk performance considerably.

✦ To squeeze more stuff onto a disk, use DriveSpace to compress the disk. For larger drives (up to 2 GB when compressed), use DriveSpace 3, discussed in Appendix F.

✦ To optimize return-to-application time after starting a print job, make sure you're using the EMF file format with any non-PostScript printers. To get to the file format, open My Computer, double-click the Printers folder and right-click a printer. Choose Properties⇨Details⇨Spool Settings and set the Spool Data Format to EMF.

✦ ✦ ✦

Taking Care of Business

P A R T

IV

◆ ◆ ◆ ◆

In This Part

Chapter 13
Brave New
Officeware

Chapter 14
Printers, Fonts,
and Pictures

Chapter 15
Choosing and
Installing a Modem

Chapter 16
PC Faxing and
Telephony

◆ ◆ ◆ ◆

Brave New Officeware

This chapter is about the way that things are evolving in PC business computing in general. The trend, of course, is to keep giving users more and more power, and at the same time to make the PC easier to learn and use. Windows 95 certainly is a big step in that direction.

But Windows 95 is only one "gene" in this evolutionary trend. Following in Windows 95's footsteps will be a new generation of office-productivity tools. In this chapter, I take the focus off Windows 95 and look at the parallel trends in officeware.

The Monoliths Are Fading

You may hear computer jocks refer to the great application programs of yesteryear as *monolithic apps.* The name comes from the fact that each of these programs was designed to do one thing. A word processing program, for example, is for typing. A spreadsheet program is for performing quick math calculations for forecasting and trying out "what-if" scenarios. A database program is for keeping records.

Those monolithic programs are, of course, still as great and as useful as they ever were; I'm not trying to discredit them by referring to them in the past tense. But some problems exist with the monolithic approach to creating programs.

Problem one is that not everybody on the planet has a job that can be facilitated with one application. In a huge corporation that has typists (word processors) and financial managers (spread-sheets), monolithic apps are OK. But the opposite of the corporation is the self-employed person who plays the roles of president, janitor, and everything in between. That person probably needs the capabilities of many apps.

Monolithic apps tend to be overkill for the vast majority of users. Sure, it may be great that your word processing program can do columns, fonts, and typesetting. And yeah, it's cool that your spreadsheet program can do the Einstein equations. But what if you only need *some* word processing capability (such as basic formatting and spell checking), *some* spreadsheet capability (math and charts), and *some* database capability (managing customer lists and orders)?

The 800-pages-plus instruction manuals that accompanied each app represented another formidable problem. Newer programs provide much more on-screen support and access to help.

To further complicate matters, each app has its own commands and style, so there was no guarantee that anything you learned in the first app would apply to the next one. To top it all off, it often was difficult — if not outright impossible — to get data from one application to another (especially in the DOS era).

Lack of interaction among the apps was a problem even for advanced programmers and power users. A WordPerfect and Lotus 1-2-3 macro maven, for example, could automate all kinds of things within one program or the other, but no in-between language could take advantage of the capabilities of both programs. A WordPerfect macro couldn't open a 1-2-3 worksheet, yank out a chart, and put it in the current document; each macro language functioned only within its own environment.

The Birth (and Death) of the Suites

All the problems with monolithic apps are just now starting to fade away. In fact, the apps themselves are fading away into office suites. Initially, a *suite* (such as Microsoft Office) was just a way to bundle several programs together and sell them at a discount.

But there's a lot more to modern suites than shrink-wrapping. There's a new level of integration within those apps that makes them behave more like a single app that contains many tools. A "regular Joe" can use a pinch of word processing, a smidgen of spreadsheet, and a dash of database to get some work done.

New languages are evolving that allow power users to call upon the capabilities of all the apps in a suite. When you use Visual Basic for Applications in Office 95, for example, you can write a program that plots a graph from today's database data, places a copy of that graph in a word-processed report, and places another copy in today's slide-show presentation. The person who uses that program can just click on a button to accomplish all those tasks.

The integration between Windows 95 and Office 95 is so tight that the whole kit and caboodle feels like one product — sort of a complete virtual office squeezed onto a screen.

This is the general trend, but it's still in an early stage of its evolution. Rumor has it that the Taligent operating system (currently under construction) will eliminate the monolithic apps and even the suites; all those tools will be built into the operating system. The user just picks from the desktop whatever tool is appropriate to whatever he or she wants to do at the moment. Power users will be able to automate anything and everything with a single programming language (or macro language, stack, or whatever they decide to call it).

What I'm Showing You Here

The Taligent operating system doesn't exist yet, of course, but you can see some definite progress in that direction in the new office suites for Windows 95. In this chapter, I'll use Microsoft Office 95 to present some examples. Please understand that I'm not endorsing Office 95 or in any way discrediting the competing products; I just happened to have the beta software for Office 95 when I wrote this chapter. I'm sure that competing suites will have many (if not all) of the same features.

Also understand that *beta software* is software that's in the latter stages of testing and refinement. Microsoft can change anything that I discuss in this chapter before the product goes to market. So please don't hold me — or Microsoft — to any specifics that I present in these examples. I'm assuming (and hoping) that Microsoft Office 95 will be on the store shelves by the time you read this book; I needed to use the prerelease software to write this chapter.

That Documentcentric Thing

Although Microsoft Office 95 consists of several applications — Word, Excel, PowerPoint, Schedule +, and perhaps Access — absolute beginners don't really need to know that, because Office 95 is more documentcentric than its predecessors. That is to say that the interface is geared toward documents rather than apps.

Perhaps you're familiar with the Office toolbar that appears in Microsoft Office 4.2 and 4.3. The toolbar contained a button for each application in the suite: *W* for Microsoft Word, *X* for Excel, and so on. The assumption was that the person sitting at the keyboard would know what each button was for and what each application was for — or that he or she could figure everything out from the icons. (Yeah, right.)

The new Microsoft Office toolbar, shown at the top of the screen in Figure 13-1, has no buttons for specific apps. In fact, the tooltips for the default buttons are (from left to right in the figure) simply Office, Start a Document, Open a Document, Make an Appointment, Add a Task, and Add a Contact. Hmmmmmmmmm.

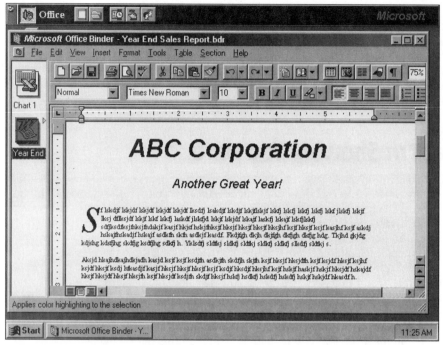

Figure 13-1: The Office 95 toolbar and the binder displaying a Word document.

The window below the toolbar is called the *binder*. The binder acts much like a real-world binder in that you can stick all the documents for any project into a single binder. The binder is very documentcentric. At the left edge of the binder in Figure 13-1, you see icons for a couple of documents that I added to that binder. One document, named Chart 1, has an Excel icon. The other document, named Year End, has a Word icon.

Remember that I'm showing beta software in this chapter. The toolbar, binder, and icons may have changed by the time you read this book.

If I click on a document's icon, that document appears inside the document area of the binder. In Figure 13-1, the Word document named Year End is selected, and the contents of that document are displayed in the binder's document area. The menu bar and toolbar at the top of the binder are actually Microsoft Word's menu bar and toolbar.

Now suppose that I click on the Chart 1 document icon. No big application launch occurs; no new window appears; not many changes take place on-screen. The Excel document simply replaces the Word document in the binder, and Excel's menu bar and toolbar replace Word's (see Figure 13-2). Now I have access to all of Excel's capabilities, with that app's menu bar and toolbar on-screen. This approach is much less confusing and intimidating to beginners and casual users.

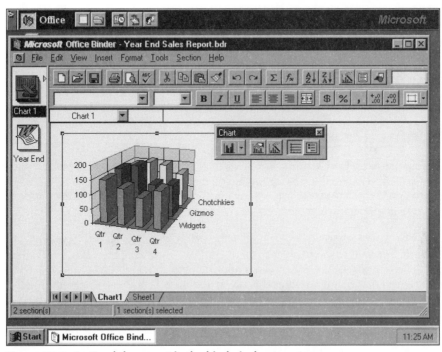

Figure 13-2: An Excel document in the binder's document area.

Not so sure about that binder?

If you're an experienced Office user, the binder may seem to be an inconvenience rather than an aid. Not to worry — the binder is optional. You can work in Office 95 exactly the way that you're accustomed to working in earlier versions of Office.

On the other hand, if you work with users who are less savvy than yourself, think what a great convenience the binder can be to them. You can pass a group of documents, neatly pack-aged in a binder, to another worker. That person can open the binder and then open any document within the binder just by clicking on it. You'll spend less time explaining what each document is and where to find it.

Also, you're not stuck with the default toolbar buttons described in this chapter. You can add whatever buttons you want, just as you can in the earlier versions of Office.

So managing documents in the binder is pretty darn easy; you don't have to look around much. And when a document comes to the screen, it brings the appropriate tools with it.

You may be thinking, "Yeah, but if you can see only one document at a time, how can you drag and drop objects between documents?" Glad you asked.

Awesome Drag-and-Drop

As you saw in earlier chapters, Windows 95 has made many inroads toward universal drag-and-drop capability. For example, you can drag folders and files to the Recycle Bin to delete them; you can print many kinds of documents by selecting their icons and dragging them to a printer icon.

Universal drag-and-drop is evolving in Office 95 as well. The goal is a general rule that says, "If you want to move object x to document y, just drag the object to its destination." The person sitting there with mouse in hand shouldn't have to worry about a zillion rules that define whether this particular object can be dragged into that particular document. The person just drags the object, and it works.

Scraps

Scraps are the solution to the problem of dragging and dropping when only one document is visible on-screen at a time. Suppose that I'm looking at my Excel chart in the binder and want to put that chart in my Word document. To get started, I need to shrink the binder window a little to make room on the desktop. Then I can click on the chart and drag it to the desktop. A scrap appears on the desktop, as shown in the lower-left corner of Figure 13-3.

Now I can click on the icon for the Word document on the left side of the binder. My written document instantly appears in the binder's work area again, replacing the chart that was there. All I have to do is drag the scrap from the desktop into my Word document. My document now contains a copy of the chart, as shown in Figure 13-4.

If you think about it, this method is very natural and intuitive. No menu commands are involved; no window navigation is required; no mysterious invisible Clipboard is used. The process is like cutting and pasting printed documents with scissors and glue.

 Puzzled?

If you're wondering why my screen shots in this chapter are so cluttered, it's because I'm using 640 by 480 resolution; that resolution makes it possible to see small objects in these tiny black-and-white printed screens. In real life, I'd do this work at 800 by 600 or higher resolution, which would give me a lot more elbow room.

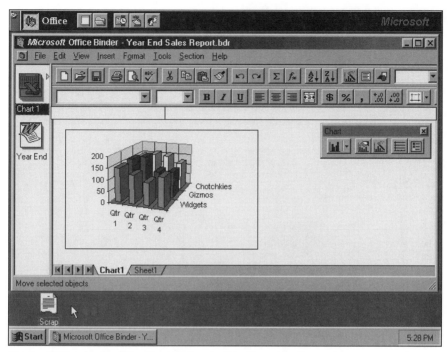

Figure 13-3: I dragged the chart to the desktop to create the scrap.

In-place editing

After an object is embedded in a document, you can edit that object in two ways: click on the object's button in the binder bar at the left (that is, click on the Chart 1 icon in Figure 13-3). Or you can double-click on the object in its container document to perform *in-place editing*. In in-place editing, the complete document remains on-screen, and the tools from the other application (Excel, in this example) appear for use in the document.

As you make changes in the object, you see exactly how the changes will look within the container document. To save the edited object, click on any spot in the document outside the object. The Excel tools disappear.

OLE ain't what it used to be

Some of you may be thinking, "Hey, most of what you just described is called OLE, and we've had it since Windows 3.1." True. Only the scraps are new to Windows 95 and Office 95. But since I've brought up the subject of OLE, I may as well discuss how it fits into the Windows 95/Office 95 scheme of things.

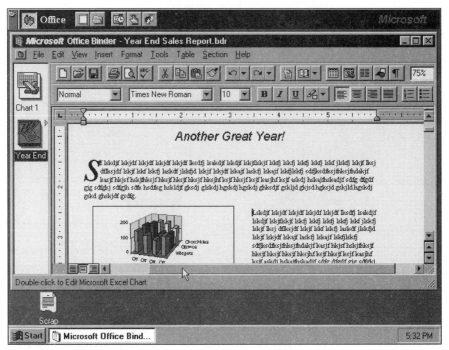

Figure 13-4: The Excel chart now is part of my Word document.

As you may know, *OLE* stands for *object linking and embedding* — at least, it used to. If you were to ask a Microsoft employee what OLE stands for now, she'd probably say, "Nothing. It's just *olay.*"

OLE could be a first — an acronym that doesn't stand for *anything*.

Why remove the meaning from an acronym? Because *object linking and embedding* no longer does justice to the many capabilities of OLE. Linking and embedding are just a couple of end-user capabilities of OLE; we now have OLE automation as well. As you'll see in the following section, OLE automation brings an enormous amount of power and flexibility to the people at the high end of the nerd scale: application developers and power users. In a nutshell, OLE automation enables you to manipulate an application's objects from outside the application.

One OOP Does It All

As I mentioned earlier, a big problem with the early monolithic apps for power users was the fact that their macro languages could drive only one app. In Office 95, the problem has been fixed by Visual Basic for Applications (VBA). The way that VBA works is elegant, simple, and very powerful.

You have one language, VBA, that *sees* Office 95 as though it were one program. A single VBA program can contain commands that control Microsoft Word, Microsoft Excel, Microsoft Access, Microsoft PowerPoint, and Microsoft Schedule Plus. VBA can use just about any capability, no matter how large or small, from any app to get a job done; it also can move and copy things from one app to another.

Although the *one language drives all* concept itself is simple, mastering VBA is not so simple. You can't learn it overnight; there's a lot to know, and I certainly can't teach you all there is to know in this chapter. But I can give you an idea of how VBA works.

In a sense, VBA is like two languages. On one hand, VBA has the standard Visual Basic commands, which resemble the BASIC commands of yesteryear. In the sample VBA code shown in Figure 13-5, you see the If...Then...Endif, Sub, and Exit commands from traditional Visual Basic (if such a thing as *traditional* exists in this ever-changing industry). You use those commands to control what happens and when it happens.

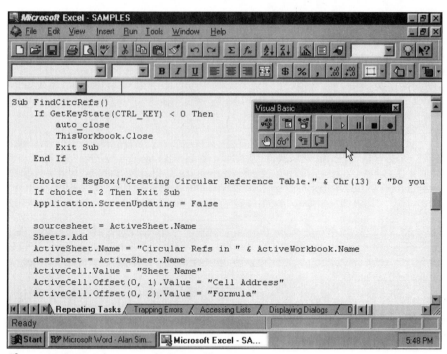

Figure 13-5: Sample VBA code from Office 95.

On the other hand, VBA has an object-oriented programming (OOP) language. Unlike the regular Visual Basic commands, the OOP commands enable you to manipulate objects directly. The OOP commands use *dot* syntax, such as ThisWorkbook.Close and ActiveCell.Value = "Sheet Name" in Figure 13-5. (I'll talk about that syntax more in a moment.)

In some cases, the OOP commands are similar to earlier macro languages, in that you can create them by recording some action in a macro. Open the resulting macro, and voilà — you have your OOP code, ready to place in your custom VBA program.

Objects, properties, and methods

The key to understanding VBA is realizing that just about everything in Office 95 is an object. Excel is an object. A chart within Excel is an object. An Excel worksheet is an object. Even a single cell in a worksheet is an object. As a colleague of mine eloquently put it after his moment of realization, "Every-stinkin'-thing is an object!"

Each object has its own unique set of properties and methods. An object's *properties* are things such as its color and size — how it looks on the screen or printed page. An object's *methods* are things that the object can do — or, more precisely, things that an outside program can make the object do. (For example, you can open, save, print, and close many objects by using the Open, Save, Print, and Close methods.) In a sense, properties are nouns (describing an object), whereas methods are verbs (describing an action).

When you're doing day-to-day work on the screen, you can right-click on almost any object to display a pop-up menu, which lists several things you can do with that object. Most of the actions listed in that pop-up menu are methods. Typically, the pop-up menu also includes a Properties option. When you choose the Properties option, you go to a dialog box that allows you to change the properties of that particular object.

Basically, VBA enables you to do the same things from within code — that is, VBA can do all those things automatically, behind the scenes, without your having to click on anything. You don't need to see the pop-up menu, the object, or even the object's application on-screen.

The syntax for manipulating objects from within code is based on object names and actions, separated by dots. To make an object take some action, you use the following simple syntax:

```
objectname.method
```

In the following example, MyChart is the name of an object (most likely, an Excel chart). When executed, the command copies that object to the Windows Clipboard.

```
MyChart.copy
```

Object exposure

The objects that you can manipulate from outside an application are called that application's *exposed objects*. The idea is that the application exposes certain of its objects to VBA so that programs outside the application can manipulate those objects.

Probably the most formidable task in becoming a fluent VBA programmer is learning which objects each application expose and what properties and methods each object offers. Learning these things is tough, because Excel and Access each expose hundreds of objects, and every object has its own unique set of properties and methods.

If you do start learning VBA, make sure that you learn about the *Object Browser* early in your learning curve. Object Browser is a big help in determining what objects are available and what properties and methods each object provides.

A little forewarning: in an amazing stroke of counterintuitiveness, Microsoft Word exposes only one object, named WordBasic. But WordBasic is a heck of a thing to expose, because that object is, literally, the entire Word Basic language. Funky.

To change one of an object's properties, you typically use this syntax:

```
objectname.property = setting
```

The following command refers to an object named MyCell (which presumably is some cell in a worksheet) and sets the font for that cell's contents to boldface:

```
MyCell.font.bold = True
```

Notice that the command contains no procedure, as in older languages. You don't have to go through a series of commands to make something happen to the object; rather, you name the object and specify what you want it to do or how you want it to look.

If you're steeped in traditional procedural programming language, this new object-oriented approach feels very strange at first, but once you get the hang of it, it's pretty slick.

What you need to create custom VBA programs

If you want to create custom VBA programs, you need several things, the first and foremost of which is knowledge. Programming is not a skill that you can learn overnight. And before you can even think about programming, you need to be very familiar with the capabilities of all the Office 95 applications that your programs will address.

In terms of tools, what you need depends on what you want to do. If you're developing a custom Office program for in-house use, you don't need anything extra; Microsoft Office 95, by itself, is all you need. You can create your custom program within any

Office app, such as Excel or Access, or you can spread your app's code across several objects. It really doesn't matter which app the VBA program starts from, because when the program gets going, it has access to everything in all the Office 95 programs.

On the other hand, if you're thinking about developing a custom Office app to sell, you'll probably want to buy Microsoft's Visual Basic for Applications. That product allows you to put all your code in an .EXE file that you can distribute to anyone who has Office 95. Users would treat your custom app the way they would any other program — they install it, and when they want to run it, they double-click on its icon.

It's important to understand, though, that if your .EXE file calls upon Word, Excel, Access, or PowerPoint to do something, that program needs to be on the user's machine. The process is not like distributing a classic .EXE file that will run an any Windows PC; on the contrary, the person who uses your custom application must have whatever Office apps your custom program calls upon.

The last little point is a bummer, because it narrows your potential customer base to Office 95 users. But remember that this is simply where we are right now in this evolving technology. Eventually, all that Office stuff will be built right into the operating system, along with multimedia, video, Internet access, and so on. When we get to the Taligent point, techno artists will be able to create tiny programs that do huge and amazing things just by calling on built-in capabilities in new and interesting ways. The PC will be a household appliance; the custom programs that you create will be simple plug-ins that make the appliance do great things.

Yowza

Whew! In this chapter, I tried to cover a lot of ground, explaining how things are evolving and where we are in that evolution. Some sections were geared toward advanced users who have considerable programming experience, and I apologize if I went over your head. But no more of that for a while. Starting in the next chapter, I'll get back to specific Windows 95 issues, with just a little digression into related issues.

Summary

Lots of new things are happening in the world of basic business/office software:

✦ Individual monolithic applications are being replaced by suites, where all programs are well integrated and can act more as a unit.

✦ The documentcentric approach to working is forcing the programs out of the limelight and into the background.

✦ Drag-and-drop is becoming the standard technique for doing just about anything and everything.

✦ In-place editing lets you edit an object that's embedded in a document, without leaving that document.

✦ A single programming language can control all the data and programs in a suite of programs.

✦   ✦   ✦

Printers, Fonts, and Pictures

Windows 95 comes with hundreds of new 32-bit printer drivers to make your print jobs faster and smoother than ever before. But more that the operating system, advances in printing technology, fonts, clip art, paper stock, and color have made printing something of an art form in and of itself. In this chapter, I discuss all the tools that enable you to do some awesome printing of your own.

Installing a Printer

Installing a printer is easy. Just follow these steps:

1. Gather up your original Windows 95 floppy disks or CD-ROM, as well as any disks that came with your printer.

2. If you are connecting to a network printer (a printer that has already been installed and shared on some other PC in the LAN), skip to Step 7.

3. Shut down Windows and shut down your PC.

4. Plug the printer into the computer and into the wall; then turn the printer on.

5. Restart your PC.

6. If your printer is Windows 95 plug-and-play-compatible, Windows detects that fact during startup and helps you install the drivers.

   Follow the instructions on-screen, and skip the remaining steps.

Whenever you're given the choice to install a Windows 95 driver or the manufacturer's driver, always try the Windows 95 driver first. Click on the Have Disk button only if the printer has no Windows 95 driver and you need to use the manufacturer's.

7. Click on the Start button and choose Settings⇨Printers.

8. Double-click on the Add Printer icon.

    You see the first page of the Add Printer Wizard (see Figure 14-1).

9. Follow the instructions on-screen.

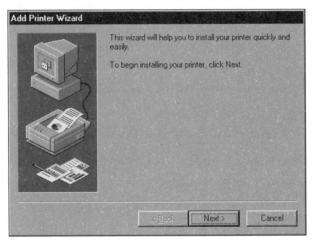

Figure 14-1: First page of the Add Printer Wizard.

When you're given a choice between Local and Network printer installation, choose Local unless the printer is *not* physically attached to the PC. Use the Network option only to install shared printers that are on some other PC in the LAN. See Chapter 26 for more information on network printing.

 To minimize return-to-application time when you use a non-PostScript printer, use the EMF data format; see "Optimizing Print Speed" in Chapter 12.

Every installed printer on your PC is represented by an icon in the Printers folder. To open the Printers folder, simply click on the Start button and choose Settings⇨Printers.

Figure 14-2 shows a sample Printers folder from one of my PCs.

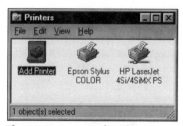

Figure 14-2: Sample Printers folder open on the desktop.

Printing Documents

After your printer is installed, you can use any of these techniques to print most documents:

✦ *To print from a program:* Open the document by double-clicking on it or by choosing File⇨Open. When the document is open, choose File⇨Print.

✦ *To print from the desktop:* Browse to the document that you want to print. Then right-click on the document's icon and choose Print from the pop-up menu that appears.

 Not all document types support right-clicking and drag-and-drop printing, but you can use the Registry to add those methods to many document types. See Chapter 31 for details.

✦ *To print several documents:* Open the Printers folder; browse to and select the documents that you want to print. Then drag the selected documents to the printer's icon in the Printers folder.

You can use the last technique to drag the selected documents to a printer's desktop shortcut icon. Figure 14-3, for example, shows a shortcut to my HP LaserJet printer, which I created by using the techniques discussed in Chapter 4. Then I browsed to the folder named Windows 95 Bible. Within that folder, I clicked on the Type column heading (in Details view) to group all the Microsoft Word documents. Then I selected all those Word documents. In the figure, I'm dragging the selected icons to the printer's shortcut icon to print them all in one fell swoop.

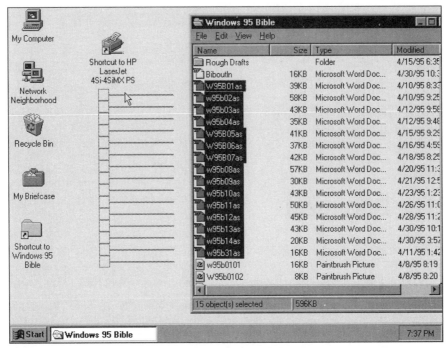

Figure 14-3: Dragging selected icons to a printer's shortcut icon.

Managing Printers and Print Jobs

The icon for a printer doubles as the Print Manager for that printer. When you want to check the status of the printer or manage ongoing print jobs, double-click on the printer's icon in the Printers folder or any shortcut icon for that printer. You go to a dialog box like the one shown in Figure 14-4.

You can choose options from the Printer menu to control the print queue. Choose Printer➪Pause Printing to pause the entire print queue, for example, or choose Printer➪Purge Print Jobs to clear all the documents that are waiting to be printed. To manage individual documents in the print queue, select a document by clicking on it; then choose an option from the Document pull-down menu.

To view jobs that have been sent to a network printer, you need to go to the server (the PC that is physically connected to the printer) and double-click on the printer's icon there.

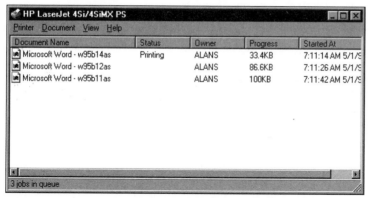

Figure 14-4: A queue of documents waiting to be printed.

Choosing a default printer

If you have access to several printers from your PC, you can specify the one that you use most often as the default printer. That way, when you start a print job without specifying a particular printer, the job is sent to the default printer.

To define a default printer, follow these steps:

1. Click on the Start button, and choose Settings⇨Printers.

2. Double-click on the icon for the printer that you want to make the default printer.

3. Choose Printer⇨Set as Default.

Changing printer properties

Every printer has its own unique set of properties, which you can change. Regardless of what settings your printer offers, you can follow these simple steps to get to those properties:

1. Click on the Start button, and choose Settings⇨Printers.

2. Right-click on the icon for the printer that you want to make the default printer.

3. Choose Properties to get to the properties sheets.

 If you right-click on the shortcut icon for a printer, choosing the Properties option from the pop-up menu takes you to the shortcut's properties, not the printer's properties. Make sure that you go through the Printers folder.

Figure 14-5 shows a sample properties sheet for a printer. Be aware that the properties that appear on your screen depend entirely on your printer. For more information about the available properties, you need to refer to the manual that came with your printer.

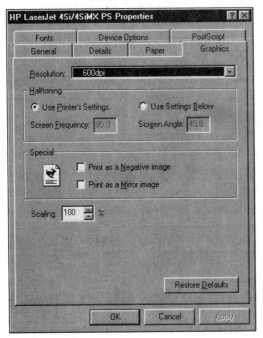

Figure 14-5: Properties for an HP LaserJet 4Si/4SiMX printer.

Using Fonts

A *font*, simply stated, is a style of print. This text is in one font; the heading above this paragraph is in a different font. Any font can be printed in a variety of weights. What you're reading right now is the regular (or roman) weight. **This is the boldface (or bold) version of this font.** *And here is the italic weight for this font.*

The size of a font is measured in *points*; 1 point equals roughly $1/72$ inch. Normal-size text (such as this) usually ranges from 8 to 12 points. Letters printed at 36-point size are around a half-inch tall, and letters printed at 72 points are around one inch tall.

The three main classes of fonts are serif, sans serif, and decorative. *Serif* fonts have little curlicues at the end of each letter to minimize eyestrain when reading small print. This font and the Times New Roman font shown in Figure 14-6 are serif fonts.

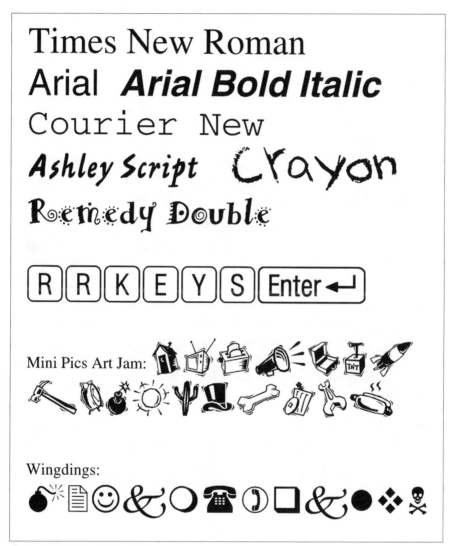

Figure 14-6: Examples of fonts.

Sans-serif fonts don't have the little curlicues and generally are used for large text. The Arial font shown in Figure 14-6 is a sansserif font, as are the fonts that appear on most street signs.

Decorative fonts are used to call attention to something or to set a mood. Most of the fonts shown in Figure 14-6 are decorative. These fonts sometimes are used for headlines, advertisements, and signs, usually to call attention to a single word or short phrase. Some decorative fonts (for example, the last two in Figure 14-6) contain little clip-art images and symbols.

After a font is installed, the way that you apply it to text depends on the program that you're using. In most programs, you select the text to which you want to apply the font and then choose Format⇨Font. In some cases, you can choose a font from the toolbar. Figure 14-7 shows a Microsoft Word document; I'm using the Font drop-down list in the formatting toolbar to apply a font to selected text.

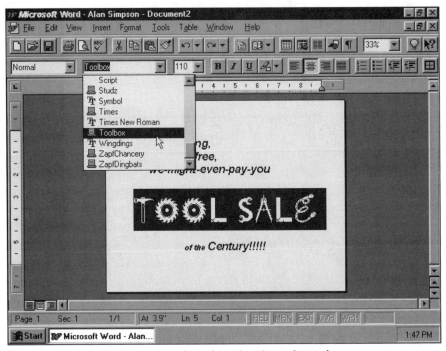

Figure 14-7: Choosing a font for selected text in Microsoft Word.

Expanding your font collection

Thousands of fonts are available in the marketplace. When buying fonts, you'd do well to limit yourself to TrueType and PostScript Type 1 fonts, both of which are fully compatible with Windows 95. TrueType, however, offers a few advantages over PostScript. For one thing, TrueType fonts are fully supported by virtually all Windows programs and utilities and by all printers that can print graphics. The tools for managing TrueType fonts are built into Windows 95.

The downside to TrueType is that most professional typesetting and printing services support PostScript fonts, rather than TrueType. If your printing needs often take you beyond the desktop, you may want to ask your printing service which fonts it prefers; chances are that the choice will be PostScript. If you lean more toward PostScript fonts, you'll need to buy a PostScript printer or add PostScript capability (if available) to your current printer.

You can find TrueType and PostScript fonts at computer stores; the fonts also are advertised in many computer and desktop-publishing magazines. One of my favorite sources of fonts is Image Club, which will gladly send you its catalog. Contact Image Club Graphics, Inc., c/o Publisher's Mail Service, 10545 West Dognes Court, Milwaukee, WI 53224-9985. The phone number is (800) 387-9193; the fax number is (403) 261-7013.

Managing TrueType fonts

You can review, add, and remove TrueType fonts via the Fonts folder. To get there, follow these steps:

1. Click on the Start button, and choose Settings⇨Control Panel.
2. Double-click on the Fonts icon.

An icon for each installed font TrueType font appears, marked with a TT symbol. The folder also lists older raster fonts, which are included with Windows 95 to maintain compatibility with earlier versions.

✦ *To select a view,* pull down the View menu and choose any command, or click on one of the view-option buttons in the toolbar.

✦ *To see what a font looks like,* double-click on its icon. When the font's window appears (refer to Figure 14-8), you can click on Print to print the font sample or click on Done to close the window.

✦ *To delete a font,* click on its icon and choose File⇨Delete.

✦ *To view similar fonts,* choose View⇨Fonts by Similarity. Then choose a font from the List fonts by similarity to drop-down list.

✦ *To close the Fonts folder,* click on its Close (X) button.

Notice that you don't use the Fonts folder to apply a font to text. Rather, you apply fonts to text within whatever program you happen to be working with at the moment, as described earlier in this section.

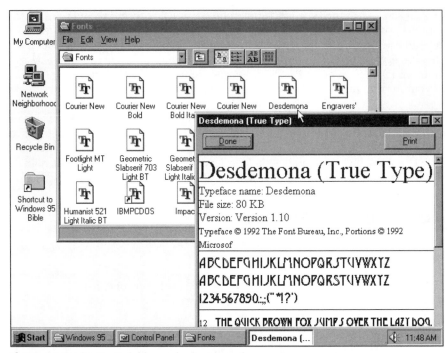

Figure 14-8: The Fonts folder and a font sample on-screen.

Installing TrueType fonts

New TrueType fonts that you purchase typically are delivered on floppy disk or CD-ROM. Before you can use a TrueType font, you need to install it. Follow these steps:

1. Insert the floppy disk or CD-ROM that contains the font(s) into a drive.

2. Click on the Start button, and choose Settings⇨Control Panel.

3. Double-click on the Fonts icon to display the Fonts folder.

4. Choose File⇨Install New Font.

5. Use the Drives and Folders options to navigate to the disk that contains the fonts you want to install.

   In Figure 14-9, I've navigated to the floppy disk in drive A.

6. In the List of fonts box, select the font(s) that you want to install.

   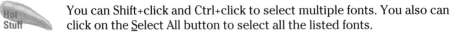 You can Shift+click and Ctrl+click to select multiple fonts. You also can click on the Select All button to select all the listed fonts.

7. Click on the OK button.

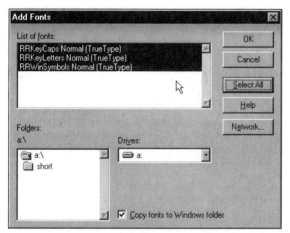

Figure 14-9: Ready to install a new TrueType font from a floppy disk.

Copying the fonts to your hard disk takes a few moments. When that process finishes, you return to the Fonts folder; the new fonts will be listed there. To verify the font installation, close the Fonts and Control Panel windows, start any Windows program, and look at your font options within that program.

 If the fonts are compressed, you may need to follow the manufacturer's instructions to get them decompressed and onto your hard disk. You also may need to follow the installation instructions in this section to install the decompressed files.

Managing PostScript Type 1 fonts

Windows 95 has no built-in capability to manage PostScript fonts; instead, you use Adobe Type Manager (ATM) to install and manage PostScript fonts. Typically, when you buy a set of PostScript fonts, a copy of ATM comes with the fonts on a disk labeled ATM Program Disk (or something to that effect). You have to install that program before you can use PostScript fonts.

Installing Adobe Type Manager

You install Adobe Type Manager as you would any other program, and you need to install it only once. ATM is updated from time to time, however, so when you get a new copy of ATM, you may want to try installing it. If the version that you are about to install is *not* newer than the version you already have installed, a message on the screen tells you so, and you can cancel the installation.

To install ATM, follow these steps:

1. Save any work in progress, and close all open program windows.

2. Insert the Adobe Type Manager program disk or CD-ROM into the floppy or CD-ROM drive.

3. Click on the Start button, and choose Settings⇨Control Panel.

4. Double-click on Add/Remove Programs.

5. Click on the Install button.

6. Follow the instructions on-screen.

 If Add/Remove Programs doesn't find an INSTALL or Setup program, perhaps the disk that you're using contains only fonts — not the ATM program. Look for the disk labeled Program Disk, and try again.

When the installation process starts, you go to a window that looks something like Figure 14-10 (depending on what version you happen to be installing). You can accept the suggested folders for storing the fonts (C:\PSFONTS and C:\PSFONTS\PFM) and then click on Install. After the fonts have been copied to your hard disk, you're prompted to restart Windows; do so. Remove the ATM disk from its drive after you restart Windows 95.

ATM Installer

Adobe *Type Manager*™

Installer Version: 2.51

ATM Installer will install the following:
* ATM System files.
* ATM Control Panel (into the Main group).
* Fonts included with ATM.

Target directory for PostScript outline fonts:

    c:\psfonts

Target directory for font metrics files:

    c:\psfonts\pfm

[Install] [Cancel]

Figure 14-10: Ready to install Adobe Type Manager.

From now on, ATM loads automatically whenever you start Windows 95. The Adobe icon will appear (briefly) in the lower-left corner of the screen while Windows 95 is starting.

Managing PostScript fonts

When you want to review, delete, or add PostScript fonts, you need to open the ATM Control Panel. Typically, you do that by following these simple steps:

1. Click on the Start button, and point to Programs.

2. Point to Main, and click on ATM Control Panel.

You are taken the Adobe Type Manager Control Panel, shown in Figure 14-11. If you don't see a program group called Main, look through other program groups to see whether you can find the icon for the ATM Control Panel. If you still can't find the icon and are sure that you have installed ATM, see the sidebar in this section titled "Where's my ATM Control Panel?"

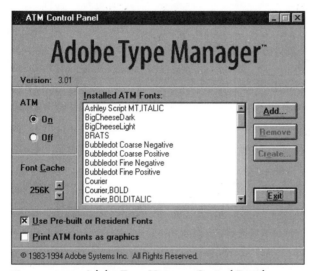

Figure 14-11: Adobe Type Manager Control Panel.

The list in the center of the ATM Control Panel shows the PostScript fonts that you already have installed. To remove a font, select the font name and then click on the Remove button. When you finish reviewing or deleting PostScript fonts, click on the Exit button.

In the ATM Control Panel, always make sure that the On option in the ATM section is selected. If you select Off, ATM won't load at startup, and your PostScript fonts won't display on-screen.

Where's my ATM Control Panel?

If you are certain that you have installed Adobe Type Manager but can't find its Startup icon anywhere in your Programs menu, you can create a shortcut. Here's the basic procedure:

1. Right-click on the Start button, and choose Open.

2. Double-click on the Programs icon.

3. Click on the Start button again, and choose Find⇨Files or Folders.

4. Type **atmcntrl**, and click on Find Now.

   The icon that you're looking for is repre-sented by a lowercase *a*. Move and size the Find and Programs windows so that you can see the atmcntrl icon and the folders in the Programs menu.

5. Right-drag the atmcntrl icon into any folder in the Programs folder.

6. Release the right mouse button, and choose Create Shortcut(s) Here.

7. Close all open windows.

To start the ATM control panel in the future, click on the Start button, point to Programs, point to whatever program group you dragged the atmcntrl icon to, and then click on the ATM Control Panel icon.

Installing PostScript fonts

When you purchase new PostScript fonts, they're delivered to you on floppy disk or CD-ROM. You need to use the ATM Control Panel to install those fonts on your hard disk before you can use them. Follow these steps:

1. Insert the floppy disk or CD-ROM that contains the fonts you want to install.

2. Start the ATM Control Panel, as described in the preceding section ("Managing PostScript fonts").

3. Click on the Add button.

4. Navigate to the drive and folder that contain the fonts you want to install.

   In many versions of ATM, you need to scroll to the bottom of the Directories list and then double-click on a drive letter, such as [-a-] for drive A. Then, if neces-sary, you choose the appropriate folder from the Directories list.

5. Select the font(s) that you want to install.

 You can Shift+click and Ctrl+click to select multiple fonts.

6. Click on the Add button to begin the installation.

7. Follow the instructions (if any) that appear on-screen.

When installation is complete, you return to the ATM Control Panel. Click on the Exit button. To verify that the PostScript fonts are now available, start any program that supports fonts, and check out your selection of fonts within the program. If the PostScript fonts that you just installed aren't available, you may need to restart Windows. Click on the Start button, and choose Shut Down⇨Restart the computer?⇨Yes. Then try again when you get back to the desktop.

Add a Little Art to Your Life

Clip art is a great way to spruce up newsletters, reports, brochures, and other printed material. You can buy clip-art collections at most computer stores, and also from mail-order houses that advertise in computer and desktop-publishing magazines. Figure 14-12 shows a few examples, ranging from the fun and funky images of Art Parts to the photographic realism of Oswego's Illustrated Archives.

Sharing PostScript fonts on a LAN

If you have a LAN, it's not always easy to ensure that every PC on the LAN has exactly the same set of fonts installed. Also, if your collection of fonts takes up a great deal of disk space, storing the same fonts on every PC in the LAN wastes disk space. You can solve both problems by installing fonts on only one PC in the LAN and then sharing the folder that contains the fonts.

To do this, first choose one PC in the LAN to hold the PostScript fonts. Install the PostScript fonts on that PC, using ATM as usual. After installing the fonts, share the folder that contains the fonts (typically, c:\psfonts).

Next, go to any other PC in the LAN, and use Network Neighborhood to map a drive letter to the shared folder that contains the PostScript fonts. Choose Reconnect at Logon, while you're at it. For example, let's suppose that you decide to map the drive letter **t:** to that shared folder. (For more information on sharing folders and mapping drive letters, see Chapter 26.)

After mapping the drive letter, stay at this PC, and start ATM. Click on the Add button, and make sure that Install without copying files is selected. Then use the Directories list to browse to the shared folder that contains the PostScript fonts (**t:**, in this example). Select the fonts that you want to use, and click on the Add button.

In the future, you can use the PostScript fonts normally from this PC, so long as you're connected to that shared folder (drive **t:**, in this example).

Figure 14-12: Sample clip art.

Windows 95 supports all popular PC clip-art formats including .CGM, .TIF, .PCX, .BMP, .WMF, and .GIF. The real compatibility issue, however, is between the program in which you plan to use the clip art and the format of the clip art. You should check the help file or documentation for your word processing, desktop publishing, or graphics program to see which formats are supported.

Some professional clip-art packages deliver their files in Encapsulated PostScript (EPS) format. You can print those images only on PostScript printers.

Many clip-art collections are delivered on CD-ROM, so you won't need to use a great deal of hard disk space to store them. I always keep a little collection of frequently used clip art on my hard disk. As I discussed in Chapter 8, I keep all the clip art in one folder and organize the art, by theme, in subfolders. That clip-art folder is shared on my LAN, so I can get to it from any PC in my LAN (or by phone, if I happen to be away).

A good clip-art browser is a tool well worth having. One of these browsers, called the Microsoft Clip Art Gallery, is built into Office 95. The Gallery enables you to organize clip art by theme and displays thumbnails of each piece of art within a theme, as in the example shown in Figure 14-13.

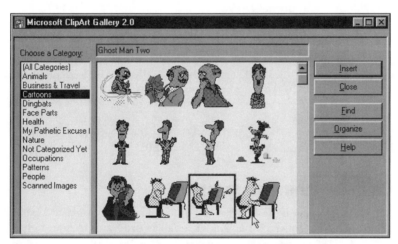

Figure 14-13: Microsoft Clip Art Gallery comes with Office 95.

The Gallery is simple to use. When I want to pop a piece of art into a Word (or whatever) document, I choose Insert⇨Object⇨Microsoft Clip Art. The Gallery appears, and I choose a category from the left column. Then I double-click on a thumbnail picture, and that picture pops into my document.

Printing the screen (screen dump)

If you're familiar with DOS, you may remember the days when you could press the Print Screen (Prt Scr) key to print a copy of whatever was on-screen. In Windows, pressing Print Screen sends a copy of the screen to the Clipboard, rather than to the printer, so you have to take a few extra steps to actually print the screen. To take it from the top, follow these steps:

1. If you haven't already done so, arrange the screen so that it looks the way you want it to look in print.

2. To capture the entire screen, press Print Screen.

   To capture only the active window, press Alt+Print Screen.

Puzzled? Some PCs require you to press Shift+Print Screen or Alt+Shift+Print Screen to capture the screen.

3. Click on the Start button, and choose Programs⇨Accessories.

4. Click on the Paint icon.

5. Choose Edit⇨Paste or press Ctrl+V.

6. To print the image immediately, choose File⇨Print⇨and then click on the OK button.

This method is fine for the occasional screen shot. But if you need to manage many screen shots, or if you need to crop, size, add borders, and embed the screen shots in other documents, you'd do well to buy a program that's designed for that purpose.

To create the screen shots for this book, I used Collage for Windows, published by Inner Media Inc., 60 Plain Road, Hollis, NH (603) 465-3216.

Image Color Matching support

Windows 95 is the first version of Windows to support Image Color Matching (ICM). This technology, licensed from Eastman Kodak, enables programs to offer better consistency between the colors displayed on-screen and the colors that come out of the printer.

Because ICM is built in, there's nothing that you, personally, need to do to take advantage of it. Instead, when you purchase new software and hardware for printing color, you want to look for a product that supports ICM. When installed, the product creates a profile in the Windows\System\Color folder. When you use the product, Windows 95 automatically performs the appropriate color transformation to ensure consistent color representation across all display and printing devices.

Awesome Papers

Your printer can do a lot more than just print text and graphics on 8 1/2- by 11-inch paper. The following sections examine ways that you can expand your horizons by printing labels, cards, checks, and more.

Printing checks and business forms

You can use your printer to print on preprinted checks and business forms. Just keep in mind that if you want to print on carbon-paper forms, you really should use a *forms printer* (which basically is a heavy-duty dot-matrix printer). Carbonless (single-sheet thickness) forms and checks can be printed on either a laser printer or a dot-matrix printer.

To check out your options, request a catalog or brochure from the following companies:

Designer Checks
P.O. Box 13387
Birmingham, AL 35202
Phone: (800) 239-4087
Fax: (800) 774-1118

Nebs
500 Main Street
Groton, MA 01471
Phone: (800) 225-6380
Fax: (800) 234-4324

Cards, stickers, transparencies, and slides

Most laser printers can print on mailing labels, floppy disk labels, file-folder labels, and a wide variety of stickers. You can find stock for printing on those items, as well as for printing business cards, invitations, greeting cards, file cards, and gatefold mailers. Most laser printers even enable you to print on the transparencies used with overhead projectors. But don't trust just any paper or transparency to your laser printer; instead, find stock that's specifically designed to handle the high heat that laser printers produce.

The Avery label company offers a large selection of laser-printer labels, stickers, and transparencies. You can find these products at most large office-supply and computer stores. Alternatively, contact Avery at the following address:

Avery Laser Products
P.O. Box 5244
Diamond Bar, CA 91765-4000
Phone: (800) 462-8379
FaxFacts: (818) 584-1681

For cards and predesigned labels, see the catalogs mentioned in "Color from black-and-white printers" later in this chapter.

Label printers

If you get tired of switching between regular stock and labels in your printer, consider purchasing a dedicated label printer. Typically, you can plug the label printer into a serial port, so that it doesn't conflict with your main printer.

Seiko Instruments makes a couple of nice label printers, which you can find at most computer stores. I use a CoStar label printer, and I'm pleased with it. For more information on that label printer, contact the company at the following address:

> CoStar Corporation
> 100 Field Point Road
> Greenwich, CT 06830-6406
> Phone: (800) 4-COSTAR or (203) 661-9700
> Fax: (203) 661-1540

CoStar also makes a label printer that can print bar codes and POSTNET bar codes.

35mm slides

Printing on 35mm slides for a slide show requires special equipment. The most cost-effective means of creating and printing 35mm slides is presentation software such as Microsoft PowerPoint, which comes with the Office 95 suite. Within that program, you'll find instructions for sending your work to a service center that will create the slides for you.

Color from black-and-white printers

Even if you don't have a color printer, you still can use color to spruce up your letterhead, brochures, mailing labels, postcards, business cards, newsletters, and other items. Just purchase predesigned colored stock for laser printers. The selection of designs, paper sizes, and label formats is fantastic, and you can buy coordinated sets to give your documents a consistent, professional image. Contact the following companies, and ask them to send you a catalog; you'll be glad you did.

> Image Street
> P.O. Box 5000
> Vernon Hills, IL 60061
> Phone: (800) 462-4378
> Fax: (800)329-6677

On Paper
P.O. Box 1365
Elk Grove Village, IL 60009-1365
Phone: (800) 829-2299
Fax: (800) 595-2094

Premier Papers
P.O. Box 64785
St. Paul, MN 55164
Phone: (800) 843-0414
Fax: (800) 526-3029

Queblo
1000 Florida Ave.
P.O. Box 1393
Hagerstown, MD 21741-9893
Phone: (800) 523-9080
Fax: (800) 554-8779

Troubleshooting Printers and Fonts

If you have any trouble with printing or fonts, the Troubleshooter can help you. Follow these steps:

1. Click on the Start button, and choose <u>H</u>elp.

2. Click on the Contents tab.

3. Double-click on the Troubleshooting book.

4. Double-click on If you have trouble printing.

5. Follow the steps on-screen.

If you have trouble with PostScript fonts, first make sure that ATM is loaded. To do that, open the ATM Control Panel, and make sure that ATM is on. Exit ATM, and restart the computer.

If PostScript fonts aren't included in your list of available fonts, check the program's help file or documentation for information on fonts. Some applications and utilities, such as Microsoft WordArt, do not support PostScript fonts. (I just hate it when that happens!)

Finally, if your PostScript fonts are on another PC in a LAN, use Network Neighborhood to map a drive letter to the shared folder. Be sure to use the same drive letter that you used to install the fonts (such as T:) to reconnect to that shared folder.

Summary

Here's a quick recap of the important points about printing:

✦ To install a printer, connect it to your PC per the manufacturer's instructions. Then to install the Windows 95 drivers, click Start, choose Settings⇨Printers, double-click the Add Printer icon, and follow the instructions on the screen.

✦ To print the document that's currently open and visible on the screen, choose File⇨Print from the program's menu bar.

✦ To print a document that isn't open, right-click the document's icon and choose Print. Or drag the document's icon to a printer icon.

✦ To manage print jobs in progress, double-click the printer's icon. Use the Printer and Document commands in the menu bar that appears to manage print jobs.

✦ To install and manage TrueType fonts, click the Start button and choose Settings⇨Control Panel. Then double-click the Fonts icon.

✦ To install and manage PostScript Type 1 fonts, you need to purchase and install the Adobe Type Manager program, available wherever fonts are sold.

✦ To apply a font to selected text, use commands in whatever program you're working with at the moment. Typically, you just need to select text, then choose Format⇨Font from the program's menu bar.

✦ Clip art is a great way to spruce up printed documents. Learn to use a clip art browse, such as the ClipArt Gallery that comes with Microsoft Office to get the most from your clip art collection.

✦ Remember that you're not limited to plain white 8.5 x 11 inch paper. There are hundreds of sizes and colors of papers to choose from.

✦   ✦   ✦

Choosing and Installing a Modem

In the next chapter, I'm going to talk about PC faxing and telephony. In later chapters, I'll discuss using information services, transmitting files via phone lines, and dial-up networking. All these options require a modem. So right now seems to be a good time to discuss modems in general and how you install one on your Windows 95 PC.

Choosing a Modem

A *modem* is a gadget for hooking your computer to a telephone. Dozens of modems are on the market, each with its own strengths and weaknesses. Choosing a modem can be a little tricky, because you have so many options. The following sections explain the key features to consider.

Major features of modems

Before you buy a modem, you should consider which features you need. Some modems are strictly data modems; some modems have auto-answer capabilities; still others offer fax and voice-mail capabilities. Here, in a nutshell, are the reasons why you might want these features:

   ◆ *Data modem.* You use this basic modem to connect to cyberspace: the Internet, CompuServe, America Online, The Microsoft Online Network, bulletin-board systems (BBSs), and other PCs.

✦ *Auto-answer modem.* If you plan to use dial-up networking (see Chapter 19), you need a modem with auto-answer capability. You'll also need this capability if you want to accept incoming calls from other PCs.

✦ *Fax/modem.* A fax/modem enables you to send a fax directly from your PC, without printing it. The majority of fax/modems actually are fax/data modems; they can fax and do all the stuff that a data modem can do.

✦ *Cellular modem.* A cellular modem is a fax/data modem that fits into the PCMCIA slot of a laptop computer and connects to a cellular phone. This modem allows you to make fax/data transmissions on the road (that is, from your car or in a plane).

✦ *Telephony board.* A telephony board is a combination of a data modem and fax modem with sound that can act as an answering machine and/or voice-mail system. Some telephony boards even support fax on demand and fax back (see Chapter 16).

Internal, external, and PC Card modems

You can buy modems in three main configurations: internal, external, and PC Card. No real difference exists among the types in terms of performance. The following list summarizes the types of modem configurations:

✦ *External modem.* Up side: Easy hookup; you don't have to disassemble the computer. Down side: You must have a spare serial (COM) port, and the modem takes up a little space on your desktop.

✦ *Internal modem.* Up side: The modem stays inside your PC and doesn't take up any space. Down side: You need to disassemble the computer to install the modem, and you may need to mess with IRQs and all that.

So many gizmos, so few phone numbers

Pop quiz: Suppose that you have several phone gadgets, such as an answering machine, fax machine, data modem, and regular voice telephone, but you have only one phone number. How do you handle incoming calls — that is, how do you keep the modem from answering when someone is calling you to talk? And how do you get the fax machine to pick up the call when someone is sending you a fax?

One simple answer is a telephone line-sharing device, such as the ComShare devices made by Command Communications Inc. A line-sharing device automatically determines whether an incoming call is a fax, a PC, or a human being and then directs the call to the appropriate gadget. Check out these devices at your local computer store, or contact the manufacturer at (303) 751-5000 or fax (303) 750-6437.

For more information on IRQ settings and installing hardware, refer to Chapter 10. For more information on PCMCIA slots, see Chapter 19.

◆ *PC Card.* A PC Card (PCMCIA) modem fits into the PCMCIA slot. Most modern laptops have at least one PCMCIA slot. When you buy a PCMCIA modem, make sure that it's compatible with your PCMCIA slot type. Chapter 19 discusses PCMCIA in depth.

Performance considerations

Modem speed determines how long it takes to send and receive files over telephone lines. The general rule of thumb is simple: the higher the baud rate, the less time you spend waiting. The going baud rate at this writing is 28.8K. Most online services support at least 14.4K. So if you're going to buy a modem, 14.4 or 28.8 is the way to go.

Some modems also have what people call the *v-dot* standard. Again, the higher the number, the faster and more capable the model is. At this writing, v.34 is the latest standard.

A fast modem may pay for itself quickly if you download files from services that charge for connect time. A file that takes 60 minutes to download at 9600K baud, for example, might take 30 minutes to download at 14.4K. Half the connect time means half the cost.

Most modems are downwardly compatible — that is, if you buy a state-of-the-art 28.8K, v.34 modem, you'll still be able to access older (slower) modems. You can, for example, use your 28.8K modem to dial into CompuServe, which at this writing supports speeds up to 14.4K. A good modem detects the slower speed of the modem at the other end of the line and adjusts itself accordingly. This feature is called *auto-negotiation*.

Choosing a modem based on performance is simply a matter of deciding how much money you want to spend. A state-of-the-art modem always costs more than yesterday's model, but the return on your investment is less waiting time (and, usually, better reliability).

Windows 95 compatibility

Modems that bear the "Designed for Windows 95" plug-and-play logo are the easiest to install; you just plug the modem in and go. Windows 95 also comes with built-in 32-bit drivers for many non-plug-and-play modems. If you want to see which non-plug-and-play modems Windows 95 has drivers for, follow these steps:

1. Click on the Start button.
2. Choose Settings⇨Control Panel.
3. Double-click on the Modems icon.

4. Do one of the following things:

  ✦ If — and *only* if — you see a dialog box rather than the Install New Modem wizard, a modem already is installed on your PC.

  ✦ If you want to look at drivers for other modems, click on the Add button.

5. In the Install New Modem wizard, select the check box for the option Don't detect my modem; I will select it from a list.

6. Click on Next.

  You are taken to the window shown in Figure 15-1.

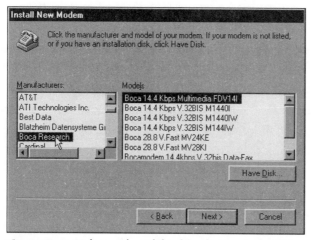

Figure 15-1: Makes and models of modems supported by Windows 95.

7. Click on any modem manufacturer in the left column.

  The right column shows you the specific models that Windows 95 supports directly. Browse at your leisure.

8. When you finish, click on Cancel.

Be sure to click on Cancel in step 8 because at this point, you're just looking at makes and models of supported modems, not actually installing the modem. If you already have a modem installed, click on the Close button in the dialog box that displays that modem name to get back to the Control Panel without disturbing the existing modem installation.

Installing the Modem

The first step in installing a modem is actually installing the modem hardware. Follow the modem manufacturer's instructions to do that. But *don't install any DOS or Windows 3 drivers.* Just physically install the modem in your PC or connect it to a serial port and then connect the modem to a telephone wall jack.

 If your modem has a jack labeled Phone, use that jack *only* if you are using one wall jack and one telephone number for both your modem and voice telephone. The jack labeled Phone always connects to a voice telephone — never to the wall jack.

When your modem is installed, turned on, and connected to the phone jack, and your PC is up and running, you're ready to install the modem drivers. If Windows 95 detects the new modem at startup, it may install the correct drivers automatically. But even if the modem appears to have been installed, there's no harm in checking to make sure. Even if you think that the modem drivers already are installed, complete at least the first four of the following steps:

1. Gather up your original Windows 95 floppies or CD-ROM.

   Keep any disks that came with the modem handy, too, in case you need to install the manufacturer's drivers. (You install those drivers only if Windows 95 has no driver for your modem.)

2. Click on the Start button.

3. Choose <u>S</u>ettings⇨<u>C</u>ontrol Panel.

4. Double-click on the Modems icon.

   If your modem already is installed, the Modem Properties window appears. Click on the Cancel button, because you don't need to re-install the same modem.

   If your modem is not installed, you see the Install New Modem Wizard, shown in Figure 15-2.

5. Click on the Next button.

6. Follow the instructions on the screen.

The wizard guides you through the process of installing your modem. When you finish, you return to the Windows 95 desktop.

 If your modem has a built-in sound card for voice, the Add New Hardware wizard may install everything without activating the modem. Follow the preceding steps to verify installation or, if necessary, to install the modem.

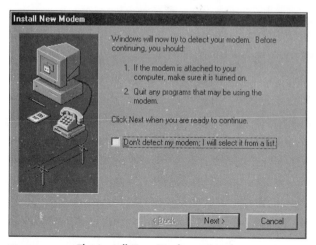

Figure 15-2: The Install New Modem wizard.

Use Your Modem for Speed Dialing

Windows 95 comes with a handy little phone dialer. Like the speed dialer on some phones, this device lets you to keep a list of frequently called numbers and to dial those numbers with the click of a button. Phone Dialer is especially handy if your modem shares the same phone number as your voice phone, because you can use Phone Dialer to dial out. When the connection is made, an on-screen message tells you to pick up the receiver and click on the Talk button:

 More Info If Phone Dialer isn't in your Accessories menu, you can install it now. See "Installing Missing Windows Components" in Chapter 9. When you get to the Windows Setup tab, click on the Communications component and then click on the Details button to find Phone Dialer.

To use Phone Dialer, follow these steps:

1. Click on the Start button.

2. Choose Programs⇨Accessories.

3. Click on Phone Dialer to display its dialog box (see Figure 15-3).

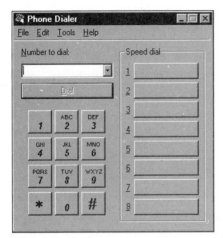

Figure 15-3: The Windows 95 Phone Dialer.

Phone Dialer is fairly self-explanatory after you're in it. But I'll discuss the basic options in the following sections.

Adding numbers to the speed dialer

Adding a new phone number to the speed dialer is easy: just click on any blank button and fill in the blanks that appear. Include the area code, even if the phone number is within your own area code. Suppose that your phone number is (619) 555-4321 and that the number you want to speed dial is (619) 555-1234. You would type the number as follows:

```
(619)555-1234
```

When you speed dial the number, Phone Dialer automatically omits the area code. So why include it in the first place? You'll see when you get to "Changing Phone Dialer's dialing properties" later in this chapter.

The only time you need to omit the area code from a phone number is when you're predialing some number to get a discounted local rate. For example, my phone company promises that if I dial 10+ATT before I dial a local number, the call will cost me less. I can use 10+ATT only when I'm dialing a number within my area code, so I have to omit the area code. If I want the speed dialer to dial, say, 10+ATT and then 555-9876, I would type the number to dial like this:

```
10288,555-9876
```

The comma is optional; it just causes a slight pause in the dialing sequence. I include the comma only so that I can hear that pause when the modem is dialing, as a reminder that 10+ATT is activated. That way, if I use the speed dialer on my laptop from another area code, and the call doesn't go through, the pause reminds me that I have to dial 1 and the area code, rather than 10288, from my current location.

You can add up to eight speed dial numbers. If you need to change an entry later, choose Edit⇨Speed Dial from within Phone Dialer, and follow the simple instructions on-screen.

Changing Phone Dialer's dialing properties

Phone Dialer's properties sheet enables you to define where you're dialing from and how to dial. That feature is especially handy if you use Phone Dialer on the road, because you need to change only the dialing properties — not all your speed dial numbers — to dial each number correctly. But even if you don't take your PC traveling, you should set up the dialing properties for your permanent location. Follow these steps:

1. If you haven't already done so, open Phone Dialer.

2. Choose Tools⇨Dialing Properties.

3. Fill in the blanks for your default location.

    If you need more information about an option, click on the Question-mark button and then click on the option.

    Don't use the options in the How I dial from this location section to dial a 1 before dialing an area code; that procedure is taken care of behind the scenes. I'll show you when those options are useful in a moment.

4. Choose OK when you finish.

Figure 15-4 shows the options in the Dialing Properties dialog box set up for me to use at my default location (home) in San Diego, which is in the 619 area code.

Using Phone Dialer

To use Phone Dialer, follow these steps:

1. Open Phone Dialer, as described earlier in this chapter.

    If you use Phone Dialer often, create a desktop shortcut icon for it (refer to Chapter 4).

On the road with Phone Dialer

When you're using Phone Dialer on a laptop, and you're outside your own area code, you can set up a new set of dialing properties for your current location. Open Phone Dialer (if you haven't already), and choose Tools⇨ Dialing Properties. Click on the New button, and enter a name for your new location. (The name of the city would do, or perhaps even a hotel name and city.) Choose OK, and fill in the dialog box for your current location.

In Figure 15-5, I set up properties for dialing from a hotel in the San Francisco area. Notice that the area code is shown as 415. The instructions on the hotel room's phone told me that I must first dial 8 to dial a local number or 9 to dial a long-distance number, so I set the How I dial from this location options accordingly. I also opted to use my calling card from the new location.

The cool thing is that when you go back home, you don't need to mess with all the dialing properties. Instead, open the Dialing Properties dialog box again, and select your current location from the I am dialing from drop-down list. If you go back to that hotel in San Francisco, simply choose your San Francisco-area properties from the same drop-down list.

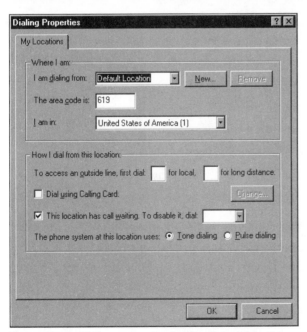

Figure 15-4: Dialing properties for the default location.

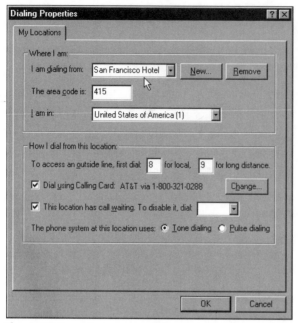

Figure 15-5: Dialing properties set for a San Francisco hotel room.

2. If you've changed your location since the last time you used Phone Dialer, choose (or create) dialing properties for your current location.

3. To speed dial a number, click on its speed dial button.

   If you don't have a speed dial button, use any of the following techniques:

   ✦ If you dialed the number recently, you may be able to select it from the Number to dial drop-down list.

   ✦ In the Number to dial text box, type the number that you want to dial.

   You can omit parentheses, hyphens, and spaces in Phone Dialer numbers. You can type 6195551234, for example, rather than (619)555-1234.

   ✦ Click on the dialing buttons as though you are dialing on a touch-tone phone.

4. Click on the Dial button.

5. Follow the instructions on-screen.

Using Phone Dialer is easy and convenient, after you get the hang of it. But you can do more with your modem than just dial the phone, as you'll learn in upcoming chapters.

Troubleshooting a Modem

If you have any problems with your modem, use the Troubleshooter to track down and correct the problem. Follow these steps:

1. Click on the Start button.

2. Click on Help.

3. Click on the Contents tab.

4. Double-click on the Troubleshooting book.

5. Double-click on the If you have trouble using your modem option.

6. Follow the instructions on-screen to diagnose and solve the problem.

If you're using a PC Card (PCMCIA) modem, see Chapter 19 for more information.

Removing a Modem

If you plan to remove an external or internal modem, you should first remove its driver and free whatever resources the driver is using. To do so, repeat steps 1–4 in "Installing the Modem" earlier in this chapter to display the Modem Properties dialog box. Click on the name of the modem that you want to remove; then click on the Remove button. Shut down Windows and turn off the PC before you remove the modem.

Summary

Here are the main points to keep in mind when choosing and installing a modem:

✦ The most important factor in choosing a modem is speed. The faster the better. If you plan to purchase a modem, be sure to get one that supports at least 14.4 BPS transmission speeds.

✦ When installing a modem, follow the manufacturer's instructions for installing the hardware only. Don't install any DOS or DOS/Windows 3 drivers for the modem.

✦ After you've physically installed the modem, install the Windows 95 drivers. To do so, click the Start button and select Settings⇨Control Panel. Double-click the Modems icon and follow the on-screen instructions.

✦ Once your modem is installed, you can use the Windows 95 Speed Dialer. Click the Start button, point to Programs⇨Accessories, then click on Phone Dialer.

✦   ✦   ✦

PC Faxing and Telephony

The capability to send faxes directly from your PC has several advantages over sending faxes on a standard fax machine. For one thing, if you compose the fax on your PC, you don't have to print it and feed it through the fax machine. For another, you can broadcast the fax to several people at the same time, if you want.

You also can receive faxes on your PC without a fax machine. Documents sent from a regular fax machine are stored as "photographs" that you can view on your screen and print at your convenience. As you'll learn in this chapter, if both the sending and receiving machines use Microsoft Fax, you also can send an editable file via fax. For example, you can fax a Microsoft Word document (.DOC) to someone. The recipient can open the faxed document, edit it normally with Word, and then fax it back to you.

In this chapter, I'm going to talk about Microsoft Fax, the faxing tool that's built right into Windows 95. I'm also going to talk about general telephony, such as voice mail and fax-on-demand. None of these capabilities is actually built into Windows 95. But you can add those capabilities to your Windows 95 PC by purchasing the appropriate hardware and software.

Is Microsoft Fax Installed Yet?

If you've never used Microsoft Fax, it may not have been installed on your PC yet. Following is a quick and easy way to determine whether you need to install Microsoft Fax:

1. Click on the Start button.

2. Choose Programs➪Accessories.

3. If you see a Fax option in the Accessories menu, you're in luck. Click anywhere outside the menus and then go straight to the section titled "Setting Up Your Fax Properties."

If you did not see a Fax option in your Accessories menu, you need to install Microsoft Fax, as described in the following section.

Installing Microsoft Fax

Be sure to install your fax/modem, as discussed in Chapter 15, before you install Microsoft Fax. Testing the modem with Phone Dialer first is a good idea, just to make sure that you're getting a dial tone. When your modem is installed, you can follow the steps to install Microsoft Fax. Be aware that Microsoft Fax uses Microsoft Exchange to handle incoming and outgoing faxes. But don't worry about that. If you've never installed Microsoft Exchange, these steps will install and set up Exchange for you as well.

 Microsoft Exchange is a program that handles all your incoming and outgoing messages and faxes. But you don't need to know anything about Exchange to use Microsoft Fax. Windows 95 automatically sets up Exchange for you, and makes it available when you need it. For now, it's best to stay focused on Microsoft Fax and just those aspects of Exchange that are discussed in this chapter.

1. Gather up your original Windows 95 floppy disks or CD-ROM; then put Disk #1 in the floppy drive or the CD-ROM in the CD-ROM drive.

2. Click on the Start button.

3. Choose Settings⇨Control Panel.

4. Double-click on Add/Remove Programs.

5. Click on the Windows Setup tab.

6. Select Microsoft Fax (so that it has a check mark).

7. If you've never installed Microsoft Fax *or* Microsoft Exchange, you'll see a message indicating that you need to install both. That's OK; choose Yes to proceed.

8. Click on the OK button.

9. Follow the instructions on-screen.

If you are installing Exchange for the first time, the installation wizard asks which information services you want to install. For now, you just need to choose Microsoft Fax, as shown in Figure 16-1; then click on the Next button. You can install other information services later, at your convenience.

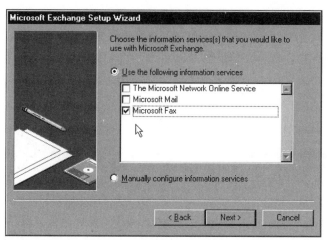

Figure 16-1: Installing both Microsoft Exchange and Microsoft Fax.

The installation wizard may ask some questions about your modem, fax number, and so on. If you see that wizard, proceed through the dialog boxes and answer questions as best you can until you get to the Congratulations! screen. Then click on the Finish button.

Don't worry if the installation wizard doesn't appear; you'll be checking and refining all your fax settings. When you get back to the Control Panel, close it. You should see a new shortcut icon, named Inbox, on your desktop. As you'll see later in this chapter, Inbox takes you to Microsoft Exchange, where you can see all your received messages, including faxes.

Setting Up Your Fax Properties

Before you use Microsoft Fax for the first time, take a few minutes to get all your settings shaped up. As you do for most items on your PC, you go through the Settings menu and Control Panel to set up your fax. You may be surprised to see that you actually have to go through yet another program — Microsoft Exchange — to get to your fax settings. This situation occurs because Microsoft Fax actually is an information service within Microsoft Exchange. The arrangement is a bit confusing at first, but if you can remember that Microsoft Fax *is* an information service, like e-mail, you'll get used to going through Exchange to handle faxes.

To set up your fax properties, follow these steps:

1. Click on the Start button.

2. Choose Settings⇨Control Panel.

3. Double-click on the Mail and Fax icon.

You see a dialog box titled MS Exchange Settings Properties.

The Mail and Fax icon in Control Panel is strictly for configuring your information services. To actually send and read messages, you use the Inbox icon.

4. To tweak your fax settings, click on the Microsoft Fax service and then click on the Properties button.

You go to the Microsoft Fax Properties dialog box, shown in Figure 16-2. Notice that this dialog box has four tabs. The sections that follow explain how to set up your options within each tab.

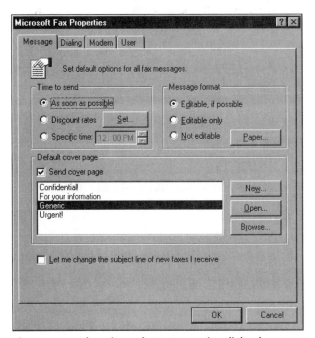

Figure 16-2: The Microsoft Fax Properties dialog box.

Remember that you are choosing default settings for all future faxes here. You're choosing the most likely settings for each future fax so that you don't have to make the same selections with each fax that you send. When you actually send a fax, you have ample opportunity to override any of the default settings for that fax, if you want.

As always, you can get more information about an option on-screen. Click on the Question-mark button and then click on the option you're wondering about.

The Message tab

The Message tab describes how your faxes will be sent. The Time to send option lets you determine when to send faxes. You can send each fax as you complete it, or you can opt to have Exchange hold on to all outgoing faxes until the phone company's discount rates kick in (or until a specific time of your choosing).

In the Message format section, you almost certainly will want to choose Editable, if possible. This setting lets you send editable documents to other PCs by using Microsoft Fax (or any version of Microsoft At Work). If the receiving device is a fax machine, you obviously can't send the document as an editable file; Microsoft Fax automatically sends it as a regular fax that prints out on the recipient's fax machine.

In the Default cover page section, select (check) the Send cover page option if you want each fax to be preceded by a cover page. For starters, use the Generic cover page. Under "Creating a Custom Cover Page" later in this chapter, I'll show you how to create your own cover page.

If you want to be able to change the subject line that appears in the faxes that you receive on the PC, choose the corresponding option. As you'll see later in this chapter, you can arrange received faxes in alphabetical order, by subject, so having the freedom to change the subject line can help you organize your faxes.

Faxing editable files

Windows 95 supports Microsoft At Work fax capability, meaning that it can send a file in its native format. By "native format," I mean the format that's on your PC—for example, a .DOC file for a Microsoft Word document. For this reason, you want to choose the Editable, if possible option as a default.

When you attach a file to a fax message, Windows automatically detects what type of device is receiving the fax. If that receiving device supports Microsoft At Work (as Windows 95 does), the attached file is sent in its native format. When the recipient opens your fax message, he or she sees an icon in the body of the message. The recipient can double-click on that icon to open the document in the appropriate program, ready for editing, printing, or whatever.

If the receiving device is a fax machine or a PC that does not support Microsoft At Work, Windows detects that fact as well. In either case, Windows automatically renders and sends a standard "photographic" fax image of your document. The recipient can open, view, and print that document with her Fax Viewer, but she cannot edit the document (unless she then uses OCR software to convert the faxed image to text, as described in "Converting bitmaps and paper to editable text" later in this chapter).

The Dialing tab

The Dialing tab records important information needed to send your faxes. Click on the Dialing Properties button and choose the default location from which you send faxes. Fill in any other information, as appropriate; then choose OK to save your new settings.

If any prefixes within your own area code require long-distance dialing, click on the Toll Prefixes button and add those prefixes to the list.

In the Retries section, define how many times you want Microsoft Fax to try sending a fax in case an attempt fails (if it gets a busy signal after dialing the fax number, for example). You also can specify how long you want Microsoft Fax to wait between attempts.

The Modem tab

The Modem tab lets you specify which modem to use for sending faxes. This capability is especially useful if you have two or more modems installed on your PC. Click on the name of the modem that you want to use for faxing, and then click on the Set As Active Fax/modem button.

You also can set your answering options, speaker volume, and other preferences in the Modem tab. Click on the Properties button and make your selections in the Fax/modem Properties dialog box, shown in Figure 16-3. Don't forget that if you prefer to receive faxes on your fax machine, you need to set Answer mode to Don't answer. When you finish, choose OK to return to the Microsoft Fax Properties dialog box.

If you're on a LAN, you can use the Modem tab to share your fax/modem with other LAN members. Chapter 26 covers sharing resources on a LAN in depth.

The User tab

The User tab lets you set up the information that will appear on each fax cover page. In the blanks, type whatever information you want the fax recipient to see.

Remember that after you make your selections in each of the four tabs, you can click on the OK and Close buttons to work your way back to the desktop. If you decide to change any of the default settings, repeat the steps in "Setting Up Your Fax Properties" earlier in this chapter.

Setting Up Your Personal Address Book

You probably will send many faxes from your PC. Wouldn't it be convenient to have a list of fax numbers that you call frequently? When you want to send a fax to someone, you just select that person's name from a list; you don't have to look up the fax number or even dial the phone.

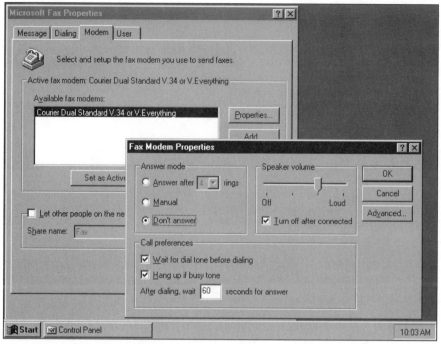

Figure 16-3: The Fax Modem Properties dialog box.

The Personal Address Book feature in Microsoft Exchange gives you that capability. This feature is your "little black book," storing the names, addresses, and phone numbers of people whom you contact often. You can use Personal Address Book in many settings — to send a fax or an e-mail message, for example, and (in some programs) even to write a letter.

 Personal Address Book is accessible from many areas in Windows 95, not just from Microsoft Fax. You can get to your Personal Address Book from many Office 95 programs.

Like Microsoft Fax, Personal Address Book is an information service within Microsoft Exchange, so to get to it, you must first go into Microsoft Exchange. Follow these steps:

1. Double-click on the Inbox icon on the desktop, or click on the Start button and then choose Programs➪Microsoft Exchange.

   You see the Inbox for Microsoft Exchange, shown in Figure 16-4.

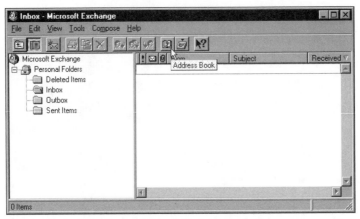

Figure 16-4: The Inbox - Microsoft Exchange window.

2. Click on the Address Book button, or choose Tools➪Address Book from Exchange's menu bar.

   You go to the Address Book window.

3. To add a new name and address, click on the New Entry button in the toolbar or choose File➪New Entry.

   The New Entry dialog box appears.

4. In the Microsoft Fax section, click on Fax; then click on OK.

   The New Fax Properties dialog box appears, as shown in Figure 16-5.

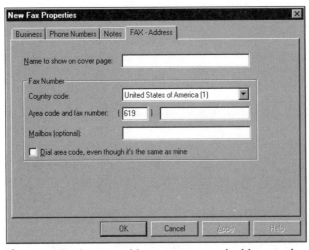

Figure 16-5: About to add a new name and address to the Address Book.

5. Fill in the text boxes, as appropriate.

   Optionally, you can enter some notes about the person in the Notes tab.

6. After you fill in as much information as you have for the person, click on the OK button.

7. Repeat steps 3–6 for each name and address that you want to add now (you can add more names and addresses at any time).

8. When you finish adding names and addresses, close the Address Book by clicking on its Close (X) button or by choosing File⇨Close.

In the next section you'll see how you can look up people in your Personal Address Book. For now, keep in mind that any time that you need to add more names and addresses, you can repeat the preceding steps. You also can add names and addresses on the fly as you compose faxes and other messages; simply click on the Address Book button wherever you happen to see it.

Composing and Sending a Fax

When you have all your fax stuff set up, you're finally ready to start sending faxes. Follow these steps:

1. If you're at the desktop, click on the Start button, choose Programs⇨Accessories⇨Fax, and then click on Compose New Fax.

   If you're in the Inbox - Microsoft Exchange window, choose Compose⇨New Fax.

   Whichever method you use, the Compose New Fax wizard starts.

2. First you'll be given the option to choose the location you're dialing from. If you're not on the road, just click the Next > button. Then you'll come to the wizard screen shown in Figure 16-6. Type the recipient's name and fax number.

   Alternatively, click on the Address Book button, click on a name, click on the To button, and then click on OK.

   To send your fax to several people who are listed in the Address Book, Shift+click or Ctrl+click on each name and then click on the To button. Alternatively, click on a name, click on To, click on another name, and so on. Optionally, you can create a list of people to send a fax to, as discussed under "Create Your Own Distribution Lists" later in this chapter.

3. After you select one or more recipients, click on the Next button to display the next wizard screen, and specify whether you want to use a cover page by choosing Yes or No cover page (see Figure 16-7).

   If, for this particular fax, you want to override the default properties that you set earlier, click on the Options button and make additional selections.

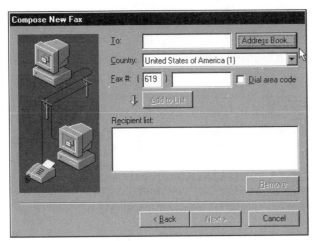

Figure 16-6: The Compose New Fax wizard.

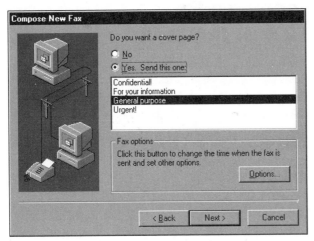

Figure 16-7: Select a cover page and other options.

4. Click on the Next button and type a Subject and your Message.

5. Click on the Next button and select any files that you want to send along with your fax.

   If you want to include a file, click on Add File, browse to and select the file(s) that you want to include with your fax, and then click on Next.

The documents that you attach in Step 5 are the ones that will be sent in editable format, if possible. When the recipient opens your fax message, he or she sees an icon that represents each attached document. Double-clicking on the icon opens the document, ready for editing or printing.

6. In the last Wizard screen, select the location from which you're dialing (if it's different from the location shown), and then click on Finish.

You're done. Exchange takes a little time to put the fax together and then send it. When Exchange actually sends the fax, a little telephone icon appears in the lower-right corner of the screen, perhaps with a message box. If you choose As soon as possible as your default Time to send option, you may not see any activity right away. You can always check the current status of a fax you sent, as discussed under "Checking the status of outgoing faxes" a little later in this chapter.

A couple of cool fax shortcuts

This section describes a couple of quick and easy alternative ways to fax a document to someone. First, you create a shortcut icon for the Microsoft Fax printer. Follow these steps:

1. Click on the Start button.

2. Choose Settings➪Printers.

3. Right-drag the Microsoft Fax printer icon to the desktop.

4. After you release the right mouse button, choose Create Shortcut(s).

Now you can browse to the document(s) that you want to fax, using the My Computer, Windows Explorer, or Find browsing tool. When you find the file that you want to send, simply drag its icon to the Shortcut to Microsoft Fax icon (shown near the lower-left corner of Figure 16-8). The Compose New Fax wizard starts to help you address and send off the fax.

An even easier route is available for some document types. Use My Computer, Explorer, or Find to get to the document's icon. Then right-click on that icon and choose Send To➪Fax Recipient (refer to Figure 16-8). The Compose New Fax wizard starts.

Sending a fax from a program

If you're in a program and want to fax out the document that you're working on, you can use this method:

1. If you plan to send the document that you're currently working on, choose File➪Save to save that document.

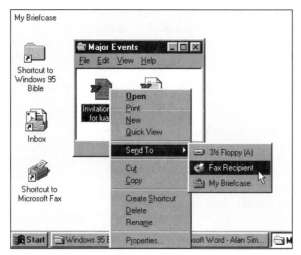

Figure 16-8: Drag a document to the Microsoft Fax
icon or right-click and choose Send To.

2. Pull down the File menu in your program, and then do one of the following things:

   ✦ If you see a Send option in the File menu, select it, and then follow the
   instructions on-screen to send your fax.

   ✦ If you don't see a Send option, choose Print from the File menu. When you
   get to the Print dialog box, select the Microsoft Fax (or similarly named)
   printer, click on the Print button, and then follow the instructions on-screen.

In case you're wondering, the Microsoft Fax icon was put in your Printers
folder automatically when you installed Microsoft Fax.

Notice that the latter method is exactly like printing to a printer. But because you
chose the fax printer icon, the document gets "printed" to the fax card; it doesn't
actually get put on paper until it gets to the recipient's fax machine. The process is
kind of like using the other person's printer instead of your own.

Checking the status of outgoing faxes

If you want to see the status of your outgoing faxes, just follow these simple steps:

1. If you're not already in Microsoft Exchange, double-click on the Inbox icon on
   the desktop, or click on the Start button and then choose Programs⇨Microsoft
   Exchange.

If you don't see a left pane in your Microsoft Exchange screen, choose View⇨Folders.

2. In the left pane, click on the Outbox folder.

The right pane lists all the outgoing faxes (and other messages), as in the example shown in Figure 16-9.

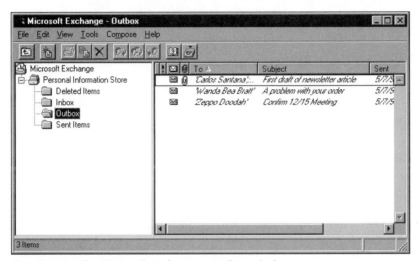

Figure 16-9: The Microsoft Exchange - Outbox window.

While you're in the Outbox, you can do any of the following things to manage your outgoing messages:

✦ If you don't see a toolbar, choose View⇨Toolbar.

✦ To sort messages by priority (!), recipient name (To), or whatever, click on the appropriate column heading in the right pane of the window.

✦ To select a message, click on it. You can Ctrl+click and Shift+click to select multiple messages.

✦ To deliver selected message(s) immediately, choose Tools⇨Deliver Now.

✦ To delete selected messages(s), click on the Delete (X) button in the toolbar or press the Delete key.

You can get on-screen help with Microsoft Exchange, Fax, and Mail by choosing Help from Exchange's menu bar (not from the Start button).

✦ To view the contents of, and full list of recipients for, an outgoing fax message, double-click on it in the right pane. Close the window when you finish viewing the message.

Creating a Custom Cover Page

Windows 95 comes with the Fax Cover Page Editor, which lets you view, change, and even create fax cover pages. To get started with the cover-page editor, follow these steps:

1. Click on the Start button.

2. Choose Programs➪Accessories➪Fax➪Cover Page Editor.

3. To open an existing cover page, click on the Open button in the toolbar or choose File➪Open.

4. Browse to the Windows folder on your C drive (or wherever you keep fax cover pages).

5. Double-click on the name of the fax cover page that you want to open.

Figure 16-10 shows an example in which I opened the GENERIC.CPE cover page. Notice that some of the information on the page is inside curly braces, such as {Recipient Name} and {Recipient's Company}. Those items are placeholders that are filled in automatically when a fax is sent. The information comes from entries that you made when you defined your fax properties and from the selections that you made in the Compose New Fax wizard.

You can modify the cover page on your screen. First, you save your version under some new name (so that in case you mess up, the original cover page will be available under its original name). Choose File➪Save As and enter your own name for the cover page (such as **My Fax Cover Page**). If you want to start from scratch, you can choose File➪New.

Next, set up the window for editing. Use the options in the View menu to hide or display toolbars, the status bar, and grid lines (useful for aligning things on the page). Then you can use the techniques described in the following sections to add, delete, and change elements of the page.

Changing and deleting objects

If you're going to create your custom cover page by modifying an existing page, you probably will want to start by changing and deleting things that are already on the page. Use these standard editing techniques:

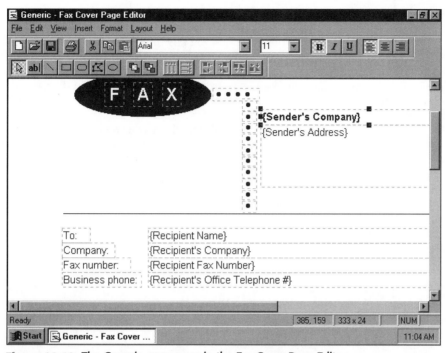

Figure 16-10: The Generic cover page in the Fax Cover Page Editor.

✦ To select an item, click on it. To select multiple items, Ctrl+click on them or drag a frame around them. To select every object on the page, choose Edit⇨Select All or press Ctrl+A.

✦ To delete the selected item(s), press Delete. If you do this by accident, choose Edit⇨Undo.

✦ To move the selected item, point to its frame until you see the four-headed mouse pointer, and then drag the item to its new location.

✦ To size the selected item, drag one of its sizing handles.

✦ To change the text in the selected item, click wherever you want to put the insertion point. Then type your new text and/or delete old text with the Backspace and Delete keys. Click outside the box to save your changes.

✦ To change the font and/or size of the text in a selected box, select a font and/or size from the drop-down lists in the formatting toolbar.

✦ To align selected items, click on one of the alignment buttons in the toolbar, or choose Layout⇨Align Objects and then choose an alignment option.

✦ To space the selected objects evenly, choose Layout⇨Space Evenly and then choose Across or Down.

✦ To center the selected item on the page, choose Layout⇨Center on Page.

Inserting new objects

You can add new objects to your cover page at any time. To insert new text, click on the Text (ab|) button in the toolbar. In the body of the document, create a frame that indicates the space that you want the text to occupy; then type your text. To change the font of the text, select a font and size from the drop-down lists in the toolbar or choose Format⇨Font.

To insert a placeholder, click on approximately where you want the placeholder to appear, choose Insert from the menu bar, select the type of information that you want to insert (Recipient, Sender, or Message), and then select a placeholder for specific information (such as Fax Number).

To insert a picture, such as a scanned bitmap image of your company logo, click about where you want the object to appear in the cover sheet. Then choose Insert⇨Object⇨Create from File. Browse to the file name of the object that you want to insert. Click on that filename and then click on the Insert and OK buttons.

Scan your signature without a scanner

If your fax/modem is set up to receive faxes, you can use any fax machine as a simple black-and-white scanner. This method is an inexpensive way to scan your signature into a bitmap file that you can import into word processing and other documents. To get started, sign your name, using a black felt-tip pen, on plain white paper; then fax that page from any fax machine to your PC's fax/modem. When you get back to your PC, open your Inbox, and double-click on the fax that you sent yourself. You'll see your signature in Fax Viewer. Rotate and zoom the image until your signature (roughly) fills the Fax Viewer screen. Then press Alt+Print Screen to capture the entire Fax Viewer window in the Clipboard.

Next, start Microsoft Paint (choose Start⇨Programs⇨Accessories⇨Paint). Maximize the Paint window, and then choose Edit⇨Paste. In Paint, use the Select tool to drag a frame around your signature. Choose Edit⇨Cut to cut out your signature, choose File⇨New⇨No

to start a new document, and then choose Edit⇨Paste to paste in your signature.

Now choose Edit⇨Copy To, and choose a monochrome bitmap format for the picture. Enter a folder and file name that you'll be able to remember later, and choose OK. Then exit Paint without saving the rest of the image (choose File⇨Exit⇨No). You also can exit Fax Viewer and Exchange.

Now your signature is a bitmap file that you can import into any document. To bring your signature into a Microsoft Word document, for example, choose Insert⇨Picture, browse to the folder and file that contain the signature, and double-click. Your signature appears in your document.

For more information and related topics, see "Printing the Screen (Screen Dump)" in Chapter 14, the help screens in Microsoft Paint, and your word processing documentation (for information on importing pictures and graphics).

When you finish, exit the Fax Cover Page editor and save your work. The next time you send a fax, the Compose New Fax wizard will include your new cover page for selection. To make your new cover page the default, use the methods described in "Setting Up Your Fax Properties" earlier in this chapter.

Create Your Own Distribution Lists

If you often need to send a fax to the same group of people, you can save some time by creating a distribution list. That way, when the time comes to send off the fax, you can choose the list rather than individual recipients.

The easiest way to create a distribution list is to first put everyone in your Personal Address book, using the method described in "Setting Up Your Personal Address Book" earlier in this chapter. Then follow these steps:

1. If you aren't already in Microsoft Exchange, open it (double-click on the Inbox icon or choose Start⇨Programs⇨Microsoft Exchange).

2. Open the Address Book (click on its toolbar button or choose Tools⇨Address Book).

3. Click on the New Entry button or choose File⇨New Entry.

4. In the Microsoft Fax section, choose Personal Distribution List; then click on OK.

5. In the Name text box, type a descriptive name for the entire group.

    In Figure 16-11, I named my group Agents and Publishers.

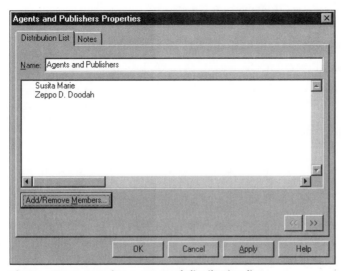

Figure 16-11: Creating a personal distribution list.

6. Click on the Add/Remove <u>M</u>embers button.

7. In the left column, select the names of the people to be included in the list.

   You can Ctrl+click and Shift+click, as usual, to select multiple names.

8. Click on the Members button to copy the selected names to the right column.

9. Choose OK twice.

10. Close the Address Book and Microsoft Exchange.

When you want to send a fax to everyone in the list, begin by composing your fax in the usual manner. When the Compose New Fax wizard asks who you want to send the fax to, click on the Address Book button, select your distribution list, click on the T<u>o</u> button, and then click on OK. You can leave the Fax # option blank and then proceed through the wizard in the usual manner.

Receiving Faxes

If you want to use your PC to receive faxes, you need to make sure that your fax/modem answers incoming calls. Follow these steps to check (and, optionally, change) the modem settings:

1. Click on the Start button.

2. Choose <u>S</u>ettings⇨<u>C</u>ontrol Panel.

3. Double-click on the Mail and Fax icon.

4. Click on Microsoft Fax; then click on <u>P</u>roperties.

5. Click on the Modem tab; then click on the name of the modem that you're using to answer incoming calls.

6. Be sure to click on Set as active <u>f</u>ax/modem; then click on <u>P</u>roperties.

7. In the Answer mode section, choose one of the following options:

   ✦ *Answer after x rings.* If you choose this option, the fax/modem always answers the phone after the number of rings that you specify. This option is good if your modem is connected to a dedicated fax number that never will receive voice calls.

   ✦ *Manual.* The fax/modem never answers, but a dialog box appears on-screen when the phone is ringing. You have to click on the Answer Now button in that dialog box to answer the phone.

8. After making your selection, choose OK to work your way back to the desktop.

You're done. Your PC now can receive incoming faxes. You'll probably hear some modem activity when a fax comes in, and a small dialog box will tell you what's going on. You can read the fax at any time after it's been fully received and the phone has disconnected.

All the faxes that you receive will be stored in your Microsoft Exchange Inbox. Remember that to open the Inbox, you double-click on the Inbox icon on your desktop, or you click on the Start button and then choose Programs⇨Microsoft Exchange. If you don't see incoming messages, perhaps you're just looking in the wrong box. Click on the Inbox icon in Exchange's menu bar.

To print a message, click on it and then choose File⇨Print. Be sure to select a regular printer (not your fax printer) in the Name section. If you want to print any files that are attached to the message, choose the Print attachment option. Then click on the OK button.

To look at a fax, double-click on it. If the fax was sent from a regular fax machine, it appears in Fax Viewer, as in the example shown in Figure 16-12. You can choose File⇨Print within Fax Viewer to print the message.

Figure 16-12: Inbox and Fax Viewer.

Converting bitmaps and paper to editable text

Any fax that's sent to you from a fax machine or non-Microsoft At Work PC is stored in a noneditable bitmap file. You can, however, get the text of that message into a document file that you can edit. Instead of typing the text into the file from scratch, you can use an OCR (optical character recognition) program. An OCR program converts the text that's hidden in a bitmap "photograph" file to a document that you can edit with your favorite word processor.

If the text that you want to get into your PC is on paper, you need both OCR software and some kind of scanner. A flatbed scanner is best. You also can buy a device that allows your fax machine to act as a simple scanner.

For a simple all-in-one method of turning printed text into editable text, look at Visioneer's PaperPort, a full-page scanner that's small enough to fit between your monitor and keyboard. The device comes with OCR software. You just feed in a sheet of a paper, and PaperPort copies it to a document file that you can edit. The cost is less than $400. Ask your computer dealer for a demo, or contact Visioneer at (800) 787-7007, Division PM.

If the fax was delivered as an editable document, it automatically opens in a different window used for messages. Any document that was attached to that fax appears as an icon within the message portion of the fax. To open the document, double-click on its icon in the message. The appropriate program starts and displays the document. Now you can use that program to print or edit the document. You also can choose File⇒Save As to save the document to a folder and file of your own choosing.

You can use all the tools that Microsoft Exchange offers to manage your incoming faxes along with other messages that you receive. Chapter 30 discusses the full range of Exchange's capabilities in more depth.

Fax Troubleshooting

If you have problems with faxes, the troubleshooter in Microsoft Fax (not the desktop troubleshooter) can help you. Follow these steps:

1. Start Microsoft Exchange by double-clicking on the Inbox icon or choosing Start⇒Programs⇒Microsoft Exchange.

2. From Exchange's menu bar, choose Help.

3. Choose Microsoft Fax Help Topics.

4. Click on the Contents tab.

5. Double-click on the Troubleshooting book to open it.

The troubleshooter will guide you the rest of the way through the troubleshooting process.

 Both Microsoft Exchange and Microsoft Fax have their own online help systems, which are not immediately accessible from the desktop. To get to the help systems for those programs, start Microsoft Exchange and then click the Help option in Exchange's menu bar.

If the Microsoft Fax Troubleshooter and help screens don't help, the problem may be in Microsoft Exchange. In Exchange, choose Help⇨Microsoft Exchange Help Topics to explore the possibilities.

Secured Faxing

If you need to fax a "for your eyes only" message to someone, you can encrypt your faxes so that only the intended recipient can open the fax. Be aware, however, that you can secure only faxes that are sent to another PC. If you send a secured fax to a regular fax machine, the recipient sees your fax cover sheet and subject, but the message section will be blank. (There's no way for someone to enter a password on a sheet of fax paper.)

Simple password protection

The quick-and-easy way to protect a faxed message is to use a password. Follow these steps:

1. Start composing your fax message to get into the Compose New Fax wizard.

2. When you get to the screen that asks about a cover page, click the Options button in the Fax options section.

3. Click on the Security button (see Figure 16-13).

4. Choose Password Protected and click on OK.

5. Type a password; then type it again to confirm it.

   Pay careful attention to whether you're using uppercase or lowercase letters (especially because you can't see them on-screen).

 Passwords are case-sensitive. The recipient must use the exact uppercase and lowercase letters that you used when you typed your password. To avoid confusion, always use a particular case — type all passwords in lowercase letters, for example.

6. Choose OK twice.

7. Proceed through the rest of the wizard screens as you normally do.

Figure 16-13: The Security option in the Compose New Fax wizard.

Don't forget to tell the recipient what the password is. When the recipient receives your fax, his or her Inbox will display the message `<Encrypted>Password pro-tected!` When the recipient tries to open the message, a dialog box pops up, requesting the password. The recipient has no way to open or print the document without typing the proper password.

Advanced fax security

Microsoft Fax also offers more-advanced security measures: key-encryption and digital signatures. This type of security requires some time to implement, because the sender and receiver need to swap *public keys* — computer-generated passwords that allow you to read each others' faxes. You never actually see the public key. It's just a string of 154 characters that you typically swap via floppy disk.

Advanced security works only for faxes transmitted to and from Microsoft Fax and Microsoft At Work-compatible fax programs. You can't use advanced security with a regular fax machine.

You'll also create a *private key* — a password that you keep to yourself to ensure that nobody else can alter your public keys. The private key gives you the capability to create a new set of public keys at any time. If you don't want Johnny D. Crook to read your key-encrypted faxes anymore, just change your public key and send the new key to everyone except Johnny D. Crook.

Step 1: Creating your keys

The first step in implementing advanced key-encryption security is getting everyone who will participate to create a set of keys. To create the keys, follow these steps:

1. Stick a label on a blank, formatted floppy disk.

2. Start Microsoft Exchange by double-clicking on the Inbox icon or choosing Start➪Programs➪Microsoft Exchange.

3. Choose Tools➪Microsoft Fax Tools➪Advanced Security.

   You go to the dialog box shown in Figure 16-14.

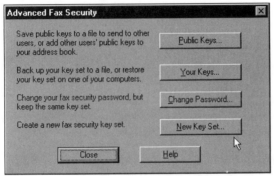

Figure 16-14: Advanced Fax Security dialog box.

4. Click on the New Key Set button.

5. Follow the instructions on-screen to type and confirm your password; then choose OK.

   Remember to keep the password private, because it lets you manage both your public and private keys.

Don't forget that passwords are case-sensitive — watch your *P*s and *q*s. Also keep in mind that the password is *not* the key. Rather, the password is your secret code for creating, changing, and deleting your automatically generated public and private keys.

6. Now, to create a set of public keys to exchange with recipients, insert a floppy disk into drive A or B.

7. Click on Save, click on To, and then click on OK.

8. When you are prompted, enter a location and filename (with the .AWP extension) for your public-key set.

   I would name mine A:\Alan Simpson.Awp, for example.

The extension .AWP stands for *at-work public password.* The advanced security features discussed in this section are part of the entire Microsoft At Work product line, which is supported by Windows for Workgroups and Windows NT as well as Windows 95.

9. Click on the Save button.

10. Follow any instructions on-screen.

When copying is complete, repeat steps 6 thru 10 to create more public-key disks (one for each recipient). When you finish, click on Close and exit Exchange to work your way back to the desktop.

You should write on each disk's label something that describes the disk's contents. I might label my disks *Alan Simpson's Public Key Set,* for example.

Now you can mail a copy of your public-key set, on floppy disk, to each of your intended recipients and wait to get their public keys, also on floppy disk, in the mail.

Step 2: Installing other people's public keys

When you receive another person's public-keys floppy disk, you must import those keys into your copy of Microsoft Exchange. Follow these steps:

1. Put the floppy disk that contains the other person's public keys in a floppy drive.

2. Start Microsoft Exchange by double-clicking on the Inbox icon or choosing Start⇨Programs⇨Microsoft Exchange.

3. Choose Tools⇨Microsoft Fax Tools⇨Advanced Security.

4. Choose Public keys.

5. As you are prompted, type your private-key password and choose OK.

    This step prevents "just anyone" from messing with your keys.

6. Choose Add.

7. Choose the Look in option to browse to the floppy drive that contains the other person's public keys.

8. Click the .AWP file name.

9. Choose Open.

10. Follow the instructions on-screen to install the other person's public keys.

When both people have installed each other's public keys, you're ready to start using advanced security.

Step 3: Sending secured faxes

After two or more parties install each other's public keys, anyone can send an encrypted fax to any (or all) parties. Follow these steps:

1. Start composing your fax, using whatever technique you want.

2. When you get to the wizard screen that asks whether you want to include a cover sheet, click the Options button in the Fax options section.

3. Click on the Security button.

4. Choose either or both of the following options:

   • *Key-encrypted*. This option ensures that only people who have your public key can read the fax message.

   Danger Zone

   Digital signatures are legally binding. Use them with care.

   • *Digitally sign all attachments*. This option allows the recipient to verify that the purported sender is the actual sender, and that the fax has not been altered during transmission. The digital signature is created automatically from your public and private keys.

5. Choose OK.

6. Proceed normally through the Compose New Fax wizard screens.

   If you need to change your keys, make a new set, or whatever, then go back to the Advanced Security dialog box, as described in previous sections. This dialog box contains options for adding, changing, and deleting keys.

Retrieving Faxes from Online Services

Microsoft Fax can retrieve documents, software updates, drivers, and images from any information service that supports Group 3 poll-retrieve capability. If you know of such a service, follow these steps to download (retrieve) from it:

1. Open Microsoft Exchange by double-clicking on the Inbox icon or choosing Start⇨Programs⇨Microsoft Exchange.

2. Choose Tools⇨Microsoft Fax Tools⇨Request a Fax.

3. Follow the instructions presented in the wizard.

Any documents that you retrieve will be stored in your Inbox.

If you want to offer fax-on-demand to your customers, you need a telephony board that supports that capability. See the following section.

Telephony

One of the latest buzzwords in PC-land is *telephony*, which is a general term for all kinds of computer/telephone integration. You've probably been on the calling end of telephony before. Perhaps you called a phone number, and a computerized voice started giving you options such as "If you know your party's extension..." and "If you want to check on your order..." That kind of telephony is called *voice mail*.

Another form of telephony that's become popular recently is fax-on-demand (also called fax back, fast facts, fax facts, and so on). As a caller, you use such a service to get more information about a product or answers to frequently asked questions (FAQs). The information then is sent to your fax machine automatically.

Historically, telephony has been the turf of huge corporations that have complex PBX systems. A year or so ago, for example, I inquired about buying a voice mail/fax-on-demand system for my little office. The price was a mere $10,000. (Needless to say, I stuck with my $100 answering machine.)

More recently, I bought a modem that supports all the voice mail and fax-on-demand capabilities that the $10,000 machine offered. The modem even came with the necessary software, and it works in just about any PC. A single phone line is all you need, and your existing phone number will do. The price of this board and the software was less than $200 — a considerably more wallet-friendly figure.

How do you pronounce *telephony*?

Telephony is such a new technology that people really haven't come to a consensus about how to pronounce the word. Some people pronounce it *TELL-a-phony*; others pronounce it more like *te-LEH-phone-ee*. If the Official Board of Pronunciations for New Technical Terms has not already stamped its blessing on one or the other, I vote for the latter. The *TELL-a-phony* pronunciation just sounds weird to me, for some reason.

To confuse things, of course, some people refer to the whole thing as CTI, for computer/telephone integration. I'm not so sure that we need yet another three-letter acronym in the PC world, so I'm still holding out for the *te-LEH-phone-ee* pronunciation. Maybe I should set up a 900 number and put it to a vote.

The reason why I'm telling you all this is that I know there's a lot of confusion about telephony. You may hear that Windows 95 supports telephony and TAPI (the Telephony Applications Programming Interface). You may be overwhelmed by discussions of telephony in some of the literature. But as a consumer, you really don't need to know any of the technical stuff.

As a consumer, you can just think of TAPI as being a tool for modem manufacturers and programmers who write communications programs; this tool makes it much simpler for them to create modems and programs that you, the consumer, can install and use on your own PC. And because TAPI is easier for the manufacturers and programmers, it ends up being a lot cheaper — and easier — for you.

The hardware that you need goes by a couple of names. Some manufacturers call the hardware *telephony boards*; others call their products *modem+voice* boards. Basically, the necessary hardware is a modem with sound-card capability that can record and play back human speech.

If you have a full-function telephony board, you don't need a fax machine, an answering machine, or even a telephone. The board will send and receive faxes, and take voice messages. Many boards also let you plug in a headset or speakerphone for normal telephone conversations.

New boards are appearing on the market all the time, so you may want to check your local computer store to see what's available. Following are a couple of boards that I'm familiar with, both of which offer voice mail and (to some extent) fax-on-demand:

Why DSP Costs More

When you're shopping for a telephony board, you might notice that there's a price hike of at least $100.00 when going from a ASIC board to a DSP board. ASIC (application-specific integrated circuit) boards cost less but have a distinct disadvantage. When new and better modem standards come along, you either have to throw away the modem and get a new one, or at least upgrade the chips on the modem.

DSP (digital signal processing) boards and Mwave boards (IBM's version of DSP) let you upgrade to new standards through software.

So when new, faster modem standards and better voice compression schemes come along, you just have to run a program to update your existing hardware.

Performance-wise, the ASICs boards are better able to handle multiple sound tasks concurrently, because they use separate chips for separate functions. So, for example, if you use your PC to answer the phone, and play multimedia titles, you'll get better performance from the ASICs board.

✦ ACE (Best Data) supports voice mail and limited fax-on-demand. The caller must be calling from a fax phone to receive fax-on-demand documents.

✦ SoundExpression 14.4 VSp (Boca Research) supports full voice mail and fax-on-demand. The caller need not be calling from a fax phone; he or she can instead provide a number where faxes can be sent.

Both of these products are widely distributed through computer stores and mail-order houses that advertise in the computer magazines. I should warn you that installing these boards can be pretty hairy — not recommended for the technologically timid. But by the time you read this book, plug-and-play telephony boards designed for Windows 95 may be available, and those boards should be much easier to install.

If you haven't bought a PC yet, consider buying one with pre-installed telephony. Check out selected models from the AST Advantage!, AT&T Globalyst, Compaq Presario, IBM Aptiva and Thinkpad, NEC Ready, and Packard Bell Multimedia Pentium lines at your local computer store.

Summary

You may have read this chapter and are wondering how a topic as simple as faxing could become so complicated when you throw a PC into the works. But actually, most of the headaches occur during installation and setup. Once that's over with, you just need to remember these important points:

✦ To send a fax, click on the Start button and choose Programs⇨Accessories⇨Fax⇨Compose New Fax, and let the wizard guide you.

✦ To check on received faxes, double-click on the Inbox icon on the desktop.

✦ To change your fax/modem properties, click on the Start button, choose Settings⇨Control Panel, double-click on the Mail and Fax icon, click on Microsoft Fax, and then click on the Properties button.

✦ To determine whether or not you want your fax/modem to answer the phone and accept incoming faxes, go to the fax/modem properties, choose the Modem tab, click the name of the modem you want to use, click on Set As Active Fax/modem. Then click the Properties and choose an option under Answer Mode.

✦ To check on the status of an outgoing message, double-click the Inbox icon. Then click the Show/Hide Folder List or choose View⇨Folders until you see the list of folders. To review faxes waiting to be sent, click the Outbox folder. To check on faxes you've already sent, click the Sent folder.

✦   ✦   ✦

Mobile Computing

Road Warrior Tools and Techniques

Hardware for mobile computing has evolved tremendously over the past few years. Laptop computers now rival desktops in storage and processing capability. PC Cards (PCMCIA) are credit-card-size boards that you can install and remove on the fly. Docking stations make it easy to use a laptop as both a desktop and a mobile PC.

On the software side of the coin, things didn't change quite so much. Operating systems really didn't offer anything new to take advantage of the advances in portable hardware. Things do, however, change (eventually). And as you'll see in this chapter and the next few chapters, Windows 95 offers many goodies that can help you get the most from your portable PC.

Summary of Mobile-Computing Features

Many features in Windows 95 make mobile computing much easier. Some of the new features are specifically designed for newer laptops that have the special plug-and-play BIOS and power-management capabilities. But if you're one of the many millions who bought a laptop before these new hardware options became available, don't fret — plenty of new features help you compute on the road regardless of what type of laptop PC you own.

Following is a summary of these features:

- ✦ Hot docking and flexible configurations
- ✦ Power management

✦ Deferred printing

✦ Dial-from settings that you can change on the fly

✦ The Briefcase (see Chapter 18)

✦ Improved PC Card (PCMCIA) support (see Chapter 19)

✦ Dial-up networking (see Chapter 20)

✦ Direct cable connection to a LAN or PC (see Chapter 20)

Many of these features are installed automatically when you install Windows 95 and choose Portable as your computer type. If you don't find a particular component, you may be able to install it via Windows Setup, as discussed in Chapter 9. If you can't find a particular component, your hardware may not support it. For more information, check the documentation that came with your laptop computer.

Hot Docking and Flexible Configurations

A *docking station* (also called a *port-replicator* more recently) is an optional device that connects a laptop to a desktop PC or to a desktop-size monitor, keyboard, mouse, and other peripherals. The idea is to give you the storage, display, and extensibility options of a desktop PC without sacrificing portability. For example, a docking station or port replicator might connect to a CD-ROM drive, multimedia device, a large monitor, a LAN, and so forth.

Consider packing these items whenever you take your laptop on the road: your power cord and extension cord, a two-prong to three-prong adapter, extra batteries, and two phone cords with RJ-11 jacks. If you'll be connecting to other PCs on the road, be sure to bring your network card, network connector cables, and/or direct connect cable.

If you are traveling abroad, you need a plug adapter for the power cord (often best purchased on arrival) and an adapter for local phone jacks. You should also carry a phone cord fitted with alligator clips on one end to attach to wires inside a telephone's mouthpiece. (Better yet, get an acoustic coupler for the handset. Hotels in London usually do not provide phone jacks and accessible handsets.)

To become mobile, the user simply needs to disconnect his or her PC from the docking station. Unfortunately, disconnecting hasn't been as easy as it sounds. The job required manually changing configuration files, such as `Config.Sys` and `Autoexec.Bat`, before disconnecting or reconnecting — a time-consuming and technically challenging endeavor for many laptop users. Windows 95 offers two new features that simplify the process: hot docking and flexible configurations.

Hot docking

Many laptops that ship with Windows 95 support *hot docking*, which allows you to dock and undock the laptop without even turning it off. This capability is both a hardware and software thing, so you probably need to check the manual that came with your laptop computer for specific instructions.

In general, though, you should be able to undock your laptop just by clicking on the Start button and choosing Eject PC. Windows 95 automatically detects the impending hardware changes, takes care of any potential problems with open files on an external drive, and loads or unloads any appropriate drivers.

To redock, simply put the laptop back into the docking station. Windows 95 once again loads the appropriate drivers automatically. If you used deferred printing while your laptop was undocked, Print Manager starts automatically and prompts you to print any documents that you "printed" while the laptop was undocked.

Not-so-hot docking

If you have a pre-Windows 95 laptop, you can't count on hot docking; you need to power down your PC before connecting to, or disconnecting from, the docking station. You can simplify matters, however, by creating two separate hardware configurations: one for docked status and the other for undocked status.

In this section, I show you how to create these configurations, starting with the laptop already docked to a port replicator. Figure 17-1 shows how the screen of my laptop looks while the machine is docked. Notice that the My Computer window shows that my laptop is connected to a CD-ROM drive (D) and to drives E, P, and W on my local area network.

While the laptop was in this docked state, I created two hardware configurations: one named Docked Configuration and the other named Undocked Configuration. Following is the quick-and-easy way to create these configurations:

1. Click on the Start button.

2. Choose Settings⇨Control Panel.

3. Double-click on the System icon.

4. Click on the Hardware Profiles tab.

5. Click on the Original Configuration option and then click on the Copy button.

6. Name the new configuration Docked Configuration.

7. Click on the Original Configuration option again and then click on the Copy button again.

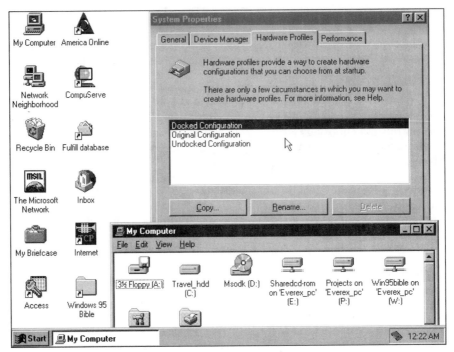

Figure 17-1: My docked laptop has drives D, E, P, and W.

8. Name this new configuration Undocked Configuration.

9. Choose OK to leave the System Properties dialog box.

Now you have three identical hardware configurations, named Original Configuration, Docked Configuration, and Undocked Configuration. (You can delete Original Configuration, if you want to; I keep it around as a safety net.) I'll show you how to make each configuration unique in a moment. First, however, you need to know the proper way to dock and undock your laptop.

Cold docking and undocking

Whenever you want to dock or undock your laptop, follow these steps:

1. Click on the Start button.

2. Choose Shut Down.

3. Choose Shut down the computer and then click on Yes.

4. When the screen says that it's safe to do so, turn off the laptop.

5. Dock or undock the laptop.

When you restart the PC later, keep an eye on the screen. You'll see something like the following before the Windows 95 desktop appears:

```
Windows cannot determine what configuration your computer is in.
Select one of the following:
1. Original Configuration
2. Docked Configuration
3. Undocked configuration
4. None of the above
Enter your choice:
```

Type the appropriate item number (2 if you're docked, 3 if you're undocked, and so on) and then press Enter.

The first time that you use Undocked Configuration, Windows 95 may complain about some missing hardware, but you should be able to work your way through any error messages until you get to the Windows 95 desktop.

The following section shows you how to customize your configurations.

Customizing hardware configurations

Much of the work needed to customize your docked and undocked configurations may have been done automatically when you restarted your PC and chose Undocked Configuration.

Examine the My Computer window in Figure 17-2, which shows how my PC looks when I start it with Undocked Configuration. The icon for drive D is gone; that drive is a CD-ROM drive that hooks into my docking station and that is not available when my laptop is undocked. Icons for network drives E, P, and W still appear, but a big red *X* through each icon reminds me that my laptop is not hooked up to the drives (because I removed my network card before undocking).

You can refine your hardware settings for a particular configuration by following these simple steps:

1. Click on the Start button.

2. Choose Settings⇨Control Panel.

3. Double-click on the System icon.

4. Click on the Device Manager tab.

5. Click on the plus sign (+) next to any device type to see devices within that category.

6. Double-click on a specific device to see its properties.

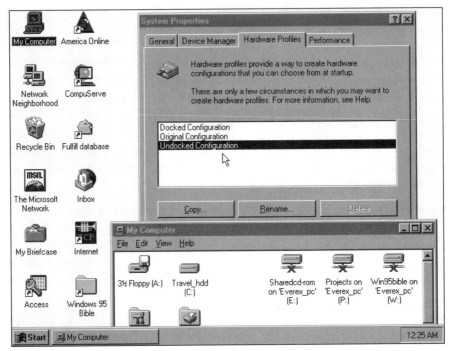

Figure 17-2: No drive D, and network drives unavailable when undocked.

7. At the bottom of the dialog box that appears (see Figure 17-3), select the hardware configurations that you want to use for the device and deselect configurations that you don't want to use for the device.

8. Repeat Steps 5–7 for as many devices as you want.

9. Choose OK and Close to work your way back to the desktop.

The preceding steps work only with virtual-mode drivers — the 32-bit Windows 95 drivers discussed in Chapter 10. Real-mode drivers (namely, those loaded via CONFIG.SYS) attempt to load, regardless of which configuration you chose. If such a driver causes a problem, you can use the techniques in the following section to bypass the driver at startup.

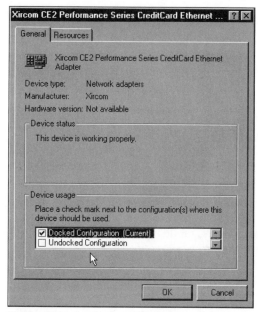

Figure 17-3: Docked Configuration selected for a device.

Bypassing real-mode drivers

Eventually, you'll want to replace all your DOS/Windows real-mode device drivers with Windows 95 virtual drivers. But if you're stuck with a real-mode driver and can't get through startup without having problems with it, follow these steps to load drivers individually at startup:

1. Start your PC as usual, but keep your eyes on the screen.

2. When you see the `Starting Windows 95` message, press the F8 key.

3. Choose 5. Step-by-step confirmation.

You'll see options that let you process the Registry and to step through CONFIG.SYS and AUTOEXEC.BAT. Choose Yes at each prompt. When you get to a real-mode driver that you don't want to install, press Esc to bypass it.

Comfort settings

The hardware configurations discussed so far in this chapter work for hardware devices. You also may want to carry more-refined "comfort settings" from one configuration to another — for example, you may want to use one set of screen colors and mouse properties when your laptop is docked and another set when the machine is undocked.

The hardware configurations don't keep track of personal preferences. But you can create multiple user profiles for yourself, perhaps named Docked and Undocked. Thereafter, when you log in, you can choose whichever user profile is appropriate at the moment. For more information, see "Enabling Multiple User Profiles" in Chapter 11.

Power Management

Battery life is a major concern for many mobile-computer users. Windows 95 supports Advanced Power Management (APM) 1.1, a new standard for modern laptop computers. If — and only if — your laptop hardware supports APM, you can use the following new features of Windows 95:

✦ Battery indicator in the taskbar

✦ Capability to put your laptop in Suspend mode by clicking on the Start button and choosing the appropriate option from the menu

✦ Capability to configure power management to shut down your PC when you shut down Windows 95

To configure power management (assuming that your laptop supports the AMP 1.1 standard), follow these simple steps:

1. Click on the Start button.

2. Choose Settings⇨Control Panel.

3. Double-click on the Power icon (if available).

4. Select your options.

The disk spin-down power-saving feature can slow your PC. Consider disabling that feature when you're not relying on battery power. See your laptop manual for directions.

There's more to APM 1.1 than meets the eye. APM lets software developers design programs that are sensitive to the power state and remaining battery life. Soon, you'll be installing battery-aware programs that can make smart decisions about whether to undertake a demanding task based on the amount of battery power left. You won't need to worry about sudden power-downs.

If possible, use nickel metal hydride (NiMH) rather than nickel cadmium (NiCad) batteries. NiMH batteries charge faster and hold more power than NiCad batteries do, and they are immune to memory loss caused by premature charging.

Deferred Printing

Deferred printing is a great new feature for computer road warriors. This feature lets you "print" a document even when your laptop is not connected to a printer. More specifically, the feature does everything that's necessary to prepare a file for printing.

If you're in a hotel room with your laptop and fax modem but don't have a printer with you, send a copy of the document to yourself via the hotel's fax machine — instant hard copy. You also can use the hotel's fax machine to scan documents into your PC. Fax the hard copy to your hotel room, and have the portable PC answer the phone.

Suppose that you're not connected to a printer at the moment, but you want to be sure to print a document when you get to a printer. No problem — go ahead and print the document, using any of the techniques discussed in Chapter 14. A message appears, telling you that the printer isn't available but that you can work in offline mode. When you choose OK, the document is prepared for printing and sent to the selected printer's queue.

When a printer is available offline, its icon is dimmed in the Printers folder, but you still can drag icons to that dimmed icon for printing.

Now you can forget about that document. You can do all your other work normally, exit Windows, turn off the computer, whatever. When you reconnect to the printer later, you see a message something like the example shown in Figure 17-4. To start printing, choose <u>Y</u>es.

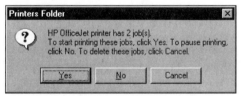

Figure 17-4: Deferred print jobs are ready to be printed.

Managing Multiple Dial-From Locations

Another traditional headache associated with mobile computing is dialing out from the PC. When you're dialing from outside your own area code, you have to dial 1 plus the area code for numbers that used to be local. When you're in a hotel room, you may need to dial 8 to get an outside line or to dial 9 before dialing long distance.

The Windows 95 modem properties greatly simplify matters by enabling you to change dial-out settings on the fly. You need to install your modem first, as discussed in Chapter 15. Then, whenever you want to change the location you're dialing from, follow these steps:

1. Click on the Start button.

2. Choose Settings⊏⊅Control Panel.

 An alternative to the Control Panel route is to double-click on My Computer and then double-click on the Control Panel icon.

3. Double-click on the Modem icon.

4. Click on the Dialing Properties button to display the dialog box shown in Figure 17-5.

5. To set new dialing properties, click on the New button, and type a name for the settings that you're about to create.

   If you're dialing from the 714 area code, for example, you can name the settings 714 Area Code. If you're dialing from a specific hotel, you can enter a name such as Honolulu Hilton.

6. Choose OK.

7. Fill in the Dialing Properties dialog box with information that describes where you're dialing from and how to dial.

   If you're outside your normal area code, for example, type the current area code. If you need to dial a special number to get an outside line, set the appropriate options for local and long-distance dialing.

8. When you finish, choose OK.

After you create the dialing settings, you need not recreate them; the settings that you choose stay in effect until you go back into Control Panel and choose different dialing properties.

To use the dialing settings again, open the Control Panel, double-click on the Modems icon, click on the Dialing Properties button, select your current location from the I am dialing from drop-down list, and choose OK to begin working your way back to the desktop.

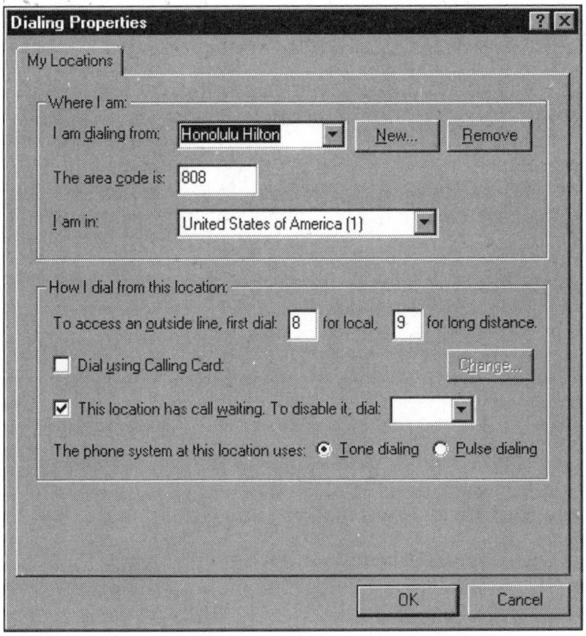

Figure 17-5: Dialing properties.

Portable voice mail

Near the end of Chapter 16, I mentioned a couple of data/fax/voice cards that can turn your desktop PC into a complete voice-mail and fax-on-demand communications center. By the time you read this book, many credit-card-size modems with the same capabilities (or similar capabilities) undoubtedly will be available. You can pop such a modem into your PCMCIA slot and convert your laptop to a voice-mail system.

One PC card for Windows 3.x — the SMART ST1414L Fax & Voice modem — already supports these capabilities, both for standard phone lines and cellular phones. I haven't had a chance to try the card with Windows 95; I simply saw it advertised in the *PCs Compleat* catalog (call (800) 669-4727 for information). You may want to hold out for a voice/fax PC card that's designed for Windows 95 plug-and-play compatibility.

Even More Great Goodies

In the next three chapters, I'll talk more about the mobile-computing features of Windows 95. First, I want to point out a few built-in gems and general ideas:

✦ When you change configurations, Windows 95 automatically detects and activates whichever mouse is available in that configuration.

✦ When you take your laptop to a meeting, get to the conference room early and take a seat next to a wall outlet, so that you can plug in your laptop rather than rely on its batteries.

✦ When you disconnect from an external monitor at 800×600 or higher resolution, Windows 95 automatically reverts to 640×480 resolution, which is ideal for most laptop screens.

✦ Quick Viewers lets you view a document even if the appropriate application isn't installed. Right-click on the document name, and choose Quick View (if it's available for that document) from the pop-up menu.

 For more information on Quick Viewers and on customizing the pop-up menu, see Chapter 31.

✦ You can buy a cellular modem to fit in a PCMCIA slot, which in turn connects to a cellular phone. This arrangement lets you send and receive faxes and e-mail and to connect to online services even when you're not near a phone line (when you're on a plane or boat, for example).

✦ Don't forget that when you're on the road, you still have access to Microsoft Exchange, which in turn gives you access to Microsoft Fax (Chapter 16), information services (Chapters 21 – 23), and even the PC that you left at the office (Chapter 20).

✦ A new set of wireless infrared drivers are being developed for release with future versions of Windows 95. These drivers will be a great boon to mobile computing, because they'll provide immediate access to other people's hardware. To hook up to some other company's printer, modem, or local area network, you'll simply put your laptop in the same room as that device.

Summary

Hardware for mobile computing has evolved beautifully over the past few years. But until now, not much was happening in the software world to take advantage of those developments. Windows 95 is the first operating system to offer special features for mobile computerists:

✦ Hot docking lets PCs with the Plug-and-Play BIOS connect and disconnect from a docking station or power replicator without powering down.

✦ Even if your portable PC doesn't have the Plug-and-Play BIOS, you can use flexible hardware configurations to simplify startup after docking or undocking

✦ If your portable PC supports APM 1.1 power management, you can use Windows 95 to manage battery power.

✦ Deferred printing lets you "print" a document while you're away from the printer (so you don't forget to do so later.) When you re-connect to a printer, the actual print job will begin automatically.

✦ To use your modem on the road, you just need to define your current dialing location. Windows 95 will take care of the "details" such as when, and when not, to dial 1 and an area code before dialing a number.

✦   ✦   ✦

The Virtual Briefcase

Many people use their portable PC as sort of a virtual briefcase. Perhaps you generally do your work on a desktop PC. To take your work on the road, you copy the appropriate files from the desktop PC to your laptop. For a while, you edit those files on your portable PC. When you get back to the office, you copy the updated files from the portable PC back to the desktop PC.

The one problem is that things can get confusing. After a while, you may lose track of which PC — the desktop or the laptop — contains the latest version of a file. Before long, you're comparing dates and times of files, trying to keep track of which file to copy where and when. Fortunately, the Windows 95 Briefcase helps reduce the confusion and simplify the entire process. Briefcase keeps tracks of the dates and times of multiple copies of a file and tells you which files need to be copied and where. In fact, Briefcase even copies the files for you.

Preparing for Briefcase

Before you use Briefcase, you need to have the My Briefcase icon on one of the computers. If neither computer shows the My Briefcase icon on the desktop, use the techniques described in "Installing Missing Windows Components" in Chapter 9 to install Briefcase on one of your PCs. If your portable is attached to the desktop PC via a docking station or cable, install Briefcase on the portable PC. If the two computers are not connected by any kind of cable, install Briefcase on the desktop PC.

When you're in Windows Setup, you'll find Briefcase in the Accessories set of components.

Briefcase relies entirely on your computer's internal calendar and clock to determine which version of a document is the most current version, so make sure that your clocks are in sync. Double-click on the little time indicator in the lower-right corner of the screen, and set the date and time on both the desktop and laptop PC.

If you don't see the time indicator on your desktop, you can search the online Help index for the word *date*. The help window for changing the system date takes you to the Date/Time Properties dialog box.

The general idea behind using Briefcase is simple, as the following list explains:

✦ When you want to take work on the road, you simply drag that work into Briefcase.

✦ To use a Briefcase document on the road, open the Briefcase and double-click on the document name. Then perform your work, close, and save the document normally.

✦ When you get back to the office, unpack Briefcase by opening My Briefcase and choosing Briefcase⇨Update All.

Using Briefcase is simple if your portable and desktop PCs are connected with a cable or LAN cards. The procedure gets a bit more complicated if the machines aren't connected, because you have to use a floppy disk to move files from one PC to the other. To prevent any unnecessary confusion for those of you who have achieved floppy-free living, I've broken the instructions for using Briefcase into the following sections:

✦ If the portable and desktop PCs are physically connected via a LAN, direct-cable connection, or dial-up networking, skip to "Using Briefcase Without Floppies" now.

✦ If the portable and desktop PCs are not physically connected by a cable, you need to use a floppy disk to transport the My Briefcase icon between the desktop and portable PCs. Skip to "Using Briefcase With Floppies" now.

There's nothing wrong with setting up a simple LAN even if you have only two PCs; a LAN is worth the relatively small investment of time and money required. And as you'll learn in Part VII of this book, you probably can set up the LAN yourself.

Using Briefcase Without Floppies

As mentioned, if the desktop and portable PCs are connected via a LAN or some other cable connection, you can use Briefcase without fumbling with floppies. When you're just about ready to hit the road, all you have to do is pack your Briefcase.

When you're ready to hit the road

To pack Briefcase, drag the files that you want to take on the road into the My Brief-case icon on your portable PC. Follow these steps:

1. On the portable computer, use Network Neighborhood, My Computer, Explorer, or Find to locate any document that you want to put into Briefcase.

2. If you want to put several documents into Briefcase, select them by Ctrl+clicking and/or Shift+clicking.

3. Drag the documents to the My Briefcase icon.

   Alternatively, right-click on the selected documents, choose Send To, and then choose My Briefcase.

Figure 18-1 shows an example in which I browsed to and selected three files to put in my Briefcase. I could drag those files over to the My Briefcase icon, near the left edge of the screen. Alternatively, I could right-click on a selected file and then choose Send To➪My Briefcase.

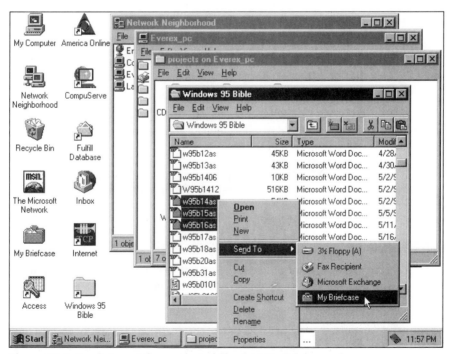

Figure 18-1: Ready to put three selected files into My Briefcase.

When Windows 95 finishes copying files, the hard disk in the portable PC will have its own copies of the files that you want to take on the road. Then you can shut down the portable and disconnect it from its docking station or network card.

While you're on the road

While you're on the road, remember one simple thing: whenever you want to work on a Briefcase document, get it from Briefcase. You can retrieve the document in either of the following ways:

✦ Double-click on the My Briefcase icon on the desktop and then double-click on the document you want to work with (see Figure 18-2).

Name	Sync Copy In	Status	Size	Type
w95b14as	W:\	Up-to-date	54.0KB	Microsoft Word D
w95b15as	W:\	Up-to-date	37.5KB	Microsoft Word D
w95b16as	W:\	Up-to-date	65.5KB	Microsoft Word D

3 object(s)

Figure 18-2: My Briefcase open on the desktop.

✦ If you're already in a program, choose File⇨Open to display the Open dialog box. In the Look in drop-down list, select My Briefcase (see Figure 18-3). Then double-click on the name of the file that you want to open.

Now you can go about your business normally. When you finish, close the document and exit the program normally. The edited copy of your document is stored in Briefcase automatically.

When you return from the trip

When you get back from your road trip, you want to unpack Briefcase — that is, get the documents that you left behind in sync with the newer copies that are on your portable PC's hard disk. Follow these steps:

1. Re-dock (or reconnect) the portable PC to the docking station, LAN, or cable that hooks it to the desktop PC.

If your laptop supports hot docking, My Briefcase may launch automatically as soon as you reconnect to the docking station.

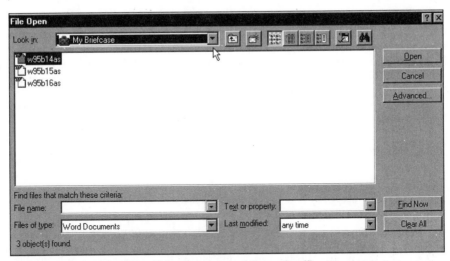

Figure 18-3: The File Open dialog box from a Microsoft Office 95 program.

2. Start Windows 95, and double-click on the My Briefcase icon.

3. Choose Briefcase➪Update All.

   You see a dialog box like the one shown in Figure 18-4, with an arrow pointing from the new version of the file to the old version.

4. To update, click on the Update button.

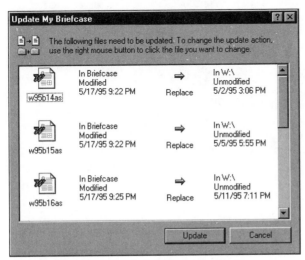

Figure 18-4: Three files in Briefcase need to be synchronized.

When you finish, the files still are in Briefcase, and the copies of those files on the desktop PC match them. If you think that you'll be working on the same documents off-site again soon, you can leave them in Briefcase. Just remember that if you change the documents on the desktop PC, you need to update Briefcase before you hit the road again. Follow the preceding steps, and Windows 95 automatically copies the latest versions of the files back into Briefcase.

If you don't think that you'll be working with the same files again off-site, you can delete them from Briefcase. Select the files that you want to delete, and then press Delete or choose File⇨Delete.

Using Briefcase With Floppies

You can use Briefcase even if the portable and desktop computers are not connected by any sort of cable. The down side to this approach is the fact that you have to use a floppy disk as your virtual briefcase, which means that your storage is limited to 1.4MB (or 2.5MB). If you work mainly with word processing and spreadsheet documents, however, that limit may be plenty roomy.

 As mentioned in "Maximize Your Disk Space" in Chapter 12, you can use DriveSpace to increase the capacity of a 1.4MB floppy to about 2.5MB.

What if both copies change?

Suppose that you load a document into Briefcase and edit that document on the road. While you're away, somebody (let's say Harry) opens the document that you left behind and changes it. When you return, Harry may not be too thrilled at the prospect of your replacing his copy of the document with the one in your Briefcase. You and Harry may have to figure out who did what while you were away and then reconcile the differences. If you're lucky, the program that both of you used to edit the document can reconcile the differences automatically.

Windows 95 supplies programmers with a set of tools called *Reconciliation APIs*. This means that the people who create your favorite programs now can hook into Briefcase, and their programs automatically reconcile the differences between two copies of a document that changed while one document was away in Briefcase. When you start upgrading to Windows 95 versions of your favorite programs, check the manuals or online help systems for information on reconciling documents. Your days of negotiating with Harry may be over.

Before you begin

Before you launch into the sections that follow, peek at the Windows 95 desktop on your larger (desktop) PC. If you see the icon named My Briefcase, grab a floppy disk and label it My Briefcase. Then skip to "Packing the floppy Briefcase" later in this chapter.

If My Briefcase is on your portable PC, read the next two sections to learn how to create your virtual briefcase and move it from the portable to the desktop PC.

Creating a "My Briefcase" floppy disk

Step 1 in using Briefcase with floppies is creating a floppy disk that acts as your virtual briefcase. Follow these steps:

1. Grab a blank floppy disk, and label it My Briefcase.

2. Go to the portable PC, which has the My Briefcase icon on its screen, and put the floppy disk in drive A.

3. Open My Computer so that you can see the icon for drive A.

   Move and size the My Computer window, if necessary, so that you also can see the desktop icon for My Briefcase.

4. Drag the My Briefcase icon to the icon for drive A.

The briefcase moves to the floppy disk, and its icon disappears from the Windows desktop. Don't worry about that; you're just going to move the icon to the desktop PC.

Putting Briefcase on the desktop PC

Now you need to put Briefcase on the desktop PC (the one containing the files that you plan to take on your trip). Follow these steps:

1. Take the floppy disk labeled My Briefcase to the desktop PC (which, presumably, contains the latest versions of the documents that you want to take with you).

2. Put the floppy disk in drive A.

3. Double-click on My Computer.

4. Double-click on the icon for drive A.

   You should see the My Briefcase icon in the window that opens.

5. Drag the My Briefcase icon from drive A to the Windows 95 desktop.

At this point, Briefcase is on the desktop PC only. The floppy disk is empty, because you moved Briefcase — you didn't copy it. This is good, because this will be your starting point whenever you plan to use Briefcase. Take a break. Go to lunch. Forget all about that little floppy-disk shuffle that you just did; you won't need to do it again.

I realize that moving Briefcase can be confusing, but you have to do this only once. Still, the real solution is to set up a little LAN between the two computers, as you'll learn in Part VII.

Packing the floppy Briefcase

Suppose that you're about to go on a trip and want to take a couple of documents from the desktop PC with you. Follow these steps:

1. At the desktop PC, use My Computer, Explorer, or Find to get to any document that you want to put into Briefcase.

2. Select the documents that you want to take by Ctrl+clicking and/or Shift+clicking them.

3. Drag the documents to the My Briefcase icon.

Now the My Briefcase icon on your desktop PC contains copies of the files that you want to take on your trip. You need to take those copies with you, so now you need to move the filled Briefcase from the desktop PC to a floppy disk. Follow these steps:

1. Insert the floppy disk that you labeled My Briefcase into drive A of the desktop computer.

2. Open My Computer, and move and size its window so that you can see both the icon for drive A and the icon for My Briefcase.

3. Drag the My Briefcase icon from the Windows 95 desktop to the icon for drive A.

Windows 95 moves Briefcase to the floppy disk, so you won't see the My Briefcase icon on the desktop computer's screen anymore. Don't worry. Just pack that floppy disk with your portable PC; you'll be using that floppy as your virtual briefcase while you're on the road.

On the road with a floppy Briefcase

When you're on the road with your portable PC and floppy briefcase, follow these steps to work on your documents:

1. Insert the My Briefcase floppy into drive A of your portable PC.

If you don't want to work from floppies on the road, you can drag the files from My Briefcase on the floppy disk to your portable PC's hard disk. Then you can edit directly from the hard disk. When you finish editing, put the My Briefcase floppy disk in drive A, open My Briefcase on that floppy, and choose Briefcase⇨Update All.

2. Double-click on the My Computer icon.

3. Double-click on the icon for drive A.

4. Double-click on the My Briefcase icon.

5. Double-click on the name of the document that you want to work with.

Now you can work on the document normally. Just don't take that floppy out of its drive while you're working.

When you finish working with the document, exit the program and save your work normally. Windows automatically saves the modified version in its original location: My Briefcase on drive A.

Unpacking the floppy Briefcase

When you get back to the home office, your best bet is to move the My Briefcase icon back to the Windows 95 desktop of your desktop PC and then update files from there. Follow these steps:

1. Insert the My Briefcase floppy into drive A of the desktop PC.

2. Double-click on My Computer.

3. Double-click on the icon for drive A.

4. Drag the My Briefcase icon to the Windows 95 desktop.

At this point, the floppy disk is empty again, and Briefcase is back on the desktop PC. You can see the Briefcase icon on the Windows 95 desktop.

To get the documents that are on the desktop PC in sync with the copies in Briefcase, follow these steps:

1. Double-click on the My Briefcase icon on the desktop.

2. Choose Briefcase⇨Update All.

3. To update all the files, click on the Update button, and follow the instructions on-screen.

When you finish, you can go back to editing the files outside Briefcase. You need to use the files inside Briefcase only when you're on the road. If you don't think that you'll be editing the same files on the road again, you can regain some space by deleting them from Briefcase. Double-click on the My Briefcase icon, select the files that you want to delete, and then choose File⇨Delete.

When you're ready to go on another road trip, you can repack Briefcase and move it to a floppy by repeating the steps in "Packing the floppy Briefcase" earlier in this chapter.

Other Briefcase Goodies

Briefcase has most of the same capabilities that My Computer has. The Under menu within Briefcase, for example, offers many common options for changing your view of files. The File and Edit menus offer commands for deleting, renaming, and copying files within Briefcase. You also can do the following handy-dandy things with files that are inside Briefcase:

✦ To check the status of a file, select its name in My Briefcase, choose File ⇨Properties, and then click on the Update Status tab. You can click on the Find Original button in that dialog box to locate the original version of the file.

✦ You can get help with My Briefcase in either of two ways. If you're at the desktop PC, click on the Start button, choose Help, click on the Index tab, and search for *briefcase*. If you're already in My Briefcase, click on the Help command in its menu bar.

✦ To update only a few files in Briefcase, select the files that you want to update and then choose Briefcase⇨Update Selection.

✦ To split a file off from Briefcase, select its name in My Briefcase and then choose Briefcase⇨Split from Original. The original copy of the file becomes an *orphan*, meaning that it no longer will be altered when you synchronize files from Briefcase.

Summary

Briefcase is a handy tool for road warriors, because it helps you keep track of which document is which when you're taking copies of your work on the road:

✦ Briefcase is automatically copied to your hard disk when you install Windows 95 and choose Portable as the installation method.

✦ If your portable PC is attached to your desktop PC via a LAN card or cable, keep the My Briefcase icon on your portable PC at all times. When you're ready to go on the road, just drag the files that you want to take with you from My Computer into the My Briefcase icon.

✦ If your portable PC is not attached to the desktop PC, it makes more sense to keep the My Briefcase icon on the desktop PC. When you're ready to go on the road, drag documents into the My Briefcase icon. Then drag the entire My Briefcase icon onto a floppy disk.

✦ While you're on the road, edit documents that are in the My Briefcase icon. For example, you can double-click on the My Briefcase icon then double-click on the document you want to edit. Or you can choose File⇨Open from your program's menu bar, and specify My Briefcase as the place to Look In.

✦ When you've finished editing a Briefcase document, just close and save the document normally.

✦ When you return from your trip, you need to update the Briefcase on your desktop PC. If you used a floppy disk while on the road, first move the My Briefcase icon from the floppy disk onto the Windows 95 desktop of the desktop (stationary) PC.

✦ To update (synchronize) the files, double-click on the My Briefcase icon and choose Briefcase⇨Update All.

✦   ✦   ✦

The Dreaded PCMCIA Slot

Some of you probably read this chapter title and wondered, "What's a PCMCIA slot, and what did it do to deserve my dread?" So I'm going to start this chapter with a brief history lesson.

If you're into computer hardware, you probably know what the boards that you add to your computer are like. The boards usually are anywhere from 4 to 12 inches long, and they have all their little circuits and chips exposed. These boards have a few negatives: to the technologically timid, they're kinda scary-looking; they're usually hard to install; they come with instruction manuals that assume that you have a Ph.D. in electrical engineering; and, perhaps worst of all, they don't fit into portable computers. But zillions of these boards are on the market nonetheless.

Enter PCMCIA — a clever idea in which the board actually is a credit-card-size card called, simply, a PC Card. The circuits aren't exposed, so the card looks kind of like a fat credit card. The card's size makes it much more portable than the older boards. And you install the card from outside the computer. You don't have to take the PC apart to install the thing; you can pop it in when you want to use it and yank it out when you're done. Sounds great, no?

The PC Card *is* a great idea, but until recently, it's been a poorly realized idea. People who have been using their PCMCIA slots have had to contend with many problems. Standards changed (Type I, then Type II, and then Type III). You never were quite sure whether a particular card would work in your system. You had to jump through all kinds of hoops involving card drivers and socket services to get the thing to work. Inserting, installing, configuring, and even removing cards usually was a headache. For many portable-PC users, the very thought of sliding a PC Card into the PCMCIA slot was scary.

But the procedure has become fairly easy. The plug-and-play architecture of Windows 95 really shines in the PCMCIA department. You can insert and remove true plug-and-play cards without powering down the PC. And even cards that don't bear the "Designed for Windows 95" plug-and-play logo are much easier to get along with than ever before. (I know that this sounds like a sales pitch, but it's not. The truth is that I really hated messing with PCMCIA slots before Windows 95. Now I hardly give it a second thought.)

Types of PC Cards

You can put a wide variety of cards and devices into a PCMCIA slot, including the following:

✦ *Fax/modems.* If your portable PC doesn't have a built-in fax/modem, you can pop one into the PCMCIA slot. Most of these devices provide full faxing and data support for e-mail.

✦ *Cellular modems.* Same as fax/modems, except that these devices plug into a cellular phone for wireless communications.

✦ *Digital-video boards.* These boards enable you to hook your portable PC to a VCR or video camera to view, capture, and edit video.

✦ *Sound cards.* If your system has no built-in sound card, you can add a sound card via the PCMCIA slot.

✦ *Network cards.* Ethernet and Token Ring PC cards enable you to connect your portable PC to an existing LAN (local area network) so that you can share files, printers, modems, and other resources.

✦ *CD-ROM drives.* Many portable CD-ROM drive units are available, including some with built-in sound for full multimedia capability. You can attach one of these devices to the PCMCIA slot of your portable.

✦ *Flash memory, ATA drives, and SRAM.* These cards enable you to add more memory and more disk storage to your portable PC via the PCMCIA slot.

 If you plan to install SRAM or flash memory, search the Windows 95 help index for *SRAM* or *flash*, as appropriate, for more information.

Some portables allow you to insert two or more PCMCIA cards at a time, so you're not limited to one. Keep in mind that many CD-ROM and hard disk drives can be driven from the parallel port as well. When I'm at home, I keep an Ethernet card in my PCMCIA slot to connect my portable to my desktop PCs. I also plug a CD-ROM drive into the portable's parallel port.

Installing PCMCIA Support

PCMCIA support is available only if your PC has a PCMCIA slot. When you installed Windows 95, the software would have detected a PCMCIA slot automatically. To install PCMCIA services, follow these steps:

1. Click on the Start button.

2. Choose Settings➪Control Panel.

3. Double-click on the PC Card (PCMCIA) icon.

   If you haven't already installed PCMCIA services, a wizard appears to help you replace existing real-mode drivers (if any) with the new 32-bit virtual drivers.

4. Follow the instructions presented by the wizard.

5. After you install the 32-bit drivers, double-click on the PC Card icon.

   The PC Card (PCMCIA) Properties dialog box appears, as shown in Figure 19-1.

Figure 19-1: The PC Card (PCMCIA) Properties dialog box.

As you see in Figure 19-1, the dialog box is simple. If you want to remove a PCMCIA card from your system, click on its name and then click on the Stop button.

The following sections discuss inserting and removing cards.

If you already have a card in the PCMCIA slot, you can double-click on the little PC Card indicator near the lower-right corner of the screen to display the PC Card (PCMCIA) Properties dialog box.

Adding a PCMCIA slot to a desktop PC

You can add a PCMCIA slot to your desktop computer. This slot can be handy if you buy a PC Card that you want to use in both your desktop and portable PCs. You may want to use a digital-video card in both PCs, or you may want to use a PCMCIA hard disk to transfer files between your portable and desktop PC without the need for floppies.

Several companies manufacture PCMCIA slots for desktop PCs. I recently purchased one called the SwapBox, manufactured by SCM Microsystems (phone (408) 395-9292). Installation was a breeze. I installed the hard-

ware per the manufacturer's instructions. Then I ignored the instructions for installing DOS/Windows drivers (called card services and sockets). Instead, I fired up Windows 95 and ran the Add New Hardware wizard (refer to Chapter 10). Windows found the device and installed it correctly.

When the Add New Hardware wizard finished, I opened Control Panel and double-clicked on the PCMCIA icon to load the Windows 95 PCMCIA drivers. The process was surprisingly easy.

Inserting and Removing PC Cards

With the release of Windows 95 will come a new breed of PC Cards that support hot swapping. But you should perform hot swapping only if the manufacturer's instructions specifically tell you that it's OK to do so. In this situation, you need to check the instruction manual that came with the PC Card for specific instructions. The following sections summarize the general procedures for hot and not-so-hot swapping.

 The first time you install a PC Card, have your original Windows 95 disks or CD-ROM and the manufacturer's disks (if any) handy. The Add New Hardware wizard may ask for one of those disks — bad news if you're on the road and didn't bring the disks with you.

Hot swapping

PC Cards that are specifically designed for Windows 95 support hot swapping. That means you can simply pop in a PC Card while the computer is running. Windows 95 detects the card and loads the appropriate drivers automatically for true plug-and-play compatibility.

If you're removing a hot-swappable card, you should stop the card before you yank it out of the slot so that Windows has a chance to gear up for the coming hardware change. To stop a device, click on the PC Card indicator in the lower-right corner of the screen and then choose the Stop option. Alternatively, double-click on the PC Card icon, choose a device from the list, and then click on the Stop button. Wait for the instruction that tells you when it's safe to remove the card.

Not-so-hot swapping

If you're not certain that a particular card supports plug-and-play compatibility, you should power down before inserting the card. If you're replacing a card that's already in the slot, stop that card first. Follow these steps:

1. If you are removing a card, first click on the PC Card indicator in the lower-right corner of the screen; then click on the appropriate option to stop that card.

   Alternatively, you can double-click on the PC Card indicator and then use the PC Card (PCMCIA) Properties dialog box to stop the card.

2. When you see the message `You may safely remove this device`, click on OK.

3. To play it extra-safe, click on the Start button and choose Sh<u>u</u>t Down; when you are asked whether you want to shut down the computer, choose <u>Y</u>es.

4. When you're told that it's safe to do so, shut down the PC.

5. Remove the PC Card from its slot.

6. Insert into the PCMCIA slot the PC card that you want to use.

7. Turn the power back on.

   Most likely, Windows will detect the new device at startup, and install the appropriate drivers for it.

If Windows does not detect the new device, or if you have problems using the device when you get to the Windows 95 desktop, use the Add New Hardware wizard (refer to Chapter 10) to install the driver for that particular PC Card. You also may need to shut down Windows, power down the PC, and restart.

Using the installed device

After you successfully install the PC Card, Windows treats the device for that card like any other device in that category. If you installed a CD-ROM drive or hard disk drive, for example, an icon for that drive appears when you open My Computer, Windows Explorer, or any other dialog box that allows you to browse through drives.

If you installed a modem, it should be available wherever the dialing properties are available. If you want to make sure (or if you have trouble with the modem), click on the Start button, choose <u>S</u>ettings⇨Control Panel, and then double-click on the Modems tab. If you don't see the new modem, click on the <u>A</u>dd button and use the wizard to install the modem. After installation, the modem will be listed like any normal modem, but it will have a PC Card icon rather than a telephone icon, as shown in Figure 19-2.

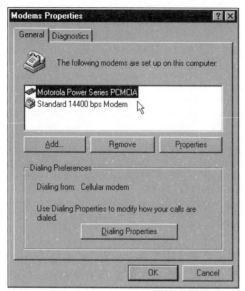

Figure 19-2: The Modems Properties dialog box recognizes a Motorola PCMCIA cellular modem.

If you have a regular built-in modem and later install a cellular modem, you need to tell programs which modem you want to use. To tell Microsoft Fax which one to use, open the Control Panel, double-click on Mail and Fax, click on an information service, and then click on Properties. Choose Set as active fax/modem in the Modem tab to choose one of your available modems. If you need more information, refer to Chapters 15, 16, and 23.

Remember that if you change hardware configurations on your PC frequently, you may find it convenient to create multiple hardware configurations, as discussed in "Not-so-hot docking" in Chapter 17. In that section, I described docked and undocked configurations. But you can create as many configurations as you want.

Summary

This chapter has been about the PCMCIA slot featured on most portable PCs and some desktop PCs. Following are the main points:

✦ The card that you can slide into a PCMCIA slot is sometimes called a *PC Card*, or *credit-card sized adapter*, or perhaps a *PCMCIA Card*.

✦ To ensure that you're using the 32-bit Windows 95 PCMCIA drivers, click the Start button, choose Settings⇨Control Panel, and double-click the PC Card (PCMCIA) icon. If you need to update your drivers, a wizard will help you do so.

✦ Many new "Designed for Windows 95" PC Cards will support hot-swapping, which means you can pop a PC Card into the PCMCIA slot without powering down the PC.

✦ To insert a card that doesn't support hot swapping, shut down Windows, power down the PC, insert the card, then restart the PC.

✦ To remove a PC Card, double-click the PC Card indicator in the taskbar, click the card you plan to remove, then click the Stop button. Then you can physically remove the card from the slot.

✦   ✦   ✦

Dial-Up Networking and Direct Cable Connection

Direct cable connection is a way to connect your portable PC to a desktop PC, or even to a network of PCs, by using just a cable (no network cards). You use this method to connect to a PC that's within a few feet of your portable PC, even if you don't have LAN (local area network) cards in either PC. When the PCs are connected, you can transfer files back and forth without using floppy disks.

Dial-Up Networking is a way to connect your portable to a desktop PC or LAN anywhere in the world. For this type of connection, both computers must have a modem. The stationary PC must be configured as a *dial-up server*, and the portable must be configured as a *dial-up client*.

Direct cable connection and Dial-Up Networking, and all the associated "how-tos," are the topics of this chapter. (Which is a good thing, because if I suddenly started writing about some unrelated topic instead — say, a clambake — I bet you'd be displeased).

I'm going to be using my trusty laptop to illustrate some things in this chapter. Be aware that in this chapter I'm using my laptop without its LAN card. Network cards are *not* required to make these kinds of connections.

 Toward the end of the Windows 95 beta test, I'd heard that in order to set up your Windows 95 PC as a dial-up server, you'd need to purchase the Microsoft Plus! program. See "Configuring the Dial-Up Server" later in this chapter for more information.

Before You Do Anything Else: Network Neighborhood

Whether you plan to use dial-up or direct cable connection, you need to ensure that Network Neighborhood is installed on both PCs. Look at the Windows 95 desktop. If you do not see Network Neighborhood on the desktop, you must install it, as described in the following section.

When you're certain that both PCs have Network Neighborhood installed, you can skip to the "Direct Cable Connection" or "Dial-Up Networking" section later in this chapter.

Installing Network Neighborhood

Network Neighborhood is installed automatically if your PC has a network card or if you install a network card and then run the Add New Hardware wizard (refer to Chapter 10). But if the PC that you plan to use has no network card, you need to install Network Neighborhood by following these steps:

1. Gather up your original Windows 95 floppy disks or CD-ROM.

2. Open Control Panel by choosing Start➪Settings➪Control Panel.

3. Double-click on the Network icon.

4. Click on the Add button.

5. Click on Protocol and then click on the Add button.

6. In the Manufacturers list, choose Microsoft.

7. In the Network Protocols list, choose IPX/SPX-compatible Protocol.

8. Click on OK.

9. When you are asked to select a device, choose OK.

10. Choose Client for Microsoft Networks from the Primary Network Logon drop-down list.

11. Click on the File and Print Sharing button.

12. If you want the other PC to be capable of copying files to or from this PC, choose the first option, I want to be able to give others access to my files.

I suggest that you always select both checkboxes in the File and Print Sharing dialog box. By doing so, you give yourself the option to share resources later, if you want to; you're not giving other computers free rein over your PC.

13. If you want the other PC to be capable of using this PC's printer, choose the second option, I want to be able to allow others to print to my printer(s).

14. Choose OK.

15. Click on the Identification tab in the Network dialog box.

16. In the Computer name box, type a name of up to 15 characters, with no blank spaces.

    You can use any name you want, but each PC must have a unique name. You could name this PC Office_PC, for example, and name the other Travel_PC.

Jot down, on a piece of paper, the exact name that you type in the Network dialog box. You may need to know that name later when you try to connect.

17. In the Workgroup box, type a name of up to 15 characters, with no spaces.

    If you don't belong to a workgroup, you can make up a workgroup name. For example, I use the workgroup name ALANS_OFFICE on my PCs.

Only PCs that have the same workgroup name can share resources. Make up a name that will be easy to remember, and make sure that you spell it the same way every time you type it.

18. Optionally, you can type a brief description of this computer.

    Figure 20-1 shows how I identified one of the computers that I'll be using in this chapter.

19. Choose OK.

20. Follow the instructions on-screen.

When you finish, your Windows 95 desktop displays the Network Neighborhood icon near the My Computer and Recycle Bin icons. Don't forget that both computers in the planned connection must have Network Neighborhood installed.

Make up one arbitrary password, such as *pinkcat*, that you'll never forget; never tell it to anyone. Then use that password in every situation in which you're allowed to create your own password. Remember to use all lowercase letters (or all uppercase letters), because passwords often are case-sensitive.

You probably will be instructed to restart the computer; follow that direction. When the computer restarts, you'll be asked to provide a user name and password. Use a separate user name for each PC. You can use the same password for each PC; just don't forget what that password is. Remember to always use all same case letters so that you don't get confused trying to remember which letters should be uppercase and which should be lowercase.

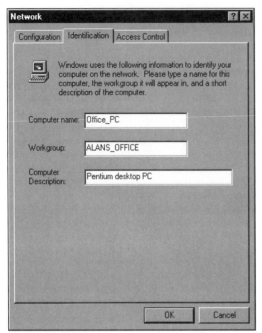

Figure 20-1: Example of identifying a PC.

Changing Network Neighborhood

If you need to view or change to your network protocol or identification settings, follow these steps:

1. Right-click on the Network Neighborhood icon.

2. Choose Properties.

3. Make your selections in the tabbed dialog boxes.

4. Choose OK.

5. Follow the instructions (if any) that appear on-screen.

Sharing resources

Whether you plan to use direct cable connection or Dial-Up Networking, you need to decide which resources will be shared (If you don't share any resources, the connection won't be worth making). In general, you need to share resources only on the stationary PC.

✦ If you're setting up direct cable connection, share resources on the host.

✦ If you're setting up Dial-Up Networking, share resources on the dial-up server (the PC that will answer the phone).

The following sections show you how to share resources:

If you want to share a printer

If you want both PCs to be capable of using one printer, you first need to share that printer. Follow these steps:

1. On the PC to which the printer is physically connected, choose Start⇨ Settings⇨Printers.

2. Right-click on the icon for the printer that you want to share.

3. Click on Sharing.

4. Click on Shared As.

5. Type a name (or accept the suggested name).

6. Choose OK.

   In the Printers folder, a little hand appears below the icon for that printer, indicating that the printer is shared.

7. Close the Printers folder.

If you want to share files

If you want to move or copy files from one PC to the other, you first need to share the disk drive, or at least specific folders, on the stationary PC. Follow these steps:

1. On the stationary PC, double-click on the My Computer icon.

2. Right-click on the icon for hard disk drive C.

3. Click on Sharing.

You can share a CD-ROM drive as well. You also can open a drive and choose specific folders to share on that drive. Right-click on the device that you want to share, click on Sharing, and complete Steps 4–7 for that drive or folder.

4. Click on Shared As.

5. In the Share Name box, type a short name, using no spaces.

   Optionally, type a longer descriptive name.

6. If you want to be able to move and copy files in both directions (to and from the portable PC to this PC), select Full in the Access Type section.

If you accept the default Access Type setting, Read Only, the guest/client PC can only copy files from this PC.

If you plan to permit other people to connect to this PC and don't want them to be able to put things on or take things off your PC, you may want to choose Read Only or <u>F</u>ull with a password.

7. Choose OK.

Now that you've set up Network Neighborhood and defined something to share on the stationary PC, you can set up direct cable connection, Dial-Up Networking, or both. The following sections discuss each topic independently.

Direct Cable Connection

Direct cable connection is the type that you use when (1) you want to connect two PCs without using network cards, (2) the PCs are close enough to each other to be connected by a cable, and (3) you already have the appropriate cable for the job. Before you connect the PCs, you need to do some setup on both PCs. You need to go through this setup procedure only one time, so if you've already done that, skip to "Making the direct cable connection" later in this section.

Installing the direct cable connection

The following sections outline the steps involved in getting set up for a direct cable connection.

Step 1: Get the right cable

The first thing that you need for direct cable connection is the appropriate type of cable. You specifically want the type of cable that goes by the name file-transfer cable, null-modem cable, LapLink cable, InterLink cable, or Serial PC to PC File Transfer cable. Trust me — you really, really want to get the right cable. Otherwise, you're likely to spend hours and hours trying to get the connection to work, with no positive result whatsoever.

Direct cable connection also supports ECP and UCM parallel cables. But the ECP cable works only with ECP parallel ports that have been enabled in BIOS.

Before you buy the cable, check to see what kinds of serial ports are available (or can be made available) on both PCs. These ports often are labeled COM 1 and COM 2, or perhaps Serial Port 1 and Serial Port 2. The ports should be male (the prongs stick out) and may be 9-pin or 25-pin. When you buy the cable, make sure that it has the correct-size plug on each end.

Try to get a two-headed file-transfer cable — one that has both a DB-9 and DB-25 plug on each end — so that you can plug the cable into whichever port is available. You also can buy gender changers to convert male ports to female ports (and vice versa).

Step 2: Connect the PCs

The second step is to connect the two PCs. I strongly suggest that you shut down Windows and power down both PCs before you make the connection. Pay attention to which port you're using on each PC; you can use COM 1 on one PC and COM 2 on the other. After the PCs are connected, power up each PC.

While you wait for the PCs to power up, decide which one will be the host and which one will be the guest, based on the following criteria:

✦ *Host.* The computer that has the resources that you want to use (i.e., an attached printer or shared folder) is the host. Usually, the larger, stationary computer plays the role of host.

✦ *Guest.* The computer that wants access to resources is the guest. Typically, this computer is the portable PC.

When both PCs are running, you're ready to complete the connection.

Step 3: Set up the host

Now it's time to get the host PC ready to connect. Go to the computer that will act as the host, and follow these steps:

1. Choose Start⇨Programs⇨Accessories⇨Direct Cable Connection.

   Assuming that Direct Cable Connection has been installed, you go to the Direct Cable Connection wizard. The first time that you use direct cable connection, that wizard looks like Figure 20-2.

If Direct Cable Connection isn't available in your Accessories menu, you need to install it. For instructions, refer to "Installing Missing Windows Components" in Chapter 9. The Direct Cable Connection component is in the Communications group.

2. Click on Host.

3. Click on the Next button.

4. Follow the instructions presented by the wizard, clicking on Next after you complete each screen.

5. In the last wizard screen, you can set a password, if you want.

6. Click on the Finish button when you finish.

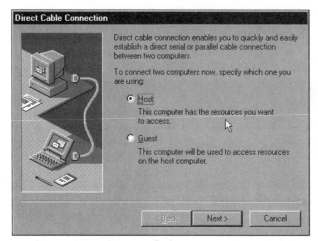

Figure 20-2: Setting up the host in direct cable connection.

The host PC displays a message, telling you that it's ready for the guest PC to drop in, but there's no hurry (I think that the question Is the guest computer running? **is** a rhetorical one. Don't answer). If you want, you can close the dialog box for now; first, you need to decide what this host PC is going to share.

Don't forget that you also need to define what you're going to share on the host PC. If you haven't done that yet, refer to "Sharing resources" earlier in this chapter.

Step 4: Set up the guest

When the host PC is set up and you've shared the items that you want the guest to have access to, you're ready to set up direct cable connection on the guest. Go to the guest (portable) PC, and follow these steps:

1. Choose Start⇨Programs⇨Accessories.

2. Click on Direct Cable Connection.

If Direct Cable Connection isn't available in the Accessories menu, you need to install it. Bummer, I know, but you have to do it only one time. Refer to "Installing Missing Windows Components" in Chapter 9.

3. Click on Guest.

4. Click on the Next button.

5. Follow the instructions on-screen to complete the wizard.

When you finish, you see a message indicating that the guest is trying to make a connection. You can close that dialog box for now, if you want.

The following sections show you how to connect the two PCs from now on (after you complete all this setup business).

Making the direct cable connection

Fortunately, after you finish the setup and your cable is in place, connecting the two PCs is easy. Follow these steps:

1. On the host PC, choose Start⇨Programs⇨Accessories.

2. Click on Direct Cable Connection.

3. If Windows needs more information, you'll be asked to fill in some wizard screens; do so.

4. When you get to the wizard screen shown in Figure 20-3, click on the Listen button.

5. On the guest PC, choose Start⇨Programs⇨Accessories⇨Direct Cable Connection, and complete the wizard screens.

6. When you get to the wizard screen shown in Figure 20-4, click on the Connect button.

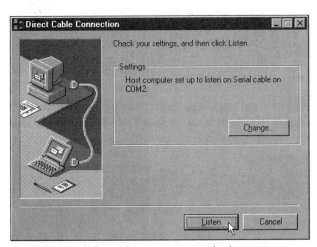

Figure 20-3: Click on Listen to prepare the host PC.

You see some activity in the dialog boxes on-screen as the two PCs connect. If the guest PC complains that it can't display the shared folders of the host computer and asks for a computer name, provide that name. If you don't remember exactly what you named the host PC, go to the host, right-click on Network Neighborhood, click on Properties, click on the Identification tab, and look at the entry in the Computer name box. Click on Cancel to close the Network Properties dialog box. Now go to the guest PC, type the name, and choose OK.

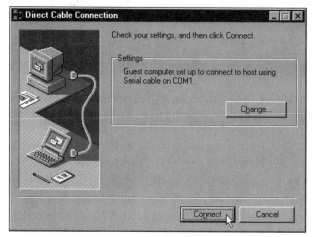

Figure 20-4: Click on Connect on the guest PC.

When the connection is made, the small Direct Cable Connection status dialog box appears on both screens, displaying the message `Connected via Serial cable on COMx`. The computers remain connected until you click on the Close button on either the host or guest PC.

Some people opt for this method of connecting two PCs because they assume that setting up a LAN is too complicated. In truth, setting up a LAN probably is easier, and a LAN connection definitely is easier to work with than a cable connection is.

The guest PC displays a window of shared drives or folders that are available on the host PC (if not, click on the View Host button on the guest PC). Figure 20-5 shows the screen of my guest PC (my portable PC) after the connection was made.

Notice the window titled Office_pc. The folders in that window represent two resources that I shared on the host: a hard disk drive (Office_hdd) and a CD-ROM drive (Office_cd), each represented as a folder on this PC (the guest). So even though I'm looking at the screen on my portable PC, I have full access to the hard drive and CD-ROM drive on the larger desktop PC (the host).

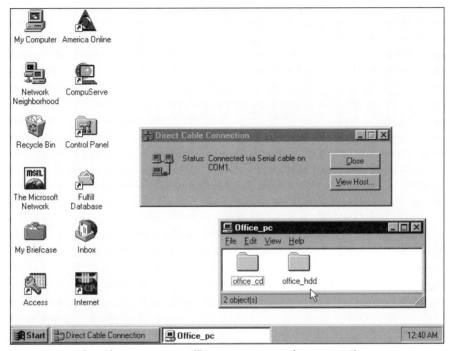

Figure 20-5: Shared resources on Office_pc appear on the guest PC's screen.

Transferring files via direct cable connection

To transfer files between connected PCs, use exactly the same techniques that you always use. Follow these steps:

1. On the guest PC, use the host PC window (Office_pc, in my example) to browse to the folder that contains the files that you want to move or copy.

2. Also on the guest PC, use My Computer, Windows Explorer, or Find to browse to the folder on this PC that contains the files that you want to move or copy.

3. In either window, select the files that you want to move or copy, and right-drag those files to the destination window.

4. Release the mouse button and then choose <u>M</u>ove Here or <u>C</u>opy Here, depending on what you want to do.

If you find that the connection is too slow, you can crank up the baud rate on both PCs, as described in "Troubleshooting a direct cable connection" later in this chapter.

Installing programs from a shared CD-ROM drive

Here's an all-too-common scenario for many portable PC owners. You buy a program that's on CD-ROM and want to install it on your portable PC, but only your desktop PC has a CD-ROM drive. How do you use the desktop PC's CD-ROM drive to install a program on your portable PC's hard disk? Installation is easy if you can connect the two PCs with a cable.

On the host PC, follow these steps:

1. Insert the CD-ROM into the CD-ROM drive.

2. Double-click on the My Computer icon.

3. Right-click on the icon for the CD-ROM drive.

4. Click on Sharing.

5. Click on Shared As, and type a name (such as CDROM).

6. Choose OK.

7. Close My Computer.

8. Choose Start⇨Programs⇨Accessories⇨ Direct Cable Connection⇨Listen.

On the guest PC, follow these steps:

1. Choose Start⇨Programs⇨Accessories⇨ Direct Cable Connection⇨Connect.

2. If necessary, type the host computer's name (Office_pc, in my example).

3. Choose OK.

4. When you see the shared resources on the host PC, click on the icon for the shared CD-ROM drive.

5. Choose File⇨Map Network Drive.

6. Select any available drive letter (for example, D).

7. Choose OK.

8. Choose Start⇨Settings⇨Control Panel.

9. Double-click on Add/Remove Programs.

10. Click on the Install button.

11. Click on the Next button to start the search.

If the wizard doesn't find an install program, click on the Browse button in the wizard, select the shared CD-ROM drive (D, in my example) from the Look in drop-down list, and double-click on the name of the install or setup program that you need.

12. When you locate the install program, click on the Finish button and proceed through the installation normally.

Using a shared printer via direct cable connection

If you want to use the host PC's printer to print something from the guest PC, follow these steps:

1. On the guest PC, go to the window that shows shared resources from the host PC.

2. Click on the name of the shared printer from the host PC.

3. Choose File⇨Install.

4. Work your way through the wizard to make the connection.

Now the host PC's printer is just like any other printer. If you want to print from a particular program on the guest PC, run that program, load the document that you want to print, and choose File⇨Print. When you're asked to choose a printer, select the name of the printer on the host; then choose OK.

Optionally, you can use drag-and-drop printing if the documents that you want to print support that feature. On the guest PC, choose Start⇨Settings⇨Printers. Arrange the printer icons in the window so that you can see the icon for the printer on the host. Then, staying on the guest PC, browse to and select the files that you want to print, and drag those files to the host PC's printer icon just as though you were printing on a local printer.

Closing the connection

To close the direct cable connection between two PCs, click on the Close button in the Direct Cable Connection status dialog box on either PC.

Troubleshooting a direct cable connection

Many factors are involved in making a successful direct cable connection between two PCs. The built-in troubleshooter offers some help. If you have any problems making the connection, however, I suggest that you first go through the following process:

1. On both PCs, right-click on Network Neighborhood and then choose Properties.

2. Make sure that both PCs have at least one network protocol in common (such as IPX/SPX-compatible Protocol).

   If not, click on the Add button to add a common protocol.

3. On the host PC, click on the File and Print Sharing button in the Network dialog box; make sure that the PC can share printers and files; and then choose OK.

4. On both PCs, click on the Identification tab in the Network dialog box; make sure that each PC has a unique computer name; make sure that both PCs have the same workgroup name; and choose OK to close the Network dialog box.

5. On both PCs, choose Start⇨Settings⇨Control Panel; double-click on the System icon; click on the Device Manager tab; and click on the plus sign (+) next to Ports (COM and LPT). Double-click on the icon for the port to which the cable is connected on this PC (COM1 or COM2), click on the Port Settings tab, and make sure that each port uses the same settings (Bits per second = same, Data Bits = 8, Parity = None, Stop Bits = 1, Flow Control = Xon/Xoff). Then close the Communications Port and System Properties dialog boxes on both PCs.

You can crank the baud rate (Bits per second) up to 115200 on both PCs to maximize the speed of transfers across the cable.

6. On the host PC, use My Computer to verify that the drives (or folders) and printers that you want to share have been shared (a little hand appears below the icon for a shared resource). If a resource that you want to share is not shared, right-click on that resource, click on Sharing, and share the resource.

7. On both PCs, close all open windows, and choose Start⇨Shut Down⇨Shut down the computer⇨Yes. When you're told that it's OK to do so, turn off each PC.

8. Make sure that the cable is properly connected to each PC, and make sure that you know which port each computer is using (COM1 or COM2). Losing track of which PC is using which port is a common (and very frustrating) mistake.

9. Power up both PCs again.

10. When you get to the Windows 95 desktop, try the connection again, as described in "Making the direct cable connection" earlier in this chapter.

If you still have problems, try using the Windows 95 Troubleshooter. Choose Start⇨Help, click on the Contents tab, double-click on the Troubleshooting book, and then double-click on If you have trouble using Direct Cable Connection.

Also check for and resolve any hardware conflicts, as described in "Using the Hardware Troubleshooter" and "Using Device Manager to Resolve Conflicts" in Chapter 10.

Dial-Up Networking

Dial-Up Networking enables you to connect to a PC via a modem. When you go on a trip, you can use Dial-Up Networking to access files that you left behind on your office or home PC. Dial-Up Networking requires the following:

✦ Both PCs must have a modem installed.

✦ Both PCs must display the Network Neighborhood icon on the Windows 95 desktop.

You don't use Dial-Up Networking to connect to a BBS (bulletin-board system), the Internet, or a commercial service such as CompuServe. Use the techniques described in Part VI of this book instead.

✦ Both PCs must have the Windows 95 Dial-Up Networking component installed.

✦ Unless Microsoft changes its plan, the PC that answers the phone must have Microsoft Plus! (Appendix F) installed so that it can be configured as a dial-up server.

✦ Any device that you want to access over the phone lines must be shared on the dial-up server PC.

✦ The PC that places the call must be configured as the dial-up client.

In the following sections, I'm going to assume that the first two items are taken care of on both PCs. If you haven't installed modems on both PCs, install them, following the directions in Chapter 15. If the Network Neighborhood icon isn't visible on the Windows 95 desktop, install it as described in "Installing Network Neighborhood" earlier in this chapter. Remember that both PCs must display the Network Neighborhood icon.

The theory behind Dial-Up Networking

Dial-Up Networking can be confusing if you don't understand the theory behind it. To illustrate the theory, I'll use an example from my home office. As you may recall, I keep all my current ongoing projects in one folder, named Projects, on one PC. I share that folder so that other PCs in my local area network (LAN) can have access to all the files in that folder. That way, regardless of which PC I happen to be sitting at, I always know that I'm working with the original files in the Projects folder. I don't need to be moving and copying files from one PC to another — a procedure that, as you may know, can be very confusing and subject to errors.

While I'm in the home office, my portable PC is connected to that LAN via a network card that lives in the PCMCIA slot, so my portable has all the resources of the LAN. Namely, I can access the Projects folder to work on current projects.

When I take the portable PC on the road, I can't take my network card with me, because it's connected to the LAN with cables. So when I open My Computer on my portable PC, I see what you see in Figure 20-6. The icon for drive P (the Projects folder on the Pentium PC) is marked out with an *X*. I don't have access to that shared folder, because I'm disconnected from my LAN.

The theory behind Dial-Up Networking is simple. While I'm traveling with my portable PC, I can use my modem to dial up the LAN that I left behind. As soon as the dial-up connection is made, I once again have access to any shared folders. In Figure 20-7, I've completed a dial-up connection. I have access to the shared Projects folder (P), so I can work with my original files even though I may be several thousand miles away. Notice that the icon for that drive no longer is marked out with an *X*.

Mind you, the modem and phone lines aren't as fast as LAN cables, so operations are a little slower. But slow access to my Projects folder (and any other shared resources) is better than no access.

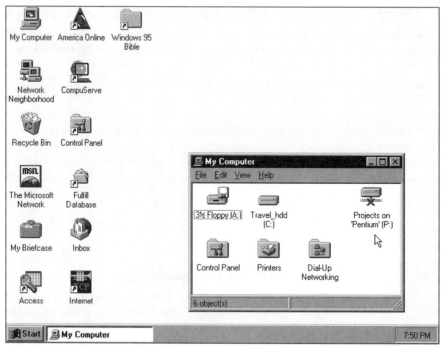

Figure 20-6: I can't use the Projects folder (P) when I'm disconnected from the LAN.

To make the original connection to the Projects folder, I chose <u>F</u>ile➪Map <u>N</u>etwork Drive in Network Neighborhood on the portable PC while the computer was physically connected to the LAN with a network card. Chapter 26 explains in detail how to map a drive letter to a shared folder.

I realize that some of you will want to use Dial-Up Networking to connect to an office PC from your portable, even if those PCs normally are not connected via a LAN at the office. If so, you need to know the Universal Naming Convention (UNC) for the resource to which you want to gain access. I'll explain how you determine that name when I show you how to share a resource on the dial-up server PC.

Installing Dial-Up Networking

To use Dial-Up Networking, both PCs must have the Dial-Up Networking component installed. If you're not sure whether that component has been installed, choose Start➪Programs➪Accessories. If you see an icon for Dial-Up Networking, the component is installed, and you don't need to reinstall it. Skip to the following section, "Configuring the dial-up server."

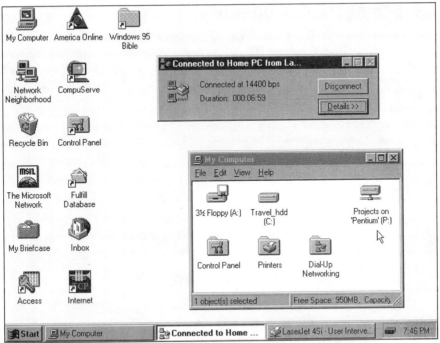

Figure 20-7: Dial-Up Networking gives me access to the shared folder.

To install the Dial-Up Networking component, follow these steps:

1. Gather up your original Windows 95 floppy disks or CD-ROM.

2. Choose Start⇨Settings⇨Control Panel.

3. Double-click on Add/Remove Programs.

4. Click on the Windows Setup tab.

5. Click on Communications.

6. Click on the Detail button.

7. Click on the Dial-Up Networking checkbox (so that it has a check mark).

8. Choose OK twice to begin the installation.

9. Follow the instructions on-screen.

You probably will need to restart the computer after Add/Remove Programs completes the installation. Don't forget that the Dial-Up Networking component needs to be available on both PCs.

Configuring the dial-up server

For some strange reason, Microsoft has been contemplating removing the dial-up server capability from Windows 95, and putting it into the Microsoft Plus! program. As I write this chapter, I'm still not certain if Plus! is required. If you don't see a Dial-Up Server option on the Connections menu when you get to Step 3 below, I guess that means you have to go out and purchase Microsoft Plus! (Don't blame me – it wasn't my idea.) Once you install Plus!, that Dial-Up Server option should be available as pictured in Figure 20-8 below. Anyway, when you're ready to set up the dial-up server (that is, the PC that will answer the phone), just follow these steps:

1. Double-click on My Computer.

2. Double-click on Dial-Up Networking.

   The Dial-Up Networking dialog box appears.

   If a wizard screen appears, click on Cancel to close it; the wizard isn't designed to help you set up the server.

3. Choose Connections⇨Dial-Up Server (see Figure 20-8).

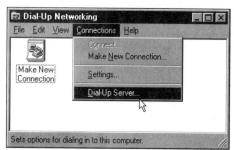

Figure 20-8: Ready to set up the dial-up server.

4. Click on Allow Caller Access.

   Optionally, click on Change Password and then enter a new password and confirmation. (Don't forget that password!)

   If you choose Allow Caller Access, the modem will answer all incoming calls to this phone number. If you want to channel voice calls to an answering machine or telephone, you need a sharing device. See the sidebar titled "So many gizmos, so few phone numbers" in Chapter 15.

5. Click on the Server Type button.

6. From the drop-down list, select PPP: Windows 95, Windows NT 3.5, Internet.

7. Set up the other options as shown in Figure 20-9.

8. Choose OK twice to return to the Dial-Up Networking dialog box.

9. Close that dialog box by clicking on its Close button.

Figure 20-9: Configuring the dial-up server.

 The Point-to-Point Protocol (PPP) for networking over phone lines is built right into Windows 95. You don't need any extra software to use PPP with Dial-Up Networking.

Remember that when you dial into the computer, you have access only to shared resources. In a moment, I'll show you how to access the entire hard disk of this PC while you're away. First, you need to set up the other PC, as described in the following section.

Configuring the dial-up client

Now you need to go to the portable PC (the dial-up client) and define the connection that you'll be making to the dial-up server (the PC that will answer the phone). Follow these steps:

1. Double-click on My Computer.

2. Double-click on Dial-Up Networking.

3. Double-click on the Make New Connection icon.

4. In the first wizard screen, enter a name for this connection (see Figure 20-10).

   If you have more than one modem installed, select that modem in the Select a modem drop-down list.

5. Click on Next.

6. Type the number that you'll use to phone the dial-up server's modem.

7. Click on Next to go to the last wizard screen.

8. Click on Finish.

   The Dial-Up Networking dialog box now includes an icon for the connection that you just defined (see Figure 20-11). Before you use it, however, you need to check some other settings.

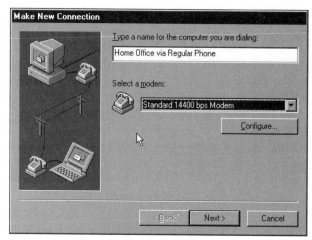

Figure 20-10: First screen of the Make New Connection wizard.

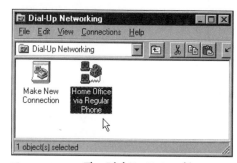

Figure 20-11: The Dial-Up Networking dialog box with some connections defined.

9. Right-click on the icon for the connection that you just created.

10. Click on Properties.

11. Click on the Server Type button.

12. In the Dial-Up Server drop-down list, select PPP: Windows 95, Windows NT 3.5, Internet.

13. Set the other options as shown in Figure 20-12.

14. Choose OK twice to save your settings.

15. Close the Dial-Up Networking dialog box.

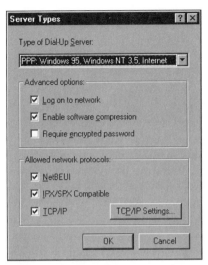

Figure 20-12: The dial-up client needs some information about the server that you'll be calling.

Everything is set up to make connections. Before you go anywhere, though, don't forget that you can connect only to shared resources while you're away. I've talked about this topic already, but a new issue, called Universal Naming Conventions, may come into play with Dial-Up Networking. The following section shows a new example of sharing a resource with Dial-Up Networking.

Sharing resources on the dial-up server

When you make a connection with Dial-Up Networking, you do not have free rein over the computer that you dialed into; you have access only to shared resources on that PC. So before you leave town, make sure that you have shared the resources that you'll need access to while you're away.

With Dial-Up Networking, you can't just browse the server and make connections on the fly. To connect to a shared resource while you're away, you may need to enter the UNC (Universal Naming Convention) for that resource. This section shows you how to share a resource on the dial-up server and how to determine that resource's UNC.

Suppose that you're going on a trip and want to have access to every file on the entire hard disk of the PC that you'll leave behind. You need to define that hard disk as a shared resource and also determine the UNC for that resource. Follow these steps:

1. On the dial-up server (the computer that you're leaving behind), right-click on the Network Neighborhood icon.

2. Click on P̲roperties.

3. Click on the Identification tab.

4. Write down the Computer n̲ame entry, preceded by two backslashes.

   The computer name of my PC is Office_pc, so I would write \\Office_pc.

5. Choose OK to close the Network dialog box.

6. Double-click on My Computer.

7. Right-click on the resource that you want to share.

8. Click on S̲haring.

9. Click on S̲hared As.

10. Type a name up to 15 characters long, with no spaces.

    I used Office_hdd (hdd is an abbreviation for hard disk drive).

11. Next to the computer name that you wrote down in Step 4, write the name that you entered in Step 10, preceded by one backslash.

    I would write \\Office_pc\Office_hdd.

    What you just wrote down is the UNC for the resource that you shared.

12. If you want to be able to read from and write to that drive while you're away, select F̲ull as the Access Type, as shown in Figure 20-13.

13. Choose OK.

    You return to My Computer, where you see a little hand below the icon for the item that you just shared. The share name that you assigned does not appear; the original local name stays intact. You use the share name when you access the shared resource from another PC.

Simply stated, the UNC for a device is *computer name**share name*. To find the computer name, right-click on Network Neighborhood, click on P̲roperties, and click on the Identification tab. To find a shared resource's share name, right-click on the icon for the shared resource and then click on S̲haring.

Of course, you can repeat Steps 7–13 to share other resources — for example, the entire CD-ROM drive, so that you have access to whatever CD-ROM is in that drive while you're away.

This example shows you how to give yourself access to an entire hard disk. But as you learn in Chapter 26, you can share individual folders instead. This procedure may be useful if you allow other people to dial into your PC and you want to limit the folders that those users can access.

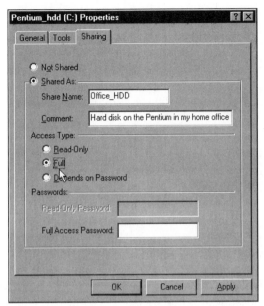

Figure 20-13: Giving myself full access to the hard disk that I'm leaving behind.

When you go on the road, don't forget to take the UNC that you jotted down; you may need it to connect to the shared resource when you dial in.

Making the dial-up connection

By the time you get to this section, you should have installed Dial-Up Networking on both the server (the PC that answers the phone) and the client (the portable PC). You also should have shared the resources that you need to have access to while you're away. Leave that PC running and its modem on, of course, so that the PC can answer the phone when you dial in. (You can turn off the monitor on the server, if you want.) Now you're far away with your portable PC, all hooked up to a modem and ready to dial out.

Follow these steps to make the connection:

1. Double-click on My Computer.

2. Double-click on the Dial-Up Networking icon.

3. Double-click on the icon for the connection that you defined for dialing in to your dial-up server.

   You can leave the Password box blank unless you assigned a password when you set up the dial-up server.

4. If you need to dial the area code, country code, or whatever from this location, click on the Dialing from button and/or the Dial Properties button to define where you're calling from.

5. Click on the Connect button.

You should see some activity on-screen and may hear the modem as your portable PC connects to the dial-up server. When you're connected, you see a message like the one shown in Figure 20-14.

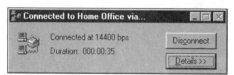

Figure 20-14: The dial-up connection to the home-office PC is successful.

If you go back to My Computer, any connections that you made previously via the LAN (or whatever) will be restored, as in the examples shown in Figures 20-6 and 20-7. If so, skip the rest of the steps and resume work normally. You are, for all intents and purposes, back on the LAN. (You just happen to be using a modem rather than a LAN card at the moment.)

6. If you need to connect to a shared resource, double-click on Network Neighborhood and wait for the Entire Network option to appear.

7. In Network Neighborhood's toolbar, click on the Map Network Drive button.

8. Select any available drive letter (I'll use D in this example).

9. In the Path box, type the UNC for the resource to which you want to connect.

In my example, I would type **Office_pc\Office_hdd**.

 When you're physically connected to your LAN with a network card, you can double-click on Entire Network to browse around the LAN. Dial-Up Networking doesn't support that capability, however, because the modem connection is too slow. For this reason, you need to know the UNC for the resource to which you want to connect.

10. Choose OK.

Most likely, a window for browsing that drive appears immediately, just as though that hard disk was part of the PC that you're using right now.

To see things from the My Computer perspective, you can close the browsing window that just opened (if any), and go back to the My Computer window. In that window, choose View⇨Refresh and perhaps View⇨Arrange Icons⇨By Drive Letter. You should see an icon for the shared drive.

Preflight checklist for Dial-Up Networking

When you're away from your dial-up server PC, you can't easily change any settings that you forgot to change before you left. You'll be high and dry until you get back unless someone at the home office can set everything up for you. Your best bet is to make the necessary changes on the PC that you'll be leaving behind. Check the following things:

✦ Make sure that you can get a dial tone on the PC that will be answering the phone. Start Phone Dialer (choose Start⇨Accessories⇨Phone Dialer), type any phone number, and click on Dial. If the modem can dial out, it can answer your incoming calls.

✦ Open My Computer, double-click on Dial-Up Networking, close the wizard, and choose Connections⇨

Dial-Up Server. Make that sure Allow Caller Access is selected. Check your password (if any) and server type (it should be PPP for dialing in from a Windows 95 client). Then choose OK twice.

✦ Use My Computer to make sure all the resources you'll need are shared; if they're not, be sure to share them before you go. Remember to write down the UNC names; you may need them on the road.

✦ Close all open windows, and leave the server PC running with just the Windows 95 desktop showing. You can turn off the monitor, if you want, but don't turn off the PC or modem.

Figure 20-15 shows an example in which I dialed in to my home-office PC. The My Computer window now shows an icon for the shared resource that I left at home: Office_hdd on 'Office PC' (D:).

While you're connected, you can treat that drive as though it really is a hard disk drive named D on your portable PC. To browse the shared drive, double-click on its icon in My Computer. To copy things to and from folders in that shared drive, select items and drag them to or from whatever folders you want. You can use the shared resource for as long as you want.

Disconnecting a dial-up connection

When you finish using a dial-up connection, you can click on the Disconnect button. To play it safe, though, I suggest that you go through the following ritual to make sure that you don't leave any unfinished work behind:

1. Save all work in progress.

2. Close all windows except the Connected To dialog box.

3. Click on the Disconnect button in the Connected To dialog box.

When you are disconnected, you can shut down the portable PC, if you want. All your work is safe and sound on whichever drive you stored it on.

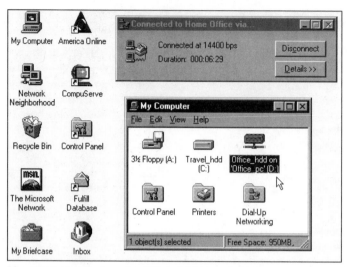

Figure 20-15: The icon for Office_hdd is available in My Computer during dial-up connection.

Disabling Dial-Up Networking

When you return from your trip, you may want the modem on the dial-up server to stop answering the phone. Follow these steps:

1. On the dial-up server, double-click on My Computer.

2. Double-click on the Dial-Up Networking icon.

3. If a wizard screen appears, click on Cancel to bypass it.

4. In Network Neighborhood, choose Connections⇨Dial-Up Server.

5. Select No Caller Access, as shown in Figure 20-16.

6. Choose OK.

7. Close the Dial-Up Networking dialog box.

After you perform these steps, nobody (including you) can dial in to the dial-up server. If you want to regain access to this PC on your next trip, remember to complete the entire procedure described in the "Preflight checklist for Dial-Up Networking" sidebar earlier in this chapter.

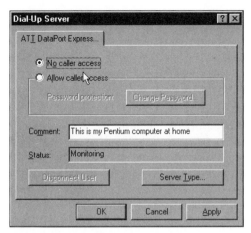

Figure 20-16: Modem won't answer incoming calls anymore.

Troubleshooting Dial-Up Networking

Many factors go into Dial-Up Networking — which, unfortunately, means that many little things can go wrong and make the whole thing unworkable. If you have two phone lines in your office, I strongly suggest that you plug the dial-up server into one line and the portable PC into the other. Then dial the server from the portable right there in the office. That way, you'll have access to both PCs while you troubleshoot.

Following are some basic troubleshooting tips for Dial-Up Networking:

✦ If you didn't complete the checklist on the server, you can do absolutely nothing until you get back to the server and prepare it to answer the phone and share resources.

✦ If you're on the road, make sure that you're using the correct dialing properties. See Chapter 15 for more information on that topic.

✦ If you're sure that the server is prepared but you still can't connect from the client, try using the Windows 95 Troubleshooter. Choose Start⇨Help, click on the Contents tab, double-click on the Troubleshooting book, and select If you have trouble using Dial-Up Networking.

If you can't solve the problem through these means, try the following procedures when both computers are within immediate reach:

✦ On both PCs, right-click on Network Neighborhood, and click on Properties. Make sure that both PCs have at least one network protocol in common (for example, IPX/SPX-compatible Protocol); if not, click on the Add button to add a common protocol.

✦ On the host PC, click on the File and Print Sharing button in the Network dialog box. Make sure that this PC can share printers and files. Then choose OK.

✦ On both PCs, click on the Identification tab of the Network dialog box. Make sure that each PC has a unique computer name and that both PCs have the same workgroup name. Then click on the OK button to close the Network dialog box.

✦ On both PCs, choose Start⇨Settings⇨Control Panel, double-click on the Modems icon, and make sure that the modem is installed properly. See Chapter 15 for more information on installing modems and setting up your dialing properties.

Dialing into non-Windows 95 servers

Throughout this chapter, I assume that both the dial-up client and the server (the one that answers the phone) are using Windows 95. A Windows 95 dial-up client can, however, dial in to any of the following:

✦ Windows for Workgroups Version 3.11 RAS (Remote Access Services)

✦ Windows NT 3.5

✦ Windows NT 3.1 with RAS protocol

✦ Novell NetWare connect server

✦ Shiva LanRover or NetModem/E remote access servers

Techniques for setting up both the server and the client for these other operating systems are included in the *Windows 95 Resource Kit*, published by Microsoft Press ((800) MS-PRESS). I don't want to repeat all that information here, because if you're working in an environment that supports those systems, you probably need that resource kit anyway. The book is written specifically for corporate users and others who have a large investment in big-time legacy hardware and software.

You also can find more information on Dial-Up Networking in the help screens. For the broadest selection of topics, choose Start⇨Help, click on the Find tab, and search for *dial-up*.

Summary

Dial-Up Networking and direct cable connection let you share resources on two PCs without fumbling with floppy disks. To recap:

✦ Both direct cable and dial-up connections require that both PCs in the LAN have Network Neighborhood installed.

✦ In direct-cable connection, the PC that has the resources to share is called the host. The PC that wants access to those resources is called the guest.

✦ In Dial-Up Networking, the PC that has the resources and answers the phone is called the *dial-up server*. The PC that dials in is called the *dial-up client*.

✦ The guest or client PC can gain access to *shared resources* on the host/server PC only.

✦ In Dial-Up Networking, it's important to share resources on the server *before* you leave town. Otherwise, you won't be able to get at those resources while you're on the road.

✦   ✦   ✦

Hopping On the Info Superhighway

Cruising the Microsoft Network (MSN)

This chapter describes the Microsoft Network (MSN), Microsoft's entry into the online services arena.

What Is MSN?

Physically, the Microsoft Network (MSN) is a huge room that's stacked to the ceiling with dozens and dozens of Pentium computers, all hooked together to act like one huge computer. That room in turn is connected to a veritable phone company that's capable of managing a zillion telephone calls at a time. Although I haven't actually seen all this myself, I hear it's quite a sight.

From our perspective, MSN is a place to ask questions, mingle with people of similar interests, meet celebrities, catch up on the news, and send documents to one another. Access to MSN is built into Windows 95, so getting onto the service is a matter of double-clicking on some icons and forking over your credit-card number. (I didn't say the service was free.) The billing rates, terms, and conditions are explained on-screen when you sign up for an account.

When you're connected, you'll find that most of MSN is organized like the rest of Windows 95, with folders and icons. As you cruise MSN, you'll come across the following kinds of services:

✦ *Bulletin boards.* Bulletin boards (BBSs) offer discussions and postings of recent information from specific companies that act as *content providers.*

✦ *Chat rooms.* Chat rooms offer online conversations with other users, as well as special events featuring celebrities and captains of industry.

✦ *File libraries.* These libraries contain freeware and shareware programs, add-in utilities, and drivers that you can download (copy) to your own PC.

✦ *Electronic mail (e-mail).* You can send e-mail messages to anyone else on MSN, and those people can send messages to you. E-mail is especially good for mobile computing, because you can pick up your messages from wherever you happen to be at the moment.

✦ *Internet access.* You can access the Internet's worldwide e-mail system and newsgroups.

You may find all or some of these services within a single topic area, be it art, business, games, or whatever. Figure 21-1 shows an example of the Computer Games folder on MSN.

Figure 21-1: The Computer Games folder on MSN.

Establishing An Account

Before you can use MSN, you need to establish an account. Before you do that, however, do the following:

✦ If you haven't already done so, install a modem, as described in Chapter 15.

✦ Think up a member ID (also called an *alias*) that will identify you to other users on the network. No spaces are allowed. You can use your real name with no spaces (for example, *WilmaWangdoodle*). If you want to be anonymous, make up a "handle," such as *WildWoman* or *Godzilla_Breath*.

✦ Think up a password for logging in, and keep it secret to prevent other people from logging in under your user ID. The password can be up to 15 characters long, with no spaces. If you have a universal password for all your PC access, you can use that password.

✦ Grab your local phone book, and find the page that tells you which prefixes you can dial for free.

✦ Grab a credit card.

To establish your account, follow these steps:

1. Double-click on the MSN icon (titled The Microsoft Network) on your desktop..

   Alternatively, choose @Start⇨Programs⇨Microsoft Network.

    If you can't find an icon for the Microsoft Network, first choose Start⇨Programs⇨Accessories⇨Online Registration. If that procedure doesn't work, you need to install the Microsoft Network from Windows Setup in Add/Remove Programs. See Chapter 9.

2. Follow the instructions on-screen to set up your account and to choose a phone number for dialing in.

    If possible, choose a phone number with a prefix that you can dial for free.

You need to establish an account only one time. After you complete the necessary steps, you can log in at any time by following the steps in the next section.

Getting in to MSN

When you have an account with MSN, logging in to the service is kind of a no-brainer. Follow these steps:

1. Double-click on the MSN icon on the desktop.

   The Sign In dialog box appears (see Figure 21-2).

2. Type in your member ID and password.

   If you don't share your PC with other people and aren't concerned that other people will log in under your member ID, you can check the Remember my password option so that you don't have to type the password every time you log on.

3. If you're calling from someplace other than your normal location, or if you're using a different modem (such as your cellular modem), click on the Settings button, and then select the local Access Number, Dial Helper, and Modem Settings that are appropriate for your current situation.

Figure 21-2: The Microsoft Network Sign In dialog box.

4. Click on the Connect button, and wait for the connection.

5. If any instructions appear on-screen, follow them.

If you have any new mail waiting, a message informs you of this fact. Click on Yes to check your mail now or No to check it later. If you choose Yes, Microsoft Exchange starts; then you can double-click on any message that you want to read. (Microsoft Exchange is a central repository for all incoming and outgoing messages and faxes, as you'll learn in Chapter 30.) When you finish reading your mail, you can close the Inbox and access the other features of MSN.

When you're connected, a small MSN indicator appears in the taskbar, most likely near the lower-right corner of your screen. That indicator stays there as long as you're connected. You can right-click on the indicator to jump to someplace special within MSN.

Getting Around MSN

The Microsoft Network is sort of an extension to Windows 95. The MSN interface has the same elements as the desktop: toolbars, shortcuts, command buttons, menus, and a Close (X) button in the upper-right corner of windows. When you first log on, you probably will see MSN Today and MSN Central (see Figure 21-3).

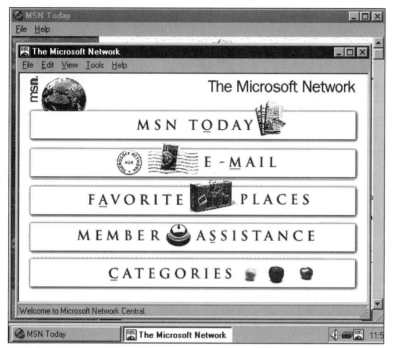

Figure 21-3: MSN Central (front window) and MSN Today.

The following are the basic skills that you need to go exploring:

✦ To go someplace that looks interesting, click on its name or button, or double-click on its shortcut icon.

✦ If you feel stuck at any point, click on Member Assistance, The MSN Lobby, or the Go To MSN Central button (whichever is available at the moment) to display more options.

✦ While you're connected to MSN, you can right-click on the MSN indicator in the taskbar (near the lower-right corner of your screen), and choose a destination from the pop-up menu that appears.

 Toolbars are useful in MSN. If you don't see a toolbar in the current window, choose View➪Toolbar (if available).

✦ To exit, click on the window's Close (X) button; or the Up One Level button in the toolbar.

✦ To exit a series of windows, hold down the Shift key and click on the Close button of the last window you opened.

✦ If you find a place that you want to revisit later, click on the Add to Favorite Places button in the toolbar.

✦ To return to a place that you sent to Favorite Places, click on the Go To Favorite Places button in any toolbar, in MSN Central, or in the pop-up menu that appears when you right-click on the MSN button in the taskbar.

Using Find on MSN

The basic skills listed in the preceding section get you on the path to discovering what's available in MSN. If you have a specific goal in mind, you can use Find. Choose Tools⇨Find⇨On The Microsoft Network in any window that offers a Tools menu. Alternatively, click on Start⇨Find⇨On The Microsoft Network. Then fill in the blanks as instructed on-screen. In Figure 21-4, I typed **chat** as the topic that I want to look up.

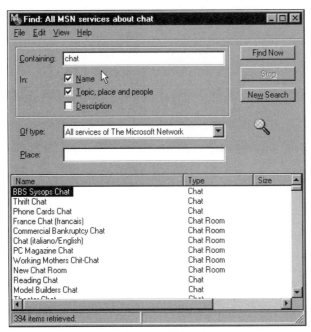

Figure 21-4: Using Find to search for chat rooms.

After clicking on Find Now, I see a long list of chat rooms. I can double-click on one of those rooms to go there. Notice that Find in MSN works much like Find on the desktop (refer to Chapter 2) — that is, searches are cumulative unless you click on New Search to cancel the preceding search.

When Find locates all the topics for the word(s) that you searched for, you can click on Name at the top of the column to alphabetize the list.

What's with the fade-in pictures?

You may notice that when you get into MSN, certain pictures (especially photos) appear to be terribly out of focus. But if you wait, the picture sort of fades in and becomes clear. The reason is that sending a picture from one PC to another over telephone lines takes a long time. Telephone lines were, after all, invented to transport voices, not pictures. So MSN sends a little bit of the picture at a time.

The advantage to you is that if you don't feel like waiting around to see a picture, you don't have to. Just go about your business and forget about the picture. As soon as you jump to another window, MSN stops spending time and resources getting the picture to you.

Using MSN E-Mail

The Microsoft Network's e-mail service is tightly integrated with Microsoft Exchange, which means that all your messages coming from MSN are listed along with your incoming faxes and local e-mail. In addition, you can compose new messages within Exchange and then use your Personal Phone Book or the MSN Phone Book to address those messages.

Creating an MSN e-mail message

Suppose that you want to write an e-mail message to someone else on MSN. Follow these steps:

1. If you haven't already done so, connect to MSN.

2. Right-click on the little MSN indicator in the taskbar, and choose <u>S</u>end Mail.

Hot Stuff

To reply to a message that you've received, click on the Reply to Sender button in Microsoft Exchange's toolbar.

3. In the T<u>o</u> box, type the recipient's name.

Alternatively, click on the T<u>o</u> button, and choose a name from your Personal Address Book. Within the Address Book, choose Microsoft Network from the <u>S</u>how Names drop-down list. Then, where indicated, start typing the name of the person to whom you want to send the message so that you can jump to that part of the list (see Figure 21-5).

4. If you want to send the same message to several people, select the appropriate names from the list, or type the names, separated by semicolons (;).

5. Type a brief subject (to appear in the recipient's Inbox) and the main body of your message.

Figure 21-6 shows an example.

6. Click on the Send button in Exchange's toolbar, or choose File⇨Send.

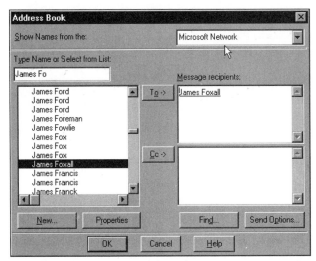

Figure 21-5: Looking up a name in the Microsoft Network Address Book.

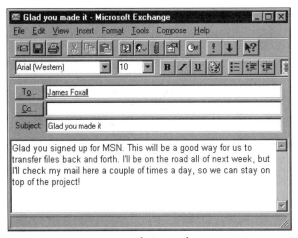

Figure 21-6: Message ready to send.

Your message is sent immediately and appears in the recipient's Inbox the next time he or she opens Microsoft Exchange. If you want to verify that the message has been sent, turn on the folder list in Microsoft Exchange (click on the Show/Hide Folder List or choose View⇨Folders); then select the Sent Items folder. If your message isn't listed there, click on the Outbox folder; click on your message; and choose Tools⇨Deliver Now.

Sending a file via MSN

If you want to send a document to someone on MSN, you can attach it to a message by completing the steps in the preceding section. But before you send your message, click on the Insert File button in Exchange's toolbar or choose Insert⇨File. In the Look In drop-down list, browse to the drive, folder, and file name of the document that you want to send. Then double-click on the document's file name. The file appears as an icon in your message, as shown in Figure 21-7. The recipient simply double-clicks on that icon to open the attached file.

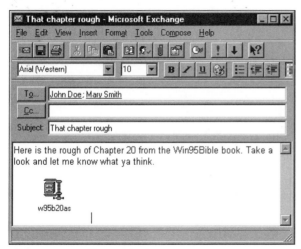

Figure 21-7: A file attached to a message appears as an icon.

In Exchange's Inbox, messages marked with a little paper-clip icon are the ones that contain attached files.

Sending a message to other services

When you want to send an e-mail message to someone who isn't on MSN, you can use that person's Internet, CompuServe, America Online, or Prodigy account. Compose your message normally within MSN and Microsoft Exchange. In the To box, address the message, using the appropriate format listed in Table 21-1.

Table 21-1
Formats for Addressing Messages to Other Services

Service	Format of To Address	Example
America Online	*username*@aol.com	SimpsonAC@aol.com
CompuServe	*nnnnn.nnnn*@compuserve.com	72420.2236@compuserve.com
Internet	*username*@*domainname*	alan@coolnerds.com
Prodigy	*userID*@prodigy.com	JohnDoe@prodigy.com

Notice in Table 21-1 that when you type a CompuServe ID, you use a period (.) where you normally would type a comma. If you forget that period, your message won't be delivered.

Should you ever need a reminder on how to address a message to another service, choose Help⇨The Microsoft Network Help within Exchange and then use the Index tab to search for the service you're interested in (America Online, CompuServe, Internet, or Prodigy).

Your new e-mail address

If you want someone to send you an e-mail message from MSN, that person needs to look up your name in the Microsoft Network Address Book. You also have an Internet address now; that address is your user ID followed by @msn.com. If your user ID in MSN is WildWoman, for example, your Internet address would be wildwoman@msn.com.

A person who sends you mail from the Internet or America Online uses that address. A person who sends you e-mail from CompuServe uses that service's standard Internet addressing scheme (INTERNET:WildWoman@msn.com). Regardless of where the sender sends the message from, it ends up in your Microsoft Exchange Inbox.

MSN and the Internet

While we're on the topic of the Internet, I should point out that MSN offers access to Internet e-mail as well as to the popular Internet newsgroups. But more features are coming down the pike. By the time you read this book, MSN may offer even more ways to access the Internet.

Microsoft Plus! (see Appendix F) includes Internet Explorer, which gives you access to the World Wide Web and FTP, right from your MSN account.

Rather than guess how things will pan out in this arena, I'll just tell you how to find the latest information on accessing the Internet from Microsoft Network. Follow these steps:

1. Choose Start⇨Find⇨On the Microsoft Network.

2. Type **internet**.

3. Click on Find Now.

   After a minute or so, the bottom of the Find dialog box lists all kinds of Internet-related topics (see Figure 21-8). You can click on the Name button at the top of the list to alphabetize the topics. To read a topic, double-click on it.

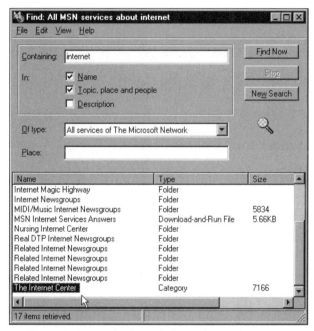

Figure 21-8: To get the latest information on MSN Internet access, search for *internet.*

If you want to get totally wired into the Net, see the next chapter for information about getting direct access to the Internet.

Creating MSN Shortcuts

One of MSN's best features is its capability to create shortcuts. Just as you can create a shortcut to any file, folder, or program on your PC (refer to Chapter 4), you can create a shortcut to any place on MSN. Shortcuts are really great, because you sometimes find something that you want to share with other people, but forgot how you got there. No problem — just drag an icon to that place on your desktop, or drag the icon into an e-mail message to whomever you want to share your discovery with.

The Favorite Places described earlier are shortcuts, in a sense, but they're accessible only from the Favorite Places area of MSN. The shortcuts that I describe in this section can go right on your desktop or into e-mail messages that you send to someone else.

Suppose that you're on MSN, and you come to some place that you want to be able to find again easily and/or share with other users. Follow these steps:

1. If you're in the area to which you want to create a shortcut, click on the Up One Level button in the toolbar, or choose File⇨Up One Level.

   Now you see the icon that took you to where you are.

2. Move and size windows so that you can see any portion of the Windows 95 desktop.

3. Drag the icon to your desktop.

Figure 21-9 shows an example in which I dragged the icon for the Computer Games File Library file from its folder in MSN to my desktop.

Figure 21-9: Desktop shortcut to the Computer Games File Library on MSN.

If you want to send a shortcut to someone else, you can drag it from its original location or drag a copy of the shortcut from your desktop to an e-mail message. In Figure 21-10, I created an e-mail message by right-clicking on the MSN indicator in the taskbar and choosing Send Mail. Then I addressed and typed the message normally. Finally, I dragged the Shortcut to Computer Games File Library icon from my desktop into the body of the message.

Figure 21-10: MSN shortcut dragged into an e-mail message.

Now I can send that message, using the usual techniques. When the recipient gets the message, he or she can double-click on the shortcut icon to go right to the Computer Games File Library on MSN or drag that icon to his or her desktop to create a permanent shortcut.

Downloading Files from MSN

You can download programs and other files from any MSN file library or BBS. *Downloading* means copying something from the host PC (MSN) "down" to your personal computer. (*Uploading* means the opposite: copying something from your PC "up" to the host PC.)

I've also put shareware copies of WinZip and PKZIP on the companion CD-ROM in the back of this book.

This section demonstrates how to download a file named WinZip for Windows 95. (You can use the steps to download any file from MSN.) Suppose that you have cruised through Categories to Computers and Software to Computer Games to Computer Games File Library to Utilities. You find WinZip for Win95 & NT near the top of the list shown in Figure 21-11.

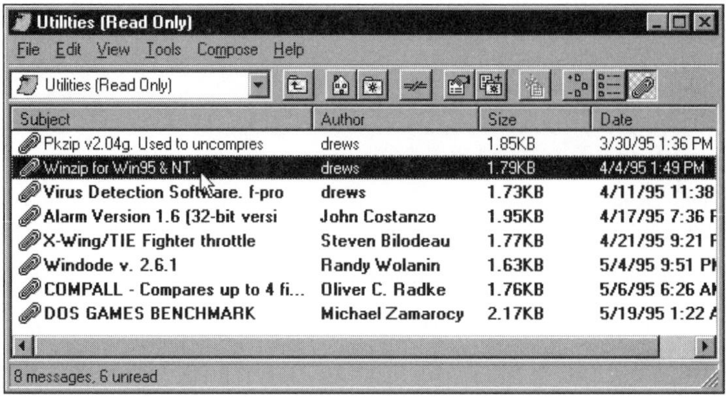

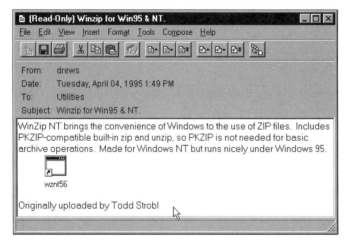

Figure 21-11: You want to download the second file to your own PC.

To download that file to your own PC, follow these steps:

1. Choose View⇨Attached Files to limit the list to files that you can download.

2. Double-click on the name of the file that you want to download.

   You should see some instructions and an icon for the file that you want to download, as shown in Figure 21-12. If you want to print the instructions, click on the Print button in the toolbar.

Figure 21-12: After double-clicking on the Winzip for Win95 & NT message.

3. Click on the icon for the file that you want to download.

   A border appears around the icon to indicate that you selected it.

4. Choose File⇨Save.

5. Click on the Attachments radio button.

6. In the Folders section, browse to the drive and folder on your own PC where you want to save the file.

   In Figure 21-13, I chose a folder named Zippers on my drive C.

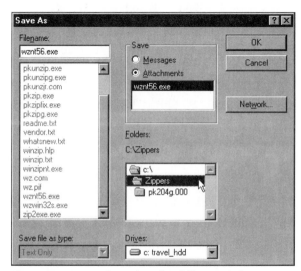

Figure 21-13: Ready to download file to C:\Zippers.

7. Choose OK.

   The File Transfer Status dialog box appears. The odometer and timer at the bottom of that dialog box indicate how long the transfer will take.

You need not wait for the entire transfer; you can minimize that window and go about your business. Just remember not to disconnect from MSN until all the downloads are completed. The little modem indicator probably will flash red and green while the download is in progress. To check the progress of the download at any time, click on the File Transfer Status button in the taskbar.

 More Info If you need a reminder on how to copy a file to your PC, search MSN's help system for *download*.

Dealing with Zipped Files

Files on information services such as MSN often are compressed, or *zipped*. Files are zipped for two reasons: the sender can combine many files in one zipped file, and a zipped file is compressed to speed its transfer over phone lines. When you download a zipped file to your own PC, you can get several files in one comparatively brief transfer.

The catch, of course, is that the downloaded zipped file is useless until you decompress it. Exactly how you decompress depends on the format of the zipped file. The two most likely formats are .EXE and .ZIP (based on the extensions assigned to the file names). The following list explains the difference:

✦ *.EXE.* If a compressed file is self-extracting, it has the .EXE file extension. To decompress this type of file, you must run the .EXE file just as you would run any other program. Choose Start⇨Run, and browse to the .EXE file.

✦ *.ZIP.* These files are not self-extracting. You must have — and know how to use — an unzipping utility such as WinZip.

The latter files are a bit of a problem if you don't own and know how to use an unzipping utility. Unfortunately, I can give you only rough instructions, because WinZip is a third-party shareware program, and could change by the time you read this book. In general, most people get an unzipping utility such as WinZip by downloading a copy from an information service. (I used the downloading of WinZip as the example in "Downloading Files from MSN" earlier in this chapter.)

 If you have a CD-ROM drive, you can get WinZip and PKZIP shareware from the companion CD-ROM in the back of this book.

I can't even say for certain where you'll find WinZip; the owners of BBSs are free to organize and reorganize files however they want. But I will tell you where I found the copy that I used in the MSN example. Starting at MSN Central, I used the following buttons and icons, in this order:

Categories⇨Computers and Software⇨Computer Game⇨Computer Games File Library⇨Utilities folder

WinZip itself usually is stored as a self-extracting (.EXE) file. After you download the file to your PC, you need to run that .EXE file and then follow the instructions on-screen to decompress it. Then you can open the file named ReadMe on the floppy disk for installation instructions.

 When you get WinZip running on your PC, you can press F1 to get help information for it.

After you successfully install WinZip, you can launch the program by choosing Start⇨Programs⇨WinZip⇨WinZip for Windows (or whatever it's called). Typically, you see a sign-on screen; then WinZip starts on your PC.

To unzip a .ZIP file, use My Computer, Find, or Windows Explorer to get to the icon for the .ZIP file, and then drag that file into the WinZip window. You see the names of the files that are inside the zipped file. In Figure 21-14, I used Find to locate a .ZIP file and then dragged that file into the WinZip window. The README.TXT and RNASERV.DLL files shown inside WinZip's window are the compressed files inside RNA456.ZIP.

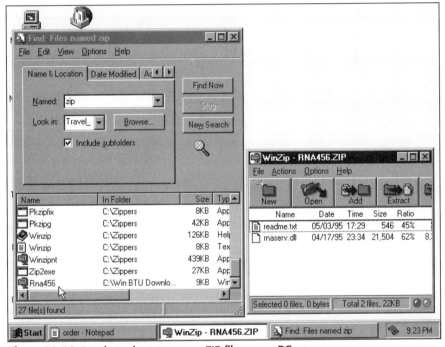

Figure 21-14: Ready to decompress a .ZIP file on my PC.

To decompress the files, I would click on the Extract button in WinZip's toolbar, select a destination, and then click on Extract again. The extracted files would reside in whatever folder I specified after clicking on Extract, and would be normal (uncompressed) files.

To compress files, you do pretty much the same thing. Use My Computer, Find, or Windows Explorer to get to the files that you want to compress. Press Ctrl+click or Shift+click to select those files, run WinZip, and drag the selected files into the WinZip window. Click on the New button, type a folder and file name for the .ZIP file, and then click on Add to put the files into the .ZIP file. When WinZip finishes, you can attach that .ZIP file to any e-mail message that you send.

As mentioned earlier, I can give only rough instructions here. By the time you read this book, a completely new and different WinZip 95 may be available from MSN. Keep in mind that after you get WinZip running, you can press the F1 key for help at any time.

Disconnecting from MSN

As long as you see the MSN indicator in the taskbar, you're connected to MSN. (You may be racking up connect time and Ma Bell charges until you disconnect.) To disconnect from MSN, do any of the following things:

✦ Right-click on the MSN indicator in the taskbar, and choose Sign Out.

✦ Click on the Sign Out button in any MSN toolbar.

✦ Choose File➪Sign Out in any MSN window.

You'll be given an opportunity to change your mind. Click on the Yes button to sign off and disconnect from MSN.

Summary

Microsoft Network (MSN) is a great online service for newbies and experienced Internauts alike. Here are some salient points to mull over:

✦ Before you can connect to MSN, you need to install a modem, as discussed in Chapter 15.

✦ Your first trek into MSN requires that you establish an account. Grab a credit card, click the Start button, choose Programs➪The Microsoft Network. Follow the on-screen instructions that appear.

✦ While you're connected to MSN, a tiny MSN indicator appears in the taskbar (perhaps to remind you that you're spending money!).

✦ If you get lost in MSN, just right-click the tiny MSN indicator in the taskbar and choose a more familiar location.

✦ To create and send an e-mail message in MSN, right-click the MSN indicator in the Taskbar and choose Send Mail.

✦ Establishing an MSN account automatically gives you an Internet e-mail address — your Member ID followed my @msn.com.

✦ To disconnect from MSN, right-click the MSN indicator and choose Sign Out.

✦ To fully explore and use the Internet from your MSN account, consider purchasing Microsoft Plus!, discussed in Appendix F.

✦   ✦   ✦

Hooking into Cyberspace (the Internet)

You have no doubt at least heard of the Internet. Everybody's talking about it, and millions of people are "doing it." If you're not quite sure what the Internet is, let me just say that it's a huge network of computer networks spanning the globe. About 30 to 40 million people have access to the Internet, and for some the access is even free of charge. You may have to pay an Internet Service Provider (ISP) to keep you connected, and if you can't get a local dial-in number, you may have to pay Ma Bell for the phone time. But no per-unit charge applies for sending e-mail or downloading most files. So while you're on it, most of the Internet itself is free of charge.

How the Internet came to be is an interesting story in itself. The Net started back in the Cold War days, when the U.S. government was concerned that someone might drop a bomb in some strategic location and wipe out the desperately needed communications capabilities of the Department of Defense computers. The DoD wanted to set up a network of computers that was not dependent on any single computer. If a message needed to get from Washington, D.C., to California, for example, it had to get there, no matter how many computers in the link were down. The message had to reach its destination; finding a way to get the message through was up to the computers. That scheme was known as *dynamic rerouting*. If the computers in Denver were down, the message would have to be routed through whatever computers in a different region were available.

The research paid off. Now, 20 years later, with the threats of the Cold War waning and the popularity of personal computers growing, opening this taxpayer-created network to the people who paid for it — the tax-paying public — made sense. And this network *is* open — a huge worldwide network of computers that can talk to one another, with nobody in charge and no central committee governing what can and cannot be done. The Internet really is cyberspace in the sense that it's a wide-open frontier with a life of its own, governed by nature (human nature, that is) rather than by people; it's uncensored, unedited, and uncontrolled . . . so far, anyway. Jumping into the Net is always an adventure, because you never know what you'll find next.

Microsoft Plus! provides Internet Explorer, which gives you access to a wide range of Internet Features, using Microsoft Network (MSN) as your Internet Service Provider. For more information on Microsoft Plus!, see Appendix F.

Getting on the Net

Most of the major online services, including the Microsoft Network (MSN), CompuServe, and America Online, require only four things: a PC, a modem, an account, and a program for interacting with the service. Accessing the Internet also requires those four things, as well as an Internet Service Provider (ISP). An ISP is a company that provides the service of connecting PCs to the Internet.

You already may have an ISP via your company or school. Following are the possibilities:

✦ If you're connected to MSN, America Online, CompuServe, or just about any other commercial service, that service can act as an ISP for Internet e-mail and perhaps for some other Internet services. Check with that service for information on Internet access.

✦ If you work for an organization that already has Internet access, your company is, in essence, your ISP. Just ask your local Internet guru to set you up with a connection to the Net.

✦ You can go to your local computer store and buy an "Internet-in-a-box" product that comes with ready-to-go access. Your ISP likely will be a national company with an 800 number that you can dial to get on to the Internet toll-free.

✦ You can establish an account with a local ISP to get direct PPP (Point-to-Point Protocol) connection to all (or at least most of) the Internet's services.

The first three methods of connecting to the Internet are by far the easiest. You just need to search your existing information service for information on the Internet, have your local Internet guru get you connected, or follow the directions that came with the kit. After you're connected, you can explore to your heart's content, interact with newsgroups, and use the e-mail service. If you're just getting started with the Internet, I suggest that you take one of these approaches, because they give you the quickest, easiest, and least expensive access.

Internet on the road

If you're a mobile computerist who needs Internet access from wherever you happen to be at the moment, consider getting an access provider that offers toll-free or local-number access. You'll still have to pay for connect time, but you won't be racking up big bills with Ma Bell. Following are some possible sources (the numbers given are regular voice lines):

Alternet: (800) 258-4035

CERFnet: (800) 876-2373

Computer Witchcraft (WinNET Mail): (800) 589-5999

Netcom Online Communications Services: (800) 501-8649

Performance System International's InterRamp: (800) 827-7482

After you're on the Net, you may want to check out a couple of mobile-computing sites:

Mobile Planet (http://www.mplanet.com)

Mobile Office Magazine (http://www/mobileoffice.com).

Cruising the Internet

When you're able to access the Internet, you need certain Internet programs to take advantage of its features. The following sections talk about the most popular Internet features and the kinds of programs that you need to access those features. If you're going through an online service such as MSN, CompuServe, or America Online, however, some of these features may not be available to you.

Dial-up access

The first step in cruising the Internet is making your modem connection. You should already have set up some kind of account so that you can dial in. If you're using a kit or an Internet Service Provider, you have been provided with a dial-up program.

I use a shareware program called Trumpet Winsock to connect to my ISP, which in turn connects me to the Internet. All I do is double-click on an icon. The modem dials in; I hear some phone noise; and a message appears, telling me that I'm connected. The Trumpet Winsock program shrinks to a button in the taskbar. That button is my clue that I'm hooked into the Internet and now can use any of the Internet programs available on my system.

Using Internet e-mail

If you use your MSN account as your Internet e-mail address, all your Internet mail comes in through Microsoft Exchange. Likewise, if you use a CompuServe or America Online account as your Internet address, your mail will come in via that service.

If you set up your own Internet account, you need to get hold of an e-mail program to send and receive messages. In this section, I demonstrate a shareware program named Eudora. When I want to check my e-mail or send some out, I open my Eudora program (see Figure 22-1). Notice the Trumpet Winsock button in the taskbar, which tells me that I'm connected to the Net.

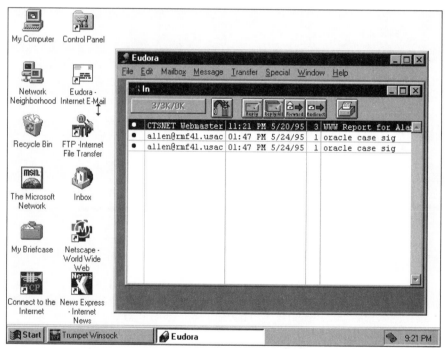

Figure 22-1: Eudora is one of many Internet e-mail programs.

When I have Eudora up and running, sending and receiving messages is a breeze. To check unread mail, I choose File⇨Check Mail. To create and send e-mail, I choose Message⇨New Message, type my message, and type the recipient's e-mail address (for example, **homer@simpson.com**).

I can do many other neat things with Eudora, but I won't get into them here because you may well be using a different e-mail program. When I finish with e-mail, I exit Eudora. Doing so does not disconnect me from the Internet, so I can use my other programs without logging back in.

Using Internet FTP

FTP is an acronym for *file transfer protocol*. I use my FTP program to upload files from my computer to another computer or to download files from another computer to my computer. Suppose that I learn that Microsoft Corporation has many files available for downloading via FTP, including a written index of all those files. Following is the information that I have:

✦ Microsoft's FTP address (`ftp.microsoft.com`)

✦ File that I want to download (`/Softlib/index.txt`)

To download that file, I start my FTP program and tell it to connect to `ftp.microsoft.com` (see Figure 22-2). FTP makes the connection, and after a couple of minutes, I see a list of directory names at `ftp.microsoft.com`. I double-click on the Softlib directory name, and — lo and behold — I find the INDEX.TXT file that I'm looking for (see Figure 22-3).

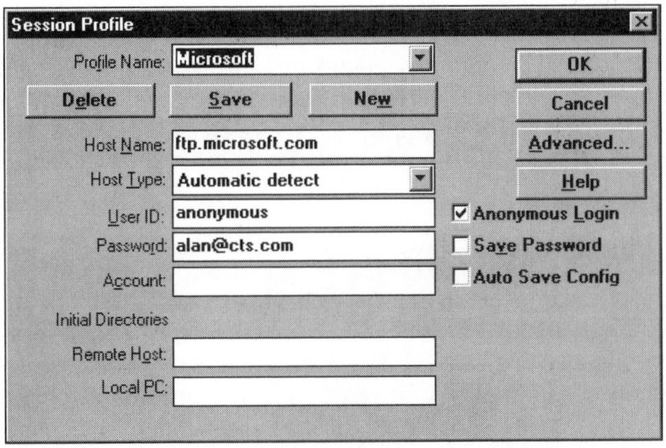

Figure 22-2: Getting ready to connect to ftp.microsoft.com.

I simply double-click on the name of the file that I want to download and wait for the progress meter that appears to tell me that the download is complete. Then I can download other files, explore other FTP sites, or close my FTP program.

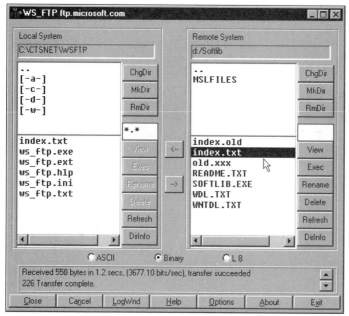

Figure 22-3: Connected to ftp.microsoft.com (displayed in the title bar).

FTP's only weakness is that it's not particularly glamorous. After you're connected to the remote computer, you have to use a DOS-like interface to navigate through directories and files. If you're looking for ease of use and a pretty interface, the World Wide Web will be your favorite Internet browsing tool.

Using the World Wide Web

The World Wide Web (WWW) is an extremely popular and easy-to-use feature of the Internet. The Web basically is a worldwide collection of documents, cross-referenced by means of *hypertext links*. To use the World Wide Web, you need a *Web browser* in addition to your Internet account. Many Web browsers are available — perhaps the best-known being Mosaic and Netscape Navigator. Most likely, your ISP will provide a Web browser when you sign up for your account.

The Internet Explorer that comes with Microsoft Plus! provides easy access to the Internet's World Wide Web and FTP sites, right from your MSN account. See Appendix F for more information.

To view a document on the Web, you open your Web browser and connect to the appropriate URL (*Universal Resource Locator*). Suppose that everyone tells me that if I'm just getting started on the Web, the Global Network Navigator (GNN) is a good place to start. The URL for GNN is `http://gnn.com/gnn/gnn.html` — not the kind of address one is likely to remember off the top of one's head!

After you get on the World Wide Web, you can point and click your way from one place to another without knowing the URLs. Nonetheless, I have to start somewhere. So I fire up my Web browser (Netscape Navigator, in this example) and type the URL next to the Go to: prompt. After I press Enter and wait a couple of minutes, I see GNN's *home page*, shown in Figure 22-4.

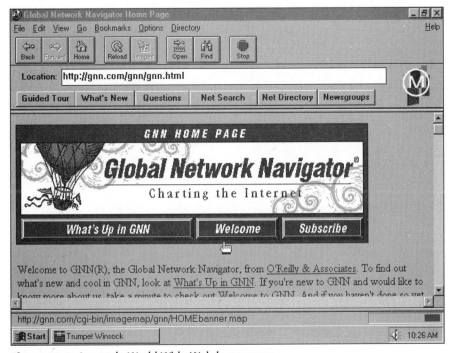

Figure 22-4: A sample World Wide Web home page.

You may look at the sample home page in Figure 22-4 and think, "Big deal!" But the cool thing about the home page is that now that I'm on the Web, I can jump from place to place just by clicking on buttons or underlined text. When I click on the Welcome button, for example, I jump to the home page shown in Figure 22-5. This home page seems to be quite friendly; I may be able to learn more about the Web from the home page, even as a beginner.

Now that I'm on the Web, I have access to thousands of home pages containing information on every conceivable topic. All I need to do to get from one page to another is click on a hot spot on the screen. Whether the home page that you click on is in New York City or New Delhi, it pops up on your screen instantly.

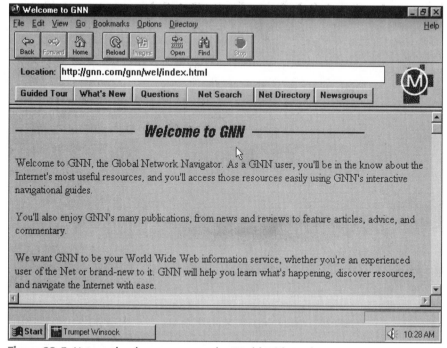

Figure 22-5: Yet another home page on the World Wide Web.

Appreciating everything that the Web has to offer is difficult until you've used it for a while. If you think of the Web as giving you one-click access to all the knowledge in the world, you're pretty much on target.

I could go on and on about the World Wide Web and other Internet services, but this, of course, isn't a book about the Internet per se. Still, read the following section, which tells you how to go about creating an Internet site — a place for Internauts to discover.

Cool Web sites

When you get connected to the World Wide Web, you can visit many fun places with your Web browser. If you're just getting started, check out the Electronic Frontier Foundation at http://www.eff.org. For a catalog of Web sites, check out the WWW Virtual Library at http://info.cern.ch/hypertext/DataSources/bySubject/Overview.html.

Are you interested in a virtual shopping spree? Take a peek at the Hall of Malls at http://nsns.com/MouseTracks/HallofMalls.html. Looking for that special someone? See the Virtual MeetMarket at http://wwa.com:1111. Or get a little culture at the Internet Art Museum at http://www.artnet.org/iamfree.

Web-crawling infobots

No, this sidebar isn't about an Ed Wood monster flick. A *Web crawler* is a solution to a problem that the World Wide Web has imposed on users — how do you keep up on what's new in a global information network that grows by leaps and bounds daily, finding the information that you need when you need it?

A Web crawler (also called a Web worm or Web spider) is a program that goes out and searches the Web all by itself. A good example is Lycos, from Carnegie-Mellon University. Lycos runs around the Web, copies every document that it finds, and reduces each document to an abstract of the original document. The program eliminates graphics, video, and binary files; extracts the title, headings, subheadings; and hyperlinks; pulls out the 100 most important words and the first 10 lines of the document; and then adds the abstract to its database, which you can search by keyword.

A couple of other popular Web searchers are WebCrawler and World Wide Web Worm. To learn more about these programs, get on the Web and cruise to http://pubweb.nexor.co.uk/public/cusi/cusi.html.

Gaining a Presence on the Net

After you get a little experience lurking on the Net, you may want to go a step further; rather than be a passive onlooker, you may want to create a presence on the Net. If you find the right Internet Service Provider, you can set up your own World Wide Web site and your own FTP drop box, and even get your own domain name.

This section assumes that you're not a huge corporation with money to burn, but a small business that wants to set up shop on the Net to promote or actually sell products and services. You have no intention of buying a ton of equipment or of hiring a staff to manage it; you just want the most bang for your buck.

To set up your own account on the Internet, you definitely need to go through an Internet Service Provider. When you choose an ISP, you have many things to consider. The following considerations probably are the most important:

✦ *Cost.* How much does the ISP charge?

✦ *Phone charges.* You don't want to tack long-distance charges on to the rest of your Internet charges, so find an ISP that can provide a phone number in your local dialing area (or an 800 number). Check your local phone book for exchanges (three-digit phone prefixes) within your area that you can dial for free.

✦ *PPP connectivity.* As a Windows 95 user, you probably will want to use Point-to-Point (PPP) protocol to connect to the Net, so you should choose an ISP that supports PPP.

You don't *have* to go through an ISP to create your own Web site. You can create a Web site by using Windows NT 3.51 or Windows 95 with the Website program from O'Reilly and Associates (707) 829-0515. Be forewarned, however — doing it yourself involves all the managerial headaches of running a site 24 hours a day, seven days a week.

✦ *Your own Web site.* If you plan to open shop on the Web, you want your own Web site. Be sure to find an ISP that can provide one.

✦ *Your own FTP drop box.* If you want to be able to send and receive files over the Web, you need File Transfer Protocol (FTP) capability. If you want people to be able to send files to you while you're away from your PC, find an ISP that can provide you an FTP drop box.

✦ *Your own domain name.* If you want to get your own *domain name* (the last part of your e-mail address, after the @ symbol), you need to find an ISP provider that offers Domain Name Service (DNS).

Consider this example of a domain name. I originally signed up with an ISP named CTS, and my e-mail address was alan@cts.com. But I wanted something a little more original than that — something that people in my field might remember. Because my ISP offered DNS, I applied for a new domain name. I figured that I'd compose a domain name from the two most overused words in computer literature, which other people in the field might remember. Now my official e-mail address is alan@coolnerds.com.

Types of ISP connections

Your ISP may offer several types of connections, which can be confusing. Table 22-1 lists some common connection types, which (as you can see) vary greatly in price.

Table 22-1
Connection Types Offered by Internet Service Providers

Type	Speed	Approximate Cost
PPP/SLIP	Your modem speed	$20–$30 per month
Dedicated PPP/SLIP	Your modem speed	$200–$300 per month
56K	56,000 bps	$150–$300 per month
PPP ISDN	128,000 bps	$70–$100 per month, plus equipment
T1	1,500,000 bps	$1,500–$2,000 per month
T3	45,000,000 bps	$65,000–$80,000 per month

I'm sure that 99.999 percent of you will need only the basic PPP connection, even if you're getting an FTP and World Wide Web site from your ISP. The ISP will have the T1 or higher connection to manage calls coming into your Web site; you just need a PPP connection to manage your Web site on the ISP's equipment. A simple PPP site gives you complete access to the entire Internet from standard telephone lines at a reasonable cost.

Finding an Internet Service Provider

You can find an ISP in your area in several ways:

✦ Watch your local newspaper for ads.

✦ Check the Computer Networking section of your local yellow pages.

✦ Refer to Appendix C of this book for the names and phone numbers of service providers in (or near) your area code.

In addition, listings of ISPs appear all over the Internet, but that's kind of a Catch-22 situation: you need to be connected to the Internet before you can look for service providers in your area.

The ISDN debacle

The one thing that you'll discover about the Internet via a PPP connection is that it's s-l-o-o-o-o-w. Even with a high-speed modem, a simple graphic may take a long time to appear on your screen. The promised solution to this slowness is ISDN (Integrated Services Digital Network). In addition to giving you faster Internet access, ISDN will support digital videoconferencing.

What's the debacle? Getting ISDN service in most areas is like trying to pull teeth from a cranky crocodile. The fact that you need special hardware on the telephone poles, at your site, and in your computer is only part of the headache.

In the spring of 1995, the Federal Communications Commission got involved and decided to essentially double the rates of the service. The justification? An ISDN line gives you two phone lines: your original analog line plus the digital (ISDN) line. So the FCC decided that charging on a per-subscriber basis made more sense than charging on a per-ISDN-line basis, just to make sure that nobody got an unfair bargain on phone rates. Bell Atlantic and Pacific Bell have filed petitions, but we all know how these things go. Affordable ISDN may not be available to the computing masses for quite a while.

In the long run, though, this debacle may not matter much. Intel is designing Fast Ethernet — the most likely medium for tomorrow's information superhighway — to run on the existing cable-TV infrastructure. Also, rumor has it that Microsoft is researching two-way satellite communications as an alternative to cable-TV lines.

What you'll get from your ISP

After you set up an account with an ISP, the provider will give you some of the information listed in Table 22-2. You'll get only information that's relevant to your account and the services you ordered, not necessarily everything that's shown in the table, and you may get more information than the table shows.

Table 22-2 Information That You'll Get from an ISP	
Information	*Example*
ISP name	YourISP
PPP access phone number	555-1234
IP address	123.45.67.890
Gateway IP address	980.765.432.987
Netmask (or submask)	255.255.255.240
Name server 1	123.456.78.90
Your host name	Babs1
Domain name	yourisp.com
E-mail user name	Babs
E-mail password	stinkyturtle
POP3 e-mail	mail.yourisp.com
SMTP relay host	smtp.yourisp.com
E-mail address	babs@yourisp.com
Default Mosaic host	www.yourisp.com
Default Gopher host	gopher.yourisp.com
Default news host	news.yourisp.com
Anonymous FTP	ftp/yourisp/com
WWW presentation address	http://www.yourisp.com/~babs

You should make a printed copy of whatever information you get from your service provider and store it in a safe place, where finding it again will be easy. You'll need that information from time to time as you expand your collection of Internet programs and expand your presence on the Net.

Along with the information presented in Table 22-2, your ISP will provide information on how to use the services that you ordered. If you got a Web site, for example, the ISP will explain how to create and load your Web pages. You also can find many, many books about the Internet and even on Web publishing (a good one is *Creating Cool Web Pages with HTML* by Dave Taylor, published by IDG Books, 1995). Because this book is about Windows 95, however, we need to get back to the topic at hand.

Good luck getting that Internet connection set up, and happy cruising. If you get a chance, drop me an e-mail message at alan@coolnerds.com.

Summary

This chapter has covered the much-talked-about Internet. My main goal in this chapter was to help those of you who are not connected get connected. The main points:

✦ The Internet is a world-wide collection of interconnected computers. Some people call it *the Net*, others call it *cyberspace*.

✦ There are many ways to connect to the Net. Many of the popular services like CompuServe, America Online, and Microsoft Network (MSN) can give you direct access to Internet e-mail and other Internet services.

✦ The Internet Explorer that comes with Microsoft Plus! (Appendix F) offers Access to the Internet's popular World Wide Web and FTP sites, right from you Microsoft Network (MSN) account.

✦ To gain a presence on the Web (that is, become a web site or FTP site), you'll probably need to sign up with an Internet Service Provider (ISP) that can provide those services. Refer to Appendix C for an ISP in or near your area code.

✦   ✦   ✦

Connecting to a Bulletin Board System (BBS) or PC

All the big commercial online services offer custom front ends. When you sign up with America Online, CompuServe, or the Microsoft Network (MSN), for example, you use a program that's specifically designed for interacting with that service. A smaller bulletin-board system (BBS) has no custom front end. Instead, you communicate with the small BBS by using general communications software. This chapter discusses HyperTerminal, the general communications program that comes with Windows 95.

How to Connect to a BBS

When you see an ad or listing for a BBS, the least information that you'll find is the phone number that you use to dial in. You may (or may not) see a string of other numbers after the bulletin board's name. Following is an example:

> Everybaudy's BBS   (610) 668-2983   28.8 n-8-1

The phone number is probably all you need to know. The 28.8 part is the fastest possible baud rate you can use with that BBS. The n-8-1 part stands for the settings Parity = None, Data Bits = 8, and Stop Bits = 1. Usually, you don't need to concern yourself with those settings. Your modem will just automatically use the fastest baud rate that the BBS allows. And n-8-1 is the default setting for HyperTerminal and most BBSs.

So in most cases, all you need to know is the BBS's phone number. To set up a connection to the BBS, follow these steps:

1. Choose Start⇨Programs⇨Accessories⇨HyperTerminal.

   You go to the folder for the HyperTerminal program.

2. Double-click on the Hypertrm icon.

   You see a wizard screen titled New Connection.

3. Type the name of the BBS that you're going to contact, and choose an icon for that service, as in the example presented in Figure 23-1.

Figure 23-1: Identifying the BBS that you plan to call.

4. Choose OK.

5. In the next wizard screen, enter the country code, the area code, the phone number, and the modem that you plan to use to make the connection (see Figure 23-2).

6. Choose OK.

7. In the next wizard screen, modify the number that you're calling or select your own dialing properties, if necessary; then click on the Dial button.

   You should hear the modem dial in, and you'll be connected.

If no activity occurs on-screen after you hear all the dialing and buzzing sounds, press the Enter key once or twice (the universal "Hey, you; I'm here" signal in modem communications).

If you still have trouble connecting, check out all of your settings. To do so, click on File in HyperTeminal's menu bar, and choose Properties. Click the Configure button in the dialog box that appears to get to more advanced settings such as baud rate, parity, data bits, and so forth. Make any changes that the BBS requires, then try again.

Figure 23-2: Phone number and other information for the BBS you want to call.

After you're connected, you're on your own. Every BBS is different, so you'll have to rely on the screen to navigate the BBS.

If you see weird characters on-screen when you connect to the BBS, try using a different font. Choose View⇨Font, and try the Terminal font first. If that font doesn't work, try some others.

Capturing and printing BBS text

Most BBSs are *text-based*, which means that after you connect to a BBS, you interact with it by reading text and answering questions or by choosing items from menus (perhaps typing the letter or number of the option that you want and then pressing Enter).

Often, the text from a BBS scrolls by quickly. Even if the text scrolls by a screen at a time, the document may contain too much information for you to absorb at one sitting. To give yourself time to think, you can capture text as it goes by on-screen, either straight to your printer or into a file that you can open and print later.

Use either of the following techniques:

✦ To capture incoming text in a file, choose Transfer⇨Capture Text and then type a file name, or choose Start to use the suggested filename (CAPTURE.TXT). The Capture indicator lights in HyperTerminal's status bar.

✦ To capture incoming text to the printer, choose Transfer⇨Capture to Printer. The Print Echo indicator lights in HyperTerminal's status bar.

Top 12 BBSs

Each year, *Boardwatch Magazine* conducts a Reader's Choice contest to find America's favorite BBSs. Following are some of the winners of the 1994 contest. To try one of these BBSs, use HyperTerminal to dial the number.

Software Creations: entertainment software; (508) 368-7139

EXEC-PC: largest shareware BBS; (414) 789-4360

Monterey Gaming System: custom interactive gaming; (408) 655-5555

Blue Ridge Express: many files and CD-ROMs; (804) 790-1675

Deep Cove BBS: news, publications, shareware, and Internet e-mail; (604) 536-5885

America's Suggestion Box: shareware and Usenet newsgroups; (516) 471-8625

Prodigy Genealogy: information on, and help with, searching for people; (800) 775-7714

Chrysalis: online publications and 34 CD-ROMs; (214) 690-9295

The Spa: family BBS with access to 4,000 Usenet newsgroups; (413) 536-4365

DSC: full Internet and Usenet access; (215) 443-7390

Wizards Gate BBS: no fees, full access, and 12GB; (614) 224-1635

Windows Online: largest Windows BBS; (510) 736-8343

Now you can go about your business normally. Be aware, however, that only new text that scrolls by after this point will be captured. Your printer may not start printing until its buffer is filled. You may scroll through several screens of text before you hear any printer activity. When you want to stop capturing text, do either of the following things:

✦ To stop capturing to the file, choose Transfer⇨Capture Text⇨Stop.

✦ To stop capturing to the printer, choose Transfer⇨Capture to Printer⇨Stop.

The file that was capturing your text closes. To see the contents of that file later, simply browse to it. If you used the default name, the file will be in the same folder as HyperTerminal; if you don't find the file there, use Find to search for CAPTURE.TXT (or whatever file name you used). Double-click on the icon to open the file. To print the file, choose File⇨Print in the program that opens. You also can open and edit the file in any text editor or word processing program.

When you stop capturing to the printer, your printer probably will eject all captured text.

Downloading files from a BBS

The exact steps that you follow to *download* (copy a file from) from a BBS to your own PC depend on what type of BBS you're connected to at the moment. The typical scenario is to work your way to the BBS's file area or file library and then use whatever tools are available to locate the file that you want.

When you find the file that you want, follow these steps to download it:

1. Choose Download from the BBS's menu system, and follow any instructions.

   You may, for example, be told to type the number (on-screen) of the file that you want to download.

2. If you are asked which protocol to use, choose Zmodem, Kermit, or Xmodem.

 HyperTerminal supports the Xmodem, Ymodem, Zmodem, and Kermit protocols. Zmodem generally is the fastest protocol for modern modems, but you can use any protocol that's available. *Both PCs must be using the same protocol, or the transfer will fail.*

3. Keep following the instructions on-screen until you see an instruction such as Receive, Receive Files, or Download.

4. What you do next depends on what happens on-screen, as follows:

   • If you see a dialog box like the one shown in Figure 23-3, HyperTerminal started the download automatically. You don't need to do anything (except wait).

   • If HyperTerminal doesn't kick in automatically, choose Transfer⇨Receive File, fill in the requested information, and make sure that you select the same protocol that you chose in Step 2. Then click on the Receive button.

Zmodem file receive for The Daily Planet BBS

Receiving:	WAM14.ZIP
Storing as:	C:\Program Files\Accessories\HyperTermi	Files: 1
Last event:	Receiving	Retries:
Status:	Receiving	

File:	▮▮▮▮▮	75k of 570K
Elapsed: 00:00:47	Remaining: 00:05:14	Throughput: 1610 cps

[Cancel] [Skip file] [cps/bps]

Figure 23-3: HyperTerminal receiving a file.

The indicator in the dialog box gives you a sense of how long the download is going to take. If you have a long wait ahead and want to do something else, minimize — but don't close — the HyperTerminal window. Then you can use some other program(s), occasionally reopening HyperTerminal's window to check the progress of your download.

When you finish downloading, the BBS is back in control, and you need to choose options from its menus. The file that you downloaded is stored in the same folder as HyperTerminal unless you specified some other folder for the download. If the file is zipped (has a .ZIP extension), you need to unzip it before you can use it. If you don't have a clue as to what I'm talking about here, refer to "Dealing with Zipped Files" in Chapter 21.

WinZip and PKZIP are on the companion CD-ROM in the back of this book.

Uploading to a BBS

Whether you can *upload* (send files to) to a BBS and, if so, exactly how you do it depend on the BBS. If the BBS's menu system contains an upload option, you typically select that option and follow any instructions on-screen. Then, when the BBS is ready to receive, you choose one of the following options from within HyperTerminal:

✦ If you're sending a program or document, or if you're not sure how the file is formatted, choose Transfer⇨Send File, and follow the instructions on-screen.

✦ If you're certain that the file you're sending is pure ASCII text, choose Transfer⇨Send File, and follow the instructions on-screen.

Any problems that you encounter are most likely to be on the receiving (BBS) end. You need to send a message to, or page, the *sysop* (system operator) for assistance.

Disconnecting from a BBS

When you finish exploring the BBS and/or downloading files, follow these steps to disconnect:

1. Exit or log off, as the BBS instructs.

2. Click on the Disconnect button in the toolbar or choose Call⇨Disconnect (just to make sure that you hang up the phone on your end).

3. Choose File⇨Exit from within HyperTerminal.

   If you just connected to the BBS for the first time, you have a chance to save those settings. Choose Yes if you think that you'll contact the same BBS in the future.

When you return to the HyperTerminal folder, you see an icon for the BBS that you just dialed, as shown in Figure 23-4. To contact this BBS in the future, all you need to do is double-click on that icon.

Figure 23-4: After you save
a BBS's settings, double-click
on its icon to reconnect.

Create Your Own BBS

Creating and managing your own BBS is no small undertaking. The job is expensive, time-consuming, and (as most entrepreneurial sysops have discovered) a labor of love rather than profit — all of which is fine if that's what you expect when you go in.

If you're thinking about starting your own BBS, the first thing that you'll want to do is shop around for BBS software. I suggest that you go to your local computer store and pick up the latest issue of *Boardwatch Magazine* or *BBS Magazine*. You'll find out about the latest products and get the inside scoop on the BBS industry.

When you look for BBS software, be aware that most of it still is text-based DOS stuff. Frankly, that kind of BBS isn't going to attract many users anymore — not when you have to compete with the likes of the Microsoft Network, America Online, and other graphical systems. (I hate to sound like a curmudgeon, but I've got to tell the truth as I see it; that's my job.)

An alternative to creating a do-it-yourself BBS is setting up a BBS on the Microsoft Network (MSN). For information on becoming a *content provider*, call (800) 4MSNFAX (that's (800) 467-6319). Also consider going on the Internet by getting a Web site and an FTP drop box (refer to Chapter 22).

As I write this chapter, I know of only four Windows-based BBS software packages that are actually on the market (or close to release). Those packages are:

Excalibur BBS
Excalibur Communications, Inc.
4410 East 80th Place
Tulsa, OK 74136
Voice: (800) 392-2522
      (918) 488-9801
Modem: (918) 496-8113

MediaHost
MediaHouse Software, Inc.
32 Eardley Road
Aylmer, Quebec, Canada J9H 7A3
Voice: (819) 682-9737
Modem: (819) 682-3330
Fax: (819) 685-0994

Power BBS
Power Computing
35 Fox Court
Hicksville, NY 11801
Voice: (800) 242-4775
       (516) 938-0506
Modem: (516) 822-7396

WorldGroup
Galacticomm
4101 S.W. 47th Avenue, Suite 101
Fort Lauderdale, FL 33314
Voice: (800) 328-1128
Modem: (305) 583-7808
E-mail: sales@gcomm.com or http://www.gcomm.com

PC-to-PC File Transfers

The easiest way to send files from one PC to another is through an information service to which both PCs can connect. When I finish writing a chapter, for example, I zip the text and figures for that chapter into a file, and I send that file to the editor's CompuServe account. The editor downloads the file from CompuServe at his or her leisure, unzips it, makes his or her editorial pass, zips everything back up, and sends the file back to my CompuServe account. We send things back and forth that way until it's time to actually start printing.

You can, of course, get into a situation in which the two parties who want to transfer files don't have a common online service. In that case, you can send files directly from one PC to the other by using HyperTerminal. This kind of transfer can be tricky, however, because one of the PCs has to answer the incoming call, and getting a modem to do that isn't always easy. Nonetheless, the following sections lay out the basic procedure and then leave you to your own devices.

Step 1: Get your modems in sync

The sender and receiver need to get their modems on the same wavelength. Each user must install a modem (refer to Chapter 14 for instructions) and then choose similar settings. To synchronize modem settings, follow these steps:

1. Choose Start⇨Settings⇨Control Panel.

2. Double-click on the Modems icon.

3. Select the modem that you'll be using for this transfer and then click on the Properties button.

4. Click on the Connection tab.

5. Set the Connection preferences as follows: Data bits = 8, Parity = None, and Stop Bits = 1.

6. Choose OK to return to the Control Panel.

7. Close the Control Panel by clicking on its Close button (X).

Now proceed to the appropriate Step 2 section, depending on whether your PC will dial out or answer the incoming call.

Step 2: If your PC will be dialing out...

If your PC is the one that will dial out, follow these steps to set up your end of the connection:

1. Choose Start⇨Programs ⇨Accessories ⇨HyperTerminal.

2. Double-click on the Hypertrm icon.

   The first New Connection wizard screen appears.

3. Type a descriptive name (for example, **Elizabeth's PC**), select any icon, and then choose OK.

4. In the next wizard screen, type the area code and phone number of the PC that you want to dial; then choose OK.

5. In the last wizard screen, click on the Modify button, click on the Settings tab, and then click on the ASCII Setup button.

6. Select Send line ends with line feeds so that its checkbox is checked.

7. Select Echo typed characters so that its checkbox is checked (see Figure 23-5).

8. Choose OK twice.

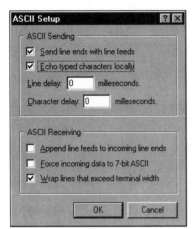

Figure 23-5: ASCII settings for connecting to another PC.

Proceed to "Step 3: Make the connection."

Step 2: If your PC will be answering...

If your PC will be answering the phone, you need to set up bogus dial-out settings so that you can get your settings in sync with the caller's PC. Follow these steps:

1. Choose Start➪Programs➪Accessories➪HyperTerminal.

2. Double-click on the Hypertrm icon.

   The first New Connection wizard screen appears.

3. Type **Answer incoming calls** as the descriptive name, select icon, and then choose OK.

4. In the next wizard screen, type your own area code and phone number (the number of the phone line that your modem uses), and then choose OK.

   (I know that this step sounds strange, but you need to specify some kinds of settings, and HyperTerminal won't allow you to leave the phone number blank.)

5. In the last wizard screen, click on the Modify button, click on the Settings tab, and then click on the ASCII Setup button.

6. Select Send line ends with line feeds so that its checkbox is checked.

7. Select Echo typed characters so that its checkbox is checked (refer to Figure 23-5).

8. Choose OK twice.

9. Click on the Dial button.

Because you're dialing your own phone number, you get a busy signal.

10. Click on Cancel, and wait.

You should see a dialog box titled Answer incoming calls — HyperTerminal.

Proceed to the following section, but start with Step 2 rather than Step 1.

Step 3: Make the connection

By this time, the two parties are in sync. To proceed, follow these steps:

1. If your PC is the one that will be dialing out, give the other PC a minute or so to get prepared; then click on the Dial button.

2. If your PC is the one that will be answering, wait for the phone to ring, for the words RING RING to appear on-screen, or for the AA (Automatic Answer) indicator light on the modem to blink. When one of those things happens, type **ata** and press the Enter key.

After some modem yelping, you should see a message indicating that you are connected.

3. If your PC answered the call, type a message (such as **Are you there?**), press Enter, and wait a few seconds.

4. If your PC dialed out, wait to see the message from the person at the other end. When you see the message, type a message back (something like **Yeah, I'm here. I can't believe this worked!**), and press Enter.

If you can see each other's messages, your PCs are connected, and you can type messages back and forth for as long as you want. I suspect, however, that your real motivation for making the connection was to transfer files from one PC to another. To do that, follow these steps:

1. The person who will send the file should type a message to the recipient, telling him or her the name of the file, and then press Enter.

The sender may type a message like the following:

I am going to send mydocument.zip.

2. The sender should choose Transfer⇨Send File, Browse to the file to be sent, choose Zmodem as the protocol, and click on the Send button.

You should see a dialog box like the one shown in Figure 23-6.

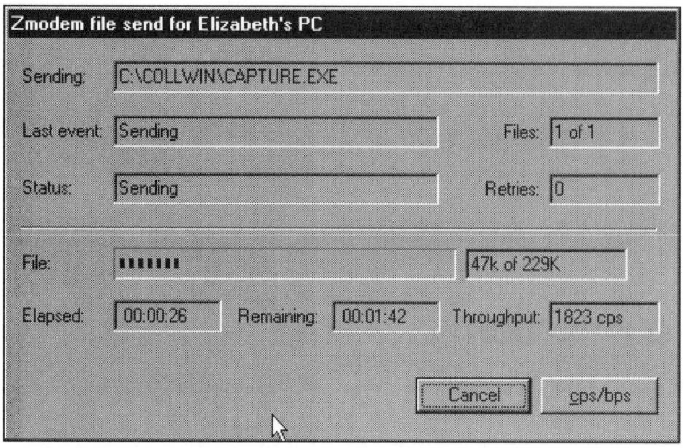

Figure 23-6: The sender is sending a file.

3. The recipient should wait to see whether the dialog box for receiving the file appears automatically.

   If the dialog box appears, the recipient simply waits for the transfer to complete.

   If the dialog box doesn't appear, the recipient needs to choose Transfer⇨Receive File and fill in the dialog box that appears.

You can send as many files back and forth as you want. When you're ready to disconnect, both parties need to click on the Disconnect button or choose Call⇨Disconnect.

The recipient should be aware that unless he or she specified a different directory when receiving, the files received will be in the HyperTerminal folder. To get to that folder via My Computer, double-click on your hard-drive's icon; then choose Program Files⇨Accessories⇨HyperTerminal.

Remember that the method described in the preceding sections is sort of a *kludge* (something thrown together quickly). If you need to transfer files often, you should use an intermediary online service, such as CompuServe or MSN. Use a compression program to compress files before you send them (refer to Chapter 21).

If you need to connect to your home PC while you're on the road, you'll want to use dial-up networking (refer to Chapter 20) rather than HyperTerminal.

Summary

Most of the big commercial online services have their own custom *front ends*, programs you use to connect to and interact with the service. To connect to a smaller "local" bulletin board, you need to use a generic communications program.

✦ HyperTerminal, which comes with Windows 95, is a good general communications program for connecting to small BBS's and other PCs.

✦ To get to HyperTerminal click the Start button and choose Programs⇨Accessories⇨HyperTerminal.

✦ If you want to reconnect to a BBS that you've connected to previously, just double-click the icon for the BBS you've saved settings for.

✦ To create a new connection, double-click the HyperTrm icon. Then follow the instructions on the screen to describe the BBS. When you get to the end of the questions, click on the Dial button.

✦ Once you're connected, you need to follow whatever instructions the BBS presents on your screen in order to get around, and download files.

✦ To disconnect from a BBS, enter the BBS's "Quit" or "Goodbye" command (often **Q** or **G**) and press Enter. Then click the Disconnect button in HyperTerminal's toolbar, or choose Call⇨Disconnect from HyperTerminal's menu bar.

✦   ✦   ✦

Local Area Networking (LANs)

Why Bother with a LAN?

If you have two or more PCs in your office or home, the best thing that you can do for yourself is hook them together as a *local area network* (LAN). You may think, "Yeah, right. Like I'm really gonna create a LAN just to hook my portable PC to my desktop." You're thinking that because you assume that creating a LAN is a big, expensive, complicated undertaking. You think you'll need to shell out big bucks to have someone set it up, and that you'll be at that person's mercy every time the LAN goes down. Or worse, you'll have to hire someone full-time just to babysit the LAN.

Put all such thoughts out of your head. LANs were a big complicated mess when DOS was in the picture. But things have gotten much, much easier now that Windows 95 (and Windows NT and Windows for Workgroups) have built-in networking capabilities. You no longer have an operating system (DOS) that's fighting a LAN every step of the way. Instead, you have an operating system that supports and embraces a LAN, and that even has all the software you need built right into it.

Advantages of a LAN

Even though setting up a LAN is easier than ever, some investment of time and money still is involved, so you need some justification. Perhaps one of the following advantages of a LAN will solve a problem for you:

+ If only one PC in the LAN has a printer, CD-ROM drive, or fax/modem, every PC in the LAN can use that hardware.

+ If several people work on the same document, they can use the documents on one PC without copying and transporting files via floppy disk. In many cases, several people can work on the same document at the same time.

✦ If several people work with the same data — such as a customer list, inventory list, or orders — all that information can reside on one PC. Each user in the LAN will have access to that always-up-to-date data.

✦ You can set up local e-mail, whereby users can send messages to one another via PC.

✦ Any portable PCs that are connected to the LAN can regain access to the resources of the LAN even while they're away, thanks to dial-up networking.

A *WAN* (wide area network) consists of PCs that are connected by modems and phone lines, because they're too far apart to connect by any other means. A LAN (local area network) consists of PCs that are connected to one another directly, because they're close enough to be connected that way.

In short, if you find yourself using floppy disks to transport files from one PC to another — whether to print, fax, modem, or whatever — you need a LAN. You'll quickly earn back the time and money that you invest in creating the LAN by not having to fumble with floppies anymore.

Why LANs Seem to Be So Complicated

When you read about LANs, you usually are inundated by so many acronyms, technical terms, and product names, you have difficulty understanding what's really involved in setting up a LAN. Maybe I can clear up some confusion about this topic.

Any PC that has Windows 95, Windows NT, or Windows for Workgroups on it can hook into the LAN without any third-party software. You don't need Novell NetWare, Banyan-Vines, Microsoft LAN Manager, Lantastic, or other network programs.

If you have relatively few computers (15 or fewer), a simple peer-to-peer LAN probably will work perfectly for you. You won't need to worry about client/server terminology.

The written documentation for LANs often is one of the most confusing elements of networking. Often, when you look up the solution to a problem, the documentation tells you to ask your network administrator — not much help if you *are* the network administrator. Another problem with the written documentation is that step 1 in the instruction manual says something like this: "Make sure that the LAN is up, running, and working perfectly, and that you have full administrative rights, before you do anything else. If you have any problems, ask your network administrator."

Isn't this situation a catch-22? You're expecting to set up a LAN, and the instructions tell you to set it all up and grab your local full-time network guru before you do anything else.

In this book, I make no such assumptions. For all intents and purposes, you *are* the network administrator, even if you don't know diddly-squat about LANs at the moment. And I am not assuming that the LAN is set up and ready to go. I'm just assuming that you have two or more PCs that you want to connect in a LAN.

What You Really Need to Know

I don't mean to imply that a computer novice should be setting up a LAN. The job calls for some prerequisite skills and knowledge, summarized in the following list:

✦ You need to know how to use My Computer or Windows Explorer to browse around a PC.

✦ You need to know how to open a computer case and install a board. If the PC that you're connecting to the LAN has an available PCMCIA slot, you need to know how to insert and remove PC Cards.

✦ You should get a little practice with Device Manager (refer to Chapter 10) so that you can find available resources and tweak some settings if the need arises.

If you don't meet those criteria, you may be better off hiring a pro to do the job. Just make sure that this person understands that you want to set up a peer-to-peer LAN, using the network capabilities built into Windows 95 (or Windows NT, or Windows for Workgroups). Explain that you're not looking for a dedicated server just yet and don't need third-party software, such as NetWare. The installer may grumble because this approach seems to be too easy. But easy is good. Trust me — the simpler, the better.

Planning the LAN

Phase one in setting up a LAN is planning your equipment purchase. You have to choose among several types of cables and network cards. In the interest of keeping things simple, I'm going to narrow your choices to the items that have emerged as industry standards and that offer the simplest and most flexible solutions to the problem.

Choosing a cable type

The first decision is the kind of cable to use. You have several choices, but you'd do well to stick with TPE cable. This type of cable has many names, including 10BaseT, 10BT, Twisted Pair, Twisted Pair Ethernet, TPE, and RJ-45. But you can recognize the cable by the fact that the plugs at the ends look like slightly oversize telephone plugs. The cable looks sort of like the cable that connects your telephone to the wall.

This type of cabling requires an Ethernet hub (also called a Ethernet concentrator) to which each PC in the LAN will connect, as shown in Figure 24-1.

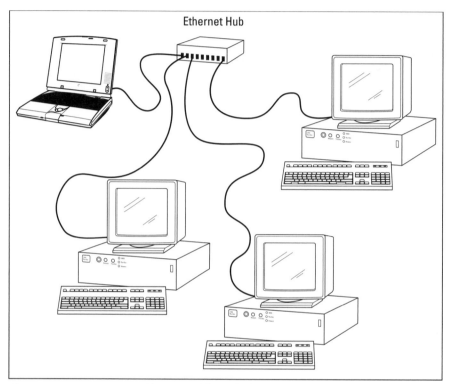

Figure 24-1: PCs connected by TPE cable and a hub in a star configuration.

This type of arrangement, in which each PC plugs into a hub, sometimes is called a *star configuration*. I guess that the name arose because if you put the hub smack in the middle and spread the PCs around evenly, the configuration would look like a giant asterisk (*), and an asterisk sometimes is called a star. (Now we're *really* getting technical, eh?)

After you decide to use the TPE cable, you need to decide where you want to put the hub. Some hubs actually require their own power and, therefore, must plugged into a wall outlet. You probably should plan to put the hub near a standard power outlet (the same kind that you use for a lamp).

Next, you need to measure the distance from each PC to the hub. Take into the consideration the fact that you need to run the cable in such a way that people aren't likely to trip over it. Always round up when you make your calculations. If one PC is just a few feet from the hub, you need a 2-foot or 4-foot cable for that connection. If another PC is about 10 feet from the hub, you need about a 12-foot cable for that connection. You need one cable for each PC that you plan to connect to the LAN.

A cable that's too long still is usable; a cable that's too short is not.

Choosing a network card

In addition to cable, you need one network interface card for each PC in the LAN. This card is a piece of hardware that allows you to connect one PC to a LAN. Like cables, network cards go by several names, including network adapter card, Ethernet card, and NIC. Choosing a network card is fairly easy if you follow these guidelines:

- ✦ Make sure that the card is an Ethernet card.

- ✦ Make sure that the card will fit in the slot that you have available — typically, ISA on a desktop PC, an ISA or PCI slot on a Pentium, or a PCMCIA slot on a portable computer.

- ✦ Choose a card that supports the type of cable that you're using (TPE). The hole into which the TPE cable plugs sometimes is called an RJ-45 connector.

- ✦ The easiest card to install is one that bears the "Designed for Windows 95" plug-and-play logo.

- ✦ The second-easiest card to install is one for which Windows 95 has a built-in driver and that the program can detect and install automatically. The Windows 95 Hardware Compatibility List includes supported Ethernet adapters.

- ✦ A 32-bit card is faster (and more expensive) than a 16-bit card but not worth fretting over if the LAN is fairly small.

You can mix and match brands and models of network cards however you want, as long as all of them are Ethernet cards. But for simplicity's sake, you may want to buy the same make and model of network card for each PC in the LAN. (You can buy network cards in packs of 5 and 10.). Any laptop PCs that you want to hook to the LAN require PC Cards (PCMCIA) rather than traditional internal cards.

Making the Buy

Before you go to the local Comput-O-Rama to buy the stuff for your LAN, you should have your shopping list ready to go. You need to know the following things:

- ✦ How many ISA (or PCI) Ethernet cards you need, and how many PCMCIA Ethernet cards you need.

- ✦ What type of plug you need on each Ethernet card (most likely, the RJ-45 plug for TPE cable).

✦ How many Ethernet cables you need and how long each cable should be. Make sure that the cables have the proper plugs on each end (the plugs that fit into the RJ-45 socket).

✦ How many slots you need in your Ethernet hub. Allowing for growth never hurts. If you plan to link, say, four computers in your LAN, consider getting a hub that has six connection slots.

Figure 24-2 shows an example of a shopping list for connecting four PCs in a LAN. I need four Ethernet cards. But because one of the PCs in my LAN is a laptop, one card must be a PCMCIA-style card. I need four cables (one for each card) and a hub with at least four connection slots.

```
             Things to Pick up at Comput-O-Rama


    3     Ethernet cards for desktop PCs [ISA slots]

    1     Ethernet card for laptop PC [PCMCIA slot]


    2     6-foot TPE cables
    2     12-foot TPE cables


    1     Ethernet hub with at least 4 slots [6 to allow growth]
```

Figure 24-2: Shopping list for equipment needed to set up a four-PC LAN.

After you buy all that stuff and get it back to where your PCs are, you're ready to move to the next chapter, in which you actually set up that LAN.

Summary

If you have two or more PCs in one location, you should seriously consider hooking them together in a local area network (LAN).

✦ Computers in a LAN can share resources—printers, drives, CD-ROM drives, folders, and modems.

✦ LANs, which once required highly specialized knowledge, are relatively easy to set up and maintain in Windows 95.

✦ All the networking software you need is built right into Windows 95.

✦ You do need additional *hardware* to set up a LAN. In particular, you need a network card and Ethernet cable for each PC in the LAN, and an Ethernet Hub to connect all the cables to.

✦ When buying a network card, try to find one that bears the "Designed for Windows 95" logo for quick-and-easy installation.

✦   ✦   ✦

Create Your Own LAN

After you purchase all the hardware that you need to turn those independent PCs into a working team, you're ready to start installing. Be forewarned that this process can take a few hours; try to do it when people are not working on the PCs that you want to link. Get ready to concentrate. Take the phone off the hook. If other people are around, put a big sign on your back that says, "Do not talk to me." Your brain is going to be tied up for a few hours.

Installing the LAN Hardware

At this point, you have hardware (cards and cables) and perhaps software (disks that came with the network cards) in hand. This part is a little tricky. You may have Ethernet cards that were designed for DOS/Windows, or you may have plug-and-play Ethernet cards designed for Windows 95. If you're adding a portable PC to the LAN, you may have a PCMCIA Ethernet card. In the sections that follow, I'll try to cover all the possibilities. But you also will have to rely on the card manufacturer's instructions in addition to my instructions.

> **More Info** If the card manufacturer's documentation includes instructions for installing software in DOS or Windows 3.x, you want to *ignore* that section of the documentation. You don't want to use the old real-mode 16-bit drivers if you can avoid them. Instead, you want to use the 32-bit drivers that are built into Windows 95.

Step 1: Check available resources

Whenever you install new hardware in your PC, you're likely to be asked to choose an Interrupt Request (IRQ) for that device. You also may have to provide an Input/Output (I/O) address. Network cards are no exception.

What is an IRQ?

An Interrupt Request (IRQ) is a channel that's allowed to interrupt whatever the processor is doing at the moment and request immediate attention. The keyboard is a perfect example. Suppose that you start some long process and then decide to finish it later. When you press the Esc key, you don't want the processor to ignore you and keep doing what it's doing; you want the processor to stop what it's doing and pay attention to whatever key you happen to be pressing.

Some standards exist for assigning IRQs to devices. IRQ 1, for example, is used for the keyboard on virtually every PC. IRQ 2 is used for the system timer, and IRQs 3 and 4 are for the serial ports (COM 1 and COM 2). The IRQs that generally are left free are 5, 7, 9, 10, and a few others.

Every time you install some new internal device, such as a sound card or modem, you may need to give that device its own IRQ, so the available ones start getting used up. Remembering which IRQs are used and which are available at any given time is tough, so use Device Manager to check for available IRQs before you install any new hardware device.

Before you shut down a PC to install the card, take a moment to jot down (or print) the resources that are available on the PC. Follow these steps:

1. Choose Start⇨Settings⇨Control Panel.

2. Double-click on the System icon.

3. Click on the Device Manager tab.

   If this computer is connected to a printer, click on the Print button, select System summary, and then choose OK. You get a printed summary of the used IRQ and I/O ports, as well as other information.

4. Double-click on Computer at the top of the list and then click on the Interrupt request (IRQ) option button.

   The screen shows installed devices, listed by the IRQs that the devices are using (see Figure 25-1).

5. Write down any IRQs that are not already taken — that is, IRQs that do not appear in the list.

   By looking at Figure 25-1, for example, I could write "Available IRQs on this PC: 05, 07, 09, 10."

6. Your network card may want its own area in memory for input/output (I/O), so click on the Input/output (I/O) option button to see what's available.

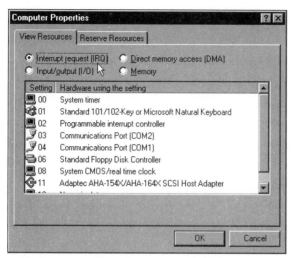

Figure 25-1: Installed devices, listed by IRQs.

7. Scroll about a third of the way down the list until you see the range 00F0-00FF (see Figure 25-2).

Your network card probably will want an address range below that number, but above 03A. Typically, only a few ranges are already taken, so writing down the ones that are *not* available may be easier. By looking at Figure 25-2, I would write "NOT available I/O ranges: 02F8-02FF, 0330-0333, 0378-037A."

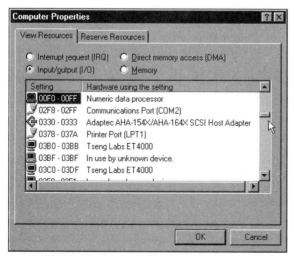

Figure 25-2: I/O addresses above 00FF that already are in use.

8. Choose OK twice.

9. Close the Control Panel by clicking on its Close button.

Keep in mind that the settings that you wrote down (or printed) apply only to this PC, so don't let your notes drift too far from this PC. Also make sure that you don't confuse these settings with those of any of the other PCs that you plan to add to the LAN. While working with each PC, you'll need to refer to the settings several times.

Step 2: Set the board's IRQ

Some ISA cards (not PCMCIA or PCI cards) require you to set dip switches on the board to tell the board which IRQ to use. Now you're getting into a tricky area. You really need to look at the instructions for the Ethernet card that you're installing to determine whether you have to set an IRQ yourself — and if so, how you should go about setting that IRQ. Following are the possibilities:

✦ If the card's instructions say that you don't have to set anything, skip to "Step 3: shut everything down" later in this chapter.

✦ If the card has dip switches that you can adjust manually, and if the directions tell you how to set those switches, follow those instructions to set the dip switches to an available IRQ (in my example, 05, 07, 09, or 10). Then skip to "Step 3: shut everything down."

✦ If the card requires you to run a program to set the IRQ, do so, following the Ethernet card's instructions to do that. *Make sure that you follow only the instructions for setting the dip switches; do not install the DOS or Windows 3.x drivers.* Then read on.

Running the little program that sets dip switches may be somewhat tricky. Most likely, the program will be a DOS program, and you may not be able to run it from a DOS window. Furthermore, you may be required to run the program twice: before you install the board in the PC and after you physically install the board. If you need to run the program before you install the card, follow these steps:

1. Insert into drive A or B the floppy disk that came with the Ethernet card, according to the manufacturer's instructions.

2. If you must run the program from a DOS prompt, first try choosing Start⇨Programs⇨MS-DOS Prompt.

3. Type the command that the instructions tell you to type (for example, **a:\softset2**), and press Enter.

4. If the program complains that it cannot be run from a DOS window, type **exit** and press Enter to return to Windows. Then choose Start⇨Shut Down⇨Restart the computer in MS-DOS mode⇨Yes. Again type the command that you typed in step 3, and press Enter.

At this point, you need to rely on the Ethernet card manufacturer's instructions to set the IRQ. The screen may tell you how to set the dip switches or jumpers to select a specific IRQ. If the program tells you that the best choice is an IRQ that's already taken, don't believe the program — choose an IRQ that you know for sure is not taken (in my example, 05, 07, 09, or 10).

If you set the board to a specific IRQ now, write down that setting on a piece of paper. You may be asked for the setting later, and you may forget if you don't jot it down. You can write something like "I set the Ethernet card's IRQ to 5" (replacing the 5 with the actual setting that you used).

When you complete the manufacturer's instructions on what to do before you install the board, exit the program, if necessary. Type **exit** and press Enter at the C> prompt to return to the Windows 95 desktop.

Step 3: Shut everything down

Before you install the card, you should shut down everything on this PC (and I do mean everything). Follow these steps:

1. Choose Start⇨Shut Down.
2. Click on Shut down the computer?, and click on Yes.
3. When the screen says that it's safe to do so, shut down the PC and all peripherals that are attached directly to the PC (monitor, printer, external modem, external CD-ROM drive, and so on).

Why it's so confusing

If you read this chapter, you may think that all of this is terribly complicated and confusing. The reason is that networking hardware and software have been evolving from the takes-a-genius technology of the '80s to Windows 95 plug-and-play simplicity.

How complicated things are really depends on the age of your hardware. If you buy plug-and-play cards designed for Windows 95 or PCMCIA cards, you don't have to mess with IRQs. Also, if you have a Pentium computer with an available PCI slot, you can buy a PCI Ethernet card for that computer, which is easier to install than the legacy ISA cards. A PCI card is easier to install because it can detect an available IRQ and set itself to use that IRQ.

Older cards require *you* to do all those things. Your goal is to find an IRQ that's not being used by any other device. Set the Ethernet card to that IRQ (assuming that you can somehow set the IRQ right on the board). The trick is to always specify that IRQ whenever any prompt asks you which IRQ to use for the network card, or which IRQ the network is using. (Ugh!)

Step 4: Install the Ethernet card

With everything shut down, you are ready to install the Ethernet hardware. Once again, you should follow the manufacturer's instructions, but the general procedure will be something like the following:

1. If you're installing an internal card (not a PCMCIA card), remove the case from the system unit.

2. Put the card in an available slot.

   If the board contains dip switches, be careful that you don't change the dip-switch settings accidentally.

3. Replace the cover.

4. Connect one end of an Ethernet cable to the slot on the Ethernet card, and the other end to your Ethernet hub.

Step 5: Set the IRQ (if you haven't already)

You probably can ignore this step if you already set the IRQ on the board by setting dip switches. If the board has no dip switches, the hardware manufacturer may require you to run a program to set those switches. Most likely, the instructions will tell you to run the program from DOS, before Windows starts up. Windows 95, of course, has no DOS. But if the card requires you to run a setup program from the DOS prompt to set IRQ switches, you need to carefully follow these instructions:

1. Remove any floppies from the floppy disk drives.

2. Turn on the monitor, and give it a few seconds to warm up.

3. Turn on the PC, put a finger near the F8 key, and keep your eyes on the screen.

4. As soon as you see the message `Starting Windows 95`, press the F8 key.

5. Choose Command prompt only by typing **5** and pressing Enter.

6. When you get to the `C>` prompt, follow the manufacturer's instructions to set the board's IRQ.

   You may need to put a floppy disk in drive A, type **a:\softset2**, and press Enter, for example.

Keep in mind that if the program you're running suggests using an IRQ that you know is already in use, *do not* use that suggested setting. Instead, pick an IRQ that you know is available (in my example, 05, 07, 09, or 10).

You also may need to provide an I/O address. Make sure that you don't to pick an address that's already in use. I determined that I/Os 02F8-02FF, 0330-0333, 0378-037A were not available on my PC, so I would choose any suggested range except one of those.

After you set the IRQ (and optionally, the I/O address), jot down the settings you chose. You may write something like "I set my board to IRQ = 5, I/O address = 0210-021F."

Again, don't let your notes wander away from this PC; keep the notes right there, because they have no bearing on any other PC in the LAN. I know that I'm harping on this point, but it's not purely a neurotic compulsion. Getting this IRQ and I/O stuff squared away as early in the process as possible is important. Most networks fail simply because the IRQ setting on the board doesn't match the IRQ setting that Windows expects, or because the IRQ setting that you chose for the network card conflicts with the IRQ setting for some other device that's installed in the PC. Going back and fixing the mistake can be a lengthy process.

The address range may be expressed without the leading zero and followed by h, which stands for *hexadecimal*. Therefore, the address range 210-21Fh is the same as 0210-021F. (Dreadfully confusing, I know.)

Follow the instructions to complete and exit the manufacturer's program. When you get to the C> prompt, you can shut down the PC again. Trying to test the card or the LAN makes no sense until at least two of the PCs have their cards installed and are connected to the Ethernet hub.

Step 6: Repeat Steps 1–5 on each PC

The best thing to do now is repeat the process for each PC in the LAN, starting with "Step 1: Check available resources." The process takes a while. But if you properly install all the network hardware and connect every PC to the Ethernet adapter now, getting everything working right will be much easier later. I've spent many frustrating, hair-pulling hours trying to set up LANs in a hurry. The technique that I'm giving you here is slow and cautious, but in the long run, it produces satisfactory results faster.

Telling Windows 95 That You're on the LAN

After you install all the Ethernet cards and hook every PC to the Ethernet hub, you need to fire up Windows 95 and tell it, "Hey, look — we're on a LAN now." As long as all the hardware is in place and at least two PCs are connected to the Ethernet hub, Windows 95 will say, "Hey, yeah, cool. Let me install my networking software for you."

This part usually is easy. You need to complete the following procedure on each PC in the LAN (one PC at a time, of course):

1. Gather up your original Windows 95 floppy disks or CD-ROM.

2. Turn on all the peripherals (monitor, printer, external modem, external CD-ROM drive, and so on) for any PC in the LAN.

3. Remove any floppy disks from the floppy drives.

4. Turn on the computer, sit back, and watch the screen.

What you do next depends on what happens on-screen. Windows 95 may detect the new piece of hardware in your PC. If so, follow the instructions on-screen and skip to "Identifying this PC on the LAN" for further information.

If you got all the way to the Windows 95 desktop and Windows didn't detect the new Ethernet card, follow these steps:

1. Choose Start⇔Settings⇔Control Panel.

2. Double-click on the Add New Hardware icon.

3. Read the instructions, click on Next, choose Yes when you're asked about auto-detection, and then click on Next again.

4. Follow the instructions on-screen.

If the Add New Hardware wizard says that it didn't find any new devices, you need to install the device. Click on the Next button, click on Network adapters, click on Next again, and select the Manufacturer and Model of your network card. If you can't find your make and model, put the manufacturer's drivers disk in drive A, click on Have Disk, choose OK, and follow the instructions on-screen.

Windows 95 probably will install many files from the floppy disks or CD-ROM and then ask you to restart the computer. Follow whatever instructions appear on-screen. Then proceed to the following section.

Identify this PC on the LAN

No matter which route you take to install your Ethernet card, you eventually return to the Windows 95 desktop. You may be prompted to enter a user name and password along the way. Type a user name — typically, a person's first name, followed by the first letter of the last name, with no spaces (e.g., AlanS). Also type a password of up to 15 characters, with no spaces.

 Remember that passwords often are case-sensitive. The password Snorkel, for example, is not the same as snorkel or SNORKEL. Pay attention to the Caps Lock key when you type your password.

Write both the user name and password on a piece of paper, and keep that paper near the PC; you'll need to refer to it in the near future. You can change the user name and password later if you want, but you need to know the password that you typed originally.

Any time that you're not sure how to respond to a prompt, you can click on the Question-mark button in that window and then click on the item you're confused about. Additional information pops up on-screen.

When you get to the desktop, you should see an icon titled Network Neighborhood; typically, that icon is below the My Computer icon. If you don't see the icon, close all open windows, right-click on the desktop, and choose Arrange Icons⇨by Name.

 If you still don't see the Network Neighborhood icon after arranging the desktop windows, something didn't install correctly. Make sure that the hardware (card and cable) are hooked up; then choose Start⇨Settings⇨Control Panel, and double-click on the Network icon. Click on Add, click on Adapter, click on Add again, and follow the instructions on-screen to install your network adapter card.

Your final step is to identify this PC on the LAN and adjust a few settings. Right-click on the Network Neighborhood icon, and choose Properties. The Network dialog box appears (see Figure 25-3).

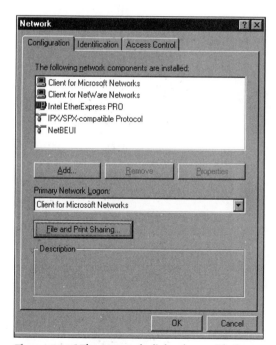

Figure 25-3: The Network dialog box, with the Configuration tab selected.

Notice the three tabs near the top of the Network dialog box, named Configuration, Identification, and Access Control. Read the following sections carefully for instructions on setting up this PC to run on the LAN.

The Configuration tab

The Configuration tab on your screen should show at least the five options shown in Figure 25-3. If an option is missing, click on Add; select Client, Adapter, or Protocol (depending on which type of component is missing); select the missing component; and then follow the instructions on-screen to install that component.

In the Primary Network Logon drop-down list, select Client for Microsoft Networks.

Last — and this step is important — click on the File and Print Sharing button. I suggest that you choose both options in the File and Print Sharing dialog box: I want to be able to give others access to my files and I want to be able to allow others to print to my printer(s), as shown in Figure 25-4. (All that you're doing here is giving yourself the option to share things from this PC later; you're not giving anything away.) Then choose OK to close the dialog box.

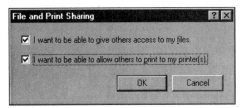

Figure 25-4: Give yourself the option to share stuff later.

The Identification tab

When you finish with the Configuration tab, click on the Identification tab. You see a dialog box that looks something like Figure 25-5.

The following list explains how to fill in the blanks:

✦ *Computer name.* Give the computer a unique name of up to 15 characters, with no spaces. You can use any name that identifies the computer or use the name of the person who uses this computer most often. In Figure 25-5, I named the PC CD_Master because I mainly use this PC to create masters of CD-ROM discs.

✦ *Workgroup.* Giving each PC in the LAN the same workgroup name is extremely important, because only PCs that have the same workgroup name can share resources. The name can be up to 15 characters long, with no spaces. In my

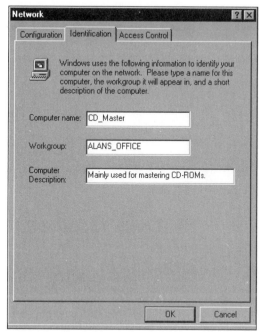

Figure 25-5: The Identification tab of the Network dialog box.

example, every PC belongs to a workgroup named ALANS_OFFICE; you, of course, can make up your own workgroup name. Just make sure that you type the name exactly the same way on each PC.

✦ *Computer Description.* You can type any description for this computer; no particular rules apply. Just type a brief description that you think will further identify this PC to someone on the LAN.

The Access Control tab

The Access Control tab (see Figure 25-6) defines security on this PC.

I strongly suggest that you select Share-level access control, which is by far the easiest type of control to manage. If, after using the LAN for a few weeks, you feel that you need to tighten security, you can change this setting. But unless you're allowing total strangers to dial in to your network, I seriously doubt that you'll ever need User-level access control. User-level control is a hassle, because you have to list the name of every LAN member who's allowed to use every shared device.

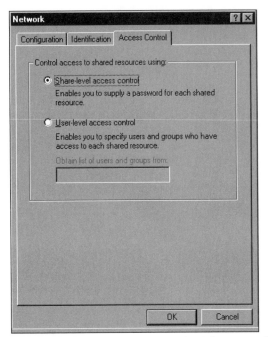

Figure 25-6: The Access Control tab of the Network dialog box.

Save the network settings

After you complete all three tabs of the Network dialog box, you're ready to save your choices; simply click on OK at the bottom of the Network dialog box. Depending on your selections, you may need to insert some of the original Windows 95 floppy disks or the CD-ROM. Just follow the instructions on-screen.

You probably will be prompted to restart the PC as well. Remove any floppy disks from the floppy drives, and follow the instructions to restart the PC.

Know what you get to do next? You get to gather up all those original Windows 95 floppies (or the CD-ROM), and carry them (or it) to the next PC in the LAN. When you get to that PC, start over again, from "Telling Windows 95 That You're on the LAN" to this paragraph. Then repeat the process for every PC that's connected to the LAN.

Read my instructions carefully at each PC. If you forget certain little steps, they'll come back and bite ya later, and figuring out what you forgot to do is hard.

When you get to the Identification-tab step, remember to give each PC a different computer name, but the same workgroup name.

After you set up every PC in the LAN, you're ready to test the network.

Testing the LAN

By the time you get to this section, you should have set up the network hardware on every PC in the LAN and identified each PC in the LAN. Every PC is running, showing the Windows 95 desktop, and each desktop shows a Network Neighborhood icon. (It's late at night, your eyes are tired, your brain is fried, and you wish I'd hurry up and get this over with, right?)

To test your new LAN, follow these steps:

1. Go to any PC in the LAN.
2. Double-click on the Network Neighborhood icon.
3. Repeat steps 1 and 2 for every PC in the LAN.

If everything went well, you see a little icon for every PC in the LAN. In Figure 25-7, for example, you see the four PCs in my little LAN: Cd_master, Comm_center, Pentium_pc, and Travel_pc. Your screen, of course, should list the computer names that you assigned to the PCs in your LAN.

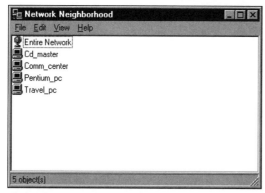

Figure 25-7: Each PC in the workgroup appears in Network Neighborhood.

If you don't see the names of the PCs in your LAN, first try double-clicking on the Entire Network option. That action may be enough of a wake-up call to get things going. When you can close the Network Neighborhood folder, reopen the folder, and immediately see all the PCs on your LAN, you're finished. You're ready to move on to Chapter 26 and start sharing resources on the LAN.

If you can't get the network going, or if some PCs refuse to appear inside Network Neighborhood, try the troubleshooting techniques in the following section.

Troubleshooting the LAN

As you've seen, setting up a LAN is a complicated ritual that involves many settings and options. Any little wrong setting can cripple the network. The following sections examine possible solutions to various problems that may arise.

You have no Network Neighborhood icon

If one of your PCs doesn't have a Network Neighborhood icon on its desktop, first make sure that the icon isn't just hidden. Close all open windows, right-click on the desktop, and choose Arrange Icons⇨by Name. Typically, this action puts the Network Neighborhood icon right below the My Computer icon.

If that procedure doesn't work, something isn't installed — the LAN hardware, the LAN software, or both. Make sure that you installed the LAN hardware and that the cable from the PC is connected to the Ethernet hub. Then repeat the installation instructions, beginning with "Telling Windows 95 That You're on the LAN" earlier in this chapter.

Network Neighborhood is empty

If nothing appears when you open Network Neighborhood, try the following semi-superstitious ritual on each PC:

1. Close all open windows.

2. Choose Start⇨Shut Down.

3. Select Shut down the computer? and then click on Yes.

4. When the screen says that it's safe to do so, shut down the PC and all attached peripherals — monitor, printer, external CD-ROM drive, everything.

Next, check the cable that attaches the PC to the Ethernet hub. Make sure that the cable is properly plugged into the PC's network card and properly plugged into the hub. If the hub has its own power, make sure that the hub is plugged into the wall and turned on. (See the manual that came with the hub for any additional instructions.)

When you're sure that everything is plugged in correctly, follow these steps:

1. Go to any PC in the LAN, and turn on all of its external peripherals (monitor, external CD-ROM drive, and so on).

2. Turn on the PC.

3. Watch the screen for any error message that may give you a clue as to what's wrong.

4. When you're prompted, log in, using the appropriate user name and password for that PC.

Logging in to the LAN with a valid user name and password is very important. If you just make up a user name and password, Windows will allow you to go to the desktop but not to the LAN. This situation will make it appear as though the LAN isn't working when, in fact, it may be working perfectly.

5. Repeat Steps 1–4 on each PC in the LAN.

After all the PCs are turned back on, double-click on the Network Neighborhood icon on each PC again. You should see an icon for every PC in the LAN. If so, you're finished, and you're ready to start sharing resources on the LAN. Proceed to Chapter 26.

A PC is missing

If Network Neighborhood shows some, but not all, of the PCs in the LAN, you need to troubleshoot the missing PCs. Go to any PC that is not listed (but should be), and follow these steps:

1. Shut down Windows.
2. Shut down the entire PC system, including all external peripherals.
3. Make sure that the cable is properly plugged into the LAN card on the PC and properly connected to the Ethernet hub.
4. Restart all the external peripherals, restart the PC, and go to the Windows desktop.
5. Open Network Neighborhood on the current PC and on some other PC in the LAN.

If you see the names of both PCs in Network Neighborhood, you're finished. You're ready to move to Chapter 26 and start sharing resources.

If you're still having a problem with one PC, follow these steps on that PC:

1. Right-click on Network Neighborhood, and choose P̲roperties.

Make sure that the workgroup name on the Identification tab for this PC is spelled exactly like the workgroup name for other PCs in the LAN.

2. Check everything on all three tabs, as discussed in "The Configuration tab," "The Identification tab," and "The Access Control tab" earlier in this chapter, for instructions on setting up this dialog box.
3. After you review all three tabs, choose OK.
4. Follow any instructions that appear on-screen.

If you changed any settings, you probably need to restart this PC and possibly feed it some disks. When you get back to the Windows 95 desktop, open Network Neighborhood again on this PC and on some other PC in the LAN. If you *still* can't see this PC in the LAN, you may have a hardware conflict with your Ethernet card. This problem can be the nastiest of all to solve, which is why I was so obsessed with getting the IRQs right to begin with. To diagnose and solve this problem, follow these steps:

1. Right-click on Network Neighborhood, and choose Properties.

2. Double-click on the icon for the network adapter card.

   This icon looks like a tiny board with a letter *P* on it and should show the make and model of your network card. If you see an icon named Dial-Up Adapter, ignore it; it's for dial-up networking only.

3. If your network card has a configurable IRQ and/or I/O address range, you see a tab labeled Resources. Click on that tab.

   If you don't see a Resources tab, skip to Step 6.

4. Look at the current Interrupt (IRQ) and/or I/O address range settings.

5. What you do now depends on what you see.

   - If a pound sign (#) appears before the IRQ and I/O settings, as shown in Figure 25-8, those settings are not the problem. Go to Step 6.

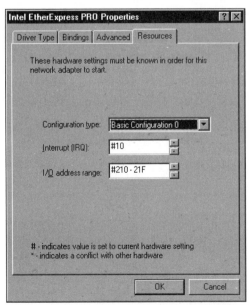

Figure 25-8: The Resources tab of a network card's Properties dialog box.

- If the IRQ setting does not match the setting that you wrote down for this computer way back in "Installing the LAN Hardware" earlier in this chapter, use the spin boxes to select the appropriate IRQ. (If the IRQ option is dimmed and unavailable, first set the Configuration type to Basic Configuration 0.) When you choose the right IRQ, you may see a # sign before that setting, but only if the card has dip switches or some kind of program for setting the IRQ.

- If an asterisk (*) appears for either the IRQ or I/O setting, you have a conflict between this piece of hardware and some other piece. Proceed to Step 6, and then read the section "If you have a hardware conflict."

6. Choose OK until you get back to the desktop.

If you have a hardware conflict

If you discover a hardware conflict, you'll have to change the IRQ setting on either the network card or on the device that's conflicting with the network card. You can use the Troubleshooter to help with that process. Follow these steps:

1. Choose Start⇨Help.
2. Click on the Contents tab.
3. Double-click on the Troubleshooting book.
4. Double-click on If you have a hardware conflict.

   Alternatively, if you think that something else may be the trouble, double-click on If you have trouble using the network.

5. Follow the instructions on-screen.

If you still can't seem to get the network working, you may have to start from scratch. Follow these steps:

1. Choose Start⇨Settings⇨Control Panel.
2. Double-click on the System icon.
3. Click on the Device Manager tab.
4. Click on the plus sign (+) next to the Network Adapters option (if any).
5. Click on the name of the adapter card that's giving you grief.
6. Click on the Remove button to remove all drivers for that card.
7. Follow the instructions on-screen.

8. Go back to the Windows 95 desktop, shut down everything, remove the network card from the computer, and start all over with "Installing the LAN Hardware" near the start of this chapter.

This time, pay very close attention to the IRQs that you choose, and be sure to write down *everything* as you go. If possible, repeat the entire process with a different IRQ this time. If IRQ 5 let you down on the first go-around, for example, use IRQ 7, 9, or 10 (if any of those settings is available) on the second try.

 Chapter 10 discusses general techniques for installing hardware and troubleshooting hardware conflicts.

If all else fails, you may need to call the manufacturer. Alternatively, study closely the instructions that came with the board and the instructions that came with the Ethernet hub. Good luck, and hang in there — I'm sure that you'll get everything working.

Summary

This chapter has been all about installing network hardware and getting your LAN up and running. The main points are:

✦ Before you install *any* hardware, use Device Manager to check, and perhaps print, information on used and available IRQs and I/O addresses.

✦ If you're installing a network card that requires you to set an IRQ and other settings right on the board, be sure you do so before installing the card. Refer to the manufacturer's instructions.

✦ You should install the actual card as per the manufacturer's instructions. But ignore any instructions about installing DOS/Windows 3 drivers for the card.

✦ As you specify IRQ and other settings, be sure to jot down notes. You may be asked for this information several times as you proceed through the installation.

✦ After you've installed all the LAN hardware, in all the PCs, you can start setting up the LAN software. Turn on all peripherals and PCs. Then start up each PC. If Windows 95 doesn't detect the new hardware automatically, you can run the Add New Hardware wizard to install the appropriate software.

✦ When identifying PCs on the LAN, be sure to give each computer a unique computer name, but give each computer *the same* workgroup name.

✦ When configuring the LAN software, be sure to click the File and Print Sharing button, and enable file and print sharing if you plan to share either anywhere down the road.

✦ After installing all hardware, setting up the software, and restarting each PC in the LAN, you should be able to double-click the Network Neighborhood icon on any PC, and see the names of all PCs in the LAN.

✦   ✦   ✦

Sharing Resources on a LAN

By the time you get to this chapter, you should already have set up your LAN, as described in Chapters 24 and 25. Sharing resources on a LAN makes no sense until you can see the PCs listed in Network Neighborhood.

Sharing a Printer

When you share a printer on a LAN, any other PC on the LAN can use that printer. The printer, of course, needs to be physically connected (by a cable) to one PC on the LAN. *Which* PC you use doesn't matter. Throughout this chapter, I refer to whichever PC you use for printing as the *print server*. Mind you, this computer need not be dedicated to printing; it can be anyone's PC on the LAN. If two or more PCs in the LAN have a printer attached, you can share all those printers.

On the print server

Before you can use another PC's printer, you need to go to the PC to which the printer is physically attached, make sure that the printer is installed locally at that machine, and then share that PC. Follow these steps:

1. Go to the PC that the printer is plugged in to and open My Computer (double-click on its icon).

2. Double-click on the Printers folder.

3. If the printer that you want to share already has an icon in the Printers folder, skip to Step 5.

4. If you haven't already installed the printer on this PC, go ahead and do so, using the Add Printer icon.

When the wizard asks, be sure to tell it that you're install-ingalocalprinter(aprinterthat'sconnectedtothisPCbyacable).Whenyoufinishwiththewizard, proceed to Step 5.

5. Right-click on the icon for the printer that you want to share and choose Sharing.

If you don't see Sharing as an option when you right-click on a printer icon, chances are that you just forgot to allow printer sharing on this PC. See "Troubleshooting File and Printer Sharing" later in this chapter.

6. Choose Shared As; then type a brief name for the printer and a description, as in the example shown in Figure 26-1.

Optionally, if you want to limit the sharing of this printer to people who know a password, you can type that password.

7. Choose OK.

A little hand appears below the printer's icon, indicating that the printer can be shared.

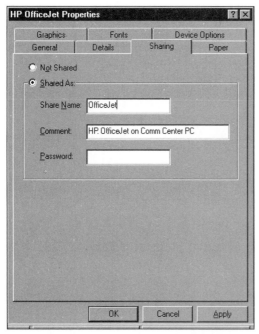

Figure 26-1: Sharing a printer named OfficeJet.

On any printer client

Any other PC in the LAN now can act as a *printer client*. By printer client, I mean any PC in the LAN that the printer is not directly plugged in to. But before you can print from a particular PC to the shared printer, you need to install a driver for that printer. Follow these steps:

Gather up your original Windows 95 floppies or CD-ROM for this procedure; you may need them to install a driver for the network printer.

1. Go to any PC that needs access to the shared printer.

   Remember that this printer can be any printer in the LAN *except* the PC that the printer is physically plugged in to.

2. Open My Computer (double-click on its icon).

3. Double-click on the Printers folder.

4. Double-click on the Add Printer icon.

5. Click on Next.

6. In the second page of the wizard, choose Network printer, as shown in Figure 26-2.

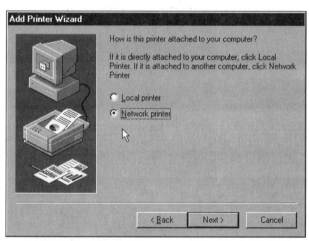

Figure 26-2: Ready to connect to a printer that's connected to some other PC in the LAN.

7. Click on Next.

8. Click on the Browse button, double-click on the name of the PC to which the printer is attached, and then click on the name of the shared printer, as shown in Figure 26-3.

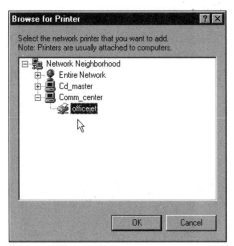

Figure 26-3: Connecting to the shared printer named OfficeJet.

9. Choose OK.

10. Click on Next.

11. Type a name for the printer.

    Optionally, if you want to use this printer as the general default printer when you print from this PC, also choose Yes.

12. Click on Next.

13. Complete the remaining options and instructions that the wizard presents.

    When you finish, an icon for the shared printer appears in the Printers folder.

You needn't repeat this process in the future. The newly installed network printer will be available whenever you use this PC (provided the printer and the print server are running at the moment).

Keep in mind, however, that you have connected only this PC to the network printer. If you want to connect other PCs to that printer, you must go to that PC and Steps 2–3.

Printing a document

After you install the driver for a network printer, using that printer is no different from using a printer that's physically attached to your computer. You can do the following things:

✦ To print from the program that you're currently using, choose File⇨Print in that program. If necessary, you can select a specific printer in the Print dialog box that appears (exactly how you do that depends on the program that you're using).

✦ You can print documents by dragging their icons to the printer's icon.

 For more information on printing, refer to Chapter 14.

If the network printer happens to be busy printing someone else's document, your print job waits in the queue until the printer is available. You can go about your business normally, right after you start the print job.

Network printer tips

As mentioned earlier, you can share several printers on a network. To specify which printer you want to use as the default printer for any PC, open the Printers folder (by double-clicking on it in My Computer or by choosing Start⇨Settings⇨Printers). Then click on the printer that you want to use as the default and choose File⇨Set as Default.

When you print from within a program, the program assumes that you want to use the default printer. Most programs, though, allow you to choose a different printer on the fly. After you choose File⇨Print, select a printer by using the Name drop-down list, the Select Printer button, or whatever tool is available for that purpose.

If you have a problem with a print job, check the print queue on your local printer; open the Printers folder and then double-click on the icon for the printer that's causing the problem. Most likely, the print job still is in your local print queue. You can use commands in the Printer and Document menus to pause or cancel the print job.

Deferred network printing

If, for whatever reason, a network printer becomes unavailable, the icon for that printer is dimmed, but still available. Any print jobs that you send to the printer are held in your local print queue until the network printer becomes available. When that printer becomes available, your print jobs start.

Sharing an Entire Hard Disk

You can share an entire hard disk from any PC in the LAN. When you do, every other PC in the LAN has access to everything on that hard disk. This setup is useful when security is not an issue. If you're setting up a LAN between a portable PC and a desktop PC, for example, you may want to share the desktop computer's entire hard disk. That way, you can get to all of its contents from the portable even while you're on the road, if you use Dial-Up Networking (refer to Chapter 20).

Sharing a hard disk is like sharing any other device. Two steps are involved: going to the server (the PC which contains the hard disk that you want to share) and sharing the disk. Then you can go to any client (any other PC in the LAN) and get to that drive via Network Neighborhood. You also can map a drive letter to the shared drive, as discussed a bit later in this chapter.

On the hard-disk server

The first step in giving multiple computers access to another computer's hard disk is to actually perform the sharing. Follow these steps:

1. Go to the PC that contains the hard disk that you want to share.

2. Open My Computer (double-click on its icon).

3. Right-click on the icon for the drive that you want to share, and choose Sharing.

If you don't see Sharing as an option when you right-click on a drive's icon, chances are that you forgot to allow file sharing on this PC. See "Trouble-shooting File and Printer Sharing" later in this chapter.

4. Choose Shared As and give the drive a name.

5. Choose Full if you want to be able to add, change, and remove files from this drive (see Figure 26-4).

6. Choose OK.

   A little hand now appears below the icon for the drive, indicating that the drive is shared.

From this point on, any other PC in the LAN can connect to that drive.

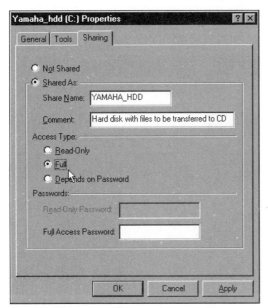

Figure 26-4: Sharing an entire hard disk drive (HDD).

On any hard-disk client

The easiest way to access a shared hard drive from a *client* (a client being any other PC in the LAN) is to start by mapping a drive letter to that shared drive. Follow these steps:

1. Go to any client PC, and double-click on Network Neighborhood.

2. Double-click on the name of the PC that contains the shared drive.

    You see a list of all the shared resources on that PC.

3. Click on the name of the shared drive and then choose File⇨Map Network Drive.

    Alternatively, right-click on the icon for the shared drive and then choose Map Network Drive (see Figure 26-5).

4. In the dialog box that appears, choose any available drive letter to represent this shared drive.

    If you want to re-establish this connection whenever you log on in the future, choose the Reconnect at logon option (see Figure 26-6).

5. Choose OK.

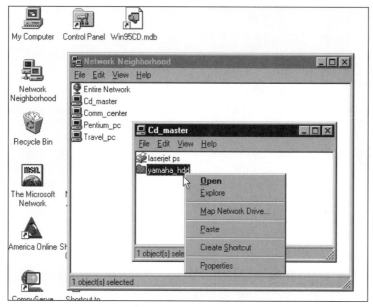

Figure 26-5: Mapping a drive letter to a shared hard disk.

Figure 26-6: Mapping the drive named Y to a shared hard disk on another PC.

You can close the Map Network Drive and Network Neighborhood windows now, if you want. You don't need these windows to use the shared drive; you needed them only to establish the connection.

Sharing floppy, removable, and zip drives

You can use the techniques described in "Sharing an Entire Hard Disk" to share any type of drive: a floppy drive, a removable Syquest or Bernoulli drive, a zip drive, and even a CD-ROM drive. Then go to any other PC in the LAN and map a drive letter to that shared drive.

When you double-click on the icon for the shared drive in My Computer, you see the contents of whatever disk happens to be in that drive. If you gave yourself full permission, you also can create folders on that drive and copy files to those folders — a great way to

make backups of specific folders on many PCs in the LAN.

You also can install programs from the shared drive. Suppose that the drive you shared is a floppy drive or CD-ROM drive and that you mapped the drive letter G to that drive. To install a program from that shared drive, go to the PC on which you want to install the program, click on the Start button, choose Run, and launch the appropriate startup program from drive G (for example, G:\SETUP or G:\INSTALL).

Using the shared hard drive

After you map a drive letter to a shared drive, you can treat the drive as though it were connected directly to the current PC. The fact that the drive happens to be housed inside some other PC becomes, essentially, irrelevant. When you open My Computer, for example, the drive to which you mapped a letter appears just like the hard disk that's really on your computer, but with a little network cable below the icon (see Figure 26-7). You can move and copy files to this drive just as though it were inside this PC.

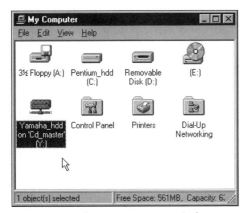

Figure 26-7: The My Computer window after you map a drive letter (Y) to a shared network drive.

If I double-click on the icon for the Y drive, for example, I see the folders and some files within that drive. Now suppose that I size that window and move it to the right, double-click on the icon for my local C drive, and then size and move that window to the left. Now I can now see the contents of both drives (see Figure 26-8). I can right-drag folders, or files within folders, from one drive's window to the other's to move and copy files at will.

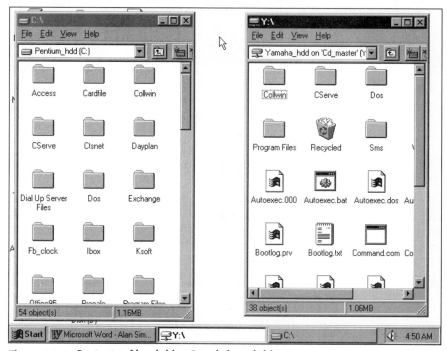

Figure 26-8: Contents of local drive C and shared drive Y.

You have all your normal viewing and browsing options in both windows. You can, for example, choose an option from the View menu to change your view of the icons in either window. To see the contents of a folder on either drive, just double-click on the folder.

If you start to lose track of which window represents which drive, choose View⇨Options in My Computer, click on the View tab, and then choose Display the full MS-DOS path in the title bar. Each window's title bar now includes the drive letter.

Sharing a CD-ROM Drive

You can share, and connect to, a CD-ROM drive by using exactly the same techniques that you use to share and connect to an entire hard disk. A few minor differences exist, however, in the way that you use the shared CD-ROM drive:

✦ Because a CD-ROM drive is, by definition, read-only, allowing full access to the drive has no advantage.

✦ What's shared and available at any given moment is the CD-ROM that happens to be in the CD-ROM drive at that moment.

✦ Some CD-ROMs have an installation procedure that copies one or more programs to your hard disk. You can install those programs on the local hard disk after you map a drive letter to the shared CD-ROM drive.

Consider this example of using a shared CD-ROM drive. I tend to keep the Microsoft Bookshelf CD-ROM in the CD-ROM drive of my main Pentium computer, for the simple reason that Bookshelf is a good resource for writers. Now suppose that I want to be able to access Bookshelf from some other PC in the LAN (or all other PCs in the LAN).

The first step is to share the CD-ROM drive. I go to the Pentium computer that houses the CD-ROM drive, open My Computer, right-click on the icon for the CD-ROM drive, and choose S̲haring. Then I choose S̲hared As, give the drive a name (PentiumCDROM, for this example), select R̲ead-Only as the access type (see Figure 26-9), and choose OK.

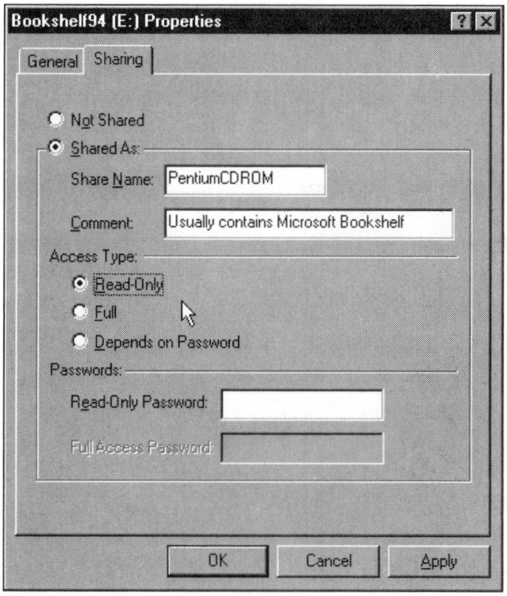

Figure 26-9: Sharing the CD-ROM drive on my Pentium PC.

Connecting to the shared CD-ROM drive

Now I can go to any other PC in the LAN and map a drive letter to the shared CD-ROM drive. I go to my portable PC, open Network Neighborhood, and double-click on the icon for the Pentium computer. When the shared objects from that computer appear, I right-click on the PentiumCDROM icon and choose _M_ap Network Drive. I specify any available drive letter (M, for example) and opt to reconnect at logon. Then I choose OK and close all the remaining open windows.

Installing programs from the shared CD-ROM drive

Before I can actually use the Microsoft Bookshelf CD-ROM from the shared CD-ROM drive, I need to install some of its programs to the portable computer's hard disk. That procedure is simple enough. Follow these steps:

1. Choose Start⇨_S_ettings⇨_C_ontrol Panel.

2. Double-click on the Add/Remove Programs icon.

3. Click on the Install button.

4. Click on Next, and see whether the wizard finds the appropriate program.

   In my example, the program would be on drive M, because that's the drive letter that I mapped to the shared CD-ROM drive.

5. If the wizard finds a setup program on some other drive before it gets to the appropriate drive (M, in this case), click on the _B_rowse button; select the shared CD-ROM drive in the Look _i_n drop-down list; and then click on the setup or install program on that drive, as shown in Figure 26-10.

6. Choose _O_pen.

   The Run Installation wizard window states that the PC is about to run the selected program (M:\SETUP, in this case), as shown in Figure 26-11.

Figure 26-10: Ready to run Setup from the PentiumCDROM drive.

7. Click on the Finish button.

8. Follow any instructions on-screen.

Figure 26-11: Ready to run the setup program on CD-ROM drive M.

From now on, I can access Microsoft Bookshelf from either the Pentium PC or the portable PC, so long as the Bookshelf CD-ROM is in the Pentium's CD-ROM drive. All I need to do is click on the QuickStart buttons that come with Bookshelf. Alternatively, I can choose Start⇨Programs⇨Microsoft Multimedia⇨Bookshelf 95 on whichever PC I happen to be using.

The example of running Microsoft Bookshelf from several PCs is not an endorsement for software piracy. Many programs require special licensing for concurrent use on a LAN, or individual use on multiple PCs. Read your software license agreement for more information. Then comply!

I can repeat the preceding steps on all the PCs in my LAN, if I want, so that I can get to the Bookshelf CD-ROM from wherever I happen to be. I can even have all the PCs access Microsoft Bookshelf at the same time.

Sharing a Folder

Sharing drives is great in some situations, but it can be confusing in other situations. Also, you may want to share some stuff on your hard disk but keep other people away from other stuff. The simple solution is to share individual folders rather than an entire drive. Other users can map a drive letter to that folder. When they browse the drive letter, the "drive" that they see is just that folder, including any subfolders within that folder.

As mentioned earlier, I keep all my ongoing work in a folder named Projects. I keep that folder on one PC and share it. Then, from every other PC in the LAN, I map a drive letter (P) to that folder. When I'm not at my main computer, I always know where to look for a document for some current project: in the P drive.

On the folder server

Technically, a PC that shares folders or files is called a *file server*. But that term can be a little misleading in this context, because it implies that just one PC is acting as the server and that all the other PCs are clients. In the peer-to-peer type of network discussed in this chapter, any PC can share a folder, and any other PC can connect to that shared folder. So a more accurate term may be *folder server*, which means "whatever PC the folder happens to be on."

The technique for sharing and connecting to a folder is exactly the same as the procedure for sharing and connecting to a drive; you just have to navigate a little deeper. To share a folder, follow these steps:

1. Go to the PC on which the folder is actually stored.

2. Use My Computer or Windows Explorer to browse to the folder that you want to share.

3. When you see the icon for the folder that you want to share, right-click on that icon and choose S̲haring.

If you don't see S̲haring as an option when you right-click on a drive's icon, you probably forgot to allow file sharing on this PC. See "Troubleshooting File and Printer Sharing" later in this chapter.

4. Choose S̲hared As, and type a brief, descriptive name for the folder.

   You can type a longer description in the Comment box.

5. Select the access type that you want to use: R̲ead-Only (other users can see and copy files but not change, move, or delete them), F̲ull (other users can view, change, copy, move, and delete files), or D̲epends on Password (you can define one password to limit some people to read-only access and define another password to give other people full access.

   Figure 26-12 shows an example in which I'm allowing full access to my Projects folder.

6. Choose OK.

   A little hand appears below the icon for the folder, indicating that the folder is shared.

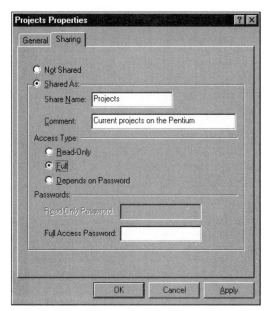

Figure 26-12: Full access to my Projects folder is granted to other LAN members.

On any folder client

Now you can get to the shared folder, via Network Neighborhood, from any PC on the LAN. To simplify future access to this shared folder, you can assign a drive letter to the folder by following these steps:

1. On any PC in the LAN (other than the PC on which the folder is actually stored), double-click on Network Neighborhood on the Windows 95 desktop.

2. Double-click on the name of the PC that contains the shared folder.

3 In the dialog box that appears, right-click on the name of the shared folder and then choose Map Network Drive (see Figure 26-13).

4. In the Map Network Drive dialog box, select any available drive letter.

   Optionally, you also can specify whether you want to reconnect to this folder automatically in future logons.

5. Choose OK.

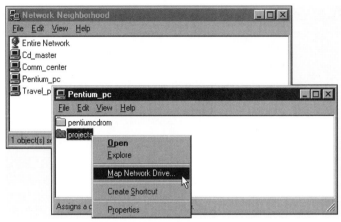

Figure 26-13: About to map a drive letter to a shared folder.

You can close all open windows now, if you want.

Using the shared folder

After you connect to a shared folder, you can think of that folder as being its own little drive, from the perspective of the PC that you're using. This concept may be confusing at first, but if you think of the drive letter as being sort of a nickname for the folder, understanding it becomes easier.

Whenever I'm on a PC in my LAN, for example, I know that drive P really is just the nickname for my Projects folder. The folder's real name is \\Pentium_pc\projects; remembering P is easier. And that's the beauty of being able to assign a drive letter to a shared folder.

Any shared resource on the LAN to which you've mapped a drive letter appears with a network-drive icon in My Computer. You have no separate icon for a connected CD-ROM drive or a connected folder.

After you map that drive letter, you can treat the shared folder as you would any drive that's physically connected to your PC. When you open My Computer, you see a network-drive icon for the shared folder (see Figure 26-14). You can double-click on that icon to browse the shared folder and to open, copy, move, rename, and delete files normally (assuming that you have full access to the shared folder).

Yet another advantage to having all your ongoing projects in a single folder is the simplicity of making backups. Rather than use a slow, noisy tape-backup machine to back up your entire hard disk, you can install a removable hard disk, or zip drive. To back up all your current work, drag the Projects folder to the icon for that drive.

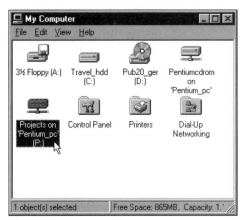

Figure 26-14: The shared folder is drive P, from this computer's perspective.

You also can get to the drive through all the other traditional means of browsing your computer. The connected folder appears as a network-drive icon in Windows Explorer, for example. When you're in a program and choose File⇨Open or File⇨Save As, you can use the Drives or Look in icon to navigate to the connected folder.

Figure 26-15 shows the Open dialog box in Microsoft Word. I've opened the Look in: drop-down list and am about to open P (my Projects folder) to look for the document that I want to open.

You can share as many folders as you want on as many PCs as you want. Just remember that first, you have to go to the PC that the folder is stored on and share the folder from there. Then you can go to any other PC in the LAN and use Network Neighborhood (or Windows Explorer) to map a drive letter to the shared folder.

You even can share a subfolder that's within a shared folder. This form of sharing may seem to be a little strange, because that folder is accessible already. But if you share the subfolder on its own, you can map a drive letter to it and then have easy one-click access to that folder.

Figure 26-16 shows the Windows Explorer window on my Pentium PC, on which the Projects folder resides. Notice that the Projects folder is shared, as always. In addition, I have shared the Windows 95 Book folder within that folder.

After sharing that subfolder, I can go to any other PC in the LAN and, using Network Neighborhood or Windows Explorer, map a different drive letter to that subfolder. Suppose that I map the drive letter W to that folder. From then on, whenever I'm in My Computer, Windows Explorer, a program's Open dialog box, or whatever, I can refer to drive W when I specifically want the folder for this book. In other words, I've given the subfolder its own nickname: W (see Figure 26-17).

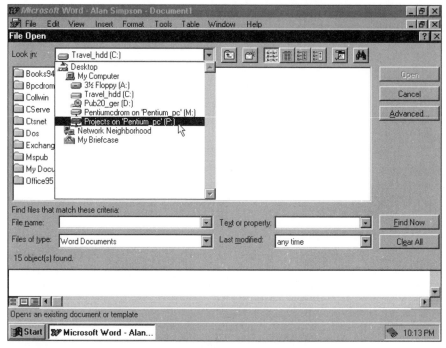

Figure 26-15: Switching to drive P from Word's Open dialog box.

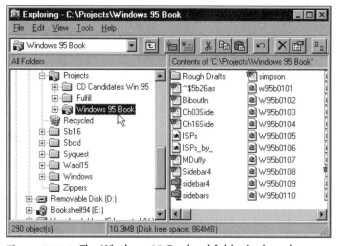

Figure 26-16: The Windows 95 Book subfolder is shared.

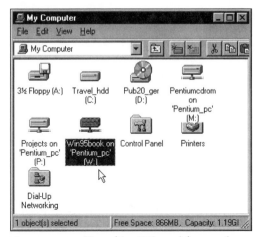

Figure 26-17: Now drive W is a nickname for the Windows 95 Book folder on my Pentium.

This kind of freedom and flexibility takes some getting accustomed to, especially if you've been fighting with floppy disks or dealing with a restrictive dedicated-server type of LAN for a few years. If you remember that you can get to any folder from any drive on any PC in the LAN, however, you'll soon find new ways to organize your materials for quick and efficient access.

Disconnecting from a Shared Resource

If you want to disconnect from a shared printer, drive, or folder, follow these steps:

1. Go to the client PC — the one that's connected to the resource via the network, not physically connected to the source.

2. Open My Computer (double-click on its icon).

3. Do one of the following things:

   - To disconnect from a shared drive or folder, right-click on the appropriate network-drive icon and choose <u>D</u>isconnect.

   - To disconnect from a shared printer, double-click on the Printers folder. Then right-click on the icon for the printer from which you want to disconnect and choose Disconnect.

4. Close My Computer.

The resource itself remains shared, and any other PCs that were connected to the resource still are connected. If you want to stop sharing the resource, see the following section.

Stopping Resource Sharing

To stop sharing a resource, follow these steps:

1. Go to the resource server — the PC to which the printer is physically attached or the PC that contains the shared drive or folder.

2. Open My Computer (double-click on its icon).

3. Do any of the following things:

    • To stop sharing a drive, right-click on the drive's icon (the sharing hand appears below it) and choose Sharing.

    • To stop sharing a folder, double-click on the icon for the drive that contains the shared folder, browse to the shared folder, right-click on the folder's icon, and choose Sharing.

    • To stop sharing a printer, double-click on the Printers icon, right-click on the icon for the shared printer, and choose Sharing.

4. Choose Not Shared from the dialog box that appears.

 When you stop sharing a device, you disconnect all users from that device. Disconnecting users from a shared drive or folder can destroy any work that they have in progress. Don't do it!

5. If any users are connected to that shared device, you see a warning that you're about to disconnect them; choose No to leave them connected (recommended).

You should disconnect users only if you're sure that they're not working on documents stored on the shared drive or folder; otherwise, you run the risk of ruining any work that the other users have in progress. Your best bet is to go to each client PC in the network, save any outstanding work, and disconnect that PC from the shared resource first. Then, when you get back to the PC that's playing the role of server for the shared resource, you can stop sharing the resource without destroying some colleague's hard work.

Shutting Down LAN PCs

After you connect a PC to a LAN, never turn that PC off — unless, of course, you have to shut it down to install some new hardware. In that case, you should warn other users to save all their work so that you don't cut them off from a folder that they may be using.

But in general, you don't want other users to lose access to any shared resources that may be on the PC. So if the person who works at that machine is going home for the evening, he or she should turn off the monitor and leave everything else on. The monitor, even if it's just displaying a screen saver, is the biggest power hog in the system. So shutting down the monitor if you're going to be away from the PC for any length of time is a good idea.

Troubleshooting File and Printer Sharing

If you can remember these important points, you should be able to troubleshoot any problems that you have sharing resources on a LAN:

✦ Before you can share a resource, you must allow sharing from the PC to which the resource is connected. If you can't share a particular resource, right-click on Network Neighborhood and choose Properties. Then activate file and printer sharing in the Configuration tab (refer to Chapter 25).

✦ Remember that only PCs that have the same workgroup name can share resources in Network Neighborhood. To check (and, optionally, change) a PC's workgroup name, right-click on Network Neighborhood on that PC, and then use the Identification tab.

✦ Network Neighborhood displays only resources that are shared. Before you can connect to a shared resource, you must go to the PC to which the resource is connected and share the resource from there.

✦ To simplify access to a shared drive or folder, you can right-click on the resource's icon in Network Neighborhood and map a drive letter to that resource. From then on, the resource appears as a network-drive icon in that PC's My Computer window.

Committing these important points to your brain will help prevent many potential problems and make troubleshooting problems on the fly easier. But other factors also come into play. If you need help with a problem in sharing a resource or connecting to a shared resource, try the Troubleshooter. Follow these steps:

1. Click the Start⇨Help.

2. Click on the Contents tab.

3. Double-click on the Troubleshooting book.

4. Double-click on If you have trouble using the network.

5. Follow the instructions on-screen.

The Troubleshooter is very good at helping you define and isolate a problem, as well as taking you right to the settings that you need to change to make the problem go away.

Sharing a Fax/Modem

If you have more PCs than fax/modems in your office, you can share any fax/modem so that you can send a fax from any PC in the LAN without moving or copying files to another PC.

Sharing a fax/modem is a little trickier than sharing other devices. Before you even attempt to share a fax/modem, you need to do three things:

✦ Choose one PC in the LAN to act as the fax server and install the fax/modem on that PC, as discussed in Chapter 15.

✦ Install Microsoft Fax and Microsoft Exchange, as discussed in Chapter 16, on all PCs that will use the fax/modem.

If you have problems installing Microsoft Fax on a PC that doesn't have a modem yet, you can install a standard modem (even though no physical modem may even be attached to the PC). Later, you can delete the fake modem and attach the PC to the shared fax/modem.

✦ You need to have the entire LAN set up and working, as discussed in Chapters 24 and 25.

When the three preliminary tasks are out of the way, you can proceed with the tasks in the following sections.

On the fax server

I'll refer to the PC that the fax/modem is physically connected to as the *fax server*. Your first step in sharing that fax/modem is to make the modem available for sharing. Follow these steps:

1. Go to the fax server — the PC to which the fax/modem is connected.

2. Double-click on the Inbox icon on the desktop or choose Start⇨Programs⇨Microsoft Exchange to get into Microsoft Exchange.

3. Choose Tools⇨Microsoft Fax Tools⇨Options.

   The Microsoft Fax Properties dialog box appears.

4. Click on the Modem tab.

5. Click on the name of the modem that you plan to share and then click on the Set as Active Fax Modem button.

6. Near the bottom of the dialog box, select Let other people on the network use my modem to send faxes.

7. Click on the Properties button, choose Shared as, and type a brief name and description for the fax.

   Optionally, you can type a password if you want to limit access to your fax/modem to people who know the password.

8. Choose OK.

   You return to the Microsoft Fax Properties dialog box, in which the fax name appears, dimmed, next to Share name (see Figure 26-18).

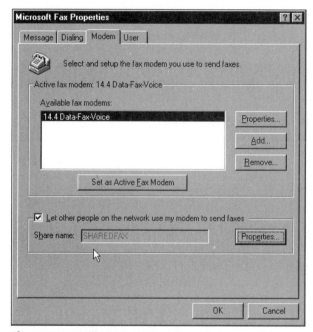

Figure 26-18: Sharing a fax/modem.

9. Optionally, if you want to double-check other settings on this shared modem, click on the Properties button near the fax/modem name, check your settings, and then choose OK.

10. Choose OK.

   You return to the Microsoft Exchange window.

11. Click the Close (X) button to close Exchange.

Even though you may not be prompted to do so, I've found that restarting the computer at this time is a good idea. Choose Start⇨Shut Down⇨Restart the Computer?; then click on the Yes button. Wait for the Windows 95 desktop to come back on-screen before you try connecting to the shared modem from another PC in the LAN.

On any fax client

To give another PC in the LAN access to the shared fax/modem, you first need to know the name of the computer on which the fax/modem is installed and the name of the fax/modem. You can see the computer's name in Network Neighborhood. In my case, the computer that's acting as fax server is named Comm_ctr. The name of the fax/modem is whatever you entered in the Microsoft Fax Properties dialog box (refer to Figure 26-18). The official name that you'll need to know is two backslashes, followed by the computer name, followed by one backslash and the fax/modem name. In my example, that name comes out as \\Comm_ctr\SharedFax.

Jot the name down on a piece of paper and take it with you to any PC that you want to give access to that shared modem. Then follow these steps:

1. On any PC that you want to give access to the shared modem, open Microsoft Exchange (double-click on the Inbox icon or choose Start⇨Programs⇨Microsoft Exchange.

2. Choose Tools⇨Microsoft Fax Tools⇨Options.

   The Microsoft Fax Properties dialog box appears.

3. Click on the Modem tab.

4. Click on the Add button.

5. Choose Network Fax/modem from the little list that appears.

6. In the next dialog box, you must type the computer name and fax-modem name, as discussed earlier.

   In my case, I would make the entry shown in Figure 26-19.

7. Choose OK.

   You return to the Microsoft Fax Properties dialog box.

8. Click on the name of the shared modem to which you just connected; then on click the Set As Active Fax/modem button.

9. Choose OK to return to Microsoft Exchange.

10. Close Exchange.

If you previously had to install a driver for a fake modem, you can get rid of the driver now. Open Control Panel (choose Start⇨Settings⇨Control Panel), double-click on the Modems icon, click on the name of the fake modem driver, and click on the Remove button. Then choose Close and close Control Panel.

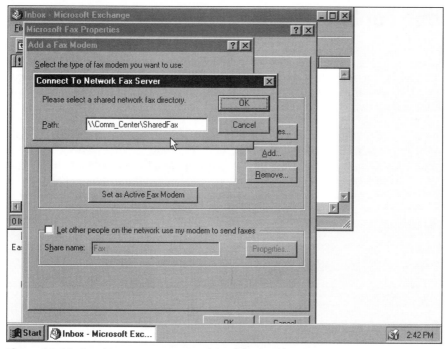

Figure 26-19: Ready to connect to my shared fax/modem.

Using the shared fax/modem

The shared fax/modem now is your default modem for sending faxes from this PC. Use the standard technique described in Chapter 16 to create and send a fax at any time — that is, choose Start⇨Programs⇨Accessories⇨Fax⇨Compose New Fax.

 Chapter 30 discusses Microsoft Exchange in more detail. Chapter 16 discusses faxing in particular.

Your new fax message is added to the Outbox in Microsoft Exchange and sent when the modem becomes available. To check on a fax that you sent, open Exchange, and check the Outbox and Sent Items. If the fax still is in the Outbox, you can choose Tools⇨Deliver Now Using⇨Microsoft Fax to send it right away (assuming that the fax/modem isn't busy at the moment).

Sharing Fonts

Fonts can get to be a pain on a LAN, because different PCs may have different fonts installed. Suppose that Bertha creates a nice document using her cool Avalon Quest font. Then Ellen opens that document on her PC. But Ellen doesn't have the Avalon Quest font on her PC, so Windows replaces that font with something else, such as Times Roman, which doesn't have quite the look and feel that Bertha intended.

One way around this problem is to create a single font repository on one PC in the LAN. Figure 26-20 shows one of the PCs, named Comm_ctr, in my LAN. On that computer is a folder named NetFonts. When you open the NetFonts folder, you see that it contains two subfolders: one named TrueType and one named Psfonts. The TrueType folder contains TrueType fonts, all of which all have the file extension .TTF. The Psfonts folder contains PostScript Type 1 fonts. (A subfolder named PFM within the Psfonts folder contains PostScript Metric fonts.)

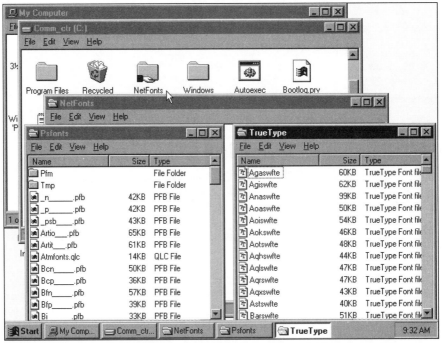

Figure 26-20: TrueType and Psfonts folders in the NetFonts folder on one PC.

You need at least version 3.0 of Adobe Type Manager to share PostScript Type 1 fonts on a LAN. Also, that version does not support long folder names. To keep things simple, give your shared fonts folder a DOS-style name, such as NETFONTS (eight characters, no spaces).

How you get all your fonts into these two folders is something for which I can't give you step-by-step instructions, because different font companies have different installation procedures. But I can give you the following pointers:

✦ Any time that you purchase and install a new font, install the font files in the appropriate folder within the NetFonts folders. Later, you can install fonts from that shared folder.

✦ To move existing PostScript fonts into the shared folder, move all the fonts that currently are in your Psfonts and Psfonts\PFM directory into the Psfonts and Psfonts\PFM subfolders within the NetFonts folder.

✦ If you want to move existing TrueType fonts into the shared folder, move only the .TTF files from the \Windows\Fonts directory, and or \Windows\System directory into that TrueType subfolder in the NetFonts folder. Keep the non-TrueType fonts (fonts that don't have the .TTF file extension) in the Windows\Fonts folder.

✦ Also keep in the Windows\Fonts folder the basic TrueType font files (.TTF) that come with Windows 95, so that if you're disconnected from the network, you still have those basic fonts to work with.

Table 26-1 lists the fonts that you should store in Windows\Fonts.

Table 26-1
Minimum Fonts in Your Local \Windows\Fonts Folder

Font Name	Normal	Bold	Bold Italic	Italic
Arial	ARIAL.TTF	ARIAL.TTF	ARIALBI.TTF	ARIALI.TTF
Courier New	COUR.TTF	COURBD.TTF	COURBI.TTF	COURI.TTF
Symbol	SYMBOL.TTF			
Times New Roman	TIMES.TTF	TIMESBD.TTF	TIMESBI.TTF	TIMESI.TTX
Wingdings	WINGDING.TTF			

Whew! (If you don't have a ton of fonts, going to all this trouble may not be worthwhile.) After you set up your NetFonts folder and subfolders and then install (or move) font files into those files, read the following sections for instructions on installing fonts from those shared folders in Windows.

Installing the TrueType fonts

Getting the .TTF font files into a folder on your hard disk is just the first step in installing a font. Again, I can't give you specific step-by-step instructions, because the procedure depends on how the font manufacturer distributes its fonts.

Once again, I'm not endorsing software piracy here. Before you share a set of fonts, check your license agreement for information on network and concurrent-use details.

The second step is making Windows 95 aware that the .TTF fonts are there — a confusing situation, because this step also is called "installing the fonts." I can give you step-by-step instructions. I'm assuming that the .TTF file for the font that you want to install already is on the hard disk in the NetFonts\TrueType folder.

Installing TrueType fonts on the font server

On the PC that's playing the role of font server, you need to install TrueType fonts from the local NetFonts\TrueType directory. Follow these steps:

1. Choose Start⇨Settings⇨Control Panel.

2. Double-click on the Fonts icon.

3. Choose File⇨Install New Font.

4. Browse to the folder that contains the .TTF files (`c:\NetFonts\TrueType`, in my example), and then deselect the Copy fonts to Fonts folder option, as shown in Figure 26-21.

5. Select the fonts that you want to install by Shift+clicking, Ctrl+clicking, or clicking on the Select All button.

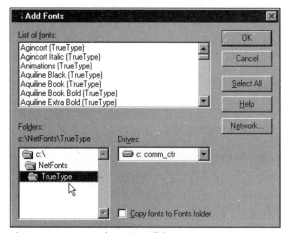

Figure 26-21: Ready to install fonts from C:\NetFonts\TrueType.

6. Choose OK.

7. Follow any instructions on-screen.

When you finish, a shortcut symbol appears on fonts that you added from the NetFonts\TrueType folder (when you're in Large Icons view). Before you leave this PC, don't forget that you need to share that folder named NetFonts if you want other PCs on the LAN to have access to these fonts. To share a folder, browse to it in My Computer, right-click on the NetFonts icon, and choose Sharing, as discussed earlier in this chapter.

Installing TrueType fonts on any client PC

Now suppose that you want to make the same TrueType fonts accessible from some other PC in the LAN. The first thing that you need to do is map a drive letter to the NetFonts folder. Follow these steps:

1. Go to the PC that will serve as a client to the shared fonts, and double-click on Network Neighborhood.

2. Double-click on the name of the PC that contains the shared fonts.

3. Right-click on the name of the shared folder that contains the shared fonts, and choose Map Drive Letter.

4. Assign a drive letter.

   I chose F in Figure 26-22.

5. Choose the Reconnect at logon option.

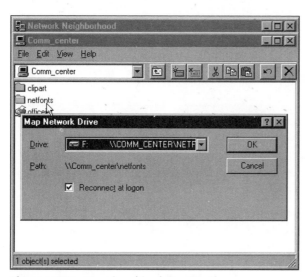

Figure 26-22: Mapping drive letter F to the NetFonts folder.

6. Choose OK.

7. Close all open windows.

If you want to make certain that you mapped a drive letter correctly, open My Computer on the current PC. You should see a network-drive icon for the NetFonts folder.

The next phase is to tell Windows 95 that the TrueType font files (.TTF) are on the shared folder and then install those fonts so they'll be accessible to all programs on this PC. Follow these steps:

1. Choose Start⇨Settings⇨Control Panel.

2. Double-click on the Fonts icon.

3. Choose File⇨Install New Font.

4. Browse to the drive and folder that contains the .TTF files (F:\TrueType, in my example), and deselect the Copy fonts to Fonts folder option; you don't need another copy of those .TTF files on this PC.

   Figure 26-23 shows an example of this procedure on a PC on my LAN.

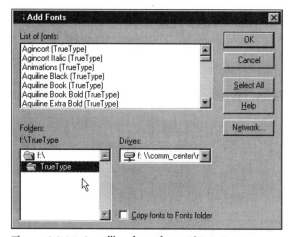

Figure 26-23: Installing fonts from F:\TrueType.

5. Select the fonts that you want to install by Ctrl+clicking, Shift+clicking, or clicking on the Select All button.

6. Choose OK.

7. Follow the instructions on-screen (if any).

You may see a message saying that you're pointing to a folder that may not be available later, because you're installing from a network drive. That's OK in this case; you're trying to avoid copying all the .TTF files to every PC in the LAN. Choose OK, and proceed with the installation.

When you finish, you can close all open windows. To test your success, open any program that supports fonts, such as Microsoft Word; then choose a font from that program (in Word, choose Format⇨Font). Your font list should include all the newly installed fonts.

Remember that if you want every PC in the LAN to have access to the same fonts, you need to go to each PC, map a drive letter, and then install the fonts as described in the two preceding sets of steps.

Installing the PostScript fonts

To use PostScript Type 1 fonts, you need a copy of the Adobe Type Manager (ATM) program on every PC that will use the Type 1 fonts. Typically, when you buy a set of Type 1 fonts, you get a copy of the ATM program disk with those fonts.

 Only ATM Version 3.0 or later allows you to install fonts without copying them. Also, you must be licensed to use Type 1 fonts on multiple PCs. For more information, contact Adobe at (800) 833-6687.

To find out whether you need to install ATM on a PC, follow these steps:

1. Choose Start⇨Programs⇨Main.

2. If you don't find the ATM icon, choose Start⇨Find, and search for `atmcntrl`.

3. If you still don't find the ATM logo and `atmcntrl` file, you need to install ATM on this PC.

You need to install ATM only one time, so if you found it by using the preceding steps, you do not need to install ATM on this PC. But if you didn't find the program, you'll need to get a copy of the program and install it on your hard disk before you can do anything with Type 1 fonts. The program usually is shipped with any PostScript Type 1 fonts that you purchase and often is labeled the ATM Control Panel Program Disk. Typically, you just need to insert that disk into drive A, click on the Start button, choose Run, and then run A:\INSTALL.EXE. Remember that you need to install a copy of the ATM Control Panel on every PC in the LAN.

Installing PostScript fonts on the server

When you buy a new PostScript Type 1 font, you want to install it on your font server. So go to the PC that acts as your font server and follow these steps:

1. Open the ATM Control Panel window (by double-clicking on its icon in the Main program group or by using Find to locate its icon and then double-clicking on that icon).

2. In the ATM section, make sure that the On option is selected, as shown in Figure 26-24.

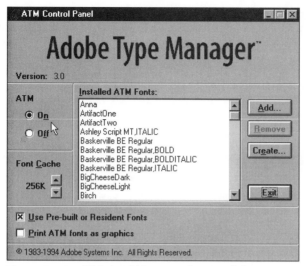

Figure 26-24: ATM should be turned on at all times.

3. Insert into drive A or B the floppy disk containing the fonts that you want to install.

4. Click on the <u>A</u>dd button.

   The Add ATM Fonts dialog box appears.

5. In the Directo<u>r</u>ies list, double-click on the drive name for the floppy from which you're installing the fonts.

6. Near the bottom of the dialog box, make sure that you specify your shared fonts folder before the psfonts and psfonts\pfm folder names.

   In Figure 26-25, I'm installing the new fonts in `c:\netfonts\psfonts` and `c:\netfonts\psfonts\pfm`.

When you're installing fonts to the server, you *do* want to copy files to that PC's hard disk. So make sure the *Install without copying files* check box is *not* selected. In other words, make sure that check box is empty as in Figure 26-25.

7. Select the fonts that you want to install.

8. Click on the <u>A</u>dd button.

9. After the fonts have been installed, click on the E<u>x</u>it button and close Adobe Type Manager.

The fonts now are ready for use on this PC (the one that's acting as the font server). To make the same fonts accessible to other PCs in the LAN, you need to tell ATM, on each PC, that the new fonts are in the shared-fonts folder.

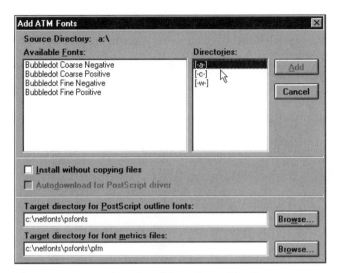

Figure 26-25: Ready to install fonts from drive A to
c:\netfonts\psfonts.

Installing PostScript fonts on any client PC

Following are a couple of things that you need to do on the client PC, if you've never
done them before:

✦ Map a drive letter to the shared-fonts directory (NetFonts, in my example), as
discussed in "Installing TrueType fonts on any client PC" earlier in this chapter.

✦ Install a copy of ATM Control Panel version 3.0 or later on this PC.

Assuming that the client PC now has access to drive F (which really is the shared-
fonts directory) and that you can start ATM on this PC, follow these steps:

1. Start ATM by choosing Start➪Programs➪Main➪ATM Control Panel or by using
Find to locate atmcntrl and then double-clicking on the ATM icon.

2. In the ATM Control Panel, make sure that ATM is turned On.

3. Click on the Add button.

4. You don't want to copy the font files to the client PC. So do select the check box
for the Install without copying files option, as I did in Figure 26-26.

5. In the Directories list, browse to drive F (or whatever drive letter you created for
your shared-fonts folder).

6. Browse to the \psfonts\pfm folder on that drive, as shown in Figure 26-26.

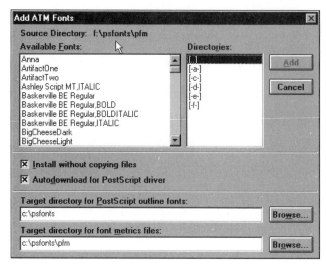

Figure 26-26: Ready to install fonts without copying them to this PC.

7. Select the fonts that you want to install (you can click the first one and then Shift+click the last one to select them all).

8. Click on the <u>A</u>dd button.

9. Follow the instructions on-screen, if any.

If the current PC already has a font that's installed on the shared network drive, for example, you see a message to that effect. Click on Cancel if you just want to keep the reference to the local copy of the font intact.

PostScript fonts will not show up in the Fonts folder; only TrueType fonts live there. So to verify the installation, you need to open a program that supports Type 1 fonts, such as Microsoft Word. Get to the fonts list (choose Format⇨Fonts), and you see the PostScript fonts marked with a printer symbol (or some symbol other than *TT* for TrueType; it depends on what program you're using). Figure 26-27 shows an example where the fonts named Anna and ArtifactOne are PostScript fonts. The others are TrueType.

Wow — I'll bet you didn't know that you could do so much with a small LAN! The next chapter examines another great advantage of LANs: the capability to send e-mail to other PCs in the LAN.

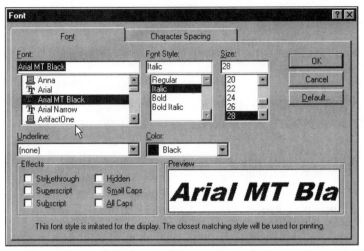

Figure 26-27: TrueType and PostScript fonts in Word's font list.

Summary

This chapter has been all about using your LAN after you've installed all the appropriate hardware and configured Windows 95 accordingly. In a nutshell:

✦ You can share a printer, drive, folder, or fax modem on any PC in the LAN.

✦ The computer that the shared resource is on or connected to is called the *server*. For example, the PC that has a printer hooked to its parallel port is the *print server*.

✦ Before other LAN members can access a shared resource, you must go to the server of that resource and share the resource. You can do that in My Computer.

✦ Any other PC in a LAN that can uses a shared resource is called a *client* to the resource. For example, every PC in the LAN *except* the one that a printer is connected to is a *print client*.

✦ Before a client can use a shared resource, that PC needs to connect to the shared resource. You can use Network Neighborhood to connect to most shared resource.

✦   ✦   ✦

Setting Up
Local E-Mail

Yet another advantage to connecting PCs in a LAN is
local e-mail, which is an easy-to-set-up type of e-mail that
allows members of a workgroup to send messages to one
another. Windows 95 comes with the Microsoft Mail Postoffice
Workgroup Edition, which is all you need to set up workgroup e-
mail. Your incoming local e-mail messages are stored in your
Microsoft Exchange Inbox, right along with your MSN (Microsoft
Network) messages, incoming faxes, and other types of messages. So managing your local e-mail along with the rest of your
messages is easy.

But before you even *think* about setting up local e-mail, make
sure that you've set up your LAN, as described in Chapters 24
and 25, and that everything is working. You need to do some
folder-sharing as well, so you should be familiar with at least that
topic from Chapter 26. On top of all that, you have to do some
planning, as the following section explains.

Phase I: Planning Local E-Mail

You need to go through the following preliminary steps before
you set up your mail system:

  ✦ Decide who will be the postmaster

  ✦ Decide which PC will be the post office

  ✦ List the names of all the people in the workgroup

These decisions generally aren't too tough to make.

Deciding who will be postmaster

Somebody needs to administer the electronic post office. The responsibilities of this job include the following:

✦ Adding new workgroup members to the post office

✦ Changing information about users

✦ Replacing forgotten passwords

✦ Occasionally checking the status of various post-office folders

✦ Occasionally backing up the post office on tape or disk

Deciding where to put the post office

The second choice that you have to make is where to put the central electronic post office. Every message that is sent over the local e-mail system will be stored on the post-office PC, so choose a PC that has a great deal of available disk space.

Also, if you've decided on a postmaster, you want to make sure that he or she can get to the post-office PC easily when necessary. Ideally, you would use the postmaster's PC as the post office.

Getting a list of workgroup members

The postmaster needs to get an e-mail name and password for each person in the workgroup who will be using the local e-mail system. I suggest that for starters, all users just use the names and passwords with which they log in. I log in with the name AlanS and the password sesame, for example, so I would use those names as my mailbox name and password.

You also can mark down each person's role in the workgroup, although only one person will be the postmaster and everyone else will be a user. Figure 27-1 shows an example of a four-person workgroup in which Susita Schumack is the postmaster (administrator).

Grab your original Windows 95 disk(s)

You may need to install some items from your original Windows 95 disks or CD-ROM, so keep the disks or the CD-ROM handy. If you need to install programs from the CD-ROM and don't have a CD-ROM drive on every PC in the workgroup, share your CD-ROM drive; then map a drive letter from each PC to that CD-ROM drive so that you can install programs from that drive. See Chapter 26 if you need help with this procedure.

Name	Mailbox Name	Password	Role
Susita Schumack	SusanS	honcho	Postmaster
Ashley Marie	AshleyM	sesame	User
Alec Fraser	AlecF	sesame	User
Alan Simpson	AlanS	sesame	User

Figure 27-1: A list of e-mail users, mailbox names, and passwords.

 More Info   If your PC is missing any of the components discussed in this chapter, you can install them by using the Microsoft Exchange item in Windows Setup. See "Installing Missing Windows Components" in Chapter 9.

Phase II: Setting Up the Post Office

When you have your plans written down on paper, you're ready to set up your workgroup post office. As usual, setup is the most time-consuming and complicated part of the process, but you have to go through it only one time. When you finish, sending and receiving e-mail messages will be a cinch.

To set up the post office, follow these steps:

1. On the PC that will act as the post office, choose Start➪Settings➪Control Panel.

2. Double-click on the Microsoft Mail Postoffice icon.

 Danger Zone   Make sure that you create only one post office, on one PC, for the entire workgroup.

3. In the first wizard screen, choose Create a new Workgroup Postoffice (see Figure 27-2).

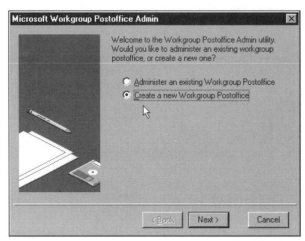

Figure 27-2: Ready to create the workgroup post office.

4. Click on the Next button.

5. In the next wizard screen, type **c:** (your local hard disk) as the post-office location, as shown in Figure 27-3, and then click on the Next button.

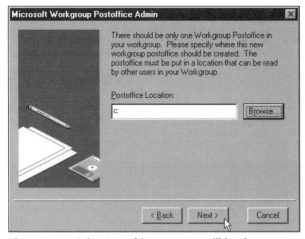

Figure 27-3: Drive C on this computer will be the post-office location.

6. The next wizard asks whether it should create C:\WGPO0000; click on Next to accept.

   The strange name is short for *workgroup post-office* number 0000.

7. In the next wizard screen, type the postmaster's name, his or her mailbox name, a password that only the postmaster will know, and any of the optional information.

   In Figure 27-4, Susita Schumack is listed as the postmaster.

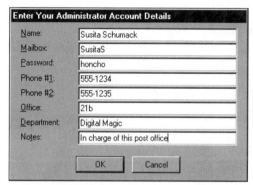

Figure 27-4: Postmaster (workgroup mail administrator) defined.

8. Choose OK.

9. You see a reminder about sharing the post-office folder; choose OK.

10. Close the Control Panel by clicking on its Close button (X), if you want.

Phase III: Sharing the Post-Office Folder

Now that the wizard has created a post-office folder for you (most likely, C:\WGPO0000), you have to decide how to share it and give other LAN members unrestricted access to that folder. Follow these steps:

1. On the PC on which you just created the post office, open My Computer (double-click on its icon).

2. Double-click on the icon for hard disk drive C.

3. Choose View⇨Arrange Icons⇨by Name to put the folders in alphabetical order.

4. Right-click on the wgpo0000 folder and choose Sharing.

If Sharing isn't an option in your pop-up menu, you probably forgot to allow file sharing on this PC. You need to right-click on Network Neighborhood, choose Properties, and turn on File and Print Sharing, as discussed in Chapter 25.

5. Choose Shared As, enter a share name (you can use wgpo0000), type a comment, and choose Full in the Access Type section, as shown in Figure 27-5.

Make sure that you leave the boxes in the Passwords section blank.

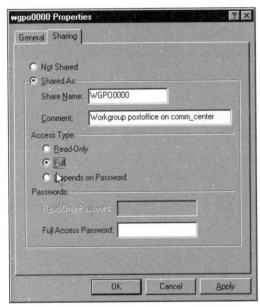

Figure 27-5: Sharing the new wgpo0000 folder, with full access granted.

6. Choose OK.

A little hand should appear below the wgpo0000 folder icon, indicating that the folder is shared.

7. Close all open windows now, if you want, by clicking their Close buttons.

Your post office is almost open for business.

Phase IV: Setting Up User Accounts

Now the postmaster needs to set up an account for each member of the workgroup. If you're not the postmaster, you may want to go get that person and help him or her through this process. The postmaster has to go through this procedure each time anyone joins the workgroup LAN, deletes an account, or changes a password.

To set up user accounts, follow these steps:

1. On the PC that's acting as the post office, choose Start⇨Settings⇨Control Panel.
2. Double-click on the Microsoft Mail Postoffice icon.
3. Choose Administer an existing Workgroup Postoffice and then click on the Next button.
4. Click on the Next button to select the suggested wgpo0000 folder.
5. The postmaster needs to enter his or her mailbox name and password.

   In my example, the postmaster enters **SusitaS** and **honcho**. The password appears as asterisks, as shown in Figure 27-6.

Figure 27-6: Only the postmaster can get past this point.

6. Click on the Next button.

   The Postoffice Manager dialog box appears (see Figure 27-7).

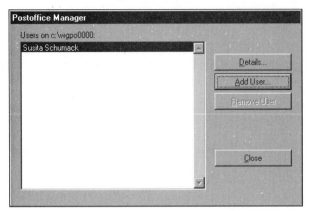

Figure 27-7: The Postoffice Manager dialog box.

When you reach the Postoffice Manager dialog box, follow this procedure:

1. Click on the Add User button.

2. Fill in the Name, Mailbox, and Password box for one person in the workgroup, using the information that you jotted down earlier (refer to Figure 27-1).

3. Optionally, fill in other boxes (see Figure 27-8), and choose OK.

Add User	
Name:	Ashley Marie
Mailbox:	AshleyM
Password:	sesame
Phone #1:	555-2123
Phone #2:	555-2234
Office:	22-C
Department:	Digital Magic
Notes:	ALANS_OFFICE workgroup

OK   Cancel

Figure 27-8: One user added to the workgroup post office.

4. Repeat Steps 1–3 for each person who will be sending and receiving workgroup e-mail.

   When you finish, the list in the Postoffice Manager dialog box should include the postmaster's name and the name of each user, as shown in Figure 27-9. (You don't have to add all users at this time, of course. You can stop at any time and repeat the procedure in this section to add more people later.)

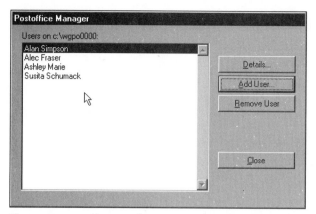

Figure 27-9: My four workgroup members listed in Postoffice Manager.

5. To save your new users, click on the Close button.

6. Close the Control Panel, if you want.

Phase V: Setting Up E-Mail on Every PC

Microsoft Exchange handles all incoming and outgoing local e-mail messages, along with other types of messages.

Setting up Microsoft Exchange

To set up Exchange to use local e-mail, you need to follow these steps:

1. Choose Start⇨Settings⇨Control Panel.

2. Double-click on the Mail and Fax icon.

3. If Microsoft Mail is already listed in the information-services list box, skip to Step 13.

4. If Microsoft Mail isn't listed as an information service (see Figure 27-10), click on the Add button.

5. In the Add Service to Profile dialog box that appears, click on Microsoft Mail.

If Microsoft Mail is not available on this PC, click on Cancel; click on Cancel again to return to Control Panel; and go straight to "Installing Microsoft Mail" later in this chapter.

6. Click on the OK button.

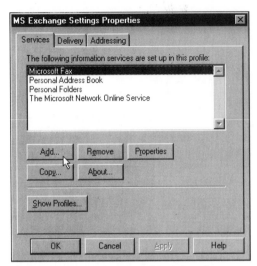

Figure 27-10: Microsoft Mail isn't listed as an information service here.

7. If you are on the post-office PC, skip to step 8.

   If you are not on the post-office PC, click on the <u>B</u>rowse button, double-click on Network Neighborhood in the list that appears, double-click on the name of the post-office PC (Comm_center, in my example), and then click on the wgpo0000 folder name (see Figure 27-11).

Figure 27-11: Default settings for Microsoft Mail in an Exchange profile.

8. Choose OK three times to return to the Control Panel; then close the Control Panel.

9. To identify this particular PC on the LAN, double-click on the Inbox icon on the desktop, or choose Start⇨Programs⇨Microsoft Exchange.

   A dialog box appears, asking for the mailbox name and password for this PC.

10. Type the appropriate information from the list that you made earlier, as shown in Figure 27-12.

Figure 27-12: Identifying this particular PC's e-mail address.

11. Choose OK.

    You go to Microsoft Exchange.

12. Close Exchange.

13. Repeat this procedure on every other PC in the LAN that will send and receive electronic mail.

 If you're not prompted to identify this PC's e-mail address, check to make sure that the information already entered is correct. Click on Start, choose Settings⇨Control Panel, then double-click the Mail and Fax icon. Click on Microsoft Mail then click the Properties button. Check the Connection and Logon tabs, and fill in the appropriate entries. Use the same format that I used in Figure 27-12 to enter the path to the Postoffice, mailbox name, and password.

When you complete these steps on every PC in the LAN, your post office is open for business. Skip to "How to Send Local E-Mail" later in this chapter.

Installing Microsoft Mail

Some PCs in the LAN may not have Microsoft Mail installed. To install Microsoft Mail on a PC, first gather up your original Windows 95 disks, or share a CD-ROM drive on the LAN and put your Windows 95 CD-ROM in that drive. (Remember that to install Windows components from a shared CD-ROM drive to another PC, you must map a drive letter to the CD-ROM drive, as discussed in Chapter 25.)

After you collect the original Windows 95 disks or share the CD-ROM drive, follow these steps:

1. Choose Start⇨Settings⇨Control Panel.

2. Double-click on the Add/Remove Programs icon.

3. Click on the Windows Setup tab.

4. Click on Microsoft Exchange and then click on the Details button.

5. Select both Microsoft Exchange and Microsoft Mail Services, as shown in Figure 27-13.

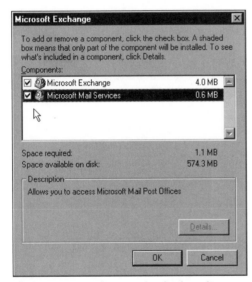

Figure 27-13: Make sure that both Exchange and Mail are selected.

6. Choose OK twice.

7. Follow the instructions on-screen.

When you get back to the Control Panel, follow the procedure in "Phase V: Setting Up E-Mail on Every PC" earlier in this chapter.

How to Send Local E-Mail

After the local e-mail system is set up and installed in Microsoft Exchange as an information service on every PC, sending and receiving local e-mail messages is a breeze. Just follow these steps:

1. Double-click on the Inbox icon, or choose Start⭢Programs⭢Microsoft Exchange.

2. Choose Compose⭢New Message.

3. If you know the recipient's mailbox name, type it in the To box, and skip to Step 4.

   Alternatively, to ensure that you have a valid name, click on the To button. If you don't see e-mail recipients' names listed, drop down the Show Names from list and select Postoffice Address List. Then select any number of recipients by clicking on each name and then clicking on the To button. When you finish, choose OK.

   In Figure 27-14, for example, someone on the LAN is addressing a message to Alan Simpson.

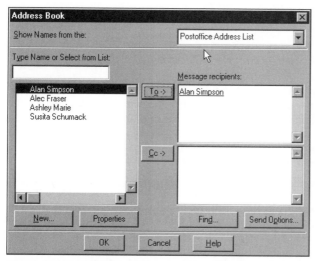

Figure 27-14: Sender has chosen Alan Simpson from the Postoffice Address List.

4. Type a subject and your message, as in the example shown in Figure 27-15.

   Remember that the subject is the brief line that the recipient sees in his or her Inbox before opening your message.

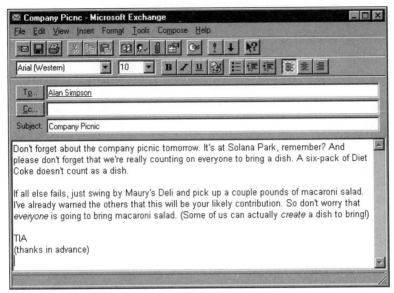

Figure 27-15: Subject and message.

5. When you finish typing your message, click on the Send button in the toolbar (the first button from the left) or choose File⇨Send.

Your message is on its way. If you want to make absolutely sure that the message was sent, stay in Exchange (or reopen it) and make sure that you can see the folder list. (Click on the Show/Hide Folder List button in the toolbar if you don't see the folder list.) Then click on the Sent Items folder. If you don't see your message, perhaps the post office hasn't delivered it yet. To try again, click on the Outbox folder, click on the message that you want to send, and choose Tools⇨Deliver Now.

If you have any problems with your e-mail, try running the Inbox Repair Tool. Click the Start button, point to Programs⇨Accessories⇨System Tools and choose Inbox Repair Tool. Click its Help button for information.

Reading Your Local E-Mail

Reading your e-mail messages is the same as reading any other kind of message. Follow these steps:

1. Double-click on the Inbox icon on your desktop or choose Start⇨Programs⇨ Microsoft Exchange.

2. The Inbox opens, displaying all newly received messages.

When I open the Inbox on my PC, for example, I may see a message sent to me by Ashley Marie (see Figure 27-16).

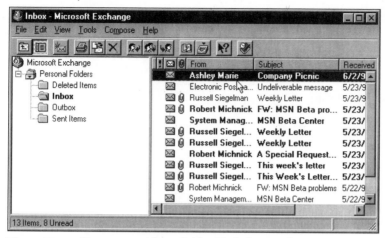

Figure 27-16: Message sent from Ashley Marie in my Inbox.

3. To read a message, double-click on it.

While you read the message, you can click on the buttons in the toolbar to print, delete, reply forward the message, and so on. Chapter 30 discusses these options, which apply to all messages that you receive on your PC.

Changing Your Mail Password

I've been pretty lax about security in telling you how to set up your mail system. As this system is designed, anyone who can log on under your name also can read your mail messages. If you need tighter security, you can change your own password and/ or require the user to enter that password before any messages can be opened.

To change your mail password

To change your existing mail password, follow these steps:

1. Open Microsoft Exchange by double-clicking on the Inbox icon or choosing Start⇨Programs⇨Microsoft Exchange.

2. Choose Tools⇨Microsoft Mail Tools⇨Change Mailbox Password.

3. Type your old password.

4. Type your new password twice (once for confirmation).

5. Choose OK.

To require a password

If you want to ensure that only people who know the password (you) can get to your messages, follow these steps to make Microsoft Mail prompt you for a password every time:

1. Choose Start⇨Settings⇨Control Panel.
2. Double-click on the Mail and Fax icon.
3. Click on Microsoft Mail.
4. Click on the Properties button.
5. Click on the Logon tab.
6. Clear the checkbox titled When logging on, automatically enter password (see Figure 27-17).

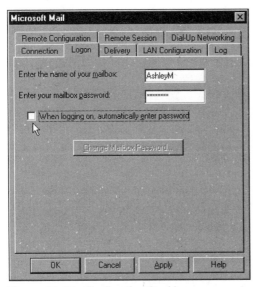

Figure 27-17: Clearing the checkbox ensures that Mail always prompts for a password.

7. Choose OK twice to return to the Control Panel.
8. Close the Control Panel.

From now on, whenever you open Microsoft Exchange, you are prompted for a password. You will not be allowed to open your Inbox until you type the password and choose OK.

If you change your mind and don't want to be prompted for a password every time you open your Inbox, click the Remember Password option after you type your mail password and before you click OK.

For most users on the LAN, knowing how to send and read messages is sufficient. You can do many other things with Microsoft Mail, however, especially if you're the postmaster and/or network administrator. The following section talks about basic postmaster responsibilities; Chapter 30 discusses advanced Mail techniques.

Adding, Changing, and Deleting Mail Users

Only the postmaster has the capability to add users, delete users, and change information about users in the workgroup post office. Follow these steps:

1. On the post-office PC, choose Start⇨Settings ⇨Control Panel.

2. Double-click on the Microsoft Mail Postoffice icon.

3. Choose Administer an existing Workgroup Postoffice and then click on the Next button.

4. Click on the Next button to accept the suggested post-office folder (C:\WPGO0000, for example).

5. Type the postmaster password, and click on Next.

6. Select any user name in the list, as shown in Figure 27-18; then click on Details to change the user information or click on Remove User to delete the user.

   Alternatively, to add a user, click on the Add User button and then fill in the form that appears, as discussed earlier in this chapter.

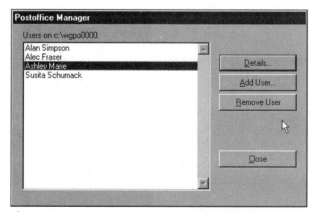

Figure 27-18: The postmaster can add, delete, or change Microsoft Mail users in this dialog box.

7. When you finish making your changes, click on the Close button to return to the Control Panel.

8. Close the Control Panel, if you want.

Don't forget that if you added a new PC to the LAN, you also need to set up e-mail on that PC, as discussed in "Phase V: Setting Up E-Mail on Every PC" earlier in this chapter.

Summary

✦ To set up local e-mail for a workgroup, you first must decide which PC will play the role of post office.

✦ Then you need to create a workgroup post office on that PC and share the directory that the post-office wizard creates.

✦ Next, a person designated as postmaster must create an account for each member of the workgroup.

✦ On each PC, Microsoft Mail must be added to Microsoft Exchange's list of information services.

✦ To send local e-mail, open Microsoft Exchange and choose Compose⇨ New Message.

✦ To read local e-mail, open your Inbox.

✦   ✦   ✦

More Cool LAN Tricks

This chapter explains some features and tricks that you can try on your own LAN. Everything discussed in this chapter is optional — you don't have to do any of these things to set up or use a LAN — so feel free to read this chapter at your leisure.

Pop-Up Messages

WinPopup is a handy built-in utility that enables network users to send immediate messages to one another. Unlike e-mail messages, which are stored in the Inbox, pop-up messages appear in the recipient's taskbar immediately.

To set up WinPopup on a PC, you need to install WinPopup from the original floppy disks or CD-ROM (if you haven't already done so). Then drag the WinPopup icon to the Startup folder so that the utility starts automatically when you start Windows.

Installing WinPopup

If you're not sure whether WinPopup is on your PC yet, follow these steps to find out and to install it, if necessary:

1. Choose Start⇨Settings⇨Control Panel.

2. Double-click on the Add/Remove Programs icon.

3. Click on the Windows Setup tab.

4. Click on Accessories, click on the Details button, and then scroll down to see if Win Popup is installed.

5. If WinPopup is installed, click on the Cancel button and skip to "Adding WinPopup to your Startup folder" later in this chapter.

   If WinPopup isn't already installed, select it so that its checkbox is checked.

Figure 28-1: WinPopup is already installed in this example.

6. Gather up your original Windows 95 program disks or CD-ROM, and click on OK.

7. Follow the instructions on-screen.

After WinPopup is installed on your PC, proceed to the following section.

Adding WinPopup to your Startup folder

The best way to use WinPopup on a LAN is to make sure that all LAN members have the utility up and running at all times. The simplest way to do this is to go to each PC and add WinPopup's icon to the Startup folder. Follow these steps:

1. Choose Start⇨Find⇨Files or Folders.

2. Type **winpopup.exe** as the file to look for.

3. Click on the Find Now button.

    When the file is found, it should have a little jack-in-the-box icon.

You can put a WinPopup shortcut right on your desktop. Right-drag the Jack-In-The-Box icon to the desktop, release the mouse button, and choose Create Shortcut(s) Here.

4. Right-click on the Start button, and choose Open.

5. Double-click on the Programs icon.

6. Move and size the windows so that you can see both the icon for the Startup icon and the icon for WinPopup, as shown in Figure 28-2.

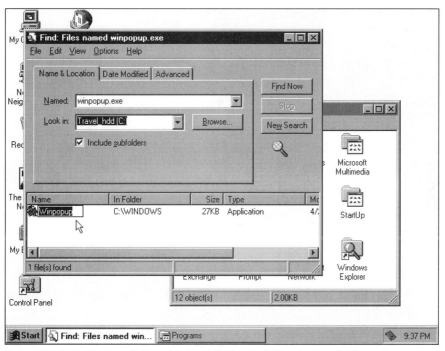

Figure 28-2: Getting ready to right-drag WinPopup to the Startup folder.

7. Holding down the right mouse button, drag the WinPopup icon so that it covers the Startup folder's icon.

8. Release the mouse button, and choose Create Shortcut(s) Here.

9. Close all open windows.

To ensure that WinPopup starts, restart your PC; choose Start⇨Shut Down⇨Restart the computer?⇨Yes.

Don't forget that you need to go to each PC in the LAN and repeat this procedure, so that all PCs start with WinPopup ready to go.

WinPopup appears on-screen already open, as shown in Figure 28-3. But you can click on its Minimize button to reduce it to a taskbar button when you want it out of the way.

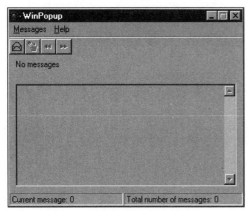

Figure 28-3: WinPopup fully opened.

Sending a pop-up message

To send a pop-up message to someone in your workgroup, follow these steps:

1. Open the WinPopup window, if it isn't open already.

   (By this point, you should be able to click on the WinPopup taskbar button to open it.)

2. Choose Messages⇨Send, or click on the envelope button in WinPopup's toolbar.

3. To send the message to a specific person or computer, type that person's log-in name (such as **AshleyM** or **AlanS**) or the name of the computer (for example **\\comm_center**).

   To send the message to the entire workgroup, click on the Workgroup option button; the name of your workgroup appears automatically.

4. Type your message, as in the example shown in Figure 28-4.

5. Choose OK to send the message.

6. Choose OK to respond to the prompt that your message has been sent.

You could minimize the WinPopup window now, but don't close it yet; you want to leave it open so that you can receive messages.

Figure 28-4: A pop-up message to AshleyM in my LAN.

Reading pop-up messages

When somebody sends you a pop-up message, the WinPopup button in your taskbar informs you that you have a message. Just click on that taskbar button to view your message. After reading the message, you can use the various toolbar buttons and the commands in the Messages menu to respond, as follows:

✦ To send a reply, click on the Send button.

✦ To delete the message, click on the Delete button.

✦ If you have several messages in your bin, click on the Previous and Next buttons to scroll through the messages.

When you finish reading your messages, minimize the WinPopup window. But don't close the window if you want to continue getting pop-up messages from other workgroup members.

Personalizing WinPopup

If you want to change the way WinPopup behaves when it receives a message, choose Messages⇨Options from within WinPopup. You see the simple dialog box shown in Figure 28-5. Make your changes and then choose OK.

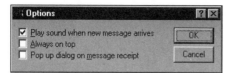

Figure 28-5: Options for personalizing WinPopup.

Cutting and Pasting Between PCs

Scraps (refer to "You'll Love These Scraps" in Chapter 4) are great ways to get stuff from one document into another, and using them is fun and easy. But consider the following scenario, using two new LAN members as the example.

Homer is working next to Marge, and he sees something on her screen that he wants to paste into his own document. How does Marge cut or copy that object in such a way that enables Homer, on the other PC, to paste it into his document? When you find out, please drop me a line, because I'd like to know myself. (Ha, ha — just kidding.)

The answer is, "It depends." For starters, define the goal simply as follows:

Marge (has it)⇨Homer (wants it)

If the document that Marge is using is in a shared folder (such as the Projects folder that I'm always talking about), Marge can choose File⇨Save to save her work to disk. Homer can browse to the shared folder, via Network Neighborhood, and double-click on the name of Marge's document. A copy of Marge's entire document now appears on Homer's screen. Homer can select whatever he wants and then choose Edit⇨Copy to copy the selection into his own Clipboard, even if the document opens as read-only on his PC. When Homer has the stuff in his Clipboard, he can choose Edit⇨Paste to paste that object into any document on his PC.

This solution is the simplest, but it works only if the document in question is in a shared folder. If Marge's document isn't in a shared folder, she can copy the document and send it to a shared folder, from which Homer can retrieve the copy. Marge can press Ctrl+A to select her entire document, press Ctrl+C to copy to her Clipboard, press Ctrl+N to create a new blank document, and then press Ctrl+V to paste the selection into that new blank document.

Next, Marge can choose File⇨Save As to save the new copy. In the Save As dialog box that appears, she needs to browse to a shared folder that Homer can access, enter a file name (such as Homer's Copy), and choose OK. Then Marge can choose File⇨Close to get rid of the copy she made for Homer and go back to working on her original document. Now Homer can go to the shared folder, open Homer's Copy, and do with it as he pleases.

If Homer frequently bugs Marge for scraps, a third method may be called for. In this method, Marge creates a shared folder on her own PC, named (for example) Marge's Scraps. Homer maps a drive letter from his PC to the Marge's Scraps folder. Marge can drag any scrap into that shared folder at any time. Homer can go to the Marge's Scraps folder at any time, and cut and paste scraps from that folder into any document of his own. The following sections show you how Homer and Marge would set up and use the shared scraps folder.

Creating a shared scraps folder

Marge wants to be able to cut or copy any portion of any document that she's working on to a shared folder named Marge's Scraps. Follow these steps to create that shared folder:

1. On the PC that you'll be cutting or copying from (Marge's PC, in my example), double-click on My Computer.

2. Double-click on the icon for drive C.

3. Choose File⇨New⇨Folder.

4. Type a name for the folder (**Marge's Scraps**, for this example).

5. Click just outside that new folder icon to save the new name.

6. Right-click on the new folder (Marge's Scraps), and choose S̲haring.

 If S̲haring isn't available in the pop-up menu after you right-click, you probably didn't allow for file sharing when you set up this PC. You need to right-click on Network Neighborhood, choose Properties, and use the Configuration tab to allow file sharing. See Chapter 25 (in the neighborhood of Figure 25-3) if you need more information.

7. Choose S̲hared As.

8. Type a brief Share N̲ame (**MargeScraps**, for this example).

9. Optionally, type a C̲omment, choose what type of access you want to offer, and enter a password.

   Figure 28-6 shows my example.

   Read-only access if fine if you want other users to be able to read from this folder but not take anything out of it.

10. Choose OK.

11. To create a desktop icon for this folder, right-drag the folder to the Windows 95 desktop, release the mouse button, and choose Create Shortcut(s) Here.

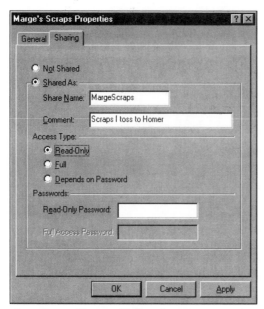

Figure 28-6: Marge will share her new scraps folder.

Within My Computer, you should see your folder with a little sharing hand below it. On the desktop, you should see a shortcut to that folder, as in my example shown in Figure 28-7.

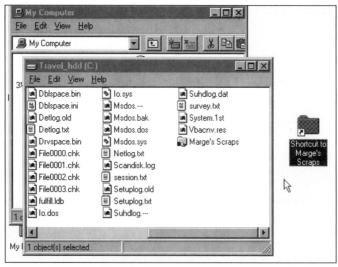

Figure 28-7: New shared Marge's Scraps folder and desktop shortcut.

Now Marge can close all her open windows and rearrange desktop icons in alphabetical order (by right-clicking on the desktop and choosing Arrange Icons⇨by Name). And now she has a place to toss scraps to Homer.

Next, you need to set up the other PC so that you can get at the scraps quickly and easily. Follow these steps:

1. On Homer's PC (or any other PC in the LAN that needs Marge's scraps), double-click on Network Neighborhood.

2. Double-click on the name of the PC on which you created the shared scraps folder.

3. Click on the name of the shared scraps folder (Marge's Scraps, in this example).

4. Right-drag the folder to the desktop.

5. Release the mouse button, and choose Create Shortcut(s) Here.

6. Close all open windows.

7. If you want, you can rename the new shortcut by right-clicking on its icon and choosing Rename.

In Figure 28-8, I named the shortcut to the shared folder Marge's Scraps; you can, of course, give the shortcut any name that you want.

Figure 28-8: Shortcut to Marge's Scraps on Homer's PC.

Cutting and copying to the scraps folder

How does Marge get a scrap from whatever document she's working on to the shared folder? She drags it there — that is, she selects the object that she wants to share and then drags that object from its current position to the shortcut icon for the shared folder.

In Figure 28-9, Marge selected text from a Word document and dragged that text to the open window for the Marge's Scraps folder.

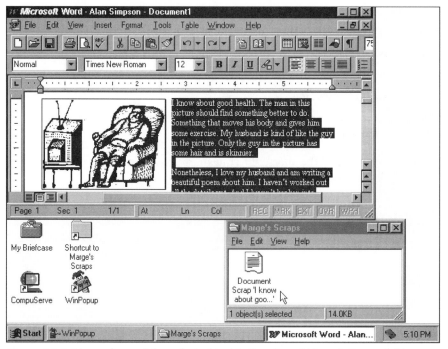

Figure 28-9: Marge dragged the selected text to the shared Marge's Scraps folder.

Pasting from the scraps folder

To get a scrap into your Clipboard so that you can paste it wherever you want, follow these steps:

1. On your own PC, open the window for the Marge's Scraps folder.

You may be able to skip Steps 2–4, depending on the program into which you plan to paste the scrap. Some programs allow you to drag a scrap icon into an open document; you may want to try this simpler method first.

2. To open the scrap, double-click on it (see Figure 28-10).

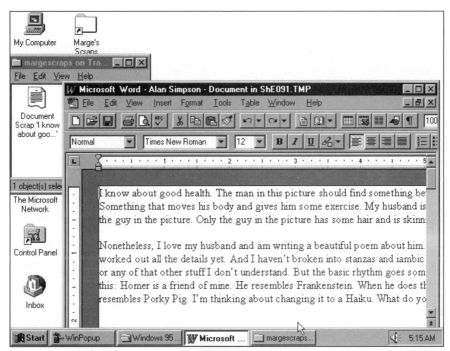

Figure 28-10: Double-clicking on a scrap to open it.

3. Choose Edit⇨Select All to select everything within the scrap.

4. Choose Edit⇨Copy to copy the selection to the Windows Clipboard on your PC.

Now that the scrap is in Homer's Clipboard, Homer can open any document, place the insertion point wherever he wants to put the scrap, and choose Edit⇨Paste to paste the Clipboard contents at the current insertion-point position.

This scenario is just an example of how two people can cut and paste between their PCs. You simply want to get whatever Person X wants from Person Y's PC to a shared folder. When the object is in a shared folder, Person X can navigate to that shared folder, using Network Neighborhood; then he or she can open, copy, or move the document from that shared folder to his or her own PC or document.

Long-distance cutting and pasting

If you need to send an object long-distance over phone lines, your best bet is to first save the object as a file. You can use several methods, depending on the application that you're using; some applications allow you to select text or graphics and then choose File⇨Save As or Edit⇨Copy To to save the selection to a file. Alternatively, you can select an object and choose Edit⇨Copy to copy the object to the Clipboard. Then open the Clipboard Viewer (choose Start⇨Programs⇨Accessories⇨Clip-

board Viewer) and choose File⇨Save As from within Clipboard Viewer to save the Clipboard contents to a file.

Regardless of how you get the selection into a file, the next step is to address e-mail to the intended recipient and attach the file to the message that you're sending. To see how you do this with the Microsoft Network (MSN), see Chapter 21. You can send mail to the Internet, CompuServe, and America Online from MSN.

Finding Things on the LAN

Finding things on a single-user PC can be challenging for beginning and casual users, because they need to understand (and keep track of) drives, folders, and file names. Throw a LAN into the picture, and you add a new dimension — now you also have to know which PC a particular thing is on. You can, however, use several techniques to find things on a LAN, as you'll learn in the following sections.

Browsing for computers and shared resources

If your LAN is fairly small, you probably will find that browsing around with Network Neighborhood is sufficient to find whatever resource you're looking for. Double-click on the Network Neighborhood icon; initially, you see a list with Entire Network at the top, followed by a list of PCs in your workgroup. To check out the shared resources on any PC in your own workgroup, double-click on the name of the computer that you want to browse.

If your workgroup is connected to other workgroups, you can double-click on Entire Network to see what other workgroups are available. (Figure 28-11 shows an example in which I have two workgroups going: one named ALANS_OFFICE and the other named MEDIA_LAB.) To explore another workgroup, just click on the workgroup's name.

If you find a drive or folder to which you want to connect, you can map a drive letter to it on the spot. Right-click on the name of the drive or folder, and choose Map Network Drive from the shortcut menu that appears.

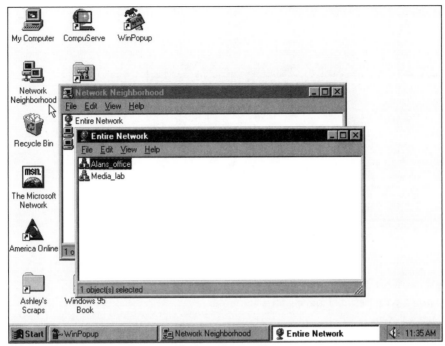

Figure 28-11: Double-clicking on Entire Network shows the names of other workgroups.

 If you need a reminder on the details of mapping a drive letter, see "Sharing an Entire Hard Disk," "Sharing a CD-ROM Drive," or "Sharing a Folder," as appropriate, in Chapter 26.

Finding a specific computer

If your workgroup has hundreds of computers, browsing for a specific computer can be time-consuming. If you know even part of the name of the computer that you're looking for, you can use Find, rather than Network Neighborhood, to locate a specific computer faster. Follow these steps:

1. On any PC in the workgroup, choose Start⇨Find.
2. Click on Computer.
3. Type the name (or part of the name) of the computer that you're looking for.
4. Click on the Find Now button.

   After the little magnifying glass stops spinning around, you see a list of computers that match the requested name.

In Figure 28-12, I searched for *comm*. Find located a computer named Comm_center on my LAN.

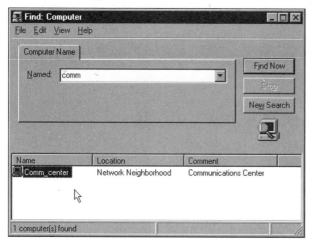

Figure 28-12: Result of looking for a computer named Comm.

To explore shared resources on that computer, I would double-click on the icon for that PC. Then, to map a drive letter on that PC, I would right-click on the appropriate file name and choose Map Network Drive.

Searching for a folder or file

At some point, your LAN may have thousands of folders and files, so searching for something by browsing can take a l-o-o-o-o-o-ng time. But you can speed the process by using the My Computer option with Find. That way, Find will look through your local hard disk and CD-ROM drive (if any), as well as all shared resources to which you mapped a drive letter. Follow these steps:

1. Choose Start⇨Find.

2. Click on Files or Folders.

3. Type all or part of the folder or file that you're looking for.

4. In the Look in list, select My Computer.

5. Click on Find Now.

    The search may take a while, especially if you mapped drive letters to many different resources. But when Find finishes, you see exactly where the folder or file is stored.

Figure 28-13 shows an example in which I searched for a file containing the word
mailing. Find located a file containing that word in the drive named P. To open that
file, I double-click on its icon, as usual.

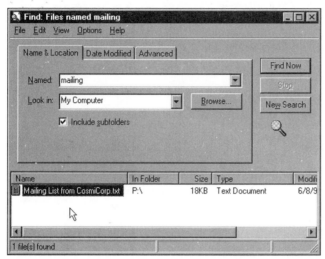

Figure 28-13: Searched My Computer for file with *mailing* in
the file name.

Managing Other PCs From Your Own PC

Remote Administration enables you to manage other PCs in the LAN from your own
PC. Specifically, you can share or unshare folders on some PC other than your own
without getting out of your chair. On a larger scale, if you set up all the PCs in the LAN
for remote administration, you can share and unshare any folder on any PC in the LAN
from whichever PC you happen to be using.

In a sense, all the drives and folders on the LAN become yours to do with as you please.
You no longer are limited to accessing shared resources on the LAN; you can access
any folder, shared or not. You become the grand wazoo of virtually every file and folder
on the LAN (the official title is *network administrator* rather than *grand wazoo*).

Before I go into any great detail on remote administration, let me give you this
warning: Remote Administration can be fairly simple and straightforward, or horren-
dously complicated. In this chapter, I'll stick with the not-so-complicated stuff that 98
percent of you are likely to find sufficient for your needs. What you learn between
here and the end of this chapter, although fairly simple, can make you the grand
wazoo of every folder and file on the LAN.

Allowing a PC to be managed remotely

Before you can administer a PC remotely, you have to set up that PC so that it *can* be administered remotely. This step is a safety net that prevents any person on the LAN from messing with any PC that he or she feels like messing with. So your first step is to complete the following steps:

1. On the PC that you want to be able to manage remotely, choose Start⇨Settings⇨Control Panel.

2. Double-click on the Passwords icon.

3. Click on the Remote Administration tab.

4. Select the Enable Remote Administration of this server option.

5. Type a password (twice) that will allow this PC to be managed from another PC.

   As usual, the password appears in asterisks, as shown in Figure 28-14.

6. Choose OK.

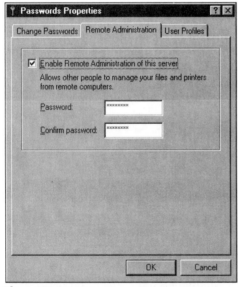

Figure 28-14: This PC can be managed from any other PC in the LAN.

If this PC (the one that you're sitting at right now) is not set up to allow file sharing, you won't be able to share anything on it from any PC. If you're unsure about the sharing status of files on this PC, right-click on Network Neighborhood, choose Properties, click on the Configuration tab, and then click the File and Print Sharing button. If necessary, refer to Chapter 25, starting with the section titled "The Configuration Tab."

This procedure takes care of the PC that you're using right now. If you want to manage the hard disk of another PC on this LAN, you need to go to that PC and repeat the procedure. You can assign the same password to each PC, if you want, so that you need to remember only one password to get to any PC in the LAN.

Managing a PC remotely

Whenever you're ready to put on your grand-wazoo robe and take control of another PC's drive(s), follow these steps:

1. On your PC (or whatever PC you happen to be using), double-click on the Network Neighborhood icon.

2. Right-click on the name of the PC that you want to manage, and choose Properties from the shortcut menu.

3. Click on the Tools tab in the dialog box that appears.

4. Click on the Administer button.

5. When you are prompted, type your password for managing that PC and then choose OK.

   You see all the shared resources on that PC, with a new item called C$ included in the list, as shown in Figure 28-15.

That little C$ is your ticket to the remote PC's hard drive. Double-click on C$, and you get a view of the entire hard disk on that PC. Figure 28-16 shows an example.

Remember that if you disconnect someone from a shared folder that he or she is using, you can destroy his or her work. Exercise extreme caution when you unshare a shared folder.

If you accidentally disconnect another user from his work, and he has trouble reopening the file that he was working on when you disconnected him, go to the PC that holds the shared folder, and run ScanDisk on that PC, as discussed in "Find and Repair Disk Errors" in Chapter 11.

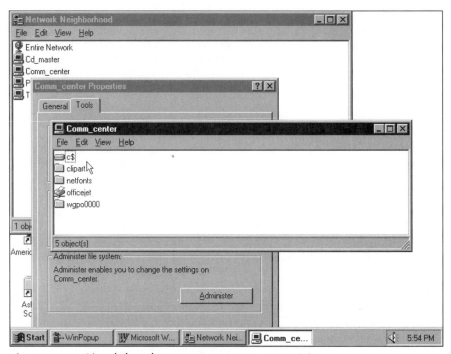

Figure 28-15: C$ and shared resources on comm_center PC.

Figure 28-16: Opening C$ shows folders on the remote PC's hard drive.

To share or unshare a folder on that PC, right-click on the folder and choose Sharing. Fill out the dialog box in the usual manner. If you need help with this procedure, see "Sharing a Folder" in Chapter 26. Remember that your action affects everyone in the LAN. After you share a folder, any member of the LAN can connect to that folder and map a drive letter to it. Conversely, when you stop sharing a folder, you disconnect everyone from that folder.

Summary

Following is a review of the main techniques discussed in this chapter:

✦ To send a pop-up message to another LAN member, open WinPopup, click on the envelope button, address the message, type the message, and choose OK.

✦ When you receive a pop-up message, open WinPopup to read the message. To reply, click on the envelope button. To delete the message, click on the trash-can button.

✦ Remember that after you close WinPopup, you won't get messages anymore. A better idea is to minimize WinPopup only when you want it out of the way.

✦ The trick to cutting and pasting between PCs is creating a shared folder that both PCs can access. A LAN member can save folders or scraps to the shared folder; then any other LAN member can open and copy objects in that folder.

✦ You can use Network Neighborhood to browse for shared objects on your network.

✦ You can choose Start⇨Find⇨Computer to locate a particular PC in your workgroup.

✦ You can tell Find to conduct a search of My Computer when you want to search all local and mapped network drives for a folder or file.

✦ If you want to be able to share folders from a PC without actually going to that PC, you need to activate Remote Administration on that PC. Choose Start⇨Settings⇨Control Panel, double-click on the Passwords icon, and use the Remote Administration tab to set up a password.

✦ To manage a PC's folders remotely, double-click on Network Neighborhood, right-click on the name of the PC you want to manage, and choose Properties from the shortcut menu. Click on the Tools tab, click on the Administer button, and then double-click on the C$ drive to gain access to that PC's entire hard disk.

This chapter about wraps it up for networking. I know that if you're in a large corporation, your LAN probably is more complicated than the ones discussed in this part of the book; you may have dozens of PCs and workgroups on the LAN, as well as several full-time network administrators. But most of the techniques discussed in this part of the book work on any LAN, large or small.

✦   ✦   ✦

Windows 95 Potpourri

Modern Multimedia

All the earliest programs used one communications medium: text. Text appeared on-screen. You typed text at the keyboard.

Multimedia brings other communications media into the fray — namely pictures, sound, animation, and video. These media allow programmers and multimedia producers to create far more interesting programs for the rest of us to enjoy. But problems have occurred along the way.

Multimedia is something of an irony. Installing and using a multimedia program can be the simplest thing in the world: just slide the CD-ROM into the CD-ROM drive and sit back. On the other hand, if you've been around the block a few times, you probably know that multimedia also can be the most frustrating experience: slide the disc into the CD-ROM drive and fight for hours trying to get the thing to work.

Many of the problems in multimedia are caused by one simple fact: PC multimedia is too new. PCs were introduced in the late 1970s, so we probably can say that PC technology is in the toddler stage of development. The first sound cards and video for Windows programs were introduced in 1991 and 1992. By comparison with PCs, multimedia is in the infant (or, perhaps, zygote) stage of development.

Like real-life zygotes, multimedia has grown rapidly, to say the least. In fact, multimedia hardware and software have been the fastest-growing segments of the PC industry since about 1993. Millions of people just like you are tearing their hair out, trying to get that #$%*$@# game to make some sound.

What Windows 95 Brings to Multimedia

I wish I could say that Windows 95 takes care of all the problems posed by multimedia, but no operating system can take care of all the problems. The hardware involved and the ever-changing standards don't allow a single operating system to take care of every conceivable problem.

But although Windows 95 can't solve all the problems, it can increase the likelihood of success. Following are some of the features of Windows 95 that can improve your experience with multimedia:

✦ A built-in CD-ROM File System (CDFS) and cache ensure that data from a CD-ROM is read as quickly as possible, allowing for a richer, smoother multimedia presentation.

✦ Better use of memory allows even memory-hungry DOS-based multimedia games to run without requiring you to make elaborate changes in the CONFIG.SYS and AUTOEXEC.BAT files.

✦ Built-in support for a wide variety of *codecs* (compression/decompression methods) increases the likelihood that a new multimedia title will run correctly the first time you use it.

✦ Device Manager (see Chapter 10) facilitates diagnosing and correcting the hardware conflicts that cripple multimedia hardware.

The future for multimedia looks much brighter. As the "Designed for Windows 95" logo finds its place on sound cards, video capture boards, and multimedia titles, you'll be assured that any multimedia title will run correctly on your hardware — assuming that you have the right hardware. The following section discusses the right hardware for today's and tomorrow's multimedia applications.

What to Look for in a Multimedia PC

Right off the bat, I can say with certainty that older PCs don't have the horsepower needed to run sophisticated multimedia titles. When you're buying a multimedia PC or hardware to upgrade an existing PC, you need to look at all the factors on which modern multimedia titles rely. Those factors are:

✦ *Local bus or PCI video.* Historically, one of the biggest constraints on multimedia has been the video subsystem. When you purchase a multimedia PC, be sure to get one that supports local bus video or PCI, so that you get the best possible multimedia performance.

✦ *2x or greater CD-ROM speed.* Many new multimedia titles assume that you have at least a *2x* (double-speed) CD-ROM drive. If possible, consider getting a 4x drive now.

✦ *SVGA with 16-bit color.* The old 640×480 VGA with 16 colors doesn't quite cut it for new titles. Many titles assume that you have at least SVGA (Super VGA) capable of displaying at 800×600 resolution and even 16-bit (HighColor) or 24-bit color (TrueColor).

✦ *16-bit audio with MIDI.* Audio cards must be 16-bit and should support MIDI. Very few modern multimedia titles run on the old 8-bit sound cards.

If you're the power-hungry type, you may be tempted to get the biggest, fastest CPU and tons of RAM when you buy a multimedia PC, but those features are not major factors in multimedia. Multimedia playback places more demand on other components of the system, especially graphics capability and the CD-ROM drive. If you have to budget, you'd be better off to spend more for local bus or PCI graphics and a fast CD-ROM drive, and to skimp a little in the CPU and RAM departments.

At the Simpson home and Workaholics Anonymous bunker (aka Hair-Tearing Central), our family multimedia PC is a 486/66 with 8MB of RAM, which I think is considered to be an entry-level machine these days, but it's sufficient for running all of our multimedia titles and games. Sure, we have a few titles that refuse to cooperate (and lately, I've been too busy to find out why). But all in all, the 486/66 CPU, 8MB of RAM, 16-bit sound card, 2x CD-ROM drive, and local-bus video graphics on that machine do the trick.

Playing With Sound

To do anything with sound, you need to install a sound card. You have to consider tons of options when you buy a sound card, but the most important factor is getting a 16-bit (or better) sound card. If you need to upgrade from an 8-bit card or still haven't gotten around to putting a sound card in your system, consider purchasing a "Designed for Windows 95" plug-and-play-compatible board. Such a board greatly simplifies installation and use of that card.

Adjusting the volume

The first thing that you need to do with sound is adjust the volume, so that you don't blast your eardrums. On the other hand, you want to make sure there is some volume. Otherwise, when you don't hear any sound from your speakers, you might assume something is wrong and waste a lot of time trying to "fix" your sound card.

You can control volume in six ways. I suggest that you try the following methods, in this order, until you get the volume that you want:

✦ If your speakers have their own volume control, adjust the volume on the speakers.

✦ Click on the speaker icon in the taskbar, and adjust the slider.

✦ If you're using a multimedia program, search its menus or help system for options that control the volume.

✦ Double-click on the speaker icon in the taskbar, and use your installed mixer to adjust the volume (see Figure 29-1).

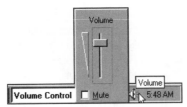

Figure 29-1: Click on the taskbar's speaker button to adjust the volume.

✦ Choose Start⇨Programs⇨Accessories⇨Multimedia⇨Volume Control.

✦ Choose Start⇨Settings⇨Control Panel; then double-click on the Audio Control (or similar) icon, if it's available.

If you have powered speakers and are having trouble getting the volume and clarity just right, try setting the volume with the speaker power turned off.

Playing a sound clip

If you want to play a sample sound clip, use My Computer, Explorer, or Find to browse to any file with the .WAV (*wave*) or .MID (*MIDI*) extension; then double-click on that file's icon. In Figure 29-2, for example, I've opened a couple of folders that contain wav files (which have a speaker icon) and MIDI files (which have a musical-note icon). I copied these files from the CD-ROM that came with my sound card.

Double-clicking on a wave file launches the Windows 95 Sound Recorder (also visible in Figure 29-2). Double-clicking on a MIDI file launches the Windows 95 Media Player program.

Assigning sound effects to events

You can assign sounds, stored in .wav files, to various events that occur in Windows. You can play one sound when Windows starts, another when an error message appears on-screen, and so on.

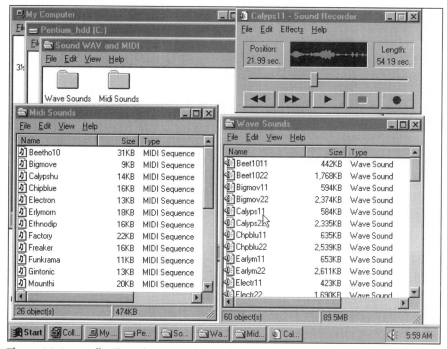

Figure 29-2: A collection of wave and MIDI files on my PC.

To assign system sounds, follow these steps:

1. Choose Start➪Settings➪Control Panel.

    Remember that you also can get to the Control Panel by double-clicking on the My Computer icon and then double-clicking on the Control Panel icon.

2. Double-click on the Sounds icon.

   You see the Sounds Properties dialog box, shown in Figure 29-3.

3. Optionally, choose a predefined sound scheme from the Schemes drop-down list near the bottom of the dialog box.

4. Select the name of any event to which you want to assign a sound.

   Events that have speaker icons already have sounds assigned to them, but you can change the sounds, if you want.

5. Assign a sound to the selected event by choosing a sound from the Name drop-down list or by clicking on the Browse button and then navigating to the wave file of your choosing.

6. To preview a sound, click on the Play button next to the Preview box.

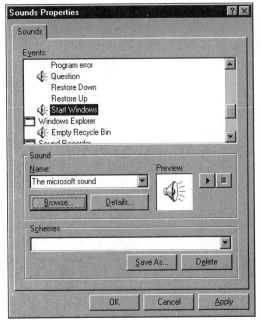

Figure 29-3: The Sounds Properties dialog box.

7. For details on a particular sound, click on the Details button.

8. Repeat Steps 4–7 to assign sounds to as many events as you want.

9. If you want to save your current mix of sounds, choose Save and then enter a file name.

10. When you finish, choose OK to return to the Control Panel.

11. Close the Control Panel, if you want.

The next time one of the events to which you assigned a sound occurs, you'll hear that sound.

You can install some fun sound schemes from your original Windows 95 disks or CD-ROM disc. Go to Windows Setup (Chapter 9), click on Multimedia, click the Details button, and select the sound schemes you want to install. The Desktop Themes in Microsoft Plus! (Appendix F) also have built-in sound schemes of their own.

Recording, editing, and playing sounds

Sound Recorder, which comes with your Windows 95 program, enables you to record, edit, and play wave sounds. To start Sound Recorder, you can do either of the following things:

◆ Double-click on any wave file's icon.

◆ Choose Start⇨Programs⇨Accessories⇨Multimedia⇨Sound Recorder.

Figure 29-4 shows how Sound Recorder looks with a sound in its clutches.

Figure 29-4: Sound Recorder.

Recording a sound

To record a sound with Sound Recorder, you need to hook up a microphone or other input device. I can't give you exact instructions on that procedure, because it depends on your sound card; check the manual that came with the sound card. In general, however, if you want to record from a microphone, you plug the microphone into the Mic plug on the sound card. If you want to record from a cassette-tape player or audio CD player, you connect that player's Line Out plug to the sound card's Line In plug, using whatever cable is appropriate for your hardware.

 You can permanently damage sound hardware by plugging in an unacceptable device or by plugging a device into the wrong plug. Refer to your sound-card manual for specific instructions before you plug in any device.

Next, you may need to use your mixer or the Windows 95 Volume Control tool to specify the device from which you want to record. The way that you perform this step varies from one sound card to the next; refer to your sound-card documentation if you run into any problems. On my systems, I've been able to get to the mixer in two ways: by double-clicking on the speaker icon in the taskbar and by choosing Start⇨Programs⇨Accessories⇨Multimedia⇨Volume Control.

Within the mixer, go to the recording controls (or input controls, as opposed to output or playback controls), and crank up the volume on the input device that you plan to use. Then mute or crank down all other devices. In Figure 29-5, which shows the mixer for my Sound Blaster card, I selected Line In as the input and cranked up the volume a little. I left all other input devices unselected so that they won't contribute anything to the sounds I want to record.

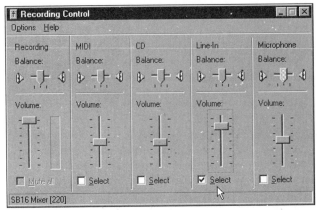

Figure 29-5: Ready to record from the Line In port (only).

If you're using a Sound Blaster mixer and don't see the input controls, don't fret; just choose Options⇨Properties⇨Recording.

When you have your input device ready to go, display Sound Recorder and then follow these steps to record a sound:

1. Choose Edit⇨Audio Properties.

   The Audio Properties dialog box appears, as shown in Figure 29-6.

2. Make sure that the recording volume is turned up at least halfway.

3. In the Preferred Quality section, choose one of the following options:

   • *CD Quality.* High-quality sound; produces large wave files

   • *Radio Quality.* Medium-quality sound; produces medium-size wave files

   • *Telephone Quality.* Lower-quality sound; produces small wave files.

4. Choose OK to close the dialog box.

5. In Sound Recorder, choose File⇨New.

6. To start recording, click on the Record button (red circle).

   The wave indicator should show the sound as it's being recorded.

7. When you're ready to stop recording, click on the Stop button (black square).

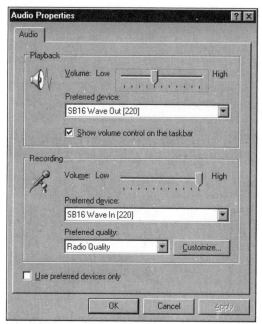

Figure 29-6: Audio Properties dialog box.

8. To save the recording, choose File⇨Save and then enter a file name.

Sound Recorder automatically adds the .wav extension to whatever file name you type.

The recording stays in Sound Recorder for the time being, so you can play it back and edit it as described in the next two sections.

Playing a sound

After you record a sound (or open a sound file by choosing File⇨Open), you can play it back easily. Use the control buttons in Sound Recorder as you use the buttons on a tape player. To rewind to the beginning of the sound, for example, click on the Seek to Start button; to play the sound, click on the Play button. If you're not sure which button is which, point to any button and wait for the tooltip to appear.

Editing a sound

When you have a sound in Sound Recorder, you can have some fun playing with the options in the Effects menu (see Figure 29-7).

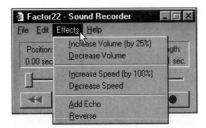

Figure 29-7: Options for editing a sound file.

Experiment on your own with these options. Choose any option from the menu; then rewind and click on the Play button to hear that effect.

The effects are cumulative. If you choose Effects ➪Add Echo one time, for example, you hear a little echo. If you choose Effects➪Add Echo five times, you get five times as much echo.

Playing audio CDs

Your PC can double as a player for the regular audio CDs that you use in your stereo system. To play an audio CD, follow these steps:

1. Put the audio CD in your PC's CD-ROM drive.

2. Choose Start button➪Programs➪Accessories➪Multimedia➪CD Player.

   The CD Player dialog box appears.

3. If you want to listen to specific tracks (songs), choose Disc➪Edit Play List; click on the Remove and Add buttons to add and remove playlist tracks (as in the example shown in Figure 29-8); and then click on OK.

4. Click on the Play button in CD Player.

5. If you need to adjust the volume, choose View➪Volume or click on the speaker icon in the taskbar.

Figure 29-9 shows CD Player playing an audio CD. I have the volume cranked up SO LOUD THAT I CAN HARDLY HEAR MYSELF THINK.

When CD Player gets going, you can play with some of the settings in its menu bar. CD Player also has its own help file, so if you need help, choose Help from the menu bar or click on the Question-mark button and then click on the item that you need help with.

You can resume your normal work while CD Player is running. If you want to get the CD Player window out of the way, click on its Minimize button. The window shrinks to a taskbar button, and the CD continues to play.

Figure 29-8: Selecting specific tracks on an audio CD.

Figure 29-9: The Windows 95 CD Player.

Windows 95 comes with built-in support for CD+, a new standard that will allow audio CDs to be played in a stereo system or a PC. Under CD+, a CD played in a PC also displays song titles and other useful information.

To stop playing a CD, click on the Stop button (black square) in CD Player, or close the CD Player window by clicking on its Close button (X).

Media Player and MIDI

MIDI (Musical Instrument Digital Interface) is electronic sheet music of a sort that can mimic the sounds of many musical instruments. When you play games or use multi-media titles that have great-sounding audio, chances are that you're actually listening to MIDI files.

You may have received some sample MIDI sound clips when you purchased your sound card. You can play a MIDI clip simply by double-clicking on its icon in My Computer, Windows Explorer, or Find, just as you can play a wave file (as discussed in "Playing a sound clip" earlier in this chapter.) Alternatively, you can play a MIDI clip from Media Player by following these steps:

1. Choose Start➪Programs➪Accessories➪Multimedia.

2. Click on Media Player to launch that program.

3. Choose Device➪3 MIDI Sequencer.

4. Browse to any folder that contains MIDI clips.

5. Double-click on any MIDI (.mid) file.

   In Figure 29-10, I've opened a MIDI file named Freaker from my Sound Blaster CD-ROM.

Figure 29-10: Media Player with MIDI file open.

6. Click on the Play button (tooltips are provided for the buttons).

You can play wave (.wav), MIDI (.mid), and video (.avi) files from Media Player's Open dialog box.

As you can in Sound Recorder, you can control the volume from your mixer (choose Device➪Volume Control from within Media Player) or by clicking on the speaker icon in the taskbar. You can use your computer to do other things while the MIDI file is playing.

Features to look for in MIDI boards

If you're just getting into MIDI or are considering upgrading your sound/MIDI card, look for the following factors, which enable you to take advantage of Windows 95's new MIDI features:

✦ Be sure to purchase a card that has *general MIDI support*, so that your MIDI card plays the right instrument at the right time.

✦ Look for a *standard MIDI port*, into which you can plug any MIDI device (as well as a joystick).

✦ A board that supports *polyphony* provides rich sound. Look for a board that can handle 16-voice to 20-voice polyphony.

✦ *Sampled sounds* provide much better acoustics than wavetable synthesis does. A sampled sound is a recording of the actual instrument, whereas wavetable synthesis produces a mathematical approximation of the instrument's sound.

✦ Support for *MIDI streams* relieves the CPU of some of the burden of playing MIDI; that burden is transferred to the sound card. The result is much better multimedia performance.

Any sound card that bears the "Designed for Windows 95" plug-and-play logo is easier to install than an older, non-plug-and-play board.

Recording MIDI

MIDI recording usually is done by professional musicians with MIDI-input hardware and special software. The input device, which usually looks like a piano keyboard, plugs into the MIDI/Game port slot of the sound card.

Windows 95 supports the *general MIDI specification*, to which all MIDI devices adhere, so just about any input device will work. Also worthy of mention is the fact that Windows 95 uses a new 32-bit technology called *MIDI streams support* that allows more music to be played through the PC, with less CPU use. This feature allows music developers to create more advanced music, mixing more instruments. And that capability, in turn, allows multimedia developers to include more complex music in their multimedia games and software titles.

In your volume-control box or mixer (refer to Figure 29-5), MIDI input and output volume is controlled by the MIDI, or Synth, channel. You also can control MIDI output volume from the speaker icon in the taskbar.

Advanced MIDI options

If you are a professional musician, and if you plan to create some MIDI files of your own, you should be aware of all the settings that influence MIDI in Windows 95. You can get to these settings through the Control Panel. Choose Start⟹Settings⟹Control Panel, and double-click on the Multimedia icon. Then click on the MIDI tab (see Figure 29-11) to set up custom configurations or add new instruments, or click on the Advanced tab to choose and enable MIDI drivers (see Figure 29-12).

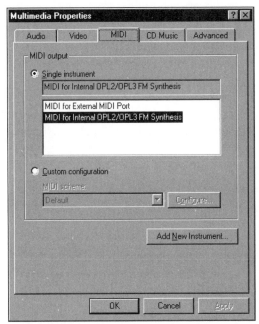

Figure 29-11: MIDI properties are accessible from the MIDI tab.

To see the properties of a specific MIDI file, browse to the file, right-click on its icon, and then choose Properties from the shortcut menu. You can preview the MIDI file from the Properties dialog box that appears (see Figure 29-13).

Digital Video

Windows 95 comes with built-in video-playback capability. In most situations, you'll see digital video played in multimedia titles. Figure 29-14 shows a screen from the movie *Casablanca* in Microsoft's Cinemania 95. Click on the Play button below the picture of Ingrid Bergman to play a short clip from the movie.

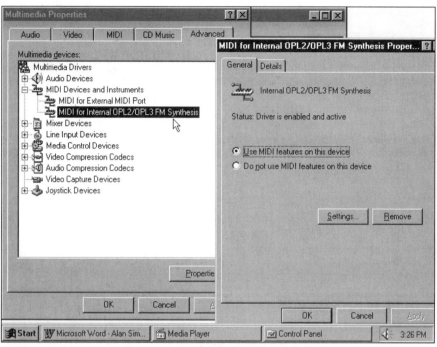

Figure 29-12: The Advanced tab enables you to configure MIDI drivers.

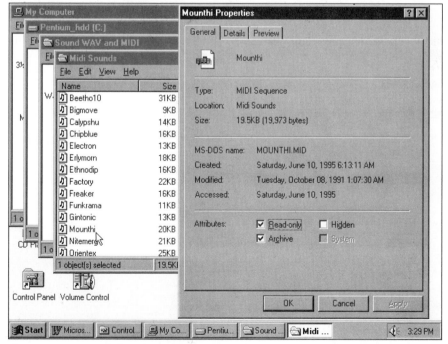

Figure 29-13: Properties of a MIDI file.

Figure 29-14: Sample video clip from Microsoft Cinemania 95.

You also can buy video clips or download them from many information services. A file that contains a video clip typically has the file extension .avi, Video Clip as its description, and a video-camera icon. In Figure 29-15, I browsed to a collection of video clips on a CD-ROM that contains sample clips from Microsoft and then double-clicked on the filename cool to watch the video. The video is paused in the figure, but the mouse pointer is touching the Play button. To restart the video, I just need to click on that button.

You also can launch a digital video clip from Media Player. Follow these steps:

1. Choose Start➪Programs➪Accessories➪Multimedia.

2. Click on Media Player.

3. Choose Device➪1 Video for Windows.

4. Browse to a video-clip file.

5. Double-click on any video-clip file.

   The first frame of the clip appears in a window.

6. Click on the Play button in Media Player.

   The clip plays in its small window.

7. To open another clip, choose File➪Open.

Figure 29-15: Digital video (.avi) clips, one of which is playing.

Adjust the brightness and contrast buttons on your monitor to fine-tune video playback. Your display settings (refer to Chapter 6) also affect the quality of playback.

Controlling video-playback size

Normally, a video clip plays in a small window. You can adjust the size of that window by dragging any corner. Alternatively, you can have Windows 95 launch the video at a specific size by following these steps:

1. Choose Start➪Settings➪Control Panel.

2. Double-click on the Multimedia icon.

3. Click on the Video tab.

4. Choose an option from the Window drop-down list or click on the Full Screen option button, as shown in Figure 29-16.

5. Click on the OK button.

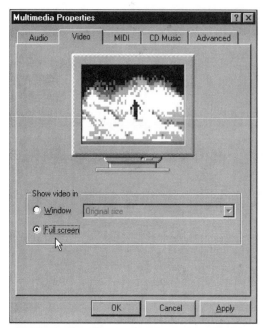

Figure 29-16: Video properties set for full-screen playback.

Any video clips that you play, whether by double-clicking on the file names or by using Media Player, display in the new size.

Video graininess and jerkiness

When you start playing video at larger sizes, you probably will start to see some degradation in the image. Graininess, or "blockiness," is caused by the fact that the images must be compressed to fit on a computer disk. If video were stored in an uncompressed format, a single frame of digital video would require an entire megabyte of disk space — and entire CD-ROM would be required to store even a short clip. Furthermore, that CD would need to spin at an awesome speed to feed the data to the PC.

Jerkiness in videos is caused by the speed of the video subsystem, the speed of the CPU, or the speed of the CD-ROM drive. If any of those devices is too slow, the device becomes a bottleneck in getting the huge stream of data into the CPU, decompressed, and out through your screen and sound card.

In terms of software, you can't do a whole lot about graininess and jerkiness; the 32-bit multimedia system in Windows 95 is decompressing and playing the video as fast as the hardware allows it to. (When you start buying 32-bit multimedia titles and video clips, however, those elements will run more smoothly.) In terms of hardware, you can throw money at the following options to minimize the problems:

✦ Get the fastest CD-ROM player possible; at least 300KB per second is recommended. A fast CD-ROM drive reduces both graininess and jerkiness.

✦ A fast 486 or Pentium CPU provides quicker decompression and less jerkiness.

✦ Be sure to get a computer that has a local-bus or PCI graphics subsytem.

✦ A display card that has a DCI (Display Control Interface) provider provides the best video performance.

Also, I should point out that running digital video over a network is likely to produce extremely poor results. Most network hardware and software simply aren't designed to carry the amount of data required to run multimedia digital video smoothly. While I was writing this chapter, though, I came across a review of IBM's Multimedia Server — a machine that's designed specifically to act as a file sharer in a LAN and to serve up data at a speed that would support multimedia on several workstations. I suspect that by the time I write the second edition of this book, dozens of brand-name multimedia servers will be available.

Capturing and editing video

Windows 95 offers no built-in features for capturing (recording), compressing, or editing digital video; you need to buy specialized hardware and software for those purposes. At the time I wrote this book, I didn't know of any 32-bit "Designed for Windows 95" hardware and software for capturing, compressing, or editing video. But I do know which two products are the most popular — and the most highly praised by critics — in the 16-bit world of Windows 3.x.

On the hardware side of the equation, Intel's VideoRecorder Pro consistently gets rave reviews in the industry press. On the software side of the equation, Adobe Premiere 4.0 causes many a reviewer to gush. For putting all the pieces of a multimedia production together, Macromedia Director has been enormously popular. Check out these products at your local computer store.

Adding AutoPlay to your CD-ROM production

Windows 95 now offers AutoPlay, a magical feature that allows a user to slide a disc into the CD-ROM drive, sit back, and enjoy the show. No browsing for setup or startup programs is required.

To add AutoPlay to the software that you distribute on CD-ROM, you simply need to add the text file named AUTORUN.INF to the CD-ROM's directory. Three lines are all that's required, as follows:

```
[autorun]
open=pathname\filename.exe
paramteers
icon = filename.ico
```

Replace the italicized parameters with actual names from your CD-ROM. For more information, see the *Windows 95 Resource Kit*, published by Microsoft Press.

Writing to CD-ROM

Windows 95 offers no built-in software for mastering (writing to) a CD-ROM disc. CD-ROM is strictly read-only memory, unless you buy special CD-ROM mastering hardware and software. Many such products are available, but machines that cost less than $2,000 have appeared only recently.

Be forewarned that saving to a CD-ROM is not at all like saving to a hard disk. On a hard disk, you can store and erase files easily, at will. On a CD-ROM, however, you have to get everything right the first time, because you can't erase what you put on the disc. Having a hard disk with 680M of free space helps. You can store the entire contents of the CD-ROM on the hard disk first, and when you're happy with what's on the hard disk, you can copy the full 680M (or whatever) to a CD-ROM.

Windows 95 Codecs

Wave sound (including voice), MIDI, and digital video use some kind of compression/decompression (abbreviated *codec*) scheme to store information on computer disks. Compression is necessary, because audio and video data require huge amounts of storage. Without compression, a single frame of digital video could take up a megabyte of storage. Therefore, a CD-ROM could hold about 680 frames, which represents a short video clip.

Currently, a CD-ROM holds about 680MB of data — roughly equivalent to about 500 floppy disks. Soon, you're likely to see the next generation of CD-ROMs, which will hold 3GB of data — the equivalent of about 3,000 floppies. Next will come 7GB CD-ROMs, which probably will be able to hold a full-length motion picture with no compression (and, hence, no graininess).

Windows 95 comes with many popular codecs built right in. To see which codecs are currently installed and to tweak their settings, follow these steps:

1. Choose Start⇨Settings⇨Control Panel.

2. Double-click on the Multimedia icon.

3. Click on the Advanced tab.

4. To view video codecs, click on the plus sign (+) next to Video compression codecs.

    To view audio codes, click on the plus sign (+) next to Audio compression codecs.

Figure 29-17 shows an example. If you want to explore or change the settings for a particular codec, click on the codec and then click on the Properties button. After you explore and/or make changes, click on OK to work your way back to the Control Panel, and follow the on-screen instructions (if any).

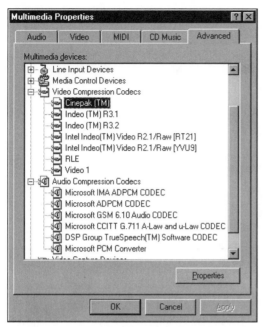

Figure 29-17: Installed codecs.

If you buy a hardware device that requires a codec that you don't have, you easily can add the appropriate codec to your list. If you buy a video capture board that uses JPEG compression, for example, you can add JPEG to Windows 95. Follow these steps:

1. Choose Start⇨Settings⇨Control Panel.

2. Double-click on the Add New Hardware icon.

3. Click on the Next button.

4. When you are asked about detecting new hardware, click on No.

5. Click on the Next button to display the list of device categories.

6. Click on the Sound, Video, and Game Controllers option, as shown in Figure 29-18.

7. Choose one of the codec options from the Manufacturers list.

   You can choose Microsoft Audio Codes or Microsoft Video Codecs, for example. Optionally, to install another manufacturer's codec, click on Have Disk.

8. In the Models section, click on the codec that you want to install (see Figure 29-19).

9. Click on the Next button.

10. Follow the on-screen instructions.

Figure 29-18: About to install a codec, via the Add New Hardware wizard.

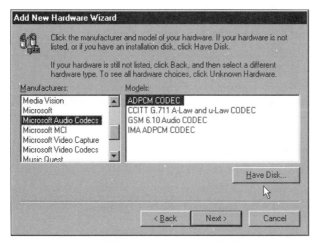

Figure 29-19: Installing a codec via the Add New Hardware wizard.

Troubleshooting Multimedia

Multimedia is one of the more difficult things to troubleshoot on a PC. One reason is the simple fact that multimedia involves a great deal of hardware and software, and you can adjust the volume and picture quality in many places. Furthermore, different multimedia programs use different techniques to display animation, video, sound, and so on; it's hard to tell whether the problem is in your settings or in the program that you're trying to use. Nonetheless, if you're having trouble with multimedia, the following checklist can help you diagnose (and perhaps solve) the problem:

✦ If you're having a problem with a specific multimedia program, you may want to set it aside and try a different program. (The troublesome program may be incompatible.)

✦ Make sure that all hardware is properly installed and connected properly, per the manufacturers' instructions.

✦ Check the volume of devices outside the PC (such as the volume knobs on your speakers).

✦ Check the status and output volume of all devices in your mixer (choose Start⇨Programs⇨Accessories⇨Multimedia⇨Volume Control).

✦ Check the volume control in the taskbar (click on the speaker icon).

If problems persist, use the Device Manager and the hardware-conflict Troubleshooter (discussed in Chapter 10) to diagnose and solve any conflicts between your multimedia hardware and other devices on your PC.

Remember that multimedia will get better for everyone. Soon, you'll be able to purchase "Designed for Windows 95" hardware and software, feeling confident that you can just plug everything in and go.

Summary

Following is a recap of the main points discussed in this chapter:

✦ Like most new technologies, multimedia is plagued with problems that affect both multimedia producers and consumers.

✦ Windows 95 has many built-in features that are designed to make multimedia richer and easier to use. But even Windows 95 needs speedy modern hardware to do its job.

✦ Most multimedia elements that you play probably will be embedded in a game or title that's stored on a CD-ROM drive.

✦ You can manage small multimedia clips with Windows 95. To play a sound (.WAV), MIDI (.MID), or video (.AVI) clip, you can double-click on its file name.

✦ You can control the volume of sound in multimedia in many ways. You can use the volume controls on the speakers, the taskbar's speaker icon, and perhaps controls within the program that you're using at the moment.

✦ Use the Sounds Properties dialog box to assign custom sounds to Windows events. Choose Start➪Settings➪Control Panel, and double-click on the Sounds icon.

✦ Use Sound Recorder to record, edit, and play wave (.WAV) sounds: Choose Start➪Programs➪Accessories➪Multimedia➪Sound Recorder.

✦ Use CD Player to listen to audio CDs. Choose Start➪Programs➪Accessories➪Multimedia➪CD Player.

✦ Use Media Player to play MIDI (.MID) sound files and video clips (.AVI files). Choose Start➪Programs➪Accessories➪Multimedia➪Media Player.

✦   ✦   ✦

Using Microsoft Exchange

I feel compelled to start this chapter with a confession: when I started using Microsoft Exchange, I quickly became totally lost and confused. Within minutes of starting Exchange, I would have absolutely no idea what was going on. I'm making this confession because I want you to know that if you have this problem yourself, I can relate.

Figuring out the secret of Microsoft Exchange took me a while. That secret is: ignore Microsoft Exchange for a few weeks or a few months. That's right — pretend that Exchange isn't even there for a while. I know that this advice sounds strange. But after I explain what Exchange really is and how to learn about it, my advice may make some sense to you.

What Is Microsoft Exchange?

Microsoft Exchange is simply a place to store and manage incoming and outgoing messages. Exchange is called into play automatically whenever you use one of the following Windows 95 information services:

+ Faxes sent and received by Microsoft Fax (refer to Chapter 16)

+ Electronic mail from the Microsoft Network (refer to Chapter 21)

+ Electronic mail from your local area network (refer to Chapter 27)

I recommend that you ignore Microsoft Exchange for a few weeks because you'll find it much easier to install and use any of the preceding three services first. For directions, refer to the chapter listed with each service.

As you use whichever service(s) you install, you'll automatically be introduced to the various components of Exchange that are relevant to that service. While you're learning to do something useful, such as sending and receiving faxes, you'll also be learning about Microsoft Exchange in general. But you'll be learning in a practical, productive manner — which (I think) is the easiest way for most people to learn things.

After you learn to use Microsoft Fax, the Microsoft Network (MSN), Microsoft Mail (local e-mail), or any combination thereof, the techniques and concepts described in this chapter will make much more sense to you. You'll have some practical experience to which you can anchor the more abstract aspects of Microsoft Exchange.

Starting Microsoft Exchange

You can start Microsoft Exchange in many ways — a fact that adds to the confusion that this program seems to generate. In some situations, Microsoft Exchange starts automatically. If you log on to MSN and have e-mail waiting, for example, you have the opportunity to open Exchange and read those new messages. You also can fire up Exchange on your own whenever you want to check your messages, using either of the following techniques:

✦ Double-click on the Inbox icon on the desktop.

✦ Choose Start⇨Programs⇨Microsoft Exchange.

A dialog box appears, telling you that Microsoft Exchange is starting. Then that dialog box is replaced by the Inbox for Microsoft Exchange, which looks something like Figure 30-1.

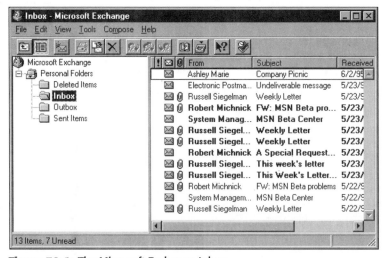

Figure 30-1: The Microsoft Exchange Inbox.

What's on the screen

To see all the items shown in Figure 30-1, make sure that you select the same view options. Choose View from the menu bar, and then select Folders, Toolbar, and Status Bar, as necessary. This chapter also talks about the Show/Hide Folder List, New Message, Address Book, Inbox, and various Reply toolbar buttons, so take a moment to point to (don't click on yet) each button in the toolbar, just to familiarize yourself with them.

You should be looking at a two-pane view of Exchange now. The left pane lists your personal folders — the folders where your messages are stored. The folder names describe the type of messages that they contain, as follows:

✦ *Deleted Items:* contains messages that you deleted from one of the other three folders. These "deleted" copies are maintained as backups until you're sure that you want to delete the messages permanently.

✦ *Inbox:* stores new messages that you've received.

✦ *Outbox:* stores messages that you've written but have not yet sent.

✦ *Sent Items:* stores copies of all the messages that you've sent.

The right pane shows the contents of whatever folder is open. When you click on the Inbox folder name, for example, the pane on the right shows the messages that you've received. Seven columns appear across the top pane (although in Figure 30-1, the last column is scrolled out of view). The columns are:

✦ *! (exclamation point):* marked if the message is marked "Urgent"

✦ *(envelope):* marked if the message contains a written message, not just an attachment

✦ *(paper clip):* marked if the message contains, or is, an attachment (a file)

✦ *From:* sender's name, if known

✦ *Subject:* the subject line that the sender typed

✦ *Received:* the date and time when the message was received

✦ *Size:* the size of the message, in kilobytes (KB)

You can sort messages by any column instantly, simply by clicking the appropriate column heading. If you sort by the From column, for example, messages are alphabetized by sender.

In the Inbox, messages that you have not read yet are boldfaced.

Managing received messages

The real purpose of Microsoft Exchange is to give you a central place from which to view, respond to, and send messages. Exchange certainly excels in that department, because it enables you to whip through your messages. To read a message, double-click on it. The message appears in a larger window called the *message viewer*, as in the example shown in Figure 30-2.

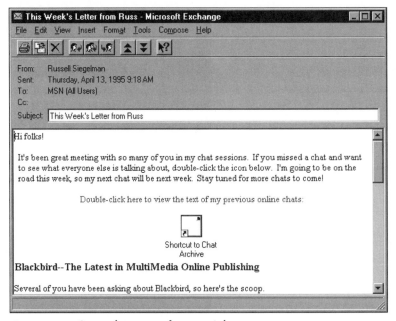

Figure 30-2: Opened message from my Inbox.

You can use the toolbar buttons to manage the message, as follows:

✦ To print a message, click on the Print button.

✦ To reply to the sender, click on the Reply to Sender button.

✦ To reply to the sender and all the original recipients, click on the Reply to All button.

✦ To forward the message to someone else, click on the Forward button.

✦ To delete the message, click on the Delete button. The message goes into your Deleted Items folder.

✦ To move the message to some folder other than Deleted Items, click on the Move Item button.

✦ To move to the following message, click on the Next button.

✦ To move to the preceding message, click on the Previous button.

✦ To close the message viewer, click on its Close button (X).

The following sections examine the ways in which you can compose and send messages.

Composing and Sending Messages

You can use Microsoft Exchange as a central area for composing and sending all types of e-mail messages and faxes. Follow these easy steps:

1. If you're not already in Microsoft Exchange, double-click on the Inbox icon or choose Start⇨Programs⇨Microsoft Exchange.

2. Do either of the following things:

   ✦ If you want to reply to a message in your Inbox, click on the Reply to Sender or Reply to All button in the toolbar.

   ✦ If you want to compose a message from scratch, click on the New Message button or choose Compose⇨New Message.

Either way, you end up at the New Message window, shown in Figure 30-3.

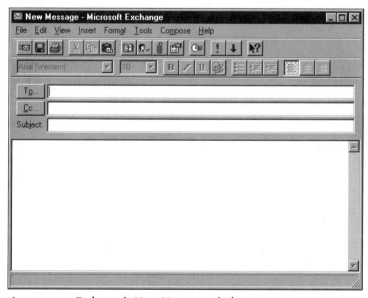

Figure 30-3: Exchange's New Message window.

This small New Message window offers a ton of features that make quick work of addressing, typing, and sending an e-mail message. The following sections talk about those features. If you're in a hurry, however, a great deal of help is available from the New Message window. You can turn the toolbars on and off by choosing the appropriate commands from the View menu. You can point to any toolbar button to display its tooltip. And if you want an explanation of some item in the New Message window, click on the Question-mark button and then click on the item that you want help with.

If you want to type and send a quick fax, you can use the Compose New Fax wizard. If you're in Exchange, choose Compose⇨New Fax; if you're at the desktop, choose Start⇨Programs⇨Accessories⇨Fax⇨Compose New Fax. See Chapter 16 for more information.

The New Message window also offers a direct route to many of your installed information services. Click on the Help command in the menu bar, and choose whichever topic you want help with (see Figure 30-4).

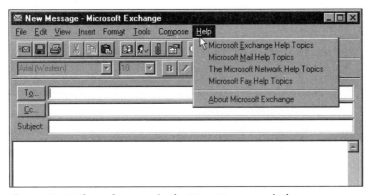

Figure 30-4: The Help menu in the New Message window.

Addressing a message

If you're replying to someone else's message, your new message is already addressed to that person. If you're creating a message from scratch, you can click on the To button to address your message. Follow these steps:

1. Click on the To button.

2. In the drop-down list to the right of Show names from, select an address book.

   The options that are available depend on which information services you have installed, as follows:

✦ *Personal Address Book:* your personal "little black book" of names and addresses. You need to maintain this book yourself, using the general techniques described in "Setting Up Your Personal Address Book" in Chapter 16.

✦ *Microsoft Network:* names and addresses of MSN members, maintained automatically by MSN.

✦ *Postoffice Address Book:* members of your local e-mail system, maintained automatically by Microsoft Mail.

3. If the list of names is long, type the first few letters of the recipient's name to jump to the appropriate part of the list, and click on the To button when you find the recipient's name.

4. Optionally, to send a copy to another person, select that person's name in the list and then click on the Cc button.

If you accidentally copy the wrong name to the recipient column, click on that name and then press the Delete key to remove the name from the column.

5. Repeat Steps 3 and 4 to select as many recipient and copy-recipient names as you want, as shown in Figure 30-5.

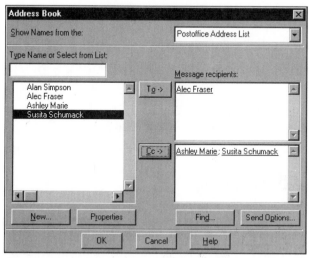

Figure 30-5: Recipient names selected.

6. When you finish selecting names, choose OK.

You return to the New Message window. The To and Cc portions of the window now contain the names of all the recipients.

You also can send blind carbon copies of messages. To activate this feature, choose View➪Bcc in the New Message window.

Filling in the subject

Whatever you type in the Subject line is what appears in the recipient's Inbox. Keep this line brief and to the point, so that the recipient has some idea what the message is about before he or she opens the message.

Figure 30-6 shows an example in which I'm ready to type the body of the message.

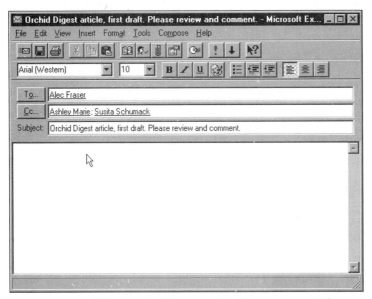

Figure 30-6: Recipients and subject typed in the message window.

Typing and editing the message

The large text box is where you type the actual message. You can use all the standard Windows text-editing tools and techniques. You can select text by dragging the mouse pointer through it or by holding down the Shift key while you tap the arrow keys. After you select text, you can apply any of the formatting features to that text: Font, Size, Bold, Italic, Underline, Color, Bullets, Decrease Indent, Increase Indent, Align Left, Center, or Align Right.

If the formatting features aren't visible, choose View➪Formatting Toolbar in the New Message window.

Attaching a file to the message

You can attach any file, or combination of files, to a message. The file can be a program, a document, or another message, for example. When you attach a file, the attachment appears in the message as an icon. When the recipient receives the message, he or she sees the icon. Generally, you should include brief instructions, telling the recipient how to use the icon.

Most people center the descriptive text and the icon in a message. If you want to format your message that way, follow these steps:

1. Move the insertion point to the place in your message where you want the descriptive text to appear.

   If you need to insert a blank line, press Enter once or twice.

2. Type the descriptive text, as in the example shown in Figure 30-7.

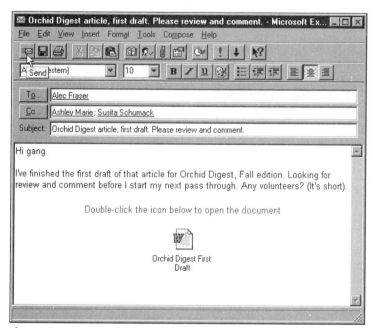

Figure 30-7: Descriptive text and attachment icon in an outgoing message.

3. If you want to center the descriptive text, click on the Center button in the formatting toolbar.

4. To make room for the attachment, press the End key to move to the end of the descriptive-text line; then press Enter to move down a line.

5. Click on the Insert File (paper-clip) button in the toolbar.

6. Browse to and select the file that you want to insert.

7. Choose OK.

Both the descriptive text and the icon now appear in your message, as shown in Figure 30-7.

If you want to add more text, you can press Enter once or twice to insert blank lines. To align the new text with the left margin, click on the Align Left button.

 You can insert text from a file, an object, or another message into the body of your message by choosing options from the Insert menu. For more information, choose Help⊅Microsoft Exchange Topics in the New Message window; then use the Index and Find tabs to search for the topic *insert*.

Assigning properties to a message

You can assign several properties to a message before sending it. Click on the Properties button in the toolbar or choose File⊅Properties in the New Message window; choose options in the dialog box that appears (see Figure 30-8); and then choose OK.

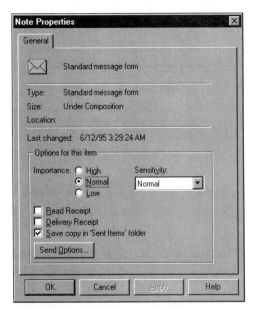

Figure 30-8: Properties assigned to a message.

Sending a message

When you're ready to send the message, click on the Send button in the toolbar. Exactly when the message is sent depends on how you set properties for the specific information service that you're using to send the message. You can check the status of a message, however, and send it immediately, if need be. Follow these steps:

1. If you closed Microsoft Exchange, reopen it by double-clicking on the Inbox icon or choosing Start⇨Programs⇨Microsoft Exchange.

2. If the Folder List isn't visible, choose View⇨Folders or click on the Show/Hide Folder List button.

3. Click on the Outbox folder.

   Any items listed in the Outbox are waiting to be sent.

4. To send one of the Outbox items immediately, click on its name and then choose Tools⇨Deliver Now Using.

5. Select the service that you want to use to send the message.

After a message has been sent, it no longer appears in the Outbox; instead, it appears in your Sent Items folder.

Clearing Out Old Messages

As mentioned earlier, Exchange keeps copies of all the messages that you send and receive. Eventually, all these messages start eating up disk space, so you need to clear out old messages from time to time. Follow these steps:

1. Open your Inbox by double-clicking on the Inbox icon or choosing Start⇨Programs⇨Microsoft Exchange.

2. Make sure that you can see the folder list (choose View⇨Folders or click on the Show/Hide Folder List button).

3. Click on the Inbox folder.

4. Select any messages that you want to get rid of.

   You can Ctrl+click and Shift+click to select multiple messages.

5. Click on the Delete button in the toolbar.

6. Click on the Sent Items folder.

7. Select any messages that you want to get rid of (Shift+click or Ctrl+click to select multiple messages).

8. Click on the Delete button to delete the selected messages.

9. Click on the Deleted Items folder.

   The messages in this folder have been deleted from some other folder but remain on your disk as backups.

10. Select any messages that you want to delete permanently (Shift+click or Ctrl+click to select multiple messages).

11. Click on the Delete button.

    You see a warning, as shown in Figure 30-9.

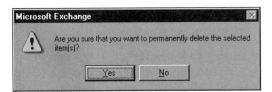

Figure 30-9: Final warning about deleting messages.

12. If you're sure that you want to delete these messages permanently and reclaim the disk space that they're using, choose Yes.

Understanding Exchange Profiles

One aspect of Microsoft Exchange that confuses many people is the difference between *information services* and *profiles.* Following are definitions of these terms:

✦ *Information service:* a service to which Exchange gives you access, such as Microsoft Fax, Microsoft Mail, Microsoft Network, and Personal Address Book.

✦ *Profile:* a collection of information settings for a single user of the PC.

If two or more people share a PC, chances are that each person will want to set up his or her own Exchange profile, because buried within the profile is information such as your return address, phone number, and cover sheet.

The easiest way to set up a profile is to have one user create his or her own information-service, fax, address-book, MSN, and local-e-mail profile, as discussed in the chapters on those topics (Chapters 16, 21, and 27). When that profile is set up, another user can copy that profile to a new profile under his or her name and then tweak the profile to suit his or her needs.

To copy an existing profile, follow these steps:

1. Choose Start⇨Settings⇨Control Panel.

2. Double-click on the Mail and Fax icon.

3. In the first dialog box that appears, click on the Show Profiles button.

4. To copy the existing profile, click on it and then click on the Copy button.

5. Type a name for the new profile.

6. Choose OK.

   The new profile appears in the list of profile names.

In Figure 30-10, I copied the original MS Exchange Settings to Ashley's Exchange Profile. Notice that within the same dialog box, you can specify which profile serves as the default profile.

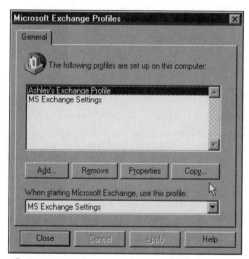

Figure 30-10: Two Exchange profiles are on this computer.

To tweak the settings in Ashley's Exchange Profile, click on her profile name in the list and then click on the Properties button. A list of information services included in Ashley's profile appears (see Figure 30-11). In this example, Ashley's profile contains the same information settings as the MS Exchange Settings profile, because I copied that profile to create Ashley's profile.

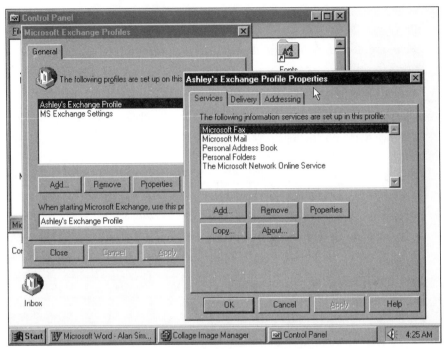

Figure 30-11: Ready to start tweaking Ashley's Exchange Profile.

Click on any information in Ashley's Exchange Profile (Microsoft Fax, Microsoft Mail, and so on) and then click on the Properties button to view the settings and tailor them to Ashley's profile. When you finish, click on OK and Close, as appropriate, to work your way back to the Control Panel. (You also can close the Control Panel, if you want.)

Now that you have more than one profile defined on this PC, you probably will want Windows to prompt you for which profile to use at any given moment. Follow these steps:

1. Open Microsoft Exchange (double-click on the Inbox icon or choose Start⊏>Programs⊏>Microsoft Exchange).

2. Choose Tools⊏>Options.

3. In the When starting Microsoft Exchange section, choose Prompt for a profile to be used, as shown in Figure 30-12.

4. Choose OK.

From now on, whenever you open Microsoft Exchange, you'll be prompted to choose a profile, as shown in Figure 30-13. Select a profile from the drop-down list and then choose OK.

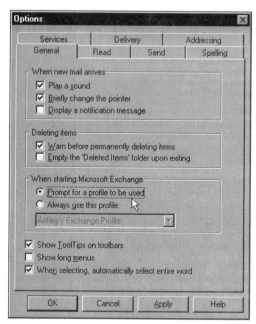

Figure 30-12: Telling Exchange to prompt for a profile.

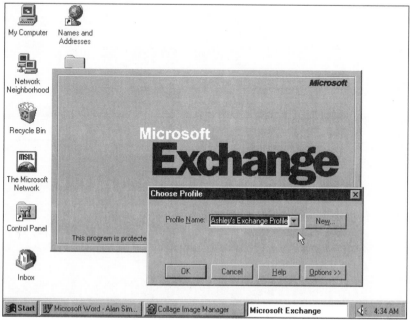

Figure 30-13: Exchange prompting for a profile.

Summary

Following are the main points to remember from this chapter:

✦ Microsoft Exchange is a central area for managing incoming and outgoing messages.

✦ The messages are handled by different information services within Exchange: Microsoft Fax, Microsoft Mail (local e-mail), and Microsoft Network (MSN).

✦ To open Exchange, double-click on the Inbox icon on the desktop or choose Start⇨Programs⇨Microsoft Exchange.

✦ The Inbox in Exchange shows the messages that you've received. Double-click on any message to read it.

✦ To reply to a message, click on one of the Reply buttons in the toolbar.

✦ To create a message from scratch, click on the New Message button in Exchange.

✦ If several people share a PC, each person can create a separate Microsoft Exchange profile.

✦   ✦   ✦

Dealing with
the Registry

This chapter explores the Windows 95 Registry. If you skipped several chapters to get here, I should warn you that this chapter probably is the only chapter in the book that you can ignore. Virtually everything that you can do within the Registry, you can do more easily, and more accurately, *outside* the Registry. To prove this fact to myself, I wrote the first 30 chapters of this book without even looking at the contents of the Registry.

So if you're not an experienced programmer, please don't be intimidated by the information presented in this chapter. In all likelihood, you'll never need to modify, or even look at, the Registry yourself. Maintaining the Registry is Windows' job, not yours. All the wizards and dialog boxes discussed in Chapters 1–30 are there so that you *don't* have to mess with the Registry. In other words, about 99.9 percent of the people who read this book can ignore this chapter.

What Is the Registry?

Windows needs to keep track of many, many settings that you make as you use your PC. When you're changing settings via the Control Panel, for example, Windows needs to keep track of your selections. When you install new hardware, Windows needs to keep track of the settings required by that device. When you install new programs, Windows needs to keep track of information about that program and the documents that it supports. All the information that Windows keeps track of is stored in a database called the Registry.

For the most part, the Registry is invisible — and for good reason. Windows 95 is responsible for creating, maintaining, and deleting Registry entries automatically as you change settings and add or delete hardware and software. The information in the Registry isn't in very human-readable form and doesn't need to be; Windows 95 uses the Registry itself to get your computer started and keep track of your preferences.

Nonetheless, you occasionally may want to change the way that a document is registered to its program; this chapter explains how to do that. Also, if you're an experienced programmer, you may need to explore the Registry to locate specific keys and values that you need to access from a program that you're writing. This chapter shows you how to fire up RegEdit so that you can explore the Windows 95 Registry.

Managing Program and Document Associations

One job of the Registry is to keep track of the way that documents are associated with programs. The Registry determines, for example, what program is launched when you double-click on a document icon. The Registry also defines what appears in the shortcut menu when you right-click on a document icon and what happens when you choose an option from the shortcut menu.

You can change the default settings that determine the way that a document is associated with a program. You don't have to open the Registry directly to make these changes. Instead, you can follow these steps:

1. Double-click on the My Computer icon.

2. Choose <u>V</u>iew⇨<u>O</u>ptions.

3. Click on the File Types tab.

   You go to a list of registered file types.

4. To see how a specific file type is registered, click on the appropriate document icon.

In Figure 31-1, for example, I clicked on Microsoft Word Document. In the bottom portion of the dialog box, you see that the file extension for Microsoft Word documents is DOC and that the program opened for that file type is WINWORD.

The following sections discuss how to create new associations, edit existing associations, and delete associations. Each section assumes that you're starting from the dialog box shown in Figure 31-1.

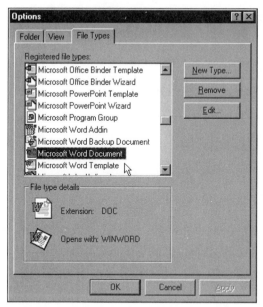

Figure 31-1: Microsoft Word document's file extension and associated program.

Creating a new association

You can use the <u>N</u>ew Type button to create a new association. Suppose that I want to assign the extension .LET to letters that I write. So when I double-click on a file that has the .LET extension, I want that document to open in Microsoft Word. My job is to associate .LET with Microsoft Word by following these steps:

1. Click on the <u>N</u>ew Type button.

   The Add New File Type dialog box appears.

2. Type a brief description for this type of document and then type the three-letter extension (without the leading period).

   In Figure 31-2, I'm preparing to make an association with files that have the .LET extension.

3. To see if the extension you typed is already registered, click on the OK button.

   If you see a warning message like the one shown in Figure 31-3, skip to step 11.

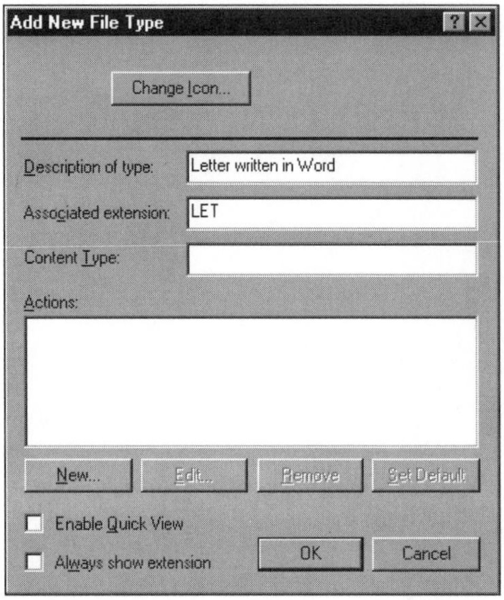

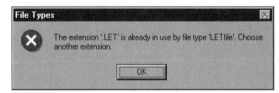

Figure 31-2: About to associate the .LET extension with a program.

Figure 31-3: Whoops — .LET is already registered.

If you don't see an error message, your new description appears, highlighted, in the list of registered types.

4. Click on the Edit button.

5. Click on the Change Icon button .

6. In the dialog box that appears, select an icon for this document type.

If you have your own collection of icons, you can click on the Browse button to choose an icon. You also can click on the Browse button to go to the program's folder and look for icons in that folder. I got the icon shown in Figure 31-4 from the C:\OFFICE95\WINWORD\WINWORD.EXE file.

7. In the Actions section, click on the New button.

8. Type a brief description of the action that you're defining.

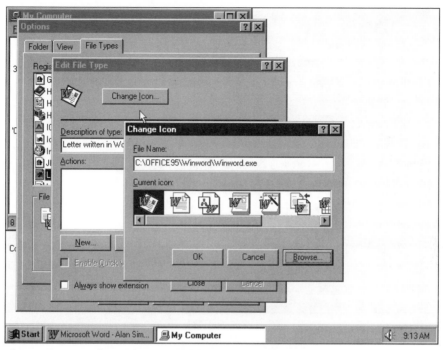

Figure 31-4: Icon from C:\OFFICE95\WINWORD\WINWORD.EXE.

9. Click on the Browse button to select the program with which you want to associate this extension.

   In Figure 31-5, I typed **open** as the action and selected C:\OFFICE95\WINWORD\WINWORD.EXE as the application to be used to perform the action.

10. Choose OK and click on Close to work your way back to the desktop; ignore step 11.

11. If you got to this step, you're trying to create an association for an extension that already exists. Choose OK; click on Cancel; and then delete or edit the existing association as discussed in the sections that follow.

From now on, when you save a Microsoft Word document, you can add the extension .LET to whatever filename you provide. Later, when you're browsing around the folders and come across a .LET file, you can double-click on its icon to open that document in Microsoft Word.

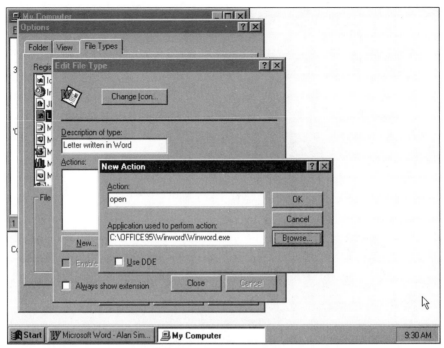

Figure 31-5: C:\OFFICE95\WINWORD\WINWORD.EXE will open .LET files.

Changing an association

 To see which program a file extension is associated with, choose Start➪Find to locate a file that has that extension and then double-click on the file's icon. Whatever program opens is the associated program.

To change an existing association, follow these steps:

1. If you're not already in the list of registered file types, open My Computer; choose View➪Options; and click on the File Types tab.

2. Click on the file type that you want to change.

   The program and extension for the selected file type appear in the File type section at the bottom of the dialog box.

3. Click on the Edit button.

4. In the Description of type text box, type a new description for this file type.

5. To change an action, click on the action that you want to change and then click the Edit button.

Use the Browse button to locate the program that you want to initiate the current action.

In Figure 31-6, I changed what originally was called the Paintbrush file type (the program associated with the .PCX extension) to C:\COLLWIN\IMGMGR.EXE, which is the Image Manager program that I use for screen shots.

6. Click on OK and Close as necessary to work your way back to the desktop.

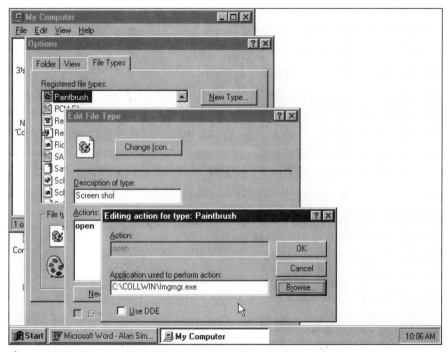

Figure 31-6: Changing the old Paintbrush file type to Screen shot.

Deleting an association

In some cases, you may want to delete an association between a file extension and a program. Rather than edit an existing association, you may want to delete the existing association and then create a new one from scratch.

To delete an association, follow these steps:

1. If you're not already in the list of registered file types, open My Computer; choose View➪Options; and click on the File Types tab.

2. Click on the file type that you want to delete.

   Remember that the program and extension for the selected file type appears in the File type details section at the bottom of the dialog box.

3. Click on the <u>R</u>emove button.

   A warning message appears.

4. Click on <u>Y</u>es to proceed.

5. Repeat Steps 2–4 to delete as many associations as you want.

6. When you finish, click on the OK button to return to My Computer.

Customizing a file type's shortcut menu

When you right-click on a document icon in My Computer, Windows Explorer, or Find, you typically see a shortcut menu of things that you can do with that document type. In Figure 31-7, for example, I right-clicked on a document icon that I browsed to via My Computer. Notice that the first option in the shortcut menu is boldface, which indicates the default action for that document type. The default action is the one that occurs when you double-click (rather than right-click) on that type of document.

Figure 31-7: Shortcut menu for a document icon.

The shortcut menus in most documents contain an <u>O</u>pen option. Some documents' shortcut menus include other options, such as <u>P</u>rint and <u>N</u>ew. The actions at the top of those menus actually are defined in the Registry. You can change these actions or add new ones.

Some "Designed for Windows 95" programs add multiple shortcut menus automatically. When I associate the .LET extension with Microsoft Word for Windows, for example, Windows 95 automatically adds the <u>O</u>pen, <u>P</u>rint, and <u>N</u>ew options to the shortcut menu for .LET documents.

The trick is finding the proper startup switch or DDE command for getting a program to do something other than open the document. Unfortunately, no standards exist, and you have no hope of guessing what the command may be. The only way to find the required information is to dig through the program's help files or printed documentation for topics such as startup, switches, and DDE.

When you find the information, follow the steps in "Changing an association" earlier in this chapter to get to the file type's actions. Then you can click on the <u>N</u>ew button and define a new action, or select an existing action and click on the <u>E</u>dit button. You go to the dialog box that enables you to create or edit the action. Type the action as a single word (for example, **print**). Then define the action in the Appl<u>i</u>cation used to perform action box.

If you need to send a DDE command to initiate a specific action, you can choose <u>U</u>se DDE to expand the dialog box to include DDE information. Figure 31-8 shows an example in which I'm viewing the Print action for the Microsoft Word Document file type.

Use extreme caution when you create or modify actions. You're poking directly into the Registry, and no early-warning system will notify you if you make a mistake. When in doubt, press the Escape key or click the Cancel button to back out of a dialog box without saving any changes.

Editing the Registry with RegEdit

For the truly advanced user, Windows 95 offers a program named RegEdit, which allows you to open the Registry directly and tweak its settings. Professional programmers also can use RegEdit to get the information required for getting information from the Registry into a program written in C++ or some other language.

All the information that's stored in the Registry comes from the selections that you make in the Control Panel. Always try to use the Control Panel to choose settings for your PC. Use RegEdit only as a last resort, such as when you have instructions from a hardware or software manufacturer telling you exactly what to put into the Registry.

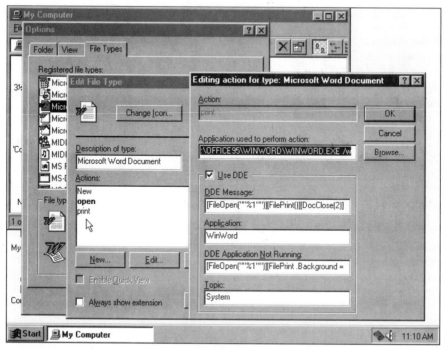

Figure 31-8: Sample action defined by using DDE.

No icon or menu command leads to RegEdit; it's far too dangerous a tool for nonprofessionals, and Microsoft wants to be sure that nobody stumbles upon it by accident. So to open RegEdit, you need to follow these steps:

1. Choose Start⇨Run.

2. Type **regedit**.

3. Choose OK.

   The Registry Editor window opens, as shown in Figure 31-9.

Each folder in the left pane is called a *key* and contains a collection of settings. To open a key, click on the plus sign (+) next to the key. The following list summarizes the information stored within each key:

✦ *HKEY_CLASSES_ROOT.* This key contains essential information required for OLE, file document/program associations, and drag-and-drop operations. This information is created and maintained automatically whenever you add or remove programs.

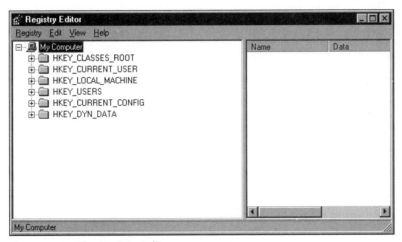

Figure 31-9: The Registry Editor.

✦ *HKEY_CURRENT_USER.* This key contains information about the person who is currently using the PC. You use the Applicable only if you've allowed multiple user profiles under the Passwords icon in Control Panel.

✦ *HKEY_LOCAL_MACHINE.* This key contains hardware settings appropriate to this particular PC. This information, maintained by the Add New Hardware wizard, reflects the options that you chose through the Control Panel.

✦ *HKEY_USERS.* This key retains information about every person who logs on to this computer. This information is maintained by the log-on box that appears when you start Windows.

✦ *HKEY_CURRENT_CONFIG.* This key maintains information about the current configuration. This information is managed automatically by hot docking, hot swapping, and multiple hardware profiles. These topics are discussed in Chapter 17.

✦ *HKEY_DYN_DATA.* This key maintains information about "Designed for Windows 95" plug-and-play devices. Windows 95 maintains this information automatically.

When you activate (open) a key, you're likely to find more subfolders within that key. As you drill down, you eventually come to a folder that has no subfolder (has no + or – sign next to it). When you open this folder, you see the information stored within that folder. In Figure 31-10, for example, I drilled down to Colors in the HKEY_USERS key.

The right pane of the Registry Editor contains the *value entries* that the subfolder maintains. In Figure 31-10, you see the color settings for all the various doodads on the screen. The numeric values are the actual settings, in the format in which Windows stores them. 128 128 128, for example, actually is the color gray.

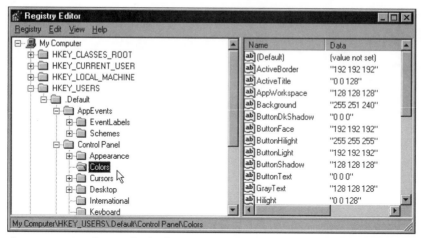

Figure 31-10: Value entries in the right pane of the Registry.

Ideally, that last example helps drive home the point about not using RegEdit to change settings. The numbers 128 128 128 have meaning only to Windows, not to human beings. As a human being, you'd be much better off choosing a color setting without RegEdit. Just right-click on the desktop, choose Properties, click on the Appearance tab, and choose your colors there.

Summary

✦ The Registry is a database of settings that Windows 95 manages automatically.

✦ A registered document type is a file extension that's associated with a program.

✦ To change an association between a document type and program, you can modify the Registry by using the File Types tab in My Computer's Options dialog box.

✦ Windows 95 comes with a program named RegEdit, which professionals can use to view and modify the Registry database directly.

✦   ✦   ✦

Corporate Considerations

I realize that some of the people who are reading this book are MIS managers and similar professionals who are responsible for dozens, perhaps hundreds, or even thousands of PCs. And I'm well aware of the fact that in a large corporation, upgrading from Windows 3.x to Windows 95 isn't quite as simple as sticking a disk into a drive and running SETUP.EXE. In this chapter, I discuss some of the challenges and solutions Windows 95 presents to corporate MIS manages.

Why a Corporate Upgrade?

At Microsoft's Tech Ed conference, back in about March 1994, I attended a presentation on Windows 95. During the question-and-answer period at the end of the session, an attendee stood and posed the following scenario and question:

> "We currently have about 600 users of PCs in our enterprise. Most PCs are running Windows for Workgroups, which we recently upgraded to from Windows 3.1. It took several months, and considerable resource expenditure, to make the relatively 'simple' switch from Windows 3.1 to Windows for Workgroups.

> "But we did it, and now all our PCs are working, people are trained, and everybody seems to be getting the job done without daily crisis intervention from the MIS staff. My question is this: Are you suggesting that we now go back, tear all that down, and replace it with Windows 95? And if you *are* suggesting that, could you write a list of specific advantages that would justify the enormous expenditure of resources that this yet-another-upgrade is going to require?"

I was happy *not* to be the speaker who had to respond to this question. The speaker at that session did come up with a fairly good list of justifications, however, which are summarized in the following sections. (I won't try to *sell* you on the idea, though. That's Microsoft's job, not mine!)

Reduced support costs

One potential benefit of switching to Windows 95, even in a large organization, is reduced support costs, as described in the following list:

✦ The intuitive nature of the Windows 95 user interface makes users more independent and therefore reduces support costs.

✦ Plug-and-play also reduces support costs by simplifying the hardware-installation process.

✦ The 32-bit operating system offers greater reliability and performance, thereby taking some of the load off support personnel.

✦ Built-in networking allows Windows 95 to work seamlessly with all major networks, including Novell NetWare and Windows NT, so network administration is less costly.

More control of desktop PCs

A second justification for large-scale upgrades to Windows 95 centers on the fact that MIS managers will have more control of all the PCs in the enterprise, as described in the following list:

✦ User profiles allow multiple users to share a single PC without getting in one another's way.

✦ System policies can be implemented to reduce a user's ability to change configuration settings.

✦ Support for remote administration tools and agents is built into Windows 95.

✦ Support for centralized pass-through security, log-on scripts, and validated logon with NetWare and NT Server networks also is built in.

Improved user productivity

A third reason for a corporation to upgrade to Windows 95 is increased user productivity. Workers will be more productive for the following reasons:

✦ Faster 32-bit processing means that more work gets done in less time.

✦ Preemptive multitasking allows multiple hardware devices — such as a printer, a modem, and a floppy disk drive — to work simultaneously.

✦ Dial-Up Networking and Briefcase make it easier for users to work from home or on the road.

✦ Centralized messaging via Microsoft Exchange enables users to take care of incoming and outgoing messages more quickly.

Built-in support for smooth migration

Finally, Microsoft has gone to great lengths to make the transition from Windows 3.x to Windows 95 as smooth, painless, and easy as possible, as described in the following list:

✦ The setup program for Windows 95 automatically detects hardware and installs drivers, so that upgrading a single PC is quick and easy.

✦ The setup procedure can be scripted to choose options automatically as the installation proceeds.

✦ *Push installation* allows multiple computers to be upgraded from a server. The administrator need not even go to the PC that's being upgraded.

The Resource for MIS Professionals

Microsoft offers the *Windows 95 Resource Kit*, which is specifically directed to MIS professionals. That book covers, in great depth, the technical information required for large-scale installation and support. The 1,200+–page book includes technical information on using Windows 95 with legacy hardware and networks, as well as corporate-planning, deployment, and implementation guides. To purchase the book, contact Microsoft Press at (800) MSPRESS.

Summary

Large-scale upgrades from Windows 3.x to Windows 95 are bound to be time-consuming and resource-draining undertakings. To encourage such upgrades, Microsoft offers the following justifications:

✦ Support costs are reduced, because users are more independent.

✦ MIS managers have more control of desktop PCs and therefore can minimize problems caused by inexperienced users fussing with settings.

✦ Workers are more productive, because Windows 95 is faster and offers support for preemptive multitasking.

✦ Microsoft has built-in tools for custom, hands-on, and push installations from a server.

✦ Microsoft Press sells *The Windows 95 Resource Kit* to support MIS professionals.

✦   ✦   ✦

Appendixes

Installing Windows 95

If you just purchased your PC, and it came with Windows 95 preinstalled, you don't have to do anything in this appendix — you can go straight to Chapter 1 and start enjoying the new Windows.

I suspect that most of you, however, currently have DOS and perhaps Windows 3.x on your PC, and you now need to install Windows 95. This appendix is written for you.

System Requirements for Windows 95

To use Windows 95, your PC must meet *at least* the following specifications:

Processor	386, 486, or Pentium
Memory (RAM)	4MB (8MB preferred)
Available hard disk space	30MB (40MB preferred)
Video display recommended	VGA minimum; SVGA

Preinstallation Housekeeping

If you've been using your PC for a while with DOS or DOS/Windows 3.x, now may be a good time to do a little spring cleaning and get rid of any old junk that's taking up space on your hard disk. Don't delete DOS or your existing version of

Windows, however, and don't delete any programs that you want to use after you install Windows 95. Delete only old projects that you don't need anymore and any programs that you no longer use. The process is sort of like moving to a new house; take this opportunity to get rid of some unnecessary clutter and extra baggage.

When you've whittled down your hard disk to DOS, Windows 3.x, programs that you use frequently, and works in progress, consider doing the following things. (If you don't know how to do these things, you can look them up in your DOS manual or just skip them.)

✦ If you know how to modify CONFIG.SYS and AUTOEXEC.BAT, comment out any commands that load TSR programs, such as antivirus utilities, pop-up tools, undelete utilities, screen savers, and any other extra goodies that use memory but aren't required to make your system run.

To comment out a command, type **rem**, followed by a space, at the beginning of the line.

✦ After you modify CONFIG.SYS and AUTOEXEC.BAT, shut down your PC and then restart it to activate those changes and get a fresh start.

✦ If your computer has any time-out features, such as the suspend features used on portable PCs, disable those features now.

✦ Make sure that any external devices (modems, external CD-ROM drives, and so on) are connected and turned on, so that Windows 95 can detect them during installation.

✦ Run SCANDISK or CHKDSK to tie up any loose ends caused by dangling file fragments.

✦ Run DEFRAG with full optimization to maximize the efficiency of your hard disk.

✦ If possible, back up the entire hard disk at this point.

✦ Run MSD, and make sure that your system has what it takes to install and use Windows 95.

✦ If your PC is connected to a local area network (LAN), check to make sure that you're connected to the LAN properly, so that Windows 95 can see your LAN during installation.

If you discover that your system doesn't meet the minimum system requirements, don't try to install Windows 95 until you upgrade your computer to meet the requirements. If you need help upgrading, contact your local computer dealer or repair service.

Starting the Installation

Now you're ready to begin the installation procedure. Gather up your Windows 95 installation disks or CD-ROM, and (if you haven't already done so) start your computer in the usual manner. Then follow these steps:

1. If you have any programs running, close them; if you know of any TSR programs that are running and know how to terminate them, do so now.

2. If you are installing from floppy disks, put Windows 95 Disk 1 in drive A or B of your PC.

   If you're installing from a CD-ROM, put the Windows 95 compact disc in the CD-ROM drive.

3. If you are installing from a DOS-only PC (a PC that has no version of Windows on it), ignore the following steps; skip to "Installing on a DOS-only PC" later in this chapter.

4. If you haven't already done so, start Windows in the usual manner (type **win** at the DOS command prompt).

5. When you get into Windows, close all open windows *except* Program Manager.

6. Choose File⇨Run.

7. Type **x:\setup**, in which *x* is the location of your Windows 95 disk.

   If you're installing from a floppy disk in drive A, for example, type **a:\setup**. If you're installing from a CD-ROM in CD-ROM drive D, type **d:\setup**.

8. Press Enter or click on OK.

Start reading the on-screen instructions, and skip to "The routine-check phase" later in this chapter.

Installing on a DOS-only PC

If you're installing Windows 95 on a PC that doesn't have Windows 3.x on it, follow these steps to get started:

1. Make sure that the DOS command prompt (C>) is on your screen and that Windows 95 Disk 1 is in drive A or drive B or that the Windows 95 CD-ROM is in the CD-ROM drive.

2. Switch to the drive that contains the Windows 95 disk.

   If Windows 95 Disk 1 is in drive A, for example, type **a:** and press Enter; you should see an A> prompt. If the Windows 95 CD-ROM is in drive D, type **d:** and press Enter; you should see a D> prompt.

3. Type **setup** and press Enter.

Start reading the on-screen instructions, and proceed with the following section.

The routine-check phase

In the first phase of the installation, the Setup program makes a routine check of your system. If you already ran SCANDISK and DEFRAG, this phase goes by quickly. If Setup finds any problems during this phase, you need to respond to any prompts that appear.

If you're installing from floppy disks, you probably will be prompted to remove and insert floppies after the routine check is complete. Just follow the on-screen instructions.

About the Setup wizard

After copying some files to your hard disk, Setup starts the Setup wizard. The wizard handles most of the installation procedure. Various wizard screens ask questions and keep you informed as the installation proceeds, as in the example shown in Figure A-1.

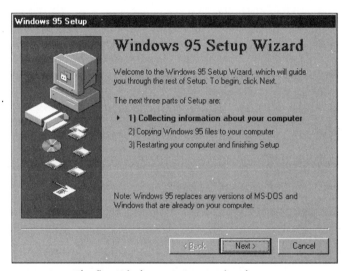

Figure A-1: The first Windows 95 Setup wizard screen.

Most of the wizard screens contain buttons labeled Back and Next. In general, you want to read each screen, follow any instructions, make any selections presented on each screen, and then click on the Next button. Click on the Back button only if you need to go back to a previous screen and change some earlier selections.

The installation procedure has several phases. The following sections describe each of these phases. For actual instructions on what to do next, always do what the screen tells you to do.

The Information-Collection Phase

The first step that the wizard performs involves gathering information about you and your PC. The wizard screens are self-explanatory, but the following sections discuss your options in various screens.

Choosing a directory

When you are asked to choose a directory (see Figure A-2), you should choose C:\WINDOWS to replace your current version of Windows (if any).

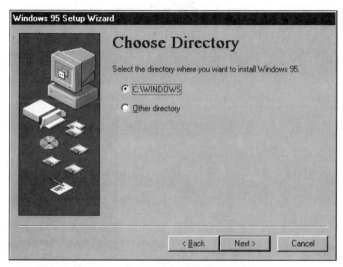

Figure A-2: Choose a directory for Windows 95.

I know that you'll be tempted to keep the "old Windows" until you're sure about the new version, and indeed, you can choose Other directory and put Windows 95 in its own directory (such as Win95). But my experience has been that trying to keep two operating systems — or two versions of an operating system — on one hard disk is more trouble and more confusion than it's worth. I suggest that you just accept the suggested directory (C:\WINDOWS) and then click on Next.

Setup takes a moment to prepare the directory and to check for installed components and available space.

Providing setup options and user information

You'll be given a choice of options for setting up Windows 95, as in the example shown in Figure A-3.

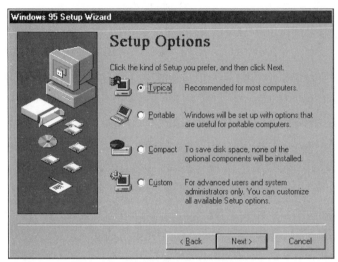

Figure A-3: Choose a Typical (desktop) or Portable (laptop) installation.

The options are self-explanatory. You probably will want to choose Typical if you're installing on a desktop PC. If you're installing on a laptop PC, choose Portable. You don't really need to worry about which components are installed right now; you can go back and add components at any time, as discussed in "Installing Missing Windows Components" in Chapter 9 of this book.

After you click on Next, you are prompted to type your name and (optionally) your company name. Fill in the text boxes as they appear, and click on Next to proceed through the wizard screens.

Analyzing your computer

Eventually, you reach the wizard screen that begins the hardware-analysis phase (see Figure A-4). You may see a list of hardware components. If you have any of the listed components, click on the appropriate checkboxes. Then click on Next to start the hardware analysis.

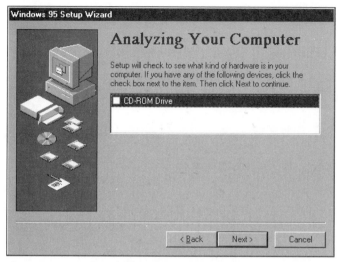

Figure A-4: Ready to begin hardware analysis.

The hardware analysis may take several minutes. Read the instructions on-screen during that phase to learn what you need to do in case problems arise.

Getting connected

When the hardware analysis is complete, the Get Connected wizard screen appears (see Figure A-5).

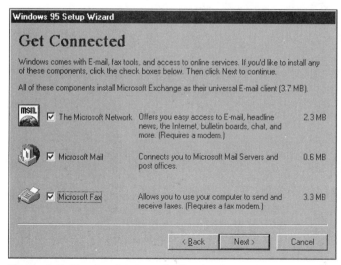

Figure A-5: The Get Connected wizard screen.

You should choose options for which you have the appropriate hardware, as summarized in the following list:

✦ If you have a modem, choose The Microsoft Network.

✦ If you are on a local area network (LAN), choose Microsoft Mail.

✦ If you have a fax modem, choose Microsoft Fax.

Click on the Next button to proceed.

Specifying Windows components

The next wizard screen (see Figure A-6) enables you to decide which components to install. Chances are that you'll be better off making those decisions after you learn about all the various optional components. Installing components at any time in the future is easy. So you can safely choose Install the most common components (recommended) and then click on Next to move on.

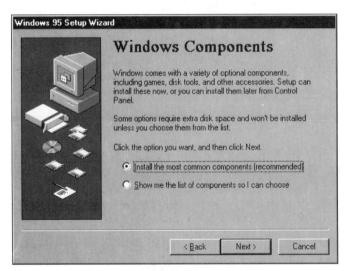

Figure A-6: Choose optional components, or just move on.

Identifying the PC

You may be prompted to identify your computer on the network. If so, the following list explains how to fill in the blanks:

✦ *Computer name.* Type any name that you feel like giving this PC — a brand name, pet name, your name, whatever.

✦ *Workgroup.* If you're a member of a LAN and also a member of a workgroup (a local departmental LAN), you must type the correct workgroup name. If you're unsure of your workgroup name, ask your network administrator. If you're not a member of a workgroup, you can leave this box blank or type **Workgroup**.

✦ *Computer Description.* Type any description that you want to use.

Click on the Next button after you fill in the blanks.

Creating a startup disk

If you have a blank floppy disk handy, creating an emergency startup disk is a good idea. That way, if your hard disk ever crashes, you can start your PC from the floppy.

To create the startup disk, choose the Yes option, and follow the instructions on-screen. When the startup disk is complete, I suggest that you label it Windows 95 Startup and store it in a safe place.

If you don't have a floppy handy right now, you can create a startup disk later. For now, you can choose the No option and then click on Next to move on. Try to remember to create the startup disk soon, though, because if you ever need it, you'll *really* need it. And by then, you won't be able to create a new startup disk. The section titled "Making an Emergency Startup Disk" in Chapter 9 tells you how to create a startup disk at any time after the installation is complete.

The File-Copying Phase

After the information-gathering and startup-disk phases are complete, you move to phase 2, which involves copying files (see Figure A-7).

Click on the Next button, and follow the on-screen instructions. This phase takes several minutes. If you're installing Windows 95 from floppy disks, you'll be instructed to remove and insert disks as you go along.

Finishing Setup

After all the files have been copied, you're ready to start phase 3 of the installation. Remove the floppy disk, if any, from the disk drive, and click on Finish in the last wizard screen (see Figure A-8).

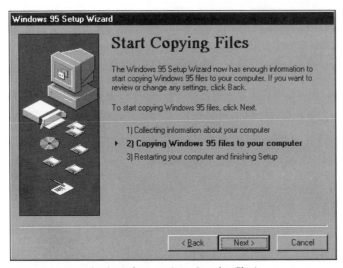

Figure A-7: Beginning phase 2 (copying the files).

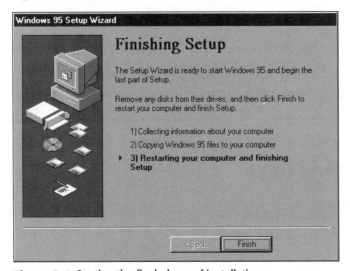

Figure A-8: Starting the final phase of installation.

Windows 95 may take several minutes to start and to set up all your programs, the help system, and so on. Be patient.

You'll be given the opportunity to specify your time zone; do so, as the screen instructs you.

Toward the end of the installation, Windows 95 attempts to detect and install your hardware, and it may ask questions about specific items. If you can answer those questions, do so. If you are unsure about any hardware item, don't panic, and don't guess — just choose the Not Installed option. You can always install a hardware device later, after you gather information about that device. For information on installing hardware, see Chapter 10 — *after* you finish installing Windows 95 and have read the basics in Chapters 1–5 or so.

When you get to the Welcome to Windows 95 window (see Figure A-9), the installation process is complete. Congratulations — you're in for some fun.

Figure A-9: Windows 95 is installed!

If you're a former Windows 3.x user who wants a summary of what's new and different in Windows 95, read Appendix B. If you're ready to get right into the program, start with Chapter 1.

Upgrading from Windows 3.x

To upgrade your Windows 3.x PC to Windows 95, follow the installation instructions in Appendix A. This appendix provides a more general discussion of upgrading, presented in question-and-answer format.

Changing from one operating system to another can be scary. I hope that this appendix will answer any questions that you have, and bolster your confidence to "go for it." I did, and I'm glad.

Before the Upgrade

If you haven't already upgraded to Windows 95, you may be wondering whether it's worth doing so. What new advantages — and new headaches — are likely to result from this upgrade? The questions and answers in this section deal with those questions.

What is Windows 95?

Windows 95 is more of a replacement for the DOS and Windows products that you probably use now than an upgrade of those products. Windows 95 is a completely new and separate product, and also a major improvement (in my opinion). Earlier versions of DOS/Windows were tied to the early 16-bit PC and AT (286) computers. Windows 95 is a clean break from all that, taking advantage of the 32-bit technology offered in the 386, 486, and Pentium microprocessors.

What benefits will I get from upgrading?

Upgrading offers many benefits, and I suspect that within a couple weeks of doing so, you'll wonder how you ever got along without Windows 95.

One immediate improvement is an easier, more intuitive interface (when you get the hang of it). Multitasking also is better; you can print, format a disk, and download files with your modem at the same time. Better multimedia is almost guaranteed. Plug-and-play technology means that you can buy new gadgets and gizmos, plug them in, and use them — all without the conventional headaches involved in installing new devices.

Will my existing hardware and software work?

If you currently use DOS and Windows 3.x, the answer to this question almost certainly is yes. You can check the hardware requirements at the beginning of Appendix A if you're not sure. But most likely, if your PC runs Windows 3.x now, it'll run Windows 95 just fine.

Windows 95 pledges to be compatible with all existing DOS and Windows programs as well. My experience during the beta-test phase (a testing period before public release of the product) tended to support that pledge. I did find, however, that some products that migrated from the Mac (Adobe PhotoShop, Macromedia Director, and so on) and also ran under Windows 3.x would not run at all under Windows 95 (or NT, for that matter). If you are concerned, ask the program manufacturer or your computer dealer whether a certain program works under Windows 95.

Soon after the release of Windows 95, a slew of new 32-bit "Designed for Windows 95" programs and hardware will come on the market. Those products, of course, will work well under Windows 95 and probably will dance circles around your existing 16-bit versions of the same programs. Gradually, the 16-bit versions of programs will fade out altogether, and 32-bit versions will become the norm.

What about my local area network?

Windows 95 is compatible with most existing LAN software, including Windows networks and Novell networks. If your PC is connected to a LAN, you should leave it connected to the LAN when you install Windows 95. That way, Windows 95 can detect your LAN hardware and software, and adjust to it automatically. You'll still be on the LAN after you complete the upgrade.

If you don't have a LAN but are considering setting one up, Windows 95 is a *must-have* product. You probably will be able to set up the LAN yourself, using the built-in LAN capabilities (no extra programs are required!).

Is Windows 95 OK for laptop PCs?

Windows 95 is the operating system of choice for portable PCs. A special installation option is designed for portables, and many new features make portable computing easier and more productive. (Part V of this book is about portable computing.)

A couple of options for portable computers require special hardware. On-screen power management, for example, requires Advanced Power Management 1.1 (APM 1.1). If you don't have APM 1.1, however, your existing power-management tools will still work. Hot docking, which is the capability to dock and undock a portable PC without powering down, requires a special plug-and-play BIOS. If your PC doesn't have the fancy BIOS, don't fret. You'll find that docking and undocking your PC are much easier under Windows 95; you'll just need to power down to do so.

What is plug-and-play?

The phrase *plug-and-play* has been around for a while, even though it has never been very meaningful. (I remember buying a plug-and-play network card that promised that I could plug it in and forget it. After fighting with that card for hours, I realized that the promise really was "Plug it in and forget you ever bought it, 'cause it ain't gonna work — ever.")

Microsoft is trying to formalize a plug-and-play specification that really *is* plug-and-play. That is, when you buy a new piece of hardware — such as a modem, network card, scanner, CD-ROM drive, or sound card — you'll be able to literally plug it into your PC and start using it. You won't have to hassle with complex installations, CONFIG.SYS and AUTOEXEC.BAT files, and IRQs.

Because the term *plug-and-play* has been used loosely for several years, Microsoft had to come up with a special logo to identify products that really are Windows 95 plug-and-play-compatible. These devices bear a logo that specifically says "Designed for Windows 95."

Will plug-and-play devices work on my existing PC?

You do not need to buy an entirely new PC to use "Designed for Windows 95" plug-and-play devices. When you install a plug-and-play device in your existing PC, you still get the benefits of easy, automatic installation.

How does Windows 95 compare with Windows for Workgroups?

Windows for Workgroups (version 3.11) was a successor to Windows version 3.1, the major difference between 3.11 and 3.1 being that the 3.11 version offers built-in networking. Versions 3.1 and 3.11 require DOS and are the older 16-bit operating systems. Windows 95 is a 32-bit operating system and does not require DOS.

Windows 95 offers the same built-in Windows networking that Windows for Workgroups offers. If you have PCs connected in a Windows for Workgroups network now, you can add a Windows 95 PC to your existing LAN or upgrade any PC on the LAN.

How does Windows 95 compare with Windows NT?

Windows NT is geared toward high-end workstations that have a great deal of RAM (at least 16MB) and disk space (200MB just for the operating system). The product works with high-end processors, such as those in the Dec Alpha and MIPS machines. NT also offers symmetric multiprocessing, which means that if your PC has several processors, NT uses all of them at the same time.

Windows 95 is the operating system of choice for modern desktop and portable PCs. The product runs only on PCs that sport 386, 486, and Pentium microprocessors. The hardware requirements of Windows 95 are much more modest; about 4MB of RAM (although 8MB is recommended) and about 40MB of extra hard disk space (for the operating system) will do the trick.

How did we get to version 95?

For years, I've been asking software manufacturers, "Why don't we stop with the random version-numbering system and start using the year, the way we do with cars?" Under that system, the version number would be a point of reference. We all know how old a '76 Volkswagen is, for example, but how old is QuasiCalc 6.01?

Nobody ever listened to me, of course. But someone at Microsoft apparently came up with the same idea, so we now have year numbers instead of version numbers. (No, this change does not mean that an upgrade will come out every year — I asked. Microsoft may very well skip some years.)

After the Upgrade

After you upgrade to Windows 95, a new crop of questions may arise as you explore the new terrain. This section deals with those issues.

What happened to Program Manager?

Program Manager, in Windows 95, is set up more like a menu than a window. If you click on the Start button and then point to (or click on) Programs, you should see your original program groups. To open one of those groups, point to it or click on it. To start a program, click on its icon in the menu.

You may miss your old buddy Program Manager for a few days, but I recommend that you get used to the new Start-button method of launching programs. Two clicks launch virtually any program. And as Part I of this book explains, you can set up shortcuts to programs that you use frequently.

You'll also learn to appreciate the Documents menu and the entire documentcentric approach, both of which enable you to forget about programs. If you want to open and edit an existing document, choose that document from the Documents menu or double-click on the document's icon. I never use the old method of opening a program and then choosing File⇨Open to open a document. Now, every document is just one or two clicks away.

What happened to File Manager?

File Manager has been replaced by Windows Explorer. To launch Explorer, click on the Start button, point to Programs, and click on Windows Explorer. You'll see the similarity with File Manager right away.

Windows 95 also has a couple of great alternatives to Explorer: My Computer and Find. The latter is especially good, because you don't even need to know where a particular file is to open it; you can type part of the name of the file that you want, and Find will find it for you. Double-click on the document's icon, and bingo — it's open and ready for editing.

What happened to DOS?

Windows 95 has no DOS to start up from and no DOS to exit to. When you want to shut down your PC, click on the Start button, choose Shut Down, click on Shut down the computer?, and then click on Yes. Wait a few seconds. When all your work is saved, a big message on-screen tells you that it's safe to turn off the PC.

If you need to get to a DOS command prompt, click on the Start button, point to Programs, and choose MS-DOS prompt. From the C> prompt that appears, you can use whatever DOS commands you're familiar with. When you want to return to Windows, type **exit** and press Enter.

If you come across a DOS program that absolutely refuses to run from a window, you'll have to take a different route to the C> prompt. Click the Start button, click on Shut Down, click on the option titled Restart the computer in MS-DOS mode?, and then click on Yes. You should be able to run that feisty DOS program from the C> prompt that appears. (Use this method as a second resort. You'll get better performance if you can run the DOS program by using the first method.)

Should I really learn to use this new interface?

Yes, you really should learn the new user interface. You no doubt will have many temptations to bring the old Program Manager back to your desktop, but I think that you'll be much better off learning to use the new Start-button technique of launching documents and programs. From there, you can start learning about creating shortcuts to things that you access often.

What happened to directories?

Directories still exist, but they're called folders now. In Explorer and other browsing tools, folders are identified by a little manila-file-folder icon. (I think that a file-drawer icon would be a better analogy, though, because a folder may contain several files.)

How do I use those long file names?

In case you haven't heard, Windows 95 no longer limits you to those dinky eight-character file names. Now you can use up to 255 characters, including spaces, to identify a folder or file. Instead of naming a file QTR01TXS.XLS, for example, you can name it `First Quarter Taxes.xls`.

Only 32-bit programs (programs designed for Windows 95 and Windows NT) allow you to type these long file names, however. When you use the 16-bit version of a program, you still are limited to typing eight-character file names, with no spaces.

Internet Service Providers

This appendix presents some Internet Service Providers (ISPs), organized by U.S. area code. Service providers vary in services available and cost, so I suggest that you shop around. If you need mobile access to the Internet, check out the service providers listed in the sidebar titled "Internet on the road" in Chapter 22.

If you're an Internet Service Provider and would like to be included in this list in the next edition of this book, send me your information at alan@coolnerds.com or fax it to me at (619) 756-0159.

Area Code	Provider	Voice Phone
202	CAPCON Connect	331-5771
204	MBnet	474-9727
205	Nuance Network Services	533-4296
206	InterServ	447-0800
	Townsend Communications	385-0464
212	Echo	255-3839
	Panix	787-6160
	The Pipeline	267-3636
213	EarthLink Network, Inc.	644-9500
214	On-Ramp Technologies, Inc.	746-4710
	Texas Metronet, Inc.	705-2900
215	VoiceNet/DSC	674-9290

(continued)

Area Code	Provider	Voice Phone
301	Express Access	220-2020
	IMS Intercom	856-2706
	SURAnet	982-4600
302	SSNet	378-1386
303	Colorado Internet Cooperative Assn.	443-3786
	Colorado Supernet, Inc.	273-3471
	ENVISIONET, Inc.	770-2408
	Internet Express	758-2656
305	Acquired Knowledge Systems	(800) 930-6398
	CyberGate, Inc.	428-4283
306	SASKnet	585-4132
312	MCSNet	248-8649
313	CICNet, Inc.	998-4754
	ClarkNet	(800) 947-4754
	Merit/MichNet	764-9430
	MSEN	998-4562
315	NYSERNET, Inc.	453-2912
317	CIOE Corporation	743-3487
	IndyNet	251-5208
401	IDS World Network	884-7856
	RISCnet	885-6855
402	MIDnet	472-7600
403	CCI Networks	450-6787
405	Questar Network Services (QNSnet)	848-3228
408	NETCOM	345-2600
	Portal Information Network	973-9111
	Santa Cruz Community Internet	457-5050
410	Clark Internet Services	(800) 735-2258
412	PREPnet	268-7870
	Telerama	481-3505

Area Code	Provider	Voice Phone
415	BARRNet	725-1790
	CRL Network Services	837-5300
	Institute for Global Communications/ IGC Networks	442-0220
	InterNex Information Services, Inc.	473-3060
	The Little Garden	487-1902
	North Bay Network, Inc.	472-1600
416	ONet	978-5058
	UUNet Canada, Inc.	368-6621
	UUNorth, Inc.	225-8649
503	RAINet, Inc.	227-5665
	Teleport	223-4245
508	DMConnection	568-1618
510	CCNet Communications	988-0680
	Holonet	704-0160
512	Real/Time Communications	451-0046
	Zilker Internet Park	206-3850
514	Communications Accessibles, Montreal	931-0749
	RISQ	398-1234
516	Network-USA	543-0234
602	Data Basix	721-1988
	Evergreen Internet, Inc.	230-9330
	Internet Direct	274-0100
	Opus One	324-0494
603	MV Communications, Inc.	429-2223
604	BCNet	291-5209
	Island Net	479-7861
609	Global Enterprise Services, Inc.	897-7300
612	MRNet	342-2570

(continued)

Area Code	Provider	Voice Phone
614	OARnet	728-8100
617	CENTnet, Inc.	868-1198
	Channel1	864-0100
	NEARNET	873-8730
	North Shore Access	593-3110
	Pioneer Global	375-0200
619	CERFnet	(800) 876-2373
	CTSNET	637-3637
703	AlterNet	204-8000
	ANS (Advanced Networks and Services)	758-7700
	Performance Systems International (PSI)	904-0300
704	Vnet	(800) 377-3282
708	American Information Systems, Inc.	413-8400
	Aquila	820-0480
	InterAccess Co.	(800) 967-1580
	netIllinois	866-1804
	Worldwide Access Services	367-1870
	XNet Information Services	983-6064
709	NLNet	737-8329
713	Neosoft	684-5969
	Sesquinet	527-4988
	South Coast Computing Services, Inc.	661-3301
714	KAIWAN Corporation	638-2139
718	ZONE 1 Network Exchange	549-8078
719	CNS Internet Express	(800) 748-1200
	Internet Express	520-5000
	Old Colorado City Communications	636-2040
800	Internet MCI	(800) 779-0949
801	Internet Direct	531-9708
	XMission	539-0852

Area Code	Provider	Voice Phone
804	Global Connect, Inc.	229-4484
	InfiNet, L.C.	622-4289
816	Tyrell Corporation	(800) TYRELL-1
817	Texas Metronet, Inc.	543-8756
901	Magibox	757-7835
902	PEINet, Inc.	892-7346
905	Hookup Communications	847-8000
914	Cloud 9 Internet	682-0626
919	Interpath	890-6300

Using the Companion CD-ROM

The first thing that I want to say about the CD-ROM that comes with this book is that it's entirely optional. I don't make references to the CD-ROM throughout the book, because I wanted to be sure that you could use the book independently. Many of you don't have CD-ROM drives, and there's no reason to feel left out if you never use the CD-ROM. I like to think of the CD-ROM as being a little bonus for people who own CD-ROM drives. But I also like to think that the book has merit of its own, even if you never use the disc.

I also felt that it was important for the CD-ROM to be a stand-alone product — something that you can use when you don't have the book nearby. If your portable PC has a CD-ROM drive and you want to explore the disc during a plane trip, for example, you can do so without lugging the book along. The disc has its own little setup program and its own on-screen documentation.

Finally, I got to thinking that if some space was left in the book after all else was said and done, I should say something about at least some of the products on the CD-ROM. So I decided to include portions of the README files from most of the shareware and demo products on the companion CD-ROM, so that you can browse around those products on paper to see what might be interesting to install and explore.

The pages that follow contain portions of the actual README files for many of the shareware programs on the disc. Each README file is printed pretty much *as is* — that is, neither I nor the publisher altered the material significantly, although I did condense for space considerations. So you'll be reading exactly what each shareware author has to say about his or her own product.

Using the CD-ROM

The CD-ROM disc that accompanies this book contains about 60 shareware, demo, and catalog programs. Each program is in its own folder. To view the contents of the disc

1. Insert the CD-ROM disc into your CD-ROM drive.
2. Open My Computer, and then double-click on the icon for your CD-ROM drive.

You should see a few files and lots of folders, as in Figure D-1.

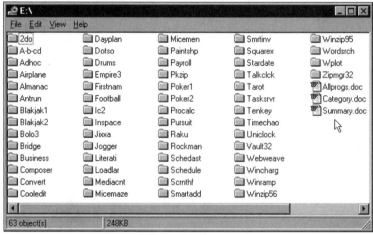

Figure D-1: Each folder contains a program.

The sections that follow in this chapter describe the various programs on the CD. If you don't happen to have the book handy while you're exploring the CD, you can double-click on any of the document files listed after all the folder names to review information on the screen, or to print it.

About Shareware and Demos

For those of you who are new to the shareware game, I'll explain some things. Shareware generally is distributed via online networks such as CompuServe, the Internet, and independent bulletin boards. The idea behind shareware is to allow you to "try before you buy." If you use a shareware program for a while and like it, you must register the program with its author. That part costs money, of course. But in return, you get a complete version of the product and information on updates; in some cases, you also may get a printed manual.

More important, however, you'll be supporting the entire shareware industry. Many talented programmers and digital artists are producing excellent products but don't have the resources required to flood the international market with "cereal box" shrink-wrapped products. So they make their products shareware.

Every product on the CD-ROM — shareware, a demo, a catalog, freeware, whatever — is offered as is, with no warranty of any kind. The best attitude to carry into the shareware industry is "we're all in this together." The programmers and artists have the talent to create these great products, but they need your feedback, tolerance, and support to grow their products into ever-better and more reliable versions.

So enjoy — and please be tolerant of bugs and any other problems that you may encounter. Shareware authors don't have the resources to perform large-scale beta testing. In a sense, *you* are the beta tester when you take a shareware program for a spin. If you find a bug, report it to the author of the program; he or she probably will correct the problem in the next release of the product.

Summary List of Programs on the CD

Here's a quick alphabetical summary of programs on the CD-ROM.

Name	Folder on CD	Category
2DO	\2Do	Personal
A-B-CD for Windows	\A-B-CD	Multimedia
Access to Business	\Business	Business
Ad Hoc Database	\AdHoc	Business
Almanac for Windows	\Almanac	Personal
Ant Run	\AntRun	Games
Bolo Adventures III	\Bolo3	Games
Casino Verite BlackJack	\Blakjak1	Games
Conversion Master	\Convert	Math, Science
Cool Edit	\CoolEdit	Multimedia
CyberTarot	\Tarot	Personal
Day Plan	\DayPlan	Personal
Dotso	\Dotso	Games
Double-DownVideo Poker	\Poker1	Games
Drums Professional	\Drums	Multimedia

(continued)

Name	Folder on CD	Category
Employee Scheduling Assistant	\SchedAst	Business
First Name Almanac	\FirstNam	Personal
Football Clock	\Football	Utility
Heavy Water Jogger	\Jogger	Games
IC2 version 3.01	\IC2	Business
Jasc Media Center v2.01	\MediaCnt	Multimedia
Jixxa Version 1.1	\Jixxa	Games
Judy's TenKey	\TenKey	Business
Literati Lite for Windows	\Literati	Games
Loader Larry	\LoadLar	Games
Medlin Payroll	\Payroll	Business
Mice Maze	\MiceMaze	Games
MVP Bridge for Windows	\Bridge	Games
MVP WordSearch for Windows	\WordSrch	Games
NoteWorthy Composer V1.20	\Composer	Multimedia
Operation: Inner Space	\InSpace	Games
Paint Shop Pro v3.0	\Paintshp	Graphics
PKZip 2	\Pkware	Communications
Poke-It! Poker	\Poker2	Games
PROcalc V1.0	\Procalc	Business
Pursuit	\Pursuit	Business
Raku Master	\Raku	Games
RockMan	\RockMan	Games
Scheduling Employees for Windows	\Schedule	Business
Screen Thief for Windows	\ScrnThf	Graphics
Smart Address	\SmartAdd	Personal
SmartTracker Inventory v2.5	\SmrtInv	Personal
Squarex	\Squarex	Games
StarDate 2140.2: Crusade in Space	\StarDate	Games
Talking Clock 2	\TalkClck	Utility
TaskServer	\TaskSrvr	Utility

Name	Folder on CD	Category
The Greatest Paper Airplanes	\Airplane	Games
The Mice Men	\MiceMen	Games
Time & Chaos	\TimeChao	Personal
Uniclock	\Uniclock	Utility
Vault 32	\Vault32	Personal
Video BlackJack	\Blakjak2	Games
Web Weaver v4.0b	\WebWeave	Communications
WinCharging v1.1	\Wincharg	Personal
WinRamp Lite	\WinRamp	Communications
WinZip 5.6	\WinZip56	Communications
WinZip 95 (Beta)	\WinZip95	Communications
World Empire III	\Empire3	Games
WPlot	\Wplot	Math, Science
Zip Manager v. 5.2	\ZipMgr32	Communications

Categorized List of Programs on the CD

Here are the same programs broken down into categories.

Business programs

Name	Folder on CD
Access to Business	\Business
Ad Hoc Database	\AdHoc
Employee Scheduling Assistant	\SchedAst
IC2 version 3.01	\IC2
Judy's TenKey	\TenKey
Medlin Payroll	\Payroll
PROcalc V1.0	\Procalc
Pursuit	\Pursuit
Scheduling Employees for Windows	\Schedule

Communications programs

Name	Folder on CD
PKZip 2	\Pkware
Web Weaver v4.0b	\WebWeave
WinRamp Lite	\WinRamp
WinZip 5.6	\WinZip56
WinZip 95 (Beta)	\WinZip95
Zip Manager v. 5.2	\ZipMgr32

Games

Name	Folder on CD
Ant Run	\AntRun
Bolo Adventures III	\Bolo3
Casino Verite BlackJack	\Blakjak1
Dotso	\Dotso
Double-Down Video Poker	\Poker1
Heavy Water Jogger	\Jogger
Jixxa Version 1.1	\Jixxa
Literati Lite for Windows	\Literati
Loader Larry	\LoadLar
Mice Maze	\MiceMaze
MVP Bridge for Windows	\Bridge
MVP WordSearch for Windows	\WordSrch
Operation: Inner Space	\InSpace
Poke-It! Poker	\Poker2
Raku Master	\Raku
RockMan	\RockMan
Squarex	\Squarex
StarDate 2140.2: Crusade in Space	\StarDate
The Greatest Paper Airplanes	\Airplane
The Mice Men	\MiceMen
Video BlackJack	\Blakjak2
World Empire III	\Empire3

Graphics programs

Name	Folder on CD
Paint Shop Pro v3.0	\Paintshp
Screen Thief for Windows	\ScrnThf

Math, science programs

Name	Folder on CD
Conversion Master	\Convert
WPlot	\WPlot

Multimedia programs

Name	Folder on CD
A-B-CD for Windows	\A-B-CD
Cool Edit	\CoolEdit
Drums Professional	\Drums
Jasc Media Center v2.01	\MediaCnt
NoteWorthy Composer V1.20	\Composer

Personal productivity programs

Name	Folder on CD
2DO	\2Do
Almanac for Windows	\Almanac
CyberTarot	\Tarot
Day Plan	\DayPlan
First Name Almanac	\FirstNam
Smart Address	\SmartAdd
SmartTracker Inventory v2.5	\SmrtInv
Time & Chaos	\TimeChao
Vault 32	\Vault32
WinCharging v1.1	\Wincharg

Utilities

Name	Folder on CD
Football Clock	\Football
Talking Clock 2	\TalkClck
TaskServer	\TaskSrvr
Uniclock	\Uniclock

2DO

2DO Personal Task Manager version 1.2 for MS-Windows. 2Do is a robust yet easy to use Personal Information Manager (PIM). Software Creations calls it "a powerful PIM with considerable depth." Windows Sources states that "2Do provides users with task-management solutions that are unequaled by any commercial PIM." by William P. Anderson. <ASP>

Category: Personal
Type: Shareware
Location on CD: \2Do
To install: Run d:\2Do\SETUP.EXE
To run: Click on Start > Programs > 2Do > 2Do

Windows Shareware. Tutorial and Registration Information is available in help. No snags installing or running.

Documentation excerpt

Welcome to the 2Do™ Personal Task Manager™. All of the documentation for the application is in the online help file. You can read the contents of the help file by selecting topics from the Help menu. You can also get context-sensitive help on any menu or dialog box by pressing the F1 key while highlighting the menu or pressing the Help button in the dialog box.

There are several topics that will be particularly helpful in providing you with an introduction to 2Do and instructions on how to use it:

✦ Overview: provides an introduction to 2Do and describes the basic concepts used in the application.

✦ Features: lists the features of 2Do.

✦ Tutorial: provides a quick lesson on how to use the basic features of 2Do.

✦ How Do I: lists answers to frequently asked questions on how to use 2Do.

✦ Registration: lists the benefits of and instructions for registering your copy of 2Do.

All of these topics can be accessed through the Contents panel of the online help file. To access the Contents panel, select the Contents command from the Help menu. When the panel is displayed, click on the name of the desired topic. Refer to the *Microsoft Windows User's Guide* for more information on how to use the Windows Help program.

A-B-CD for Windows

A-B-CD 2.8 (16-bit and 32-bit versions). Super CD player and database for Windows. If you enter the CD and song titles, they are automatically remembered each time you use that CD again. You can even rearrange song order or remove unwanted songs from the album! Windows 95 compatible.

Category: Multimedia
Type: Shareware
Location on CD: \A-B-CD
To install: Run d:\A-B-CD\SETUP.EXE
To run: Click on Start⇨Programs⇨MMS Multimedia⇨A-B-CD-32-bit

You need only install the 32-bit version. Excellent product!

Access to Business

Multimedia Catalog of products for business, vertical markets, home, and software development. Products for order fulfillment, time and billing, project management, contact management, merchant point of sale, accounting, shipping, check-writing, job costing, catalog production, human resources, chiropractic, medical patient records, funeral home, auto repair, long term care, legal evidence, benefits, and more. Presented by Access to Business 1-206-644-5977. Fax 1-206-641-9271.

Category: Business
Type: Catalog
Location on CD: \Business
To install: None, run directly from CD-ROM disc
To run: Click on Start⇨Run⇨d:\Business\ATOBCAT.EXE

Soon to offer programs for child care, church membership, drug/alcohol rehab, florist, HMO billing, water utility billing, convenience store, farm, real estate office, law offices, training scheduling, employee scheduling, estimates/bids, construction, and orthodontist.

Ad Hoc Database

Ad Hoc Database Manager, ver 1.2f. A visual relational database manager for Windows. With Ad Hoc, you can interactively design data entry forms, browse lists, reports, and on-screen queries. Import/export data from/to other applications. Powerful WYSIWYG Report Editor lets you design and preview many types of reports and labels. Use for simple data files or complex database applications.

> **Category**: Business
> **Type**: Shareware
> **Location on CD**: \AdHoc
> **To install**: Run d:\Adhoc\INSTALL.EXE
> **To run**: Click on Start⇨Programs⇨Ad Hoc⇨Ad Hoc

No snags — installs and runs without a hitch.

For ordering, contact, registration, and more detailed information, see the appropriate file for this program on the companion CD-ROM.

Almanac for Windows

Almanac for Windows, Version 3.5b. Calendar, Scheduler, To-Do List Manager, Phonebook, Notes, and more in one easy-to-use package. The SETUP32.EXE program sets up the 32-bit version for Windows 95. Distributed by Impact Software, (909) 590-8522.

> **Category**: Personal
> **Type**: Shareware
> **Location on CD**: \Almanac
> **To install**: Run d:\Almanac\SETUP32.EXE
> **To run**: Click on Start⇨Programs⇨Almanac⇨Almanac

Install the 32-bit version. It's awesome!

Registration

Almanac is not free software. It is released as shareware, which provides the opportunity for the program to be evaluated before it is purchased. We hope that after you try Almanac you will like it so much that you will want to register. By doing so, you are voting with your pocketbook for us to continue developing high-quality Windows shareware.

Complete information on how to register Almanac is included in the REGISTER.TXT file. Customers who have registered a previous version of Almanac should refer to the UPGRADE.TXT file for upgrading information.

Compatibility

This version of Almanac has been specifically created for use with Windows NT version 3.5 or higher 32-bit Windows platform. If you are running standard Windows, a 16-bit version of Almanac is available from Impact Software.

Note: This product runs on Windows 95.

Updating a previous Almanac installation

Almanac's Setup utility has been enhanced to update a previous installation automatically. Version 3.5 of Almanac may be installed over version 3.0 or 3.1. Setup will update the program and help files, and will not overwrite any existing data files on your hard disk.

If you specifically want Setup to replace any release files, such as the sample overlay files, delete them from your installation before running Setup.

Foreign language option

Although it would be difficult for us to create and distribute our shareware in multiple languages, it is important to try to meet the needs of the many customers who would enjoy such a capability. Almanac 3.5 has been designed to provide the option of customizing the text that appears on the menu, as well as the text of calendar displays and prints.

Almanac 3.5 will look for the file ALMSTR.TXT in the directory that it is executed from. This file contains the foreign language equivalents for specific text that is used on Almanac's menus and displays.

If your Windows installation is configured for either the French, German, or Spanish language, Almanac's Setup utility will ask you if you would like it to install the appropriate language information for you.

If you are running any other language than these or English, Setup will direct you here for more information.

You can build your own ALMSTR.TXT file by first copying the ALMENG.TXT file from your release disk into your Almanac directory. (Setup does not install this file — you should only copy it from the release package onto your hard disk if you intend to customize Almanac for a language other than English.) This file is a sample language template that contains the English text used in Almanac's menus and displays. You can edit this file with Windows Notepad or other ASCII text editor to create your own ALMSTR.TXT file. Simply replace the English text with the appropriate text of the language you would like. It is important that you do not add or delete any lines from this file. Each line of the file contains text that Almanac will substitute for a specific area in the program.

Menu items contain an ampersand (&) character in front of the letter of the text that will be underlined and used for Alt-key selection. Hot keys, such as Ctrl-P for printing, cannot be changed from their English derived defaults.

Almanac will automatically use the new text in ALMSTR.TXT the next time it is executed. Be careful to leave the first line of ALMSTR.TXT unchanged. This contains the major and minor version of Almanac so that later versions can avoid using the file if changes to the contents of the file must be made.

We welcome any new language files that you would like to send us, as well as any corrections that you think we should make to the files we are distributing!

For ordering, contact, registration, and more detailed information, see the appropriate file for this program on the companion CD-ROM.

Ant Run

Ant Run v2.1 (DOS game). Race against the clock as you rotate tunnels for the ant to run through. Quick thinking and fast reflexes are required to keep the ant scurrying through the ant hill passageways. Gain extra points for bonus tunnels and other objects as you try for the top ten high scores. Keep your ant on the move with various strategies for really high scores. Warning: VERY ADDICTIVE!

> **Category:** Games
> **Type:** Shareware
> **Location on CD:** \AntRun
> **To install:** No installation program provided. You'll need to copy all the files from d:\AntRun to a folder on your hard disk
> **To run:** Run the ANTRUN.EXE file on your hard disk

Like the programmer says, this one can be very addicting! (DOS game.)

Ant Run directions

Objective
The objective of Ant Run is to keep the ant running through the ant hill tunnels as long as possible before it reaches a dead end.

Game play
At the beginning of the game there is a game board filled with different shaped passageways. At the top of the screen there is a red ant which will move towards the top hole. The ant takes 10 seconds to reach the hole.

After the ant reaches the hole, the ant will appear on the board from the grid marked *Start*. Using your mouse, you can click on any grid to rotate it clockwise. Your objective is to create a continuous path for the ant to crawl through.

For the first 10 seconds you can also rotate the Start grid, yet once the ant emerges from it, it will remain stationary.

Reset and inches crawled

As ants move through the tunnels, they will turn yellow and you will not be able to use them again. The only exception is the crossing path grid which can be used more than once. You can have the ant go Off The Board in any direction. It will then appear from the opposite side.

On the right side of the screen there is an Inch Meter. This measures the distance the ant has traveled. If you can get the ant to travel 20 inches and can reach one of the sides of the board, (providing the entrance on the other side is open) then the grids, which were yellow, will reset themselves and you can continue to keep the ant moving by rotating the grids.

Every time that you are able to reset the board, a single black grid will appear which can never be removed. The starting gate, if present on the board, will now be removed and a passageway grid will take its place.

Fast button

On the left side of the board there are several buttons. One is the Fast button. If you press the Fast button while the ant is on the game board, then the ant will speed through the tunnels at a much faster rate. After the ant reaches the sides of the board and reappears on the other side, it will automatically slow down again.

This Fast button is very important because when the ant is running in Fast mode, you get double the points for the distance it travels. If you have set up a long series of tunnels that go off and on the board, then use the Fast key to get more points. This assumes you have already established a consecutive path for the ant ahead of time.

Scoring

At the beginning of each level there is a Points Needed total shown at the bottom of the screen. To proceed to the next level, you must reach or surpass this point total to continue the game.

If you don't reach this point total by the time your ant reaches a dead end, then the game will be over. The points needed for each level is determined by this formula:

```
100 + (10 * LEVEL) + (plus previous score)
```

Points are scored for each few steps it takes through the tunnels. An extra 3 points are given every time you can get the ant to exit the board and re-enter it. These will be stored in the Bonus Point total and will be added to your score at the end of the level.

There are also Green Bonus Tunnels which will sometimes appear on the board. If you can get the ant through these, you will earn 20 extra bonus points.

Bonus Rounds

Every 2,500 points scored, you will be awarded a special bonus round. You can only gain points during this round, however you must have completed the previous level with the required points needed to continue.

Multiple Starting Gates

On the higher levels, the game board might contain more than one starting grid. You will not know which start grid the ant will emerge from, so you'll have to plan ahead for each starting grid.

Ending Grid

On some levels there will also be a Red Ending Grid. This means you must get the ant to end in this grid or the game will be over no matter how many points you score for that level. This Ending grid can be rotated even after the ant starts to move on the game board.

REMEMBER WHEN YOU SEE A RED ENDING GRID, YOU MUST END THE ANT THERE OR THE GAME WILL BE OVER NO MATTER HOW MANY POINTS YOU SCORED FOR THAT LEVEL.

Buttons

The mouse buttons on the left side of the game board can be accessed at any time during the game.

SCORE : Show the Ten Top High Scores

SOUND : Toggles Sound On or Off

HELP : Ant Run Directions

FAST : Speed Ant through the maze for Double Points!

QUIT : Quits Ant Run

Note: Windows 3.x users

Running Ant Run from Windows 3.x may cause unexpected results. The game should be played by loading it directly from the DOS prompt or the DOS window in Windows 95.

About Soleau Software

Ant Run is distributed as shareware. You are welcome to give this game to your friends or local BBS. If you like Ant Run and continue to use it, we ask you to register the game with us. Soleau Software depends on your registrations in order to continue providing an alternative to expensive commercial software.

The registered version of Ant Run greatly speeds up the loading and exiting of the program, plus gives you unlimited levels of play!

Your $12.00 registration of Ant Run will instantly make you a Soleau Software Member. All members receive special discounts on our other games through special bonus package offers sent with your disk.

Members also have the option to include an extra $6.00 for our Member Game Pack which has eight of our most popular Shareware EGA/VGA games on a high density floppy disk.

Ant Run Sequel & Spider Run special offer

If you register Ant Run for $12.00, you can get the registered version of Spider Run for only $10.00 more. The description of this sequel to Ant Run can be found in the SOLSOFT.DOC file. This offer is only for those who first register Ant Run.

We at Soleau Software thank you for your support and hope you will continue to enjoy this as well as our other Shareware products.

Sincerely,

William Soleau
President, Soleau Software
163 Amsterdam Avenue, Suite 213
New York, NY 10023

For ordering, contact, registration, and more detailed information, see the appropriate file for this program on the companion CD-ROM.

Bolo Adventures III

Bolo Adventures III v2.0 is a challenging strategy game where the objective is to get Mr. Bolo out of 15 rooms of mind-boggling puzzles. Each room is filled with obstacles such as lasers, crates, water, boxes, and more! Unlike arcade games, Bolo Adventures isn't a contest of how fast your reflexes are, it's a test of your resourcefulness. A must for all serious gamers. Great animated graphics!

Category: Games
Type: Shareware
Location on CD: \Bolo3
To install: No installation program provided. You'll need to copy all the files from d:\Bolo3 to a folder on your hard disk.
To run: Run BOLO3.EXE from your hard disk

Hint: Lasers and water are not good for Mr. Bolo's health. DOS game.

Objective

The objective of Bolo Adventures III is to reach the Red Stairs located in each of the puzzle rooms.

Game play

Select one of 15 puzzles by pressing the Select Puzzle key. The puzzle will load itself onto the game board and Mr. Bolo will then enter the room.

To move him around the puzzle, use the <Arrow Keys>. There are many different objects which he can use to help him reach the stairs. Each object has different properties, which you will have to utilize in order to create his escape. To solve the puzzle, you must come up with a unique strategy using the objects which are available when the puzzle begins.

Objects

These are the various objects you might see in the puzzles: BALLS, BOXES, CRATES, HOLES, WATER, LASERS, WALLS, BUTTON(S), STAIRS.

There are also some special invisible grills. The grills are not invisible, but once Mr. Bolo crosses one, he will not be visible to you on the game board.

BALLS: Can be rolled by Mr. Bolo. They can be pushed in front of lasers, they can float in water, they can ???

BOXES: Can be pushed by Mr. Bolo. They can be pushed in front of lasers, they make walkways through water, they can ???

CRATES: Cannot be moved by Mr. Bolo. They block lasers, and are sometimes removed by pushing the Special Purple Button.

HOLES: Cannot be passed over by Mr. Bolo. They can be filled up by pushing a ball into it, they can be removed by ???

WATER: Can flow in any direction. Mr. Bolo never was too good at swimming, so he can't go into it. He can use balls and boxes and ??? to help him through water.

LASERS: Are definitely not good for Mr. Bolo's health! However, he can block them with other objects.

SPECIAL BUTTON: This purple button in most cases will help you to reach the stairs by affecting the game board in some way. The button sometimes removes crates, balls, boxes, changes water flow direction, and much more!

STAIRS: The red stairs is Mr. Bolo's objective in all the puzzles.

Key definitions and solutions

All key commands are shown at the bottom of the game board at all times. The <O>ption key brings up a special Option menu where you can toggle the Sound (On/Off), access the Directions, find out more about Soleau Software Logic Games, and access the aolutions to the first three puzzles if you need them.

Demo Puzzle

There is a special demo puzzle you can run by selecting Demo Puzzle from the <S>elect Puzzle menu. This demo will take you through a simple puzzle showing you some basic aspects about the game play and the various objects you'll encounter.

If you're new to the game, you should run the demo first.

Bolo Adventures III is a pure logic game in Soleau Software's Logic Game series. Your problem solving abilities are put to the test. So jump right in and see if you can solve all 15 of these logic puzzles. Mr. Bolo is waiting . . .

Note: Windows 3.x users

Running Bolo Adventures III under Windows 3.x may cause unexpected results. The game should be played by loading it directly from the DOS prompt or the DOS window in Windows 95.

About Soleau Software games

REGISTERED VERSION AND SOLEAU SOFTWARE MEMBERSHIP

This game is distributed as shareware and may be passed along to your friends or local BBS. A registration fee of $12.00 is requested if you find this game is a worthy addition to your game collection. The registered version of Bolo Adventures III comes with all the solutions, plus 15 more mind-bending puzzles.

Register Bolo Adventures III and become a Soleau Software Member!

All members receive special discounts on our other games through special bonus offers sent with your disk. Members also have the option to include $6.00 for our Member Game Pack containing eight of Soleau Software's most popular Shareware games! Please See the BOL3_REG.DOC or the closing screen for details.

Get three other exciting logic puzzle games fully registered for only $24.00. See the BOL3_REG.DOC or the final screen within the game for details on this offer.

Soleau Software creates a wide variety of problem-solving games that give hours of fun, challenging enjoyment. We have arcade, strategy, board, word, and maze games. Designed with varying levels of difficulty, new users can quickly master a game's objectives and then progress at their own speed to the more detailed complexities and strategies of each game.

Soleau Software is committed to the shareware concept and to bringing the consumer quality software at reasonable prices. If you enjoy our games, please show your support of us through your registration. Your support of our products allows us to continue producing our logic games as shareware.

We at Soleau Software thank you for your support and hope you will continue to enjoy this as well as our many other Shareware products.

Sincerely,

William Soleau
President
Soleau Software
163 Amsterdam Avenue, Suite 213
New York, NY 10023

For ordering, contact, registration, and more detailed information, see the appropriate file for this program on the companion CD-ROM.

Casino Verite BlackJack

Casino Verite Blackjack v1.3. Rated the best BJ game software by *Blackjack Forum Magazine*, *Dalton's BJ Review*, *BJ Confidential Magazine*, and *Win Magazine*. Over 300 rule and play variations (trillions of combinations), database with 477 real casino rule sets (from LV & AC to Kathmandu), SVGA graphics, ultra-realistic casino play. Registered version contains over 300 card-counting tables.

Category: Games
Type: Shareware
Location on CD: \Blakjak1
To install: Run d:\Blakjak1\SETUP.EXE
To run: Click on Start⇨Programs⇨ Casino Verite⇨Casino Verite Blackjack

Documentation excerpts

This is the shareware version of Casino Vérité™ Blackjack. The card counting strategy tables have not been included.

The shareware version of CV is a beta test release. Registered users receive the completed version with over 300 strategy tables, update information, technical support, and a version of the code without the annoying shareware screen. If you decide not to register, you must remove all copies of this software from your system. I apologize for being a pain about this. Fact is, for some reason, many people believe that software developers do not need money to live.

I have included the Features and Quick Start sections of the manual below which should provide enough information to use the basic features of CV. You may print this file by using FILE-PRINT. Use the online Help for the more advanced features.

Installation

Put the ZIP file (CVBJS.ZIP) into its own directory and unzip it, then use Windows Program Manager File, Run command and type in the directory name and setup to install. If any of the files cannot be installed, shut down Windows, and from DOS, enter the following command:

```
xxx\CLEANUP C:\WINDOWS
```

where xxx is the directory where you have unzipped CVBJS. Then try again. Note: CVBJ supports 16, 256 and true color graphic cards. If your card is set to 64K colors, you must change the setting to 256 colors.

Order information

For ordering, contact, registration, and more detailed information, see the appropriate file for this program on the companion CD-ROM.

Features

The main thrust of CV is practice under realistic casino conditions. Toward this end, many unusual features have been implemented. This section gives a brief rundown of some of these features.

Included:

Rule variations - Over 100 Blackjack rule and play variations exist which can be independently set in literally trillions of combinations.

Casinos - A casino file exists containing 801 rule sets in 477 actual casinos. You can set the game's rules by selecting a casino instead of setting each of the rules manually.

Maps - Simple maps of Las Vegas and Atlantic City allow casino rule display or selection by casino location.

Search Function - A casino file search function is provided to locate actual casinos with unusual rules.

Statistics - Extensive logs, graphs, and statistics are supported.

Counting Drills - You can practice card counting with cards thrown at you in different combinations of number of cards, card placement, and orientation.

Flashcard Drills - The Flashcard drills present you with selectable situations to which you must respond correctly according to the selected strategy. These drills are designed to practice strategic play.

Discard Tray Drills - These drills are used to practice calculations based on estimations of the discard tray depth.

Strategies - You can select from basic or card counting strategies. The Flashcard drills and actual play can be tested against these strategies.

Customized Strategies - You can modify one of the standard strategies or define your own.

Warning on Strategy Error - This option allows testing of your play against the selected strategy.

Tournament Play - This feature simulates a Blackjack tournament. Here, you play against the other players, not against the dealer.

Multi-Player - Play with up to three humans is supported.

Unusual Games - New variations of Blackjack, like Multi-action, Over/Under 13, Double Exposure, and Bust Out are supported.

Improving the Odds - Expert methods, like peeking at the dealer down card, "Wonging" and team play are supported.

Voice Commands - If you have the Microsoft Sound System, support is included for play by voice command.

Unusual Features - To increase realism, features like tipping, dealer errors, face up or down dealing, players coming and going, and the dealer playing for you in obvious situations are included.

Table Formats - To increase realism, different table orientations are provided. You can sit at the center or at either end of the table. The table is rotated and cards are dealt sideways and upside down to give you a more realistic perspective.

Normal Movements - To increase realism, play can be performed with natural casino hand movements instead of using buttons.

Full Table Support - A full seven seats and split up to four hands is supported with all hands on the table displayed at once. Also, up to 18 chip stacks in one seat can be displayed for unusual betting situations.

Window Sizes - Three window sizes are supported. Graphics are not stretched, but are generated at different resolutions.

Player File - Multiple people can be registered as users of CV339 parameter, option and status settings are saved for each player. Separate logs are also kept by user and session.

Not Included

Simulation - Simulation is a valuable tool for determining strategies against new rules. I have not included this because I do not feel that anyone should trust software that they have not written themselves for this purpose. If you are interested in this function, you can try RWC Analyzer or Blackjack Analyzer which can be ordered from RGE Publishing (510-465-6452) or Gambler's Book Club (800-522-1777).

Bouncy Cocktail Waitresses - Sorry, Trump Castle 3 by Capstone (IntraCorp) has this feature if that is what you are looking for.

Quick start

This section provides a quick method of understanding the use of CV. Ideally, you should start CV and watch its operation as you read this section. Start CV now by double-clicking on the CV icon on the Windows Program Manager. Note: CV uses only the left mouse button. Actions are taken by positioning the mouse over an object and clicking this button.

Who are you?

The first screen that you see is used for player identification. You may register any number of players. CV will remember over 100 options and settings for each player. This allows you to exit CV (or trip over the power cord) and then to restart it later and continue from where you left it. Normally, when you start CV, the name of the last person using CV will appear at the top of the player list. Clicking the mouse on Play (or pressing the Enter key) will continue that session. If you want to register a new player, type the name of the player and click on New Player. Pressing New Session will start the game with the selected player with a new Blackjack session. Sessions are described later. Reset will reset all options for the selected player and start the game over. Since you are a new player, type your name now and press New Player.

Casinos

Next, because you are a new player, you must select a casino. You can change the casino at any time. CV includes the rule sets for 801 Blackjack games in 477 casinos. Two methods are available for casino selection. Forty-eight of the casinos can be selected by map location. All can be selected by region and name at the bottom of the screen. You can examine the rules before selection if you wish. The rules screens are fully described later in this manual. As a new player, if you wish to start quickly, click the mouse on Las Vegas in the box at the lower left. In a few seconds, a scrollable list of the Las Vegas casinos will appear in the box on the lower right. Now click the mouse on Generic Casino at the top of this list. Now press OK to select this casino. This will load the casino rules for an average Las Vegas strip casino without any unusual rules.

Select table

The Select Table screen is now displayed. Most casinos have more than one set of rules. If you have selected Generic Casino, you will see two rule sets: one for a single-deck game and one for a six deck game. The Select Table screen is fully described later in this manual. For now, select the six deck game using the mouse and press Select. This will load the rule set for that game. If you select the single deck game, the cards will be dealt face down which is a bit more confusing for a new player.

Table format

Because you are a new player, you must now select a table format. CV supports six general table formats and three specialty game table formats. This screen is fully described later in the document. It is suggested that you select the simplest table format - a six seat table with the dealer at the top of the screen. Select this format by clicking the mouse on the picture in the upper left corner.

New player introduction

For new players, an introduction screen is now displayed. This screen allows you to preview some of the features of CV. You can preview features by pressing buttons at the left. This will enter the selected feature and allow you to experiment. Descriptions of these features can be found later in this manual. If you are tired of the New Player start up procedure, select Play at the bottom of the screen with the mouse.

Entering the game

When you have finished with the New Player procedure, the screen will go to gray while the graphics are generated for the format that you have chosen. This will take from 3 to 40 seconds depending on CPU speed, screen size, and options. When completed, the Blackjack table is displayed. The dealer then shuffles the cards and waits for bets. If you do not make any bets, the dealer will eventually ignore you and deal to other players. You can watch the game play itself to get an idea of play. You can jump in anytime by laying bets on either or both of the two hands with $0 in the player chip box. However, you should read on before proceeding.

The table

Options are selected using standard drop down menus at the top of the screen. For example, you can select the table format by using the Options - Table Format menu. The table is described here.

There are six normal table formats. The cards are dealt very differently on each format. Three formats are six seat tables and three are seven seat tables. Seat one is directly to the dealer's left (your right). Seats are numbered clockwise, one through five, six, or seven. Two formats allow play at seats 1 and 2, two others allow play at seats 3 and 4, and the final two allow play at the last two seats. Note, your hands are always in front of you (bottom middle of screen). The table, the dealer, and the other players' hands are rotated to give you a sense of being at a different seat. I suggest sticking with seats 3 and 4 in a six seat table until you get used to CV.

In the upper right or left of the screen (depending on format) you will see a "shoe" that contains the cards that have not yet been played. As cards are dealt, you will see the number of cards in the shoe decrease and the "cut card" move toward the end. Shuffling occurs the hand after the cut card reaches the end and flies across the table.

To the dealer's right is the table limit sign. You can change the limits by clicking on this sign with the mouse. The Limit Table that will be displayed is generated from the selected casino. The casinos Limit Table can be modified from menu Options - Settings, Limits/Bonuses folder.

If you have SuperVGA capability, table size can be changed from menu - Options - Table Size. The graphics are not stretched, they are regenerated for the desired resolution and improve substantially at higher resolution.

Bankroll

Your chips are in the lower right corner for seats 3 and 4 play and the dollar value of these chips is displayed at the left of the chips. Other table formats place the chips at the far left or right of the screen. The denominations of chips provided depend on the table limits. For example, if the minimum bet is $100, the game will not display $1 and $5 chips unless it must. As you play, change is made automatically to ensure that you do not have empty stacks. If necessary, half dollar coins will also be displayed and can be bet. If you have more than $18,000, only $18,000 in chips will be shown. However, the number in the chipbox will show your actual bankroll. If you run out of chips, a Marker button will appear in the chip box for borrowing money. You can also select menu File - Markers to buy and sell multiple markers.

Sessions

Blackjack play is divided into sessions. There may be several sessions in one execution of CV or one session covering several executions over months. Logs are kept by session/by player. Selecting File - Log Maintenance provides tracking and controlling of these logs. New sessions are created from the startup screen or from menu File - New Session.

Seats, hands, chip stacks

You can play zero, one, or two seats, and up to five computer players can use the other seats. Other players are set from menu Options - Settings, Speeds/Parms folder (explained further below). Each of your seats can be split into up to four hands. Each of these hands can have up to ten cards. As a result, a huge number of cards can be placed on the table at one time. As in a real casino, the dealer may move cards around to make certain that all cards are visible in crowded conditions. Your seat can also have up to 14 chip stacks for each hand including: original bet, double down bet, win stack, double down win stack, Blackjack bonus stack, side bet stacks, tip, tip win, insurance, and multi-action bets. These will all be described later. Additional stacks can exist at a seat for split hands including split bets, split payoffs, double down after split bets, and payoffs and tips on split hands. These can exist for up to eight of your split hands. Again, as in a real casino, the dealer may move around chip stacks when conditions become very crowded.

Normal play

You may control play with buttons, the mouse, the keyboard, or voice (more on this later). The game was designed to work primarily with the mouse as this is the quickest, easiest, and most realistic. Besides, when was the last time that you saw a casino table with buttons? If you do wish to use buttons, they will be provided by using the Show Buttons option on the Options - Settings menu, Environment folder. Showing the buttons, even if you do not use them, does have an advantage for novice players as they indicate which plays are valid at any given time.

Mouse actions are designed to mimic normal casino movements as follows:

You bet by moving chips from the chipbox to one of the player bet boxes. The bet boxes are the light green semicircles with a small black "$0". You can bet in either of your two seats, in both, or in neither. Click on the chip that you wish to move, drag it to the player box by moving the mouse while pressing the left mouse button, and then release the chip by letting go of the button. You may grab several chips at once by selecting into the chip stack instead of selecting a chip from the top of the stack. The chip stack that you are creating is the original bet chip stack. You can add more chips by repeating the above. To keep the chip stack at a reasonable height, change will automatically be made to the smallest number of chips possible. You can also drag chip stacks from one spot to another.

To remove a chip stack from the table, just click it with the mouse once. Dragging is not necessary.

To hit a hand, scratch the table vertically. That is, push down the mouse button somewhere on the table and drag the mouse vertically up, down, or both then release the mouse button. The distance moved can be anywhere from one inch up to the full screen.

Standing is performed by waving the hand; push the mouse button and move the mouse horizontally, once or back and forth, and then release.

Double down and split are performed by adding more chips from the chipbox to the bet box. When a double down or split is allowed, press the mouse button anywhere in the chipbox and the correct number of chips will be grabbed. Drag these to the desired bet box and release.

Insurance is handled in the same way; but, drag the chips to the Insurance line of the bet. This is the line that says 2 To 1 – Insurance Pays – 2 To 1. The bet must be released directly above the player bet box on this line. You can insure both of your hands quickly by clicking on the black box that says Insurance?

Surrender is performed by clicking once on the bet to be surrendered.

At the end of play, many chip stacks may be left on the table. You can take them off of the table by clicking on them, or you can add to the original bet chip stack. When the deal is started, all stacks that are left will be combined into one stack per seat.

To begin deal, just wait, or click the shoe, or double-click on the table. Note, if you do not wish to have the dealer deal automatically, you can turn this feature off by de-selecting the Dealer doesn't wait for bet option on the Options - Settings menu, Dealer Actions folder. The feature is temporarily turned off whenever you select any menu. You must click on the shoe or double-click on the table to restart play.

Note, the reason that hand movements are required in a casino instead of voice commands has little to do with the noise level. Casino play is monitored via closed-circuit monitors and catwalks above the ceiling. The observers can read hands, but not lips.

Summary
This is the end of the Quick Start section. You now have enough information to play basic Blackjack. The online Help discusses over 300 additional features and options.

Complete strategy list

The full version (registered users) contains over 300 strategy tables. See the CD for a complete list of the strategies supported by the full version. DAS stands for double down after split allowed, NHC indicates European no hole card, and H17 indicates dealer hits on soft 17. These tables are supplied in the full version with permission of the following copyright holders: Arnold Snyder, Dr. Lance Humble, Stanford Wong, Bryce Carlson, Stanley Roberts, Richard Canfield.

Conversion Master

Copyright © 1994 by Roger L. Moseby.

MS Windows Conversion Master Engineering Calculator (CM).

> **Category:** Math, science
> **Type:** Shareware
> **Location on CD:** \Convert
> **To install:** Run d:\convert\SETUP.EXE
> **To run:** Click on Start⇨Programs⇨Conversion Master — 3.0⇨Conversion Master

If installation complains that other Visual Basic apps are running, you should close everything and restart Windows before you try to install this program again.

Documentation excerpts

MS Windows Conversion Master Engineering Calculator (CM) v3.0 is here! Many enhancements have been added. The best just keeps getting better. The most powerful dimensional and conversion calculator available. Accepts input formats in Feet-Inches-Sixteenths, Meters, and Decimal.

CM can convert between formats at the click of a button! CM solves Right Triangles discerningly. CM's use of dual displays enable you to view more information at one time. CM has 3,200 conversions arranged in 14 categories for easy access.

There are many online examples to get you up to speed on its potential. CM has a glossary full of usefull information and excellent program documentation all available online in CM help file. CM received a trophy rating from ZiffNet publications. ZiffNet calls it a "superb program." Featured in *U.S. News & World Report,* Jan. 16, 1995, Conversion Master "will delight the intellectually curious." This is much more than just another unit conversion program. CM is an excellent tool that can find a home in almost everyone's software library.

For ordering, contact, registration, and more detailed information, see the appropriate file for this program on the companion CD-ROM.

Cool Edit

Cool Edit v.1.50 is a Waveform Editor with features such as Echo, Flange, Reverb, Stretch/Pitch Change, Compress, Brainwave Synchronizer, Noise Reducer, Envelope, Filter, Distortion, and more. Supports most every file format. Cue and Play list. View waves as amplitude or frequency plots. Analyze component frequencies. Scripts let you play back complex operations.

> **Category:** Multimedia
> **Type:** Shareware
> **Location on CD:** \CoolEdit
> **To install:** Create a folder on your hard disk (for example, CoolEdit). Then copy all the files from d:\CoolEdit into this new folder.
> **To run:** Browse to the folder that contains CoolEdit, and double-click on COOL.EXE

A cool Editor for sound files.

CyberTarot

CyberTarot(TM) version 2.3a is a complete Tarot reading system for Microsoft Windows 3.1 or later. You can choose from any of three spreads or card layouts, shuffle and select your own cards, and view individual cards on a large screen. Comprehensive online help system includes interpretations of individual cards and information about spreads and card positions. Minimum configuration requires 256 color VGA. CyberTarot also requires VBRUN300.DLL. Copyright (c) 1994 AxisMundi, Inc.

> **Category:** Personal
> **Type:** Shareware
> **Location on CD:** \Tarot
> **To install:** No need to install to hard disk
> **To run:** Click on Start➪Run➪d:\tarot\TAROT.EXE

Day Plan

Day-to-day planning tool.

> **Category:** Personal
> **Type:** Shareware
> **Location on CD:** \DayPlan
> **To install:** Run d:\DayPlan\INSTALL.EXE
> **To run:** Run c:\dayplan\dayplan

A simple day planner, and handy tool for day-to-day shopping lists and so forth. Doesn't create a program group. But if you like this program, register (via Help). And then you can make a quick shortcut from your desktop!

© 1995 3C Computer Systems

General use of Day Plan

Day Plan is for making a list of tasks to be done during one day. The list can be printed for carrying with. The list can be saved under any name desired. For instance a standard task list could be made up and saved. The saved list can be loaded back in and edited. Any number of days can be made up and saved or printed. Day Plan is a flexible, useful tool for keeping track of daily lists of tasks.

Print day
When clicked, the currently displayed day plan is sent to the printer. This selection is in the File menu.

Load day
When clicked, a dialog box is displayed allowing the selection of a file in any subdirectory. The file must have previously saved in Day Plan. This is in the File menu.

New day
When clicked, the day plan text area is cleared and the date's reset to the current day. This is in the File Menu.

Save day
When clicked, a dialog box is displayed allowing the selection of the name of the file, an existing one from any directory or a new one. The currently displayed Day Plan text is saved. This is in File menu.

Export plan to clipboard
When clicked, all of the text in the Day Plan is copied to the clipboard for exporting into any other application (such as a word processor) that can paste from the clipboard. This command is commonly in the Edit menu with the caption of Paste.

For ordering, contact, registration, and more detailed information, see the appropriate file for this program on the companion CD-ROM.

Dotso

DOTSO v1.1. Play against the computer in this classic game of 'connect the dots.' This strategy game adds new twists and features. Multiple difficulty levels are provided so that all ages will be challenged. Each time you play Dotsos the board setup will be different, so it will challenge you every time!

Category: Games
Type: Shareware
Location on CD: \Dotso
To install: No installation program provided. You'll need to copy all the files from d:\Dotso to a folder on your hard disk.
To run: After copying all files, run DOTSO.EXE on your hard disk

Another Brain Buster from Soleau Software. DOS game.

DOTSO directions

The objective of Dotso is to create boxes by drawing four sides of a box. Each player takes turns drawing a line either horizontal or vertical on the game board. The player with the most boxes created at the end of the game is the winner.

Dotso is played like the classic game, Connect the Dots. At the start of the game, the computer will generate a random board with some lines already drawn on it. Each player will take turns placing down one line (between dots).

If a player can make a box by adding its fourth side, then it will be colored in with their tile marker. If you make a box, your turn continues until the line you draw will not form a new box. The computer will automatically fill any other boxes which can be created once you have captured your first box for that turn.

Color tiles

This shareware version of Dotso pits you against the computer. Your color will be yellow and the computer will play the red. At the start of the game, there may occasionally be gray tiles on the game board. These tiles cannot be captured and will remain on the board for the duration of the game.

Drawing lines

When play begins, the computer will randomly select who will take the first turn. The color of the border around the game grid will turn to the color of the player who is about to play.

In the upper left-hand corner of the game board, there will be the yellow line icon. Using your arrow keys, move the line to the place you want to draw a line. You can change toggle the line icon between horizontal and vertical by pressing the Spacebar.

A line cannot be drawn on top of a line already on the game board. When you have found the place where you want to draw a line, press the Enter key. If a box was not created by that line, then the play will pass to the opponent.

Options

At the bottom of the screen, there are several keys which you can use to change the features of the game.

<D>irections <O>ptions <N>ew Game <Q>uit

<D>irections : Game Instructions

<N>ew Game : Begins a new game. Can be pressed at any time during a game.

<Q>uit : Quits Dotso

By pressing the <O>ption Key, a special Option Menu will appear.

The Options are:

1 = Toggle Sound (On/Off)

2 = Change Opponent Level (Beg/Adv/Exp)

3 = Soleau Software (Information)

4 = Change Opponent (Computer/Human Reg.Ver.)

Opponent level

There are three different levels of play for the computer opponent. They are Beginner, Average, and Expert. The default for the game is set to Average strength. The Level icon is located on the right side of the game board. This will tell you at which strength the computer is playing.

Strategy

The game is easy to play but requires a lot of strategy and observation to win. After the first few moves by each player, the game board will soon have no more places to safely draw a line without the opponent being able to create a box on their turn.

The trick is to limit the number of boxes your opponent will create by choosing the right location on the game board to draw your line. The game is over when all boxes have been colored in. The computer will tabulate the scores and determine the winner. All score totals are visible on the screen during the game.

Keys

Arrow Keys: Moves Line Icon

Spacebar: Toggles between Horizontal & Vertical

Enter Key: Draws the line

Note: Windows 3.x users

Running Dotso under Windows 3.x may cause unexpected results. The game should be played by loading it directly from the the DOS prompt or the Windows 95 DOS window.

For ordering, contact, registration, and more detailed information, see the appropriate file for this program on the companion CD-ROM.

Double-Down Video Poker

Exciting casino-style action in a truly spectacular, feature-rich video poker game. Complete with a double-down option. Outstanding graphics with 3-D effects, icons, buttons animation, and online help. Full mouse and keyboard support, as well as music and sound effects. A must have!

> **Category**: Games
> **Type**: Shareware
> **Location on CD**: \Poker1
> **To install**: None required. You can run shareware right from the CD
> **To run**: To try it out, just run d:\poker1\DDVP.EXE

Great DOS casino game from SNR Software. If you register, you'll get info on other casino and card games from SNR.

Documentation excerpts

If you experience problems getting Double-Down Video Poker to operate correctly load the help me file by typing HELPME at the DOS prompt.

Complete documentation is available within the program via online Help.

To print the registration form, load the file ORDER.FRM into your favorite word processor and print it. Alternatively, at the DOS prompt type: COPY ORDER.FRM PRN

Thank you for evaluating Double Video Poker and enjoy the game!

For ordering, contact, registration, and more detailed information, see the appropriate file for this program on the companion CD-ROM.

The Drums Professional

The Drums Professional v.1.10. Real-time, pattern-based editor sequencer for drum parts. Compatible with any MIDI device driver or sound card. Shareware. Registration fee $30. By Fabio Marzocca.

> **Category:** Multimedia
> **Type:** Shareware
> **Location on CD:** \Drums
> **To install:** Run d:\Drums\INSTALL.EXE
> **To run:** Click on Start⇨Programs⇨The_DrumsPro⇨The_Drums Professional

Employee Scheduling Assistant

Employee Scheduling Assistant v.1.07. <ASP> Designed for institutions with mostly full-time employees. An easy-to-use scheduler with flexibility and control that will save time and effort to keep track of items, such as vacations and shift assignments. Auto install and an example department with fictitious employees. Distribution graphs display the hour by hour coverage for each day. Many other features. From Guia International.

> **Category:** Business
> **Type:** Shareware
> **Location on CD:** \SchedAst
> **To install:** Run d:\SchedAst\SETUP.EXE
> **To run:** Click on Start ⇨Programs⇨Employee Scheduling⇨Employee scheduling

See "Scheduling Assistant for Windows" later in this Appendix for information on this and another scheduling program from Guia International.

First Name Almanac

Makes a commercial quality printout of "The Meaning of More Than 14,500+ First Names." In calligraphy script — suitable for framing. Designed for the entrepreneur who wants to sell a unique printout at swap meets, fairs, or in a small business setting. Now supports color printers! Requires 3MB free hard disk space. VBRUN300.DLL required. Make money with this! From Ken Kirkpatrick. <ASP>

Category: Personal
Type: Shareware
Location on CD: \FirstNam
To install: Run d:\FirstNam\INSTALL.EXE
To run: Click on Start⇨Programs⇨ Ken Kirkpatrick Software⇨First Name Almanac

Requires a printer.

Documentation excerpts

This is a shareware Try-Before-You-Buy copy; you have not bought it.

Note: This program requires a Windows Compatible printer. If no printer is detected, the program will route you to Control Panel so that you may select or install a default printer.

Should you encounter any problems or bugs please help me help you by bringing them to my attention! Click on Help/About for my Phone & address.

Thank you so much for trying our Shareware product!

Ken Kirkpatrick, <ASP> Ken Kirkpatrick Software

For ordering, contact, registration, and more detailed information, see the appropriate file for this program on the companion CD-ROM.

Football Clock V4.1 (FOOTBALL)

By Timothy L. Hirtle 4/24/95. All Rights Reserved.

Football Clock will allow you to have a clock of your favorite team's logo on your desktop. You may switch teams anytime. The clock is designed to stay on top of any application that you may have running, so it will always be seen. You may still use other applications while Football Clock is running. The program will also allow users to preset their favorite team to automatically load upon program execution using the "Auto Execute" command. The user can display either a digital or an analog clock. Football clock has full sound capabilities for systems with compatible sound boards. The clock can be set to chime hourly using many different sound choices. The clock has an alarm capability for user reminders.

Category: Utility
Type: Shareware
Location on CD: \Football
To install: Run d:\Football\INSTALL.EXE
To run: Click on Start⇨Programs⇨Football Clock V4.1⇨ Football Clock

Requirements

✦ Windows 3.x

✦ VBRUN300.DLL installed in your Windows or System directory (See below)

Installation should will placed the following files in the identified directories:

✦ FB_CLOCK.EXE in the install directory you specified.

✦ FB_CLOCK.TXT in the same directory as the executable file.

✦ LLATSNI.EXE and LLATSNI.INF in the same directory as the executable file.

✦ All *.WAV files in the same directory as the executable file. COOCOO.WAV, CHIME.WAV, GRANDFTH.WAV, BELLS.WAV, WHISTLE.WAV.

✦ All *.VBX files in Windows\System directory. 3DLABEL.VBX, STATBAR.VBX, VBPIC3D.VBX, VBPICBTN.VBX, WAVE1.VBX.

Distribution

✦ Football Clock is distributed as shareware. The Author maintains all rights to the program in its entirety.

✦ Football Clock may be distributed freely as long as the integrity of shareware is maintained.

✦ In the tradition of shareware, the author grants a 30 day trial period to the user to decide whether they want to keep the program. If so, a $15 donation is required. If not, then before the 30 days is up, you must delete the program from your system. The author will allow previous registered users a half-price discount for each previous registered copy of this version.

Important notice

Because of the file structure of Football Clock, users should take caution when changing and copying Football Clock files to a new directory from the original installation directory. Some files are created using the original directory. Validated users may lose their validation information. Also, Auto execution of preferred teams may be lost. Neither is a major catastrophe. Validation and Autoexecution can easily be re-established in the new directory. Validated users should write down their validation number in case they change directories.

Disclaimer

Football Clock has no expressed or implied warranty. The user accepts full responsibility for this program by loading it on their computer. At no time is the author responsible for any hardware or software malfunctions caused by Football Clock. Though the author knows of no such problems from this software, he is not liable if any should occur.

Note

The author is requesting a donation for his labor in developing the code for this program. The visual graphics of NFL team logos are *not* included in the donation request. The author cannot and will not charge a monetary fee for the graphics in this application. Any monies sent to the author is solely for the use of program code, not its graphics. The NFL team names, nicknames, helmet logos, and all other indicia are trademarks of the teams indicated. NFL is a trademark of the National Football League.

For ordering, contact, registration, and more detailed information, see the appropriate file for this program on the companion CD-ROM.

Heavy Water Jogger

Future Collector's Item. Everyone said there won't be many registrations on this one, but, hey, I like it! One, single, complete episode! Prevent total meltdown at the Three Miles Island Nuclear Plant. VGA, PC speaker sound, frustrating. Hurry, Fluke! From Viable Software Alternatives.

> **Category:** Games
> **Type:** Shareware
> **Location on CD:** \Jogger
> **To install:** No installation program provided. You need to create a folder on your hard drive (such as Jogger), then copy all files from d:\Jogger to that folder.
> **To run:** Browse to and run JOGGER.EXE after copying to your hard disk

Try not to touch the walls! Check out other Viable products on the Internet at http://delta.com/viable/viable.htm.

Documentation excerpts

Register today and you'll receive the following:

✦ The commercial version of Heavy Water Jogger that contains the Board of Superior Jogging Statistics!

✦ Our hint booklet that contains "The Saga Of Fred Fluke At Three Miles Island," and important hints to make your play easier!

✦ "Cheat" Codes — codes you enter at the beginning of the game to disable robots, remove pits, or give your self more time to complete your mission!

✦ An $8\frac{1}{2}$ by 14 full black and white Fluke Poster rendering Fred after his heroic mission at Three Miles Island!

Aw, come on, Fred, you know how it is with games like this — the less said, the better!

Just watch for the drainage pits - you can't jump from a walk! Oh, and watch for those V7734 series floating robots, you know, the ones you had installed to protect the plant from those protesters?

And try not to touch the walls!

Maybe every now and then check under those ventilation shaft covers. You've always suspected your employees of pilfering company goods and stashing them there for safekeeping.

And mark your progress, Fluke! You never know when you may need to remember whether that hallway led somewhere or not.

Maybe if you had been more interested in the real workings of your plant you would know your way around better! Or maybe this never would have happened in the first place!

HURRY, FLUKE!

Active keys

<Arrow Keys> - Used to move Fred around the plant. Press an arrow key once and you move, a second time to stop.

<SPACE> - Causes Fred to jump (ONLY WHEN HE IS RUNNING).

<R> - If Fred is walking, makes him run; if Fred is running, makes him walk.

<M> - Displays the plant map (when it is available).

<O> - Open things like doors, showers, vents, and turns showers on.

<I> - Displays Inventory (Goods Filched).

<S> - Displays the status window.

<T> - Causes Fred to take an anti-rad pill (if he has some).

<PgUp or F1> - Sets a green marker at your location.

<PgDn or F10>- Sets a red marker at your location.

<ESC> - Brings up the Main Option Menu.

V7734-series robot security system

Finally, protection at reasonable rates! No more lawsuits!

The V7724-Robot is the ultimate, state-of-the-art mechanical security guard. Just turn 'em on, let 'em go, and relax!

When the robot spots someone who doesn't belong, zing! — he's on them like glue. Provided with the most sensitive, high-tech heat sensors available, the robots will follow a trespasser using the victim's own body heat as a beacon.

Once captured the trespasser is harmlessly stunned and removed to a predetermined location, out of harm's way.

Caution: Deployment in radioactive areas can cause malfunctions in the robot's heat seeking equipment.

All robot's are provided with portable, radio-controlled Deactivators, for use by authorized personnel only, of course.

Reebuks: The Korean shoe of the century

Reebuk Inflatable Athletic Shoes are the future!

Jump further and higher than ever before in our latest foot technology.

CAUTION: Manufacturer is not responsible for accidents caused by jumping too far!

WARNING: The featherweight polyester used in the manufacturing process is vulnerable to radioactive waste. Be sure to pack an extra pair just in case.

For ordering, contact, registration, and more detailed information, see the appropriate file for this program on the companion CD-ROM.

IC2 version 3.01

Total Contact Management. IC2 is the fully-featured, workgroup-enabled contact manager designed for sales, marketing, and customer support professionals. If you need to stay on top of your customer list, you can't find a more powerful tool around. Unlimited contacts per file. Unlimited fields per file. Unlimited output: custom form letters; labels; and reports. Unlimited selections: combine simple data filters; or use SQL. Unlimited attached files to each contact Unlimited events, to-do's with reminders. Unlimited customization: change fonts; field layout; and more!

Category: Business
Type: Shareware
Location on CD: \IC2
To install: Run d:\IC2\INSTALL.EXE
To run: Click on Start⇨Run⇨Ic2-3.0⇨IC2

After you've installed and launched IC2, try out the sample database. Choose File⇨Open and open SAMPLE.MDB.

Documentation excerpts

I C 2 ™ Version 3.0

IC2 v3.0 is the best workgroup-ready contact manager for Windows! IC2 has ALL the features of pricey retail programs for a fraction of the cost — just $49! If you are looking for a full-featured contact manager, this is it!! Just received Five Star Trophy rating from ZIFF/Public Brand!.

Copyright © 1992-1995 Creativision Publishing Corp. All rights are reserved.

Program information

IC2 is the fully-featured, workgroup-enabled contact manager for $49. If you need to stay on top of your customer list, you can't find a more powerful tool than IC2:

Total contact management

✦ Unlimited contacts per file.

✦ Unlimited fields per file.

✦ Unlimited output: custom form letters, labels and reports.

✦ Unlimited selections: combine simple data filters or use SQL.

✦ Unlimited attached files to each contact.

✦ Unlimited events, to-do's with reminders.

✦ Unlimited history for each contact.

✦ Unlimited workgroup access: it's ready-to-share contact files.

✦ Unlimited customization: change fonts, field layout and more!

IC2 packs all this power into a clean interface that can be tailored to your personal style and your business needs.

Credits

IC2 is Copyright © 1992-1995 CreatiVision Publishing, all rights are reserved. (Originally released under the name of "InContact.") Written by David Balmer, Jr.

IC2 was written in Visual Basic 3.0 for the 100% IBM compatible computer running a 386 (or higher) with at least 4MB memory under Windows Version 3.1 in normal or enhanced modes.

Disclaimer and copyright notice

In no event will CreatiVision Publishing be liable to you for any damages, lost profits, lost savings, or any other incidental or consequential damages arising out of the use or inability to use this software, even if CreatiVision Publishing has been advised of the possibility of such damages, or for any claim by any other party.

This product is freely distributed as shareware with a 15-day trial license before purchase. All copyrights on the name, look-and-feel, and operations are strictly enforceable. It is illegal to change any text within the program code that would remove the copyright notice for CreatiVision Publishing. It is also illegal to change ordering information text in the program or to distort in any way the identity of the rightful copyright holder.

What's new In 3.0

Cleaner Look

✦ Get the new Windows '95 look today with IC2 3.0 . . .

✦ RMC (Right Mouse Click) menus are all over the place; they give you instant access to commonly-used actions on an item.

✦ Tabbed dialogs are everywhere; use Alt+PgUp and Alt+PgDn to move in them from the keyboard.

✦ The toolbar can be more easily edited with a new Toolbar dialog on the Options dialog.

✦ Plus a clock has been added to the status line.

Contact window

✦ The "Contact List" window has been integrated into the "Contact" window under a new tab called "Contact List".

✦ Fields may be arranged in two columns on the detail pages.

✦ The display font can be changed (as well as the color).

✦ There are four user-defined tabs and new Contact List, Attachments, and Notes tabs. The Notes field has been moved to its own tab.

✦ You can specify up to three levels of sorting.

✦ Filters on Flags, Category and Status can be created simply; a list of available choices appears in the Filter.

✦ A Locate option has been added to let you quickly find a name or company.

✦ A Contact menu has been added to provide a centralized place to manage a contact record.

✦ Options to view other windows have been moved to the Window menu to reduce confusion and shorten the View menu.

✦ Right-Click-Menus are everywhere; click on the control bar, individual fields, tabs, etc. to see context-related pop-ups.

✦ Use Alt+PgUp and Alt+PgDn to flip between field pages; this is a MS standard and it keeps strange things from happening in the Notes and Contact List tabs.

Time Manager

✦ A new view option to see upcoming events and to-do's by a contact's name.

✦ Options to view other windows have been moved to the Window menu to reduce confusion and shorten the View menu History Window.

✦ The window has a new filter system that allows you to specify a name, date range, or activity.

✦ Options to view other windows have been moved to the Window menu to reduce confusion and shorten the View menu.

File management

✦ Compress and Repair have been added; just close any open file and look in the File menu.

✦ You can select other templates for a new file (templates can be ordered from us or created with the IC2 Data Manager).

Welcome to IC2 and we hope you like it!

THE IC2 FAMILY

IC2 3.0 $49 Single-User/Workgroup enabled contact manager (this program disk)

IC2 3.0 Data Manager $29. Create custom fields and file templates and use an open SQL interface to your files.

IC2 3.0 5-User Office Pack $CALL

IC2 3.0 10-User Office Pack $CALL

IC2 3.0 Multi-User Manager $129. Add data security, user permissions, backups and a complete SQL query and update tool.

For ordering, contact, registration, and more detailed information, see the appropriate file for this program on the companion CD-ROM.

Jasc Media Center v2.01

A Windows program for multimedia file management and manipulation. Organize your multimedia files into albums of thumbnails. Catalog, search, sort by keyword, comment, or file properties. View files using the powerful slide show feature. Full file manipulation capabilities from within the program. Print high quality contact sheets. Support for over 35 file formats, removable disks, and CD-ROMs. <ASP>

Category: Multimedia
Type: Shareware
Location on CD: \MediaCnt
To install: Run d:\MediaCnt\SETUP.EXE
To run: Click on Start ⇨Programs⇨Media Center⇨Media Center

Great program for storing thumbnails of multimedia files. Just click the Help (?) button for help getting started. Purchasing details and other products from JASC Inc. are also in Help.

The user's manual

In order to keep the size of the shareware version of Jasc Media Center reasonable no user's manual is provided. You will find that all menu items and associated dialog boxes, along with general information, are provided online using the Help-Index menu option of the program. When you purchase the licensed version of Jasc Media Center you will receive the fully illustrated, perfect-bound User's Guide.

For ordering, contact, registration, and more detailed information, see the appropriate file for this program on the companion CD-ROM.

Jixxa Version 1.1

The Windows jigsaw puzzle. This package contains the shareware version of Jixxa, the premier Windows jigsaw puzzle program, plus two fun jigsaw puzzles to get you going. Includes documentation and interactive online help system. Registered version ships with four additional puzzles in various piece sizes. From Rhode Island Soft Systems, Inc. $24.95.

> **Category:** Games
> **Type:** Shareware
> **Location on CD:** \Jixxa
> **To install:** Run d:\Jixxa\Setup
> **To run:** Click on Start⇨Programs⇨Jixxa Shareware Edition⇨Jixxa

No snags. Really fun. Pretty addicting. Registration information is in Help.

Jixxa README.TXT

Hello and welcome to the Jixxa software package from Rhode Island SoftSystems, Inc.! This package contains Jixxa, the premier Jigsaw Puzzle game for Windows3.1, plus two fun jigsaw puzzles to get you going. This package contains an automated installation utility, and interactive online help. It should be noted that registered users of Jixxa receive the full retail version of Jixxa which contains everything in this shareware version plus several newgame features, and four more jigsaw puzzles!

The Jixxa puzzles in this package are intended for 256 color displays, so if you only have a 16 color display, you will not see the full beauty of the images. Of course, the game will still work, but not in the intended manner. You can verify your color setting in the Help About box.

The two puzzles in this package are made with large and small pieces. The registered version ships with additional, different piece sizes as well (medium and tiny), for more variety.

The following information will guide you through installing the Jixxafiles. Once installed, the Setup program will create a program group and install icons for the documentation files, which you can read by clicking on the document's icon.

Verification of files

At this point, please look for all of the files that belong to the Jixxa package. All of the files are listed in the file PACKING.TXT. If the PACKING.TXT file or any of the files listed in PACKING.TXT are missing, please contact us for an official copy of Jixxa — it would not be fair to either the user or Rhode Island Soft Systems, Inc. to have a user evaluate an incomplete package.

For ordering, contact, registration, and more detailed information, see the appropriate file for this program on the companion CD-ROM.

Judy's TenKey

Powerful Windows calculator with nearly every feature imaginable, including a scrolling tape you can save, print, resize, and even edit (causing the tape to automatically recalculate); selectable syntax (normal, RPN, or tenkey adding machine); financial dialogs; customizable display; keep on top option; "Tip of the Day", and much more. You will never go back to the default Windows calculator. $19.95.

> **Category:** Business
> **Type:** Shareware
> **Location on CD:** \TenKey
> **To install:** Run d:\TenKey\INSTALL.EXE
> **To run:** Click on Start➪Programs➪Judy's Applications➪TenKey

Registering this product will automatically get you the 32-bit version.

Documentation excerpts

Judy's TenKey™

This is a powerful Windows calculator with nearly every feature imaginable, including a scrolling tape you can save, print, resize, and even edit (causing the tape to automatically recalculate); selectable syntax (normal, RPN, or tenkey adding machine); financial dialogs; customizable display; keep on top option; "Tip of the Day," and much more. You will never go back to the default Windows calculator.

Judy's TenKey makes your calculations easier and more reliable. If you use the default Windows calculator, you'll find that Judy's TenKey gives you many advantages. If you're still using an old-fashioned desktop calculator, you'll love the integration Judy's TenKey gives you with your other Windows applications.

This document provides a brief description of program capabilities, installation instructions, author contact information, and version history. This document is also distributed in Windows Write format (READ_ME.WRI); you may find it easier on the eyes.

Program capabilities

SCROLLING TAPE: Records your calculations in a scrolling list which you can save, print, and resize (a real help in keeping track of your calculations). You can also modify tape entries, causing the tape to recalculate, or reuse previous entries in new calculations (saving typing and reducing errors).

SELECTABLE SYNTAX: Judy's TenKey can process numbers like a scientific calculator (RPN), an adding machine, or a normal calculator. If you are familiar with one and not another, you know how difficult and frustrating it can be to try to switch. Perfect for accountants, engineers, and you.

CUSTOMIZABLE DISPLAY: You can decide how you want your TenKey to look (selecting from tape, memory, statistics, functions, trigonometry, finance, and number pad options), enabling you to optimize screen usage. Any TenKey function can always be activated via the keyboard regardless of the current display configuration.

FINANCIAL CALCULATIONS: Judy's TenKey calculates monthly payments for most loans (e.g., cars, houses, etc.), expected investment growth, necessary retirement savings, inflation adjustment, and more. Its easy-to-use dialogs lead you through complex calculations, and records all responses on the tape (which you can later save, modify, etc.).

STATISTICS: The scrolling tape provides a natural interface for statistical calculations, including average value, sum, or even standard deviation. Simply select the desired lines, then press the appropriate statistics button.

KEEP ON TOP: You can set Judy's TenKey to stay on top of all other windows, so you quickly calculate something even when editing a document full-screen.

DECIMAL SETTING: You can set Judy's TenKey to display the number of decimal positions you prefer, ranging from 0 to "as needed". In fact, you can configure Judy's TenKey to automatically insert the decimal point for you (a real favorite with professional accountants). If you frequently deal with money, you might want to set the decimals to 2 (for cents) or 0 (for dollars).

INTELLIGENT COPY & PASTE: You can copy tape entries to other applications, including Microsoft Word, Excel, and Notepad. You can also paste input from these applications. If extraneous text and special formatting are mixed in with your numbers, Judy's TenKey uses heuristic reasoning to extract and interpret appropriate information.

EXTRA TOUCHES: Judy's TenKey remembers your favorite screen position and displays itself there every time. It also uses thousands separators (such as "1,000,000" versus "1000000"), displays negative numbers in red, and allows you to use the backspace key to edit results for further calculation. Judy's TenKey provides an extensive help system, an introductory demonstration, and a Tip of the Day feature.

BETTER PERFORMANCE: Judy's TenKey enables you to work faster and more reliably. Once you can see (and reuse!) the numbers in your calculations, you will never return to the default Windows calculator. Plus, Judy's TenKey uses a proprietary algorithm to ensure superior precision (try subtracting "750.35 - 750.30" using the Microsoft calculator: it doesn't work!). We're so sure that you'll love using Judy's TenKey that we invite you to try it for free. Simply send in the registration fee if you decide to keep it.

Program installation

REQUIREMENTS: Version 3.0 of Judy's TenKey requires Windows version 3.1 or better (a separate Windows NT version is available) and a 386 or better processor. Including the tutorial demonstration, it uses 370K of disk space.

REGISTRATION: Judy's TenKey is provided as copyrighted software; the registration fee is a modest $19.95. Registered users receive the latest version of the program, as well as a free copy of Judy's CountDown™, a fun program that helps you track important dates.

Literati Lite for Windows

Do you like Scrabble™? If so, you'll LOVE Literati Lite, the crossword board game for one to four players that will have you playing for hours. Rack up extra points with double and triple letter and word scores. Two skill levels, built-in dictionary, cool background music, and neat graphics. Written by real smart people for real smart people. By MVP Software.

> **Category:** Games
> **Type:** Shareware
> **Location on CD:** \Literati
> **To install:** Run d:\Literati\SETUP.EXE
> **To run:** Click on Start⇨Programs⇨Mvp⇨Literati Lite

Loader Larry

Loader Larry v1.2. Larry Lontrose is a part-time dock loader in his hometown of Longview. He has ambitions to be promoted up the corporate ladder. By solving the 20 mind-bending puzzle rooms, you can help Larry fulfill his dreams. Each room has objects like boxes, balloons, TNT, and much more. Using these objects and avoiding others, he must reach the doors in each room. A pure animated logic puzzle!

> **Category:** Games
> **Type:** Shareware
> **Location on CD:** \LoadLar
> **To install:** No installation program provided. You'll need to copy all the files from d:\LoadLar to a folder on your hard disk
> **To run:** After copying all the files from d:\LoadLar, run LOADLAR.EXE from your hard disk

Another knicknack for brainiacs from Soleau Software. DOS game.

Loader Larry introduction

Larry Lontrose has lived his whole life in Longview. Like his father and grandfather before him, he works for the only factory in town. Generations of Lontroses have worked hard for the factory, yet nobody in his family (except his Aunt Mable, who eventually became a Junior Vice President during the 1930s) has ever been promoted from the loading docks where most employees are put to work.

Larry, however, has bigger plans for himself. As a boy, he was told by his parents that he could achieve anything if he worked hard enough at it. Determined to make something of himself, he decides to work overtime on the night shift to impress his superiors.

Each night Larry toils away until the early morning. At exactly 6 a.m. every sunrise, the Longview church tower bells ring, telling Larry his night shift is over.

Being very tired and exhausted from the labor, he always finds himself each morning in a room where the exit doors always seem impossible to reach. This is because the other employees just leave various boxes and other objects strewn around the room. Can you help Larry reach the doorways in each room, so he can go home and get some much needed rest?

Starting out as a part-time loader, Larry knows how to lift the boxes and move them to strategic positions to help him reach the exit doors. He can jump up about four feet which is about the size of the boxes he can carry.

Objects

There are many objects Larry can use to make his way to the door in each room.
There are: Boxes, Balloons, Ladders, TNT, Walls, Steel Walls, Switch, Generators,
Wooden Bridges.

BOXES: Larry can carry and jump with boxes and place them anywhere there is
an empty space for them.

BALLOONS: Larry can jump and push balloons right, left or down. He can walk
on top of balloons and can place boxes on them. If he is not holding boxes, he
can get underneath a balloon and jump up and grab a ride upwards if the
balloon has a clear path above it. Balloons will disintegrate if pushed into
Generators. He cannot use TNT while riding balloons.

LADDERS: If Larry can reach a ladder then it will be added to his inventory. He
can use a ladder at anytime by pressing the <L>adder key. The ladder will
extend upwards as high as it can reach, and Larry can climb up and jump off it at
any point. He can also use TNT to blast through walls while on it.

TNT: If Larry can reach the dynamite, then it will be added to his inventory. If he
is not holding a box, he can use the TNT to blast through a wall. TNT cannot be
used against any other objects including Steel Walls. He can use the TNT while
on a Ladder.

WALLS: These can be blown up by using TNT.

STEEL WALLS: These are indestructible.

SWITCH: If Larry can reach the Switch, then all the Electric Generators will be
turned off and they will vanish from the room.

GENERATORS: These Generators are very dangerous if Larry touches one. They
will make balloons pop if they are pushed into them. Boxes can be placed on top
of them to help Larry avoid the deadly voltage. They can be turned off if Larry
can reach the SWITCH.

WOODEN BRIDGES: If Larry walks directly across one of these, they will crumble
and vanish from the room. He can place boxes on them to help keep them intact
if he needs them later on.

EXIT DOOR: This is Larry's final objective for each room.

Larry is hoping to be promoted from his present job as a part-time Loader. Can you
help him solve all 20 rooms?

Key functions

All Key definitions are shown on the screen at all times

Arrow Keys: -> Move Larry Right <- Move Larry Left

UP: Larry Jumps Up

DOWN: Larry Drops Package

<L>adder Larry puts up ladder if he has it in his inventory

<T>nt Larry uses TNT if he has it in his inventory

<N>ew Puzzle Select New Puzzle

<A>gain Try Same Puzzle Again

<J>ob Show Larry's Job Description List

<S>ound Toggle Sound On/Off

<?> Solutions (1-5) Shareware Version (1-40)Reg.Ver.

<Q>uit Quits Loader Larry

Solutions

Solutions to the first three puzzle rooms have been provided for you. By pressing the question mark key, you can see Larry solve the room. There can be many ways to solve a room.

Jobs/Puzzle points

Each Puzzle Room has puzzle points if it is solved. These Puzzle Points determine Larry's Job Status. This Shareware Version has 20 puzzle rooms to solve. If you can solve all of them, Larry will be promoted six times until he is the Supervisor for the Loading Dock.

Puzzle order

The puzzle rooms get harder as you go along. When you first begin Loader Larry, you can only access the first three rooms. Anytime you solve a room, the puzzle room button on the Load Puzzle menu will turn from grey to red. You will be allowed to load a puzzle number that is two higher then the highest puzzle solved. Therefore if you solved puzzle number three the first time you play the game, you would then be allowed to play 1, 2, 3, 4 or 5 the next time you load a new puzzle.

Note Windows 3.x users

Running Loader Larry from Windows 3.x may cause unexpected results. The game should be played by loading it directly from the DOS prompt or the DOS window in Windows 95.

For ordering, contact, registration, and more detailed information, see the appropriate file for this program on the companion CD-ROM.

Medlin Payroll

MWPR - Medlin Windows Payroll Writing <ASP> From Medlin Accounting Shareware. Complete, easy-to-use payroll writing program. Built-in state and federal tables. Up to four user set deductions allow for tips, 401k, medical deductions, disability insurance, local taxes, and so on. Up to three other income fields. Print reports for any period. Registered users receive W-2 printing program. $38.

> **Category:** Business
> **Type:** Shareware
> **Location on CD:** \Payroll
> **To install:** Run d:\payroll\SETUP.EXE
> **To run:** Click Start⇨Program⇨Medlin Windows Accounting⇨Medlin Windows Payroll

Remember that payroll tax tables change every year. So be sure to register this one to stay updated with Uncle Sam.

Documentation excerpts

If you've ever wished you could easily handle your payroll with a Windows program, without spending time reading a manual, then MWPR - Medlin Windows Payroll is the program for you! This program is very quick and easy to use. MWPR - Medlin Windows Payroll is a shareware program. This evaluation version includes all features of the program. You may use it for up to 30 days, without charge (see MWPR.HLP for more details). If you like the program and wish to continue using it after the evaluation period, you are required to pay for the program.

Detailed documentation is included in the package in the form of a Windows Help File, or in the Windows Write file MWPR.WRI.

Mice Maze

Mice Maze v1.0 is an adventure, arcade, and puzzle strategy game all in one! Your mission is to guide your animated little blue mouse around a maze of 36 rooms looking for your lost friend, the red mouse. Look for keys, maps, secret passageways, and much more as you try to locate your friend. Beware of the cats that are always on the prowl! Many surprises await you! Are you up to the challenge?

Category: Games
Type: Shareware
Location on CD: \MiceMaze
To install: No installation program provided. You'll need to copy all the files from d:\MiceMaze to a folder on your hard disk
To run: After copying all the files from d:\MiceMaze, run MICEMAZE.EXE on your hard disk

Another fun brain-teaser from Soleau Software. DOS game.

Mice Maze game directions

Objective

The objective of Mice Maze is to find and rescue your friend the red mouse, trapped somewhere in this puzzle maze.

Game play

In this adventure strategy game, you will be represented by the blue mouse. At the start of a new game, you will be put into a puzzle maze which consists of 36 rooms.

Use the arrow keys to move your mouse about each room. There are mouse doors on the side of the room which will allow you to exit the room and move into a new one.

When you enter a new room, a map will pop up on the game board to help identify your location. You can also press the <M>ap key to see the map at anytime during the game. The present room number is displayed to the right of the game board below the picture of the seated mouse.

Storyline

Your first objective will be to acquire 10,000 points. When you reach the 10,000 point mark, you will be given an extra life and also further instructions on how to find your friend, the red mouse. The adventure would not be an adventure if I told you what twists and turns this puzzle will take . . . you'll have to discover that for yourself.

Objects

CHEESE: Your mouse needs cheese for strength, so grab these whenever you can. If you run out of cheese the game will be over no matter how many lives you have left. Every 20 moves of your mouse or when you exit a room, one cheese will be subtracted from your cheese total.

GRILLS: These circular grills are immovable and cannot be blasted or removed with bombs.

CANS: There are green cans located in most of the rooms. These cans give you extra points if you can reach them.

CATS: In each of the rooms, there are cats on the prowl. The light yellow cats are slower and the purple cats are much faster. If you get caught by a cat, you will lose one life.

TRAPPING THE CATS: You can eliminate the cats from the room by pushing the blocks to surround them. If you can push the blocks in such a way as the cat has no where to move, then it will be removed and an extra cheese will be placed somewhere in the room. If two cats are trapped together then they will not be removed. You must trap them individually. Once you leave a room, all the cats you trapped earlier will reappear again the next time you enter that room.

BOMBS: These bombs are used to blast through the blocks. To activate a bomb, press the space bar and then press the arrow key to signify where you want to throw the bomb.

HOLES: In many of the rooms there are mouse holes that you can go into. Some-times you'll find extra items like cheese and bombs, but other times you'll find nothing. Beware . . . you can also drop some items when going into these holes.

Scoring

CHEESE: 50 POINTS (1 cheese found = 3 cheeses)

BOMB: 60 POINTS (1 bomb found = 2 bombs)

CAN: 50 POINTS

1ST TRAPPED CAT: 75 POINTS

2ND TRAPPED CAT: 150 POINTS

3RD TRAPPED CAT: 225 POINTS

4TH TRAPPED CAT: 300 POINTS

EVERY 10,000 POINTS : EXTRA LIFE

Conclusion

As you play the game you'll find you will be searching for special keys, hidden doors, secret passageways, and much more. Are you up for a challenge? Go to it and see if you can rescue your friend . . . he's/she's counting on you!

Key definitions

<ARROW KEYS> = Move Mouse up/dwn/lft/rgt spacebar = Activate Bomb (then arrow key for direction)

<H>ELP = Game Directions

<M>AP = Shows Mice Maze map

<N>EW = Start New Game. (score not recorded)

S<C>ORES = Shows Mice Maze Scoreboard

S<O>UND = Toggle sound On/Off

<S>AVE = Saves Present Game (Reg.Version Only)

<L>OAD GAME = Loads Saved Game (Reg.Version Only)

HIN<T> = Mice Maze Hints (Reg.Version Only)

<Q>UIT = Quit Mice Maze

Note: Windows 3.x users

Running Mice Maze from Windows 3.x may cause unexpected results. The game should be played by loading it directly from the DOS prompt or the DOS window in Windows 95.

For ordering, contact, registration, and more detailed information, see the appropriate file for this program on the companion CD-ROM.

MVP Bridge for Windows

The DOS version of MVP Bridge won major industry awards. Now MVP Software takes the game a step further by setting the standard for Windows card games. Added features and a special registration offer make MVP Bridge for Windows simply the best. Even if you've never played Bridge before, its online help and special hint option will have you playing like a veteran. Version 1.4 by MVP Software.

Category: Games
Type: Shareware
Location on CD: \Bridge
To install: Run d:\Bridge\SETUP.EXE
To run: Click on Start⇨Programs⇨ MVP⇨MVP Bridge

MVP WordSearch for Windows

You've seen word search games before, but none like this one. Solve any of the many included puzzles, or let the computer create one using your word list. Easy listening original sound track for your sound card, nice Windows interface, and lots of fun. Great for educational use! Updated version. By MVP Software.

Category: Games
Type: Shareware
Location on CD: \WordSrch
To install: Run d:\WordSrch\SETUP.EXE
To run: Click on Start⇨Programs⇨MVP⇨WordSearch or run c:\mvpws\ws1

NoteWorthy Composer V1.20

A Notation Processor for Windows. Provides for the creation, play back, and printing of your own musical scores. Imports and exports MIDI files. Provides selective staff print. Fast and easy Notation Editor using computer keyboard or mouse. Supports up to four lyric lines per staff sounding scores quickly and easily. From Noteworthy Artware.

Category: Multimedia
Type: Shareware
Location on CD: \Composer
To install: Run d:\Composer\SETUP.EXE
To run: Run c:\nwc12\NWC12.EXE

Serious MIDI tool! One slight snag: might hang at the end of setup. But you can use Ctrl+Alt+Del to End Task on the setup (twice). Then click on Start⇨Run and run c:\nwc12\NWC12.EXE.

Documentation excerpts

NoteWorthy Composer 1.20 Notation Processor for Windows. A shareware music composition and notation processor for Windows, providing for the creation, play back, and printing of your own musical scores. You can:

✦ Print your whole score (for a conductor's view), or just the staves you select, in several font sizes.

✦ Import and export standard MIDI files.

✦ Use the computer keyboard or mouse for notation editing.

✦ Selectively add or remove slurs, staccato, accents, beams, triplets, and accidentals through tool bar buttons.

✦ Use the included tools to automatically transpose, beam, and arrange accidentals in your score staves to make them look professional.

✦ Create up to four lyric lines per staff.

✦ Add various performance expressions, such as crescendos, fermatas, breath marks, and accelerandos that are recognized and peformed during play back.

You'll be composing, arranging, and printing in no time!

New in this version:

✦ Lyrics (up to four lyric lines per staff).

✦ Measure numbers, and a Go to Measure command.

✦ Flexible Slurs (across bar lines, rests, repeats, etc.).

✦ Many new style expressions, including Fermatas, Breath Marks, Cresc, Decresc., Accel, Legato, etc., (many of which are supported by playback).

✦ Control of both MIDI key velocity and volume from the dynamics marks, and audio support for both of these in Cresc. and Decresc. dynamic marks.

✦ Edit any existing notation or expression mark on a staff.

✦ User control of note stem directions.

✦ Chords composed of a note, or notes, and a smaller duration rest.

✦ A generic Text Expression item where you can add your own text expressions.

✦ All notation symbols now use True Type fonts, so you have much more control over the size of a score.

✦ A note beam inside of a triplet grouping.

✦ Use the copy feature from Print Preview to create a bitmap file for import into other applications (for registered users only).

✦ Several GPF fixes and maintenance features.

Registration

Upgrading to the registered version is still priced at $39. See online Help and associ-
ated order forms for details on how to order. If you wish to purchase a site license for
NoteWorthy Composer, please contact us directly for a quote. We will need to know
the number of stations which you are interested in licensing.

Minimum hardware requirements

A PC equipped with an 80386 CPU, a mouse, and 3 MB of RAM.

Hardware recommendations

A sound card or MIDI port; A Windows Supported Printer; A VGA or better color
monitor; 4 MB of RAM.

Upgrade instructions for owners of previous versions

Before installing this software, make sure you have your registration codes from the
certificate that was mailed to you. You will need your codes to re-register your system
for use with NoteWorthy Composer after installing this new version. We recommend
that you retain your existing application files until after you have successfully installed and used this new version. By default, the setup procedure will install this new
version in a directory different from the default directories used in previous versions
of NoteWorthy Composer. Once you are satisfied with the performance of this new
version, you should go ahead and remove the previous version, as described in its
original help file. You can review the file WHATSNEW.WRI if you want to find out what
is new in this release prior to installing it.

For ordering, contact, registration, and more detailed information, see the appropriate
file for this program on the companion CD-ROM.

Operation: Inner Space

Inner Space is a strategic action game made just for Windows with super fast action
on any 386 or better. Go inside your computer to capture or destroy all the icons on
your hard disk. Terrific sound, female voice-overs, music. Game also makes great
screen saver! Includes ship factory, race tracks, and battle zones. Created by the
developers of After Dark for Windows, this program is the first Windows action game
to be a Ziff-Davis Shareware Awards finalist.

Category: Games
Type: Shareware
Location on CD: \InSpace
To install: Run d:\Inspace\SETUP.EXE
To run: Click on Start⇨Programs⇨Games⇨Inner Space

If this game seems to suddenly disappear on your screen, don't panic. It's just the Inner Space screen saver kicking in. Moving the mouse or pressing a key will end the screen saver. You can right-click on the desktop and choose Properties to pick a different screen saver. Awesome!

Starting to play

Run Inner Space (INSPACE.EXE) from Windows. During the game intro, press Esc to start a new game. Select a ship to fly into Inner Space. To start playing, just use the arrow keys (Thrust=UP, Turn=LEFT, RIGHT, Brake=DOWN). Use Shift or spacebar to shoot. For more information about the game, see the online Help (press F1 or F2).

Screen savers

Inner Space comes with a configurable screen saver interface so that a changing game demonstration can be your screen saving display.

Ship Factory

With the Ship Factory, you can compare the characteristics of all the ships in the game and also make custom ships for use in Inner Space!

Tech support

We provide tech suppport by fax, e-mail, and regular mail. If you have access to CompuServe, go to Gamdpub and look in section 18 (Software Dynamics) for Inner Space upgrades, hints, and technical support. Keeping users happy with the game is top priority for us because Inner Space is shareware. We do not make any money when you download or try the game, only if you choose to order it and recommend that your friends order it, too. Please appreciate that it took years to develop the game and we work hard all the time to test and improve it, as well as field questions from users. We're really sorry when anyone experiences a problem with the game and we'll work hard to fix it. Before releasing any version of Inner Space, we rigorously test it. Some users still experience problems because there are so many combinations of computers, video drivers, sound drivers, and operating system versions, and there are so many things you could do in the game. If you report a bug to us, we will do our best to fix it, but keep in mind that the problem may occur because of an incompatible sound or video card, some other software running on your computer, or it could be a bug that depends on a subtle sequence of events. We will be more inclined and more capable to fix your bug if you tell us all the details about what you did in the game, exactly where it crashed, and provide as much detail as possible about your computer. A user might tell us "I ran it and it crashed." Obviously, such a bug report doesn't help us fix it. Upon further questioning, the user might indicate that what they meant was that one time out of 1000, the game crashed right after selecting a ship in the intro. With that, we at least have a specific part of the game to look at, but it's hard to repeat the problem. If the user then told us a sequence of events that would make it crash everytime, we could probably repeat the problem here. Any problem we can repeat, we can and will fix. If you report a bug to us, it didn't show up in our testing and we can't fix it unless you tell us how to repeat it here. Also, please do not call the order line to report bugs. We provide unlimited tech support by e-mail, fax, or our main voice number, but the toll-free line is for orders only. We will do everything possible to fix reported bugs, especially when users are considerate and provide the information we need to work on a fix.

NOTE: Bugs reported via e-mail receive top priority and make it easiest both for you to give us specific information on the problem and for us to get back to you in a timely manner.

Registered users

If you are updating a registered copy of the game, please follow the install instructions. The updater should update the game to the latest version and preserve the registered status of the game. However, we do not guarantee that specific upgrades will work for all users. After installing the upgrade, if the game seems to be unregistered, reinstall from your master disk and the game should be registered again. Try to update it again. If the updater again makes the game unregistered, reinstall from your master disk and do not try the update again. In such a case, we will replace your master disk for free, provided you send your master disk back and pay the shipping cost to send out a new master disk with the latest version ($4).

Memory

If the game halts with an error, it may be that Windows is low on memory. Please check that Windows is set up to use at least 2MB of virtual memory. To see or change Virtual Memory settings, open the 386 Enhanced item from the Windows Control Panel (CONTROL.EXE).

Video drivers

There may be problems with some video cards. We can devise workarounds for such cards if we know about the problem. If there is a crash or error when the game is loading graphics, please try to reproduce the problem and tell us so that we can get working on a fix.

MIDI music

If Inner Space's music has incorrect or missing instruments, check your MIDI mapper settings (in Windows Control Panel). For Enhanced MIDI sound cards, use channels 1-10, Basic MIDI sound cards use channels 11-16.

No sound

You need a Windows-compatible sound card to hear Inner Space's audio. If you have a sound card that works with other Windows apps, but don't hear any audio in Inner Space, you may have an older sound card which might not report itself correctly to Windows. Therefore, to force Inner Space to play audio, add AllowSound=1 to your (Inner Space) section of INSPACE.INI (in your Windows directory).

Various sound problems

Inner Space uses the Windows wavemixer to play up to eight sounds at once. The wavemixer is from Microsoft and not compatible with all systems. If you get an error referencing wavemix, or the sounds start and stop in a jerky way, set the MixChannels to 1 (in Game Setup, Audio subdialog) so that sound is played without using the wavemixer.

Deinstalling

If you need to deinstall Inner Space, just delete the Inner Space directory and all files and subdirectories of it (C:\SPACE by default). Also, make sure InnerSpace is not set as the screen saver (in Windows Control Panel). Set the screensaver to None or any other saver display to keep Windows from trying to use Inner Space as a screen saver.

For ordering, contact, registration, and more detailed information, see the appropriate file for this program on the companion CD-ROM.

Paint Shop Pro v3.0

The complete Windows graphics program for image creation, viewing, and manipulation. Features include painting with eight brushes, photo retouching, image enhancement and editing, color enhancement, image browser, batch conversion, and scanner support. Included are 20 standard filters and 12 deformations. Supports plug-in filters. Over 30 file formats supported. Winner SIA & ZiffNet awards. From JASC, Inc.<ASP>

Category: Graphics
Type: Shareware
Location on CD: \Paintshp
To install: Run d:\paintshp\SETUP.EXE
To run: Click on Start⇨Programs⇨ Paint Shop Pro⇨Paint Shop Pro 3.

Impressive alternative to the Windows 95 Paint program as a general-purpose graphics tool. No snags here. Information on purchasing, and other products is available in Help.

PKZip 2

PKZIP 2. The next generation in compression software. This is a DOS program. Shareware installation requires you to create a folder and copy PKZ204G.EXE from the \pkzip folder on the CD to the new folder on your hard disk. Then run PKZ204G.EXE on your hard disk to decompress into program (.exe and .com) and documentation (.txt and .doc) files. To run or view documentation, browse to the Pkware folder after you're copied and run the PKZ204G.EXE file.

Category: Communications
Type: Shareware
Location on CD: \Pkware
To install: This is a DOS program. To install, to create a folder named PKWare on your hard disk (c:). Copy d:\PKZip\PKZ204G.EXE to that folder. Then run c:\pkware\pkz204g
To run: Use My Computer to browse to the PKWare folder. Double-click on an icon there

PKZip is the industry standard compression/decompression program. Files that have the .ZIP extension are compacted with PKZip or a similar program (such as WinZip). PKZip and PKUnzip are both DOS programs.

Documentation excerpts

PKZIP is shareware, and if you use PKZIP regularly we strongly encourage you to register it. With registration you will receive the latest version of the software, a comprehensive printed manual, one free upgrade of PKZIP, PKUNZIP, & PKSFX, premium access to the PKWARE Support BBS, and an optional Authenticity Verification Name and Serial Number. Also included in the registered version are several utility programs not provided in the shareware version.

This file contains some answers to frequently asked questions about PKZIP 2.0, and hints for most efficient use of the software.

Q: Are PKZIP and PKUNZIP completely compatible with older versions?

A: PKZIP and PKUNZIP are completely downwardly compatible, but not upwardly. What does this mean? This means that if you compress something with PKZIP 2.0, you will need PKUNZIP 2.0 or later to extract it. However, PKUNZIP 2.0 will uncompress any .ZIP file made by any version of PKZIP 2.0 or earlier. Therefore, If you have the latest version of PKUNZIP, you need not worry about not being able to decompress any .ZIP file.

Q: I get "Warning, I don't know how to handle" when trying to extract files.

A: Most likely you are using PKUNZIP 1.1 or an earlier version to attempt to extract a .ZIP file created by PKZIP 2.0 or later. Make sure that you are using the latest version of PKUNZIP. Also be sure you do not have multiple copies of pkunzip in different areas on your machine. It may find and use an older version before it finds the newer version.

Q: How do I make self-extracting files?

A: This is a two step process. First create a .ZIP file normally with PKZIP, and then use ZIP2EXE to create a self extracting .EXE file. For example, if you have a .ZIP file called STUFF.ZIP and then entered **zip2exe stuff**, it would create STUFF.EXE, which is a PKSFX self-extracting file.

Q: I get "Bad command or Filename" when I type in PKZIP or PKUNZIP.

A: This is a DOS error message, and means that PKZIP/PKUNZIP is not in the current directory, or locatable by the DOS path variable. Consult your DOS manual for use of the path statement.

Q: I get "Error in zip, use PKZIPFIX", when attempting to compress files.

A: This may be the result of an incorrect command line. The name of the .ZIP file you are creating needs to be *before* the names of the file you want to compress. For example, if you want to compress FILE1 and FILE2 into STUFF.ZIP, use:

```
pkzip stuff file1 file2
```

and not:

```
pkzip file1 file2 stuff
```

Q: How can I use PKZIP to create full and incremental backups?

A: When creating a full backup with PKZIP, use the -a+ option. This will turn off the file's archive bit after it is compressed.

For example:

```
C:\> pkzip a:fullback -&s -a+
```

will backup the entire C: drive to a multi-disk .ZIP file called FULLBACK.ZIP on the A: drive. Then, whenever a file is updated or created by DOS, it will turn on the file's archive bit, indicating that the file has changed since it was last backed up. You can create an incremental backup set with PKZIP by using the -i switch to only compress files that have their archive bit set, and turn off the archive bit after it is compressed. For example:

```
C:\> pkzip a:incback1 -&s -I
```

will backup all the files on drive C: that are new or have been modified since the last backup was performed.

Q: What is an AV?

A: The Authenticity Verification feature allows you to create .ZIP files that PKUNZIP or PKSFX can test for authenticity while extracting. This provides for detection of tampered, hacked, or virus infected files.

Q: How do I use my AV? Where is my AV?

A: The first thing you need to do is fill out AUTHVERI.FRM included in the PKZIP distribution package with the necessary information and mail or FAX this to PKWARE. We will then process your information and send you back the information needed to use with the PUTAV to install your AV information. AV numbers are not the same as your serial number on the diskette.

Q: I ran PUTAV.EXE on the new PKZIP but it did not work; why?

A: First of all, you need to make sure that you are using the PUTAV.EXE from the registered 2.0 version. You can not use the PUTAV.EXE from 1.1, to try and install the AV numbers into version 2.0 of PKZIP. The AV process has changed and you need to use the PUTAV.EXE from version 2.0. Also, PUTAV.EXE will not work with the shareware version of PKZIP.EXE, you need to have the registered PKZIP.EXE file.

Q: I extracted a .ZIP file, but it didn't recreate the directory structure stored in the .ZIP file.

A: First make sure the files were compressed using the -rp option in PKZIP. Next, be sure you use the PKUNZIP option -d when extracting files. The -d option tells PKUNZIP to re-create stored directories on extraction.

Q: I lost the last diskette, or have errors on the last diskette in my backup set; or lost or have problems with one or more other diskettes in my backup set; or I hit Ctrl C and aborted PKZIP while I was creating the backup set. How can I recover the files that are still intact in the backup set?

A: PKZIPFIX can be used to restore the .ZIP file index after the .ZIP files on each diskette have been concatenated into one .ZIP file. Starting with the lowest number backup diskette (normally disk #001, PKZIP places the volume label PKBACK# nnn onto each disk, where nnn is the disk number), copy this file to your hard disk (or network disk). For example, say the .ZIP filename for the backup set is BACK1.ZIP, on drive B:. Enter:

```
copy b:back1.zip
```

Then, insert each diskette in ascending numerical order and enter:

```
copy/b back1.zip+b:back1.zip.
```

After you have gone through the all the disks in the backup set, then use PKZIPFIX on this file by entering: **pkzipfix back1**. This will create the file PKFIXED.ZIP which can then be extracted by PKUNZIP. Any files that were on missing or damaged diskettes will most likely have errors, but any files that were wholly contained on intact diskettes should be extractable. This procedure will also work on a subset of the backup set, if for example, you only wanted to recover the files on disks 10 through 15.

Q: When is it valid to use a '-' or '+' switch at the end of a option?

A: With PKZIP and PKUNZIP certain options may be followed by a trailing - or + to modify the original option. The basic rule to follow in knowing whether a - or + will effect the original option is, if the option can be modified in the PKZIP.CFG file, then a - or + will effect it. Below is a list of options that can be affected by a trailing '-' symbol. As always consult your manual for more information about individual switches.

Option	Meaning
-I-	Do not clear the archive attribute
-k-	Override ZIPDATE=KEEP in PKZIP.CFG
-m-	Do not remove directories after compression
-o-	verride ZIPDATE=LATEST in PKZIP.CFG
-p-	Override PATHS=ALL or PATHS=RECURSE
-q-	Override ANSI=ENABLED
-r-	Override RECURSE=ON

-(-	Override SLOWMEMCPY=ON
-&f-	Override FORMAT=ON
-&l-	Override BACKUP=LOW
-&s-	Override BACKUP=FULL
-&u-	Override BACKUP=UNCONDITIONAL
-&v-	Override BACKUP=VERIFY
-&w-	Override BACKUP=WIPE
-&-	Turns off all BACKUP= options

Here is a list of the options that can be modified by a trailing '+' symbol.

Option	Meaning
-a+	Clear archive attributes for files archived
-3+	Override 386=DISABLE
-++	Override EMS=DISABLE
—+	Override XMS=DISABLE
-~+	Override NETWORK=DISABLE
-)+	Override DPMI=DISABLE (also in PKUNZIP)

Q: What is the difference between the PKZIP option -b and the PKTMP= environment variable?

A: PKZIP creates two different types of temporary files, and allows you to specify the location of these two types separately. The two situations where PKZIP creates temp files are:

✦ When a file is being compressed by PKZIP.

✦ When an existing .ZIP file is being modified.

When PKZIP is in the process of compressing a file, it might need to create a temporary file to store information that does not fit in memory. PKZIP will create these temporary files in the directory pointed to by the PKTMP= environment variable, or in the current directory if this variable is not present.

For example, the command:

```
set pktmp=d:\
```

will tell PKZIP to create these temporary files on the D:\ drive. In general, you can get the best performance from PKZIP by having PKTMP= point to a RAM disk or very fast disk in your system, unless you are creating or updating a .ZIP file on a Novell network drive (see the question regarding Netware support earlier in this document). When PKZIP updates an existing .ZIP file, it creates a new temporary .ZIP file and copies files from the existing .ZIP file or (re)compresses files into this new file. If the PKZIP process were to be interrupted in any way, the original .ZIP file is still intact.

Once the new .ZIP file is created, PKZIP deletes the old .ZIP file and renames the new temporary .ZIP file to the original name. This, however, requires that at least twice the size of the original .ZIP file be free on the drive where the .ZIP file is. If say you had a 400K .ZIP file on a 720K diskette, you will get an insufficient disk space error when trying to modify this .ZIP file, even if you only wanted to add one small file. The -b option tells PKZIP to create the new temporary on a drive different from where the original .ZIP file is located, and then copy the new .ZIP file to the destination drive when done. For example:

```
pkzip b:stuff *.bat -bc:
```

Tells PKZIP to add the files *.BAT to the file B:STUFF.ZIP, and create the new temporary .ZIP file on drive C:. Using the -b option slows down PKZIP, but allows you to update .ZIP files that are larger than the available free space on a disk.

Q: PKZIP/PKUNZIP 2.0 have several options for DPMI, EMS, XMS, 386, NETWARE, etc. What are these things and why does PKZIP/PKUNZIP use them?

A: DPMI stands for DOS Protected Mode Interface. It is a facility that allows standard DOS programs to execute code in 32-bit protected mode, and have access to protected mode resources in the computer. Protected mode code runs faster than corresponding real mode code. PKZIP/PKUNZIP use DPMI to execute some code in protected mode for better speed. With DPMI, PKZIP/PKUNZIP can run up to 25% faster or more using 32-bit protected mode code versus using 16-bit real mode code. EMS and XMS stand for Expanded Memory Specification and Extended Memory Specification respectively. These are implemented using a memory manager on an 80386 or 80486 CPU, or using memory management hardware on an 8088 or 80286 system. EMS and XMS allows standard DOS programs to use memory outside of the conventional 640K memory space. PKZIP/PKUNZIP will use this memory in order to allow the software to run in less conventional memory. This is most useful when shelling out of other applications to run PKZIP or PKUNZIP and there is very little conventional memory free. PKZIP and PKUNZIP support 80386 and 80486 CPU's and has special code that takes advantages of these chips. This code runs fastest in protected mode with DPMI (see above). However, even when running in real mode PKZIP/PKUNZIP will use 32-bit code for better speed. Using 32-bit code can allow PKZIP/PKUNZIP to run up to 10 percent faster or more compared to executing 16-bit code. PKZIP also is Novell Netware aware. When creating or updating .ZIP files on a network drive, use of Novell functions can make PKZIP run several times faster than it would otherwise. To get maximum performance when creating or updating a .ZIP file on a network drive, make sure that the PKTMP= environment variable points to a drive in the same server as the .ZIP file; or if you do not have the PKTMP= environment variable set, that the current directory is on a drive that is in the same server as the .ZIP file.

Q: My PKZIP says it detects certain versions of DPMI, EMS, or XMS that are different than the version numbers for my memory manager or driver. Why is this?

A: There is a difference between the version number of a driver and the version of the DPMI/EMS/XMS specification that it supports. For example, QEMM version 6.02 supports version 3.00 of the XMS specification and version 4.00 of the EMS specification. QDPMI version 1.01 supports version 0.90 of the DPMI specification. The version of the specification supported affects what functions that driver will support. PKZIP/PKUNZIP display the version of the specification supported, not the version of the memory manager or driver that provides this support.

Q: PKZIP/PKUNZIP display different DPMI/EMS/XMS versions when in Windows than outside of Windows. Why is this?

A: Windows provides its own support of DPMI, EMS and XMS, regardless of any memory managers or drivers loaded prior to running Windows. The specification versions supported by Windows may be different than those supported by memory managers or device drivers loaded prior to Windows, and hence PKZIP/PKUNZIP will display different specification versions inside of Windows than in DOS.

For ordering, contact, registration, and more detailed information, see the appropriate file for this program on the companion CD-ROM.

Poke-It! Poker

Las Vegas Video Poker for Windows! From the makers of World Empire II, this immensely addictive game accurately simulates the real thing. And it's a lot cheaper! Take my word for it. I've lost on both! Note: needs VBRUN200.DLL. from Viable Software Alternatives.

> **Category:** Games
> **Type:** Shareware
> **Location on CD:** \Poker2
> **To install:** No installation program provided. You need to create a folder on your hard drive (such as Poker2), then copy all files from d:\Poker2 to that folder
> **To run:** After copying to your hard disk, browse to and double-click on POKER.EXE

Check out other Viable products on the Internet at http://delta.com/viable/viable.htm.

Documentation excerpts

Aaarghhh! Another Windows Card Game!

Note: This evaluation copy of Poke-It Poker! doesn't pay when you hit a Royal Flush . . .
Register soon!

Overview

You walk down the Strip, crowds of people passing you by, jostling you, but you don't
notice. Your mind is on one thing. You walk up to the door . . . oh, any door will do:
Caesar's Palace, Sam's Town, The Sahara, The Golden Nugget, The Flamingo . . .

You enter the casino, ooh, the din is terrible - "bing, bing, bing . . .",
"chunkachunkachunk . . .", screeches and squeals, glasses clattering . . .

Then you arrive at your favorite machine — you know — the lucky one you always
play, abandoning it for another only when it throws an unlucky tantrum. You slide
into the chair, insert your first dollar token . . .

Eeek! You are a Video Poker freak! Your wallet attests! But, after all, tonight could be
that lucky night . . .

Welcome to Poke-It Poker! The simulated Video Poker Machine!

Styled from the real thing (specifications from machine's at Sam's Town and the 7-11
at Eastern & Desert Inn Avenues - right here in Las Vegas!), Poke-It Poker will give you
hours of gambling pleasure — economically!!!

The game

We've endeavored to keep Poke-It Poker as faithful to the real machines as possible —
you can almost hear the lady walking by every twenty minutes or so, calling: "Cock-
tails!" — which are free, of course, as long as you keep popping those coins!

Two styles of Video Poker are simulated in Poke-It Poker!, Joker's Wild and regular
Draw Poker. (I prefer Draw Poker.)

Draw Poker utilizes a 52-card deck, while Joker's Wild uses the same, but with a Joker
to help you out. The payoffs differ for each game, however, and are shown at the top
of your screen.

There is a chart giving the value for each five card combination that will pay. If you
take a look, you'll see names like Full House, Royal Flush, Straight, and so on.

Winning hands available in Joker's Wild explained

Kings or Better: a pair of Kings or a pair of Aces. Pays one coin.

Two Pair: two groups of two cards showing the same number (or picture) for example, 2 of hearts and 2 of diamonds (one pair) plus Ten of Clubs and Ten of Hearts (second pair). Pays one coin.

Three Of A Kind: three cards from different suits displaying the same number, such as three Jacks. Pays two coins.

Straight: five cards in consecutive order, any combination of suits. Pays three coins.

Flush: five cards same suit. Pays five coins.

Full House: three of a kind plus a pair, such as three kings plus a pair of sixes. Pays seven coins.

Four Of A Kind: four cards from different suits displaying the same number, such as four Jacks. Pays 20 coins.

Straight Flush: five cards in consecutive order, same suit. Pays 50 coins.

Royal Flush With Joker: Ace, King, Queen, Jack, or Ten, same suit with a Joker filling the missing space. Pays 100 coins.

Five Of A Kind: Four cards from different suits displaying the same number, such as Four Jacks — but with a Joker representing the fifth card. Pays 200 coins.

Royal flush: Ace, King, Queen, Jack, ten, same suit. Pays 500 coins.

A Joker can assume the value of any card in any suit. For example, a joker and a King becomes a pair of Kings or better. A Joker and two sixes becomes Three of a kind.

Winning hands available in Draw Poker explained

Jacks or Better: a pair of Kings, Aces, Queens, or Jacks. Pays one coin.

Two Pair: two groups of two cards showing the same number (or picture) for example, Two of Hearts and Two of Diamonds (one pair) plus Ten of Clubs and Ten of Hearts (second pair). Pays two coins.

Three Of A Kind: three cards from different suits displaying the same number, such as three Jacks. Pays two coins.

Straight: five cards in consecutive order, any combination of suits. Pays four coins.

Flush: five cards same suit. Pays five coins.

Full House: three of a kind plus a pair, such as three Kings plus a pair of sixes. Pays eight coins.

Four Of A Kind: four cards from different suits displaying the same number, such as four Jacks. Pays 25 coins.

Straight Flush: five cards in consecutive order, same suit. Pays 50 coins.

Royal Flush: Ace, King, Queen, Jack, ten, same suit. Pays 250 coins.

In both games all winnings are multiplied by the number of coins played. For example, if you get Kings Or Better after playing one coin, you'll win one coin. If, however, you get Kings Or Better after playing five coins (the maximum bet allowed), you'll win five.

To play the game

You start the game with 100 credits representing $100. This is your stake.

When Poke-It Poker! appears you'll need to be aware of the following buttons:

The Bet Five Credits and Bet One Credit Buttons: In order to play the game, you need to *wager* or bet an amount that you're willing to risk. The maximum bet is five dollars. If you want to bet the maximum, press the Bet Five Credits button and then press the Deal button. To bet less, press the Bet One Credit button until the amount you want to wager on the next deal is shown on the screen, then press the Deal button.

The Deal Button: When you've wagered the amount you want, press this button to deal your first hand.

The Five Hold Buttons: After the first deal, you'll decide which cards you want to hold and which you'll discard for the second deal. Press the Hold button that corresponds to the card on the screen that you want to hold. The word Held will appear on the screen above that card. When you've held all the cards you want to, press the Deal button again and the cards you didn't hold will be replaced with newly dealt cards. NOTE: The F5 thru F9 keys also hold the corresponding card shown on the screen.

The Game button: This button controls game functions. When the Game menu appears, you'll have the following choices:

Reset Credits to 100 (does just that!)

Save Current Credits on Exit (you'll start the next time with that many)

Enable Sound (if an "X" appears in this box, the Windows Beep will augment game play. Otherwise silence will prevail)

Maximize Game Window (with an "X" here the Poke-It Poker window will fill the screen)

Okay (closes the Game Menu)

Help (displays this manual and the accompanying README file)

Exit (quits the game and returns to Windows)

Play Joker's Wild/Play Draw Poker (toggles between the two game modes)

Winning strategies

Ha! If I knew how to win this stuff I wouldn't have to write software!

Seriously, though, you've just gotta know when to hold 'em and know when to fold 'em!

These are dollar machines! So be careful, you'll go broke fast!

For ordering, contact, registration, and more detailed information, see the appropriate file for this program on the companion CD-ROM.

PROcalc V1.0

Windows printing financial calculator and adding machine. Easy to use via keyboard or with the mouse. User configurable display; print and save tally roll; full financial functions; and user definable macros for repetitive tasks. Small display mode to allow use on-screen with other applications showing. From Jupiter Software. <ASP>

Category: Business
Type: Shareware
Location on CD: \Procalc
To install: Run d:\procalc\setup
To run: Click on Start⇨Programs⇨Jupiter⇨PROcalc

PROcalc for DOS

A DOS memory resident TSR version of PROcalc is also available. This provides similar features to those contained in the Windows version but in a form that can be popped up over any DOS text based application. Please contact us or one of our agents to obtain a shareware copy of this program.

No manual!

Documentation is not normally distributed with the evaluation programs. A copy of the text of the manual is provided on the disk in a file called PROCALC.WRI. This is in Windows Write format and may be loaded and printed using that program. For your convenience, an icon will be inserted in the Jupiter program group providing quick access to the manual. The information included in the manual is also provided in the help file which can be accessed by clicking on the Help button included in the calculator displays.

Please print the contents of LICENSE.TXT before proceeding.

You may order a registered copy of the programs by completing the order form (REGISTER.TXT) and returning it to one of the organizations listed therein. Registration brings you a registered copy of the latest version of the program plus copies of our other shareware. You will also receive a printed manual and the right to download registered versions of all releases 1.xx. We will also place you on our mailing list for notification of upgrades and new products.

For ordering, contact, registration, and more detailed information, see the appropriate file for this program on the companion CD-ROM.

Pursuit

Demo version of Pursuit, a certified Microsoft Office compatible account and contact management system. Combines account, contact, and scheduling features for enterprise-wide sales and service tracking and follow-up. Integrates seamlessly with Microsoft Word, Microsoft Mail, At Work Fax, and OLE. Software Development Kit (SDK) is available for customization by experienced Microsoft Access programmers. Pursuit's minimum memory requirements are 12MB of RAM. (C) 1995 Information Management Consultants, Inc. Version 1.5.

"...an example of a real beauty of a program built in [Microsoft] Office..." *Computer Reseller News*

> **Category:** Business
> **Type:** Demo
> **Location on CD:** \Pursuit
> **To install:** Run d:\pursuit\SETUP.EXE
> **To run:** Click on Start⇨Programs⇨Pursuit⇨Pursuit Demo

This demo is identical to full retail version except that it limits the number of accounts you can have. A great example of the "Brave New Officeware" discussed in Chapter 13. Give it a try!

Documentation excerpts (from README.WRI)

Welcome to Pursuit 1.5. This version contains many new features requested by our customers, as well as performance improvements and general fixes and enhancements. In addition, this version of Pursuit is officially certified Microsoft Office Compatible. Please see below for information on features and enhancements new to version 1.5.

Every effort has been made to make Pursuit as fast and efficient as possible. To provide speedy performance while running Pursuit, we have sacrificed load time slightly. Pursuit will take a minute or two to load on some systems; this is because

Pursuit is loading commonly used objects and forms (views) so that they are immediately available when you want to use them. This is not a problem with Pursuit, simply the best approach for maximum performance while running the system.

Known issues

Selecting Print Setup from the File menu does not work properly. To change the printer that a report uses, select Print Preview for the report and then select Print Setup from the file menu. This will allow you to change the printer for the report for that time you are logged into Pursuit. You may, alternately, change your default printer and all reports will then print to that new default printer. This issue is being addressed by IMC.

Hardware requirements

In order to run Pursuit for Windows, you need the following minimum configuration:

✦ MS-DOS 3.1 or higher.

✦ Microsoft Windows 3.1, or Windows for Workgroups, Windows 95, or Windows NT version 3.1 or higher.

✦ A 386SX personal computer or faster microprocessor.

✦ At least 12 MB RAM.

✦ At least 12MB of free space on your hard drive.

✦ A $3^1/_2$" high density floppy drive (the system is not available on $5^1/_4$ diskettes).

✦ A VGA or higher resolution video adapter.

✦ A Microsoft compatible mouse.

Performance issues

Pursuit for Windows is a large database application, and like all applications of its size and complexity, Pursuit uses a significant amount of a computer's resources. Pursuit has shown excellent performance on 486/33's or faster, great performance on slower 486's and fair performance on fast 386's. Note that Pursuit requires at least a 386SX or faster processor. It should be noted, however, that Pursuit is resource intensive; if your system is not optimized, Pursuit will definitely run slower than it would on an optimized system.

If Pursuit runs slowly, or you get out-of-memory errors, your system may not have enough memory. The minimum requirements are 12 MB of main memory; however, 16 MB or more is highly recommended.

Raku Master

Raku Master v1.1. The object of the Raku is to flip all the red tiles back to gray in as few moves as possible. You can flip either diagonally, or up and down, starting at any tile. The Raku Master will tell you the exact number of moves he needs to solve the puzzle. If you don't believe him, then let him solve the first 10 of 50 puzzles for you. This game is a challenging test of your logic skills.

> **Category:** Games
> **Type:** Shareware
> **Location on CD:** \Raku
> **To install:** No installation program provided. You'll need to copy all the files from d:\Raku to a folder on your hard disk
> **To run:** After copying all the files from d:\Raku, run RAKU.EXE on your hard disk

More mental magic from Soleau Software (DOS game).

Raku Master directions: the objective

The objective of Raku Master is to flip all the tiles on the game board back to the color gray in as few moves as possible.

Game play

Select one of 50 puzzles by pressing the Select Puzzle key. The puzzle will load itself onto the game board. A yellow square will be located in the upper left hand corner of the board. Use the arrow keys to move the marker to the desired place on the board where you want to flip the tiles. To mark that tile, press the spacebar key. This will turn the yellow marker to green.

If you make a mistake and want to unmark the tile, then press the spacebar again.

To designate the direction of the flips, use the numeric keys on your computer. (Arrow keys for up/down/lft/rgt)

Starting at that tile, the other tiles in that row or column will flip over to the opposite color (red or gray).

Solving the puzzle

On top of the game board, the Raku Master will tell you how many moves you have to solve the puzzle. If you solve the puzzle in that many moves or less, the Raku Master will consider the puzzle solved and it will be recorded as *Solved* in the Status Box.

Options/keys

All key designations are shown at the bottom of the screen at all times. By pressing the <O>ption key, you get the following:

<T>oggle Sound (On/Off)

<S>olutions (Solutions for 1-10)

<G>ames by Soleau Software.

Solutions

In this shareware version of Raku Master I, we provided solutions to the first 10 puzzles. By pressing the Option key and then selecting Solutions, you will see how the Raku Master solves the current puzzle on the game board.

Raku Master puzzles get harder as you go along. You don't have to solve them in order, but by trying out the first one or two, you can get an idea how the game is played.

Note: Windows 3.x users

Running Raku Master from Windows 3.x may cause unexpected results. The game should be played by loading it directly from the DOS prompt or the DOS window in Windows 95.

For ordering, contact, registration, and more detailed information, see the appropriate file for this program on the companion CD-ROM.

RockMan

Rock Man v1.2 is an exciting logic strategy game from Soleau Software. Use your ingenuity to help Rock Man collect all the rare moths flying around each of the 15 mind-bending mountain puzzles. Use ropes, axes and other objects while avoiding dangerous lava rocks. Packed with features! Do you have what it takes solve each puzzle? A pure, animated logic puzzle for all ages!

Category: Games
Type: Shareware
Location on CD: \RockMan
To install: No installation program provided. You'll need to copy all the files from d:\RockMan to a folder on your hard disk
To run: Copy all files from d:\RockMan your hard disk, and run ROCKMAN.EXE from your hard disk

This is a very clever (and addicting) DOS strategy game. Once you get the game started, you can type **N** to choose new game, then type **D** to choose demo.

Documentation excerpts

Program by William Soleau © 1994-1995 Shareware Version

Requires: EGA/VGA & 512 Ram

Requires Files: Rockman.ov0, Rockman.ov1, Rockman.ov2, Rockman.ov3, Rockman.ov4, Rockman.ov5, Rockman.ov6, Rockman.ov7, Rockman.ov8, Rockman.ov9, Rockman.jft, Rockman1.jft

Rock Man Directions

Objective
The objective of Rock Man is to collect all the pink moths located in each puzzle. Once gathered, Rock Man must then reach the red flag to solve the puzzle.

Selecting Puzzle
Select a puzzle room by pressing the New Puzzle key. Using your arrow keys, select the puzzle you want and then press Enter to load that puzzle onto the game board.

Game Play
When the puzzle is loaded you move Rock Man by using the <Arrow Keys>. Rock Man can jump up only one rock at a time, so you will have to use your ingenuity to make it possible for him to capture all the rare moths scattered around the puzzle. Once collected, the blue flag located somewhere in the puzzle will turn to Red. This means that Rock Man must somehow reach the red flag in order to consider the puzzle solved.

Objects
Green Rocks: Rock Man can push these in any direction.

Gray Rocks: Rock Man cannot move these.

Red Rocks: Lava Rocks are dangerous if Rock Man steps on them.

Pink Moths: Rock Man must collect all these before reaching flag.

Pick Axe: Rock Man can use these to obliterate any green rock, provided that he is not on a rope or ladder. To use a pick axe, face in the direction of the green rock and then push the letter P.

Rope: Rock Man can use these to help him climb higher. He cannot use a pick axe or push any green rocks while climbing on the rope. To use a rope push the letter R. The rope will rise above Rock Man until it either hits an object or the top of the game board.

Ladders: These rope ladders have been left by previous climbers. He can use these to climb up or down. He cannot use pick axes or ropes while on the ladder. He can push green rocks while on ladder.

Bridges: These bridges will allow Rock Man to cross over them only once. After he has passed over them, they will crumble and disappear from the game board.

Smaller Green: These smaller green pebble rocks are unstable and pebble rocks will crash down on Rock Man if he walks under them. They will not fall on him if there is an object between him and these pebble rocks . . . this includes, moths, picks, and rocks.

Blue Flag: The Flag located on the game board will remain blue until all the moths have been collected. Once all the moths are gathered, it will then change to red.

Red Flag: This is Rock Man's final objective once all the moths have been collected.

Jumping
Rock Man will jump in the direction he is facing when you press the <Up Arrow> key. If Rock Man is at the side of the game board, he cannot jump up unless he is facing away from the edge of the board.

Demo puzzle
Pressing the <D>emo Key will start the Demo Puzzle. This will take you through a practice puzzle one step at a time. This will introduce you to the basic objects you'll encounter during game play.

Solutions
The solutions to the first three puzzles are provided in the Shareware version of Rock Man. Pressing <?> will show you the solutions to the puzzle loaded onto the game board. The Registered version provides solutions to all 35 puzzles!

Solving puzzle
Once a puzzle has been solved, the Main Menu Board will change that puzzle number from Gray to Green. This will allow you to see which puzzles you have not yet solved. There are a total of 15 different puzzles to choose from in the Shareware version. (There are 35 puzzles in the Registered version.)

Main menu keys

<H>ELP: Rock Man Directions

<A>GAIN: Reloads the puzzle you were playing

<N>ew: Loads Puzzle menu to try a new puzzle

<S>OUND: Toggles Sound On or Off

s<O>leau: Information on Soleau Software Games

<Q>UIT: Quits Rock Man program

Note: Windows 3.x users

Running Rock Man from Windows 3.x may cause unexpected results. The game should be played by loading it directly from the DOS prompt or the DOS window in Windows 95.

For ordering, contact, registration, and more detailed information, see the appropriate file for this program on the companion CD-ROM.

Scheduling Employees for Windows

Version 5.00. PC World (Feb.94) wrote "This program shows why Windows has become standard equipment." All time is entered by mouse with easy copy functions. Times and wages are displayed as the schedule progresses. Fictitous employees are loaded during the auto install for practice. A distribution graph displays the hour by hour coverage for each day. Many other features. From Guia International. <ASP>

> **Category:** Business
> **Type:** Shareware
> **Location on CD:** \Schedule
> **To install:** Run d:\schedule\SETUP.EXE
> **To run:** Click on Start⇨Programs⇨Scheduling Employees⇨Scheduling Employees

Documentation excerpts

Introduction

Guia International offers two Employee schedulers:

✦ This program, Scheduling Employees for Windows, was developed for those institutions that have mostly part-time help and keep an eye on the bottom line, time and labor cost as they schedule. Scheduling is done by dragging the mouse to enter working start and stop times. *PC World* magazine, in the February 1994 issue, selected this program as a best business program and commented, "This program is why Windows has become standard equipment."

✦ Employee Scheduling Assistant for Windows is designed for businesses that have for the most part full-time employees and want to do shift assignment, keeping track of vacations, sick days, etc. A shift rotation template allows easy assignments of shifts. A window for each day and for each employee, may contain appointments comments and other information. Schedules are for three years, and may start on any month for a business year. An employee's schedule for a year and a department's for a month may be viewed on a single screen.

The program Scheduling Employees for Windows is widely used in restaurants and other businesses.

The application is designed for managers to schedule personnel resources while monitoring the time and wages as the scheduling process progresses. Daily activities may be detailed by assigning Day Types. Day Types are a single characters, such as V= Vacation. Ten Day Types may be specified for the use in each department.

A graph will display the time and wage distribution for a 24-hour period for each hour and the number of employees scheduled for every 15 minutes.

The scheduling function needs a department with employees to begin scheduling. Schedules are for a one week period. You may schedule up to 150 employees in each of up to 99 departments.

To make the application more user-friendly, the user will not have to deal with directories and subdirectories. If details of a technical nature are needed, see the section entitled Technical information.

The application is divided into two parts:

1. The opening screen. It contains functions related to the application, departments and employees.
2. The Editors perform the scheduling and schedule printing functions.
3. The Graph will show the employee, time and currency distribution for a 24-hour period with the option to print these statistics.

Equipment needed

You will need:

✦ An IBM or compatible PC (286 or higher).

✦ A combination of at least one diskette drive and one fixed(hard) disk.

✦ Microsoft Windows 3.1 or later.

✦ A mouse or pointing device must be attached.

✦ A VGA Monitor.

✦ A printer to print reports and schedules, a laser printer is preferred.

Mouse tracking

Because almost all functions are directed through mouse action, it is a good idea to slow the pointer movement on the screen. To slow down the mouse tracking

1. From the Window Program Manager, select the Control Panel.

2. Click on Mouse.

3. Move the Mouse tracking speed towards Slow.

4. Move the mouse and see if the move feels comfortable.

5. Click on OK to save the setting.

Display matching

If the display does not match the setup as a VGA display, change the Video Driver in the Program Manager to Main. The resolution, should be set at 640 x 480, the character size to normal and colors to 16.

Using the menus

Scheduling Employees for Windows uses drop-down menus. Just point at the heading and press the left mouse button and a further selection can then be made.

The opening screen

The purpose of the Opening screen is to

✦ Set up new departments with Day Types.

✦ Enter, change, or delete employee records.

✦ Print reports, invoices, and this manual with page numbers.

✦ Set up options for time format, overtime, registration entry, age limit setting and day starting hour for the Editors.

✦ Help if needed.

✦ Set up Options.

✦ Exit the application.

Click on Schedule employees to go to the Editor.

The editors

Entering and changing schedules is performed in the Editors. There are two Editors;

- ✦ All Employees for one day.
- ✦ One Employee for one week.

To switch from the Main Editor to the Employee Editor, click the mouse on the employee's name on the left of the screen. To become familiar with the application, some files are added during the installation process. These files created the Example Department with fictitious names for employees and a single Schedule file based on the date of installation.

The department represents a restaurant with servers, cashiers, and cooks. Take a look at the screens, edit times in the Editor, sort based on start and stop times. Note that the Schedule filename is "Year-Month-Day.Weekday" so that when you choose a Schedule file, the oldest dates are on top.

Currency for salaried employees, is only shown as a total in the individual Editor and Schedule Reports. No adjustments are made for Overtime; the currency totals are strictly time scheduled multiplied by the hourly rate. Totals are highlighted with a red background if the totals exceed the Overtime settings under Options.

Click on Graph at the bottom of the screen, and the distribution for that day will be displayed. By clicking the mouse, Assignments you can further break this information down, and even print it.

Edit controls

Note the Scroll bars in the Editor. From left to right you may scroll, to go from midnight to midnight on the top scroll bar (Scrolling hours) or from day to day on the bottom one (Scrolling days). If you point on the arrows, the increments are one, any other place on the top bar equals six Hours; on the bottom bar three Days.

To quickly go from midnight to midnight, two controls on the bottom of the screen can be used. Nineteen employees will fit on a screen; the vertical scroll bar will only be displayed if you have more than nineteen. To quickly go from to first to the last page, use two controls on the bottom of the screen marked First page and Last page.

Display of totals

Also notice some option buttons that you can click. The column next to the Employee name will change based on these option buttons. As you progress with the scheduling process, this column will display daily or weekly accumulated totals for time or currency for employees that have an hourly pay-rate. NOTE! The daily time and currency totals displayed are for that day only, in contrast to the daily totals in the Schedule report that are the shift totals and include time after midnight if the shift started on the previous day.

The time bar

Time is entered and changed in the Editor screen. The representation of time is the Time bar. You may have up to 34 Start and Stops per week for each employee. Since the accumulated time is displayed as an option, unpaid break-times, such as a lunch break, should also be entered.

Note: An arrow is displayed under the Hour-ruler to show the current mouse position. As you enter time by dragging the mouse, a bar under the ruler will show you the progress. After the bar is completed the bar is adjusted to the nearest 15 minutes. You may choose to color of the bar under Options in the opening screen.

Making a new time bar

Start and stop times are entered by pointing the mouse at an editor line, pressing the left button and holding it down while dragging the mouse from left to right or right to left.

Move a time bar

Pointing to the bar, away from either end and while holding down the left button, will allow movement from left to right. Any conflict or override with existing bar will be resolved automatically.

Changing a time bar

Pointing the mouse to the beginning or the end of a bar will allow stretching or decreasing the bar size.

Deleting a time bar

A quick double click anywhere on the bar will delete the bar.

Pointing to the end of a bar and decreasing the bar size to less than 15 minutes will also delete the bar.

Copy an employee's day of time bars

By pointing the mouse at an employees line with time, press the right mouse button and the bars will be copied. At the same time a message will be displayed, "Holding time for copy." While the message is displayed, you can copy this time to any employee's line that has no time in it by pointing at that line and pressing the right mouse button. You may also go to other days and repeat the process. To copy a new bar, point to the Holding time for copy message and click to reset, then pick up the next bar to be copied.

Move a time bar past midnight

Example: To enter time from 11 p.m. on day one, to 3 a.m. day two. Solution: Enter four hours in day one from 6 p.m. to 10 p.m. Point the mouse to the first hour and move the beginning of the bar to 11 p.m. The remaining time will now appear in day two.

Entering and changing day types

Day Types may be changed directly by pointing the mouse and clicking at the box to the left of the edit area and pressing a valid Day Type character. You may also select DayTypes from the menu on top. All valid Day Types will be displayed for your selection. Pressing the spacebar deletes a Day Type.

Dual Assignments

For employees that consistently have dual assignments, (cook in the morning and cashiers in the afternoon), you may consider entering them twice, than schedule them after a sort on employee number to prevent overlapping time schedules.

Copy a department day schedule

After you have completed the schedule for a day, you can copy that schedule to any other day if that day has no scheduled time in it.

1. Go to the day to copy to.
2. Select Copy from the menu.
3. Select the day to copy from.

Repeat a weekly schedule

Many organizations have rotating schedules that repeat themselves every 2, 3, or 4 weeks. Make up the week one schedule by entering all the time without Day Types such as vacations and so on. Save the schedule by selecting Save as... from the menu and enter 1-1-11 as the filename. Save week two as 2-2-22. This way, these files are always listed on top of the file choices for selection. After loading the file for a new schedule, make all the changes and add vacations and so on. Save the file as the date for that week. Inactive Employees will not be loaded if they are included in a schedule from the past. They will also be filtered out and not saved on the new schedule.

The time and wages distribution graph

By clicking on the Graph button in the Editor, the Time and Wages distribution will be shown. Initially, all assignments will be displayed. By entering each assignment, the graph will show more detail. Each 15 minute period is represented with a graph line. The sequence starting with the first 15 minutes each hour is red, white, blue, black. Salaried employees are excluded from any currency calculations, only hourly Employees are reflected in the currency totals, time includes all employees. A report with the 15 minutes stats will print when you click on Print.

Flagging under-age employees

Government places limitations on the number of hours and the time of day that employees are allowed to work if the employee is below a lawful age. Under Options on the opening screen, you may set the employee age. In the Employee Individual Editor, a warning flag will advise the scheduler if the currently displayed employee is below that age, based on the current system date and the date of birth in the employee record.

Flagging overtime

Under "Options" on the opening screen, you may enter the conditions under which to warn the scheduler that overtime is scheduled. The initial settings are set to off. Click on Help for detail.

Password protection

If you are a registered user, you will have access to the password function. Passwords, once entered will restrict access to the employee and schedule files. There are two levels of password access:

✦ General Manager password

✦ Department Managers passwords (2)

The first password to enter will set the General Manager's password. The General Manager may enter up to two passwords per department, and give them to the Department Managers as a temporary password. These passwords can then be changed by the Department Manager. By entering a Department Manager password, that manager has access to only that department. The General Manager will retain access to all departments. If the General Manager makes his/her password a blank, the password function is bypassed until a new password is entered. The General Manager may hide all salaries and wages from one or both Department Managers.

Reports

Two types of report are available: one employee register that prints the employee name and other information that is requested; the other is a requested Weekly Schedule to be printed. The Schedules are printed from the Main Editor screen; all other printing is done from the opening screen.

Schedule filenames

When a schedule is saved, the name of the file is based on the Week-starting or Week-ending date (Based on option selection). In order to list the file selection in date sequence, the filename is: YY-MM-DD.dayname regardless of the International date settings in the Windows Control panel. So a filenamed 94-12-1.thu is dated December 1, 1994, which is on a Thursday, as reflected in the filename extension.

Print Schedules

Three printing formats are offered. One format will print the schedules vertically with times and currencies to the right and a format that shows the days from left to right. The three formats needs special font considerations, since the text must fit the paper to print on. You may select either Portrait or Landscape from Printer setup before starting the printing process. For most printers, a Courier font Pointsize 8 will be fine. If you select a font that does not fit, you will be advised with a message. If you print to a Matrix printer, select the Courier 17.1 font. That is the font that used to print condensed in DOS. A character-based schedule is offered to save time, especially on Matrix printers; for Laser printers it does not make that much difference. The graphic-based option has a better appearance. The smaller the font size, the more names will print on a single page! The printer must have enough memory. The print order is the same as the schedule displayed on the screen. As an option you may print time and or currency totals as part of the output. With the exception of the Bar Chart report, daily times and currencies are for shifts and include any time and wages past midnight. The Bar Chart report time is for the 24 hour period shown. The daily totals for some employees may be off slightly if partial hours are worked, causing rounding errors. Time and currency totals do not include any break times that were set up in the Editor.

No adjustments are made for Overtime, the currency totals are strictly time scheduled, multiplied by the hourly rate. At your option, you may direct your printing direct or through the Print Manager in Windows.

If you wish to print on another system, connect your printer from the current printing port (like LPT1) to File, via the Control Panel, and name the file to a floppy; then copy the file to the printer port from the floppy in the new system.

Departments

To decide the department size, consider

> A department should include all the employees that would be the responsibility
> of a Manager. Employees should consistently be a part of that Manager's
> operating unit.

The department related activity is located under menu item Scheduling Employees on
the opening screen. You may have up to 99 departments, and up to 150 employees per
department.

Employees

Employees are entered in the opening screen. While entering or changing an employee
record, use the Tab or Enter key to advance through the employee screen, or hold
down the Shift key and press the Tab key for reverse tabbing. Instructions on the
bottom will help you entering information. Employees are divided into active and
inactive employees. The Editors will only display active employees. If you display an
old schedule and an employee on that schedule was deleted or inactive, when you
save the schedule, that employee will not be included in the schedule. Seven lines are
reserved to enter the employee's availability to work. These lines are available in the
Editors to help you to schedule.

Hourly and salaried employees

The rate of pay option is divided between hourly wages and weekly salaries. Salary
totals are not related to time worked. Time worked totals include both hourly and
weekly employees.

Employee availability for work

The availability for an employee to work may be filled in when entering a new or
changing the current employee information. This information will be available as you
make the schedule. On the individual Editor it is automatically displayed. On the
Department Editor this information can be recalled by clicking the mouse on the total
box next to the employee name.

About dates

Dates entered in the employee record, conform to the International setting in the
Windows Control Panel. You may enter 2 Apr 94, or 2-Apr-94, or Apr 2, 1994, or any
combination for April 2, 1994. If the year is omitted, the current system year is
inserted. If there is an error in the date format, a message will alert you.

Technical information

This application creates directories for new departments as needed. The Example Organization is installed in directory SEW1DIR during the install process. Subsequent directories will be named automatically when new departments are installed, such as SEW2DIR, SEW3DIR etc. When a department is deleted, the directory will also be deleted and reinstalled as new department is created. The associated directory is displayed on the department Window when Change Department is selected from the menu. The files HEADING.DAT, EMPLREST.DAT and Schedule files (YY-MM-DD.day) in each directory must always be transferred or backed up together since they contain pointers. In the WINDOWS\SYSTEM directory, the following files must be present:

THREED.VBX, CSCALNDR.VBX, CSTEXT.VBX, CMDIALOG.VBX, VBRUN300.DLL, COMMDLG.DLL, QPRO200.DLL.

No files with the extension of .VBX should ever be located in the WINDOW Directory, only in the SYSTEM directory.

For ordering, contact, registration, and more detailed information, see the appropriate file for this program on the companion CD-ROM.

Screen Thief for Windows

Screen Thief for Windows v1.01. The ultimate screen capture system for Windows. Features include: Up to eight user-defined capture configurations, each with hot-key invocation; capture from desktop, active window, active application, defined area, and clipboard; send capture to disk, printer, clipboard, or MDI window; zoom in/out; crop images; auto color reduction; page preview; BMP, RLE, GIF, PCX TIFF file formats.

Category: Graphics
Type: Shareware
Location on CD: \ScrnThf
To install: Run d:\ScrnThf\SETUP.EXE
To run: Click on Start⇨Programs⇨Screen Thief for Windows⇨Screen Thief

For capturing and printing screen shots like the ones in this book. Beats the daylights out of using the PrintScreen key and Paint applet.

Documentation excerpts

Screen Thief for Windows v1.01 Copyright © 1994-1995 Nildram Software, All Rights Reserved.

README.TXT Installation notes and Errata.

Running Screen Thief for Windows.

Run as you would any other Windows application, either by clicking on the icon installed into Program Manager, or by using whatever facilities your shell, desktop manager, or file manager provides.

We suggest you should open the STWIN.HLP help file first and get to know the program. If you have the shareware Test Drive version it is essential that you read through the first topics regarding the shareware concept and the limits on use for this version, and only run Screen Thief for Windows if you agree to abide by these restrictions.

Errata and last minute changes.

The following is a list of changes or enhancements found in the Screen Thief for Windows program and Help file which did not make it into the printed documentation. Please refer to these changes by typing the given key word into the Search dialog box which is available by pressing S when the Help System first loads.

Key word subject

Delay — The text for this option entry has changed. Delay setting is now limited to the range 0-99 inclusive.

History — The full Product Release History outlining major bug fixes and changes.

Keys — The Keyboard Actions and Shortcuts - Full Screen.

View Control section — describes the new features offered from within the full screen viewing mode.

The Keyboard Actions and Shortcuts — Image View Control section describes new key combinations for scrolling and panning an image window.

MonoDemote — A new (Extended Options) entry which prevents auto colour demotion to a monochrome image.

Questions — The Questions and Answers section includes some new solutions to user queries which should be read by all new users.

For ordering, contact, registration, and more detailed information, see the appropriate file for this program on the companion CD-ROM.

Smart Address

Smart Address has been designed as an easy-to-use, yet powerful Address Book management application. Smart Address lets you create multiple address books to store different kinds of names and addresses. Includes the ability to import and export address lists. Can also auto-dial the phone. Prints envelopes, labels, and lists.

> **Category:** Personal
> **Type:** Shareware
> **Location on CD:** \SmartAdd
> **To install:** Run d:\SmartAdd\INSTALL.EXE
> **To run:** Click on Start⇨Programs⇨Smart Address⇨Smart Address V2

Registration and ordering information is in Help. Distributed in the U.S. by Insight Software Solutions.

Documentation excerpts

Smart Address is a powerful Address Management package for Windows. Features include multipage tabbed presentation with a host of fields, all with user-defineable labels, many user customisable fields, Direct Links to any WordProcessor, Mail-Merge Data File Creation, Modem Support, Envelope and Label Printing, Mail-Shot capabilities, Reminder systems, drop down point & shoot calendars, callbacks, tabbed dialogs, dialing, very user configurable, User defined notes, MDI, sophisticated searching, Import/Export, Full context sensitive Windows Help, Tooltips, and much much more! Very fast and comprehensive, but extremely easy to use.

For ordering, contact, registration, and more detailed information, see the appropriate file for this program on the companion CD-ROM.

SmartTracker Inventory v2.5

Track, organize and catalog your personal/office possessions. Track item, location, owner, worth, warranty, category, and more. Create and modify your own categories, locations, and owner lists. Advanced search facility. Complete with various reports and Report Designer. Include insurance information on reports. Flexible import and export. Advanced viewer. Formerly ISS "Track-It!".

> **Category:** Personal
> **Type:** Shareware
> **Location on CD:** \SmrtInv
> **To install:** First copy all 14 files from d:\smartinv onto a floppy disk. Then run a:\setup from the floppy disk
> **To run:** Click on Start⇨Programs ⇨ ISS Collection Series⇨SmartTracker Inventory

Needs to install from a floppy disk. (In My Computer, use View⇨Options⇨View⇨Show All Files to see all 14 files so you can select them and copy them to a floppy). Registration info is available in the Help menu.

Documentation excerpts

Track, organize, and catalog your personal possessions for insurance purposes, net worth, or just for being able to locate your belongings. Enter a multitude of information about your personal possessions in an extremely easy and straight forward fashion including the following items: Category, Location, Owner, Item, Brand, Model, Serial #, Quantity, Date Purchased, Where Purchased, ID Marks, Warranty, Warranty Expiration Date, Warranty Notes, Cost, Value, Replacement Cost, and Comments/Description. Modify the Category, Location, and Owner lists to your personal liking. Advanced search facility gives you the ability to search on the Item Name, Brand, Serial #, Description, Location, Category, Owner, and Warranty. Create one line, two line, multiline and value summary reports sorted by Item, Location, Category or Owner. Reports can be narrowed down to one category location or owner. Optionally includes insurance information on the reports, including insurance company, policy number, date of printout, and more.

Each program contains a scrollable viewer similar in appearance to a spreadsheet layout which lists the database elements. The viewer will grow and shrink with the size of the window. Configure the viewer to your personal preference. Select only those database elements that you plan on using or that you want to see to appear in the viewer. Specify the order in which they appear and specify the space to allocate to each element. Advanced search options place items matching search criteria into the viewer. ASCII delimited import/export operations are available with complete configurability on which items and in which order to import or export. Limit exports to only those items found in a search. Configure the colors for all elements of the windows for all windows or for specific windows. Design your own reports! Add as many report layouts as you like.

Select either a 90-column report for large legible reports or a 120-column report to pack as much information on the page as possible. Each database element can be spread out over a maximum of 12 lines. Place labels, blanks, and database items where you want them to be. Allocate the desired space for the labels, blanks, and database items. Optionally add up to three header lines to appear on each page. Optionally place totals which will appear after each report group and at the end of the report. Optionally place page numbers on each page. For one line reports (columns of data), optionally choose to have automatic column headers placed on the report. Choose from among any True Type font that is on your system. View reports on-screen or send to printer or ASCII file. Print one page or entire report.

For ordering, contact, registration, and more detailed information, see the appropriate file for this program on the companion CD-ROM.

Squarex

Squarex v1.1. Race against the clock in this exciting, fast-paced game where you maneuver your yellow cube around a puzzle board, capturing grids by traveling all four sides. Avoid the killer orange cubes which pursue you around the board. Strategy and logic are needed to outwit these orange devils. Reach a pink cube and go on the offensive by capturing them! Squarex is addictive fun for all ages.

Category: Games
Type: Shareware
Location on CD: \Squarex
To install: No installation program provided. You'll need to copy all the files from d:\Squarex to a folder on your hard disk
To run: After copying all the files from d:\Squarex, run SQUAREX.EXE on your hard disk

Soleau Software presents Squarex version 1.1.

Program by William Soleau © 1994-1995 Shareware Version

Requires: EGA/VGA

Requires Files: Squarex.ov1, Squarex.ov2, Squarex.ov3, Squarex.ov4, Squarex.ov5, Squarex.ov6, Squarex.ov7, Squarex.ov8, Squarex.jft, Squarex1.jft, Squarex2.jft, Squarex3.jft

Squarex directions: the objective

The objective of Squarex is to capture all the gray squares on the game board by maneuvering your yellow cube around each one.

Game play

When the game begins, your yellow cube will be blinking in the upper left-hand corner of the board. At the bottom right side of the board, there are orange cubes trying to catch you as you move around the puzzle. Use your arrow keys to move your yellow cube around the board.

You do not have to keep your hand pressing down on the arrow keys. Your yellow cube will continue in the direction you choose until it hits the side of the board or until you change its direction by pressing another arrow key. Once your yellow cube has passed an intersection, it can not change its direction until it reaches the next intersection. If your yellow cube cannot move in the direction you have selected because there is no path, then it will stop until you choose a valid direction.

When you can maneuver your cube completely around one of the gray squares, it will then change to green. To complete a level, you must keep moving around the board until you have turned all the gray squares to green.

On some levels there are blue squares. These are blank squares and do not count towards your score.

When your yellow cube moves, it will leave a red trail behind it. This will allow you to know where you have already been.

At the start of each level there will be one 100 Point Square. If you can capture this square first, then you will have 100 points added to your score. If you capture any other square before this one, it will disappear from the game board and you will not get the extra 100 bonus points.

Pink cubes

On various levels there are pink cubes which are located at different places along the passageways. The orange cubes that are chasing you cannot pass through these, but you can. When you do reach a pink cube, the orange cubes will turn light blue. As long as the orange cubes are light blue, you can capture them and get extra points. You have about 15 seconds before they will change back to orange and start chasing you again.

Orange cubes

The orange cubes will always try to catch you as you move around the board. On some levels there is only one orange cube when you begin, on others there are more. Every 30 seconds, another orange cube will emerge from the lower right hand side of the board. At the beginning levels, the orange cubes move at half the speed of your yellow cube. On higher levels, they both move at the same speed.

Bonus rounds

Every 2,500 points you will get a special bonus round. There will be no gray grids on the board, but when you make a square with your yellow cube, the square will turn to green. If you can turn all the entire black board to green squares, then a special Extra Cube square will appear somewhere on the board. If you capture this special square, then you will be given an extra yellow cube.

Yellow cubes

When you begin a new game, you will be given four cubes to start with. If you lose all your cubes, then the game will be over. At the lower left-hand side of the board, it will tell you how many extra cubes you have left, not counting the one you are playing with.

Levels/practice

You can practice any level by pressing the pra<C>tice key. This will end the present game and allow you to go directly to one of the levels. No scores are recorded while using this option.

There are a total of seven levels of play in the shareware version of Squarex. The registered version features 35 levels of play, plus a Save & Load Game feature that you access through the Option menu.

Time limit

There is a two-minute time limit on all levels. If you do not complete the level within this time, then you will lose one of your yellow cubes.

Scoring

If you complete a level you will be given 25 points for each of the green squares you captured. You will also be given Level Bonus Points which are 25 points per Level. Time Bonus Points are added to your score for each second under the two minutes it took you to complete the level (one point for each second).

When the orange cubes are changed to light blue, you get 50 points for the capturing the first cube. If you capture two light blue cubes you get 100 points for the second one, 150 points for the third one, etc.

Squarex keys

<H>ELP = Game Directions

<N>EW GAME = Begins New Game

PRA<C>TICE = Allows You to Practice A Level

<O>PTIONS = Brings Up Option Menu

<P>AUSE = Pauses Game

<Q>UIT = Quits Program

OPTION MENU KEYS

<S>OUND = Toggle Sound (On/Off)

S<O>LEAU = Games by Soleau Software

<H>IGH SCORES = Shows Squarex Scoreboard

<S>AVE GAME = Saves Present Game (Reg.Version Only)

<L>OAD GAME = Loads Saved Game (Reg.Version Only)

<E>XIT OPTION = Exits Option Menu

About Soleau Software

Please see the CD-ROM for more information about products from Soleau Software and complete information on how to order this complete shareware program. The registered version of Squarex greatly speeds up the loading and exiting of the program, plus gives you 35 levels of play! There is also a special Save & Load Game feature which allows you to save a game in progress and return to it at a later time.

StarDate 2140.2: Crusade in Space

You are the Commander in this new, interstellar conflict game for Windows. Build up your fleets, plan your strategy, and conquer the galaxy! Unless, of course, your enemies do so first. By MVP Software <ASP>.

Category: Games
Type: Shareware
Location on CD: \StarDate
To install: Run d:\StarDate\SETUP.EXE
To run: Click on Start⇨Programs⇨Games⇨Crusade In Space

During installation, this program required that I enter a new folder name. I typed in **c:\stardate** and it worked fine. Once it's running, choose Help⇨Tutorial for an overview.

Documentation excerpts

Copyright © 1994 Glacier Edge Technology

An MVP Software Production

CRUSADE is a game of *spaceploitation*, with you as the Emperor of the galaxy, commanding a force of powerful starships and land units to help to exercise your will. Your objective is simply to conquer or colonize every planet in the galaxy!

CRUSADE is shareware. You are free to evaluate this software, after which you must either register with MVP Software or delete the software from your system. Thanks for playing CRUSADE and for supporting shareware. Your honesty pays.

This is volume one of the Stardate 2410.2: Crusade in Space saga. To order the registered version, call 800-968-9684 toll-free 24 hours a day. Please have your MasterCard or Visa ready when you call. Or fill out the order form contained in the file on the CD-ROM.

Download all the latest MVP shareware games FREE

If your favorite BBS doesn't have an MVP file section, then you may be missing some great shareware. To get all the latest and greatest MVP shareware releases, call one of the leading boards included in the files on the CD-ROM.

MVP shareware is also available through major online services. See the files in the CD-ROM for complete information on downloading, ordering, and talking with the shareware authors.

Using Program Manager to install Crusade

After unzipping the shareware file, use the Program Manger in Windows to create a program item for Crusade, which should execute the STAR.EXE program.

From the Program Manager menu

1. Select FILE/NEW. Accept the Program Item setting and click OK.
2. Enter **Crusade in Space** in the Description field.
3. Select Browse. Select the disk/directory where the unzipped contents of CIS113.ZIP currently reside.
4. Select STAR.EXE from the list of files extracted from CIS113.ZIPand click on OK.
5. Enter the complete path (disk/directory) where the unzipped contents of the shareware version currently reside, in the Working Directory field.
6. Select Change Icon, select the CRUSADE icon.
7. Click OK to complete the creation of the program item.

Registration

When you register CRUSADE you will receive the CRUSADE GENERATOR, which will allow you to create an unlimited number of variably sized and populated galaxies with the Galaxy Generation Feature. It will allow you to create an unlimited number of games of various difficulty, alien mix, and to even customize the complement of forces each side receives with its Game Generation feature. You also will receive the licensed version of the CRUSADE PLAYER (which does not have finite stardates); which can play the games you generate, and the four (4) SPECIAL CRUSADES that are offered below.

Special crusades

"The Terrans Emerge!" As the Terran Emperor, you will control the development of the Terrans out into the KausKais Galaxy. What lifeforms will you encounter? What challenges face you? "Zardulan Quest" — You command the most powerful lifeform in the universe .... the mighty Zardula. All others bow before you ... or will they? Try to conquer the De'atar Galaxy if you dare. "A Tioran Test" — As the leader of the timid Tiorans, can you still manage to conquer the KausKais Galaxy against great odds? "The Cassian Challenge" — The most aggressive and powerful lifeform of the universe awaits your puny empire. Ha! Ha! You will not win this crusade into the De'atar Galaxy.

Game hint

This is a very complex game, that plays in a simple manner. It is critical to your success as an Emperor to read the online Help and Tutorial from the Main Map menu. Each important control panel, also contains specific online Help that is available by selecting the Question-mark button.

Ordering information

For ordering, contact, registration, and more detailed information, see the appropriate file for this program on the companion CD-ROM.

Talking Clock 2

Talking Clock 2 displays the current time and optionally announces the time every 15 minutes using a sound card. After starting the program, press F1 and you will be given information about running the program.

> **Category:** Utility
> **Type:** Shareware
> **Location on CD:** \TalkClck
> **To install:** Run d:\TalkClck\SETUP.EXE
> **To run:** Click on Start ⇨Programs⇨Talking Clock 2⇨Talking Clock 2

A little classic.

Required hardware and software

Microsoft Windows 95, NT, or Win32s. A sound card is optional.

Installing Talking Clock 2

Run SETUP.EXE from Windows.

Running Talking Clock 2

After starting the program, press F1 and you will be given information about running the program.

Distribution and payment

For ordering, contact, registration, and more detailed information, see the appropriate file for this program on the companion CD-ROM.

Other shareware programs from Pocket-Sized Software

Consult the online help for information about other shareware programs from Pocket-Sized Software.

Version history

VERSION 3.0: Tape allows users to insert and delete lines, modify numbers or operators, and automatically recalculate results. New dialog boxes for financial functions. "Tip of the Day" feature. Full support for Windows 3.1 common dialog boxes, such as File Open (including import of text files), Save, and Print (including the option to print only selected tape entries). Other improvements include right mouse button tape pop-up menu, ability to edit the main entry line, better keyboard shortcuts, and support for memory operations dealing with the tape.

VERSION 2.1: New proprietary algorithm for more precise calculation results, support for networked installations, and compliance with international number formats. General usability improvements: automatic decimal insertion capability, tape exit behavior now applies to all methods of closing tape, Keep on Top capability now uses Microsoft standard Always On Top, easier program registration.

VERSION 2.0: Save, restore, and print tapes, resize tape display using the mouse, reuse tape entries, copy and paste between other Windows applications, RPN syntax, statistics, transcendental, financial functions, red negatives, and keep on top.

VERSION 1.0: Configurable window display, scrolling tape, tenkey or calculator syntax, standard mathematical operations, standard functions, memory, selectable decimal display.

For ordering, contact, registration, and more detailed information, see the appropriate file for this program on the companion CD-ROM.

TaskServer

TaskServer V1.2 is a tool that allows you to start any program, batch, or command on a WIN95/ WindowsNT Workstation or WindowsNT Server, from any computer in the net. Very simple to install and use. Works with easy to create job-files. All machines that can access a shared drive on the WIN95 / Windows NT computer can start tasks. Examples of this are long print jobs, compile jobs, tosser jobs for Fido Sysops, backup of user workstations, and so on.

Nearly zero CPU stress while running idle. If you set up an FTP Server, even UNIX machines can start tasks in this way. Start jobs on the Server over a WAN (RAS) connection to ease remote administration. Optional security mode to set up user-specific job rights. Option to lock a task for a specified amount of time. Multiple task-search directories. Various logging-level options. GUI Interface for easy administration.

> **Category:** Utility
> **Type:** Shareware
> **Location on CD:** \TaskSrvr
> **To install:** Create a new folder on your hard disk, and copy all the files from d:\TaksSrvr to that new folder
> **To run:** Browse to your new folder and double-click on TSERVER.EXE

The Greatest Paper Airplanes

The Greatest Paper Airplanes v1.0g is a Windows program using full interactive 3-D animation to fold extraordinary paper airplanes. Unique notebook features simple VCR-style fold controls, color printing of decorated airplane designs, and animated tutorials on the history of flight and paper folding. From KittyHawk Software.

> **Category:** Games
> **Type:** Shareware
> **Location on CD:** \Airplane
> **To install**: Run d:\Airplane\SETUP.EXE
> **To run:** Click on Start ⇨Programs⇨Greatest Paper Airplanes⇨Greatest Paper Airplanes

Excellent interface. Shareware version comes with instructions for six planes. Gripes during install if limited extended memory, but installs and runs fine anyway. Installation modifies an INI file. So if you decide to uninstall from your hard disk, re-run setup and choose Uninstall.

The Mice Men

Soleau Software has created another exciting, fun-filled, animated strategy logic game. Try to push and pull columns of cheese blocks to get your mice to the other end of the maze before your computer opponent. Mice Men is packed with features and written in stunning, animated EGA/VGA graphics. It's an addicting logic strategy game for all ages!

> **Category:** Games
> **Type:** Shareware
> **Location on CD:** \MiceMen
> **To install:** No installation program provided. You'll need to copy all the files from d:\MiceMen to a folder on your hard disk
> **To run:** After copying all the files from d:\MiceMen, run MICEMEN.EXE on your hard disk.

DOS game.

Time & Chaos

Excerpt from Time & Chaos help screen — Our goal is to provide you with an intuituve application for managing your personal information. Our lives revolve around time and the chaos surrounding its schedules use. Our desire is that you will quickly and effectively learn to use Time & Chaos to manage your time commitments. Time & Chaos brings order to the three most common types of time-dependent information: things you need to do (to-do's); appointments you need to keep; and contacts you want to make on a regular basis. On a single screen, you can see at a glance what you need to do today, who you will be seeing, and who you might want to call or write.

> **Category:** Personal
> **Type:** Shareware
> **Location on CD:** \TimeChao
> **To install:** Run d:\timechao\SETUP.EXE
> **To run** Click on Start⇨Programs⇨Time & Chaos⇨Time & Chaos v4.06a

Winner of umpteen shareware awards. And rightly so.

Documentation excerpts

This is award-winning time-management shareware.

Please ensure that an old copy of Time & Chaos Professional (T&C) is *not* running already on your machine, before you run INSTALL.EXE. As a precaution, it is always recommended that you perform a backup of your data prior to installing an update.

T&C updates are designed to be installed in the same subdirectory as the old version. Data files will be maintained. If conversion is required, it will be automatic upon the initial startup. Previous security codes from version 4.x will be automatically maintained. If you have registered a version 4.x product, this is a no charge update.

If you are running on Windows NT or Windows 95 you should install T&C to a new subdirectory and restore your datafiles.

We have new Internet addresses: send MAIL to either support@isbister.com or sales@isbister.com. Our HOME PAGE is http://www.isbister.com/isbister (you can get updates here). FTP ftp.isbister.com - files are located in cd/pub/isbister.

Thank you all very much for your continued support!

Changes in version 4.06

Printing Enhancements include

- ✦ T&C can now utilizes the available paper. If there is room on a page for additional virtual pages, it will print them on the same page.

- ✦ Ability to print out a range of calendars. For example, three months of calendars.

- ✦ Ability to print each etter of the alphabet on a separate page.

- ✦ Ability to print a letter range such as F through M.

- ✦ Many more repeat options for ToDo's and Appointments.

- ✦ Julian Dates are now displayed on the main screen by holding down the mouse on a date.

- ✦ More secure passwords. The passwords are now stored in binary format in the database header. Your passwords will be deleted and you will need to rekey them.

- ✦ Multi-Disk Backups/Restores are now supported.

- ✦ Report Writer Enhancements include

  - • Category Sorting.

  - • Compare Field now does not need to one of the reported fields.

  - • Ability to save the report as a text file, including full notes.

  - • ALT+C will remove a Column both on the screen and on printout.

- ✦ Multiselect in the ToDo List, Appointments List, Phone List on main screen. This allows you to select multiple items for deleting, marking done, moving.

- ✦ Importing now uses a user specified file, not just IMPORT.TXT.

✦ Dragging a ToDo to the appointments will now drag with it notes, priority and description.

✦ Many more little ditty things.

Changes in version 4.05

✦ We now have very tight integration with MS Word, AmiPro, and WordPerfect for Windows.

✦ Phonebook now supports ATTACHED FILES to contacts. You can attach spreadsheets, documents.

✦ New option under preferences setup to handle EUROPE — this will have postal code print on the envelope before the city.

Changes in version 4.04b

✦ Optional Modem initialization string

✦ Allows users with very large phonebooks to define a set of phonebook categories for startup.

✦ Due to popular demand the Spinning Top has returned to the T&C icon.

✦ The bug that prevented T&C from working with Norton Antivirus has been corrected.

✦ Export from the search screen is now based on selected highlighted records.

✦ The YearView screen now supports tabs to jump to previous and next years.

Changes in version 4.04a

✦ Maintenance update that corrects all reported/confirmed bugs in v4.04.

✦ Adds small monthly calendars to the top of the ToDo List and Appointments printouts.

✦ Program no longer requires any iii*.DLL files. These may now be deleted from your chaos subdirectory if desired.

Changes in version 4.04

✦ Two new phone fields.

✦ Year View option.

✦ New Day View screens.

✦ Auto refresh frequency for LAN users.

✦ Timebar now supports scrolling over full day.

✦ Time & Chaos is now a full DDE Server Application.

✦ Now Supports Drag and Drop into future/past months.

✦ Importing now supports Tab delimited Files.

✦ Telephone Book now supports multiselect.

✦ Custom ToDo priority.

✦ Categories now support both the AND logic and OR logic.

✦ Extra Line inserted between names in telephone book printout.

✦ Weekly calendar now prints full line in one column rather than two columns.

✦ Print Layout captions now support the name of the layout.

✦ NOTES now has its own Page Layout options.

✦ Completed transition from business and home to primary and secondary Addresses.

✦ Backup will now create a directory if an non-existent directory has been specified.

✦ Backup now has an option to automatically prompt for backup on exit.

✦ The box over the phone numbers on the main screen now reflects both the company name and the contact.

✦ The button to switch between white and yellow pages on the LINKING screens has been replaced with option buttons.

✦ Autodialer screen on the ToDo items has been removed as it is now redundant.

✦ Telephone book now supports the Enter key to call up the record from the main screen.

✦ ToDo list will now stay on the last line edited rather than jumping back up to the top.

✦ Delete Key now works on front Screen to remove Appointments, ToDo's, and Phone Listings.

✦ Shortcut keys for most everything. Esc key works on all screens to close the screen.

✦ Password file is now encrypted for improved security.

Ordering information

For ordering, contact, registration, and more detailed information, see the appropriate file for this program on the companion CD-ROM.

Uniclock

Uniclock © is a utility designed to give you access to a maximum of ten time zones simultaneously. The program was designed to provide you with: fast access to the clocks; easy interface; alarms for each clock; the ability to display more then one clock at a time; and an "Always on Top" option. This handy utility will make life easier for the business person working with different time zones, or for anyone interested in communicating with people around the globe. This is a full working shareware Version. Created by University Software. We can be reached at: CompuServe 75057,1727 Internet unisoft@ios.com http://www.ios.com:80/~unisoft/. Requires VBRUN300.DLL.

> **Category:** Utility
> **Type:** Shareware
> **Location on CD:** \Uniclock
> **To install:** See notes regarding installation in the Uniclock directory on the CD.
> **To run:** Run d:\Uniclock\UNICLOCK.EXE

No setup, but you can give it a trial run right from the CD-ROM disk. Once loaded, you'll see a small UniClock Config icon above the taskbar. To see the actual clock, double-click on that button. Then select the Visible, Analog, and Big options.

For ordering, contact, registration, and more detailed information, see the appropriate file for this program on the companion CD-ROM.

The program was created by University Software, Inc.

This file is needed in your Windows/System directory to run this program. It is available from your online service provider (filename VBRUN3.ZIP).

Vault 32

Vault stores your information as an outline, organizing your information into categories and sub-categories that you specify. Vault's search command finds the information you need instantly. You can also browse the outline by expanding and collapsing items. Vault's Send command allows you to send your notes to co-workers via electronic mail. The Dial Phone command automatically dials the phone number in the current outline item.

Category: Personal
Type: Shareware
Location on CD: \Vault32
To install: Run d:\vault32\SETUP.EXE
To run: Click on Start⇨Programs⇨Vault⇨Vault

Organizes notes and other information like books and topics in Windows 95 help. Too see an example choose File⇨Open and open EXAMPLE.VLT.

Required hardware and software

Windows 95 or NT running on a 386, 486, or Pentium computer. A 16-bit version for Windows 3.1 is also available.

Running Vault and ordering information

For information on running Vault and learning about other shareware programs from Pocket-Sized Software, see Vault's online help.

For ordering, contact, registration, and more detailed information, see the appropriate file for this program on the companion CD-ROM.

Video BlackJack

Video Blackjack Version 2.0 offers exciting, casino-style action in a truly spectacular, feature-rich video blackjack game. Complete with options for split, double-down, insurance, and even money! Outstanding graphics with 3D effects, icons, buttons animation, and online help. Full mouse and keyboard support, as well as music and sound effects! A must have!

Category: Games
Type: Shareware
Location on CD: \Blakjak2P
To install: None, but you can run right from the CD
To run: Run d:\blakjak2\VBJ.EXE

Great DOS casino game from SNR Software. If you register, you'll get info on other casino and card games from SNR.

Web Weaver v4.0b

Web Weaver 4.0b. HTML editor for creating World Wide Web documents and home pages. Automated buttons and dialog boxes facilitate inserting the code into these documents.Netscape HTML extensions are available, in addition to the ability to link to a browser with the click of a button. Shareware U.S. $8 (+$2 shipping if sent by post office mail).

> **Category:** Communications
> **Type:** Shareware
> **Location on CD:** \WebWeave
> **To install:** None required — you can try it out right from the CD-ROM
> **To run:** Run d:\webweave\WEBWEV4B.EXE

A really nice editing program for creating World Wide Web pages. No setup program, but you can run directly from the CD-ROM to try it out. Registration information is in Help⇨How to Register.

Documentation excerpts

Web Weaver 4.0b Full Unregistered version. Copyright © 1995 by Mark McConnell

Web Weaver version 4.0b is an HTML editor for creating World Wide Web documents and home pages. Automated buttons and dialog boxes facilitate inserting the code into these documents. Netscape HTML extensions are available, in addition to the ability to link to a browser with the click of a button.

Web Weaver is an editor-like program which facilitates the coding of HTML documents and pages for the World Wide Web. Toolbar buttons and dialog boxes make it easier to create the code that links your text and graphics to the rest of the world.

This version (4.0b) is the *full* version of Web Weaver.

It contains the following main features:

- ✦ Easy hypertext creation (linking text to URLs, images, sounds, etc.).

- ✦ Easy inline image creation (linkable to external images, URLs, etc.).

- ✦ Easy anchor creation.

- ✦ Easy list creation (Bulleted, Numbered, Descriptive).

- ✦ Easy address information creation.

- ✦ Helpful buttons for common tasks (bold, italics, headings, <P>, etc.)

- ✦ Linking to web browsers.

- ✦ Utility to strip HTML code from your document and save the text as another file.

But...

✦ A screen reminding you to register appears in the beginning (not in the registered version).

✦ Help files are not included (only registered version).

✦ More HTML features will be added in later versions.

✦ Multiple document editing will be available in a later (registered) version.

✦ User defined toolbar will be in a later (registered) version.

Installation

Put the files WEBWEV4B.EXE and WEBWEV.INI into any directory.

Put the files CMDIALOG.VBX, THREED.VBX, and VBRUN300.DLL into your WINDOWS\SYSTEM directory.

Run WEBWEV4B.EXE from Windows and you are ready to go.

(You may have to alter the INI file to link to your browser correctly.)

How to register

To learn how to register, see the files on the CD-ROM.

Help

IMPORTANT!!! When opening an existing HTML file that was downloaded from your UNIX system, the carriage returns may not be recognized. Be sure to download/FTP it in ASCII format! Also, if the program doesn't load in your file then there may be a control character at the end of it. Open the file in Notepad, delete the control character, and save it. Then open it in Web Weaver.

The program is relatively straightforward. Creating HTML elements is simple. For example, suppose you want to bold a certain word/phrase in the HTML document. Just select the word/phrase to be bolded with the cursor and click on the BOLD button. This will place the HTML bold symbols around the text you have selected:

<B>Text or phrase here.</B>

Or, you can begin by clicking the bold button. This will place both beginning and ending HTML bold symbols at the insertion point in the document and the cursor will be placed in between them so you can begin typing the phrase you wish to have bolded. Most of the other formatting commands work the same way.

Paragraph and Horizontal Rule commands place the respective HTML symbol on the screen and then perform a carriage return to the next line. Inserting graphics and Hypertext are self-explanatory. Methods of inserting Anchors and Lists are explained on their respective dialog boxes. Cut/Copy/Paste are standard.

Viewing

Viewing documents is an easy click of a button when you specify your browser's path, filename, and caption title in the WEBWEV.INI file. A good viewer to use is SLIPKNOT available at the FTP site oak.oakland.edu in the SimTel/win3/internet directory as SLNOT110.ZIP You don't need to be connected to an outside source with this application. It can be used as just a viewer.

A little about the author

Mark McConnell is a structural engineering grad student at Tufts University in Medford, MA (in the Boston area). Mark likes photography, food, and programming on the side. If you have any comments, suggestions, bugs, etc. please e-mail them to Mark at: mmcconne@ads.cee.tufts.edu He would be glad to hear them.

For ordering, contact, registration, and more detailed information, see the appropriate file for this program on the companion CD-ROM.

WinCharging v1.1

It's the best idea yet for managing credit cards. It displays outstanding amounts; monitors credit card imits; tracks target amounts; charts, displays and prints tax summaries and card usage reports; and does much more. It can even help you if you lose your credit cards. The standard edition is $19.95; the deluxe is $24.95.

> **Category:** Personal
> **Type:** Shareware
> **Location on CD:** \Wincharg
> **To install:** Run d:\wincharg\SETUP.EXE
> **To run:** Click on Start⇨Programs⇨WinCharging⇨WinCharging

Shareware version is good for 60 day trial period. If you use credit cards, do try this one.

Documentation excerpts

WinCharging Copyright © 1994 My Little Realm Enterprises

Thank you trying WinCharging. It's the newest and best way credit card users can manage their charge accounts. WinCharging version 1.00 received a Four-Star rating from Ziff- Davis, the parent company of *PC Magazine*. That version is also a finalist in the 1995 Shareware Awards contest. This version (1.1) is even better. Its .EXE is 35,000 bytes smaller than the original. It's faster, does more, and is easier to use.

The license you agree to by evaluating WinCharging allows you to test it without charge for 60 days. After that period, you will not be able to create new records. You can, however, continue to access your existing records.

For more information about WinCharging's shareware license, read LICENSE.TXT on the CD-ROM.

The shareware edition of WinCharging is a full-featured, fully functional program. It is identical to the standard edition except for the shareware reminder screen you see when you start the program that displays the number of days remaining of your evaluation period.

Getting started

WinCharging comes with a special online Help file called MeFirst!. It's easy to read and comes with loads of graphics to simplify the setup process. When you start WinCharging the first time, it asks you if you would like to see MeFirst!. Reply yes. With both WinCharging and MeFirst! open, you can simply Alt+Tab back and forth, first reading MeFirst! about how to do something, then switching back to WinCharging to actually do it. When you no longer need MeFirst! you can delete it by simply selecting a command found on the File menu.

History

Version 1.00a: Grid Work and Details of Outstanding Bills: If you entered the edit mode for either of these forms and then clicked the scrollbar, the edit field remained on the screen. Clicking the scrollbar now ends the edit mode without saving any changes.

PDM Accounts: Changing a PDM record's amount in Grid Work would, when the record amount was greater than the account's total outstanding amount, incorrectly calculate the result.

For ordering, contact, registration, and more detailed information, see the appropriate file for this program on the companion CD-ROM.

WinRamp Lite

WinRamp Lite 2.1 for Windows, Shareware Evaluation Edition. Your personal access to the data SuperHighway. Commercial-quality communications package with RIPScrip 1.54 Emulation, VT52-220 Emulations, compilable scripts and IDE, multiple font sizes, and character sets. Customizable toolbars. Multiple terminal windows open. View GIFs during download. Supports COMt: the Telnet modem.

Category: Communications
Type: Shareware
Location on CD: \WinRamp
To install: Run d:\WinRamp\SETUP.EXE to copy files to c:\wrtemp. Then exit the DOS window, click on Start ⇨Run and run c:\wrtemp\INSTALL.EXE
To run: Click on Start⇨Programs⇨WinRamp Lite 1.21⇨WinRamp Lite 1.21

A hot modem communications package for Windows, at a very reasonable price.

Documentation excerpts

This portion of the README.1ST file contains important information that will make your installation so much easier if you read it (Really!). (Read the entire file on the CD-ROM for much more information.) Do yourself a big favor... go ahead, read it and make your day!

1. THANK YOU FOR TRYING WinRamp Lite.

   First off, the folks at Vironix NA would like to thank you for taking the time to download WinRamp Lite! We're sure you will find the application a worthwhile addition to your software collection.

2. NB! UPGRADING FROM PREVIOUS VERSIONS OF WINRAMP LITE

   If you have been running a previous version of WinRamp Lite (i.e. 1.00b, 1.01, 1.1 or 1.11) just prior to installing this new version, AND you have not closed down Windows since running the old version, it is highly likely that the WINRAMP.FON file is still in memory and may be locked. Version 1.2x added a number of new VTxxx emulation character sets to the WINRAMP.FON, so to use these new character sets the file must be upgraded. It is recommended that you first restart Windows. This will release the font file and allow the installation procedure to automatically upgrade to the new updated font file.

3. AUTHENTIC ORIGINAL DISTRIBUTION ARCHIVE

   The original distribution archives (either RMP121.ZIP or WRAMP121.ZIP) were compressed with PkWare's PKZIP Authentic Verification feature. If you obtained an archive without the -AV, it is possible that some installation files could be missing. Should your installation fail, please obtain the original archive. This can definitely be found on CompuServe in the WINSHARE and IBMCOM forums and The WinRamp Support BBS at 1-508-373-3336, or on the ftp.vironix.com (or ftp.vironix.co.za) anonymous FTP site.

4. INSTALLATION NOTES

We highly recommend that you run the INSTALL.EXE program to assist with the installation. The install program will take care of all the details such as registering the WINRAMP font file with Font Manager. Most of the files within the RMP121.ZIP or WRAMP121.ZIP archive are compressed to save space on your drive after installation. You can delete these files after installation; however, if you do this, we recommend you keep the original distribution archive. The EXTRACT.EXE utility included with the original distribution archive can be used to decompress any distribution file when required.

If you choose not to use the Installation program (we do not recommend this), remember to register the file WINRAMP.FON with the Font Manager (in Control Panel). WinRamp's terminal emulations will be severely limited if this is not done. If the Installation fails for some reason, please be sure to check the text file PACKING.LST to make sure that you have all the files necessary to run WinRamp Lite. PACKING.LST includes the addresses to online locations where you can be sure to obtain the original WinRamp Lite archive.

5. WINRAMP USER GUIDE & WR-SCRIPT REFERENCE GUIDE

As of this Version 1.21, the WinRamp User Guide and WR-Script Reference are no longer included with the SHAREWARE main distribution file set. Both manuals, in the Windows Write format, can be downloaded from the WinRamp Support BBS or by anonymous ftp from ftp.vironix.com (or ftp.vironix.co.za). The file to download/ftp is WR12DOCS.ZIP.

6. RIPSCRIP ICONS

If you will be accessing online systems that support the graphical emulation standard RIPScrip 1.x, and you do not yet have any RIP icon files on your hard-drive, you must extract (using PkWare's PKUNZIP) the archive file RIPICONS.ZIP into the following directory: <drive and WinRamp Lite directory>\RIP\ICONS

If you already have a collection of RIP icons files from a different application, you may wish to set up the WinRamp Lite RIP Terminal emulation to point to these existing icons.

7. REVISION HISTORY

All changes and revisions have been recorded within the Online Help file, and within the REVISION.121 text file. Thanks once again for trying Winramp Lite!

For ordering, contact, registration, and more detailed information, see the appropriate file for this program on the companion CD-ROM.

WinZip 5.6

WinZip 5.6 with built-in ZIP TAR gzip and compress Win32 version with long filename and UNC support. Requires Windows/NT 3.5 or Windows 95. PKZIP is not needed for basic ZIP operations. Brings the convenience of Windows to zipping. Windows 3.1 version is in WINZIP56.EXE or ZIP <ASP>.

"Should be a part of any Windows/NT user's toolkit" — *Windows Sources* 10/94

"Best Utility" —1994 Shareware Industry Awards

"Easy to use" — *InfoWorld* 4/18/94

Category Communications
Type: Shareware
Location on CD: \WinZip56
To install: Run d:\WinZip56\SETUP.EXE
To run: Click on Start⇨Programs⇨WinZip⇨WinZip for Windows_NT

This is the 32-bit shareware version of the classic WinZip compression/decompression program. Once you get it started, choose Help⇨Brief Tutorial for a basic overview. PKZip (a separate product) is also on this CD-ROM disc.

Documentation excerpts

Copyright © 1991-1995 Nico Mak Computing, Inc. All Rights Reserved

Installation

If you received this version of WinZip on a floppy disk please follow the instructions on the disk label to install WinZip. If you received this version of WinZip in a self-extracting ZIP file (for example, WINZIP56.EXE), you can install it as follows: activate the Program Manager, select Run from the File menu, type the full name of the file (for example, **C:\DNLOAD\WINZIP56.EXE**), press the Enter key, and follow the prompts. When the Setup program completes, you can delete the WinZip files in your temporary directory.

If you received this version of WinZip in a ZIP file, first extract the files to a blank floppy, then activate the Program Manager, select Run from the File menu, type **A:SETUP**, press the Enter key, and follow the prompts.

Upgrade instructions

Follow the installation instructions above. You can install this version of WinZip to the same location as a previously installed copy of WinZip.

Requirements

The Windows 3.1 version requires Windows 3.1 or Windows for Workgroups. The Win32 version requires Windows/NT 3.5 or later. Some optional features require external programs. See the documentation for details.

Documentation

For full documentation, including context sensitive help, press the F1 key at any time while running WinZip.

Win32 version

Win32 users please read the section titled "WinZip for Windows/NT" in the online help for notes on long filenames.

Self-extracting archives

The evaluation BBS version of WinZip is now distributed as a Windows self-extracting ZIP file. Nico Mak Computing, Inc. is developing a low-cost shareware product you will be able to use to create your own self-extracting ZIP files, but development is not complete at the time of this writing (January 1995) and pricing has not been set. To receive information on this product when it is available send e-mail to one of the addresses in the WinZip Help/About box.

List of files

The WinZip 5.6 package consists of the following files:

README.TXT introductory information
WINZIP.TXT product overview
*WINZIP.EXE required executable
*WZ.DLL required dynamic link library
*WZ2.DLL required dynamic link library
*WINZIPFM.DLL File Manager Extension dynamic link library
*WINZIP.HLP complete documentation in windows help format
**WINZIPNT.EXE required executable
**WZWIN32S.EXE required executable for Win32s environment
WZ.COM required executable
WZ.PIF required Program Information File
LICENSE.TXT license agreement/warranty disclaimer
ORDER.TXT order form
VENDOR.TXT information for Shareware Distributors
WHATSNEW.TXT list of changes in this version
FILE_ID.DIZ brief description for bulletin boards

* Files marked with an asterisk are part of the Windows 3.1 version and are not part of the Win32 version.

** Files marked with two asterisks are part of the Win32 version and are not part of the Windows 3.1 version. Some files are distributed with a trailing underscore or dollar sign at the end of the filename. The underscore or dollar sign is replaced with the appropriate character by the Setup program. For example, WINZIP.HL_ becomes WINZIP.HLP.

If you did not receive all these files, please contact Nico Mak Computing, Inc.

For ordering, contact, registration, and more detailed information, see the appropriate file for this program on the companion CD-ROM.

WinZip 95 (Beta)

WinZip 5.6a Beta 3 with Windows 95 features Pre-release Public Beta Test version. Brings the convenience of Windows to Zipping. External programs are not needed for ZIP, tar, gzip. Includes long filename and UNC support, and Windows 95 features. Require Windows 95 or Windows NT Release 3.5 or later. Not tested on final release of Windows 95. Try this out, and if you like it, register to get the final (non-beta) release.

Category: Communications
Type: Shareware
Location on CD: \WinZip95
To install: Run d:\winzip95\SETUP.EXE
To run: Click on Start⇨Programs⇨WinZip⇨WinZip 5.6a 32-bit beta.

This is the pre-release (beta test) version of WinZip, with specific features for Windows 95. See Help in the program for more info.

Documentation excerpts

Copyright © 1991-1995 Nico Mak Computing, Inc. All Rights Reserved

PRE-RELEASE BETA TEST VERSION

Please see whatsnew.txt for a list of recent changes, including Windows 95 specific features.

Beta Tester Note: previous versions of the 32-bit WinZip included in the file WINZIPNT.EXE. This file has been replaced by WINZIP32.EXE. You will have to delete WINZIPNT.EXE manually.

Documentation

For full documentation, including context sensitive help, press the F1 key at any time while running WinZip.

Win32 version

Win32 users please read the section titled "WinZip for Windows/NT" or "WinZip under Windows 95" in the online help for important notes on long filenames.

Self-extracting archives

The evaluation BBS version of WinZip is distributed as a Windows self-extracting ZIP file. You can use WinZip Self-Extractor, an optional add-on product, to create self-extracting ZIP files. You can download an evaluation version of WinZip Self-Extractor as WZIPSE10.EXE.

List of files

The WinZip 5.6a package consists of the following files. * Files marked with an asterisk are part of the Windows 3.1 version and are NOT part of the Win32 version. ** Files marked with two asterisks are part of the Win32 version and are NOT part of the Windows 3.1 version.

README.TXT introductory information
WINZIP.TXT product overview
* WINZIP.EXE required executable
* WZ.DLL required dynamic link library
* WZ2.DLL required dynamic link library
WINZIPFM.DLL File Manager Extension dynamic link library
WINZIP.HLP complete documentation in windows help format
** WINZIP32.EXE required executable
** WZWIN32S.EXE required executable for Win32s environment
** WZSHLEXT.DLL required dynamic link library
** WZFM32.DLL File Manager Extension dynamic link library
WZ.COM required executable
WZ.PIF required Program Information File
LICENSE.TXT license agreement/warranty disclaimer
ORDER.TXT order form
VENDOR.TXT information for Shareware Distributors
WHATSNEW.TXT list of changes in this version
FILE_ID.DIZ brief description for bulletin boards

Some files are distributed with a trailing underscore or dollar sign at the end of the filename. The underscore or dollar sign is replaced with the appropriate character by the Setup program. For example, WINZIP.HL_ becomes WINZIP.HLP. If you did not receive all these files please contact Nico Mak Computing, Inc.

For ordering, contact, registration, and more detailed information, see the appropriate file for this program on the companion CD-ROM.

World Empire III

Hegemony for the people! World Empire III For Windows v2.0 New Version. Based on the award winning DOS game, World Empire III offers 139 real world countries for your conquering pleasure. If you like Risk, you'll love this game! New graphics, expanded interface, MIDI soundtrack, and more! Reviewed as a five star program by all! Needs VBRUN300.DLL. From Viable Software Alternatives.

> **Category:** Games
> **Type:** Shareware
> **Location on CD:** \Empire3
> **To install:** No installation program provided. You need to create a folder on your hard drive (such as Empire3), then copy all files from d:\empire3 to that folder
> **To run:** Browse to and run EMPIRE.EXE after copying to your hard disk

Check out other Viable products on the Internet at http://delta.com/viable/viable.htm

Documentation excerpts

Feedback please! If you encounter any problems, please let me know.

Casey Butler, Viable Software Alternatives.

Note 1

This program is written in Visual Basic. Thus it needs the VBRUN300.DLL to run.

If you got your copy from an online service or bulletin board, take note: Some BBS Sysops remove the VBRUN300.DLL file from Windows programs that use it in order to save disk drive space.

If you are missing the VBRUN300.DLL file, log back on to the service or BBS it came from, and, if you can't easily find the VBRUN file, leave a comment to your Sysop asking how he/she allows people to acquire it.

Note 2

It has come to my attention that certain SVGA video hardware is non-compatible with the MicroSoft Visual Basic Environment and causes problems with the bitmaps (pictures) every so often in 800 x 600 mode and more often in 1024 x 768 resolution. Buttons will be misplaced in relation to maps, etc. At the moment there is one solution, which follows:

Open the Windows Setup icon and select CHANGE SYSTEM SETTINGS from the OPTIONS menu. Follow the prompts to change your video mode to a 640 x 480 or a high resolution driver using SMALL FONTS resolution driver.

The game will now run fine. When you're finished, return to Setup and re-install your original driver.

Note 3: Installing the World Empire III icon

How to install your program as an Icon with the Windows Program Manager.

1. First install the program in a DOS directory, outside of Windows.

2. Start up Windows and open the Program Manager.

3. Click once on the group in which you want the new World Empire III Icon installed.

4. Go up to the menu bar at the top of your screen and click on the word File.

5. A menu drops down. Click on New.

6. You will see a window with two choices. Select Program Item. Then click on OKAY.

7. Another window appears entitled Program Item Properties.

8. Click on the box labeled Description. Type **World Empire III.**

9. Use the Tab key or mouse and go to the box labeled Command line. Type the full name of the path to the directory where you have installed World Empire III, and the name EMPIRE.EXE. For example, if the program is in a directory called EMPIRE on the C drive, you would enter **C:\EMPIRE\EMPIRE.EXE** in the box.

10. Use the Tab key to go to the box labeled Working Directory. Type the name of the directory in which you installed World Empire III. For example, if you installed the game in a directory called Empire, then type **C:\EMPIRE**.

11. Now click on OK in the Program Item Properties Window.

You should now have the World Empire III icon installed in your Program Manager. Enjoy the program!

Program requirements

IBM Compatible Computer with an 80386, 486, or Pentium processor running Microsoft Windows 3.1 or higher. A hard disk drive. A mouse is required.

For ordering, contact, registration, and more detailed information, see the appropriate file for this program on the companion CD-ROM.

WPlot

WPLOT v1.8 Windows Plotting Software. WPLOT makes two and three-dimensional plots with linear or log axes. Data can be fit by a smooth curve, a least squares polynomial or exponential, or a Fourier series and functions can be plotted.

> **Category:** Math, science
> **Type:** Shareware
> **Location on CD:** \WPlot
> **To install:** None required
> **To run:** For a demo, run d:\wplot\wplot, then choose Help⇨Demo

Documentation excerpts

WPLOT is a Windows program that plots two and three-dimensional data. Up to 250 sets of data can be plotted on the same two-Dimensional plot, using either one or two vertical axes. There can be up to 16,000 data points per data set. Each data set can be plotted as a line plot, a smooth curve plot, a scatter plot, a step plot, or a histogram. Multiple data sets can also be plotted as a three-dimensional plots.

The plot can have linear or log axes with auto or manual scaling. Two-dimensional plots can also have cumulative normal probability axes, error bars, and descending, as well as ascending, axes. Data can be fit by a smooth curve or a least squares polynomial or exponential. The Fast Fourier Transform can be used to fit the data with a discrete Fourier series and the magnitudes of the FFT coefficients can be plotted. Mathematical transformations of the data can be performed by entering equations that operate on one or more data sets. Functions can be evaluated and plotted.

The WPLOT software comes with an auxiliary program, WFIT, which can fit a nonlinear function to data and use WPLOT to plot the fit. The WFIT program was originally written for DOS. It was compiled as a Windows program so that it could use the WPLOT program to do the plotting but it does not have a true Windows menu interface as does the WPLOT program.

Installation

The WPLOT software consists of the following files:

> WPLOT.DOC - Part of this explanatory file
>
> WPLOT.EXE - The WPLOT plotting program
>
> WPLOT.HLP - WPLOT Help file
>
> WFIT.EXE - Program that finds a nonlinear curve fit
>
> *.PLT - Example plot files that can be loaded by WPLOT
>
> *.FIT - Example curve fits that can be loaded by WFIT

To install the WPLOT software on a hard disk, make a directory that will contain the software, C:\WPLOT for example. Then copy to this directory all of the WPLOT files listed above including the example PLT and FIT files.

To install WPLOT as a Windows icon:

1. Select a Windows group.
2. Select the Program Manager's file menu item.
3. Select the New submenu item.
4. Select the Program Item option.
5. Enter the following information:

   > Description: WPLOT
   >
   > Command Line: C:\WPLOT\WPLOT.EXE
   >
   > Working Directory: C:\WPLOT

Follow a similar procedure to install the WFIT program.

To see a demo of the types of plots that WPLOT can make, start WPLOT and select the menu item File; then Load Plot Command File and load the file DEMO.PLT. The file DEMO.PLT and all of the other example PLT files must be in the working directory specified above.

You can also see the demo before installing WPLOT as a Windows icon. Use the DOS command CD to change the default directory to the directory containing the WPLOT program and example PLT files, for example:

```
CD \WPLOT
```

Then start Windows and the WPLOT program:

```
win wplot demo
```

WPLOT software license agreement and ordering information

Please see the files on the CD-ROM to read the WPLOT software software license agreement and to learn more about the program. Ordering information is also included on the CD-ROM.

Zip Manager v. 5.2

Zip Manager For Windows NT 3.5. Intel X86 Edition Version 5.2 January 26, 1995. Another approach to 32-bit Windows zipping. The README.TXT file covers important material *not* contained in the user's guide. Please read all of this information carefully! See the new features section for new features that are not covered in the help or documentation. From Software Excellence By Design Inc.

Category: Communications
Type: Shareware
Location on CD: \ZipMgr32
To install: Run d:\ZipMgr32\ZMSETUP.EXE
To run: Click on Start⇨Programs⇨Zip Manager 5.2

See the readme file on d:\ZipMgr32, and/or see Important Info! after installation. Quite a few warnings in there. But I installed and ran it on my Windows 95 PC. No snags so far.

Documentation excerpts

NOTE: This program requires Windows 95 or Windows NT version 3.5 or higher. It will not run on Windows NT 3.1.

All known bugs fixed

Version 5.2 fixes all known bugs reported to us in the last six months. All of the bugs associated with long file and directory names have been fixed. Most importantly the CD-ROM drive problem that some users reported has been fixed. The Password option has also been corrected, and your cosmetic and functional suggestions have been implemented where possible. Zip Manager fully supports NTFS; see the new features section.

Important installation directions

The install program does not accept long directory names. Enter a standard 8.3 DOS filename or accept the default directory. You can always change the name after installation.

The Zip Manager program files are in compressed format, and each file ends with an _ character. You must run the ZMSETUP program to expand them before the program can be used. You must run ZMSETUP.EXE from the Windows Program Manager. Other shells, like the Norton Desktop or PC Tools for Windows are not 100 percent compatible with our setup program, and may cause it to fail when attempting to create the Zip Manager Group.

Running the ZMSETUP program

1. From the Program Manager File menu choose Run.

2. Enter the location of the ZMSETUP Program. If the files were on your A: drive then you would enter: **A:\ZMSETUP** and press Enter or click on the OK button.

3. The Zip Manager setup dialog will be displayed.

4. The edit field will display a suggested directory.

5. Press OK to accept the default directory or enter new destination directory and press Enter or click on the OK button.

6. The setup program will create the directory for you and display the file installation progress.

7. When it has finished expanding and copying the files, it will create a new Program Manager Group and add the program files to the group. Now you can proceed with the next step.

To complete the installation

After the installation program is finished, you *must* read the installation section of the user's guide. You will see its icon in the Zip Manager group. You must set up the program's default directories and configure the program to work with your Virus Detection software.

Important information for PKZIP users only

Do not put the Zip Manager program files deep in a directory tree. Doing so may make it impossible for Zip Manager to work with the DOS programs ARJ and PKZIP. We suggest that you install Zip Manager in its own directory off of the root directory. C:\ZIPMGR, would be a good example. ZMZIP and ZMUNZIP allow Zip Manager to compress and extract files in very deep directory trees. However DOS programs are limited to 128 characters at the very most for command line arguments.

Important note for all users

Zip Manager creates its own temporary directory called zm5temp which it uses to extract and store files. Do *not* use this directory, because all of the files in it are deleted when Zip Manager ends. We wanted to be sure that you didn't set this as one of your default directories. If you did, all of your files would be gone when Zip Manager closed!

There was a bit of confusion about the usage of this directory and we wanted to make sure that you didn't lose any files accidentally.

Warning: Your data may be in danger

Never add 2.04 format files to any Zip file created with the PKZIP Version 1.10. This is the old zip file format, and if you add a file to a version 1.10 zip with either PKZIP 2.04g or Zip Manager you will corrupt the Zip file and all other files in it will be unrecoverable.

We have had a few users report this unfortunate problem, and we wanted to make you aware of it again for your safety. Zip Manager has an easy to use convert option on the Edit menu. If you are not sure if a file was created with PKZIP 1.10 or 2.04, then don't take a chance! Convert it to 2.04 format to be safe!

This potential problem with backward compatibility was never documented clearly with any other archive program. We want your data to be secure, so we felt it was worth re-documenting it here for extra safety.

Another important note

If you have the recurse directories switch checked and then select the root of your hard disk, Zip Manager will try to recurse and archive your entire drive! There may be some instance where you would need to do this, but just be aware that you will also need to have multiple volume switch set and have the target drive as either A: or B:

Important note on converting files!

Do not attempt to convert more than one file at a time! When converting a file from ZIP to ARJ or ARC to ZIP, for example, you would force the conversion process to open up more than one copy of PKZIP. This can easily result in severe data loss. The Zip Manager was designed to convert only one file at time, so please be careful.

MAPI.DLL error message warning

If you don't have an e-mail program, or one that uses the Microsoft Mail API, then the first time Zip Manager starts you *may* get a message box that says, `Error Can't Find MAPI.DLL`

To disable this error message, do the following:

1. Start the Windows Notepad program.

2. Type the following: **No mail.**

3. Choose Save from the File Menu.

4. Save the file in your Windows/System Directory with the name MAPI.DLL

5. Now when Zip Manager starts, it will see this file and disable the mail items on the menu and you will no longer get the error message.

All maintenance and minor version upgrades will be available only on our BBS. Because these releases will contain only the upgraded files, it will save you download time and keep the files on our board, where they won't inadvertently be downloaded as the complete program.

New features in version 5.2

Complete NTFS file support. Zip Manager now fully supports the NTFS file system and will handle both long filenames and long directory names.

The Short & Long Filename Buttons On the Tool Bar. In order to allow you to easily create zip files for DOS users Zip Manager has two buttons on the Tool Bar. DOS PKUNZIP wouldn't know what to do with a long filename or directory name and would report a corrupt Zip file.

✦ The L.___ Button displays long filenames only.

✦ The S.___ Button displays short filenames only.

You can press the short filename button and then be able to choose the short filename to add the a zip file. Now you can drag-and-drop only short names into a ZIP destined for DOS users.

Express Mode and alternate 8.3 names. Very important! Please note the following: Express Mode uses standard Windows list boxes, and as a result will only see long filenames and normal DOS 8.3 short filenames. It will not be able to show you the alternate short filename created by Windows NT. You will need to use Manager Mode if you need to work with alternate 8.3 names.

NTFS long name protection for DOS PKUNZIP. If you accidentally add a long filename to a zip file and then give it to a DOS user to extract, they will get the following error message from PKUNZIP: PKUNZIP you need version 3.6 to decompress this file. This was an error message that PKWARE had left in PKUNZIP for file systems other than DOS. We were able to use this to let users know that something is wrong with the ZIP file they got from you. It is nice to offer them some sort of error message other than a corrupt ZIP message.

Full PKZIP multiple-volume support. Zip Manager now fully supports creating and extracting all or selected files from a multiple-volume zip. Due to the way that a multiple-volume zip is created, you *must* place the last disk in the series in your floppy drive. The last disk is the only one that contains the needed information about all of the files contained in the ZIP file. Once the files are selected, PKUNZIP will prompt you to put in the correct disk number.

Full use of the registration database. In order to allow for multiple configurations and in keeping with the Win32 API, Zip Manager now makes full use of the registration database.

The "Easy Check Out Feature." Because Zip Manager can create a new group for you right from the menu or allow you to drag a program directly from an archive and drop it on any program manager group to add it to that group. All of these features make it very easy to check out a new program with a minimum of effort. Also remember that all you have to do to run a program is double click on it in any ZIP or ARJ file.

Self-extracting archive support. Zip Manager now fully supports self extracting EXE files as normal archive files. You double click on them to open them into the archive pane as you would any other ZIP or ARJ file. You can then perform any option available to archive files on them.

File renaming support on extraction. If Zip Manager encounters a file with the same name when extracting a zip file it gives you the option of entering a new filename. Only Zip Manager and ARJ offer users this convenient option!

Directory creation on extraction. Many users asked for this feature so that they could have a new directory created if they wanted to when the ZIP file was extracted. Zip Manager can even create a multiple level directory. For example, if you entered: **c:\test1\test2\test3,** Zip Manager would create that directory structure and extract the files into the test3 sub directory!

Drag-and-Drop server. Version 5 is now a Drag-and-Drop server, which means that you can drag files from Zip Manager and drop them on any program or other file manager for Windows to copy, move, or even add them to a Program Manager group. This functionality applies to files in archives and normal files shown in the directory pane.

. Dot and .. Double Dot support. This release supports the . and .. as target directories when creating or extracting files. You can enter a . or a .. in the target directory combo box instead of typing in the full directory name.

Virus detection programs. Note: In order for your virus detection program to work with Zip Manager it must be able to accept command line arguments. Read the user's guide (installation section) for instructions on how to determine if your program will work with Zip Manager.

Possible parameter combinations for virus detection programs.

In the Zip Manager Setup dialog box, enter the following after the program location name and directory: **X:\UTILITIES\NAVW.EXE /auto *.* /S**. This would be the correct command for the Norton Anti Virus for Windows Program.

Listed below are the (sometimes) correct switch parameters for most popular virus detection programs. You will most likely still need to experiment a little to get some of them to work. We use and recommend SCAN.EXE from McAfee and Associates.

NAVW.EXE /auto *.* /S
WNAPVIR.EXE /QM *.*
SCAN.EXE /A /nomem *.* /SUB
NAV.EXE *.* /m- /s
CPAV.EXE *.* /P
MSAV.EXE *.* /P

ZMZIP & ZMUNZIP versus PKZIP & PKUNZIP switch support cross reference

For ordering, contact, registration, and more detailed information, see the appropriate file for this program on the companion CD-ROM.

Keyboard Shortcuts Quick Reference

If you use the keyboard often in your work, you may find that you often have to take your hands off the keyboard to perform some simple mouse operation — for example, opening a drop-down list in a dialog box. In fact, however, you could press Alt+down arrow to open the drop-down list.

If you take a minute to review the common keyboard shortcuts summarized in this appendix, you may find a technique that enables you to keep your typing fingers on those home keys.

Feature/Action	Keyboard Shortcut
Accessibility: Filter Keys	Hold down right Shift key for 8 seconds
Accessibility: High Contrast	Left Alt+left Shift+Print Screen
Accessibility: Mouse Keys	Left Alt+left Shift+Num Lock
Accessibility: Sticky Keys	Tap Shift 5 times
Accessibility: Toggle keys	Hold down Num Lock for 5 seconds
Beginning of line	Home
Bottom of document	Ctrl+End
Bypass auto-play on CD-ROM	Hold down Shift while inserting CD-ROM

(continued)

Feature/Action	Keyboard Shortcut
Bypass startup programs	Hold down Shift during startup
Cancel	Esc
Check box: toggle on or off	spacebar
Close document window	Ctrl+F4
Close failed (hung) program	Ctrl+Alt+Delete
Close folder and all parent folders	Hold down Shift and click on Close (X)
Close program window	Alt+F4
Command-prompt startup	Press F8 at `Starting Windows` prompt message
Context menu	Shift+F10
Copy to Clipboard	Ctrl+C
Cut to Clipboard	Ctrl+X
Cycle through program windows	Alt+Tab
Delete	Delete
Delete; no Recycle Bin	Shift+Delete
Drag-and-drop, copy item	Ctrl+drag
Drag-and-drop, create shortcut	Ctrl+Shift+drag
Drag-and-drop, move item	Alt+drag
End of line	End
Explore object	Shift+double-click
Explorer: Collapse selection	– (gray minus key)
Explorer: Expand all below	* (gray asterisk key)
Explorer: Expand selection	+ (gray plus key)
Explorer: Go To	Ctrl+G
Explorer: Go To Parent	Backspace
Explorer: Next pane	F6
Explorer: Open combo box	F4
Explorer: Refresh	F5
Explorer: Scroll without moving selection	Ctrl+arrow key
Find	F3

(continued)

Feature/Action	Keyboard Shortcut
Help	F1
Insert/Overwrite: toggle on or off	Insert
Menu	F10
Microsoft Natural keyboard: Cycle through	Win+Tab taskbar buttons
Microsoft Natural keyboard: Explorer	Win+E
Microsoft Natural keyboard: Find Computer	Ctrl+Win+F
Microsoft Natural keyboard: Find File/Folder	Win+F
Microsoft Natural keyboard: Minimize All	Win+M
Microsoft Natural keyboard: Run	Win+R
Microsoft Natural keyboard: System Properties	Win+Break
Microsoft Natural keyboard: Undo Minimize All	Shift+Win+M
Microsoft Natural keyboard: Windows Help	Win+F1
Minimize all open windows (from taskbar or desktop)	Alt+M
New document	Ctrl+N
Next open program window	Alt+Tab
Next option in dialog box or form	Tab
Next tab of dialog box	Ctrl+Tab
OK	Enter
Open document	Ctrl+O
Open drop-down list	Alt+down arrow
Open Look In list	F4
Open property sheet	Alt+Enter or Alt+double-click
Open With: display verb list	Ctrl+right-click
Option buttons	space bar
Paste	Ctrl+V
Preceding option in dialog box or form	Shift+Tab
Preceding tab of dialog box	Ctrl+Shift+Tab
Print	Ctrl+P
Refresh	F5

(continued)

Feature/Action	Keyboard Shortcut
Rename	F2
Save document	Ctrl+S
Select All	Ctrl+A
Select text	Shift+any direction key
Select to beginning of document	Shift+Ctrl+Home
Select to end of document	Shift+Ctrl+End
Select to end of line	Shift+End
Select to start of line	Shift+Home
Start menu (open)	Ctrl+Esc
Top of document	Ctrl+Home
Undo	Ctrl+Z

Using Microsoft Plus!

Microsoft Plus! is an optional add-on to Windows 95. If you want it, you need to purchase it separately. If you want to find out more about Plus! before you buy, read this Appendix to see what Plus! has to offer, and whether or not you have the appropriate hardware. If you've already purchased Plus!, you can use the Appendix to install and use its features. Here is a brief description of the various goodies that Plus! offers:

✦ Some fun *desktop themes*, some visual enhancement features, and a 3D pinball game.

✦ *System agent* lets you schedule programs to run automatically at certain times.

✦ *DriveSpace 3* provides disk compression up to 2 gigabytes.

✦ *Dial-Up Server* allows you to access your PC from some remote location, using a portable PC and a modem.

✦ Internet *Explorer* lets you explore the Internet using the Windows 95 interface.

System Requirements for Plus!

One of the reasons that Plus! is sold as a separate product is simply because it won't work on all hardware. Before you purchase Plus!, you want to make sure your PC meets the minimum requirements:

Processor:	486, or Pentium (no 386s)
Memory (RAM):	8MB
Video display:	At least 256 colors. High Color (16-bit) recommended

Installing Microsoft Plus!

Once you have a copy of Microsoft Plus! in hand, you can install it as you would any other program:

1. Click on the Start button.

2. Point to Settings and then click on Control Panel.

3. Double-click on the Add/Remove Programs icon.

4. Click on the Install button on the Install/Uninstall tab.

5. Follow the instructions on the screen, and click on the Next button when you're ready to move onto the next screen.

If you opted to install the Internet Explorer, the Internet Setup wizard will start automatically. If you don't have all the information you need to complete the wizard, don't worry. Just choose Cancel and forget about the Internet for now. When you're ready to give the Internet a whirl, see "Exploring the Internet" later in this Appendix.

You'll also be prompted to choose a desktop theme. If you're not sure which theme you want right now, you can just click the Cancel button to keep your current desktop settings. Then you can choose a desktop theme later, following the steps under "Fun With Desktop Themes" a little later in this appendix.

Finally, if your hard disk is already compressed using DoubleSpace or DriveSpace, you'll be given some options to upgrade to DriveSpace 3. You can choose OK to upgrade right on the spot, or choose Notify me again... to leave your current compression scheme intact. To learn more about DriveSpace 3, see "Using Plus! Disk Compression" later in this Appendix.

Integrated help for Plus!

Microsoft Plus! has its own online help. But when you install Plus!, its help becomes integrated with the rest of your Windows 95 help. So you can get at the Plus! help from that Start button, as follows:

1. Click on the Start button.

2. Click on Help.

3. Click on the Contents tab.

4. You should now see a book for Microsoft Plus!. Double-click on that book to see books within the Microsoft Plus! book, as in Figure F-1.

Figure F-1: Help for Plus! added to Windows 95 help contents.

You can use the Plus! help normally now. For example, you can double-click on any book to see topics within that book. Then you can double-click on any topic to explore that topic.

The online help for Plus! is also integrated into the Index and Find tabs of the general Windows help. So let's say, for example, you use the Index or Find tab in Windows 95 to search for the word *Internet*. The results of your search will automatically include relevant topics from both Windows 95 and Microsoft Plus! If you're a little rusty on Windows 95 online help, refer to Chapter 1, starting at the section titled "Your electronic table of contents".

Fun With Desktop Themes

The desktop themes that come with Microsoft Plus! let you set up a screen saver, wallpaper, icons, sounds, and other elements, all centered around a theme. To choose a theme

1. Click on the Start button.

2. Point to Settings.

3. Click on Control Panel.

4. Double-click on the Desktop Themes icon.

You're taken to the Desktop Themes dialog box shown in Figure F-2. Use the drop-down list button next to Theme to choose a theme. If you have a 256-color display, or have limited your settings to 256 colors, choose only a 256 color theme. If you're set up for 16-bit or 24-bit color, you can choose any theme.

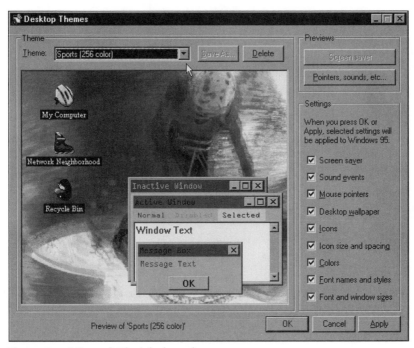

Figure F-2: Microsoft Plus! desktop themes.

 If you need to check or change your color settings, right-click on the desktop, choose Properties, and click on the Settings tab. See Chapter 6 if you need more information.

By default, Plus! will set up all elements of the theme: screen saver, sound events, mouse pointers, and so forth. If you don't want to include an element, just clear its check box. If you want to preview an element before making your selection, click on the Screen saver or Pointers, sounds, etc. button under Preview.

When you've finished making your selection(s), just click on the OK button to return to the desktop.

If you want to change a particular element of a desktop theme, such as the wallpaper or screen saver, use the standard techniques described in Chapter 6, "Personalizing the Screen." Or just follow these steps to get into the appropriate dialog box right now:

1. Click on the Start button and point to Settings.

2. Choose Control Panel.

3. Double-click on the icon for the element you want to change, and choose the appropriate tab in the dialog box that appears, as summarized below:

If you want to change...	...double-click on
Colors	Display⇨Appearance tab
Fonts	Display⇨Appearance tab
Icons	Display⇨Plus! tab
Icon Size and Spacing	Display⇨Appearance tab (Item)
Mouse pointers	Mouse⇨Pointers tab
Screen saver	Display⇨Screen Saver tab
Sound events	Sounds
Wallpaper	Display⇨Background tab

Using the Plus! Visual Enhancements

Microsoft Plus! also comes with some enhancements to improve the general appearance of your screen. When you install Plus!, options for activating these enhancements are automatically integrated into your Display Properties dialog box. To get to the options:

1. Right-click on your desktop and choose Properties. (Or click on Start⇨Settings⇨Control Panel and then double-click on the Display icon.)

2. Click on the Plus! tab in the Display properties dialog box.

The Plus! tab, shown in Figure F-3, offers the options summarized below:

✦ *Desktop icons:* Click on any of the four general desktop icons, then click on the Change Icon button to choose a different picture to represent that icon.

✦ *Show window contents while dragging:* When selected, this option assures that you can see the actual contents of any window—not just a ghost image of the window—as you drag the window to a new location on the screen.

✦ *Smooth edges of screen fonts:* When selected, this option gets rid of the *jaggies* that often give screen fonts a rough edge.

✦ *Show icons using all possible colors:* Uses whatever color capabilities your system has, rather than just 16 colors, to display icons. Makes for richer-looking icons — but consumes a little memory and slows down screen-refreshing.

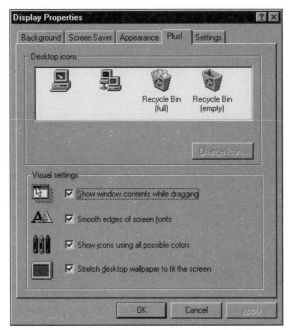

Figure F-3: Visual Enhancement options on the Plus! tab.

> ✦ *Stretch desktop wallpaper to fit the screen:* Ensures that even a small (for example, 640 x 480) screen saver will fill your 800 x 600 or greater screen. To make this work, you must also click on the Background tab in the Display Properties dialog box and choose Center under the Wallpaper options.

When you've finished making your selections, choose OK.

Scheduling Programs with System Agent

The System Agent program that comes with Microsoft Plus! lets you schedule programs to run automatically while you're away from the PC. It's especially good for ensuring that your system maintenance tasks, which we discussed back in Chapter 11, are performed on a regular basis.

When you install Microsoft Plus!, System Agent is installed and activated automatically each time you start Windows 95. Initially, System Agent appears as just a tiny indicator in the taskbar. To open System Agent, double-click that little indicator. The System Agent opens into a window and displays scheduled tasks, as in the example shown in Figure F-4.

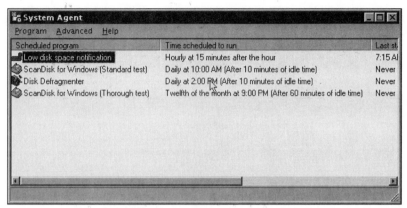

Figure F-4: The System Agent with some scheduled tasks.

If you don't see the System Agent indicator in the taskbar, you can follow these steps to open it:

1. Click on the Start button.
2. Point to Programs⇨Accessories⇨System Tools.
3. Click on System Agent.

Add a scheduled program

If you want schedule a program to run automatically at some predetermined time, you first need to know the location and file name of that program. If you don't have that information handy, here's how you can find it:

1. Right-click on the Start button and choose Open.
2. Double-click on the Programs icon. The Programs dialog box that appears contains an icon for each program group, and each program, on your Programs menu.
3. Now work your way to the Startup icon for the program you want to schedule. For example, if the program you want to schedule is right on your Programs menu (for example Microsoft Exchange), you don't need to drill down any further. However, if the program you want to schedule is in the Accessories folder, you need to double-click on the Accessories icon so you can find your program's startup icon.
4. When you see the icon for the program you want to schedule, right-click on that icon and choose Properties from the shortcut menu that appears.
5. Click on the Shortcut tab and take a look at the Target entry. That's the location and name of the program as needed by System Agent. In Figure F-5 I've zeroed in on Microsoft Exchange.

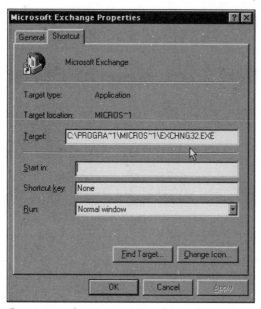

Figure F-5: The Target option shows the location and name of a program.

6. Now jot down the information in the Target box. For example, in this case I would jot down `C:\PROGRA~1\MICROS~1\EXCHNG32.EXE`.

7. Once you've jotted down the information you need, you can just back out of your previous selections. Choose Cancel and close open windows until you get back to the desktop.

Once you know the location and filename of the program you want to schedule, just follow these steps to add that program to System Agent:

1. If you haven't already done so, open System Agent.

2. Choose Program⇨Schedule a new program from System Agent's menu bar.

3. Click on the Browse button.

4. In the Browse dialog box that appears, open folders as appropriate until you find the icon for the program you want to schedule.

In my example, I would first need to click on the Up One Level button to get to drive C:, then double-click on the Program Files icon (which, in the Target box, was represented by `C:\PROGRA~1`). Then I'd double-click on the Microsoft Exchange icon (as represented by `\MICROS_1` in the Target description). Finally, I would double-click on the EXCHNG32.EXE icon.

5. Type in a Description of your own choosing. Figure F-6 shows an example using my progress on automating Microsoft Exchange.

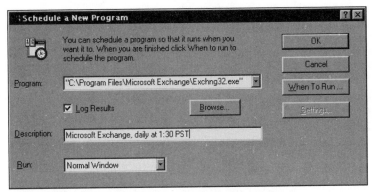

Figure F-6: Microsoft Exchange ready to be scheduled.

6. Now click on the When to Run button.

7. Choose options in the "Change Schedule..." dialog box to indicate when you want this program to run. For example, in Figure F-7 I've set up Exchange to run automatically every day at 1:30 (That'll remind me to check my e-mail before 4:30 Eastern time).

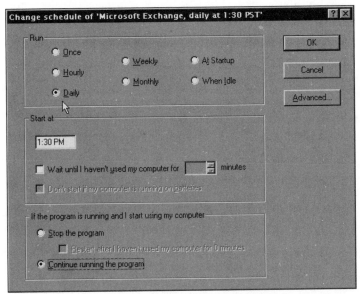

Figure F-7: Will run Microsoft Exchange daily at 1:30 PM.

8. Optionally, use the Advanced button and other options on the screen to determine how to handle the various situations that each option explains.

9. Choose OK as necessary to work your way back to the System Agent window.

The program you just scheduled will be listed with other scheduled programs. You can close System Agent, if you wish, by clicking on its Close (X) button. The program will run at the appointed time provided that your computer and System Agent are running when the time arrives.

 When I say "providing that System Agent is running . . .," I just mean that the System Agent icon needs to be visible in the taskbar. You needn't open the System Agent icon to make scheduled events occur.

Changing settings for a scheduled program

Some programs, such as DriveSpace and Disk Defragmenter, are specifically designed for use with System Agent. Those programs have special settings you can adjust to decide exactly how you want System Agent to run the program. To change those settings:

1. Open System Agent if it isn't already open.

2. Click on the program whose settings you want to change.

3. Choose Program⇨Properties from System Agent's menu bar.

4. Click on the Settings button.

5. In the Scheduled Settings... dialog box that appears, make your selections. Figure F-8 shows an example using the schedule settings for the ScanDisk program.

6. Choose OK as necessary to work your way back to System Agent.

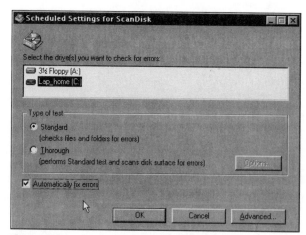

Figure F-8: Scheduled settings for ScanDisk.

Now you can close System Agent by clicking on its Close (X) button.

If a scheduled program doesn't have a simple Settings button and Schedules Settings dialog box, you may still be able to control how the program runs by passing *startup commands* to the scheduled programs. Typically a startup command is a *switch* that you add on to the end of the command, outside the quotation marks. For example, adding /a to the Program line for my Exchange program, as below

```
"C:\Program Files\Microsoft Exchange\Exchng32.exe" /a
```

would automatically start Microsoft Exchange and open the Address Book.

 To add/change a switch or setting after you've already scheduled a program, just open System Agent, right-click on the name of the program you want to change, and choose Properties.

To find out what startup switches are available for a program, you need to search that program's help or written documentation for appropriate buzzwords, such as *startup* or *switches* or *command line switches*.

To test a scheduled program and any startup options you've defined, open System Agent (if it isn't already open). Right-click on the name of the scheduled program you want to test, and choose Run Now from the shortcut menu that appears.

Change a program's schedule

To change the schedule of any program in System Agent:

1. Open System Agent.
2. Right-click the program you want to reschedule.
3. Choose Change Schedule.
4. Make your selections from the Change schedule...dialog box that appears, then choose OK.

Disable/remove a scheduled program

You can temporarily disable a scheduled program so that it does not run at its appointed time, but stays listed in the System Agent dialog box, so that you can re-enable it at some time in the future. To disable a scheduled program, open System Agent, right-click on the name of the scheduled program you want to disable, and choose Disable. The *Time scheduled to run* column in System Agent will show the word *Disabled* for that program. To reinstate the schedules program, right-click its name again in System Agent, and select the Disable option so it no longer has a check mark.

You can also remove a program from System Agent altogether. Just open System Agent, right-click on the name of the program you want to remove, and choose Remove from the shortcut menu. Or just click on the program you want to remove and choose Program ➪ Remove from System Agent's menu bar.

Disable or enable System Agent

There may be times when you don't want System Agent to run any of its programs. For example, let's say you're going to use your PC to give a public presentation, and you don't want DriveSpace or "defrag" to pop up in the middle of your presentation. No problem, here's what you do:

1. Open System Agent.

2. Choose Advanced from System Agent's menu bar.

3. Now choose one of the following:

    ✦ Suspend System Agent: Leaves the System Agent indicator in the taskbar as a reminder, but does not allow the agent to run scheduled programs.

    ✦ Stop using System Agent: Choose this option if you want to prevent all scheduled programs from running and to remove System Agent's indicator from the taskbar.

If you opted to suspend the agent, you can click on its Close button (X) to close the window. If you opted to stop the agent, you'll be asked for confirmation. Choose Yes, and the System Agent window and taskbar indicator will disappear from your screen.

If you need to re-start System Agent after removing its indicator from the taskbar, click on the Start button, point to Programs➪Accessories➪System Tools, and click on System Agent.

Using Plus! Disk Compression

Microsoft Plus! comes with two programs called DriveSpace 3 and Compression Agent. Together these two programs offer disk compression features that aren't available in the DriveSpace program that comes standard with Windows 95 (see "Maximize Your Disk Space" in Chapter 12 for more information on that program). Microsoft Plus! compression offers the following:

✦ Supports compressed drives up to 2 gigabytes (2,048 MB) in size, as compared to 512 MB in standard DriveSpace.

✦ Compression Agent allows you to compact files more tightly than DriveSpace does.

✦ You can choose settings that let you find the best balance between speed and disk space for your PC.

Compressing a drive

To compress a drive using DriveSpace 3, follow these steps:

1. Double-click on My Computer.

2. Right-click on the icon for the drive you want to compress, and choose P<u>r</u>oper-
   ties from the shortcut menu that appears.

3. Click on the Compression tab. You'll see some options like the example shown
   in Figure F-9.

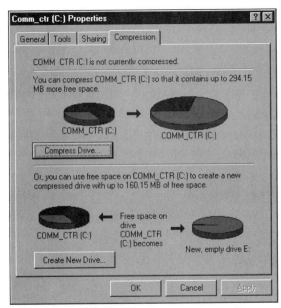

Figure F-9: Compression options for a sample
hard disk.

Notice that you have two choices. You can compress the entire drive, in which case
the entire drive will appear larger, though you'll still have only one hard drive (probably drive C). A second choice is to compress just the empty space on the current
drive and to treat that new compressed space as a separate drive. For example, if I
opted to create a new drive in Figure F-9, I'd end up with two hard disk drives, one
named C: and a new, compressed drive named E: (If you want to keep things simple,
choose the first option, Compress Drive).

It can take several hours to compress a drive, during which you cannot
use the computer at all. You may want to start the job just before leaving
work so you don't have to wait around for DriveSpace to finish the job.
Once you start compressing, do not shut down Windows or your PC until
the compression is finished.

A third possibility is that your drive is already compressed using DoubleSpace or the standard DriveSpace. In that case, clicking on the Compression tab will take you to a dialog box that will simply let you upgrade your existing compression to DriveSpace 3.

To begin the compression, just click on whichever button best describes what you want to do. Then follow instructions as they appear on the screen. After compression is complete (which might take several hours), you'll be given a choice of three compression methods:

✦ Standard compression: Compacts data to about half its normal size. This method is the fastest, but conserves the least disk space.

✦ HighPack compression: Compacts a file 10% to 20% more than the standard compression, but takes longer than standard compression.

✦ UltraPack compression: Compresses files more densely than the other two methods, but also takes the longest.

Choose whichever method seems best to you, given the density/speed trade off. For example, if keeping things running at top speed is more important than conserving hard disk space, you'll want to select Standard Compression. If disk space is a major problem, you can choose UltraPack. But do note that UltraPack requires that you also run the Compression Agent, as described next.

Using the Compression Agent

Once you've compressed a drive using DriveSpace 3, you can use the Compression Agent to compress files even further. By default, Compression Agent will compress rarely-used files using the UltraPack method. Files you use more frequently will be packed using the faster, HighPack method.

The best way to run Compression Agent is to simply let System Agent do it for you during odd hours when nobody is using the PC heavily. By default, Windows 95 will run Compression Agent at about 10 PM each night. To verify or change that setting, open the System Agent as discussed under "Scheduling Programs with System Agent." Compression Agent will be included in the list, as shown in Figure F-10.

If you want to run Compression Agent yourself, whether to force a compression now or to explore its Help screens, just click on the Start button and point to Programs⇨Accessories⇨System Tools, then click on Compression Agent.

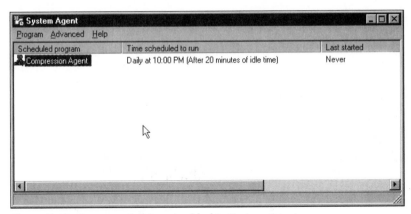

Figure F-10: Compression Agent added to System Agent.

Set Up a Dial-Up Networking Server

The Dial-Up Networking Server component of Microsoft Plus! lets you configure your Windows 95 PC as a dial-up server. That is, it lets you set up your PC so that it answers the phone when you, or someone else, call in from a Windows 95 PC running the Dial-up Server client (The client comes with standard Windows 95, so you don't need to purchase Plus! to dial into an existing server).

When you install Microsoft Plus!, it automatically adds the necessary programs and menu commands that you need to set up your dial-up server. Basically, it just adds the Dial-Up Server option to the Connections menu in the Dial-Up Networking dialog box (Figure F-11). For specific instructions on using dial-up networking, see Chapter 20. Pay special attention to the opening sections on Network Neighborhood and sharing resources, and the section titled "Dial-Up Networking."

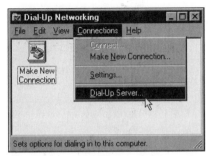

Figure F-11: The Dial-Up Server option in Dial-Up Networking.

Exploring the Internet

Microsoft Plus! also comes with a program named Internet Explorer. This is an ideal program for Internet *newbies* because it lets you learn about and use the Internet using a Windows 95 interface. Also, Internet Explorer will let you hook into the Internet via the Microsoft Network (MSN). So you don't need to go through all the hassle of getting an Internet Service Provider to get started with the Net.

Chapter 22 discusses ways of exploring the Internet *without* the Microsoft Plus! Internet Explorer. If you don't understand some of the jargon I use in this chapter, you should probably browse through Chapter 22 just to learn some basic Internet concepts.

Internet prerequisites

Before you start setting up Internet Explorer on your PC, check to make sure you've already done the following:

✦ Install a modem and test it, as discussed in Chapter 15.

✦ If you don't have an Internet account and want to use MSN as your on-ramp to the Internet, be sure to learn the basics of MSN first. See Chapter 21.

✦ If you're not at all familiar with the Internet, you might also want to browse through some of the basic concepts described in Chapter 22 (though you won't need to sign up with an ISP if you go through MSN).

Setting up Internet Explorer

When you first install Microsoft Plus!, it prompts you for information about how you want to access the Internet. If you bypassed that step, or need to make some changes to your earlier settings, you can run the Internet Setup wizard:

1. Click on the Start button.

2. Point to Programs⇨Accessories⇨Internet Tools.

3. Click on Internet Setup Wizard.

4. Follow the instructions on the screen to set up your Internet connection.

If you're new to the Internet, you might be a little unsure which options to select. If you're using the Internet for the first time, you'll almost certainly want to choose these options when the wizard asks for connection information:

✦ Connect using my phone line

✦ Use the Microsoft Network

When you've answered all the questions posed by the wizard, you can use the techniques in the sections that follow to explore the Internet.

Using Internet Explorer

Internet Explorer is the quick and easy way to explore and learn about the Internet. It's simple to get started:

✦ Double-click on the Internet Explorer icon on the Desktop

✦ Or, click on the Start button and point to Programs⇨Accessories⇨Internet Tools, then click on Internet Explorer.

You'll be taken to a World Wide Web page on the Internet. Of course, because that page is on the Internet rather than on your PC, the page is subject to change. But chances are that when you get to Internet Explorer for the first time, your screen will look something like Figure F-12.

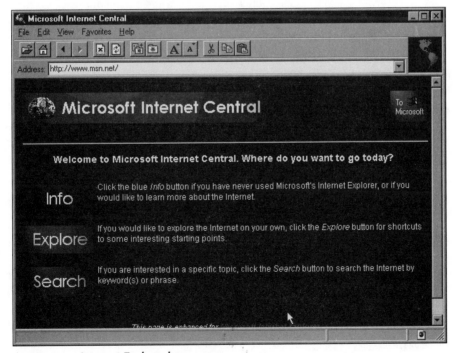

Figure F-12: Internet Explorer home page.

From this point on, the best way to learn about the Internet and Internet Explorer is by doing. Just click on the big blue Info button and let the Internet Explorer guide you through. But here's a quick overview of essential skills that'll make even the guided tour easier:

✦ Many pictures on a page are hotspots that you can click on for more information. When the mouse pointer is touching a hotspot, the pointer changes to a small hand icon.

✦ If you start to feel lost, you can click on the To Central icon in the current window, or click on the Go To Start Page button (which looks like a little house) in the toolbar.

✦ Downloading graphics can take a long time. To stop a downloading graphic image, just press the Escape (Esc) key.

✦ As with MSN, you can create a list of favorite places on the Internet. When you get to a place you'd like to visit again, just choose Favorites⇨Add To Favorites. Then click on the Add button.

✦ To return to a favorite place, click on the Favorites button and click on the name of a place from that menu. Or choose Favorites⇨Open Favorites and double-click on the place you want to go.

As you use the Internet Explorer, it will teach you more about these basic skills, and more about the Internet in general.

Entering addresses on your own

You're not limited to exploring pages that offer single-click access from Internet Explorer. You can go to any World Wide Web page, provided you know the page's address (or URL for Universal Resource Locator as it's called). Just choose File⇨Open, type in the address, and choose OK. Or type the appropriate address into the Address Bar and press Enter. If the address bar isn't visible, just choose View⇨Address Bar to display it.

As an example, let's say I hear or read about a hot Web site that has all kinds of wild graphics. All I know about this site is its address, which we'll say is `http://www.sgi.com`. No problem. I just type that address into the address bar, press Enter, and wait a few minutes. Eventually I'll come to the home page for that site, as in the example shown in Figure F-13.

Downloading files from FTP sites

You can also use the Internet Explorer to connect to FTP sites and download files. To get to an FTP site, just use File⇨Open or the address bar, as described in the previous section. For example, in Figure F-14 I've browsed jumped to the `ftp://ftp.microsoft.com` site.

Figure F-13: The home page for `http://www.sgi.com`.

Once you're in an FTP site, just browse to and double-click on the name of the file that you want to download.

Disconnecting from the Internet

When you've finished exploring, just choose File⇨Exit from Internet Explorer's menu bar. If you logged in through MSN, take a quick look at the indicators in the status bar. If the MSN indicator is still visible, and you want to hang up, double-click on the MSN indicator and choose Yes to disconnect.

Playing Pinball

After reading this grueling appendix on all the goodies that Plus! offers, you're probably ready to take a break and play a little 3D Pinball:

1. Click on the Start button.

2. Point to Programs⇨Accessories⇨Games.

3. Click on 3D Pinball to get to the window shown in Figure F-15.

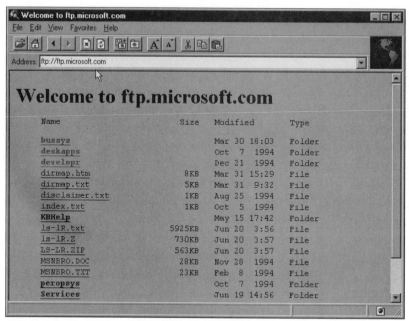

Figure F-14: To an FTP site from Internet Explorer.

Figure F-15: 3D Pinball.

4. When you're ready to play, choose Game⇨Launch Ball from the menu bar.

Now get your fingers on the Z and / keys, because those are the ones you'll use to work the flippers. I trust that you'll be able to figure out other options on your own, simply by exploring the Game, Options, and Help commands in the menu bar. I might point out, however, that if you switch to full-screen view (Options⇨Full Screen), you'll need to press the F10 key when you need to get back to the menu bar.

Glossary

:-): Your basic smiley symbol (when viewed from the side — lean your head left), often used in e-mail messages to mean "just kidding".

<g>: In an e-mail message means "grin" or "just kidding".

10BASE-T: A type of cable used to connect computers in a local area network together. Typically plugs into an RJ-45 slot on a network adapter card and ethernet hub.

16-bit: The addressing scheme used in the original IBM PC and AT (286) computers. The main reason for the old 640K limit.

32-bit: The addressing scheme used in 386, 486, and Pentium Processors. Allows a wider range of addresses, and processes data far more quickly.

256-color: The minimum number of colors that many modern programs will accept. To change your color settings, you right-click on the desktop, choose Properties, and then click on the Settings tab.

A

active window: The window that's currently capable of accepting input. The active window is said to *have the focus*. The active window can cover other windows on the desktop.

AOL (America Online): A popular information service offering e-mail, special interest groups, Internet access, and other services.

anonymous FTP: A service that allows Internet users to upload and download files freely across the Internet, without identifying themselves or typing passwords.

API (Application Programming Interface): A set of routines that programmers can call from higher-level languages. These routines access capabilities of the operating system.

ASCII (American Standard Code for Information Interchange): A standard for describing characters that allows different makes and models of computers to communicate with one another. An *ASCII file* or *ASCII text file* is one that contains only ASCII characters, no pictures or formatting codes.

associate: To tie a filename extension to a program. For example, the .doc filename extension is usually associated with Microsoft Word, so that when you double-click on a document that has the .doc extension, Windows automatically opens Microsoft Word, and opens the file you double-clicked on.

At Work: Microsoft Corporation's initiative to get all office equipment— including PCs, telephones, fax machines, and copy machines—to be able to interact with one another.

B

backward compatibility: The ability to use documents, settings, and so forth from earlier products. For example, Windows 95 is backwardly compatible with DOS and Windows 3.x.

baud: The speed of a modem. The higher the baud rate, the faster the modem.

BBS (Bulletin Board Service): A service you can contact via telephone lines using your modem and a communications program such as HyperTerminal. Most offer special interest groups, shareware, freeware, and other services.

binding: A process that establishes a communication channel between a network adapter card's driver and the driver for a network protocol. In Windows 95,

bindings are available via the Network icon in Control Panel.

BIOS enumerator: In a plug-and-play system, the BIOS enumerator identifies all hardware on the motherboard.

bps (bits per second): A measure of a modem's speed, also expressed as *baud*.

browse: To look around at drives, folders, and files using *My Computer, Windows Explorer,* or a dialog box's Browse button.

bus: A device that controls yet other devices. For example, when you plug a new board into a PC, you're actually plugging it into a bus.

byte: The amount of space required to store one character. For example, the word *cat* requires three bytes of storage. The word *Hello* requires five bytes.

C

cache: Pronounced *cash,* refers to an area in RAM where frequently-accessed data is stored, to speed up access.

CD-ROM (Compact Disc Read-Only Memory): CD-style disks used in CD-ROM readers on a PC. Unless you have special equipment, you can only read information *from* a CD-ROM. You cannot add, change, or delete files.

CDFS (Compact Disc File System): The system that Windows 95 uses to manage files stored on a CD-ROM.

character: A single letter, digit, or punctuation mark. For example, there are nine characters in the boldface text that follows: **Hello123!**.

CIS (CompuServe Information Service): A popular information service offering e-mail, special-interest forums, Internet access, and other services.

click: To press and release the main mouse button after positioning the mouse pointer onto the thing you want to click on. The main mouse button is usually the one that rests comfortable under your index finger.

client: A computer on a LAN that uses some resource shared by another computer on the LAN. The computer that the shared resource is physically connected to is called the *server*.

Clipboard: An area in memory where objects can be stored temporarily, for cut-and-paste procedures. Typically you select an object (by clicking on it) or select text (by dragging the mouse pointer to it). Then to copy to the Clipboard, choose Edit⇨Copy or press Ctrl+C. Move to wherever you want to put the object/text, and choose Edit⇨Paste or press Ctrl+V to copy the Clipboard's contents to the insertion point position. To open the Clipboard, click on start and choose Programs⇨Accessories⇨Clipboard Viewer.

close: To remove from the screen so it's no longer visible. Typically, closing an object removes it from memory (RAM) and saves the object to the hard disk.

CMOS: Memory that's maintained by a small battery within the PC. Often used to manage settings that come into play before the operating system is loaded. When you see a message such as "Press <Del> to run Setup", pressing the Delete (Del) key at that point will take you to the CMOS settings of that PC.

codec: A system for compressing/decompressing digital video and sound to minimize the amount of disk space required for storage.

computer name: The name assigned to a computer, up to 15 characters in length. To assign a name to a computer, open Control Panel, double-click on the Network icon, and click on the Identification tab.

context menu: The menu that appears when you right-click on an object. Also called a *shortcut menu* or a *pop-up menu*.

context-sensitive help: On-screen help that's relevant to what you're trying to do at the moment. In Windows 95, you typically use the Help key (F1) or Question-mark (?) button to receive context-sensitive help.

control: Any button, list, or text box within a dialog box that lets you control how the computer will behave.

Control Panel: The place in Windows 95 where you choose your own settings and preferences, add new hardware and software, and alter profiles. Click on Start and choose Settings⇨Control Panel. Or open *My Computer* and double-click on the Control Panel icon.

CTI (Computer/Telephone Integration) Using a PC in combination with the telephone system. For example, voice mail (see *telephony*).

Ctrl+Click: To hold down the Ctrl (control) key while you click objects with your mouse.

Ctrl+Drag: To hold down the Ctrl (control) key while you drag an object with your mouse.

cyberspace: A nickname for the Internet, or all the networks of the world. The place where e-mail messages travel to get from sender to recipient.

D

DDE (Dynamic Data Exchange): A means by which two separate programs can exchange data and commands. Available in early Windows, DDE has been superseded by OLE in more recent versions of Windows.

default: A selection that will be used unless you specify otherwise. For example, when you print, the job is sent to the *default printer* unless you specifically request a different printer.

default printer: The printer that's used when no other printer is specified. To define the default printer, open *My Computer,* then double-click on the Printers folder. Right-click a printer's icon and choose Set As Default from the shortcut menu. Only one printer can act as the default printer.

desktop: Basically, your entire screen when Windows 95 is running.

desktop icon: An icon that appears right on the desktop, such as *My Computer* and *Recycle Bin.* You can also add your own *shortcut* icons to the desktop.

desktop theme: A combination of sounds, wallpaper, screen saver, and icons to give your entire desktop an appearance. The Microsoft Plus! package comes with several desktop themes.

device: A general term for any gizmo or gadget that you put into a computer, or attach to a computer with a cable.

device driver: see *driver.*

dialog box: A box with options that appears on the screen, so that you can make additional selections. For example, choosing File⇨Open from a program's menu bar typically displays that program's Open dialog box.

DHCP (Dynamic Host Configuration Protocol): A protocol for TCP/IP configuration, often used for Internet connections.

digital video: Video stored in binary format on a disk rather than in the analog format of a VHS tape.

dimmed: An option of command that's grayed because it's not available in the current context. For example, Copy and Cut commands are dimmed when an object or text is selected. Paste on the Edit menu is dimmed when the Clipboard is empty.

directory: (see *folder*)

DLL (Dynamic Link Library): A file containing API routines that programmers can access using procedure calls from a higher-level language.

DMA channel (Direct Memory Access channel): A direct channel for transferring data directly between a disk drive and memory, without involving the microprocessor.

dock: To put a portable PC into a docking station or port replicator.

docking station: A unit that connects a portable computer to larger desktop accessories, such as full-sized keyboard, monitor, and disk drives.

document: Typically a file that you create while using some program. For example, when you use a word processing program to type a letter, that letter is a *document.*

document-centric: An operating system design that focuses on the *documents* that people create and use, as opposed to the programs needed to create/edit those documents.

DOS (also MS-DOS): The original Disk Operating System for the IBM PC. Purely textual interface where you type commands, rather than clicking on icons with a mouse. Still used to create many games because DOS allows quick screen updating useful in simulations and animations.

driver (also called a *device driver*): A small program that makes a hardware device work. For example, to print, you typically need a printer (hardware) and a driver (software) for that printer.

Dial-Up Networking: A service that lets a PC dial into another PC or local area network, and access its shared resources. The PC that dials is called the *dial-up client*. The PC that answers the phone is called the *dial-up server*.

domain: In Windows NT, a group of computers that share a common domain database and security policy controlled by a Windows NT Server domain controller.

domain name: On the Internet, the last part of an e-mail address. For example, in alan@coolnerds.com the coolnerds.com part is the Internet domain name.

domain controller: In a local area network, the Windows NT computer that authenticates logons, controls security, and the maintains the master domain database.

DNS (Domain Name System): A database used by Internet TCP/IP hosts for resolving host names and IP addresses. Allows users of remote computers to access one another by host names rather than IP address.

double-click: To point to an object with the mouse pointer, then press and release the main mouse button twice in rapid succession (click-click!). The main mouse button is usually the one that rests comfortably under your index finger.

drag: To hold down the mouse button while moving the mouse, usually to move an icon or selection to some new location on the screen. Right-drag means to drag using the secondary mouse button (usually the mouse button on the right side).

drag-and-drop: A mouse technique of dragging an object from one location and dropping it in another.

drop-down list: A text box with a down-arrow box attached so you can choose an option from a list rather than typing one in. To open the drop-down list, click on the drop-down list arrow, or press Alt+DownArrow.

DSP (Digital Signal Processing): A feature of modern telephony boards that allows hardware to be updated to new standards using software only. Prevents the hardware from becoming obsolete each time a new modem or compression standard comes along.

E

e-mail: Electronic mail sent over a local area network (LAN) or Wide Area Network (WAN).

e-mail address: The address that uniquely identifies you on a network, much as your street address uniquely identifies the location of your home (see Internet address).

EPS (Encapsulated PostScript): High-resolution graphics file that can only be printed on PostScript printers.

Ethernet: The most widely used network protocol for PCs.

Ethernet cable: The cable used to attach a PC's network adapter card to an ethernet Concentrator.

Ethernet Concentrator: A device that all PCs in a local area network connect to via Ethernet cables.

Ethernet hub: Another name for an Ethernet concentrator.

event: Any activity from the mouse, keyboard, or a program that the computer can detect. Mouse clicks and keypresses are events.

Explorer: A browsing tool in Windows 95 that you can get to by clicking on the Start button, pointing to Programs, and choosing Windows Explorer.

F

FAQ (Frequently Asked Questions): A document you can browse on the Internet, or download from a fax-back service, to answer common questions about a topic.

FAT (File Allocation Table): The filing system used by DOS and 16-bit versions of Windows. Windows 95 uses a 32-bit implementation of FAT called VFAT (Virtual File Allocation Table.)

file: The basic unit of storage on a disk. For example, when you create and save a letter, that letter is stored in a *file*. Each file within a folder has its own unique filename.

file sharing: Allowing multiple PCs on a local area network access to the same set of files on one PC. To allow file sharing on a PC, you need to make sure file sharing is enabled in the network properties (right-click Network Neighborhood and choose Properties). Then to actually share a drive or folder, right-click on the item's icon in My Computer, and choose Sharing.

file system: The overall structure in which files are named and organized. Windows 95 uses VFAT for the hard disk, CDFS for CD-ROM drives.

flame: To rant and rave on the Internet or some other information service.

FTP (File Transfer Protocol): A service that allows file transfers over a TCP/IP connection. Commonly used to upload/download files across the Internet.

FTP site: A place on the Internet that has files you can download to your own computer, using an FTP program.

folder: An area on the disks that contains its own set of files. Called a *directory* in DOS and earlier versions of windows.

font: A lettering style. To add, view, and remove fonts in Windows 95, click on Start, choose Settings⇨Control Panel, double on click the Fonts folder. To assign a font to text in a program, select the text. Then choose Format⇨Font from the program's menu bar.

free space: The amount of unused space on a disk. To see how much free space is available, open My Computer, click on a drive icon, and look to the status bar, or run ScanDisk on the drive. To gain free space, delete unwanted files and empty the Recycle Bin.

G

gateway: See *IP Router*

graphics: Pictures (as opposed to text).

graphics accelerator: A hardware device that speeds up complex graphics rendering on the screen.

H

hack: To get past a password or other security device. A hacker is a person who hacks into places in cyberspace. Also a general term for "programmer" or computer enthusiast.

Help key: The key labeled F1 near the top of the keyboard. Pressing F1 usually brings up context-sensitive help.

High Color: A scheme that shows near photographic-quality color on your PC. Also called 16-bit color. To change your color settings, you right-click on the desktop, choose Properties, and then click on the Settings tab. However, not all hardware supports High Color.

home page: The first page you come to when you go to a World Wide Web site on the Internet. Clicking the Home button in a web browser takes you back to the home page.

host: Any device that's attached to the Internet using TCP/IP. For example, the computer that answers the phone in dial-up networking. In direct-cable connection, the PC that has the shared resources you want to access.

hot docking: The ability to connect a portable computer to its docking station without powering down the portable PC. Requires a special plug-and-play BIOS.

hot swapping: A characteristic of some PC Cards that allows the card to be inserted/removed without powering down the PC.

HPFS (High Performance File System): The file system used by the OS/2 operating systems. Supports long filenames, but no security.

HTML (Hypertext Markup Language): A set of codes you must use in a document that you plan to present on the World Wide Web.

HTTP (Hypertext Transport Protocol): The protocol used in the World Wide Web to allow documents to call one another.

hub: Short name for an ethernet concentrator or Ethernet hub. A device into which all PC's on the local area network connect via cable.

I

Icon: Any little picture on the screen. Typically you can right-click on an icon to see its options and properties. Double-clicking on an icon usually opens it up into a window.

in-place editing: A technique that allows you to edit an embedded document without leaving the program that you're in at the moment. The tools of the object being edited come to the current program's menu bar and toolbar.

INI file: A text file that holds information necessary to initialize a program. In Windows 95, these settings are stored in the Registry, but the original INI files are maintained to support backward compatibility.

Internet: A worldwide network of computers that anyone can tap into. Home of popular services such as the World Wide Web, FTP, Usenet Newsgroups, and Internet e-mail (among others).

Internet address: A person's mailing address on the Internet. If you have an MSN account, your Internet address is your MSN name followed by *@msn.com*.

Internet Explorer: A program that comes with the Microsoft Plus! kit that allows you to explore the Internet from your Windows 95 PC. Requires a modem, Microsoft Network (MSN) account, or account with an ISP.

Internet mail: e-mail sent through the Internet via a direct ISP connection, or a connection through some other service such as MSN, CompuServe, or America Online.

Internet Service Provider: (see *ISP*)

Interrupt: A condition that disrupts ongoing processing to call attention to a process that needs processor resources.

I/O device: Any hardware device that provides input to, or output from, the central processing unit. Printers, mice, keyboards, monitors, and disk drives are all I/O devices.

IP address: An address used to uniquely identify a computer on the Internet. A series of numbers, such as 123.45.67.890, assigned by an Internet Service Provider (ISP).

IP Router: A computer that's connected to several TCP/IP networks and can route or deliver packets between networks. Also called a *gateway*.

IPX/SPX: A network transport protocol used by Novell Netware networks. In Windows 95,

the NWLINK.VXD module implements the IPX/SPX protocol.

IRQ (Interrupt Request Line): The line that a hardware device uses to call attention to the processor. Typically, each hardware device must have its own IRQ. To view IRQ usage in Windows 95, click on Start and choose Settings➪ Control Panel. Double-click on the System icon, click on the Device Manager tab, then double-click on Computer at the top of the list.

ISP (Internet Service Provider): A service that connects your PC to the Internet via your modem and telephone line (see Appendix C).

J

JPEG (Joint Photographic Experts Group): Compression/decompression scheme used for digital video. See also MPEG.

K

K or **KB** or **Kilobyte**: 1024 bytes (characters).

kernel: That part of an operating system that manages the processor.

L

LAN (local area network): Computers that are connected to one another with cables and network adapter cards, rather than by modems and telephone lines.

legacy: Older hardware devices that don't conform to the "Designed for Windows 95" plug-and-play specification.

local area network: (see *LAN*)

local printer: A printer that's physically connected, via a cable, to the current PC.

localization: Adapting software to the language and formats of a specific country or culture.

M

map a drive letter (also called *map network drive*): To assign a shortcut drive-letter name, such as M: or P:, to a shared device in a local area network. To map a drive letter, double-click on Network Neighborhood, double-click on a computer's icon. Then right-click on a shared device and choose Map Network Drive from the shortcut menu.

MAPI (Messaging Application Programming Interface): Allows programs to access the messaging capabilities of the operating system. For example, many programs offer a File⇨Send option, which interacts with the MAPI to allow you to send messages directly from that application.

memory: In PC lingo, the term *memory* generally refers to RAM, as opposed to some other type of memory (such as disk storage).

menu: A list of options. Clicking on the Start button displays the Start menu.

message box: Any box that appears on the screen to display a message.

Microsoft Network: (See *MSN*)

MIDI (Musical Interface Digital Interface): A standard for playing music on a PC's sound board.

MIME (Multipurpose Internet Mail Extensions): A protocol that allows e-mail messages to contain more that just plan text.

miniport driver: A 32-bit virtual driver that allows hardware to be added and removed easily, without rebooting the entire system. Windows 95 and Windows NT both support miniport drivers.

modem: A device that connects your PC to a telephone line.

MPEG (Motion Picture Experts Group): A modern compression/decompression scheme for digital video that may someday allow video to run as smoothly on a PC as it does on a TV/VCR.

MS-DOS: (see DOS)

MSN (Microsoft Network): An information service provided by Microsoft Corporation.

Mwave: IBM's implementation of the DSP standard that allows modem and telephony hardware to be updated via software, so that the actual hardware doesn't become obsolete when standard improve.

My Computer: A browsing tool for finding resources on your own PC. Usually the first icon on the desktop. Also displays icons for shared resources on other PCs to which you've mapped a drive letter.

N

NDIS (Network Driver Interface Specification): The interface for network drivers. All transport drivers call the NDIS interface to access network adapters.

net (the net): A slang expression for *The Internet*.

NetBEUI transport (pronounced *net buoy*): Stands for NetBIOS Extended User Interface, a local area network transport protocol provided in Windows 95.

network: Two or more computers connected to one another with cables or modems and telephone lines. A local area network (LAN) is generally PCs that are close to one another and connected without modems and telephone lines. A Wide Area network (WAN) is composed of computers that are connected with telephones and modems. A LAN can connect to a WAN.

NetBIOS (Network Basic Input/Output System): A program that allows input/output requests to be sent to, and received from, another computer on a local area network.

network adapter card: A hardware device that allows you to connect a PC to other PCs in a local area network.

network adapter driver: A small program that controls a network adapter card.

network administrator: Typically the person who is in charge of managing a local area network, including accounts, passwords, e-mail, and so on.

Network Neighborhood: A desktop icon that, when double-clicked, displays shared resources on other PCs in the same workgroup on your local area network. Network Neighborhood lets you browse shared resources on the LAN in much the same way that My Computer lets you browse resources on your own computer. If you use Network Neighborhood to map a drive letter to a shared resource, that resource will then be available in your My Computer window.

network printer: A shared printer that's physically connected to some other PC in the LAN. Opposite of a *local printer*.

NDIS (Network Driver Interface Specification): The interface for network driver adapters in all Windows networks.

NIC (Network Interface Card): Another name for a *network adapter* or *network adapter card*.

NT: The shortcut name for *Windows NT*, Microsoft's 32-bit operating system for high-end workstations and non-Intel processors, such as the Dec Alpha and Power PC.

NTFS: The file system used by Windows NT.

O

Object: An individual chunk of data that you can manipulate on the screen. Can be a chart, picture, sound, video, or chunk of text.

object-oriented: An operating system that allows chunks of data to be manipulated as individual objects, and easily moves/copies from one program to another.

object package: (see *package*)

OLE (pronounced *olay*): The acronym without words, OLE originally stood for "object linking and embedding", a feature of windows that let's you take an object from one program (such as a chart in a spreadsheet program), and link or embed that object into another program's document (such as a word processing report). OLE's capabilities extend beyond simple object embedding. So now if you ask a Microsoft person what OLE stands for, he or she is likely to say "nothing...it's just *olay*".

OOP: Object-oriented programming language used to control an object-oriented operating system.

Option button: A small, round button in a dialog box that generally lets you select only one option of many. Also called *radio buttons* (because only one can be "pushed in" at a time).

P

package (also called an object package): An icon that represents a linked or embedded object. Double-clicking the icon opens and displays the contents of the package.

packet: A chunk of information sent over a network. Typically includes a *header* describing the source and destination address, an ID number, and information used for error control.

page: 1) Internet: an electronic document in the World Wide Web or Gopher. 2) RAM: a fixed-sized chunk of memory. 3) BBS: "page the sysop" means to sound a beep on the system operator's PC.

password: A string of characters that allows you access to protected data.

path: The location of a folder described in terms of its drive folder, and subfolder. For example, in c:\winword\mydocuments\Letter to Mom.doc, the c:\winword\mydocuments\ part is the path to the file named Letter to Mom.doc. Also a DOS command used to identify directories to search, now handled by the Registry in Windows 95.

PC card: A credit-card sized adapter card that fits into the PCMCIA slot of a portable or desktop PC.

PCI (Peripheral Component Interconnect): A local bus system that allows devices to be installed quickly and easily, and supports high-speed graphics processing. Used in many Pentium and Apple Power PC computers. The successor to the older ISA, EISA, and VL bus systems.

PCMCIA (Personal Computer Memory Card International Association): A standard that defines how PC cards must be designed in order to work in the PCMCIA slot of a portable or desktop PC.

peer-to-peer network: A way of connecting several PCs into a local area network where any PC can act as either client or server.

plug-and-play: A general term for devices that are (supposedly) easy to plug into your PC and use. In Windows 95, a device that really *can* be plugged in and used immediately. The latter devices bear the *Designed for Windows 95* logo.

plug-and-play BIOS: A Basic Input/Output System capable of configuring plug-and-play devices during power up, and also during runtime.

point: To *point to* an object means to move the mouse until the mouse pointer is touching that object.

pointing device: A mouse or trackball used to move the mouse pointer around on the screen.

PPP (Point-to-Point Protocol): An industry standard method of connecting PCs through telephone lines. PPP is often used to connect a PC to the Internet, and to connect one PC to another during dial-up networking.

pop-up menu: The menu that appears when you right-click on an object. Also called a *context menu* or *shortcut menu*.

port: A slot on the back of your PC into which you plug a cable that connects to some external device. Mice, keyboards, monitors, external modems, external CD-ROM drives, printers, and all other external devices plug into a port on a PC.

port replicator: Compact-sized docking station for a portable computer that allows easy connection to full-sized keyboard, mouse, monitor, and other devices.

Postoffice: The place where an e-mail message is stored until the recipient reads the message. In a workgroup, only one PC can play the role of Postoffice.

preemptive multitasking: A scheduling technique that allows the operating system to take control of the processor at any time. Allows multiple hardware devices such as modem, printer, screen, and floppy disk to operate at the same time.

primary mouse button: On a right-handed mouse, this is typically the button on the left. If you reverse the mouse buttons for left-handed use, the primary mouse button becomes the mouse button on the right. The idea is to use whichever mouse button rests comfortably under your index finger as the primary mouse button.

printer driver: A small program that allows a PC to drive a printer (make the printer work).

printer fonts: Fonts that are built into the printer rather than stored on disk. Also called *resident fonts*.

printer sharing: Allowing your printer to be used by other members of a local area network. On the local PC (the one that the printer is connected to) print sharing must be enabled through Network Neighborhood properties. Then the printer must be installed as a local printer, and then shared via the Printers folder in My Computer. Other LAN members must then use the Add New Printer icon in their own Printers folder, and the Network Printer option, to connect to that shared printer.

private key: A password you create to manage your own *public keys*.

program: Software that makes the computer perform a specific task, or helps you to perform some job using the PC.

properties: The characteristics of an object. You can usually get to an object's properties by right-clicking on the object's icon and choosing Properties from the shortcut menu that appears.

property sheet: A specialized dialog box, or tab within a dialog box, that lets you view and change an object's characteristics. For example, right-clicking on the Windows 95 desktop and choosing Properties opens the Display Properties sheet.

protocol: An agreed-upon set of rules by which two computers can exchange information over a network. Windows 95 supports the NetBEUI, TCP/IP, and IPX/SPX protocols.

public key: Passwords shared by people who need to secure privacy in their fax and e-mail transmissions. To read someone else's private transmissions, you must get a public key from that person. To create your own secured messages, you need to create a public key, and send it to your intended recipients.

R

RAM (Random Access Memory): Super-fast memory that stores whatever programs and document you're working with at the moment. The term *memory* is often used as a synonym for RAM.

real mode: The general term for a 16-bit device driver that's loaded into memory from the CONFIG.SYS or AUTOEXEC.BAT file. Windows 95 attempts to replace all real-mode drivers with its own 32-bit virtual drivers which provide better performance.

refresh: To update something on the screen so it shows current data. Can typically be accomplished by pressing the F5 key or choosing View⇨Refresh from a menu bar.

RegEdit (Registry Editor): A program that you can use to manipulate the Registry directly, without using the Control Panel or any property sheets. To open, you must click on the Start button, choose Run, then type **regedit** and press Enter.

registered file type: A type of document file that is associated with a specific program, based on its filename extension. For example, all .DOC files are registered to (associated with) the Microsoft Word for Windows program. Extensions on registered file types are hidden unless you use View⇨Options in My Computer to turn off the option titled *Hide MS-DOS file extensions for file types that are registered.*

Registry: The place where Windows 95 stores all settings and preferences that you choose through Control Panel, and all associations between filename extensions and programs.

remote administration: The ability for a person to control sharing and other settings on someone else's PC from his/her own PC in the LAN. The PC being administered must grant this permission via the Passwords icon in Control Panel.

resource: Items that can be shared in a LAN. For example, disk drives, folders, CD-ROM drives, printers, and modems are all useful resources that can be shared.

right-click: To point to an object and then click the secondary mouse button (typically the mouse button on the right side of the mouse).

right-drag: To hold down the secondary mouse button while dragging an object across the screen.

root directory: The topmost folder on a disk, typically named just \. For example, C:\ represents the root directory of drive C:.

S

SCSI (Small Computer Standard Interface, pronounced *scuzzy*): An interface specification that allows multiple disk drives, CD-ROM drives, and other devices to be connected to one another, and then connected to a single port on the PC.

secondary mouse button: On a right-handed mouse, this is typically the button on the right. If you reverse the mouse buttons for left-handed use, the secondary mouse button becomes the mouse button on the left. The button that rests comfortably under your middle or ring finger.

select: To specify which object(s) you plan to perform some operation on. Usually you select one object by clicking on it. To select multiple objects, you can use Ctrl+Click or Shift+Click. Or you can drag a frame around the objects. To select text, drag the mouse pointer through the text.

selection: An object (or objects) that are already selected, and hence framed or highlighted in some manner.

server: In a LAN, the PC that has some resource connected directly to it. For example, if your PC has a printer attached to it, and you let other LAN users print to your printer, your PC is acting as the print server. The other PCs are *clients* to that server.

share: To allow multiple users on a local area network to use a single device, such as a printer or modem, that's attached to only one PC in the LAN. You can also share disk drives, CD-ROM drives, and folders.

shareware: Programs that you're allowed to try, and use for a while, without charge. If you like the program, the authors hope you'll *register* and send in some money. In return, you get a non-crippled version of the program, or just mailings about when bigger and better versions are available.

shortcut: 1) An icon on the desktop that lets you open a folder, document, or program without going through the Start menu. 2) An alternative to using the mouse, often called a *keyboard shortcut*.

SLIP (Serial Line Internet Protocol): A method used to connect a PC to an Internet Service Provider. PPP is preferred over SLIP when connecting to the Internet with Windows 95.

smiley: A series of characters that, when turned on its side, looks like a facial expression. For example, this is the basic **:-)** smiling face smiley. Also called *emoticon*.

snail mail: The new term for what we used to just call *mail*. Any mail that involves paper, as opposed to e-mail.

Start button: The button that appears in the taskbar, which you can click on to start a program, open a recently saved document, get help, and so forth on.

Start menu: The first menu to appear after you click the Start button in the taskbar.

status bar: The bar along the bottom of a program's window that provides information about the status of various options within that program. Can typically be turned on or off using a command on the program's View menu.

string: Textual rather than numeric data. For example, 123.45 is a number, whereas *My dog has fleas* is a string (of characters).

subfolder: A folder that's contained within another folder. The containing folder is called the *parent folder*.

subnet: Any smaller network that's connected to the Internet.

subnet mask: A value that allows the recipient of Internet packets to distinguish the network ID portion of the IP address from the ID of the host.

SVGA (Super Virtual Graphics Array): The type of display card and monitor that gives you high resolution, rich color, and graphics. An improvement over standard VGA.

system menu: A menu that you can open by clicking on the icon in the upper-left corner of a window, or by pressing Alt+Spacebar. Lets you move and size a window using the keyboard rather than the mouse.

sysop: The person who operates a bulletin board.

T

TAPI (Telephony Application Program Interface): A standardized set of procedures that programmers can use to allow their programs to interact with the modem and dialing properties on your PC.

TCP/IP (Transmission Control Protocol/ Internet Protocol): The primary communications protocol used on the Internet. Allows a Windows 95 PC to participate in Unix-based bulletin boards and other information services. Can also be used to allow a non-Windows PC (such as an OS/2 computer) to connect to a Windows local area network.

telephony: The interaction between PCs and telephones. A *telephony board* is a device that you can add to your PC to support voice mail, fax-on-demand, and similar services.

text file: A file that contains only ASCII text codes, no word-processing formatting codes. Text files should be edited with text-only editors, such as NotePad or Edit (available from the command prompt).

thread: 1) A series of messages about a topic that have been posted to an information service. 2) An executable chunk of program code that can run simultaneously with other threads in a microprocessor.

TIA (Thanks In Advance): Often used to close an e-mail message.

title bar: The colored area across the top of the window that shows the window's name, and offers the Minimize, Maximize, and Close buttons, and system menu. To move a window, you drag its title bar. You can also maximize/restore a window by double-clicking on its title bar.

toolbar: A set of buttons and other controls that provide one-click access to frequently-used menu commands. A program's toolbar usually appears just under its menu bar. In many windows you can choose View⇨Toolbar to show/hide the toolbar.

tooltip: A little label that appears below a button after you've rested the mouse pointer on that button for a couple of seconds.

tray: The name originally given to the Windows 95 taskbar.

True Color: A scheme that shows photographic-quality color on your PC. Also called 24-bit color. To change your color settings, you right-click on the desktop, choose Properties, and then click on the Settings tab. However, not all hardware supports True Color.

U

UART: Pronounced *wart,* a chip used on a modem or serial device that determines the top speed of serial communications. The latest UART, 16550A, offers the highest speeds.

UNC (Universal Naming Convention): A method of identifying a resource by its computer name, followed by a resource name. The computer name is preceded by two backslashes e.g. *Comm_Center\MyStuff*.

Unimodem: A universal driver for modems.

URL (Universal Resource Locator): A protocol on the World Wide Web that lets a web browser gain access to a variety of services.

V

VDM (Virtual DOS Machine): An environment used to run 16-bit DOS and Windows 3.x programs in Windows 95.

VESA (Video Electronic Standards Association): A group that defines standards for video displays (see VL).

VGA (Virtual Graphics Array): The type of display card and monitor that gives you rich color and graphics.

virtual driver: A 32-bit Windows 95 device driver that can be loaded into upper memory via the Registry (as opposed to a real-mode driver, which must be loaded into conventional or upper memory via CONFIG.SYS or AUTOEXEC.BAT).

virtual memory: Disk space that's used as RAM when RAM runs out.

virus: A computer program specifically designed to do damage on whatever PC it lands on. High-tech vandalism.

VL (VESA Local bus): A standard that allows high-speed connections to monitors and other devices. Often used in modern 486 computers. PCI, another standard, is used in Pentium computers.

VxD: A 32-bit Windows 95 virtual device driver, often used as a filename extension on the device driver's filename. The x indicates the type of device being driven. For example, .VPD is a printer driver. .VDD is a display driver.

W

WAOL: A Windows program for accessing the America Online information service.

wart: (see UART)

web browser: A program, such as NCSA Mosaic and Netscape Navigator, that lets you access the Internet's World Wide Web.

WinCIM (Window CompuServe Information Manager): A program used to access the CompuServe information service from a PC that uses Windows.

window: The space on a screen that holds one program or dialog box. Double-clicking on an icon typically opens that icon up into a window.

Windows NT: Microsoft's 32-bit operating system for high-end workstations and non-Intel processors. For example, computers that use the Dec Alpha, MIPS, or PowerPC chips can run the Windows NT operating system. Only Intel PCs with 386, 486, or Pentium chips can run Windows 95.

WINS (Windows Internet Name Service): A naming service that resolves Windows network computer names to Internet IP addresses.

workgroup: A collection of computers in a LAN that all share the same workgroup name. When you first open Network Neighborhood, it displays other computers in your same workgroup. You determine which workgroup a PC belongs to using the Identification tab in network properties (right-click on Network Neighborhood and choose Properties.)

workstation: A PC with unusually high processing capabilities, often used for computer-aided design and similar calculation-intensive and graphics-intensive jobs. May use a non-Intel microprocessor, such as the Dec Alpha. Or may use multiple 486 or Pentium processors.

World Wide Web: A popular place on the Internet, where you can browse through documents that contain text, graphics, and even multimedia.

Z

zipped file: A file that has been compressed to speed up transmission across telephone lines. The file must be *unzipped* on your computer after you receive it, using a program such as WinZip or PKZip (see Appendix D).

Index

D

(continued)

M

(continued)

(continued)

S

Notes

Notes

The fun & easy way to learn about computers and more!

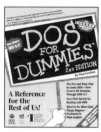

Here's a complete listing of IDG's ...For Dummies Titles

Title	Author	ISBN	Price
DATABASE			
Access 2 For Dummies™	by Scott Palmer	1-56884-090-X	$19.95 USA/$26.95 Canada
Access Programming For Dummies™	by Rob Krumm	1-56884-091-8	$19.95 USA/$26.95 Canada
Approach 3 For Windows For Dummies™	by Doug Lowe	1-56884-233-3	$19.99 USA/$26.99 Canada
dBASE For DOS For Dummies™	by Scott Palmer & Michael Stabler	1-56884-188-4	$19.95 USA/$26.95 Canada
dBASE For Windows For Dummies™	by Scott Palmer	1-56884-179-5	$19.95 USA/$26.95 Canada
dBASE 5 For Windows Programming For Dummies™	by Ted Coombs & Jason Coombs	1-56884-215-5	$19.99 USA/$26.99 Canada
FoxPro 2.6 For Windows For Dummies™	by John Kaufeld	1-56884-187-6	$19.95 USA/$26.95 Canada
Paradox 5 For Windows For Dummies™	by John Kaufeld	1-56884-185-X	$19.95 USA/$26.95 Canada
DESKTOP PUBLISHING / ILLUSTRATION / GRAPHICS			
CorelDRAW! 5 For Dummies™	by Deke McClelland	1-56884-157-4	$19.95 USA/$26.95 Canada
CorelDRAW! For Dummies™	by Deke McClelland	1-56884-042-X	$19.95 USA/$26.95 Canada
Harvard Graphics 2 For Windows For Dummies™	by Roger C. Parker	1-56884-092-6	$19.95 USA/$26.95 Canada
PageMaker 5 For Macs For Dummies™	by Galen Gruman	1-56884-178-7	$19.95 USA/$26.95 Canada
PageMaker 5 For Windows For Dummies™	by Deke McClelland & Galen Gruman	1-56884-160-4	$19.95 USA/$26.95 Canada
QuarkXPress 3.3 For Dummies™	by Galen Gruman & Barbara Assadi	1-56884-217-1	$19.99 USA/$26.99 Canada
FINANCE / PERSONAL FINANCE / TEST TAKING REFERENCE			
QuickBooks 3 For Dummies™	by Stephen L. Nelson	1-56884-227-9	$19.99 USA/$26.99 Canada
Quicken 8 For DOS For Dummies™, 2nd Edition	by Stephen L. Nelson	1-56884-210-4	$19.95 USA/$26.95 Canada
Quicken 5 For Macs For Dummies™	by Stephen L. Nelson	1-56884-211-2	$19.95 USA/$26.95 Canada
Quicken 4 For Windows For Dummies™, 2nd Edition	by Stephen L. Nelson	1-56884-209-0	$19.95 USA/$26.95 Canada
The SAT I For Dummies™	by Suzee Vlk	1-56884-213-9	$14.99 USA/$20.99 Canada
GROUPWARE / INTEGRATED			
Lotus Notes 3/3.1 For Dummies™	by Paul Freeland & Stephen Londergan	1-56884-212-0	$19.95 USA/$26.95 Canada
Microsoft Office 4 For Windows For Dummies™	by Roger C. Parker	1-56884-183-3	$19.95 USA/$26.95 Canada
Microsoft Works 3 For Windows For Dummies™	by David C. Kay	1-56884-214-7	$19.99 USA/$26.99 Canada

Title	Author	ISBN	Price

INTERNET / COMMUNICATIONS / NETWORKING

Title	Author	ISBN	Price
CompuServe For Dummies™	by Wallace Wang	1-56884-181-7	$19.95 USA/$26.95 Canada
Modems For Dummies™, 2nd Edition	by Tina Rathbone	1-56884-223-6	$19.99 USA/$26.99 Canada
Modems For Dummies™	by Tina Rathbone	1-56884-001-2	$19.95 USA/$26.95 Canada
MORE Internet For Dummies™	by John R. Levine & Margaret Levine Young	1-56884-164-7	$19.95 USA/$26.95 Canada
NetWare For Dummies™	by Ed Tittel & Deni Connor	1-56884-003-9	$19.95 USA/$26.95 Canada
Networking For Dummies™	by Doug Lowe	1-56884-079-9	$19.95 USA/$26.95 Canada
ProComm Plus 2 For Windows For Dummies™	by Wallace Wang	1-56884-219-8	$19.99 USA/$26.99 Canada
The Internet For Dummies™, 2nd Edition	by John R. Levine & Carol Baroudi	1-56884-222-8	$19.99 USA/$26.99 Canada
The Internet For Macs For Dummies™	by Charles Seiter	1-56884-184-1	$19.95 USA/$26.95 Canada

MACINTOSH

Title	Author	ISBN	Price
Macs For Dummies®	by David Pogue	1-56884-173-6	$19.95 USA/$26.95 Canada
Macintosh System 7.5 For Dummies™	by Bob LeVitus	1-56884-197-3	$19.95 USA/$26.95 Canada
MORE Macs For Dummies™	by David Pogue	1-56884-087-X	$19.95 USA/$26.95 Canada
PageMaker 5 For Macs For Dummies™	by Galen Gruman	1-56884-178-7	$19.95 USA/$26.95 Canada
QuarkXPress 3.3 For Dummies™	by Galen Gruman & Barbara Assadi	1-56884-217-1	$19.99 USA/$26.99 Canada
Upgrading and Fixing Macs For Dummies™	by Kearney Rietmann & Frank Higgins	1-56884-189-2	$19.95 USA/$26.95 Canada

MULTIMEDIA

Title	Author	ISBN	Price
Multimedia & CD-ROMs For Dummies™, Interactive Multimedia Value Pack	by Andy Rathbone	1-56884-225-2	$29.95 USA/$39.95 Canada
Multimedia & CD-ROMs For Dummies™	by Andy Rathbone	1-56884-089-6	$19.95 USA/$26.95 Canada

OPERATING SYSTEMS / DOS

Title	Author	ISBN	Price
MORE DOS For Dummies™	by Dan Gookin	1-56884-046-2	$19.95 USA/$26.95 Canada
S.O.S. For DOS™	by Katherine Murray	1-56884-043-8	$12.95 USA/$16.95 Canada
OS/2 For Dummies™	by Andy Rathbone	1-878058-76-2	$19.95 USA/$26.95 Canada

UNIX

Title	Author	ISBN	Price
UNIX For Dummies™	by John R. Levine & Margaret Levine Young	1-878058-58-4	$19.95 USA/$26.95 Canada

WINDOWS

Title	Author	ISBN	Price
S.O.S. For Windows™	by Katherine Murray	1-56884-045-4	$12.95 USA/$16.95 Canada
MORE Windows 3.1 For Dummies™, 3rd Edition	by Andy Rathbone	1-56884-240-6	$19.99 USA/$26.99 Canada

PCs / HARDWARE

Title	Author	ISBN	Price
Illustrated Computer Dictionary For Dummies™	by Dan Gookin, Wally Wang, & Chris Van Buren	1-56884-004-7	$12.95 USA/$16.95 Canada
Upgrading and Fixing PCs For Dummies™	by Andy Rathbone	1-56884-002-0	$19.95 USA/$26.95 Canada

PRESENTATION / AUTOCAD

Title	Author	ISBN	Price
AutoCAD For Dummies™	by Bud Smith	1-56884-191-4	$19.95 USA/$26.95 Canada
PowerPoint 4 For Windows For Dummies™	by Doug Lowe	1-56884-161-2	$16.95 USA/$22.95 Canada

PROGRAMMING

Title	Author	ISBN	Price
Borland C++ For Dummies™	by Michael Hyman	1-56884-162-0	$19.95 USA/$26.95 Canada
"Borland's New Language Product" For Dummies™	by Neil Rubenking	1-56884-200-7	$19.95 USA/$26.95 Canada
C For Dummies™	by Dan Gookin	1-878058-78-9	$19.95 USA/$26.95 Canada
C++ For Dummies™	by Stephen R. Davis	1-56884-163-9	$19.95 USA/$26.95 Canada
Mac Programming For Dummies™	by Dan Parks Sydow	1-56884-173-6	$19.95 USA/$26.95 Canada
QBasic Programming For Dummies™	by Douglas Hergert	1-56884-093-4	$19.95 USA/$26.95 Canada
Visual Basic "X" For Dummies™, 2nd Edition	by Wallace Wang	1-56884-230-9	$19.99 USA/$26.99 Canada
Visual Basic 3 For Dummies™	by Wallace Wang	1-56884-076-4	$19.95 USA/$26.95 Canada

SPREADSHEET

Title	Author	ISBN	Price
1-2-3 For Dummies™	by Greg Harvey	1-878058-60-6	$16.95 USA/$21.95 Canada
1-2-3 For Windows 5 For Dummies™, 2nd Edition	by John Walkenbach	1-56884-216-3	$16.95 USA/$21.95 Canada
1-2-3 For Windows For Dummies™	by John Walkenbach	1-56884-052-7	$16.95 USA/$21.95 Canada
Excel 5 For Macs For Dummies™	by Greg Harvey	1-56884-186-8	$19.95 USA/$26.95 Canada
Excel For Dummies™, 2nd Edition	by Greg Harvey	1-56884-050-0	$16.95 USA/$21.95 Canada
MORE Excel 5 For Windows For Dummies™	by Greg Harvey	1-56884-207-4	$19.95 USA/$26.95 Canada
Quattro Pro 6 For Windows For Dummies™	by John Walkenbach	1-56884-174-4	$19.95 USA/$26.95 Canada
Quattro Pro For DOS For Dummies™	by John Walkenbach	1-56884-023-3	$16.95 USA/$21.95 Canada

UTILITIES / VCRs & CAMCORDERS

Title	Author	ISBN	Price
Norton Utilities 8 For Dummies™	by Beth Slick	1-56884-166-3	$19.95 USA/$26.95 Canada
VCRs & Camcorders For Dummies™	by Andy Rathbone & Gordon McComb	1-56884-229-5	$14.99 USA/$20.99 Canada

WORD PROCESSING

Title	Author	ISBN	Price
Ami Pro For Dummies™	by Jim Meade	1-56884-049-7	$19.95 USA/$26.95 Canada
MORE Word For Windows 6 For Dummies™	by Doug Lowe	1-56884-165-5	$19.95 USA/$26.95 Canada
MORE WordPerfect 6 For Windows For Dummies™	by Margaret Levine Young & David C. Kay	1-56884-206-6	$19.95 USA/$26.95 Canada
MORE WordPerfect 6 For DOS For Dummies™	by Wallace Wang, edited by Dan Gookin	1-56884-047-0	$19.95 USA/$26.95 Canada
S.O.S. For WordPerfect™	by Katherine Murray	1-56884-053-5	$12.95 USA/$16.95 Canada
Word 6 For Macs For Dummies™	by Dan Gookin	1-56884-190-6	$19.95 USA/$26.95 Canada
Word For Windows 6 For Dummies™	by Dan Gookin	1-56884-075-6	$16.95 USA/$21.95 Canada
Word For Windows For Dummies™	by Dan Gookin	1-878058-86-X	$16.95 USA/$21.95 Canada
WordPerfect 6 For Dummies™	by Dan Gookin	1-878058-77-0	$16.95 USA/$21.95 Canada
WordPerfect For Dummies™	by Dan Gookin	1-878058-52-5	$16.95 USA/$21.95 Canada
WordPerfect For Windows For Dummies™	by Margaret Levine Young & David C. Kay	1-56884-032-2	$16.95 USA/$21.95 Canada

FOR MORE INFORMATION OR TO ORDER, PLEASE CALL ▶ 800 762 2974

For volume discounts & special orders please call
Tony Real, Special Sales, at 415. 655. 3048

Fun, Fast, & Cheap!

CorelDRAW! 5 For Dummies™ Quick Reference
by Raymond E. Werner

ISBN: 1-56884-952-4
$9.99 USA/$12.99 Canada

Windows "X" For Dummies™ Quick Reference, 3rd Edition
by Greg Harvey

ISBN: 1-56884-964-8
$9.99 USA/$12.99 Canada

Word For Windows 6 For Dummies™ Quick Reference
by George Lynch

ISBN: 1-56884-095-0
$8.95 USA/$12.95 Canada

WordPerfect For DOS For Dummies™ Quick Reference
by Greg Harvey

ISBN: 1-56884-009-8
$8.95 USA/$11.95 Canada

Title	Author	ISBN	Price
DATABASE			
Access 2 For Dummies™ Quick Reference	by Stuart A. Stuple	1-56884-167-1	$8.95 USA/$11.95 Canada
dBASE 5 For DOS For Dummies™ Quick Reference	by Barry Sosinsky	1-56884-954-0	$9.99 USA/$12.99 Canada
dBASE 5 For Windows For Dummies™ Quick Reference	by Stuart J. Stuple	1-56884-953-2	$9.99 USA/$12.99 Canada
Paradox 5 For Windows For Dummies™ Quick Reference	by Scott Palmer	1-56884-960-5	$9.99 USA/$12.99 Canada
DESKTOP PUBLISHING / ILLUSTRATION/GRAPHICS			
Harvard Graphics 3 For Windows For Dummies™ Quick Reference	by Raymond E. Werner	1-56884-962-1	$9.99 USA/$12.99 Canada
FINANCE / PERSONAL FINANCE			
Quicken 4 For Windows For Dummies™ Quick Reference	by Stephen L. Nelson	1-56884-950-8	$9.95 USA/$12.95 Canada
GROUPWARE / INTEGRATED			
Microsoft Office 4 For Windows For Dummies™ Quick Reference	by Doug Lowe	1-56884-958-3	$9.99 USA/$12.99 Canada
Microsoft Works For Windows 3 For Dummies™ Quick Reference	by Michael Partington	1-56884-959-1	$9.99 USA/$12.99 Canada
INTERNET / COMMUNICATIONS / NETWORKING			
The Internet For Dummies™ Quick Reference	by John R. Levine	1-56884-168-X	$8.95 USA/$11.95 Canada
MACINTOSH			
Macintosh System 7.5 For Dummies™ Quick Reference	by Stuart J. Stuple	1-56884-956-7	$9.99 USA/$12.99 Canada
OPERATING SYSTEMS / DOS			
DOS For Dummies® Quick Reference	by Greg Harvey	1-56884-007-1	$8.95 USA/$11.95 Canada
UNIX			
UNIX For Dummies™ Quick Reference	by Margaret Levine Young & John R. Levine	1-56884-094-2	$8.95 USA/$11.95 Canada
WINDOWS			
Windows 3.1 For Dummies™ Quick Reference, 2nd Edition	by Greg Harvey	1-56884-951-6	$8.95 USA/$11.95 Canada
PRESENTATION / AUTOCAD			
AutoCAD For Dummies™ Quick Reference	by Ellen Finkelstein	1-56884-198-1	$9.95 USA/$12.95 Canada
SPREADSHEET			
1-2-3 For Dummies™ Quick Reference	by John Walkenbach	1-56884-027-6	$8.95 USA/$11.95 Canada
1-2-3 For Windows 5 For Dummies™ Quick Reference	by John Walkenbach	1-56884-957-5	$9.95 USA/$12.95 Canada
Excel For Windows For Dummies™ Quick Reference, 2nd Edition	by John Walkenbach	1-56884-096-9	$8.95 USA/$11.95 Canada
Quattro Pro 6 For Windows For Dummies™ Quick Reference	by Stuart A. Stuple	1-56884-172-8	$9.95 USA/$12.95 Canada
WORD PROCESSING			
Word For Windows 6 For Dummies™ Quick Reference	by George Lynch	1-56884-095-0	$8.95 USA/$11.95 Canada
WordPerfect For Windows For Dummies™ Quick Reference	by Greg Harvey	1-56884-039-X	$8.95 USA/$11.95 Canada

FOR MORE INFORMATION OR TO ORDER, PLEASE CALL ▶ 800 762 2974

For volume discounts & special orders please call
Tony Real, Special Sales, at 415. 655. 3048

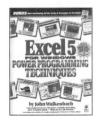

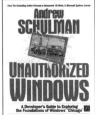
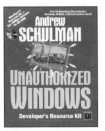